Quick Check
FOOD
GUIDE FOR
HEART
HEALTH

Quick Check
FOOD
GUIDE FOR
HEART
HEALTH

Linda McDonald, M.S., R.D., L.D.

BARRON'S

Acknowledgments

The author and publisher gratefully acknowledge the food companies listed in the Appendix for assisting with the compilations of nutritional data for this edition.

We also want to thank the American Heart Association for guidance in the development of this book and the use of the American Heart Association's Heart Check Mark (*www.heartcheckmark.org*) in our Shopping Tips.

Heart-Check Mark is a registered trademark of the American Heart Association. Used with Permission.

In addition, we gratefully thank Oldways (www.oldwayspt.org), whose mission is to guide people to good health through heritage, for the inclusion of information from two of their initiatives—the Mediterranean Food Alliance and the Whole Grain Council.

Mediterranean Pyramid: Courtesy of Oldways, *oldwayspt.org*

Whole Grain Stamp: Courtesy of Oldways and the Whole Grains Council, *wholegrainscouncil.org*

All inquiries should be addressed to:
Barron's Educational Series, Inc.
250 Wireless Boulevard
Hauppauge, New York 11788
www.barronseduc.com

ISBN: 978-1-4380-0394-8

Library of Congress Control Number: 2013029544

Library of Congress Cataloging-in-Publication Data

McDonald, Linda (Nutritionist)
  Quick check food guide for heart health / Linda McDonald, M.S., R.D., L.D. – First edition.
    pages cm
  ISBN 978-1-4380-0394-8
1. Food–Composition–Tables. 2. Nutrition–Tables. I. Title.
  TX551.M3776 2014
  664'.07–dc23

                                           2013029544

Printed in the United States of America
9 8 7 6 5 4 3 2 1

Contents

Preface

The information in this book was provided by the food manufacturers either directly from their web sites or from package labels. Additional information is based on the *USDA National Nutrient Database for Standard Reference, Release 23*, published in computer readable form by the U.S. Department of Agriculture.

For each food or beverage listed a serving size and amount per serving is given along with nutrient amounts based on the serving size. The following abbreviations are used:

> **%DV** – **% Daily Value (based on a Recommended Daily Amount for a 2000 calorie diet.)**
> **g** – **grams**
> **mg** – **milligrams**

Trans Fat is not listed because only foods with 0 grams of Trans Fat per serving are included. Since foods with less than 0.5 grams of trans fat can list 0 grams in the Nutrition Facts, be sure to check the ingredients for partially hydrogenated fats to determine if a product contains any trans fats.

About the Author

Linda McDonald, MS, RD, LD, owns SUPERMARKET SAVVY, an information and resource service focused on making healthy shopping easy. Her strategic reports, teaching tools, and website (*www.supermarketsavvy.com*) assist health professionals and consumers to shop for health.

Mrs. McDonald is a graduate of the University of Houston with a Master of Science from the University of Texas Graduate School of Biomedical Sciences. She is a preceptor for dietetic Interns from the University of Houston, Texas Women's University, and the University of Texas.

This is Mrs. McDonald's third Quick Check book. Previous books are **Quick Check Food Facts** and **Quick Check Guide to Gluten-Free Foods**. She also co-authored a series of eating-out guides and cookbooks with Houston restaurants and is a consultant for the retail food industry.

Disclaimer

The Quick Check Food Guide for Heart Health is for the consumer interested in eating heart healthy either to prevent heart disease or to alleviate the signs of heart disease. Use this book to help you make heart-smart grocery shopping and meal planning decisions.

Since there is no legal definition for a "Heart-Healthy" food, we are careful not to make that claim. The foods and beverages listed meet specific nutrient criteria listed in the introduction for each food section. This criterion is based on the standards for a "healthy" food claim (page 6) and additional Health Claims related to heart health (pages 25 to 30).

This book should be used as an aide to guide the consumer in choosing healthy food products in the supermarket. The content of this book is not medical advice and should not take the place of consulting a medical professional, such as a physician or dietitian, including the diagnosis or treatment of any health condition. Neither the author, Linda McDonald, nor the editorial staff at Barron's Educational Series, Inc. shall be held liable or responsible to any person or entity with respect to any health issues.

Every effort has been made to make this food guide as complete and accurate as possible. However, there may be errors, both typographical and in content. Therefore, this text should be used only as a general guide, not as an ultimate source of health and nutrition information.

Nutrient information in this book was provided by the food companies listed and was not confirmed by lab analysis. Food companies indicate that product and recipe ingredients may change periodically. Therefore, the consumer needs to always check the ingredients and nutrition facts on the package label of food and beverage products for the most current information. For specific questions or further information, contact the manufacturer. Check the list of food companies in this book along with contact information on pages 555 to 573.

How to Use This Book

There are several approaches to using this book that can help you plan your menus and make a shopping list depending on what area of heart health you are dealing with. Since there are so many aspects of heart health, you may want to focus on one issue and/or nutrient at a time.

- Read the introduction in the front of the book that includes information on heart disease risk factors, recommendations for dealing with risk factors, nutrients of concern for heart health, and an explanation of several food plans that are available for preventing or treating heart disease issues—high blood pressure, high cholesterol levels, diabetes, etc.

- The introduction ends with some "bottom line" tips for heart-healthy eating (pages 41 to 43) along with a sample shopping list for heart health (page 44).

- Read the recommendations for each food category for the number of servings and serving sizes. The servings given are for an adult consuming 2,000 calories per day. For a personalized food plan based on your age, sex, weight, and activity level, go to www.choosemyplate.gov.

- Make your shopping list by multiplying the number of people in your family by the recommended number of servings.

- Check the lists of foods in each category provided in this book and choose a variety of items.

- Compare nutrients within categories for the best food choices for positive nutrients such as protein, fiber, calcium, vitamins, and minerals. Also check nutrients for foods with negative nutrients such as total fat, saturated fat, cholesterol, and sodium.

- Read the shopping tips and shopping list essentials for each category, and include these suggestions into your meal planning and shopping list.

- Highlight the foods that are presently in your food plan, and use a different color highlighter for the foods you want to try. Make a goal to try a new food each week. Remember that variety is important for healthy eating.

- Take this book to the supermarket to help you find healthy foods that will benefit your heart. It will also come in handy to check on the nutrients in foods that may not have Nutrition Facts—fruits, vegetables, bulk items, meat, poultry, and fish.

Criteria for Foods in This Book

Unfortunately, the FDA does not provide a legal definition for a "heart-healthy" food. But there is a legal definition for the use of the word "healthy" on a food or beverage that includes nutrient criteria. Any food that claims it is good for heart health must meet the minimum "healthy" nutrition requirements.

The FDA requires a food that claims "healthy" to meet the following guidelines:

- Be low in total fat and saturated fat

- Limit the amount of sodium (480 mg for individual foods and 600 mg for meal-type foods). Look for lower sodium levels to help reduce high blood pressure.

- Limit the amount of cholesterol (90 mg or less).

- Provide at least 10% Daily Value of one or more of the following: vitamin A, vitamin C, iron, calcium, protein, and fiber for single-item foods. Raw, canned, or frozen fruits and vegetables and certain grain products do not necessarily need to meet this criteria. These foods can be labeled "healthy" if they do not contain ingredients that change the nutritional profile and, in the case of enriched grain products, if they conform to the standards of identity, which call for certain required ingredients (vitamins, minerals, protein, or fiber).

- Meals and entrees (those large enough to be considered a meal—6 ounces or more) need 10% Daily Value of two nutrients (main dish product) or three nutrients (meal product) of vitamin A, vitamin C, iron, calcium, protein, and fiber.

In addition to these "healthy" nutrient requirements, there are FDA-approved health claims that are based on the "healthy" claim but add additional nutrient criteria. These health claims link a food and/or nutrient with a disease such as high blood pressure, heart disease, or cardiovascular health. You can read a list of these health claims with the nutrient criteria for making each claim on pages 25 to 30. Since health claims relate to specific types of foods or nutrients, such as omega-3s found in fish, nuts, and seeds, there are additional nutrient criteria beyond those listed above for "healthy."

In the introductory remarks for each food category, you will find a list of the health claims that pertain to that group of foods. At the end of the introductory material, you will find the specific nutrient criteria used for all the foods and beverages listed in each food category.

Introduction

If you or someone in your family is trying to follow a heart-healthy diet, this book is for you. Whether you are endeavoring to prevent heart disease or are dealing with a present heart condition, you will find assistance through useful shopping tips, label reading advice, lists of foods, and general heart-healthy diet suggestions.

Warning!

This book has been prepared for the consumer interested in eating heart-healthy foods either to prevent heart disease or to alleviate the signs of heart disease. The content of this book should not be considered medical advice. If you have a medical or health problem, you should consult your physician.

Every effort has been made to make *The Quick Check Food Guide to Heart Health* as complete and accurate as possible. However, the food industry is a dynamic and constantly changing industry, with new and reformulated products hitting the supermarket shelves daily. Therefore, this book should be used as a general guide, not as the ultimate source for product information. Always check the label and ingredients to make sure a food or beverage fits your dietary needs. If you have questions, contact the manufacturer. Find contact information for food and beverage manufacturers on pages 555 to 573.

Since heart disease covers a myriad of conditions—high blood pressure, coronary artery blockages, diabetes, etc., the information given is multifaceted and the foods listed meet multiple nutrient criteria. We have endeavored to limit the foods listed to the criteria listed, but with over 2,000 listed foods, there may be some slip-ups.

In addition, the nutritional recommendations for heart health are in flux. For instance, the sodium levels for those at risk for heart disease were recently lowered from 2,400 milligrams (mg) to 1,500 mg per day. The health and food industries are in the process of addressing this issue. For instance, the American Heart Association Heart Check Mark program is revising their sodium restrictions for eligible foods. You can check out the 2014 sodium limits at *www.heartcheckmark.org* and click on "Nutrition Guidelines." The criteria used in this book for sodium are the 2013 levels since most food companies have not had time to reformulate their products to lower sodium.

Furthermore, since there is no legal definition for a "Heart-Healthy" food, we are careful not to make that claim. The information provided and list of food and beverage products meet specific nutrient criteria based on current healthy recommendations that includes FDA approved Heart Health Claims, the American Heart Association guidelines, the DASH Diet, the 2010 U.S. Dietary Guidelines, the Choose MyPlate program, and other reliable resources. Check out the specific nutrient criteria in the introduction for each food category.

What Is Heart Disease?

Heart disease (or cardiovascular disease) refers to any disease that prevents the heart from functioning normally—including coronary artery disease, heart rhythm problems, heart defects, high blood pressure, angina (chest pains), poor circulation, inflammation, oxidative stress, and cardiomyopathy—thickening or enlargement of the heart muscle. The causes of heart disease are diverse but atherosclerosis (thickening and hardening of arteries) and/or hypertension (high blood pressure) are the most common.

According to the American Heart Association, about 81 million adults in the U.S. have at least one form of heart disease—disorders that prevent the heart from functioning normally. Experts say you can reduce the risk of developing these problems with lifestyle changes that include eating a healthy diet.

Poor eating and exercise habits could be the game changer in the fight against heart disease and stroke deaths, according to the American Heart Association's "Heart Disease and Stroke Statistical Update 2013."

What Is Your Risk for Heart Disease?

There are a number of risk factors for heart disease: age, gender, high blood pressure, high serum cholesterol levels, smoking, excessive alcohol consumption, family history, obesity, lack of physical activity, diabetes, and social and psychological factors. Some of these risk factors, such as age, gender, or family history, are irreversible; however, many important cardiovascular risk factors can be modified by lifestyle changes.

Knowing your risks for heart disease is important because it is the first step in making a personal plan for prevention.

Risk Factors You Can Control

Physical inactivity/sedentary lifestyle–Your heart is a muscle and just like all muscles it needs to be exercised to stay healthy. The American Heart

Association reports that 32% of adults report no aerobic activity; 18% of girls and 10% of boys, grades 9 to 12, report fewer than an hour of aerobic activity in the past week.

High total blood cholesterol–A blood cholesterol level above 240 mg/dL combined with a low HDL cholesterol level (less than 40 mg/dL) can cause a buildup of plaque in your arteries. The American Heart Association reports that about 13% of adults have a total cholesterol level of 240 mg/dL or higher. (Refer to page 14 for a discussion on controlling blood lipids.)

Being overweight or obese–Excess abdominal fat puts strain on the heart, raises blood cholesterol and triglyceride levels, and lowers HDL cholesterol levels. More adults age 20 and over are obese (34.6%) than normal or underweight (31.8%); 68% are overweight or obese. Among children ages 2 to 19, 32% are overweight or obese. (Learn more about healthy weight on page 17.)

High blood pressure–This condition causes the heart to work harder and to enlarge and weaken. The American Heart Association reports that 33% of adults have high blood pressure; African-Americans have among the highest prevalence of high blood pressure (44%) worldwide. (See more about blood pressure control on page 14.)

Diabetes–Keeping blood sugar under control is important because people with diabetes have a higher risk of dying from a heart attack. The American Heart Association statistics show that about 8% of adults have diagnosed diabetes, and 8% have undiagnosed diabetes; 38% have prediabetes. (Learn more about blood sugar control on page 16.)

Smoking–This includes cigarette, cigar, and pipe smoking as well as exposure to secondhand smoke. Despite four decades of improvement, the American Heart Association reports that 21% percent of men and about 17% of women age 18 and over still smoke cigarettes; 18% of students in grades 9 to 12 report cigarette smoking.

(Statistics are from the American Heart Association's "Heart Disease and Stroke Statistical Update 2013," published in the American Heart Association journal *Circulation*.)

Risk Factors You Can't Control

Heredity–If you have a father or brother who developed heart disease before age 50 or a mother or sister who was diagnosed with heart disease before age 65, you are at a greater risk of developing heart disease. African Americans who are more likely to have high blood pressure also have a greater risk. Although the DNA you inherit can't be changed, an evolving science, epigenetics, is showing that your environment can alter the expression of your genes and may lower your risk of heart disease.

Age and Gender–The risk of heart disease increases for men over the age of 45 and women over the age of 55. After menopause, women's LDL cholesterol often rises.

American Heart Association Recommendations

The American Heart Association recommends you protect your heart with their "Life Check Simple Seven:"

GET ACTIVE–Get at least 30 minutes of moderate physical activity each day (like brisk walking), five times per week.

EAT BETTER–A healthy diet is one of your best weapons for fighting cardiovascular disease.

CUT CHOLESTEROL–If your cholesterol is 200 mg/dL or higher, you need to take action.

LOSE WEIGHT–If you have too much fat—especially if a lot of it is at your waist —you're at higher risk for health problems such as high blood pressure, high blood cholesterol, and diabetes.

CONTROL BLOOD PRESSURE–High blood pressure is the single most significant risk factor for heart disease. Normal blood pressure is less than 120 mmHg systolic and less than 80 mmHg diastolic, or < 120/80. Losing weight and reducing sodium intake has shown to reduce blood pressure in some individuals.

REDUCE BLOOD SUGAR–If your fasting blood sugar level is below 100, you are in the healthy range. If not, your results could indicate diabetes or pre-diabetes.

STOP SMOKING–Cigarette smokers have a higher risk of developing cardiovascular disease.

Learn more at: *http://mylifecheck.heart.org*

Warning Signs of a Heart Attack, Cardiac Arrest, and Stroke

Heart Attack:

- **Chest discomfort or pain** in the center of the chest that lasts more than a few minutes or that goes away and comes back. It can feel like uncomfortable pressure, squeezing, fullness, or pain.

- **Discomfort in other areas of the upper body** that include pain or discomfort in one or both arms, the back, neck, jaw, or stomach.

- **Shortness of breath** with or without chest discomfort.

- **Other signs** may include breaking out in a cold sweat, nausea, or lightheadedness.

- **Warning signs for men and women may differ.** Men and women's most common heart attack symptom is chest pain or discomfort. But women are somewhat more likely than men to experience some of the other common symptoms, particularly shortness of breath, nausea/vomiting, and back or jaw pain.

Cardiac Arrest:

- **Sudden loss of responsiveness**—No response to tapping on arm or shoulders or to verbal questions.

- **No normal breathing**–The victim does not take a normal breath when you tilt the head up and check for at least five seconds. Immediately call 9-1-1 and start CPR.

Stroke:

F.A.S.T. is an easy way to remember the sudden signs of stroke. When you can spot the signs, you'll know that you need to call 9-1-1 for help right away. F.A.S.T. is:

- **Face Drooping**–Does one side of the face droop or is it numb? Ask the person to smile. Is the person's smile uneven?

- **Arm Weakness**–Is one arm weak or numb? Ask the person to raise both arms. Does one arm drift downward?

- **Speech Difficulty**–Is speech slurred? Is the person unable to speak or hard to understand? Ask the person to repeat a simple sentence, like "The sky is blue." Is the sentence repeated correctly?

- **Time to call 9-1-1**–If someone shows any of these symptoms, even if the symptoms go away, call 9-1-1 and get the person to the hospital immediately. Check the time so that you know when the first symptoms appeared.

Learn the signs, but remember—minutes matter! Fast action can save lives. Don't wait more than five minutes to call 9-1-1.

Difference Between a Heart Attack, Cardiac Arrest, and Stroke

- **A Heart Attack** occurs when a coronary artery (one of the arteries that supplies blood to the heart muscle) becomes suddenly blocked. The sudden blockage robs a portion of the heart muscle of its vital blood supply, and the muscle dies. So a heart attack is the death of a part of the heart muscle.

- **Cardiac Arrest** is caused by a sudden heart arrhythmia called ventricular fibrillation. In ventricular fibrillation, the electrical signals within the heart suddenly become completely chaotic. Because these electrical signals control the timing and the organization of the heartbeat, when the signals degenerate to total chaos, the heart suddenly stops beating.

- **A Stroke** happens when blood flow to a part of the brain stops due to the blockage of an artery. If blood flow is stopped for longer than a few seconds, the brain cannot get oxygen, which results in the death of brain cells, causing permanent damage.

Why Eat Better?

When you eat a heart-healthy diet, you improve your chances for feeling good and staying healthy. However, an alarmingly high number of people are not making healthy food choices. Recent studies show that more than 90% of people fail to consistently eat a heart-healthy diet. Additionally, *Produce for Better Health* reports that more than 90% of Americans consume fewer fruits and vegetables than the daily amount recommended by the *Dietary Guidelines for Americans*, which ranges from 2 to 6½ cups. On a more positive note, whole grains are of mounting interest to the U.S. shopper. Sixty-one percent of shoppers report boosting their intake of whole grains in the past two years according to a *Health Focus Trend Report*. Poor eating habits puts you at a higher risk for heart disease, stroke, diabetes, and obesity.

What Is a "Heart Healthy" Food?

There is no legal definition for a "heart-healthy" food, although there is a legal definition for a "healthy" food. The FDA requires a food that claims to be "healthy" to meet the following guidelines:

- Be low in total fat and saturated fat.

- Limit the amount of sodium (480 mg for individual foods and 600 mg for meal-type foods). These levels are high for heart health and many hospital programs recommend lower sodium levels.

- Limited in cholesterol (90 mg or less).

- Provides at least 10% Daily Value of one or more of the following: vitamin A, vitamin C, iron, calcium, protein, and fiber (for single-item foods). Raw, canned, or frozen fruits and vegetables and certain cereal-grain products do not necessarily need to meet this criteria. These foods can be labeled "healthy" if they do not contain ingredients that change the nutritional profile, and, in the case of enriched grain products, if they conform to the standards of identity, which call for certain required ingredients (vitamins, minerals, protein, or fiber).

- Meals and entrees (those large enough to be considered a meal—6 ounces or more) need 10% Daily Value of two nutrients (main dish product) or three nutrients (meal product): vitamin A, vitamin C, iron, calcium, protein, and fiber.

Although there is no legal definition for a heart-healthy food, any food that claims it is good for heart health must meet the minimum "healthy" requirements above just because it uses the word "healthy." Another way to claim "heart healthy" is to meet the requirements for a Health Claim or Qualified Health Claim that links a food and nutrient with a disease such as high blood pressure, heart disease, or cardiovascular health. You can see a list of health claims that relate to heart disease on pages 25 to 30.

Heart-Healthy Diets

Since heart health involves a myriad of risk factors and recommendations, there are a variety of food plans that have been developed to treat and prevent heart disease. The following food plans address the issues of heart health. They have many commonalities but focus on different nutrients and foods. Choose the one that fits your needs and lifestyle. Or check out our "Bottom Line" recommendations on page 41.

The foods listed in this book will follow guidelines that take all these different recommendations into consideration, along with the information available on food labels. Each food category will give you the criteria used in choosing the foods and beverages listed in this book.

2010 U.S. Dietary Guidelines for General Health

These basic guidelines, based on scientific research, are updated every five years by the FDA. They provide nutrition criteria for general health that includes heart health. The practical application of the Dietary Guidelines is given in the MyPlate program described on page 11.

Foods and Nutrients to Reduce

- Reduce daily sodium intake to less than 2,300 mg and further reduce intake to 1,500 mg among persons who are 51 and older and those of any age who are African American or have hypertension, diabetes, or chronic kidney disease. The 1,500 mg recommendation applies to about half of the U.S. population, including children, and the majority of adults.

- Consume less than 10% of calories from saturated fatty acids by replacing them with monounsaturated and polyunsaturated fatty acids.

- Consume less than 300 mg per day of dietary cholesterol. Consuming less than 200 mg per day can further help individuals at high risk of cardiovascular disease.

- Keep trans fatty acid consumption as low as possible by limiting foods that contain synthetic sources of trans fats, such as partially hydrogenated oils, and by limiting other solid fats (hydrogenated fats).

- Reduce the intake of calories from solid fats (hydrogenated) and added sugars.

- Avoid the consumption of foods that contain refined grains, especially refined grain foods that contain solid fats, added sugars, and sodium.

- If alcohol is consumed, it should be consumed in moderation—up to one drink per day for women and two drinks per day for men—and only by adults of legal drinking age.

Foods and Nutrients to Increase

Individuals should meet the following recommendations as part of a healthy eating pattern while staying within their calorie needs.

- Increase vegetable and fruit intake.

- Eat a variety of vegetables, especially dark green, red and orange vegetables as well as beans and peas.

- Consume at least half of all grains as whole grains. Increase whole grain intake by replacing refined grains with whole grains.

- Increase intake of fat-free or low-fat milk and milk products, such as milk, yogurt, cheese, or fortified soy beverages.

- Choose a variety of protein foods, which include seafood, lean meat and poultry, eggs, beans and peas, soy products, and unsalted nuts and seeds.

- Increase the amount and variety of seafood consumed by choosing seafood in place of some meat and poultry. Eat seafood at least 2 times per week.

- Replace protein foods that are higher in solid fats with choices that are lower in solid fats and calories and/or are sources of oils.

- Use oils to replace solid fats where possible. The best oils for heart health are olive and canola oil rather than soy or corn oil.

- Choose foods that provide more potassium, dietary fiber, calcium, and vitamin D, which are key nutrients in American diets. These foods include vegetables, fruits, whole grains, and milk and milk products.

Read more about the 2010 U.S. Dietary Guidelines–
http://www.cnpp.usda.gov/dgas2010-policydocument.htm

MyPlate – U.S. Dietary Guidelines for Consumers

MyPlate is based on the 2010 U.S. Dietary Guidelines and illustrates the five food groups that are the building blocks for a healthy diet using a familiar image—a place setting for a meal. Before you eat, visualize this distribution of the major food groups on your plate. Think about the portions of foods that go on your plate or in your cup or bowl. Here are some basic MyPlate messages:

- **Balancing Calories**
    - Enjoy your food, but eat less.
    - Avoid oversized portions.
- **Foods to Increase**
    - Make half your plate fruits and vegetables.
    - Make at least half your grains whole grains.
    - Switch to fat-free or low-fat (1%) milk.
- **Foods to Reduce**
    - Compare sodium in foods like soup, bread, and frozen meals, and choose the foods with lower numbers.
    - Drink water instead of sugary drinks.

Learn more about MyPlate at *www.choosemyplate.gov*.

The Mediterranean Diet for Heart Health

Another general plan for healthy eating is the traditional Mediterranean diet that research has shown can reduce the risk of heart disease. In fact, a recent analysis of more than 1.5 million healthy adults demonstrated that following a Mediterranean diet was associated with a reduced risk of overall and cardiovascular mortality, a reduced incidence of cancer and cancer mortality, and a reduced incidence of Parkinson's and Alzheimer's diseases.

Key Components of the Mediterranean Diet

- Get plenty of exercise.

- Eat primarily plant-based foods, such as fruits and vegetables, whole grains, legumes, and nuts.

- Replace butter with healthy fats such as olive oil and canola oil.

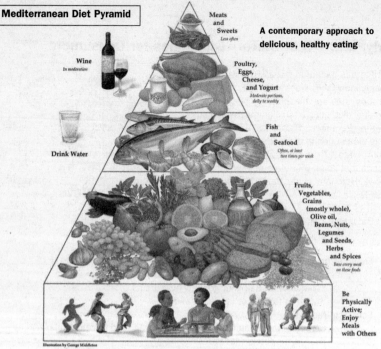

Mediterranean Diet Pyramid

A contemporary approach to delicious, healthy eating

Meats and Sweets
Less often

Wine
In moderation

Poultry, Eggs, Cheese, and Yogurt
Moderate portions, daily to weekly

Fish and Seafood
Often, at least two times per week

Drink Water

Fruits, Vegetables, Grains (mostly whole), Olive oil, Beans, Nuts, Legumes and Seeds, Herbs and Spices
Base every meal on these foods

Be Physically Active; Enjoy Meals with Others

Illustration by George Middleton

© 2009 Oldways Preservation and Exchange Trust • www.oldwayspt.org

- Use herbs and spices instead of salt to flavor foods.

- Limit red meat to no more than a few times a month.

- Eat fish and poultry at least twice a week.

- Drink red wine in moderation (optional).

- The diet also recognizes the importance of enjoying meals with family and friends.

Learn more about the Mediterranean Diet–
http://oldwayspt.org/resources/heritage-pyramids/mediterranean-pyramid/overview

DASH Diet for High Blood Pressure

DASH stands for Dietary Approaches to Stop Hypertension. The DASH diet is a life-long approach to healthy eating that is designed to help treat or prevent high blood pressure (hypertension). The DASH diet encourages you to reduce the sodium in your diet and eat a variety of foods rich in nutrients that help lower blood pressure, such as potassium, calcium, and magnesium.

What Is High Blood Pressure?

Blood pressure is the force of blood pushing against the walls of the arteries as the heart pumps out blood. High blood pressure, or hypertension, is dangerous because it makes your heart work too hard. The condition can damage your blood vessels and organs, such as your heart, kidneys, brain, and eyes. High blood pressure stretches your arteries past their healthy limit and causes microscopic tears. Your body then kicks into injury-healing mode to repair these tears with scar tissue. But, unfortunately, the scar tissue traps plaque and white blood cells, which can form into blockages, blood clots, and hardened, weakened arteries. That is why high blood pressure can lead to stroke, heart attack, kidney failure, and even heart failure.

How Do You Measure Blood Pressure?

Blood pressure includes systolic and diastolic pressures. "Systolic" refers to blood pressure when the heart beats while pumping blood. "Diastolic" refers to blood pressure when the heart is at rest between beats. You'll most often see blood pressure numbers written with the systolic number above or before the diastolic number, such as 120/80 mmHg. (The mmHg is millimeters of mercury—the units used to measure blood pressure.)

Blood pressure is considered high if it stays at or above 140/90 mmHg over time. If you have diabetes or chronic kidney disease, high blood pressure is defined as 130/80 mmHg or higher. A diagnosis of high blood pressure is based on an average of two or more properly measured, seated blood pressure readings done during two or more doctor's office visits.

Categories for Blood Pressure Levels in Adults
(measured in millimeters of mercury, or mmHg)

Category	Systolic (top number)		Diastolic (bottom number)
Normal	Less than 120	and	Less than 80
Prehypertension	120–139	or	80–89
High blood pressure			
Stage 1	140–159	or	90–99
Stage 2	160 or higher	or	100 or higher

High blood pressure can be controlled if you take these steps:

- Maintain a healthy weight.

- Be moderately physically active on most days of the week.

- Follow a healthy eating plan, which includes foods lower in sodium.

- If you drink alcoholic beverages, do so in moderation.

- If you have high blood pressure and are prescribed medication, take it as directed.

Follow the DASH Eating Plan to Reduce High Blood Pressure

Here's a look at the recommended servings from each food group for the 2,000-calorie-a-day DASH diet.

Grains: 6 to 8 servings a day

Vegetables: 4 to 5 servings a day

Fruits: 4 to 5 servings a day

Dairy: 2 to 3 servings a day

Lean meat, poultry, and fish: 6 oz or less a day

Nuts, seeds, and legumes: 4 to 5 servings a week

Fats and oils: 2 to 3 servings a day

Sweets: 5 or fewer a week

Alcohol: 2 or fewer drinks a day for men; for women one or less.

Sodium: 2,300 mg or less per day or 1,500 mg or less per day for those over 51, African-Americans, or those with high blood pressure.

Learn more about the DASH Diet Eating Plan at
http://www.nhlbi.nih.gov/health/public/heart/hbp/dash/new_dash.pdf

American Heart Association Dietary Goals for Cardiovascular Health

The American Heart Association says that a healthy diet is one of your best weapons for fighting cardiovascular disease. They emphasize foods low in saturated and trans fat, cholesterol, sodium and added sugars, and foods high in whole grain fiber, lean protein, and a variety of colorful fruits and vegetables. These are the specific recommendations for an adult consuming 2,000 calories:

- Balance calorie intake and physical activity to maintain a healthy body weight.
- Consume a diet rich in fruits and vegetables: at least 4.5 cups a day.
- Choose fiber-rich whole grains: at least three 1 oz. equivalent servings a day.
- Limit intake of saturated fat: less than 7% of total energy intake.
- Limit trans fat: less than 1% of energy intake.
- Limit intake of cholesterol: less than 300 mg per day; 200 mg if you already have heart disease.
- Limit intake of processed meats: no more than 2 servings a week.
- Include nuts, legumes, and seeds: at least 4 servings a week.
- Consume fish (preferably oily fish): at least two 3.5 oz. servings a week.
- Minimize intake of beverages and foods with added sugar: limit sugar-sweetened beverages to less than 450 calories (36 oz.) per week.
- Limit sodium: less than 1,500 mg a day.
- If consuming alcohol, do so in moderation.

Source: Circulation, 2010; 121:586-813

Look for the American Heart Association Heart-Check Mark

The Heart-Check mark makes it easy to spot heart-healthy foods in the grocery store. Simply look for the name of the American Heart Association along with their familiar red heart with a white check mark on the package or on grocery shelf hang tags. But not all red hearts you see on foods are from the American Heart Association so look for the American Heart Association name to be sure.

When you spot the American Heart Association's Heart-Check mark, you'll instantly know the food has been certified to meet the American Heart Association's guidelines for a heart-healthy food. It's a good first step in creating an overall sensible eating plan.

For more information on the Heart-Check Mark go to *www.heartcheckmark.org.*

Diabetes—Controlling Blood Sugar

What Is Diabetes?

Diabetes is a condition that affects the way your body converts sugar and starch into energy. Most of the food we eat is turned into blood sugar (glucose) that our body uses for energy. To get the blood sugar into the cells where it is needed, our bodies produce a substance called insulin. When your body stops making insulin or the insulin stops doing its job, sugar stays in the blood and your blood sugar level rises to a dangerous level. People with this condition are often tired because their cells are not getting energy. If your blood sugar level (glucose) is over 100, you should be concerned and consult a physician.

There are 2 main types of diabetes:

Type 1 – In this form of diabetes, your body does not produce insulin and you need to take daily insulin shots to get the blood sugar into your cells for energy.

Type 2 – With this type of diabetes, your body doesn't produce enough insulin or the body doesn't respond to insulin normally. About 80% of people with type 2 diabetes are overweight and blood glucose levels can be controlled through food choices, weight control, and physical activity.

What Can I Do to Reduce Blood Sugar?

If you have diabetes or prediabetes is detected, you need to look at your eating habits, control your weight, and get adequate exercise to control your blood sugar. It is critical for people with diabetes to have regular checkups, and your doctor may prescribe drugs. In general, you should:

- Reduce the consumption of added sugars that are mainly found in cereal, candy, sugary desserts, and beverages.
- Eat regular meals and always combine a moderate amount of carbohydrates along with a source of protein—meat, fish, beans, or dairy.
- Get regular exercise. Moderate-intensity aerobic activity helps your body respond to insulin.

Carbohydrate Counting to Control Blood Sugar

Carbohydrates are part of a healthy diet for everyone, but because carbohydrates—both starches and sugars—affect blood glucose levels more than any other nutrient, they need to be monitored if you have diabetes or are at risk for diabetes. A plan that sets limits on the grams of carbohydrates for each meal can help control blood sugar. For example, you might set your goal at 45 to 60 grams for each meal and 20 grams for snacks. Your carbohydrate needs will vary depending on the amount of calories you need. Use the food lists in this book that include grams of carbohydrates to help you control your blood sugar levels.

Maintaining a Healthy Weight

Too much fat, especially at your waist, makes you at higher risk for such health problems as high blood pressure, high blood cholesterol, and diabetes. Obesity is now recognized as a major, independent risk factor for heart disease. It is important for heart health to know your ideal weight and maintain that weight. A good way to tell if you need to lose weight is to calculate your body mass index.

Body Mass Index

Body mass index (BMI) is a number calculated from a person's weight and height. BMI provides a reliable indicator of body fat for most people and is used to screen for weight categories that may lead to health problems. It is a useful, indirect measure of body composition because it correlates highly with body fat in most people. If your BMI is 25 or higher, you will benefit by bringing your number down below 25. If your BMI is 30 or higher, you are at significant risk for heart health problems. You can calculate your BMI with the chart below.

Body Mass Index (BMI) Chart

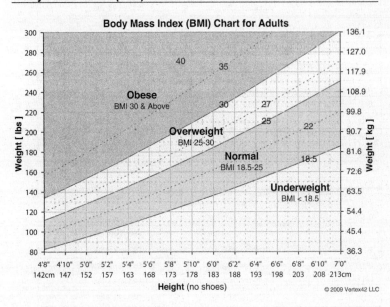

Ideal Weight Chart

Height	Ideal Male Weight	Ideal Female Weight
4'6"	63–77 lbs.	63–77 lbs.
4'7"	68–84 lbs.	68–83 lbs.
4'8"	74–90 lbs.	72–88 lbs.
4'9"	79–97 lbs.	77–94 lbs.
4'10"	85–103 lbs.	81–99 lbs.
4'11"	90–110 lbs.	86–105 lbs.
5'0"	95–117 lbs.	90–110 lbs.
5'1"	101–123 lbs.	95–116 lbs.
5'2"	106–130 lbs.	99–121 lbs.
5'3"	112–136 lbs.	104–127 lbs.
5'4"	117–143 lbs.	108–132 lbs.
5'5"	122–150 lbs.	113–138 lbs.
5'6"	128–156 lbs.	117–143 lbs.
5'7"	133–163 lbs.	122–149 lbs.
5' 8"	139–169 lbs.	126–154 lbs.
5' 9"	144–176 lbs.	131–160 lbs.
5'10"	149–183 lbs.	135–165 lbs.
5'11"	155–189 lbs.	140–171 lbs.
6'0"	160–196 lbs.	144–176 lbs.
6'1"	166–202 lbs.	149–182 lbs.
6'2"	171–209 lbs.	153–187 lbs.
6'3"	176–216 lbs.	158–193 lbs.
6'4"	182–222 lbs.	162–198 lbs.
6'5"	187–229 lbs.	167–204 lbs.
6'6"	193–235 lbs.	171–209 lbs.
6'7"	198–242 lbs.	176–215 lbs.
6'8"	203–249 lbs.	180–220 lbs.
6'9"	209–255 lbs.	185–226 lbs.
6'10"	214–262 lbs.	189–231 lbs.
6'11"	220–268 lbs.	194–237 lbs.
7'0"	225–275 lbs.	198–242 lbs.

Reading Food Labels

To follow a heart-healthy diet it is imperative that you understand and read food labels—especially nutrition and health claims. But also realize that just because a food makes a health or nutrition claim, it does not mean that a food is healthy and the best choice for your particular needs. You should always look at the Nutrition Facts and balance the claim based on the nutrition information and ingredients. A food may claim to be low fat but be higher in calories or sodium. Or it may say "reduced sodium" and still be higher in sodium than you want.

Using Nutrition Facts
(see following page)

Nutrient Content Claims

Nutrient Content Claims describe the level of a nutrient in a single serving of a food. These guidelines use the term "reference amount," which is basically a serving unless the serving is less than 30 grams, then the claim is calculated on 50 grams. These terms, defined by the FDA and USDA, ensure that they mean the same thing on every product.

FREE–An amount of a substance so small that it probably won't have an effect on the body. Synonyms for "free" are "zero," "no," "without," "trivial source of," and "negligible source of," and "dietary insignificant source of." Free claims that signal "heart healthy" are "trans-fat-free," "cholesterol free," and "saturated fat free." Since an amount less than 0.5 grams can be labeled as "Free," this means that a small amount of that nutrient may still be found in a product. This can be a concern with Trans Fat that is damaging in small amounts. Check the ingredient list for "partially hydrogenated oils" to make sure that a product is truly "Trans Fat Free."

LOW–An amount specifically defined for each term, such as "low-calorie," "low-fat," or "low-sodium." Synonyms for "low" are "little," "few" (for calories), "contains a small amount of," and "low source of." For heart health, look for "low fat," "low saturated fat," "low cholesterol," and "low sodium."

Using Nutrition Facts

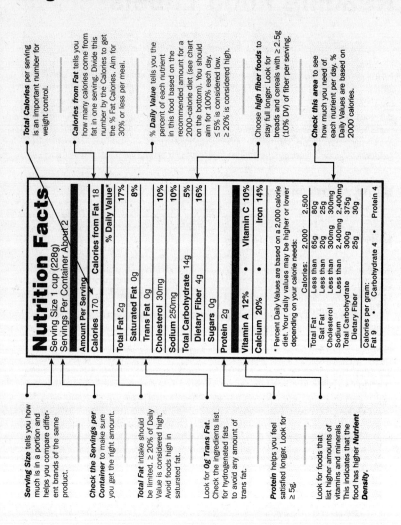

Total Calories per serving is an important number for weight control.

Calories from Fat tells you how many calories come from fat in one serving. Divide this number by the Calories to get the % Fat Calories. Aim for 30% or less per meal.

% Daily Value tells you the percent of each nutrient in this food based on the recommended amount for a 2000-calorie diet (see chart on the bottom). You should aim for 100% each day. ≤ 5% is considered low. ≥ 20% is considered high.

Choose **high fiber foods** to stay full longer. Look for breads and cereals with ≥ 2.5g (10% DV) of fiber per serving.

Check this area to see how much you need of each nutrient per day. % Daily Values are based on 2000 calories.

Serving Size tells you how much is in a portion and helps you compare differ-ent brands of the same product.

Check the Servings per Container to make sure you get the right amount.

Total Fat intake should be limited. ≥ 20% of Daily Value is considered high. Avoid foods high in saturated fat.

Look for **0g Trans Fat**. Check the ingredients list for hydrogenated fats to avoid any amount of trans fat.

Protein helps you feel satisfied longer. Look for ≥ 5g.

Look for foods that list higher amounts of vitamins and minerals. This indicates that the food has higher **Nutrient Density**.

Nutrition Facts

Serving Size 1 cup (228g)
Servings Per Container About 2

Amount Per Serving

Calories 170 Calories from Fat 18

	% Daily Value*
Total Fat 2g	17%
Saturated Fat 0g	8%
Trans Fat 0g	
Cholesterol 30mg	10%
Sodium 250mg	10%
Total Carbohydrate 14g	5%
Dietary Fiber 4g	16%
Sugars 0g	
Protein 0g	

Vitamin A 12%	•	Vitamin C 10%	
Calcium 20%	•	Iron 14%	

*Percent Daily Values are based on a 2,000 calorie diet. Your daily values may be higher or lower depending on your calorie needs:

	Calories:	2,000	2,500
Total Fat	Less than	65g	80g
Sat Fat	Less than	20g	25g
Cholesterol	Less than	300mg	300mg
Sodium	Less than	2,400mg	2,400mg
Total Carbohydrate		300g	375g
Dietary Fiber		25g	30g

Calories per gram:
Fat 9 • Carbohydrate 4 • Protein 4

REDUCED/LESS–Refers to a food with at least 25% less calories, fat, saturated fat, cholesterol or sodium than a comparable food. Synonyms for "reduced/less" are "lower" or "fewer" (for calories). Heart-healthy claims to look for are "reduced sodium," "lower in total fat," and "fewer calories." The label should also tell you the food it is less than and the difference in the amount of sodium, fat, calories, etc.

HIGH–Designates that the product contains 25% or more of the Daily Value for a given nutrient. Examples of heart-healthy high claims are "high in omega-3s," "high potassium," or "high calcium."

GOOD SOURCE–Designates that the product contains 10 to 19% of the Daily Value of the nutrient. Find this claim on nutrients that will benefit heart health—omega-3s, potassium, calcium, and fiber.

LIGHT–Designates that a food has one-third fewer calories or 50% less fat than the traditional version of the food. Find this claim on salad dressings that are lower in total fat, soups with less sodium, and ice cream with fewer calories. Look for a statement on the label that tells the product it is being compared with and the amount of the reduction.

HEALTHY–Can only be used on labels for foods that are low in total fat and saturated fats and contain specific levels of cholesterol, sodium, and other vitamins and minerals. See "What Is a Heart-Healthy" Food? on page 6.

CALORIES–These claims are especially important if you are trying to lose weight. You should balance calorie intake with physical activity to maintain a healthy body weight.

   Free: Less than 5 calories per reference amount and per labeled serving.
   Low: 40 calories or less per reference amount.

   Reduced/Less: At least 25% fewer calories per reference amount than an appropriate reference food. Reference food may not be "low calorie." Uses term "fewer" rather than "less."

   Light or Lite: If 50% or more of the calories are from fat, the fat must be reduced by at least 50% per reference amount. If less than 50% of calories are from fat, the fat must be reduced by at least 50% or calories reduced by at least 1/3 per reference amount.

TOTAL FAT—The type of fat is more important than the total fat. For heart health, it is vital to reduce the amount of saturated and trans fat in a product. Include good fats like mono and polyunsaturated fats and omega-3 fats. Remember that fat is a concentrated source of calories (9 calories in each gram), so even good fats can add to weight gain and impede weight loss.

> **Free:** Less than 0.5 grams per reference amount and per labeled serving.
> Low: 3 grams or less per reference amount (and per 50 grams if reference amount is small).

> **Reduced/Less:** At least 25% less fat per reference amount than an appropriate reference food. Reference food may not be "low fat."

> **Light:** Food must be "fat free."

SATURATED FAT—These are the bad fats that you should try to reduce. The American Heart Association recommends having less than 7% of your calories come from saturated fats. This is about 15 grams of saturated fat per day for a 2,000-calorie diet. Another form of saturated fat is trans fat. The American Heart Association recommends limiting trans fats to less than 1% of calories, which is about 2 grams a day.

Next to all saturated fat claims, the manufacturer must declare the amount of cholesterol if 2 milligrams or more per reference amount and the amount of total fat if more than 3 grams per reference amount (or 0.5 grams or more of total fat for "saturated fat–free").

> **Free:** Less than 0.5 grams saturated fat and less than 0.5 grams trans fatty acids per reference amount and per labeled serving.

> **Low:** 1 gram or less per reference amount and 15% or less of calories from saturated fat.

> **Reduced/Less:** At least 25% less saturated fat per reference amount than an appropriate reference food. Reference food may not be "low saturated fat."

> **Dietary Supplements:** Saturated fat claims cannot be made for products that are 40 calories or less per serving.

CHOLESTEROL—The American Heart Association recommends limiting cholesterol to 300 milligrams or less per day or 200 mg per day if you already have heart disease. One egg yolk contains about 200 mg cholesterol.

Cholesterol claims are only allowed when a food contains 2 grams or less of saturated fat per serving; or for meals and main dish products, claims are only allowed per labeled serving size for "free" claims or per 100 grams for "low" and "reduced/less" claims. Manufacturers must declare the amount of total fat next to the cholesterol claim when fat exceeds 13 grams per reference amount and labeled serving.

Free: Less than 5 milligrams per reference amount and per labeled serving (or for meals and main dishes, less than 2 milligrams per labeled serving). No ingredient that contains cholesterol except if the ingredient listed in the ingredient statement has an asterisk that refers to footnote (e.g., "* adds a trivial amount of fat").

Low: 20 milligrams or less per reference amount.

Reduced/Less: At least 25% less cholesterol per reference amount than an appropriate reference food. Reference food may not be "low cholesterol."

Dietary Supplements: Cholesterol claims cannot be made for products that are 40 calories or less per serving.

SODIUM—Pay attention to sodium claims because a low-sodium diet is important for high blood pressure. The current recommendation is 2,300 mg of sodium a day for the general population and 1,500 mg per day if you are over 51, have an elevated blood pressure or diabetes, or are African-American.

Free: Less than 5 milligrams per reference amount and per labeled serving. No ingredient that is sodium chloride or generally understood to contain sodium except if the ingredient listed in the ingredient statement has an asterisk that refers to footnote (e.g., "* adds a trivial amount of sodium").

Low: 140 milligrams or less per reference amount (and per 50 grams if reference amount is small).

Reduced/Less: At least 25% less sodium per reference amount than an appropriate reference food. Reference food may not be "low sodium."

Light (for sodium-reduced products): If food is "low calorie" and "low fat" and sodium is reduced by at least 50%.

Light in Sodium: If sodium is reduced by at least 50% per reference amount. Light in sodium for meals is equivalent to "low in sodium."

Very Low Sodium: 35 milligrams or less per reference amount.

Salt Free: Must meet criterion for "sodium free."

No Salt Added and Unsalted: Must declare "This is not a sodium-free food" on the information panel if the food is not "sodium free."

Lightly Salted: 50% less sodium than normally added to reference food, and if not "low sodium," it must be so labeled on the information panel.

SUGAR–Reducing sugar, especially added sugars, is important for blood sugar control for people with diabetes or prediabetes.

"No added sugars" and "without added sugars" are allowed on the packaging of foods if no sugar or sugar-containing ingredient is added during processing. The manufacturer must state if the food is not "low" or "reduced calorie." The terms "unsweetened" and "no added sweeteners" remain as factual statements.

Free: Less than 0.5 grams of sugar per reference amount and per labeled serving. No ingredient that is a sugar or generally understood to contain sugars, except if the ingredient listed in the ingredient statement has an asterisk that refers to a footnote (e.g., "* adds a trivial amount of fat"). Must disclose calorie profile (e.g., "low calorie").

Low: Not Defined. The FDA does not provide a basis for recommended intake.

Reduced/Less: At least 25% less sugars per reference amount than an appropriate reference food. This claim may not be used on dietary supplements of vitamins and minerals.

FIBER–Fiber is important for digestion and preventing conditions such as heart disease, diabetes, obesity, diverticulitis, and constipation.

High Fiber: Greater than or equal to 5 grams of fiber per serving and must meet the definition for low fat, or the level of total fat must appear next to the high fiber claim.

Good Source of Fiber: Between 2.5 and 4.9 grams of fiber per serving.

More or Added Fiber: Greater than or equal to 2.5 grams or more of fiber per serving than reference food.

FDA-approved Heart Health Claims on Food Lab

Health Claims link a food or food component with a lowered risk for some chronic disease. These claims are strictly regulated by the FDA and are supported by scientific evidence. Since including a health claim on a food label is optional, some foods that meet the criteria may not carry a claim. Read the Nutrition Facts to determine if a food is right for you. Here are the health claims that have been approved that relate to heart health—hypertension, coronary heart disease, diabetes, and stroke.

Approved Claims	Food Requirements	Claim Statements
Sodium and Hypertension *(21 CFR 101.74)*	Low sodium	*Diets low in sodium may reduce the risk of high blood pressure, a disease associated with many factors.*
Dietary Saturated Fat and Cholesterol, and Risk of Coronary Heart Disease *(21 CFR 101.75)*	Low saturated fat, Low cholesterol, and Low fat	*While many factors affect heart disease, diets low in saturated fat and cholesterol may reduce the risk of this disease.*
Fruits, Vegetables, and Grain Products That Contain Fiber, Particularly Soluble Fiber, and Risk of Coronary Heart Disease *(21 CFR 101.77)*	A fruit, vegetable, or grain product that contains fiber; Low saturated fat; Low cholesterol; Low fat; At least 0.6 grams of soluble fiber per RACC* (without fortification); and Soluble fiber content provided on label	*Diets low in saturated fat and cholesterol and rich in fruits, vegetables, and grain products that contain some types of dietary fiber, particularly soluble fiber, may reduce the risk of heart disease, a disease associated with many factors.*

*RACC – Reference amount customarily consumed as determined by FDA.

(continued on following page)

Approved Claims	Food Requirements	Claim Statements
Soluble Fiber from Certain Foods and Risk of Coronary Heart Disease (21 CFR 101.81)	Low saturated fat, low cholesterol, and low fat. *Eligible Sources of Soluble Fiber are:* 1) Oat bran 2) Rolled oats ✓ 3) Whole oat flour 4) Oatrim 5) Whole-grain barley and dry-milled barley 6) Barley beta fiber 7) Soluble fiber from psyllium husk with purity of no less than 95% The amount of soluble fiber per RACC* must be declared in nutrition label.	*Soluble fiber from foods such as [name of soluble fiber source and, if desired, name of food product], as part of a diet low in saturated fat and cholesterol, may reduce the risk of heart disease. A serving of [name of food product] supplies __ grams of the [necessary daily dietary intake for the benefit] soluble fiber from [name of soluble fiber source] necessary per day to have this effect.*
✗ **Soy Protein and Risk of Coronary Heart Disease** (21 CFR 101.82)	At least 6.25g soy protein per RACC* Low saturated fat, Low cholesterol, and Low fat (except that foods made from whole soybeans that contain no fat in addition to that inherent in the whole soybean are exempt from the "low fat" requirement)	*(1) 25g of soy protein a day, as part of a diet low in saturated fat and cho-lesterol, may reduce the risk of heart disease. A serving of [name of food] supplies __ grams of soy protein.* *(2) Diets low in saturated fat and cholesterol that include 25g of soy pro-tein a day may reduce the risk of heart disease. One serving of [name of food] provides __ grams of soy protein.*

*RACC – Reference amount customarily consumed as determined by FDA.

Plant Sterol/Stanol Esters and Risk of Coronary Heart Disease *(21 CFR 101.83)*	At least 0.65g plant sterol esters per RACC* of spreads and salad dressings, or At least 1.7g plant stanol esters per RACC* of spreads, salad dressings, snack bars, and dietary supplements. Low saturated fat and low cholesterol.	*(1) Foods containing at least 0.65g per of vegetable oil sterol esters, eaten twice a day with meals for a daily total intake of least 1.3g, as part of a diet low in saturated fat and cholesterol, may reduce the risk of heart disease. A serving of [name of food] supplies __ grams of vegetable oil sterol esters.* *(2) Diets low in saturated fat and cholesterol that include two servings of foods that provide a daily total of at least 3.4g of plant stanol esters in two meals may reduce the risk of heart disease. A serving of [name of food] supplies __ grams of plant stanol esters.*
Potassium and the Risk of High Blood Pressure and Stroke *(Docket No. 2000Q-1582)*	Good source of potassium, Low sodium, Low total fat, Low saturated fat, and Low cholesterol	*"Diets containing foods that are a good source of potassium and that are low in sodium may reduce the risk of high blood pressure and stroke."*
Saturated Fat, Cholesterol, and Trans Fat, and Reduced Risk of Heart Disease *(Docket No. 2006Q-0458)*	Low saturated fat, Low cholesterol, Contains less than 0.5g trans fat per RACC*, and Contains less than 6.5g total fat	*"Diets low in saturated fat and cholesterol, and as low as possible in trans fat, may reduce the risk of heart disease."*

*RACC – Reference amount customarily consumed as determined by FDA.

(continued on following page)

(continued from preceding page)

Approved Claims	Food Requirements	Claim Statements
Whole Grain Foods and Risk of Heart Disease and Certain Cancers *(Docket No. 1999P-2209)*	Low fat, Contains 51 percent or more whole grain ingredients by weight per RACC*, and Dietary fiber content at least: • 3.0g per RACC* of 55g • 2.8g per RACC* of 50g • 2.5g per RACC* of 45g • 1.7g per RACC* of 35g	*"Diets rich in whole-grain foods and other plant foods and low in total fat, saturated fat, and cholesterol may reduce the risk of heart disease and some cancers."*

http://www.fda.gov/Food/GuidanceRegulation/GuidanceDocumentsRegulatoryInformation/LabelingNutrition/ucm064919.htm-

Qualified Health Claims–Qualified health claims are based on emerging evidence of a relationship between a food or food component and a health-related condition or reduced risk of a disease. The scientific evidence for a qualified health claim is not as strong as that of a health claim based on scientific agreement, so it needs qualifying language. To identify a "Qualified Health Claim" look for qualifying language such as "scientific evidence suggests but does not prove," "supportive but not conclusive research," and "may."

Qualified Health Claims	Eligible Foods	Claim Statements
Nuts and Heart Disease *Docket No. 2002P-0505 07/14/2003 enforcement discretion letter*	Types of nuts eligible for this claim are restricted to almonds, hazelnuts, peanuts, pecans, some pine nuts, pistachio nuts, and walnuts. Eligible nuts may not exceed 4g saturated fat per 50g of nuts.	*Scientific evidence suggests but does not prove that eating 1.5 oz. per day of most nuts [such as name of specific nut] as part of a diet low in saturated fat and cholesterol may reduce the risk of heart disease. [See nutrition information for fat content.]*

*RACC   Reference amount customarily consumed as determined by FDA.

(continued from preceding page)

| **Walnuts and Heart Disease**

Docket No. 2002P-029
03/09/2004 enforcement discretion letter	Whole or chopped walnuts	Supportive but not conclusive research shows that eating 1.5 oz. per day of walnuts, as part of a low-saturated fat and low-cholesterol diet and not resulting in increased caloric intake, may reduce the risk of coronary heart disease. See nutrition information for fat [and calorie] content.
Omega-3 Fatty Acids and Coronary Heart Disease

Docket No. 2003Q-0401
09/08/2004 enforcement discretion letter - Wellness Petition 09/08/2004 enforcement discretion letter - Martek Petition | Conventional foods that contain EPA and DHA omega-3 fatty acids. | Supportive but not conclusive research shows that consumption of EPA and DHA omega-3 fatty acids may reduce the risk of coronary heart disease. One serving of [Name of the food] provides [ ] gram of EPA and DHA omega-3 fatty acids. [See nutrition information for total fat, saturated fat, and cholesterol content.] |
| **Monounsaturated Fatty Acids from Olive Oil and Coronary Heart Disease**

Docket No. 2003Q-0559
11/01/2004 enforcement discretion letter | EVOO

Pure olive oil and olive oil-containing foods (salad dressings, vegetable oil spreads, etc.) that contain 6g or more olive oil per RACC* are low in cholesterol and do not contain more than 4g of saturated fat per 50g.

Meal products or main dish products are not eligible for the claim. | Limited and not conclusive scientific evidence suggests that eating about 2 tablespoons (23g) of olive oil daily may reduce the risk of coronary heart disease due to the monounsaturated fat in olive oil. To achieve this possible benefit, olive oil is to replace a similar amount of saturated fat and not increase the total number of calories you eat in a day. One serving of this product contains [x] grams of olive oil. |

*RACC – Reference amount customarily consumed as determined by FDA.

29

(continued on following page)

Qualified Health Claims	Eligible Foods	Claim Statements
Unsaturated Fatty Acids from Canola Oil and Reduced Risk of Coronary Heart Disease *Docket No. 2006Q-0091* *10/06/2006 enforcement discretion letter*	Canola oil and canola oil-containing foods (vegetable oil spreads, dressings for salads, shortenings, etc.) that contain 4.75g or more of canola oil per RACC*, are low in saturated fat, are low in cholesterol, and meet the saturated fat, cholesterol, and sodium disqualifying levels** Vegetable oil spreads and canola oil-containing foods must also meet the 10% minimum nutrient content requirement.	*Limited and not conclusive scientific evidence suggests that eating about 1 1/2 tablespoons (19 grams) of canola oil daily may reduce the risk of coronary heart disease due to the unsaturated fat content in canola oil. To achieve this possible benefit, canola oil is to replace a similar amount of saturated fat and not increase the total number of calories you eat in a day. One serving of this product contains ___ grams of canola oil.*
Corn Oil and Corn Oil-Containing Products and a Reduced Risk of Heart Disease *Docket No. 2006P-0243* *3/26/2007 enforcement discretion letter*	Corn oil and salad dressings, vegetable oil blends and shortenings that contain 4g or more corn oil per RACC*, are low in cholesterol, meet the cholesterol and sodium disqualifying levels**, and do not contain more than 4g of saturated fat per RACC*.	*Very limited and preliminary scientific evidence suggests that eating about 1 tablespoon (16g) of corn oil daily may reduce the risk of heart disease due to the unsaturated fat content in corn oil. The FDA concludes that there is little scientific evidence supporting this claim. To achieve this possible benefit, corn oil is to replace a similar amount of saturated fat and not increase the total number of calories you eat in a day. One serving of this product contains ___ grams of corn oil.*

http://www.fda.gov/Food/IngredientsPackagingLabeling/LabelingNutrition/ucm2006877.htm

*RACC – Reference amount customarily consumed as determined by FDA.

** Disqualifying nutrient levels means the levels of total fat, saturated fat, cholesterol, or sodium in a food above which the food will be disqualified from making a health claim. These levels are 13g of fat, 4g of saturated fat, 60mg of cholesterol, or 480mg of sodium per RACC*.

Heart-Healthy Nutrients

Heart health is a complex issue because the heart is essential to moving nutrients in your blood to all cells in your body. Keeping your heart and arteries healthy is important for most bodily functions. Therefore, almost all the foods you eat contain nutrients important to your heart—salt and potassium affect blood pressure; fats can raise or lower cholesterol; whole grains, fiber, and phytosterols can control blood sugar; and antioxidants can affect your blood vessels. Here is an overview of the nutrients that are important for heart health. For more shopping and preparation tips to add or decrease these nutrients in your diet, refer to the food category introductions. Specifically look at:

- Whole grains and fiber in grains (page 211)

- Fats in protein and dairy foods—meats, fish, eggs, legumes, nuts, oils, cheese, etc. (Dairy: page 77; Proteins: page 309)

- Omega-3s in seafood, oils, seeds (page 311)

- Fats in oils, margarine, salad dressings (page 107)

- Potassium in dairy (page 77), vegetables (page 429) and fruits (page 151)

- Sodium in prepared foods—entrees, side dishes, soups (page 259)

- Antioxidants in fruits (page 151), vegetables (page 107), nuts, and beverages (page 45)

- Phytosterols in spreads (page 107), dairy (page 77), and orange juice (page 151)

The Right Fats Can Reduce the Risk of Heart Disease

High blood lipids—cholesterol and triglycerides—are major risk factors for heart disease. If you can keep your total and LDL cholesterol and triglyceride blood levels low, you reduce your risk of heart disease. Paying attention to the total fat and types of fat can keep these numbers low. (See page 33 for recommended blood lipid levels.)

Total Fat

Keep the total amount of fat you consume (including heart-healthy fats) to 30% or less of your calories. This is about 66 grams of fat for a 2,000-calorie diet. Fat is an essential nutrient for your body, and you should not try to eliminate it completely. Some fats are actually heart healthy. Fats are also needed for your body to digest and metabolize other essential nutrients. (See page 22 for nutrient content claims for fat.)

Saturated and Trans Fat

Limit saturated fat to less than 7% of calories, according to the American Heart Association and the National Cholesterol Education Program, and keep trans fats as low as possible. Saturated fats are found in fatty meat, poultry skin, bacon, butter, cheese, and whole-fat dairy products. Trans fats are mainly found in stick margarine and packaged foods with partially hydrogenated oils. Even if the Nutrition Facts says 0 grams trans fats, check the ingredients for the term "partially hydrogenated." Foods high in saturated fats and trans fats boost your blood cholesterol levels more than anything else. (See page 22 for nutrient content claims for saturated and trans fat.)

Cholesterol

The National Cholesterol Education Program recommends limiting dietary cholesterol to 200 mg or less if your blood cholesterol level is high. The American Heart Association recommends 300 mg or less per day for general heart health and 200 mg if you have cardiovascular disease. Cholesterol is found in egg yolks (one yolk contains about 200 mg of cholesterol), all meats but highest in fatty meat, shrimp, lobster, crab, cheese, and whole-fat dairy products. You should not eliminate all foods with cholesterol because many of these foods have other health benefits, but be sensible. Portion control of meats is an important aspect of heart health. (See page 22 for nutrient content claims for cholesterol.)

Polyunsaturated Fat

Polyunsaturated fats (PUFAs) promote lower total blood cholesterol as well as lower LDL cholesterol. Unfortunately, they may also lower the good (HDL) cholesterol. Corn oil, safflower oil, soybean oil, sunflower oils, and sesame oils contain PUFAs. Seafood also contains polyunsaturated fats. A group of polyunsaturated fats that are highly recommended for heart health are omega-3 fatty acids. (See more on omega-3s on page 33).

Monounsaturated Fat

Monounsaturated fats (MUFAs) are the best fat for lowering blood cholesterol levels—both total and LDL. They also have been shown to increase HDL cholesterol, the blood lipid you want to be high. Monounsaturated fats are found in nuts; vegetable oils such as canola oil, olive oil, high oleic safflower oil, and sunflower oil; and avocadoes. (Check out the FDA-approved Qualified Health Claim for monounsaturated fat and heart disease on page 29).

Heart-Healthy Omega-3 Fats

What Are Omega-3s?

Omega-3 fatty acids are long-chain polyunsaturated fats that have proven health benefits. They include DHA and EPA, which exist naturally in fish oil, and ALA found in flaxseed, soybeans, walnuts, and canola oil. All forms of omega-3s have been shown to be effective for treatment and prevention of cardiovascular disease and arthritis. However, only DHA is shown to be effective for brain and retina development in children, cognitive function, and risk prevention for dementia and Alzheimer's disease. This is why eating a variety of omega-3 sources is important for overall disease prevention and treatment. Omega-6 fatty acids, found in some vegetables oils (soybean, safflower, sunflower or corn); nuts; and seeds, are also a beneficial part of a heart-healthy eating plan.

Recommendations

According to the 2010 Dietary Guidelines, the ALA omega-3 recommendation is 1,600 mg for men and 1,100 mg for women. The American Heart Association's recommendation for omega-6 fats is to consume at least 5% to 10% of your total daily calories from omega-6 fatty acids. This can be done by replacing saturated fats with polyunsaturated fats, which are natural sources of omega-6 fatty acids.

Omega-3 Nutrient Claims

Package claims can be confusing. With generic terms like "good source" and "high source," it is difficult to understand what they mean. The FDA makes specific definitions for terms used on product labeling.

- A "good source" means that product contains 10 to 19% of the recommended daily intake of the nutrient. A "Good Source of omega-3s" means the product provides 100 to 190 mg of omega-3s.

- A "High" or "Excellent" source means the product contains at least 20% of the recommended daily intake of the nutrient. A "High Source of omega-3s" means the product provides at least 200 mg of omega-'3s.

Best Sources of Omega-3s (3.5 oz. portion)

Food	Amount	Food	Amount
Salmon	2,147 mg	Walnuts, 2 T	1,000 mg
Mackerel	1,848 mg	Flaxseeds (ground), 2 T	3,200 mg
Trout	936 mg	Soybeans (cooked), 1 cup	600 mg
Sea Bass	762 mg	Flaxseed Oil, 1 T	7,300 mg
Halibut	456 mg	Walnut Oil, 1 T	1,400 mg
Tuna	328 mg	Canola Oil, 1 T	130 mg
Scallop	180 mg	Firm Tofu, ½ cup	70 mg
Catfish	177 mg	Soybean Oil, 1 T	100 mg

There is a qualified health claim for omega-3s (See page 29). The FDA approves these types of claims on packaging when there is sufficient evidence to make a statement about health benefits but evidence isn't conclusive.

Tips for Increasing Omega-3 Intake

- Include a fish portion (3 oz.) 2 or more meals per week. Avoid fried fish as benefits are not as strong when fried.
- Using canned tuna or salmon will help save money. Use it as a snack with crackers or a meal on the go.
- If you are allergic to fish, look for products fortified with omega-3s.
- Buy milled flaxseed and add it to your favorite cereals, soups, sauces, and yogurt. You won't even know it's there. If purchasing a product fortified with flaxseed, make sure the ingredients say "milled" or "ground" flaxseed.
- Switch to olive and/or canola oil. It is low in saturated fat and high in monoun-saturated fats and omega-3s.
- Walnuts are a great snack. Just ¼ cup of walnuts provides 90% of your daily recommended intake of omega-3s.
- Be adventurous with your food! Try tofu. 4 ounces of tofu provides 0.4 grams of omega-3s.
- Consider grass fed beef and dairy products that are higher in omega-3 fats.

Trim Salt to Lower Blood Pressure

Eating less sodium can lower some people's blood pressure and result in a lower risk of heart disease. Sodium is an essential component of our diets, but most people get too much. Sodium is mainly found as a component of salt. Here are some tips to trim the salt in your diet.

How Much Salt Do We Need?

The basic recommendation for adults is 2,300 mg of sodium per day (about one teaspoon of salt). But for nearly half of all Americans and almost all adults, the rec-ommendation was cut to just 1,500 mg of sodium per day. Count yourself in this group if you are older than 51; African-American; or have high blood pressure, dia-betes, or chronic kidney disease.

Where is the salt in our diets?
- 80% processed foods
- 10% added salt in cooking or at the table
- 10% natural salt in foods

Use Salt-Trimming Tricks at the Supermarket:

- Look for sodium or salt claims on labels. (See sodium claims for food labels on page 23.)
- Check the % Daily Value for sodium in the Nutrition Facts box. Look for products less than 10% Daily Value.
- Choose small portions of higher-sodium foods such as lunch meats, hot dogs, bacon, and pickles.
- Cut back on condiments like mustard, ketchup, and soy sauce, or try reduced sodium versions.
- Pass up processed foods and make your own pasta sauce, salad dressings, casseroles, etc. when possible.
- Replace salty snacks, such as chips, pretzels and salted nuts, with lower salt alternatives, such as unsalted nuts and pretzels and reduced sodium chips.
- Make sure that poultry and other meats have not been infused with a solution of water and salt.

In Your Kitchen:

- Rinse canned vegetables, beans, and tuna to wash away most of the sodium.
- Use only half the seasoning packet in packaged mixes for rice, pasta, and soups.
- Reduce the amount or eliminate the salt added to the cooking water for pasta, rice, and hot cereals.
- Take the salt shaker off the table.
- Season with a squeeze of lemon or lime juice, a splash of vinegar, or a shake of a salt-free seasoning blend.

Choices make a difference!

Choose:	Rather than:	Sodium Savings *(approximate)*
chicken noodle soup, reduced sodium	Ramen noodle soup	440 mg/cup
green beans, no added salt, canned	green beans, regular, canned	380 mg/1/2 cup
nuts, dry roasted	nuts, mixed, salted	120 mg/ounce
pasta sauce, low sodium	pasta sauce, regular	150 mg/1/2 cup
pretzel, unsalted	pretzel, salted	500 mg/ounce
salad dressing, reduced salt	salad dressing, bottled	200 mg/tablespoon
tomato ketchup, no salt	ketchup, regular	190 mg/tablespoon
tomato sauce, no added salt	tomato sauce, regular	400 mg/1/4 cup
tomato soup, reduced sodium	tomato soup, regular	450 mg/1 cup
tortilla chips, lightly salted	tortilla chips, flavored	100 mg/ounce
turkey breast, sliced, low sodium	turkey breast, processed	300 mg/2 ounces

Get Enough Potassium for Your Heart

Potassium is a heart-friendly mineral. It doesn't treat or prevent heart disease, but studies have shown that getting enough potassium benefits the heart in several important ways. Potassium is an electrolyte that is essential for the body's growth and maintenance. It is necessary to keep a normal water balance between the cells and body fluids. Potassium also plays an essential role in the response of nerves to stimulation and in the contraction of muscles. Cellular enzymes need potassium to work properly.

A potassium deficiency due to increased urinary loss often occurs when medication for certain heart diseases is used to prevent sodium and water retention. To overcome this loss, physicians often suggest eating more foods high in potassium or more potassium may be prescribed as a medicine.

If you have high blood pressure, heart failure, or heart rhythm problems, getting enough potassium is especially important. Although potassium and cholesterol aren't directly related, eating a potassium-rich diet just might lower your cholesterol too.

Most people get plenty of potassium just by eating a normal American diet. The main source of potassium in our food is fruits and vegetables. Dairy products, whole grains, meat, and fish also provide potassium.

Excellent sources of potassium include:

- Potatoes
- Tomatoes
- Avocados
- Fresh fruits (bananas, oranges, and strawberries)
- Orange juice
- Dried fruits (raisins, apricots, prunes, and dates)
- Spinach and leafy green vegetables
- Beans and peas

How Much Potassium Is Necessary?

If you really feel like counting, the USDA recommends 4,700 milligrams of potassium per day. Potassium is not a required nutrient to be listed on food labels, but it is often included.

Phytosterols Can Lower Cholesterol

What Are Phytosterols?

Plant sterols and stanols (collectively called phytosterols) are the plant equivalent to the animal cholesterol found naturally in small amounts in a wide variety of foods—nuts, whole grains, vegetables, and fruits. Additionally, foods can be fortified with phytosterols in much higher amounts.

Why Eat Phytosterols?

The main benefit of adding phytosterols to your diet is to help reduce your risk for heart attack and stroke by lowering your LDL cholesterol. Because the structure of phytosterols is similar to cholesterol, phytosterols block the absorption of cholesterol in your intestines and lower the amount of cholesterol in your blood.

Check out the FDA approved Health Claim for Plant Sterols/Stanols (Phytosterol) and Heart Disease on page 27.

How Much Phytosterol Is Recommended?

	Plant sterols	Plant sterol esters	Plant stanol/ plant stanol esters
FDA Health Claim for prevention of heart disease	0.8g or more per day	1.3g or more per day	3.4g or more per day
NCEP* recommendation to lower LDL cholesterol	2g sterols or stanols per day as part of a diet low in saturated fat and cholesterol and high in soluble fiber		

*National Cholesterol Education Program

Where to Find Phytosterols?

Natural Sources of Phytosterols	Serving size	Phytosterols/serving (g)
Flaxseed	3½ oz	0.210
Wheat germ	3½ oz	0.197
Rye Bread	2 slices	0.033
Almonds	3½ oz	0.187
Pistachios	3½ oz	0.280
Pecans	3½ oz	0.150
Walnuts	3½ oz	0.113
Broccoli	3½ oz	0.049
Brussels sprouts	3½ oz	0.037
Raspberries	3½ oz	0.027
Blueberries	3½ oz	0.026

Foods Fortified with Phytosterols

Plant Sterol	Serving Size	Stanol/serving (g)
Benecol Spread	1 Tbsp	0.5
Lifetime Cheese	1 oz	0.65
Minute-Maid Heart/Wise Orange Juice	1 cup (8 oz)	1.0
Rice Dream Heart Wise Rice Milk	1 cup (8 oz)	0.65
Smart Balance Heart Right Spread	1 Tbsp	1.7
Smart Balance Heart Right Fat-Free Milk	1 cup (8 oz)	0.4

*National Cholesterol Education Program

Antioxidants Prevent Artery Damage

Antioxidants are natural substances that exist as vitamins, minerals, and other compounds in foods. They are believed to help prevent disease by fighting free radicals, substances that harm the body when left unchecked. Free radicals are formed by normal bodily processes such as breathing, and by environmental contaminants like cigarette smoke. Without adequate amounts of antioxidants, these free radicals travel throughout the body, damaging cells.

Part of this cellular damage leads to one of the major known factors in the development of heart disease—oxidation of cholesterol that leads to the buildup of fatty plaque on artery walls (atherosclerosis), which can eventually slow or block blood flow to the heart.

Although the research on antioxidants and heart disease has produced mixed results, there are several antioxidants in foods that are recommended. Antioxidants are typically concentrated in the skin of fruits and vegetables. You should not take antioxidant supplements without the advice of your physician.

Antioxidant	Food Sources
Lycopene	Tomatoes, pink/red grapefruit, watermelon, papaya
Vitamin E	Sunflower seeds, almonds, hazelnuts, turnip greens
Resveratrol	Red wine, grape skins, peanuts, berries
Phenolic Acids	Apples, pears, dates, citrus fruits, whole grains, coffee
Catechins	Green tea, cocoa, chocolate, apples, grapes
Procyanidins/ Proanthocyanides	Cranberries, cocoa/chocolate, strawberries, grapes, red wine, peanuts, tea, cinnamon, black currants
Beta carotene	Brightly colored orange and yellow foods such as carrots, squash, sweet potatoes, cantaloupe, and tomatoes

Bottom Line

Tips to Eat Better for Heart Health

- **Take small steps**–Think about planning a heart-healthy diet in a number of small manageable steps rather than one big drastic change. Purchase one new food product each week and try one new recipe each week.

- **Think smaller portions**–Check out your dinner plates and bowls. Are they super-sized? A normal portion size will look lost on a large plate or bowl. Meat, chicken, or fish portions should be about the size of the palm of your hand or a deck of cards; a slice of bread should be the size of a CD case; and a half cup of mashed potatoes, rice, or pasta is about the size of a tennis ball or a traditional lightbulb.

- **Plan heart-healthy meals with heart-healthy recipes**–There are countless heart healthy cookbooks and websites full of delicious recipes to try. See page 575 for a list of suggested cookbooks and websites. Start collecting recipes that are low in total fat, saturated fat, cholesterol, and sodium. Or modify your existing recipes by using the following suggestions:

When your recipe calls for . . .	Use this instead . . .
Whole milk	Fat-free or low-fat milk
Heavy cream	Evaporated skim milk or 1 cup low-fat yogurt
Sour cream	Fat-free sour cream
Butter (1 tablespoon)	1 tablespoon soft, trans fat free margarine or ¾ tablespoon liquid vegetable oil
Egg (1)	2 egg whites; or egg substitute (¼ cup)
Oil in baking (½ cup)	Applesauce (½ cup)

- **Stock your kitchen with healthy food**–Do a healthy kitchen checkup by going through your pantry, refrigerator, and freezer and getting rid of all foods that are high in total fat, saturated fat, cholesterol, and sodium. If it makes you uncomfortable to throw away foods, tag these foods and pair them with fresh fruits and vegetables and high-fiber, whole-grain carbohydrates.

- **Eat vegetables and fruits**–These are nutrient-rich foods that are high in vitamins, minerals, and fiber and low in calories. Eating a variety of deeply colored fruits and vegetables can help you control your weight and blood pressure.

- **Eat fiber-rich whole-grain foods**–Whole grain foods have been shown to lower the risk of heart disease, and a diet rich in fiber can help promote weight loss because fiber keeps you feeling fuller longer so you eat less. Both can also help lower blood cholesterol.

- **Eat fish at least twice a week**–Research shows that eating a 3.5 oz. serving of oily fish 2 times per week containing omega-3 fatty acids (salmon, trout, and herring) may help lower your risk of death from coronary artery disease.

- **Choose lean meats and low-fat dairy products**–For low-fat protein, choose skinless poultry and trimmed lean meats and prepare them without adding fat. Use lean cuts of meat—"choice" or "select" grades of beef rather than "prime." Choose "loin" and "round" cuts of meat, as they usually have the least fat. For poultry, choose light-meat products, such as breasts, rather than dark meat (legs and thighs). Select fat-free, 1% fat, and low-fat dairy products. Be sure to trim visible fat from meat and remove skin from chicken.

- **Try vegetarian meals a couple of times a week**–Research shows that people who follow a vegan (without animal products) diet have a lower incidence of heart disease.

- **Cut back on saturated, trans fats, and cholesterol**–Cut down on foods containing partially hydrogenated vegetable oils to reduce trans fat in your diet. Aim to eat less than 300 milligrams of cholesterol each day or 200 mg or less if you have heart disease.

- **Trim sodium and sugar**–Choose and prepare foods with little or no salt. Aim to eat less than 1,500 milligrams of sodium per day. Limit beverages and other foods with added sugar.

Heart-Healthy Cooking Methods

Avoid high-fat food preparation by using cooking methods that add little or no fat, such as these:

- **Bake** foods in covered cookware with just a little extra liquid.

- **Grill or broil** on a rack so the fat drips away from the food.

- **Microwave** meats on a rack or paper towels to eliminate the fat.

- **Poach** chicken or fish by immersing it in simmering liquid.

- **Roast** by placing meat on a rack in a pan so the meat or poultry is removed from any fat dripping.

- **Baste** with fat-free liquids like wine, tomato juice, or lemon juice rather than the pan drippings. When making gravy from the drippings, chill first to allow the fat to rise to the top so that you can skim it off with a gravy strainer or skim ladle.

- **Sauté** using a nonstick pan so you will need to use little or no oil when cooking. Use a nonstick vegetable spray to brown or sauté foods; or, as an alternative, use a small amount of broth or wine, or a tiny bit of vegetable oil rubbed onto the pan with a paper towel.

- **Steam** vegetables in a basket over simmering water. They'll retain more flavors and won't need any salt.

- **Stir-fry** in a wok. Cook vegetables, poultry, or seafood in vegetable stock, wine, or a small amount of oil. Avoid high-sodium (salt) seasonings like teriyaki and soy sauce.

Shopping List for Heart Health

VEGETABLES
☐ Fresh – tomatoes, cabbage, broccoli, spinach
☐ Leafy greens for salads
☐ Canned – low sodium or no added salt
☐ Frozen – without added butter or sauces

GRAINS (bread, cereal, rice, pasta)
☐ Whole grain bread
☐ Whole-grain breakfast cereals - oatmeal
☐ Brown or wild rice
☐ Whole wheat or whole-grain pasta
☐ Corn, barley, bulgur

OILS (margarine, salad dressings)
☐ Vegetable oil (olive, canola, peanut, sesame)
☐ Non-stick cooking spray
☐ Soft margarine with no trans fats
☐ Salad dressing – light or fat free

FRUITS
☐ Fresh – apples, oranges, pears, peaches, berries
☐ Canned fruit in 100% juice, not syrup
☐ Fruit juice – 100% juice
☐ Frozen – without added sugar

PROTEINS (meat, poultry, fish, nuts, eggs)
☐ Chicken and Turkey – white meat without skin
☐ Seafood – fish and shellfish
☐ Pork – leg, shoulder, tenderloin
☐ Beef – round, tenderloin, extra lean ground
☐ Beans, lentils, peas
☐ Egg white substitutes or omega-3 eggs (4 per week)
☐ Nuts and seeds (raw and unsalted)

DAIRY/MILK
☐ Milk – fat free or low fat (1%)
☐ Yogurt – fat free or low fat (1%)
☐ Cheese – 3 grams of fat or less
☐ Soy beverages with added calcium (soy milk)

Beverages

Why Drink Beverages?

Beverages provide hydration, and keeping the body hydrated helps the heart pump blood through the blood vessels to the muscles. Additionally, it helps the muscles remove waste so that they can work efficiently. If you are well hydrated, your heart doesn't have to work as hard. Even mild dehydration can put stress on your heart, drain your energy, and make you tired.

Find milk and milk alternatives in the Dairy section (page 77) and juice in the Fruit section (page 151).

Daily Goal

"8 by 8 rule"—drink eight 8 oz. glasses of fluid a day.
Women need about 9 cups of total fluid a day.
Men need about 13 cups of total fluid a day.
Women who are expecting or breast feeding need about 10 to 13 cups
of fluids a day.

Heart-Healthy Nutrients in Beverages

Antioxidants can help prevent artery damage by fighting products produced in the process of oxidation. The major antioxidants found in beverages are:

Antioxidant	Food Sources
Lycopene	Tomato juice
Resveratrol	Red wine
Phenolic Acids	Coffee
Catechins	Green tea
Procyanidins/ Proanthocyanides	Red wine, tea

Heart-Healthy Shopping Tips for Beverages

- Look for the AHA Heart-Check mark on dairy product labels (milk) and dairy alternatives (soy, rice, and nut milks) and juices. For more information on the Heart-Check mark, go to *www.heartcheckmark.org*.

- Plain water is best for hydration. Drink water throughout the day and even more when exercising—especially in hot, humid weather.

- Choose 100% juices rather than juice drinks. Since fruit juices are high in sugar and may increase triglycerides, use moderation (1/2 cup servings) or eat the whole fruit.

- Drink skim or fat-free milk or milk alternatives.

- Coffee and caffeine have shown mixed effects on heart disease. In most people, one to four cups of coffee per day appears safe for cardiac health. Just keep in mind that loading up your cup of coffee with cream, sugar, syrup, or whipped cream may more than cancel out any benefit you might otherwise gain from it.

- The antioxidants/flavonoids in green tea may be heart healthy, although FDA recently turned down a health claim for green tea and heart disease for insufficient scientific research.

- Red wine, in moderation, has long been thought of as heart healthy. The alcohol and certain substances in red wine called antioxidants may help prevent heart disease by increasing levels of "good" cholesterol and protecting against artery damage. Recommendation is one 4 ounce glass of wine a day.

- If you drink alcohol, do so in moderation. This means an average of one to two drinks per day for men and one drink per day for women. (A drink is one 12 ounce beer, 4 ounces of wine, 1.5 ounces of 80-proof spirits, or 1 ounce of 100-proof spirits.) Drinking more alcohol increases such dangers as alcoholism, high blood pressure, obesity, stroke, breast cancer, suicide, and accidents.

Shopping List Essentials

Bottled or filtered water
Seltzer water
Milk or milk alternatives, fat free or skim
Juice drinks, 100% juice (may elevate triglycerides)

Caution: Drinks can be high in calories and sugars. Make sure that beverages don't have added sugars. A soda that only has sugar calories is an example of an "empty calories" choice. You need water for hydration but try not to drink calories with your water.

Criteria for Beverages

- There are no FDA guidelines for Heart Health Claims for beverages other than those for milk and juice. To learn more about milk and juice beverages, go to the Dairy section (page 77) and Fruit section (page 151).

- Beverages listed are flavored waters, coconut waters, teas, and coffees. If sugar is a concern, choose the unsweetened or diet versions.

- Beverages not listed are fruit drinks with less than 100% juice and sodas. These beverages often have added sugars that are not beneficial for heart health. This does not mean that these beverages are bad. Drink them occasionally, but remember that water is the best beverage for hydration.

Coconut Water

Nature Factor, Organic Coconut Water

1 can / 10 fl oz

Amount per serving	%DV	Amount per serving	%DV	Amount per serving	%DV
Calories 50		**Cholesterol** 0mg	0%	**Total Carbohydrate** 12g	4%
Total Fat 0g	0%	**Sodium** 35mg	1%	Dietary Fiber 0g	0%
Saturated Fat 0g	0%	**Protein** 1g		Sugars 12g	
Polyunsaturated Fat 0g					
Monounsaturated Fat 0g		Vitamin A 0% Vitamin C 0%		Calcium 4% Iron 2%	

Vitacoco, 100% Pure Coconut Water

8 fl oz / 240 ml

Amount per serving	%DV	Amount per serving	%DV	Amount per serving	%DV
Calories 45		**Cholesterol** 0mg	0%	**Total Carbohydrate** 11g	4%
Total Fat 0g	0%	**Sodium** 30mg	1%	Dietary Fiber 0g	0%
Saturated Fat 0g	0%	**Protein** 0g		Sugars 11g	
Polyunsaturated Fat 0g					
Monounsaturated Fat 0g		Vitamin A 0% Vitamin C 100%		Calcium 2% Iron 0%	

Vitacoco, Pure Coconut Water with Acai & Pomegranate

8 fl oz / 240 ml

Amount per serving	%DV	Amount per serving	%DV	Amount per serving	%DV
Calories 60		**Cholesterol** 0mg	0%	**Total Carbohydrate** 16g	5%
Total Fat 0g	0%	**Sodium** 45mg	2%	Dietary Fiber 1g	4%
Saturated Fat 0g	0%	**Protein** 0g		Sugars 15g	
Polyunsaturated Fat 0g					
Monounsaturated Fat 0g		Vitamin A 0% Vitamin C 60%		Calcium 2% Iron 0%	

Vitacoco, Pure Coconut Water with Orange

8 fl oz / 240 ml

Amount per serving	%DV	Amount per serving	%DV	Amount per serving	%DV
Calories 60		**Cholesterol** 0mg	0%	**Total Carbohydrate** 16g	5%
Total Fat 0g	0%	**Sodium** 30mg	1%	Dietary Fiber 0g	0%
Saturated Fat 0g	0%	**Protein** 0g		Sugars 16g	
Polyunsaturated Fat 0g					
Monounsaturated Fat 0g		Vitamin A 0% Vitamin C 170%		Calcium 3% Iron 0%	

Vitacoco, Pure Coconut Water with Peach & Mango

8 fl oz / 240 ml

Amount per serving	%DV	Amount per serving	%DV	Amount per serving	%DV
Calories 60		**Cholesterol** 0mg	0%	**Total Carbohydrate** 15g	5%
Total Fat 0g	0%	**Sodium** 45mg	2%	Dietary Fiber 0g	0%
Saturated Fat 0g	0%	**Protein** 0g		Sugars 15g	
Polyunsaturated Fat 0g					
Monounsaturated Fat 0g		Vitamin A 0% Vitamin C 65%		Calcium 2% Iron 0%	

Vitacoco, Pure Coconut Water with Pineapple

8 fl oz / 240 ml

Amount per serving	%DV	Amount per serving	%DV	Amount per serving	%DV
Calories 60		**Cholesterol** 0mg	0%	**Total Carbohydrate** 15g	5%
Total Fat 0g	0%	**Sodium** 40mg	2%	Dietary Fiber 0g	0%
Saturated Fat 0g	0%	**Protein** 0g		Sugars 15g	
Polyunsaturated Fat 0g					
Monounsaturated Fat 0g		Vitamin A 0%	Vitamin C 75%	Calcium 2%	Iron 0%

Vitacoco, Pure Coconut Water with Tropical Fruit

8 fl oz /240 ml

Amount per serving	%DV	Amount per serving	%DV	Amount per serving	%DV
Calories 55		**Cholesterol** 0mg	0%	**Total Carbohydrate** 13g	4%
Total Fat 0g	0%	**Sodium** 24mg	1%	Dietary Fiber 0g	0%
Saturated Fat 0g	0%	**Protein** 0g		Sugars 13g	
Polyunsaturated Fat 0g					
Monounsaturated Fat 0g		Vitamin A 0%	Vitamin C 25%	Calcium 4%	Iron 0%

Teas

AriZona, Black and White Tea with Ginseng & Honey

8 fl oz / 240 ml

Amount per serving	%DV	Amount per serving	%DV	Amount per serving	%DV
Calories 50		**Cholesterol** 0mg	0%	**Total Carbohydrate** 14g	5%
Total Fat 0g	0%	**Sodium** 10mg	0%	Dietary Fiber 0g	0%
Saturated Fat 0g	0%	**Protein** 0g		Sugars 14g	
Polyunsaturated Fat 0g					
Monounsaturated Fat 0g		Vitamin A 0%	Vitamin C 25%	Calcium 0%	Iron 0%

AriZona, Black Tea with Ginseng and Honey

8 fl oz / 240 ml

Amount per serving	%DV	Amount per serving	%DV	Amount per serving	%DV
Calories 60		**Cholesterol** 0mg	0%	**Total Carbohydrate** 15g	5%
Total Fat 0g	0%	**Sodium** 20mg	1%	Dietary Fiber 0g	0%
Saturated Fat 0g	0%	**Protein** 0g		Sugars 14g	
Polyunsaturated Fat 0g					
Monounsaturated Fat 0g		Vitamin A 0%	Vitamin C 25%	Calcium 0%	Iron 0%

AriZona, Black Tea, Diet Lemon Tea

8 fl oz / 240 ml

Amount per serving	%DV	Amount per serving	%DV	Amount per serving	%DV
Calories 0		**Cholesterol** 0mg	0%	**Total Carbohydrate** 0g	0%
Total Fat 0g	0%	**Sodium** 20mg	1%	Dietary Fiber 0g	0%
Saturated Fat 0g	0%	**Protein** 0g		Sugars 0g	
Polyunsaturated Fat 0g					
Monounsaturated Fat 0g		Vitamin A 0%	Vitamin C 25%	Calcium 0%	Iron 0%

AriZona, Black Tea, Diet Peach Tea

8 fl oz / 240 ml

Amount per serving	%DV	Amount per serving	%DV	Amount per serving	%DV
Calories 0		**Cholesterol** 0mg	0%	**Total Carbohydrate** 1g	0%
Total Fat 0g	0%	**Sodium** 20mg	1%	Dietary Fiber 0g	0%
Saturated Fat 0g	0%	**Protein** 0g		Sugars 1g	
Polyunsaturated Fat 0g					
Monounsaturated Fat 0g		Vitamin A 0%	Vitamin C 25%	Calcium 0%	Iron 0%

AriZona, Black Tea, Diet Raspberry Tea

8 fl oz / 240 ml

Amount per serving	%DV	Amount per serving	%DV	Amount per serving	%DV
Calories 90		**Cholesterol** 0mg	0%	**Total Carbohydrate** 23g	8%
Total Fat 0g	0%	**Sodium** 25mg	1%	Dietary Fiber 0g	0%
Saturated Fat 0g	0%	**Protein** 0g		Sugars 22g	
Polyunsaturated Fat 0g					
Monounsaturated Fat 0g		Vitamin A 0%	Vitamin C 100%	Calcium 0%	Iron 0%

AriZona, Black Tea, Lemon Tea

8 fl oz / 240 ml

Amount per serving	%DV	Amount per serving	%DV	Amount per serving	%DV
Calories 90		**Cholesterol** 0mg	0%	**Total Carbohydrate** 25g	8%
Total Fat 0g	0%	**Sodium** 20mg	1%	Dietary Fiber 0g	0%
Saturated Fat 0g	0%	**Protein** 0g		Sugars 24g	
Polyunsaturated Fat 0g					
Monounsaturated Fat 0g		Vitamin A 0%	Vitamin C 0%	Calcium 0%	Iron 0%

AriZona, Black Tea, Peach Tea

8 fl oz / 240 ml

Amount per serving	%DV	Amount per serving	%DV	Amount per serving	%DV
Calories 70		**Cholesterol** 0mg	0%	**Total Carbohydrate** 18g	6%
Total Fat 0g	0%	**Sodium** 10mg	0%	Dietary Fiber 0g	0%
Saturated Fat 0g	0%	**Protein** 0g		Sugars 17g	
Polyunsaturated Fat 0g					
Monounsaturated Fat 0g		Vitamin A 0%	Vitamin C 25%	Calcium 0%	Iron 0%

AriZona, Black Tea, Raspberry Tea

8 fl oz / 240 ml

Amount per serving	%DV	Amount per serving	%DV	Amount per serving	%DV
Calories 90		**Cholesterol** 0mg	0%	**Total Carbohydrate** 23g	8%
Total Fat 0g	0%	**Sodium** 25mg	1%	Dietary Fiber 0g	0%
Saturated Fat 0g	0%	**Protein** 0g		Sugars 22g	
Polyunsaturated Fat 0g					
Monounsaturated Fat 0g		Vitamin A 0%	Vitamin C 100%	Calcium 0%	Iron 0%

AriZona, Black Tea, Sweet Tea

8 fl oz / 240 ml

Amount per serving	%DV	Amount per serving	%DV	Amount per serving	%DV
Calories 90		**Cholesterol** 0mg	0%	**Total Carbohydrate** 23g	8%
Total Fat 0g	0%	**Sodium** 20mg	1%	Dietary Fiber 0g	0%
Saturated Fat 0g	0%	**Protein** 0g		Sugars 23g	
Polyunsaturated Fat 0g					
Monounsaturated Fat 0g		Vitamin A 0% Vitamin C 0%		Calcium 0% Iron 0%	

AriZona, Green Tea, Asia Plum Green Tea

8 fl oz / 240 ml

Amount per serving	%DV	Amount per serving	%DV	Amount per serving	%DV
Calories 70		**Cholesterol** 0mg	0%	**Total Carbohydrate** 18g	6%
Total Fat 0g	0%	**Sodium** 20mg	1%	Dietary Fiber 0g	0%
Saturated Fat 0g	0%	**Protein** 0g		Sugars 17g	
Polyunsaturated Fat 0g					
Monounsaturated Fat 0g		Vitamin A 0% Vitamin C 25%		Calcium 0% Iron 0%	

AriZona, Green Tea, Diet Blueberry Green Tea

8 fl oz / 240 ml

Amount per serving	%DV	Amount per serving	%DV	Amount per serving	%DV
Calories 5		**Cholesterol** 0mg	0%	**Total Carbohydrate** 2g	1%
Total Fat 0g	0%	**Sodium** 20mg	1%	Dietary Fiber 0g	0%
Saturated Fat 0g	0%	**Protein** 0g		Sugars 0g	
Polyunsaturated Fat 0g					
Monounsaturated Fat 0g		Vitamin A 0% Vitamin C 0%		Calcium 0% Iron 0%	

AriZona, Green Tea, Diet Decaf Green Tea

8 fl oz / 240 ml

Amount per serving	%DV	Amount per serving	%DV	Amount per serving	%DV
Calories 0		**Cholesterol** 0mg	0%	**Total Carbohydrate** 1g	0%
Total Fat 0g	0%	**Sodium** 20mg	1%	Dietary Fiber 0g	0%
Saturated Fat 0g	0%	**Protein** 0g		Sugars 1g	
Polyunsaturated Fat 0g					
Monounsaturated Fat 0g		Vitamin A 0% Vitamin C 25%		Calcium 0% Iron 0%	

AriZona, Green Tea, Diet Green Tea with Ginseng and Honey

8 fl oz / 240 ml

Amount per serving	%DV	Amount per serving	%DV	Amount per serving	%DV
Calories 0		**Cholesterol** 0mg	0%	**Total Carbohydrate** 1g	0%
Total Fat 0g	0%	**Sodium** 20mg	1%	Dietary Fiber 0g	0%
Saturated Fat 0g	0%	**Protein** 0g		Sugars 1g	
Polyunsaturated Fat 0g					
Monounsaturated Fat 0g		Vitamin A 0% Vitamin C 25%		Calcium 0% Iron 0%	

AriZona, Green Tea, Diet White Cranapple Green Tea

8 fl oz / 240 ml

Amount per serving	%DV	Amount per serving	%DV	Amount per serving	%DV
Calories 5		**Cholesterol** 0mg	0%	**Total Carbohydrate** 2g	1%
Total Fat 0g	0%	**Sodium** 20mg	1%	Dietary Fiber 0g	0%
Saturated Fat 0g	0%	**Protein** 0g		Sugars 0g	
Polyunsaturated Fat 0g					
Monounsaturated Fat 0g		Vitamin A 0% Vitamin C 0%		Calcium 0% Iron 0%	

AriZona, Green Tea, Extra Sweet Green Tea

8 fl oz / 240 ml

Amount per serving	%DV	Amount per serving	%DV	Amount per serving	%DV
Calories 90		**Cholesterol** 0mg	0%	**Total Carbohydrate** 23g	8%
Total Fat 0g	0%	**Sodium** 20mg	1%	Dietary Fiber 0g	0%
Saturated Fat 0g	0%	**Protein** 0g		Sugars 23g	
Polyunsaturated Fat 0g					
Monounsaturated Fat 0g		Vitamin A 0% Vitamin C 25%		Calcium 0% Iron 0%	

AriZona, Green Tea, Georgia Peach Green Tea

8 fl oz / 240 ml

Amount per serving	%DV	Amount per serving	%DV	Amount per serving	%DV
Calories 70		**Cholesterol** 0mg	0%	**Total Carbohydrate** 18g	6%
Total Fat 0g	0%	**Sodium** 10mg	0%	Dietary Fiber 0g	0%
Saturated Fat 0g	0%	**Protein** 0g		Sugars 17g	
Polyunsaturated Fat 0g					
Monounsaturated Fat 0g		Vitamin A 0% Vitamin C 25%		Calcium 0% Iron 0%	

AriZona, Green Tea, Green Tea with Ginseng and Honey

8 fl oz / 240 ml

Amount per serving	%DV	Amount per serving	%DV	Amount per serving	%DV
Calories 70		**Cholesterol** 0mg	0%	**Total Carbohydrate** 18g	6%
Total Fat 0g	0%	**Sodium** 20mg	1%	Dietary Fiber 0g	0%
Saturated Fat 0g	0%	**Protein** 0g		Sugars 17g	
Polyunsaturated Fat 0g					
Monounsaturated Fat 0g		Vitamin A 0% Vitamin C 25%		Calcium 0% Iron 0%	

AriZona, Green Tea, Mandarin Orange Green Tea

8 fl oz / 240 ml

Amount per serving	%DV	Amount per serving	%DV	Amount per serving	%DV
Calories 70		**Cholesterol** 0mg	0%	**Total Carbohydrate** 19g	6%
Total Fat 0g	0%	**Sodium** 20mg	1%	Dietary Fiber 0g	0%
Saturated Fat 0g	0%	**Protein** 0g		Sugars 18g	
Polyunsaturated Fat 0g					
Monounsaturated Fat 0g		Vitamin A 0% Vitamin C 25%		Calcium 0% Iron 0%	

AriZona, Green Tea, Pomegranate Green Tea

8 fl oz / 240 ml

Amount per serving	%DV	Amount per serving	%DV	Amount per serving	%DV
Calories 70		**Cholesterol** 0mg	0%	**Total Carbohydrate** 19g	6%
Total Fat 0g	0%	**Sodium** 10mg	0%	Dietary Fiber 0g	0%
Saturated Fat 0g	0%	**Protein** 0g		Sugars 18g	
Polyunsaturated Fat 0g					
Monounsaturated Fat 0g		Vitamin A 10% Vitamin C 50%		Calcium 0% Iron 0%	

AriZona, Green Tea, Red Apple Green Tea

8 fl oz / 240 ml

Amount per serving	%DV	Amount per serving	%DV	Amount per serving	%DV
Calories 70		**Cholesterol** 0mg	0%	**Total Carbohydrate** 19g	6%
Total Fat 0g	0%	**Sodium** 20mg	1%	Dietary Fiber 0g	0%
Saturated Fat 0g	0%	**Protein** 0g		Sugars 18g	
Polyunsaturated Fat 0g					
Monounsaturated Fat 0g		Vitamin A 0% Vitamin C 25%		Calcium 0% Iron 0%	

AriZona, Herbal Tea, Rx Energy Herbal Tea

8 fl oz / 240 ml

Amount per serving	%DV	Amount per serving	%DV	Amount per serving	%DV
Calories 120		**Cholesterol** 0mg	0%	**Total Carbohydrate** 31g	10%
Total Fat 0g	0%	**Sodium** 25mg	1%	Dietary Fiber 0g	0%
Saturated Fat 0g	0%	**Protein** 0g		Sugars 29g	
Polyunsaturated Fat 0g					
Monounsaturated Fat 0g		Vitamin A 25% Vitamin C 25%		Calcium 0% Iron 0%	

AriZona, Herbal Tea, Rx Stress Herbal Tea

8 fl oz / 240 ml

Amount per serving	%DV	Amount per serving	%DV	Amount per serving	%DV
Calories 70		**Cholesterol** 0mg	0%	**Total Carbohydrate** 19g	6%
Total Fat 0g	0%	**Sodium** 20mg	1%	Dietary Fiber 0g	0%
Saturated Fat 0g	0%	**Protein** 0g		Sugars 18g	
Polyunsaturated Fat 0g					
Monounsaturated Fat 0g		Vitamin A 0% Vitamin C 25%		Calcium 0% Iron 0%	

AriZona, White Tea, Blueberry White Tea

8 fl oz / 240 ml

Amount per serving	%DV	Amount per serving	%DV	Amount per serving	%DV
Calories 70		**Cholesterol** 0mg	0%	**Total Carbohydrate** 19g	6%
Total Fat 0g	0%	**Sodium** 10mg	0%	Dietary Fiber 0g	0%
Saturated Fat 0g	0%	**Protein** 0g		Sugars 18g	
Polyunsaturated Fat 0g					
Monounsaturated Fat 0g		Vitamin A 10% Vitamin C 50%		Calcium 0% Iron 0%	

Bigelow Teas, Apple Cider Herbal, Brewed, Prepared with Tap Water

8 fl oz

Amount per serving	%DV	Amount per serving	%DV	Amount per serving	%DV
Calories 0		**Cholesterol** 0mg	0%	**Total Carbohydrate** 0g	0%
Total Fat 0g	0%	**Sodium** 0mg	0%	Dietary Fiber 0g	0%
Saturated Fat 0g	0%	**Protein** 0g		Sugars 0g	
Polyunsaturated Fat 0g					
Monounsaturated Fat 0g		Vitamin A 0% Vitamin C 20%		Calcium 0% Iron 0%	

Bigelow Teas, Black Tea with Pomegranate, Brewed, Prepared with Tap Water

8 fl oz

Amount per serving	%DV	Amount per serving	%DV	Amount per serving	%DV
Calories 0		**Cholesterol** 0mg	0%	**Total Carbohydrate** 0g	0%
Total Fat 0g	0%	**Sodium** 0mg	0%	Dietary Fiber 0g	0%
Saturated Fat 0g	0%	**Protein** 0g		Sugars 0g	
Polyunsaturated Fat 0g					
Monounsaturated Fat 0g		Vitamin A 0% Vitamin C 0%		Calcium 0% Iron 0%	

Bigelow Teas, Chamomile Mango Herb Tea, Brewed, Prepared with Tap Water

8 fl oz

Amount per serving	%DV	Amount per serving	%DV	Amount per serving	%DV
Calories 0		**Cholesterol** 0mg	0%	**Total Carbohydrate** 1g	0%
Total Fat 0g	0%	**Sodium** 0mg	0%	Dietary Fiber 0g	0%
Saturated Fat 0g	0%	**Protein** 0g		Sugars 0g	
Polyunsaturated Fat 0g					
Monounsaturated Fat 0g		Vitamin A 0% Vitamin C 0%		Calcium 0% Iron 0%	

Bigelow Teas, Chamomile Mint Herb Tea, Brewed, Prepared with Tap Water

8 fl oz

Amount per serving	%DV	Amount per serving	%DV	Amount per serving	%DV
Calories 0		**Cholesterol** 0mg	0%	**Total Carbohydrate** 0g	0%
Total Fat 0g	0%	**Sodium** 0mg	0%	Dietary Fiber 0g	0%
Saturated Fat 0g	0%	**Protein** 0g		Sugars 0g	
Polyunsaturated Fat 0g					
Monounsaturated Fat 0g		Vitamin A 0% Vitamin C 0%		Calcium 0% Iron 0%	

Bigelow Teas, Chinese Oolong Tea, Brewed, Prepared with Tap Water

8 fl oz

Amount per serving	%DV	Amount per serving	%DV	Amount per serving	%DV
Calories 0		**Cholesterol** 0mg	0%	**Total Carbohydrate** 0g	0%
Total Fat 0g	0%	**Sodium** 0mg	0%	Dietary Fiber 0g	0%
Saturated Fat 0g	0%	**Protein** 0g		Sugars 0g	
Polyunsaturated Fat 0g					
Monounsaturated Fat 0g		Vitamin A 0% Vitamin C 0%		Calcium 0% Iron 0%	

Bigelow Teas, Cinnamon Apple Herb Tea, Brewed, Prepared with Tap Water

8 fl oz

Amount per serving	%DV	Amount per serving	%DV	Amount per serving	%DV
Calories 0		**Cholesterol** 0mg	0%	**Total Carbohydrate** 0g	0%
Total Fat 0g	0%	**Sodium** 0mg	0%	Dietary Fiber 0g	0%
Saturated Fat 0g	0%	**Protein** 0g		Sugars 0g	
Polyunsaturated Fat 0g					
Monounsaturated Fat 0g		Vitamin A 0% Vitamin C 0%		Calcium 0% Iron 0%	

Bigelow Teas, Cinnamon Stick Tea, Brewed, Prepared with Tap Water

8 fl oz

Amount per serving	%DV	Amount per serving	%DV	Amount per serving	%DV
Calories 0		**Cholesterol** 0mg	0%	**Total Carbohydrate** 1g	0%
Total Fat 0g	0%	**Sodium** 0mg	0%	Dietary Fiber 0g	0%
Saturated Fat 0g	0%	**Protein** 0g		Sugars 0g	
Polyunsaturated Fat 0g					
Monounsaturated Fat 0g		Vitamin A 0% Vitamin C 0%		Calcium 0% Iron 0%	

Bigelow Teas, Constant Comment Green Tea, Brewed, Brewed with Tap Water

8 fl oz

Amount per serving	%DV	Amount per serving	%DV	Amount per serving	%DV
Calories 0		**Cholesterol** 0mg	0%	**Total Carbohydrate** 0g	0%
Total Fat 0g	0%	**Sodium** 0mg	0%	Dietary Fiber 0g	0%
Saturated Fat 0g	0%	**Protein** 0g		Sugars 0g	
Polyunsaturated Fat 0g					
Monounsaturated Fat 0g		Vitamin A 0% Vitamin C 0%		Calcium 0% Iron 0%	

Bigelow Teas, Constant Comment Tea, Brewed, Prepared with Tap Water

8 fl oz

Amount per serving	%DV	Amount per serving	%DV	Amount per serving	%DV
Calories 0		**Cholesterol** 0mg	0%	**Total Carbohydrate** 0g	0%
Total Fat 0g	0%	**Sodium** 0mg	0%	Dietary Fiber 0g	0%
Saturated Fat 0g	0%	**Protein** 0g		Sugars 0g	
Polyunsaturated Fat 0g					
Monounsaturated Fat 0g		Vitamin A 0% Vitamin C 0%		Calcium 0% Iron 0%	

Bigelow Teas, Cozy Chamomile Herb Tea, Brewed, Prepared with Tap Water

8 fl oz

Amount per serving	%DV	Amount per serving	%DV	Amount per serving	%DV
Calories 0		**Cholesterol** 0mg	0%	**Total Carbohydrate** 0g	0%
Total Fat 0g	0%	**Sodium** 0mg	0%	Dietary Fiber 0g	0%
Saturated Fat 0g	0%	**Protein** 0g		Sugars 0g	
Polyunsaturated Fat 0g					
Monounsaturated Fat 0g		Vitamin A 0% Vitamin C 0%		Calcium 0% Iron 0%	

Bigelow Teas, Cranberry Apple Herb Tea, Brewed, Prepared with Tap Water

8 fl oz

Amount per serving	%DV	Amount per serving	%DV	Amount per serving	%DV
Calories 0		Cholesterol 0mg	0%	Total Carbohydrate 1g	0%
Total Fat 0g	0%	Sodium 0mg	0%	Dietary Fiber 0g	0%
Saturated Fat 0g	0%	Protein 0g		Sugars 0g	
Polyunsaturated Fat 0g					
Monounsaturated Fat 0g		Vitamin A 0% Vitamin C 0%		Calcium 0% Iron 0%	

Bigelow Teas, Cranberry Hibiscus Herb Tea, Brewed, Prepared with Tap Water

8 fl oz

Amount per serving	%DV	Amount per serving	%DV	Amount per serving	%DV
Calories 0		Cholesterol 0mg	0%	Total Carbohydrate 0g	0%
Total Fat 0g	0%	Sodium 0mg	0%	Dietary Fiber 0g	0%
Saturated Fat 0g	0%	Protein 0g		Sugars 0g	
Polyunsaturated Fat 0g					
Monounsaturated Fat 0g		Vitamin A 0% Vitamin C 0%		Calcium 0% Iron 0%	

Bigelow Teas, Earl Grey Decaffeinated Tea, Brewed, Prepared with Tap Water

8 fl oz

Amount per serving	%DV	Amount per serving	%DV	Amount per serving	%DV
Calories 0		Cholesterol 0mg	0%	Total Carbohydrate 0g	0%
Total Fat 0g	0%	Sodium 0mg	0%	Dietary Fiber 0g	0%
Saturated Fat 0g	0%	Protein 0g		Sugars 0g	
Polyunsaturated Fat 0g					
Monounsaturated Fat 0g		Vitamin A 0% Vitamin C 0%		Calcium 0% Iron 0%	

Bigelow Teas, Earl Grey Green Tea, Brewed, Prepared with Tap Water

8 fl oz

Amount per serving	%DV	Amount per serving	%DV	Amount per serving	%DV
Calories 0		Cholesterol 0mg	0%	Total Carbohydrate 0g	0%
Total Fat 0g	0%	Sodium 0mg	0%	Dietary Fiber 0g	0%
Saturated Fat 0g	0%	Protein 0g		Sugars 0g	
Polyunsaturated Fat 0g					
Monounsaturated Fat 0g		Vitamin A 0% Vitamin C 0%		Calcium 0% Iron 0%	

Bigelow Teas, Earl Grey Tea, Brewed, Prepared with Tap Water

8 fl oz

Amount per serving	%DV	Amount per serving	%DV	Amount per serving	%DV
Calories 0		Cholesterol 0mg	0%	Total Carbohydrate 0g	0%
Total Fat 0g	0%	Sodium 0mg	0%	Dietary Fiber 0g	0%
Saturated Fat 0g	0%	Protein 0g		Sugars 0g	
Polyunsaturated Fat 0g					
Monounsaturated Fat 0g		Vitamin A 0% Vitamin C 0%		Calcium 0% Iron 0%	

Bigelow Teas, Eggnogg'n Tea, Brewed, Prepared with Tap Water

8 fl oz

Amount per serving	%DV	Amount per serving	%DV	Amount per serving	%DV
Calories 0		**Cholesterol** 0mg	0%	**Total Carbohydrate** 0g	0%
Total Fat 0g	0%	**Sodium** 0mg	0%	Dietary Fiber 0g	0%
Saturated Fat 0g	0%	**Protein** 0g		Sugars 0g	
Polyunsaturated Fat 0g					
Monounsaturated Fat 0g		Vitamin A 0% Vitamin C 0%		Calcium 0% Iron 0%	

Bigelow Teas, English Breakfast Tea, Brewed, Prepared with Tap Water

8 fl oz

Amount per serving	%DV	Amount per serving	%DV	Amount per serving	%DV
Calories 0		**Cholesterol** 0mg	0%	**Total Carbohydrate** 1g	0%
Total Fat 0g	0%	**Sodium** 0mg	0%	Dietary Fiber 0g	0%
Saturated Fat 0g	0%	**Protein** 0g		Sugars 0g	
Polyunsaturated Fat 0g					
Monounsaturated Fat 0g		Vitamin A 0% Vitamin C 0%		Calcium 0% Iron 0%	

Bigelow Teas, English Teatime Decaffeinated Tea, Brewed, Prepared with Tap Water

8 fl oz

Amount per serving	%DV	Amount per serving	%DV	Amount per serving	%DV
Calories 0		**Cholesterol** 0mg	0%	**Total Carbohydrate** 0g	0%
Total Fat 0g	0%	**Sodium** 0mg	0%	Dietary Fiber 0g	0%
Saturated Fat 0g	0%	**Protein** 0g		Sugars 0g	
Polyunsaturated Fat 0g					
Monounsaturated Fat 0g		Vitamin A 0% Vitamin C 0%		Calcium 0% Iron 0%	

Bigelow Teas, English Teatime Tea, Brewed, Prepared with Tap Water

8 fl oz

Amount per serving	%DV	Amount per serving	%DV	Amount per serving	%DV
Calories 0		**Cholesterol** 0mg	0%	**Total Carbohydrate** 1g	0%
Total Fat 0g	0%	**Sodium** 0mg	0%	Dietary Fiber 0g	0%
Saturated Fat 0g	0%	**Protein** 0g		Sugars 0g	
Polyunsaturated Fat 0g					
Monounsaturated Fat 0g		Vitamin A 0% Vitamin C 0%		Calcium 0% Iron 0%	

Bigelow Teas, French Vanilla Decaffeinated Tea, Brewed, Prepared with Tap Water

8 fl oz

Amount per serving	%DV	Amount per serving	%DV	Amount per serving	%DV
Calories 0		**Cholesterol** 0mg	0%	**Total Carbohydrate** 1g	0%
Total Fat 0g	0%	**Sodium** 0mg	0%	Dietary Fiber 0g	0%
Saturated Fat 0g	0%	**Protein** 0g		Sugars 0g	
Polyunsaturated Fat 0g					
Monounsaturated Fat 0g		Vitamin A 0% Vitamin C 0%		Calcium 0% Iron 0%	

Bigelow Teas, French Vanilla Tea, Brewed, Prepared with Tap Water

8 fl oz

Amount per serving	%DV	Amount per serving	%DV	Amount per serving	%DV
Calories 0		**Cholesterol** 0mg	0%	**Total Carbohydrate** 1g	0%
Total Fat 0g	0%	**Sodium** 0mg	0%	Dietary Fiber 0g	0%
Saturated Fat 0g	0%	**Protein** 0g		Sugars 0g	
Polyunsaturated Fat 0g					
Monounsaturated Fat 0g		Vitamin A 0% Vitamin C 0%		Calcium 0% Iron 0%	

Bigelow Teas, Fruit & Almond Herb Tea, Brewed, Prepared with Tap Water

8 fl oz

Amount per serving	%DV	Amount per serving	%DV	Amount per serving	%DV
Calories 0		**Cholesterol** 0mg	0%	**Total Carbohydrate** 1g	0%
Total Fat 0g	0%	**Sodium** 0mg	0%	Dietary Fiber 0g	0%
Saturated Fat 0g	0%	**Protein** 0g		Sugars 0g	
Polyunsaturated Fat 0g					
Monounsaturated Fat 0g		Vitamin A 0% Vitamin C 0%		Calcium 0% Iron 0%	

Bigelow Teas, Ginger Snappish Herb Tea, Brewed, Prepared with Tap Water

8 fl oz

Amount per serving	%DV	Amount per serving	%DV	Amount per serving	%DV
Calories 0		**Cholesterol** 0mg	0%	**Total Carbohydrate** 0g	0%
Total Fat 0g	0%	**Sodium** 0mg	0%	Dietary Fiber 0g	0%
Saturated Fat 0g	0%	**Protein** 0g		Sugars 0g	
Polyunsaturated Fat 0g					
Monounsaturated Fat 0g		Vitamin A 0% Vitamin C 0%		Calcium 0% Iron 0%	

Bigelow Teas, Green Chai, Brewed, Prepared with Tap Water

8 fl oz

Amount per serving	%DV	Amount per serving	%DV	Amount per serving	%DV
Calories 0		**Cholesterol** 0mg	0%	**Total Carbohydrate** 0g	0%
Total Fat 0g	0%	**Sodium** 0mg	0%	Dietary Fiber 0g	0%
Saturated Fat 0g	0%	**Protein** 0g		Sugars 0g	
Polyunsaturated Fat 0g					
Monounsaturated Fat 0g		Vitamin A 0% Vitamin C 0%		Calcium 0% Iron 0%	

Bigelow Teas, Green Tea Decaffeinated, Brewed, Prepared with Tap Water

8 fl oz

Amount per serving	%DV	Amount per serving	%DV	Amount per serving	%DV
Calories 0		**Cholesterol** 0mg	0%	**Total Carbohydrate** 0g	0%
Total Fat 0g	0%	**Sodium** 0mg	0%	Dietary Fiber 0g	0%
Saturated Fat 0g	0%	**Protein** 0g		Sugars 0g	
Polyunsaturated Fat 0g					
Monounsaturated Fat 0g		Vitamin A 0% Vitamin C 0%		Calcium 0% Iron 0%	

Bigelow Teas, Green Tea w/Pomegranate, Decaff, Brewed With Tap Water

8 fl oz

Amount per serving	%DV	Amount per serving	%DV	Amount per serving	%DV
Calories 0		**Cholesterol** 0mg	0%	**Total Carbohydrate** 0g	0%
Total Fat 0g	0%	**Sodium** 0mg	0%	Dietary Fiber 0g	0%
Saturated Fat 0g	0%	**Protein** 0g		Sugars 0g	
Polyunsaturated Fat 0g					
Monounsaturated Fat 0g		Vitamin A 0% Vitamin C 0%		Calcium 0% Iron 0%	

Bigelow Teas, Green Tea w/Wild Blueberry & Acai Decaff, Brewed With Tap Water

8 fl oz

Amount per serving	%DV	Amount per serving	%DV	Amount per serving	%DV
Calories 0		**Cholesterol** 0mg	0%	**Total Carbohydrate** 1g	0%
Total Fat 0g	0%	**Sodium** 0mg	0%	Dietary Fiber 0g	0%
Saturated Fat 0g	0%	**Protein** 0g		Sugars 0g	
Polyunsaturated Fat 0g					
Monounsaturated Fat 0g		Vitamin A 0% Vitamin C 10%		Calcium 0% Iron 0%	

Bigelow Teas, Green Tea w/Wild Blueberry & Acai, Brewed With Tap Water

8 fl oz

Amount per serving	%DV	Amount per serving	%DV	Amount per serving	%DV
Calories 0		**Cholesterol** 0mg	0%	**Total Carbohydrate** 0g	0%
Total Fat 0g	0%	**Sodium** 0mg	0%	Dietary Fiber 0g	0%
Saturated Fat 0g	0%	**Protein** 0g		Sugars 0g	
Polyunsaturated Fat 0g					
Monounsaturated Fat 0g		Vitamin A 0% Vitamin C 10%		Calcium 0% Iron 0%	

Bigelow Teas, Green Tea with Lemon, Brewed, Prepared With Tap Water

8 fl oz

Amount per serving	%DV	Amount per serving	%DV	Amount per serving	%DV
Calories 0		**Cholesterol** 0mg	0%	**Total Carbohydrate** 0g	0%
Total Fat 0g	0%	**Sodium** 0mg	0%	Dietary Fiber 0g	0%
Saturated Fat 0g	0%	**Protein** 0g		Sugars 0g	
Polyunsaturated Fat 0g					
Monounsaturated Fat 0g		Vitamin A 0% Vitamin C 0%		Calcium 0% Iron 0%	

Bigelow Teas, Green Tea with Lemon, Decaffeinated, Brewed With Tap Water

8 fl oz

Amount per serving	%DV	Amount per serving	%DV	Amount per serving	%DV
Calories 0		**Cholesterol** 0mg	0%	**Total Carbohydrate** 0g	0%
Total Fat 0g	0%	**Sodium** 0mg	0%	Dietary Fiber 0g	0%
Saturated Fat 0g	0%	**Protein** 0g		Sugars 0g	
Polyunsaturated Fat 0g					
Monounsaturated Fat 0g		Vitamin A 0% Vitamin C 0%		Calcium 0% Iron 0%	

Bigelow Teas, Green Tea with Mango, Brewed, Prepared With Tap Water

8 fl oz

Amount per serving	%DV	Amount per serving	%DV	Amount per serving	%DV
Calories 0		**Cholesterol** 0mg	0%	**Total Carbohydrate** 0g	0%
Total Fat 0g	0%	**Sodium** 0mg	0%	Dietary Fiber 0g	0%
Saturated Fat 0g	0%	**Protein** 0g		Sugars 0g	
Polyunsaturated Fat 0g					
Monounsaturated Fat 0g		Vitamin A 0%	Vitamin C 0%	Calcium 0%	Iron 0%

Bigelow Teas, Green Tea with Mint, Brewed, Prepared With Tap Water

8 fl oz

Amount per serving	%DV	Amount per serving	%DV	Amount per serving	%DV
Calories 0		**Cholesterol** 0mg	0%	**Total Carbohydrate** 0g	0%
Total Fat 0g	0%	**Sodium** 0mg	0%	Dietary Fiber 0g	0%
Saturated Fat 0g	0%	**Protein** 0g		Sugars 0g	
Polyunsaturated Fat 0g					
Monounsaturated Fat 0g		Vitamin A 0%	Vitamin C 0%	Calcium 0%	Iron 0%

Bigelow Teas, Green Tea with Peach, Brewed, Prepared With Tap Water

8 fl oz

Amount per serving	%DV	Amount per serving	%DV	Amount per serving	%DV
Calories 0		**Cholesterol** 0mg	0%	**Total Carbohydrate** 0g	0%
Total Fat 0g	0%	**Sodium** 0mg	0%	Dietary Fiber 0g	0%
Saturated Fat 0g	0%	**Protein** 0g		Sugars 0g	
Polyunsaturated Fat 0g					
Monounsaturated Fat 0g		Vitamin A 0%	Vitamin C 0%	Calcium 0%	Iron 0%

Bigelow Teas, Green Tea with Pomegranate Iced Tea, Brewed With Tap Water

8 fl oz

Amount per serving	%DV	Amount per serving	%DV	Amount per serving	%DV
Calories 0		**Cholesterol** 0mg	0%	**Total Carbohydrate** 1g	0%
Total Fat 0g	0%	**Sodium** 0mg	0%	Dietary Fiber 0g	0%
Saturated Fat 0g	0%	**Protein** 0g		Sugars 0g	
Polyunsaturated Fat 0g					
Monounsaturated Fat 0g		Vitamin A 0%	Vitamin C 0%	Calcium 0%	Iron 0%

Bigelow Teas, Green Tea with Pomegranate, Brewed, Prepared With Tap Water

8 fl oz

Amount per serving	%DV	Amount per serving	%DV	Amount per serving	%DV
Calories 0		**Cholesterol** 0mg	0%	**Total Carbohydrate** 0g	0%
Total Fat 0g	0%	**Sodium** 0mg	0%	Dietary Fiber 0g	0%
Saturated Fat 0g	0%	**Protein** 0g		Sugars 0g	
Polyunsaturated Fat 0g					
Monounsaturated Fat 0g		Vitamin A 0%	Vitamin C 10%	Calcium 0%	Iron 0%

Bigelow Teas, Green Tea, Brewed, Prepared with Tap Water

8 fl oz

Amount per serving	%DV	Amount per serving	%DV	Amount per serving	%DV
Calories 0		**Cholesterol** 0mg	0%	**Total Carbohydrate** 0g	0%
Total Fat 0g	0%	**Sodium** 0mg	0%	Dietary Fiber 0g	0%
Saturated Fat 0g	0%	**Protein** 0g		Sugars 0g	
Polyunsaturated Fat 0g					
Monounsaturated Fat 0g		Vitamin A 0% Vitamin C 0%		Calcium 0% Iron 0%	

Bigelow Teas, Half Iced Tea & Half Lemonade, Brewed, Prepared with Tap Water

8 fl oz

Amount per serving	%DV	Amount per serving	%DV	Amount per serving	%DV
Calories 15		**Cholesterol** 0mg	0%	**Total Carbohydrate** 4g	1%
Total Fat 0g	0%	**Sodium** 0mg	0%	Dietary Fiber 0g	0%
Saturated Fat 0g	0%	**Protein** 0g		Sugars 3g	
Polyunsaturated Fat 0g					
Monounsaturated Fat 0g		Vitamin A 0% Vitamin C 0%		Calcium 0% Iron 0%	

Bigelow Teas, Half Iced Tea/Half Lemonade w/Pomegranate, Brewed With Tap Water

8 fl oz

Amount per serving	%DV	Amount per serving	%DV	Amount per serving	%DV
Calories 10		**Cholesterol** 0mg	0%	**Total Carbohydrate** 3g	1%
Total Fat 0g	0%	**Sodium** 0mg	0%	Dietary Fiber 0g	0%
Saturated Fat 0g	0%	**Protein** 0g		Sugars 2g	
Polyunsaturated Fat 0g					
Monounsaturated Fat 0g		Vitamin A 0% Vitamin C 0%		Calcium 0% Iron 0%	

Bigelow Teas, Herb Plus Lemon Ginger (Probiotics), Brewed with Tap Water

8 fl oz

Amount per serving	%DV	Amount per serving	%DV	Amount per serving	%DV
Calories 0		**Cholesterol** 0mg	0%	**Total Carbohydrate** 1g	0%
Total Fat 0g	0%	**Sodium** 0mg	0%	Dietary Fiber 0g	0%
Saturated Fat 0g	0%	**Protein** 0g		Sugars 0g	
Polyunsaturated Fat 0g					
Monounsaturated Fat 0g		Vitamin A 0% Vitamin C 0%		Calcium 0% Iron 0%	

Bigelow Teas, I Love Lemon & C Herb Tea, Brewed, Prepared with Tap Water

8 fl oz

Amount per serving	%DV	Amount per serving	%DV	Amount per serving	%DV
Calories 0		**Cholesterol** 0mg	0%	**Total Carbohydrate** 1g	0%
Total Fat 0g	0%	**Sodium** 0mg	0%	Dietary Fiber 0g	0%
Saturated Fat 0g	0%	**Protein** 0g		Sugars 0g	
Polyunsaturated Fat 0g					
Monounsaturated Fat 0g		Vitamin A 0% Vitamin C 100%		Calcium 0% Iron 0%	

Bigelow Teas, Jasmine Green Tea, Brewed, Prepared with Tap Water

8 fl oz

Amount per serving	%DV	Amount per serving	%DV	Amount per serving	%DV
Calories 0		**Cholesterol** 0mg	0%	**Total Carbohydrate** 0g	0%
Total Fat 0g	0%	**Sodium** 0mg	0%	Dietary Fiber 0g	0%
Saturated Fat 0g	0%	**Protein** 0g		Sugars 0g	
Polyunsaturated Fat 0g					
Monounsaturated Fat 0g		Vitamin A 0% Vitamin C 0%		Calcium 0% Iron 0%	

Bigelow Teas, Lemon Lift Decaffeinated Tea, Brewed, Prepared with Tap Water

8 fl oz

Amount per serving	%DV	Amount per serving	%DV	Amount per serving	%DV
Calories 0		**Cholesterol** 0mg	0%	**Total Carbohydrate** 1g	0%
Total Fat 0g	0%	**Sodium** 0mg	0%	Dietary Fiber 0g	0%
Saturated Fat 0g	0%	**Protein** 0g		Sugars 0g	
Polyunsaturated Fat 0g					
Monounsaturated Fat 0g		Vitamin A 0% Vitamin C 0%		Calcium 0% Iron 0%	

Bigelow Teas, Lemon Lift Tea, Brewed, Prepared with Tap Water

8 fl oz

Amount per serving	%DV	Amount per serving	%DV	Amount per serving	%DV
Calories 0		**Cholesterol** 0mg	0%	**Total Carbohydrate** 1g	0%
Total Fat 0g	0%	**Sodium** 0mg	0%	Dietary Fiber 0g	0%
Saturated Fat 0g	0%	**Protein** 0g		Sugars 0g	
Polyunsaturated Fat 0g					
Monounsaturated Fat 0g		Vitamin A 0% Vitamin C 0%		Calcium 0% Iron 0%	

Bigelow Teas, Mint Medley Herb Tea, Brewed, Prepared with Tap Water

8 fl oz

Amount per serving	%DV	Amount per serving	%DV	Amount per serving	%DV
Calories 0		**Cholesterol** 0mg	0%	**Total Carbohydrate** 1g	0%
Total Fat 0g	0%	**Sodium** 0mg	0%	Dietary Fiber 0g	0%
Saturated Fat 0g	0%	**Protein** 0g		Sugars 0g	
Polyunsaturated Fat 0g					
Monounsaturated Fat 0g		Vitamin A 0% Vitamin C 0%		Calcium 0% Iron 0%	

Bigelow Teas, Orange & Spice Herb Tea, Brewed, Prepared with Tap Water

8 fl oz

Amount per serving	%DV	Amount per serving	%DV	Amount per serving	%DV
Calories 0		**Cholesterol** 0mg	0%	**Total Carbohydrate** 1g	0%
Total Fat 0g	0%	**Sodium** 0mg	0%	Dietary Fiber 0g	0%
Saturated Fat 0g	0%	**Protein** 0g		Sugars 0g	
Polyunsaturated Fat 0g					
Monounsaturated Fat 0g		Vitamin A 0% Vitamin C 0%		Calcium 0% Iron 0%	

Bigelow Teas, Organic Breakfast Blend Decaff Tea, Brewed with Tap Water

8 fl oz

Amount per serving	%DV	Amount per serving	%DV	Amount per serving	%DV
Calories 0		**Cholesterol** 0mg	0%	**Total Carbohydrate** 0g	0%
Total Fat 0g	0%	**Sodium** 0mg	0%	Dietary Fiber 0g	0%
Saturated Fat 0g	0%	**Protein** 0g		Sugars 0g	
Polyunsaturated Fat 0g					
Monounsaturated Fat 0g		Vitamin A 0%	Vitamin C 0%	Calcium 0%	Iron 0%

Bigelow Teas, Organic Ceylon-Fair Trade Tea, Brewed, Prepared with Tap Water

8 fl oz

Amount per serving	%DV	Amount per serving	%DV	Amount per serving	%DV
Calories 0		**Cholesterol** 0mg	0%	**Total Carbohydrate** 0g	0%
Total Fat 0g	0%	**Sodium** 0mg	0%	Dietary Fiber 0g	0%
Saturated Fat 0g	0%	**Protein** 0g		Sugars 0g	
Polyunsaturated Fat 0g					
Monounsaturated Fat 0g		Vitamin A 0%	Vitamin C 0%	Calcium 0%	Iron 0%

Bigelow Teas, Organic Chamomile Citrus Herb Tea, Brewed with Tap Water

8 fl oz

Amount per serving	%DV	Amount per serving	%DV	Amount per serving	%DV
Calories 0		**Cholesterol** 0mg	0%	**Total Carbohydrate** 0g	0%
Total Fat 0g	0%	**Sodium** 0mg	0%	Dietary Fiber 0g	0%
Saturated Fat 0g	0%	**Protein** 0g		Sugars 0g	
Polyunsaturated Fat 0g					
Monounsaturated Fat 0g		Vitamin A 0%	Vitamin C 0%	Calcium 0%	Iron 0%

Bigelow Teas, Organic Chamomile Citrus Herb Tea, Brewed, Prepared with Tap Water

8 fl oz

Amount per serving	%DV	Amount per serving	%DV	Amount per serving	%DV
Calories 0		**Cholesterol** 0mg	0%	**Total Carbohydrate** 0g	0%
Total Fat 0g	0%	**Sodium** 0mg	0%	Dietary Fiber 0g	0%
Saturated Fat 0g	0%	**Protein** 0g		Sugars 0g	
Polyunsaturated Fat 0g					
Monounsaturated Fat 0g		Vitamin A 0%	Vitamin C 0%	Calcium 0%	Iron 0%

Bigelow Teas, Organic Green Decaffeinated Tea, Brewed, Prepared with Tap Water

8 fl oz

Amount per serving	%DV	Amount per serving	%DV	Amount per serving	%DV
Calories 0		**Cholesterol** 0mg	0%	**Total Carbohydrate** 0g	0%
Total Fat 0g	0%	**Sodium** 0mg	0%	Dietary Fiber 0g	0%
Saturated Fat 0g	0%	**Protein** 0g		Sugars 0g	
Polyunsaturated Fat 0g					
Monounsaturated Fat 0g		Vitamin A 0%	Vitamin C 0%	Calcium 0%	Iron 0%

Bigelow Teas, Organic Green Tea Pomegranate & Acai, Brewed with Tap Water

8 fl oz

Amount per serving	%DV	Amount per serving	%DV	Amount per serving	%DV
Calories 0		**Cholesterol** 0mg	0%	**Total Carbohydrate** 0g	0%
Total Fat 0g	0%	**Sodium** 0mg	0%	Dietary Fiber 0g	0%
Saturated Fat 0g	0%	**Protein** 0g		Sugars 0g	
Polyunsaturated Fat 0g					
Monounsaturated Fat 0g		Vitamin A 0%	Vitamin C 10%	Calcium 0%	Iron 0%

Bigelow Teas, Organic Imperial Earl Grey Tea, Brewed, Prepared with Tap Water

8 fl oz

Amount per serving	%DV	Amount per serving	%DV	Amount per serving	%DV
Calories 0		**Cholesterol** 0mg	0%	**Total Carbohydrate** 0g	0%
Total Fat 0g	0%	**Sodium** 0mg	0%	Dietary Fiber 0g	0%
Saturated Fat 0g	0%	**Protein** 0g		Sugars 0g	
Polyunsaturated Fat 0g					
Monounsaturated Fat 0g		Vitamin A 0%	Vitamin C 0%	Calcium 0%	Iron 0%

Bigelow Teas, Organic Moroccan Mint Herb Tea, Brewed, Prepared with Tap Water

8 fl oz

Amount per serving	%DV	Amount per serving	%DV	Amount per serving	%DV
Calories 0		**Cholesterol** 0mg	0%	**Total Carbohydrate** 0g	0%
Total Fat 0g	0%	**Sodium** 0mg	0%	Dietary Fiber 0g	0%
Saturated Fat 0g	0%	**Protein** 0g		Sugars 0g	
Polyunsaturated Fat 0g					
Monounsaturated Fat 0g		Vitamin A 0%	Vitamin C 0%	Calcium 0%	Iron 0%

Bigelow Teas, Organic Pure Green Decaff Tea, Brewed with Tap Water

8 fl oz

Amount per serving	%DV	Amount per serving	%DV	Amount per serving	%DV
Calories 0		**Cholesterol** 0mg	0%	**Total Carbohydrate** 0g	0%
Total Fat 0g	0%	**Sodium** 0mg	0%	Dietary Fiber 0g	0%
Saturated Fat 0g	0%	**Protein** 0g		Sugars 0g	
Polyunsaturated Fat 0g					
Monounsaturated Fat 0g		Vitamin A 0%	Vitamin C 0%	Calcium 0%	Iron 0%

Bigelow Teas, Organic Pure Green Tea, Brewed, Prepared with Tap Water

8 fl oz

Amount per serving	%DV	Amount per serving	%DV	Amount per serving	%DV
Calories 0		**Cholesterol** 0mg	0%	**Total Carbohydrate** 0g	0%
Total Fat 0g	0%	**Sodium** 0mg	0%	Dietary Fiber 0g	0%
Saturated Fat 0g	0%	**Protein** 0g		Sugars 0g	
Polyunsaturated Fat 0g					
Monounsaturated Fat 0g		Vitamin A 0%	Vitamin C 0%	Calcium 0%	Iron 0%

Bigelow Teas, Organic Rooibos w/Asian Pear Tea, Brewed with Tap Water

8 fl oz

Amount per serving	%DV	Amount per serving	%DV	Amount per serving	%DV
Calories 0		**Cholesterol** 0mg	0%	**Total Carbohydrate** 0g	0%
Total Fat 0g	0%	**Sodium** 0mg	0%	Dietary Fiber 0g	0%
Saturated Fat 0g	0%	**Protein** 0g		Sugars 0g	
Polyunsaturated Fat 0g					
Monounsaturated Fat 0g		Vitamin A 0%	Vitamin C 0%	Calcium 0%	Iron 0%

Bigelow Teas, Organic Wh w/Raspberry/Chrysanthemum, Brewed with Tap Water

8 fl oz

Amount per serving	%DV	Amount per serving	%DV	Amount per serving	%DV
Calories 0		**Cholesterol** 0mg	0%	**Total Carbohydrate** 0g	0%
Total Fat 0g	0%	**Sodium** 0mg	0%	Dietary Fiber 0g	0%
Saturated Fat 0g	0%	**Protein** 0g		Sugars 0g	
Polyunsaturated Fat 0g					
Monounsaturated Fat 0g		Vitamin A 0%	Vitamin C 0%	Calcium 0%	Iron 0%

Bigelow Teas, Perfect Peach Herb Iced Tea, Brewed, Prepared with Tap Water

8 fl oz

Amount per serving	%DV	Amount per serving	%DV	Amount per serving	%DV
Calories 0		**Cholesterol** 0mg	0%	**Total Carbohydrate** 1g	0%
Total Fat 0g	0%	**Sodium** 0mg	0%	Dietary Fiber 0g	0%
Saturated Fat 0g	0%	**Protein** 0g		Sugars 0g	
Polyunsaturated Fat 0g					
Monounsaturated Fat 0g		Vitamin A 0%	Vitamin C 0%	Calcium 0%	Iron 0%

Bigelow Teas, Perfect Peach Herb Tea, Brewed, Prepared with Tap Water

8 fl oz

Amount per serving	%DV	Amount per serving	%DV	Amount per serving	%DV
Calories 0		**Cholesterol** 0mg	0%	**Total Carbohydrate** 1g	0%
Total Fat 0g	0%	**Sodium** 0mg	0%	Dietary Fiber 0g	0%
Saturated Fat 0g	0%	**Protein** 0g		Sugars 0g	
Polyunsaturated Fat 0g					
Monounsaturated Fat 0g		Vitamin A 0%	Vitamin C 0%	Calcium 0%	Iron 0%

Bigelow Teas, Plantation Mint Tea, Brewed, Prepared with Tap Water

8 fl oz

Amount per serving	%DV	Amount per serving	%DV	Amount per serving	%DV
Calories 0		**Cholesterol** 0mg	0%	**Total Carbohydrate** 0g	0%
Total Fat 0g	0%	**Sodium** 0mg	0%	Dietary Fiber 0g	0%
Saturated Fat 0g	0%	**Protein** 0g		Sugars 0g	
Polyunsaturated Fat 0g					
Monounsaturated Fat 0g		Vitamin A 0%	Vitamin C 0%	Calcium 0%	Iron 0%

Bigelow Teas, Pomegranate Pizzazz Herb Tea, Brewed, Prepared with Tap Water

8 fl oz

Amount per serving	%DV	Amount per serving	%DV	Amount per serving	%DV
Calories 0		**Cholesterol** 0mg	0%	**Total Carbohydrate** 0g	0%
Total Fat 0g	0%	**Sodium** 0mg	0%	Dietary Fiber 0g	0%
Saturated Fat 0g	0%	**Protein** 0g		Sugars 0g	
Polyunsaturated Fat 0g					
Monounsaturated Fat 0g		Vitamin A 0% Vitamin C 0%		Calcium 0% Iron 0%	

Bigelow Teas, Pumpkin Spice Tea, Brewed, Prepared with Tap Water

8 fl oz

Amount per serving	%DV	Amount per serving	%DV	Amount per serving	%DV
Calories 0		**Cholesterol** 0mg	0%	**Total Carbohydrate** 0g	0%
Total Fat 0g	0%	**Sodium** 0mg	0%	Dietary Fiber 0g	0%
Saturated Fat 0g	0%	**Protein** 0g		Sugars 0g	
Polyunsaturated Fat 0g					
Monounsaturated Fat 0g		Vitamin A 0% Vitamin C 15%		Calcium 0% Iron 0%	

Bigelow Teas, Raspberry Royale Tea, Brewed, Prepared with Tap Water

8 fl oz

Amount per serving	%DV	Amount per serving	%DV	Amount per serving	%DV
Calories 0		**Cholesterol** 0mg	0%	**Total Carbohydrate** 1g	0%
Total Fat 0g	0%	**Sodium** 0mg	0%	Dietary Fiber 0g	0%
Saturated Fat 0g	0%	**Protein** 0g		Sugars 0g	
Polyunsaturated Fat 0g					
Monounsaturated Fat 0g		Vitamin A 0% Vitamin C 0%		Calcium 0% Iron 0%	

Bigelow Teas, Red Raspberry Herb Iced Tea, Brewed, Prepared with Tap Water

8 fl oz

Amount per serving	%DV	Amount per serving	%DV	Amount per serving	%DV
Calories 0		**Cholesterol** 0mg	0%	**Total Carbohydrate** 0g	0%
Total Fat 0g	0%	**Sodium** 0mg	0%	Dietary Fiber 0g	0%
Saturated Fat 0g	0%	**Protein** 0g		Sugars 0g	
Polyunsaturated Fat 0g					
Monounsaturated Fat 0g		Vitamin A 0% Vitamin C 0%		Calcium 0% Iron 0%	

Bigelow Teas, Red Raspberry Herb Tea, Brewed, Prepared with Tap Water

8 fl oz

Amount per serving	%DV	Amount per serving	%DV	Amount per serving	%DV
Calories 0		**Cholesterol** 0mg	0%	**Total Carbohydrate** 1g	0%
Total Fat 0g	0%	**Sodium** 0mg	0%	Dietary Fiber 0g	0%
Saturated Fat 0g	0%	**Protein** 0g		Sugars 0g	
Polyunsaturated Fat 0g					
Monounsaturated Fat 0g		Vitamin A 0% Vitamin C 0%		Calcium 0% Iron 0%	

Bigelow Teas, Spiced Chai Decaffeinated Tea, Brewed, Prepared with Tap Water

8 fl oz

Amount per serving	%DV	Amount per serving	%DV	Amount per serving	%DV
Calories 0		Cholesterol 0mg	0%	Total Carbohydrate 0g	0%
Total Fat 0g	0%	Sodium 0mg	0%	Dietary Fiber 0g	0%
Saturated Fat 0g	0%	Protein 0g		Sugars 0g	
Polyunsaturated Fat 0g					
Monounsaturated Fat 0g		Vitamin A 0% Vitamin C 0%		Calcium 0% Iron 0%	

Bigelow Teas, Spiced Chai Tea, Brewed, Prepared with Tap Water

8 fl oz

Amount per serving	%DV	Amount per serving	%DV	Amount per serving	%DV
Calories 0		Cholesterol 0mg	0%	Total Carbohydrate 0g	0%
Total Fat 0g	0%	Sodium 0mg	0%	Dietary Fiber 0g	0%
Saturated Fat 0g	0%	Protein 0g		Sugars 0g	
Polyunsaturated Fat 0g					
Monounsaturated Fat 0g		Vitamin A 0% Vitamin C 0%		Calcium 0% Iron 0%	

Bigelow Teas, Sweet Dreams Herb Tea, Brewed, Prepared with Tap Water

8 fl oz

Amount per serving	%DV	Amount per serving	%DV	Amount per serving	%DV
Calories 0		Cholesterol 0mg	0%	Total Carbohydrate 0g	0%
Total Fat 0g	0%	Sodium 0mg	0%	Dietary Fiber 0g	0%
Saturated Fat 0g	0%	Protein 0g		Sugars 0g	
Polyunsaturated Fat 0g					
Monounsaturated Fat 0g		Vitamin A 0% Vitamin C 0%		Calcium 0% Iron 0%	

Bigelow Teas, Sweetheart Cinnamon Herb Tea, Brewed, Prepared with Tap Water

8 fl oz

Amount per serving	%DV	Amount per serving	%DV	Amount per serving	%DV
Calories 0		Cholesterol 0mg	0%	Total Carbohydrate 0g	0%
Total Fat 0g	0%	Sodium 0mg	0%	Dietary Fiber 0g	0%
Saturated Fat 0g	0%	Protein 0g		Sugars 0g	
Polyunsaturated Fat 0g					
Monounsaturated Fat 0g		Vitamin A 0% Vitamin C 0%		Calcium 0% Iron 0%	

Bigelow Teas, Vanilla Caramel Tea, Brewed, Prepared with Tap Water

8 fl oz

Amount per serving	%DV	Amount per serving	%DV	Amount per serving	%DV
Calories 0		Cholesterol 0mg	0%	Total Carbohydrate 1g	0%
Total Fat 0g	0%	Sodium 0mg	0%	Dietary Fiber 0g	0%
Saturated Fat 0g	0%	Protein 0g		Sugars 0g	
Polyunsaturated Fat 0g					
Monounsaturated Fat 0g		Vitamin A 0% Vitamin C 0%		Calcium 0% Iron 0%	

Bigelow Teas, Vanilla Chai Tea, Brewed, Prepared with Tap Water

8 fl oz

Amount per serving	%DV	Amount per serving	%DV	Amount per serving	%DV
Calories 0		**Cholesterol** 0mg	0%	**Total Carbohydrate** 1g	0%
Total Fat 0g	0%	**Sodium** 0mg	0%	Dietary Fiber 0g	0%
Saturated Fat 0g	0%	**Protein** 0g		Sugars 0g	
Polyunsaturated Fat 0g					
Monounsaturated Fat 0g		Vitamin A 0%	Vitamin C 0%	Calcium 0%	Iron 0%

Bigelow Teas, White Chocolate Obsession Tea, Brewed, Prepared with Tap Water

8 fl oz

Amount per serving	%DV	Amount per serving	%DV	Amount per serving	%DV
Calories 0		**Cholesterol** 0mg	0%	**Total Carbohydrate** 1g	0%
Total Fat 0g	0%	**Sodium** 0mg	0%	Dietary Fiber 2g	8%
Saturated Fat 0g	0%	**Protein** 1g		Sugars 1g	
Polyunsaturated Fat 0g					
Monounsaturated Fat 0g		Vitamin A 0%	Vitamin C 0%	Calcium 0%	Iron 0%

Bigelow Teas, Wild Blueberry with Acai Herb Tea, Brewed, Prepared with Tap Water

8 fl oz

Amount per serving	%DV	Amount per serving	%DV	Amount per serving	%DV
Calories 0		**Cholesterol** 0mg	0%	**Total Carbohydrate** 0g	0%
Total Fat 0g	0%	**Sodium** 0mg	0%	Dietary Fiber 0g	0%
Saturated Fat 0g	0%	**Protein** 0g		Sugars 0g	
Polyunsaturated Fat 0g					
Monounsaturated Fat 0g		Vitamin A 0%	Vitamin C 0%	Calcium 0%	Iron 0%

Hansen's Natural, Tea Stix, Natural Blackberry Tea

1/2 packet / makes 8 fl oz

Amount per serving	%DV	Amount per serving	%DV	Amount per serving	%DV
Calories 5		**Cholesterol** 0mg	0%	**Total Carbohydrate** 1g	0%
Total Fat 0g	0%	**Sodium** 5mg	0%	Dietary Fiber 0g	0%
Saturated Fat 0g	0%	**Protein** 0g		Sugars 0g	
Polyunsaturated Fat 0g					
Monounsaturated Fat 0g		Vitamin A 0%	Vitamin C 100%	Calcium 0%	Iron 0%

Hansen's Natural, Tea Stix, Natural Iced Tea

1/2 packet / makes 8 fl oz

Amount per serving	%DV	Amount per serving	%DV	Amount per serving	%DV
Calories 5		**Cholesterol** 0mg	0%	**Total Carbohydrate** 1g	0%
Total Fat 0g	0%	**Sodium** 0mg	0%	Dietary Fiber 0g	0%
Saturated Fat 0g	0%	**Protein** 0g		Sugars 0g	
Polyunsaturated Fat 0g					
Monounsaturated Fat 0g		Vitamin A 0%	Vitamin C 100%	Calcium 0%	Iron 0%

Honest Tea, Assam Black Tea

8 fl oz serving / 2 per bottle

Amount per serving	%DV	Amount per serving	%DV	Amount per serving	%DV
Calories 17		**Cholesterol** 0mg	0%	**Total Carbohydrate** 5g	2%
Total Fat 0g	0%	**Sodium** 5mg	0%	Dietary Fiber 0g	0%
Saturated Fat 0g	0%	**Protein** 0g		Sugars 5g	
Polyunsaturated Fat 0g					
Monounsaturated Fat 0g		Vitamin A 0% Vitamin C 0%		Calcium 0% Iron 0%	

Honest Tea, Black Forest Berry

8 fl oz serving / 2 per bottle

Amount per serving	%DV	Amount per serving	%DV	Amount per serving	%DV
Calories 30		**Cholesterol** 0mg	0%	**Total Carbohydrate** 8g	3%
Total Fat 0g	0%	**Sodium** 5mg	0%	Dietary Fiber 0g	0%
Saturated Fat 0g	0%	**Protein** 0g		Sugars 8g	
Polyunsaturated Fat 0g					
Monounsaturated Fat 0g		Vitamin A 0% Vitamin C 0%		Calcium 0% Iron 0%	

Honest Tea, Classic Green

8 fl oz serving / 2 per bottle

Amount per serving	%DV	Amount per serving	%DV	Amount per serving	%DV
Calories 30		**Cholesterol** 0mg	0%	**Total Carbohydrate** 9g	3%
Total Fat 0g	0%	**Sodium** 5mg	0%	Dietary Fiber 0g	0%
Saturated Fat 0g	0%	**Protein** 0g		Sugars 9g	
Polyunsaturated Fat 0g					
Monounsaturated Fat 0g		Vitamin A 0% Vitamin C 0%		Calcium 0% Iron 0%	

Honest Tea, Community Green

8 fl oz serving / 2 per bottle

Amount per serving	%DV	Amount per serving	%DV	Amount per serving	%DV
Calories 17		**Cholesterol** 0mg	0%	**Total Carbohydrate** 5g	2%
Total Fat 0g	0%	**Sodium** 5mg	0%	Dietary Fiber 0g	0%
Saturated Fat 0g	0%	**Protein** 0g		Sugars 5g	
Polyunsaturated Fat 0g					
Monounsaturated Fat 0g		Vitamin A 0% Vitamin C 0%		Calcium 0% Iron 0%	

Honest Tea, Green Dragon Tea

8 fl oz serving / 2 per bottle

Amount per serving	%DV	Amount per serving	%DV	Amount per serving	%DV
Calories 30		**Cholesterol** 0mg	0%	**Total Carbohydrate** 8g	3%
Total Fat 0g	0%	**Sodium** 5mg	0%	Dietary Fiber 0g	0%
Saturated Fat 0g	0%	**Protein** 0g		Sugars 8g	
Polyunsaturated Fat 0g					
Monounsaturated Fat 0g		Vitamin A 0% Vitamin C 0%		Calcium 0% Iron 0%	

Honest Tea, Heavenly Lemon Tulsi

8 fl oz serving / 2 per bottle

Amount per serving	%DV	Amount per serving	%DV	Amount per serving	%DV
Calories 30		**Cholesterol** 0mg	0%	**Total Carbohydrate** 8g	3%
Total Fat 0g	0%	**Sodium** 5mg	0%	Dietary Fiber 0g	0%
Saturated Fat 0g	0%	**Protein** 0g		Sugars 8g	
Polyunsaturated Fat 0g					
Monounsaturated Fat 0g		Vitamin A 0%	Vitamin C 0%	Calcium 0%	Iron 0%

Honest Tea, Jasmine Green Energy Tea

8 fl oz serving / 2 per bottle

Amount per serving	%DV	Amount per serving	%DV	Amount per serving	%DV
Calories 17		**Cholesterol** 0mg	0%	**Total Carbohydrate** 5g	2%
Total Fat 0g	0%	**Sodium** 5mg	0%	Dietary Fiber 0g	0%
Saturated Fat 0g	0%	**Protein** 0g		Sugars 5g	
Polyunsaturated Fat 0g					
Monounsaturated Fat 0g		Vitamin A 0%	Vitamin C 0%	Calcium 0%	Iron 0%

Honest Tea, Just Black Tea

8 fl oz serving / 2 per bottle

Amount per serving	%DV	Amount per serving	%DV	Amount per serving	%DV
Calories 0		**Cholesterol** 0mg	0%	**Total Carbohydrate** 0g	0%
Total Fat 0g	0%	**Sodium** 5mg	0%	Dietary Fiber 0g	0%
Saturated Fat 0g	0%	**Protein** 0g		Sugars 0g	
Polyunsaturated Fat 0g					
Monounsaturated Fat 0g		Vitamin A 0%	Vitamin C 0%	Calcium 0%	Iron 0%

Honest Tea, Just Green Tea

8 fl oz serving / 2 per bottle

Amount per serving	%DV	Amount per serving	%DV	Amount per serving	%DV
Calories 0		**Cholesterol** 0mg	0%	**Total Carbohydrate** 0g	0%
Total Fat 0g	0%	**Sodium** 5mg	0%	Dietary Fiber 0g	0%
Saturated Fat 0g	0%	**Protein** 0g		Sugars 0g	
Polyunsaturated Fat 0g					
Monounsaturated Fat 0g		Vitamin A 0%	Vitamin C 0%	Calcium 0%	Iron 0%

Honest Tea, Lori's Lemon

8 fl oz serving / 2 per bottle

Amount per serving	%DV	Amount per serving	%DV	Amount per serving	%DV
Calories 30		**Cholesterol** 0mg	0%	**Total Carbohydrate** 8g	3%
Total Fat 0g	0%	**Sodium** 5mg	0%	Dietary Fiber 0g	0%
Saturated Fat 0g	0%	**Protein** 0g		Sugars 8g	
Polyunsaturated Fat 0g					
Monounsaturated Fat 0g		Vitamin A 0%	Vitamin C 0%	Calcium 0%	Iron 0%

Honest Tea, Mango Acai White Tea

8 fl oz serving / 2 per bottle

Amount per serving	%DV	Amount per serving	%DV	Amount per serving	%DV
Calories 35		**Cholesterol** 0mg	0%	**Total Carbohydrate** 9g	3%
Total Fat 0g	0%	**Sodium** 5mg	0%	Dietary Fiber 0g	0%
Saturated Fat 0g	0%	**Protein** 0g		Sugars 9g	
Polyunsaturated Fat 0g					
Monounsaturated Fat 0g		Vitamin A 0% Vitamin C 0%		Calcium 0% Iron 0%	

Honest Tea, Moroccan Mint Tea

8 fl oz serving / 2 per bottle

Amount per serving	%DV	Amount per serving	%DV	Amount per serving	%DV
Calories 17		**Cholesterol** 0mg	0%	**Total Carbohydrate** 5g	2%
Total Fat 0g	0%	**Sodium** 5mg	0%	Dietary Fiber 0g	0%
Saturated Fat 0g	0%	**Protein** 0g		Sugars 5g	
Polyunsaturated Fat 0g					
Monounsaturated Fat 0g		Vitamin A 0% Vitamin C 0%		Calcium 0% Iron 0%	

Honest Tea, Peach Oo-la-long

8 fl oz serving / 2 per bottle

Amount per serving	%DV	Amount per serving	%DV	Amount per serving	%DV
Calories 30		**Cholesterol** 0mg	0%	**Total Carbohydrate** 8g	3%
Total Fat 0g	0%	**Sodium** 5mg	0%	Dietary Fiber 0g	0%
Saturated Fat 0g	0%	**Protein** 0g		Sugars 8g	
Polyunsaturated Fat 0g					
Monounsaturated Fat 0g		Vitamin A 0% Vitamin C 0%		Calcium 0% Iron 0%	

Honest Tea, Pomegranate Red Tea with Goji Berry

8 fl oz serving / 2 per bottle

Amount per serving	%DV	Amount per serving	%DV	Amount per serving	%DV
Calories 35		**Cholesterol** 0mg	0%	**Total Carbohydrate** 9g	3%
Total Fat 0g	0%	**Sodium** 5mg	0%	Dietary Fiber 0g	0%
Saturated Fat 0g	0%	**Protein** 0g		Sugars 9g	
Polyunsaturated Fat 0g					
Monounsaturated Fat 0g		Vitamin A 0% Vitamin C 0%		Calcium 0% Iron 0%	

Honest Tea, Raspberry Fields

16 fl oz / 1 container

Amount per serving	%DV	Amount per serving	%DV	Amount per serving	%DV
Calories 70		**Cholesterol** 0mg	0%	**Total Carbohydrate** 18g	6%
Total Fat 0g	0%	**Sodium** 10mg	0%	Dietary Fiber 0g	0%
Saturated Fat 0g	0%	**Protein** 0g		Sugars 0g	
Polyunsaturated Fat 0g					
Monounsaturated Fat 0g		Vitamin A 0% Vitamin C 0%		Calcium 0% Iron 0%	

Snapple, Diet Green Tea

8 fl oz

Amount per serving	%DV	Amount per serving	%DV	Amount per serving	%DV
Calories 0		**Cholesterol** 0mg	0%	**Total Carbohydrate** 0g	0%
Total Fat 0g	0%	**Sodium** 5mg	0%	Dietary Fiber 0g	0%
Saturated Fat 0g	0%	**Protein** 0g		Sugars 0g	
Polyunsaturated Fat 0g					
Monounsaturated Fat 0g		Vitamin A 0% Vitamin C 20%		Calcium 0% Iron 0%	

Snapple, Diet Half 'n Half Lemonade / Iced Tea

16 fl oz

Amount per serving	%DV	Amount per serving	%DV	Amount per serving	%DV
Calories 10		**Cholesterol** 0mg	0%	**Total Carbohydrate** 1g	0%
Total Fat 0g	0%	**Sodium** 15mg	1%	Dietary Fiber 0g	0%
Saturated Fat 0g	0%	**Protein** 0g		Sugars 0g	
Polyunsaturated Fat 0g					
Monounsaturated Fat 0g		Vitamin A 0% Vitamin C 0%		Calcium 0% Iron 0%	

Snapple, Diet Lemon Tea

16 fl oz

Amount per serving	%DV	Amount per serving	%DV	Amount per serving	%DV
Calories 10		**Cholesterol** 0mg	0%	**Total Carbohydrate** 0g	0%
Total Fat 0g	0%	**Sodium** 15mg	1%	Dietary Fiber 0g	0%
Saturated Fat 0g	0%	**Protein** 0g		Sugars 0g	
Polyunsaturated Fat 0g					
Monounsaturated Fat 0g		Vitamin A 0% Vitamin C 0%		Calcium 0% Iron 0%	

Snapple, Diet Peach Tea

16 fl oz

Amount per serving	%DV	Amount per serving	%DV	Amount per serving	%DV
Calories 10		**Cholesterol** 0mg	0%	**Total Carbohydrate** 1g	0%
Total Fat 0g	0%	**Sodium** 15mg	1%	Dietary Fiber 0g	0%
Saturated Fat 0g	0%	**Protein** 0g		Sugars 0g	
Polyunsaturated Fat 0g					
Monounsaturated Fat 0g		Vitamin A 0% Vitamin C 0%		Calcium 0% Iron 0%	

Snapple, Diet Raspberry Tea

16 fl oz

Amount per serving	%DV	Amount per serving	%DV	Amount per serving	%DV
Calories 5		**Cholesterol** 0mg	0%	**Total Carbohydrate** 1g	0%
Total Fat 0g	0%	**Sodium** 15mg	1%	Dietary Fiber 0g	0%
Saturated Fat 0g	0%	**Protein** 0g		Sugars 0g	
Polyunsaturated Fat 0g					
Monounsaturated Fat 0g		Vitamin A 0% Vitamin C 0%		Calcium 0% Iron 0%	

Snapple, Diet Trop-A-Rocka Tea

16 fl oz

Amount per serving	%DV	Amount per serving	%DV	Amount per serving	%DV
Calories 10		**Cholesterol** 0mg	0%	**Total Carbohydrate** 0g	0%
Total Fat 0g	0%	**Sodium** 20mg	1%	Dietary Fiber 0g	0%
Saturated Fat 0g	0%	**Protein** 0g		Sugars 0g	
Polyunsaturated Fat 0g					
Monounsaturated Fat 0g		Vitamin A 0%	Vitamin C 0%	Calcium 0%	Iron 0%

Snapple, Green Tea

16 fl oz

Amount per serving	%DV	Amount per serving	%DV	Amount per serving	%DV
Calories 120		**Cholesterol** 0mg	0%	**Total Carbohydrate** 31g	5%
Total Fat 0g	0%	**Sodium** 10mg	0%	Dietary Fiber 0g	0%
Saturated Fat 0g	0%	**Protein** 0g		Sugars 30g	
Polyunsaturated Fat 0g					
Monounsaturated Fat 0g		Vitamin A 0%	Vitamin C 20%	Calcium 0%	Iron 0%

Tea, Brewed, Prepared with Distilled Water

6 fl oz / 178g

Amount per serving	%DV	Amount per serving	%DV	Amount per serving	%DV
Calories 2		**Cholesterol** 0mg	0%	**Total Carbohydrate** 1g	0%
Total Fat 0g	0%	**Sodium** 0mg	0%	Dietary Fiber 0g	0%
Saturated Fat 0g	0%	**Protein** 0g		Sugars g	
Polyunsaturated Fat 0g					
Monounsaturated Fat 0g		Vitamin A 0%	Vitamin C 0%	Calcium 0%	Iron 0%

Tea, Brewed, Prepared with Tap Water, Decaffeinated

6 fl oz / 178g

Amount per serving	%DV	Amount per serving	%DV	Amount per serving	%DV
Calories 2		**Cholesterol** 0mg	0%	**Total Carbohydrate** 1g	0%
Total Fat 0g	0%	**Sodium** 5mg	0%	Dietary Fiber 0g	0%
Saturated Fat 0g	0%	**Protein** 0g		Sugars 0g	
Polyunsaturated Fat 0g					
Monounsaturated Fat 0g		Vitamin A 0%	Vitamin C 0%	Calcium 0%	Iron 0%

Tea, Herb, Chamomile, Brewed

6 fl oz / 178g

Amount per serving	%DV	Amount per serving	%DV	Amount per serving	%DV
Calories 2		**Cholesterol** 0mg	0%	**Total Carbohydrate** 0g	0%
Total Fat 0g	0%	**Sodium** 2mg	0%	Dietary Fiber 0g	0%
Saturated Fat 0g	0%	**Protein** 0g		Sugars 0g	
Polyunsaturated Fat 0g					
Monounsaturated Fat 0g		Vitamin A 1%	Vitamin C 0%	Calcium 0%	Iron 1%

Tea, Herb, Other Than Chamomile, Brewed

6 fl oz / 178g

Amount per serving	%DV	Amount per serving	%DV	Amount per serving	%DV
Calories 2		Cholesterol 0mg	0%	Total Carbohydrate 0.5g	0%
Total Fat 0g	0%	Sodium 2mg	0%	Dietary Fiber 0g	0%
Saturated Fat 0g	0%	Protein 0g		Sugars 0g	
Polyunsaturated Fat 0g					
Monounsaturated Fat 0g		Vitamin A 0%	Vitamin C 0%	Calcium 3.5%	Iron 0%

Waters

Water, Bottled, Generic

1 cup / 237g

Amount per serving	%DV	Amount per serving	%DV	Amount per serving	%DV
Calories 0		Cholesterol 0mg	0%	Total Carbohydrate 0g	0%
Total Fat 0g	0%	Sodium 4.5mg	0%	Dietary Fiber 0g	0%
Saturated Fat 0g	0%	Protein 0g		Sugars 0g	
Polyunsaturated Fat 0g					
Monounsaturated Fat 0g		Vitamin A 0%	Vitamin C 0%	Calcium 2%	Iron 0%

Water, Bottled, Non-Carbonated, Crystal Geyser

1 bottle, 8 fl oz / 237g

Amount per serving	%DV	Amount per serving	%DV	Amount per serving	%DV
Calories 0		Cholesterol 0mg	0%	Total Carbohydrate 0g	0%
Total Fat 0g	0%	Sodium 2.5mg	0%	Dietary Fiber 0g	0%
Saturated Fat 0g	0%	Protein 0g		Sugars 0g	
Polyunsaturated Fat 0g					
Monounsaturated Fat 0g		Vitamin A 0%	Vitamin C 0%	Calcium 1%	Iron 0%

Water, Bottled, Non-Carbonated, Dannon

1 bottle, 11.2 fl oz / 331g

Amount per serving	%DV	Amount per serving	%DV	Amount per serving	%DV
Calories 0		Cholesterol 0mg	0%	Total Carbohydrate 0g	0%
Total Fat 0g	0%	Sodium 0mg	0%	Dietary Fiber 0g	0%
Saturated Fat 0g	0%	Protein 0g		Sugars 0g	
Polyunsaturated Fat 0g					
Monounsaturated Fat 0g		Vitamin A 0%	Vitamin C 0%	Calcium 1%	Iron 0%

Water, Bottled, Non-Carbonated, Dannon Fluoride to Go

1 bottle, 8.5 fl oz / 251g

Amount per serving	%DV	Amount per serving	%DV	Amount per serving	%DV
Calories 0		Cholesterol 0mg	0%	Total Carbohydrate 0g	0%
Total Fat 0g	0%	Sodium 2.5mg	0%	Dietary Fiber 0g	0%
Saturated Fat 0g	0%	Protein 0g		Sugars 0g	
Polyunsaturated Fat 0g					
Monounsaturated Fat 0g		Vitamin A 0%	Vitamin C 0%	Calcium 1%	Iron 0%

Water, Bottled, Non-Carbonated, Dasani

1 bottle, 16.9 fl oz / 500g

Amount per serving	%DV	Amount per serving	%DV	Amount per serving	%DV
Calories 0		**Cholesterol** 0mg	0%	**Total Carbohydrate** 0g	0%
Total Fat 0g	0%	**Sodium** 0mg	0%	Dietary Fiber 0g	0%
Saturated Fat 0g	0%	**Protein** 0g		Sugars 0g	
Polyunsaturated Fat 0g					
Monounsaturated Fat 0g		Vitamin A 0%	Vitamin C 0%	Calcium 0%	Iron 0%

Water, Bottled, Non-Carbonated, Evian

1 bottle, 11.2 fl oz / 331g

Amount per serving	%DV	Amount per serving	%DV	Amount per serving	%DV
Calories 0		**Cholesterol** 0mg	0%	**Total Carbohydrate** 0g	0%
Total Fat 0g	0%	**Sodium** 0mg	0%	Dietary Fiber 0g	0%
Saturated Fat 0g	0%	**Protein** 0g		Sugars 0g	
Polyunsaturated Fat 0g					
Monounsaturated Fat 0g		Vitamin A 0%	Vitamin C 0%	Calcium 3%	Iron 0%

Water, Bottled, Non-Carbonated, Pepsi, Aquafina

1 bottle, 16.9 fl oz / 500g

Amount per serving	%DV	Amount per serving	%DV	Amount per serving	%DV
Calories 0		**Cholesterol** 0mg	0%	**Total Carbohydrate** 0g	0%
Total Fat 0g	0%	**Sodium** 0mg	0%	Dietary Fiber 0g	0%
Saturated Fat 0g	0%	**Protein** 0g		Sugars 0g	
Polyunsaturated Fat 0g					
Monounsaturated Fat 0g		Vitamin A 0%	Vitamin C 0%	Calcium 0%	Iron 0%

Water, Bottled, Perrier

1 bottle, 6.5 fl oz / 192g

Amount per serving	%DV	Amount per serving	%DV	Amount per serving	%DV
Calories 0		**Cholesterol** 0mg	0%	**Total Carbohydrate** 0g	0%
Total Fat 0g	0%	**Sodium** 2mg	0%	Dietary Fiber 0g	0%
Saturated Fat 0g	0%	**Protein** 0g		Sugars 0g	
Polyunsaturated Fat 0g					
Monounsaturated Fat 0g		Vitamin A 0%	Vitamin C 0%	Calcium 3%	Iron 0%

Water, Bottled, Poland Spring

1 bottle, 16.9 fl oz / 500g

Amount per serving	%DV	Amount per serving	%DV	Amount per serving	%DV
Calories 0		**Cholesterol** 0mg	0%	**Total Carbohydrate** 0g	0%
Total Fat 0g	0%	**Sodium** 5mg	0%	Dietary Fiber 0g	0%
Saturated Fat 0g	0%	**Protein** 0g		Sugars 0g	
Polyunsaturated Fat 0g					
Monounsaturated Fat 0g		Vitamin A 0%	Vitamin C 0%	Calcium 5%	Iron 0%

Water, Tap, Drinking

1 cup, 8 fl oz / 237g

Amount per serving	%DV	Amount per serving	%DV	Amount per serving	%DV
Calories 0		**Cholesterol** 0mg	0%	**Total Carbohydrate** 0g	0%
Total Fat 0g	0%	**Sodium** 9.5mg	0%	Dietary Fiber 0g	0%
Saturated Fat 0g	0%	**Protein** 0g		Sugars 0g	
Polyunsaturated Fat 0g					
Monounsaturated Fat 0g		Vitamin A 0% Vitamin C 0%		Calcium 7% Iron 0%	

Water, Tap, Municipal

1 cup, 8 fl oz / 237g

Amount per serving	%DV	Amount per serving	%DV	Amount per serving	%DV
Calories 0		**Cholesterol** 0mg	0%	**Total Carbohydrate** 0g	0%
Total Fat 0g	0%	**Sodium** 7mg	0%	Dietary Fiber 0g	0%
Saturated Fat 0g	0%	**Protein** 0g		Sugars 0g	
Polyunsaturated Fat 0g					
Monounsaturated Fat 0g		Vitamin A 0% Vitamin C 0%		Calcium 7% Iron 0%	

Water, Tap, Well

1 cup, 8 fl oz / 237g

Amount per serving	%DV	Amount per serving	%DV	Amount per serving	%DV
Calories 0		**Cholesterol** 0mg	0%	**Total Carbohydrate** 0g	0%
Total Fat 0g	0%	**Sodium** 12mg	0%	Dietary Fiber 0g	0%
Saturated Fat 0g	0%	**Protein** 0g		Sugars 0g	
Polyunsaturated Fat 0g					
Monounsaturated Fat 0g		Vitamin A 0% Vitamin C 0%		Calcium 7% Iron 0%	

Dairy

Why Eat Dairy Products?

Consuming dairy products provides health benefits—especially improved bone health. Intake of dairy products is also associated with a reduced risk of cardio-vascular disease and type 2 diabetes, and with lower blood pressure in adults. Foods in the dairy group provide nutrients that are vital for health and maintenance of your body. These nutrients include calcium, potassium, vitamin D, and protein. Calcium is used for building bones and teeth and maintaining bone mass. Diets rich in potassium may help to maintain healthy blood pressure. Vitamin D functions in the body to maintain proper levels of calcium and phosphorous, thereby helping to build and maintain bones.

Daily Goal

Three cups for an adult on a 2,000-calorie diet.
    1 cup equivalents:
        1 cup milk
        6 oz. yogurt
        1.5 oz. hard cheese
        1/3 cup shredded cheese
        2 oz. processed cheese
        2 cups cottage cheese

Heart-Healthy Nutrients in Dairy

Potassium–Helps your heart beat as it squeezes blood through your body. If you have high blood pressure, heart failure, or heart rhythm problems, getting enough potassium is especially important. Although potassium and cholesterol aren't directly related, eating a potassium-rich diet might lower your cholesterol, too.

Good dairy sources of potassium are yogurt, milk, cottage cheese, and soy-based dairy alternatives.

Check out the FDA approved Health Claim for potassium and high blood pressure and stroke on page 27.

Plant sterols and stanols (collectively called phytosterols)–These are the plant equivalent to the animal cholesterol found naturally in small amounts in a wide variety of foods. Foods can be fortified with phytosterols in much higher amounts. The main benefit of adding phytosterols to your diet is to help reduce your risk for heart attack and stroke by lowering your LDL cholesterol. Because the structure of phytosterols is similar to that of cholesterol, phytosterols block the absorption of cholesterol in your intestines and lower the amount of cholesterol in your blood. Phytosterols are added to milk (Smart Balance), milk alternatives (Rice Dream) and cheese (Lifetime).

See the FDA-approved Health Claim for phytosterols and risk of heart disease on page 27.

Soy Protein–Soy is beneficial to overall cardio health because it is high in polyunsaturated (good) fats, low in saturated fat, and naturally cholesterol-free. When you substitute animal protein with soy proteins, you're replacing saturated fats and cholesterol with a much healthier protein for your heart. In addition, soy has been shown to improve blood vessel elasticity—a measure of how "hardened" your blood vessels are. Soy milk, soy yogurt, and soy cheese are dairy alternatives. Choose those that are fortified with calcium.

Check out the FDA-approved Health Claim for soy protein and risk of heart disease on page 26.

Heart-Healthy Shopping Tips for Dairy Products

* **Look for these FDA-approved Heart Health Claims on Dairy Products:**

Saturated Fat, Cholesterol, and Trans Fat, and Reduced Risk of Heart Disease
"Diets low in saturated fat and cholesterol, and as low as possible in trans fat, may reduce the risk of heart disease."

Foods that display this claim must be low in saturated fat (1g or less) and cholesterol (20mg or less) and contain less than 0.5g trans fat per serving and less than 6.5g total fat.

Dietary Saturated Fat and Cholesterol and risk of Coronary Heart Disease
"While many factors affect heart disease, diets low in saturated fat and cholesterol may reduce the risk of this disease."

Foods that make this claim must be low in total fat, saturated fat, and cholesterol.

Potassium and the Risk of High Blood Pressure and Stroke

"Diets containing foods that are a good source of potassium and that are low in sodium may reduce the risk of high blood pressure and stroke."

Products carrying this claim must be low in sodium, total fat, saturated fat, and cholesterol and contain a good source of potassium (350mg/10% Daily Value or higher).

Plant Sterol/Stanol Esters and Risk of Coronary Heart Disease

(1) Foods containing at least 0.65g per serving of vegetable oil sterol esters, eaten twice a day with meals for a daily total intake of least 1.3g, as part of a diet low in saturated fat and cholesterol, may reduce the risk of heart disease. A serving of [name of food] supplies __ grams of vegetable oil sterol esters.

(2) Diets low in saturated fat and cholesterol that include two servings of foods that provide a daily total of at least 3.4g of plant stanol esters in two meals may reduce the risk of heart disease. A serving of [name of food] supplies __ g of plant stanol esters.

Eligible products that carry this claim must have at least 0.65g plant sterol esters or at least 1.7g plant stanol esters per Reference Amount Customarily Consumed (RACC). They must also be low in saturated fat and cholesterol. Find this claim on dairy products that have been fortified with phytosterols.

Soy Protein and Risk of Coronary Heart Disease

(1) 25g of soy protein a day, as part of a low in saturated fat and cholesterol diet, may reduce the risk of heart disease. A serving of [name of food] supplies __ g of soy protein.

(2) Diets low in saturated fat and cholesterol that include 25g of soy protein a day may reduce the risk of heart disease. One serving of [name of food] provides __ g of soy protein.

Soy foods that carry this claim must contain at least 6.25g of soy protein per serving and be low in total fat, saturated fat, and cholesterol. Foods made from whole soybeans that contain no fat in addition to that inherent in the whole soybean are exempt from the "low fat" requirement.

- Look for the American Heart Association's Heart-Check mark on dairy product labels—milk, yogurt, and cheese products. The Heart-Check mark may also be found on dairy alternatives (such as soy, rice, and nut milks). For more information on the Heart-Check mark, go to *www.heartcheckmark.org.*

- The fat in dairy products is highly saturated, so the lower the fat content the better.

- Move from whole milk to reduced fat, to low fat, to skim or fat free gradually to let your taste buds adjust.

- Choose dairy products that provide a good source of calcium—10% Daily Value or higher.

- Use fat-free or low-fat yogurt as a snack or to make dips or smoothies. Yogurt can be high in sugar so look for yogurts that are less than 20g of sugar for a 6 oz. serving.

- Avoid milk that contains added flavorings such as vanilla, chocolate, or strawberry. They usually have added sugars and calories.

- Choose fat-free, low-fat, or reduced-fat cheeses.

- If you don't or can't consume milk, choose lactose-free products or milk alternatives.

- Look for milk alternatives that are fortified with calcium.

- If you prefer full-fat cheese, use it wisely. Choose the strongest flavor (sharp cheddar) and sprinkle it on top of dishes for the biggest impact.

- Cheese is high in sodium so look for low sodium cheese products.

Shopping List Essentials

Milk, low fat or fat free
Yogurt, low fat or fat free
Cottage cheese, low fat or fat free
Soy milk, calcium fortified
Cheese, reduced fat
Lactose-free low-fat or fat-free milk, if needed
Egg white products

Criteria for Dairy

Using the FDA guidelines for Heart Health Claims, the foods listed meet the following criteria per serving:

- Calories–130 calories or less per 8 oz. of milk or milk alternative

- Total fat–3 grams or less

- Saturated fat–1 gram or less

- Trans fat–0.5 grams or less (Trans Fat is not listed in the charts because all items report 0 grams Trans Fat. Since foods with less than 0.5 grams of trans fat can list 0 grams in the Nutrition Facts, be sure to check the ingredients for partially hydrogenated fats to determine if a product contains any trans fats.)

- Cholesterol–20 mg or less

- Beneficial Nutrients–10% Daily Value or higher of one beneficial nutrient (vitamin A, vitamin C, iron, calcium, protein, or dietary fiber)

- Sodium–240 mg or less, except for condensed or evaporated milk–(140 mg). Look for lower sodium levels to reduce high blood pressure.

- Total sugar for yogurt is limited to 20 grams or less per standard 6-oz. serving

Foods that don't meet this criteria are whole eggs (cholesterol in the yolks is above 20 mg), full-fat milk and yogurt, half and half, cream, and most cheeses (total fat over 3 grams and saturated fat is over 1 gram). Choose egg substitutes made with egg whites, low-fat or fat-free milk and yogurt, and low-fat cheese.

Milk

Borden, Fat-free Skim Milk, Refrigerated

1 cup / 240 ml

Amount per serving	%DV	Amount per serving	%DV	Amount per serving	%DV
Calories 80		**Cholesterol** 5mg	2%	**Total Carbohydrate** 12g	4%
Total Fat 0g	0%	**Sodium** 125mg	5%	Dietary Fiber 0g	0%
Saturated Fat 0g	0%	**Protein** 8g		Sugars 12g	
Polyunsaturated Fat 0g					
Monounsaturated Fat 0g		Vitamin A 10% Vitamin C 4%		Calcium 30% Iron 0%	

Horizon, Organic Fat-free Milk Plus DHA Omega-3, Refrigerated

1 cup / 240 ml

Amount per serving	%DV	Amount per serving	%DV	Amount per serving	%DV
Calories 100		**Cholesterol** 5mg	2%	**Total Carbohydrate** 14g	5%
Total Fat 0g	0%	**Sodium** 150mg	6%	Dietary Fiber 0g	0%
Saturated Fat 0g	0%	**Protein** 9g		Sugars 12g	
Polyunsaturated Fat 0g					
Monounsaturated Fat 0.5g		Vitamin A 10% Vitamin C 10%		Calcium 30% Iron 0%	

Horizon, Organic Fat-free Milk, Refrigerated

1 cup / 240 ml

Amount per serving	%DV	Amount per serving	%DV	Amount per serving	%DV
Calories 90		**Cholesterol** 5mg	2%	**Total Carbohydrate** 13g	4%
Total Fat 0g	0%	**Sodium** 130mg	5%	Dietary Fiber 0g	0%
Saturated Fat 0g	0%	**Protein** 8g		Sugars 12g	
Polyunsaturated Fat 0g					
Monounsaturated Fat 0g		Vitamin A 10% Vitamin C 2%		Calcium 30% Iron 0%	

Smart Balance, Fat Free Milk and Calcium

1 cup / 240 ml

Amount per serving	%DV	Amount per serving	%DV	Amount per serving	%DV
Calories 100		**Cholesterol** 5mg	2%	**Total Carbohydrate** 15g	5%
Total Fat 0g	0%	**Sodium** 150mg	6%	Dietary Fiber 0g	0%
Saturated Fat 0g	0%	**Protein** 11g		Sugars 15g	
Polyunsaturated Fat 0g					
Monounsaturated Fat 0g		Vitamin A 10% Vitamin C 0%		Calcium 35% Iron 0%	

Smart Balance, Fat Free Milk and Omega-3s

1 cup / 240 ml

Amount per serving	%DV	Amount per serving	%DV	Amount per serving	%DV
Calories 100		**Cholesterol** 5mg	2%	**Total Carbohydrate** 14g	5%
Total Fat 0g	0%	**Sodium** 120mg	5%	Dietary Fiber 0g	0%
Saturated Fat 0g	0%	**Protein** 10g		Sugars 14g	
Polyunsaturated Fat 0g					
Monounsaturated Fat 0g		Vitamin A 10% Vitamin C 0%		Calcium 35% Iron 0%	

Stonyfield, Fat-free Milk, Refrigerated

1 cup / 240 ml

Amount per serving	%DV	Amount per serving	%DV	Amount per serving	%DV
Calories 90		**Cholesterol** 0mg	0%	**Total Carbohydrate** 12g	4%
Total Fat 0g	0%	**Sodium** 125mg	5%	Dietary Fiber 0g	0%
Saturated Fat 0g	0%	**Protein** 8g		Sugars 12g	
Polyunsaturated Fat 0g					
Monounsaturated Fat 0g		Vitamin A 10% Vitamin C 0%		Calcium 30% Iron 0%	

Smart Balance, Lactose-Free Fat Free Milk and Omega-3s

1 cup / 240 ml

Amount per serving	%DV	Amount per serving	%DV	Amount per serving	%DV
Calories 100		**Cholesterol** 5mg	2%	**Total Carbohydrate** 14g	5%
Total Fat 0g	0%	**Sodium** 115mg	5%	Dietary Fiber 0g	0%
Saturated Fat 0g	0%	**Protein** 10g		Sugars 14g	
Polyunsaturated Fat 0g					
Monounsaturated Fat 0g		Vitamin A 10% Vitamin C 0%		Calcium 35% Iron 0%	

Stonyfield Organic, Fat Free, Organic Milk

1 cup / 240 ml

Amount per serving	%DV	Amount per serving	%DV	Amount per serving	%DV
Calories 90		**Cholesterol** 0mg	0%	**Total Carbohydrate** 12g	4%
Total Fat 0g	0%	**Sodium** 125mg	5%	Dietary Fiber 0g	0%
Saturated Fat 0g	0%	**Protein** 8g		Sugars 12g	
Polyunsaturated Fat 0g					
Monounsaturated Fat 0g		Vitamin A 10% Vitamin C 0%		Calcium 30% Iron 0%	

Yogurts

Brown Cow Farms, Blueberry on the Bottom, Non Fat Greek Yogurt, Blueberry

1 container / 4 oz

Amount per serving	%DV	Amount per serving	%DV	Amount per serving	%DV
Calories 90		**Cholesterol** 0mg	0%	**Total Carbohydrate** 13g	4%
Total Fat 0g	0%	**Sodium** 40mg	2%	Dietary Fiber 0g	0%
Saturated Fat 0g	0%	**Protein** 9g		Sugars 13g	
Polyunsaturated Fat 0g					
Monounsaturated Fat 0g		Vitamin A 0% Vitamin C 0%		Calcium 10% Iron 0%	

Brown Cow Farms, Fruit on the Bottom, Non Fat Greek, Blueberry

5.3 oz / 150g

Amount per serving	%DV	Amount per serving	%DV	Amount per serving	%DV
Calories 120		**Cholesterol** 5mg	2%	**Total Carbohydrate** 18g	6%
Total Fat 0g	0%	**Sodium** 50mg	2%	Dietary Fiber 0g	0%
Saturated Fat 0g	0%	**Protein** 12g		Sugars 17g	
Polyunsaturated Fat 0g					
Monounsaturated Fat 0g		Vitamin A 0% Vitamin C 0%		Calcium 15% Iron 0%	

Brown Cow Farms, Strawberry on the Bottom, Non Fat Greek, Strawberry

1 container / 113g

Amount per serving	%DV	Amount per serving	%DV	Amount per serving	%DV
Calories 90		**Cholesterol** 0mg	0%	**Total Carbohydrate** 13g	4%
Total Fat 0g	0%	**Sodium** 40mg	2%	Dietary Fiber 0g	0%
Saturated Fat 0g	0%	**Protein** 9g		Sugars 13g	
Polyunsaturated Fat 0g					
Monounsaturated Fat 0g		Vitamin A 0% Vitamin C 0%		Calcium 10% Iron 0%	

Dannon, Oikos, Fruit on the Bottom, Greek Nonfat Yogurt, Strawberry

1 container / 150g

Amount per serving	%DV	Amount per serving	%DV	Amount per serving	%DV
Calories 120		**Cholesterol** 5mg	2%	**Total Carbohydrate** 19g	6%
Total Fat 0g	0%	**Sodium** 50mg	2%	Dietary Fiber 0g	0%
Saturated Fat 0g	0%	**Protein** 12g		Sugars 18g	
Polyunsaturated Fat 0g					
Monounsaturated Fat 0g		Vitamin A 0% Vitamin C 0%		Calcium 15% Iron 0%	

Fage, Total 0%, Blueberry Acai Yogurt

1 container / 5.3 oz / 150g

Amount per serving	%DV	Amount per serving	%DV	Amount per serving	%DV
Calories 120		**Cholesterol** 0mg	0%	**Total Carbohydrate** 18g	6%
Total Fat 0g	0%	**Sodium** 45mg	2%	Dietary Fiber 0g	0%
Saturated Fat 0g	0%	**Protein** 13g		Sugars 16g	
Polyunsaturated Fat 0g					
Monounsaturated Fat 0g		Vitamin A 0% Vitamin C 0%		Calcium 15% Iron 0%	

Fage, Total 0%, Cherry Pomegranate Yogurt

1 container / 5.3 oz / 150g

Amount per serving	%DV	Amount per serving	%DV	Amount per serving	%DV
Calories 130		**Cholesterol** 0mg	0%	**Total Carbohydrate** 19g	6%
Total Fat 0g	0%	**Sodium** 50mg	2%	Dietary Fiber 0g	0%
Saturated Fat 0g	0%	**Protein** 13g		Sugars 16g	
Polyunsaturated Fat 0g					
Monounsaturated Fat 0g		Vitamin A 0% Vitamin C 0%		Calcium 15% Iron 0%	

Fage, Total 0%, Cherry Yogurt

1 container / 5.3 oz / 150g

Amount per serving	%DV	Amount per serving	%DV	Amount per serving	%DV
Calories 120		**Cholesterol** 0mg	0%	**Total Carbohydrate** 17g	6%
Total Fat 0g	0%	**Sodium** 50mg	2%	Dietary Fiber 0g	0%
Saturated Fat 0g	0%	**Protein** 13g		Sugars 16g	
Polyunsaturated Fat 0g					
Monounsaturated Fat 0g		Vitamin A 0% Vitamin C 0%		Calcium 15% Iron 0%	

Fage, Total 0%, Family Size, Plain Yogurt

1 cup / 8 oz / 227g

Amount per serving	%DV	Amount per serving	%DV	Amount per serving	%DV
Calories 130		**Cholesterol** 0mg	0%	**Total Carbohydrate** 9g	3%
Total Fat 0g	0%	**Sodium** 85mg	4%	Dietary Fiber 0g	0%
Saturated Fat 0g	0%	**Protein** 23g		Sugars 9g	
Polyunsaturated Fat 0g					
Monounsaturated Fat 0g		Vitamin A 0%	Vitamin C 0%	Calcium 25%	Iron 0%

Fage, Total 0%, Mango Guanabana Yogurt

1 container / 5.3 oz / 150g

Amount per serving	%DV	Amount per serving	%DV	Amount per serving	%DV
Calories 120		**Cholesterol** 0mg	0%	**Total Carbohydrate** 18g	6%
Total Fat 0g	0%	**Sodium** 45mg	2%	Dietary Fiber 0g	0%
Saturated Fat 0g	0%	**Protein** 13g		Sugars 17g	
Polyunsaturated Fat 0g					
Monounsaturated Fat 0g		Vitamin A 0%	Vitamin C 0%	Calcium 15%	Iron 0%

Fage, Total 0%, Peach Yogurt

1 container / 5.3 oz / 150g

Amount per serving	%DV	Amount per serving	%DV	Amount per serving	%DV
Calories 120		**Cholesterol** 0mg	0%	**Total Carbohydrate** 17g	6%
Total Fat 0g	0%	**Sodium** 45mg	2%	Dietary Fiber 0g	0%
Saturated Fat 0g	0%	**Protein** 13g		Sugars 16g	
Polyunsaturated Fat 0g					
Monounsaturated Fat 0g		Vitamin A 0%	Vitamin C 0%	Calcium 15%	Iron 0%

Fage, Total 0%, Raspberry Yogurt

1 container / 5.3 oz / 150g

Amount per serving	%DV	Amount per serving	%DV	Amount per serving	%DV
Calories 120		**Cholesterol** 0mg	0%	**Total Carbohydrate** 18g	6%
Total Fat 0g	0%	**Sodium** 45mg	2%	Dietary Fiber 0g	0%
Saturated Fat 0g	0%	**Protein** 13g		Sugars 16g	
Polyunsaturated Fat 0g					
Monounsaturated Fat 0g		Vitamin A 0%	Vitamin C 0%	Calcium 15%	Iron 0%

Fage, Total 0%, Single Size Plain Yogurt

1 container / 6oz / 170g

Amount per serving	%DV	Amount per serving	%DV	Amount per serving	%DV
Calories 100		**Cholesterol** 0mg	0%	**Total Carbohydrate** 7g	2%
Total Fat 0g	0%	**Sodium** 65mg	3%	Dietary Fiber 0g	0%
Saturated Fat 0g	0%	**Protein** 18g		Sugars 7g	
Polyunsaturated Fat 0g					
Monounsaturated Fat 0g		Vitamin A 0%	Vitamin C 0%	Calcium 20%	Iron 0%

Fage, Total 0%, Strawberry Goji Yogurt

1 container / 5.3 oz / 150g

Amount per serving	%DV	Amount per serving	%DV	Amount per serving	%DV
Calories 120		**Cholesterol** 0mg	0%	**Total Carbohydrate** 17g	6%
Total Fat 0g	0%	**Sodium** 50mg	2%	Dietary Fiber 0g	0%
Saturated Fat 0g	0%	**Protein** 13g		Sugars 16g	
Polyunsaturated Fat 0g					
Monounsaturated Fat 0g		Vitamin A 0% Vitamin C 0%		Calcium 15% Iron 0%	

Fage, Total 0%, Strawberry Yogurt

1 container / 5.3 oz / 150g

Amount per serving	%DV	Amount per serving	%DV	Amount per serving	%DV
Calories 120		**Cholesterol** 0mg	0%	**Total Carbohydrate** 17g	6%
Total Fat 0g	0%	**Sodium** 45mg	2%	Dietary Fiber 0g	0%
Saturated Fat 0g	0%	**Protein** 13g		Sugars 16g	
Polyunsaturated Fat 0g					
Monounsaturated Fat 0g		Vitamin A 0% Vitamin C 0%		Calcium 15% Iron 0%	

Kraft, Breyers Light Fat-Free Strawberry Yogurt

6 oz / 1 container / 170g

Amount per serving	%DV	Amount per serving	%DV	Amount per serving	%DV
Calories 80		**Cholesterol** 5mg	2%	**Total Carbohydrate** 12g	4%
Total Fat 0g	0%	**Sodium** 105mg	4%	Dietary Fiber 1g	4%
Saturated Fat 0g	0%	**Protein** 6g		Sugars 7g	
Polyunsaturated Fat 0g					
Monounsaturated Fat 0g		Vitamin A 8% Vitamin C 8%		Calcium 20% Iron 2%	

Stonyfield Organic, Fat Free, Smooth and Creamy, Plain Yogurt

170 g / 1 container

Amount per serving	%DV	Amount per serving	%DV	Amount per serving	%DV
Calories 80		**Cholesterol** 0mg	0%	**Total Carbohydrate** 12g	4%
Total Fat 0g	0%	**Sodium** 120mg	5%	Dietary Fiber 0g	0%
Saturated Fat 0g	0%	**Protein** 8g		Sugars 12g	
Polyunsaturated Fat 0g					
Monounsaturated Fat 0g		Vitamin A 0% Vitamin C 0%		Calcium 25% Iron 0%	

Yoplait Kids, Cars Vroom Vroom Vanilla

85g container

Amount per serving	%DV	Amount per serving	%DV	Amount per serving	%DV
Calories 70		**Cholesterol** 5mg	2%	**Total Carbohydrate** 13g	4%
Total Fat 1g	2%	**Sodium** 45mg	2%	Dietary Fiber 0g	0%
Saturated Fat 0.5g	2%	**Protein** 3g		Sugars 9g	
Polyunsaturated Fat 0g					
Monounsaturated Fat 0g		Vitamin A 10% Vitamin C 0%		Calcium 20% Iron 0%	

Yoplait Kids, Dora the Explorer Strawberry

85g container

Amount per serving	%DV	Amount per serving	%DV	Amount per serving	%DV
Calories 70		**Cholesterol** 5mg	2%	**Total Carbohydrate** 13g	4%
Total Fat 1g	2%	**Sodium** 45mg	2%	Dietary Fiber 0g	0%
Saturated Fat 0.5g	3%	**Protein** 3g		Sugars 9g	
Polyunsaturated Fat 0g					
Monounsaturated Fat 0g		Vitamin A 10% Vitamin C 0%		Calcium 20% Iron 0%	

Yoplait Kids, Mickey Mouse Clubhouse Strawberry Banana Adventure

85g container

Amount per serving	%DV	Amount per serving	%DV	Amount per serving	%DV
Calories 70		**Cholesterol** 5mg	2%	**Total Carbohydrate** 13g	4%
Total Fat 1g	2%	**Sodium** 45mg	2%	Dietary Fiber 0g	0%
Saturated Fat 0.5g	3%	**Protein** 3g		Sugars 9g	
Polyunsaturated Fat 0g					
Monounsaturated Fat 0g		Vitamin A 10% Vitamin C 0%		Calcium 20% Iron 0%	

Yoplait, Greek 100, Black Cherry Yogurt

1 container / 150g

Amount per serving	%DV	Amount per serving	%DV	Amount per serving	%DV
Calories 100		**Cholesterol** 5mg	2%	**Total Carbohydrate** 14g	5%
Total Fat 0g	0%	**Sodium** 45mg	2%	Dietary Fiber 0g	0%
Saturated Fat 0g	0%	**Protein** 10g		Sugars 9g	
Polyunsaturated Fat 0g					
Monounsaturated Fat 0g		Vitamin A 4% Vitamin C 0%		Calcium 10% Iron 0%	

Yoplait, Greek 100, Key Lime Yogurt

1 container / 150g

Amount per serving	%DV	Amount per serving	%DV	Amount per serving	%DV
Calories 100		**Cholesterol** 5mg	2%	**Total Carbohydrate** 10g	3%
Total Fat 0g	0%	**Sodium** 55mg	2%	Dietary Fiber 0g	0%
Saturated Fat 0g	0%	**Protein** 13g		Sugars 7g	
Polyunsaturated Fat 0g					
Monounsaturated Fat 0g		Vitamin A 4% Vitamin C 0%		Calcium 15% Iron 0%	

Yoplait, Greek 100, Mixed Berry Yogurt

1 container / 150g

Amount per serving	%DV	Amount per serving	%DV	Amount per serving	%DV
Calories 100		**Cholesterol** 5mg	2%	**Total Carbohydrate** 14g	5%
Total Fat 0g	0%	**Sodium** 45mg	2%	Dietary Fiber 0g	0%
Saturated Fat 0g	0%	**Protein** 10g		Sugars 9g	
Polyunsaturated Fat 0g					
Monounsaturated Fat 0g		Vitamin A 4% Vitamin C 0%		Calcium 10% Iron 0%	

Yoplait, Greek 100, Peach Yogurt

1 container / 150g

Amount per serving	%DV	Amount per serving	%DV	Amount per serving	%DV
Calories 100		**Cholesterol** 5mg	2%	**Total Carbohydrate** 14g	5%
Total Fat 0g	0%	**Sodium** 45mg	2%	Dietary Fiber 0g	0%
Saturated Fat 0g	0%	**Protein** 10g		Sugars 9g	
Polyunsaturated Fat 0g					
Monounsaturated Fat 0g		Vitamin A 4%	Vitamin C 0%	Calcium 10%	Iron 0%

Yoplait, Greek 100, Strawberry Yogurt

1 container / 150g

Amount per serving	%DV	Amount per serving	%DV	Amount per serving	%DV
Calories 100		**Cholesterol** 5mg	2%	**Total Carbohydrate** 14g	5%
Total Fat 0g	0%	**Sodium** 45mg	2%	Dietary Fiber 0g	0%
Saturated Fat 0g	0%	**Protein** 10g		Sugars 9g	
Polyunsaturated Fat 0g					
Monounsaturated Fat 0g		Vitamin A 4%	Vitamin C 0%	Calcium 10%	Iron 0%

Yoplait, Greek 100, Vanilla Yogurt

1 container / 150g

Amount per serving	%DV	Amount per serving	%DV	Amount per serving	%DV
Calories 100		**Cholesterol** 5mg	2%	**Total Carbohydrate** 11g	4%
Total Fat 0g	0%	**Sodium** 55mg	2%	Dietary Fiber 0g	0%
Saturated Fat 0g	0%	**Protein** 13g		Sugars 7g	
Polyunsaturated Fat 0g					
Monounsaturated Fat 0g		Vitamin A 4%	Vitamin C 0%	Calcium 15%	Iron 0%

Yoplait, Greek, Cherry Pomegranate Yogurt

1 container / 113g

Amount per serving	%DV	Amount per serving	%DV	Amount per serving	%DV
Calories 110		**Cholesterol** 5mg	2%	**Total Carbohydrate** 18g	6%
Total Fat 0g	0%	**Sodium** 65mg	3%	Dietary Fiber 0g	0%
Saturated Fat 0g	0%	**Protein** 8g		Sugars 13g	
Polyunsaturated Fat 0g					
Monounsaturated Fat 0g		Vitamin A 10%	Vitamin C 0%	Calcium 25%	Iron 0%

Yoplait, Greek, Plain Yogurt

1 container / 6oz / 170g

Amount per serving	%DV	Amount per serving	%DV	Amount per serving	%DV
Calories 120		**Cholesterol** 10mg	3%	**Total Carbohydrate** 13g	4%
Total Fat 0g	0%	**Sodium** 115mg	5%	Dietary Fiber 0g	0%
Saturated Fat 0g	0%	**Protein** 15g		Sugars 8g	
Polyunsaturated Fat 0g					
Monounsaturated Fat 0g		Vitamin A 15%	Vitamin C 0%	Calcium 40%	Iron 0%

Yoplait, Light Apple Turnover Yogurt

1 container / 6oz / 170g

Amount per serving	%DV	Amount per serving	%DV	Amount per serving	%DV
Calories 90		**Cholesterol** 5mg	2%	**Total Carbohydrate** 16g	5%
Total Fat 0g	0%	**Sodium** 80mg	3%	Dietary Fiber 0g	0%
Saturated Fat 0g	0%	**Protein** 5g		Sugars 10g	
Polyunsaturated Fat 0g					
Monounsaturated Fat 0g		Vitamin A 15% Vitamin C 0%		Calcium 20% Iron 0%	

Yoplait, Light Apricot Mango Yogurt

1 container / 6oz / 170g

Amount per serving	%DV	Amount per serving	%DV	Amount per serving	%DV
Calories 90		**Cholesterol** 5mg	2%	**Total Carbohydrate** 16g	5%
Total Fat 0g	0%	**Sodium** 80mg	3%	Dietary Fiber 0g	0%
Saturated Fat 0g	0%	**Protein** 5g		Sugars 10g	
Polyunsaturated Fat 0g					
Monounsaturated Fat 0g		Vitamin A 15% Vitamin C 0%		Calcium 20% Iron 0%	

Yoplait, Light Banana Cream Pie Yogurt

1 container / 6oz / 170g

Amount per serving	%DV	Amount per serving	%DV	Amount per serving	%DV
Calories 90		**Cholesterol** 5mg	2%	**Total Carbohydrate** 16g	5%
Total Fat 0g	0%	**Sodium** 80mg	3%	Dietary Fiber 0g	0%
Saturated Fat 0g	0%	**Protein** 5g		Sugars 10g	
Polyunsaturated Fat 0g					
Monounsaturated Fat 0g		Vitamin A 15% Vitamin C 0%		Calcium 20% Iron 0%	

Yoplait, Light Black Forest Cake Yogurt

1 container / 6oz / 170g

Amount per serving	%DV	Amount per serving	%DV	Amount per serving	%DV
Calories 90		**Cholesterol** 5mg	2%	**Total Carbohydrate** 16g	5%
Total Fat 0g	0%	**Sodium** 80mg	3%	Dietary Fiber 0g	0%
Saturated Fat 0g	0%	**Protein** 5g		Sugars 10g	
Polyunsaturated Fat 0g					
Monounsaturated Fat 0g		Vitamin A 15% Vitamin C 0%		Calcium 20% Iron 0%	

Yoplait, Light Blackberry Yogurt

1 container / 6oz / 170g

Amount per serving	%DV	Amount per serving	%DV	Amount per serving	%DV
Calories 90		**Cholesterol** 5mg	2%	**Total Carbohydrate** 16g	5%
Total Fat 0g	0%	**Sodium** 80mg	3%	Dietary Fiber 0g	0%
Saturated Fat 0g	0%	**Protein** 5g		Sugars 10g	
Polyunsaturated Fat 0g					
Monounsaturated Fat 0g		Vitamin A 15% Vitamin C 0%		Calcium 20% Iron 0%	

Yoplait, Light Blueberry Patch Yogurt

1 container / 6oz / 170g

Amount per serving	%DV	Amount per serving	%DV	Amount per serving	%DV
Calories 90		**Cholesterol** 5mg	2%	**Total Carbohydrate** 16g	5%
Total Fat 0g	0%	**Sodium** 80mg	3%	Dietary Fiber 0g	0%
Saturated Fat 0g	0%	**Protein** 5g		Sugars 10g	
Polyunsaturated Fat 0g					
Monounsaturated Fat 0g		Vitamin A 15% Vitamin C 0%		Calcium 20% Iron 0%	

Yoplait, Light Boston Cream Pie Yogurt

1 container / 6oz / 170g

Amount per serving	%DV	Amount per serving	%DV	Amount per serving	%DV
Calories 90		**Cholesterol** 5mg	2%	**Total Carbohydrate** 16g	5%
Total Fat 0g	0%	**Sodium** 80mg	3%	Dietary Fiber 0g	0%
Saturated Fat 0g	0%	**Protein** 5g		Sugars 10g	
Polyunsaturated Fat 0g					
Monounsaturated Fat 0g		Vitamin A 15% Vitamin C 0%		Calcium 20% Iron 0%	

Yoplait, Light Harvest Peach Yogurt

1 container / 6oz / 170g

Amount per serving	%DV	Amount per serving	%DV	Amount per serving	%DV
Calories 90		**Cholesterol** 5mg	2%	**Total Carbohydrate** 16g	5%
Total Fat 0g	0%	**Sodium** 80mg	3%	Dietary Fiber 0g	0%
Saturated Fat 0g	0%	**Protein** 5g		Sugars 10g	
Polyunsaturated Fat 0g					
Monounsaturated Fat 0g		Vitamin A 15% Vitamin C 0%		Calcium 20% Iron 0%	

Yoplait, Light Key Lime Pie Yogurt

1 container / 6oz / 170g

Amount per serving	%DV	Amount per serving	%DV	Amount per serving	%DV
Calories 90		**Cholesterol** 5mg	2%	**Total Carbohydrate** 16g	5%
Total Fat 0g	0%	**Sodium** 80mg	3%	Dietary Fiber 0g	0%
Saturated Fat 0g	0%	**Protein** 5g		Sugars 10g	
Polyunsaturated Fat 0g					
Monounsaturated Fat 0g		Vitamin A 15% Vitamin C 0%		Calcium 20% Iron 0%	

Yoplait, Light Lemon Cream Pie Yogurt

1 container / 6oz / 170g

Amount per serving	%DV	Amount per serving	%DV	Amount per serving	%DV
Calories 90		**Cholesterol** 5mg	2%	**Total Carbohydrate** 16g	5%
Total Fat 0g	0%	**Sodium** 80mg	3%	Dietary Fiber 0g	0%
Saturated Fat 0g	0%	**Protein** 5g		Sugars 10g	
Polyunsaturated Fat 0g					
Monounsaturated Fat 0g		Vitamin A 15% Vitamin C 0%		Calcium 20% Iron 0%	

Yoplait, Light Orange Crème Yogurt

1 container / 6oz / 170g

Amount per serving	%DV	Amount per serving	%DV	Amount per serving	%DV
Calories 90		**Cholesterol** 5mg	2%	**Total Carbohydrate** 16g	5%
Total Fat 0g	0%	**Sodium** 80mg	3%	Dietary Fiber 0g	0%
Saturated Fat 0g	0%	**Protein** 5g		Sugars 10g	
Polyunsaturated Fat 0g					
Monounsaturated Fat 0g		Vitamin A 15% Vitamin C 0%		Calcium 20% Iron 0%	

Yoplait, Light Pineapple Upside Down Cake Yogurt

1 container / 6oz / 170g

Amount per serving	%DV	Amount per serving	%DV	Amount per serving	%DV
Calories 90		**Cholesterol** 5mg	2%	**Total Carbohydrate** 16g	5%
Total Fat 0g	0%	**Sodium** 80mg	3%	Dietary Fiber 0g	0%
Saturated Fat 0g	0%	**Protein** 5g		Sugars 10g	
Polyunsaturated Fat 0g					
Monounsaturated Fat 0g		Vitamin A 15% Vitamin C 0%		Calcium 20% Iron 0%	

Yoplait, Light Raspberry Cheesecake Yogurt

1 container / 6oz / 170g

Amount per serving	%DV	Amount per serving	%DV	Amount per serving	%DV
Calories 90		**Cholesterol** 5mg	2%	**Total Carbohydrate** 16g	5%
Total Fat 0g	0%	**Sodium** 80mg	3%	Dietary Fiber 0g	0%
Saturated Fat 0g	0%	**Protein** 5g		Sugars 10g	
Polyunsaturated Fat 0g					
Monounsaturated Fat 0g		Vitamin A 15% Vitamin C 0%		Calcium 20% Iron 0%	

Yoplait, Light Raspberry Lemonade Yogurt

1 container / 6oz / 170g

Amount per serving	%DV	Amount per serving	%DV	Amount per serving	%DV
Calories 90		**Cholesterol** 5mg	2%	**Total Carbohydrate** 16g	5%
Total Fat 0g	0%	**Sodium** 80mg	3%	Dietary Fiber 0g	0%
Saturated Fat 0g	0%	**Protein** 5g		Sugars 10g	
Polyunsaturated Fat 0g					
Monounsaturated Fat 0g		Vitamin A 15% Vitamin C 0%		Calcium 20% Iron 0%	

Yoplait, Light Red Raspberry Yogurt

1 container / 6oz / 170g

Amount per serving	%DV	Amount per serving	%DV	Amount per serving	%DV
Calories 90		**Cholesterol** 5mg	2%	**Total Carbohydrate** 16g	5%
Total Fat 0g	0%	**Sodium** 80mg	3%	Dietary Fiber 0g	0%
Saturated Fat 0g	0%	**Protein** 5g		Sugars 10g	
Polyunsaturated Fat 0g					
Monounsaturated Fat 0g		Vitamin A 15% Vitamin C 0%		Calcium 20% Iron 0%	

Yoplait, Light Red Velvet Cake Yogurt

1 container / 6oz / 170g

Amount per serving	%DV	Amount per serving	%DV	Amount per serving	%DV
Calories 90		**Cholesterol** 5mg	2%	**Total Carbohydrate** 16g	5%
Total Fat 0g	0%	**Sodium** 80mg	3%	Dietary Fiber 0g	0%
Saturated Fat 0g	0%	**Protein** 5g		Sugars 10g	
Polyunsaturated Fat 0g					
Monounsaturated Fat 0g		Vitamin A 15%　Vitamin C 0%		Calcium 20%　Iron 0%	

Yoplait, Light Strawberry 'n Bananas Yogurt

1 container / 6oz / 170g

Amount per serving	%DV	Amount per serving	%DV	Amount per serving	%DV
Calories 90		**Cholesterol** 5mg	2%	**Total Carbohydrate** 16g	5%
Total Fat 0g	0%	**Sodium** 80mg	3%	Dietary Fiber 0g	0%
Saturated Fat 0g	0%	**Protein** 5g		Sugars 10g	
Polyunsaturated Fat 0g					
Monounsaturated Fat 0g		Vitamin A 15%　Vitamin C 0%		Calcium 20%　Iron 0%	

Yoplait, Light Strawberry Orange Sunrise Yogurt

1 container / 6oz / 170g

Amount per serving	%DV	Amount per serving	%DV	Amount per serving	%DV
Calories 90		**Cholesterol** 5mg	2%	**Total Carbohydrate** 16g	5%
Total Fat 0g	0%	**Sodium** 80mg	3%	Dietary Fiber 0g	0%
Saturated Fat 0g	0%	**Protein** 5g		Sugars 10g	
Polyunsaturated Fat 0g					
Monounsaturated Fat 0g		Vitamin A 15%　Vitamin C 0%		Calcium 20%　Iron 0%	

Yoplait, Light Strawberry Shortcake Yogurt

1 container / 6oz / 170g

Amount per serving	%DV	Amount per serving	%DV	Amount per serving	%DV
Calories 90		**Cholesterol** 5mg	2%	**Total Carbohydrate** 16g	5%
Total Fat 0g	0%	**Sodium** 80mg	3%	Dietary Fiber 0g	0%
Saturated Fat 0g	0%	**Protein** 5g		Sugars 10g	
Polyunsaturated Fat 0g					
Monounsaturated Fat 0g		Vitamin A 15%　Vitamin C 0%		Calcium 20%　Iron 0%	

Yoplait, Light Strawberry Yogurt

1 container / 6oz / 170g

Amount per serving	%DV	Amount per serving	%DV	Amount per serving	%DV
Calories 90		**Cholesterol** 5mg	2%	**Total Carbohydrate** 16g	5%
Total Fat 0g	0%	**Sodium** 80mg	3%	Dietary Fiber 0g	0%
Saturated Fat 0g	0%	**Protein** 5g		Sugars 10g	
Polyunsaturated Fat 0g					
Monounsaturated Fat 0g		Vitamin A 15%　Vitamin C 0%		Calcium 20%　Iron 0%	

Yoplait, Light Thick & Creamy Blueberry Pie Yogurt

1 container / 6oz / 170g

Amount per serving	%DV	Amount per serving	%DV	Amount per serving	%DV
Calories 100		**Cholesterol** 5mg	2%	**Total Carbohydrate** 21g	7%
Total Fat 0g	0%	**Sodium** 90mg	4%	Dietary Fiber 0g	0%
Saturated Fat 0g	0%	**Protein** 5g		Sugars 14g	
Polyunsaturated Fat 0g					
Monounsaturated Fat 0g		Vitamin A 15% Vitamin C 0%		Calcium 20% Iron 0%	

Yoplait, Light Thick & Creamy Cherry Cobbler Yogurt

1 container / 6oz / 170g

Amount per serving	%DV	Amount per serving	%DV	Amount per serving	%DV
Calories 100		**Cholesterol** 5mg	2%	**Total Carbohydrate** 21g	7%
Total Fat 0g	0%	**Sodium** 90mg	4%	Dietary Fiber 0g	0%
Saturated Fat 0g	0%	**Protein** 5g		Sugars 14g	
Polyunsaturated Fat 0g					
Monounsaturated Fat 0g		Vitamin A 15% Vitamin C 0%		Calcium 20% Iron 0%	

Yoplait, Light Thick & Creamy Cinnamon Roll Yogurt

1 container / 6oz / 170g

Amount per serving	%DV	Amount per serving	%DV	Amount per serving	%DV
Calories 100		**Cholesterol** 5mg	2%	**Total Carbohydrate** 21g	7%
Total Fat 0g	0%	**Sodium** 90mg	4%	Dietary Fiber 0g	0%
Saturated Fat 0g	0%	**Protein** 5g		Sugars 14g	
Polyunsaturated Fat 0g					
Monounsaturated Fat 0g		Vitamin A 15% Vitamin C 0%		Calcium 20% Iron 0%	

Yoplait, Light Thick & Creamy French Vanilla Yogurt

1 container / 6oz / 170g

Amount per serving	%DV	Amount per serving	%DV	Amount per serving	%DV
Calories 100		**Cholesterol** 5mg	2%	**Total Carbohydrate** 21g	7%
Total Fat 0g	0%	**Sodium** 90mg	4%	Dietary Fiber 0g	0%
Saturated Fat 0g	0%	**Protein** 5g		Sugars 14g	
Polyunsaturated Fat 0g					
Monounsaturated Fat 0g		Vitamin A 15% Vitamin C 0%		Calcium 20% Iron 0%	

Yoplait, Light Thick & Creamy Key Lime Pie Yogurt

1 container / 6oz / 170g

Amount per serving	%DV	Amount per serving	%DV	Amount per serving	%DV
Calories 100		**Cholesterol** 5mg	2%	**Total Carbohydrate** 21g	7%
Total Fat 0g	0%	**Sodium** 90mg	4%	Dietary Fiber 0g	0%
Saturated Fat 0g	0%	**Protein** 5g		Sugars 14g	
Polyunsaturated Fat 0g					
Monounsaturated Fat 0g		Vitamin A 15% Vitamin C 0%		Calcium 20% Iron 0%	

Yoplait, Light Thick & Creamy Lemon Meringue Yogurt

1 container / 6oz / 170g

Amount per serving	%DV	Amount per serving	%DV	Amount per serving	%DV
Calories 100		**Cholesterol** 5mg	2%	**Total Carbohydrate** 21g	7%
Total Fat 0g	0%	**Sodium** 90mg	4%	Dietary Fiber 0g	0%
Saturated Fat 0g	0%	**Protein** 5g		Sugars 14g	
Polyunsaturated Fat 0g					
Monounsaturated Fat 0g		Vitamin A 15% Vitamin C 0%		Calcium 20% Iron 0%	

Yoplait, Light Thick & Creamy Strawberry Yogurt

1 container / 6oz / 170g

Amount per serving	%DV	Amount per serving	%DV	Amount per serving	%DV
Calories 100		**Cholesterol** 5mg	2%	**Total Carbohydrate** 21g	7%
Total Fat 0g	0%	**Sodium** 90mg	4%	Dietary Fiber 0g	0%
Saturated Fat 0g	0%	**Protein** 5g		Sugars 14g	
Polyunsaturated Fat 0g					
Monounsaturated Fat 0g		Vitamin A 15% Vitamin C 0%		Calcium 20% Iron 0%	

Yoplait, Light Triple Berry Torte Yogurt

1 container / 6oz / 170g

Amount per serving	%DV	Amount per serving	%DV	Amount per serving	%DV
Calories 90		**Cholesterol** 5mg	2%	**Total Carbohydrate** 16g	5%
Total Fat 0g	0%	**Sodium** 80mg	3%	Dietary Fiber 0g	0%
Saturated Fat 0g	0%	**Protein** 5g		Sugars 10g	
Polyunsaturated Fat 0g					
Monounsaturated Fat 0g		Vitamin A 15% Vitamin C 0%		Calcium 20% Iron 0%	

Yoplait, Light Vanilla Cherry Yogurt

1 container / 6oz / 170g

Amount per serving	%DV	Amount per serving	%DV	Amount per serving	%DV
Calories 90		**Cholesterol** 5mg	2%	**Total Carbohydrate** 16g	5%
Total Fat 0g	0%	**Sodium** 80mg	3%	Dietary Fiber 0g	0%
Saturated Fat 0g	0%	**Protein** 5g		Sugars 10g	
Polyunsaturated Fat 0g					
Monounsaturated Fat 0g		Vitamin A 15% Vitamin C 0%		Calcium 20% Iron 0%	

Yoplait, Light Very Cherry Yogurt

1 container / 6oz / 170g

Amount per serving	%DV	Amount per serving	%DV	Amount per serving	%DV
Calories 90		**Cholesterol** 5mg	2%	**Total Carbohydrate** 16g	5%
Total Fat 0g	0%	**Sodium** 80mg	3%	Dietary Fiber 0g	0%
Saturated Fat 0g	0%	**Protein** 5g		Sugars 10g	
Polyunsaturated Fat 0g					
Monounsaturated Fat 0g		Vitamin A 15% Vitamin C 0%		Calcium 20% Iron 0%	

Yoplait, Light Very Vanilla Yogurt

1 container / 6oz / 170g

Amount per serving	%DV	Amount per serving	%DV	Amount per serving	%DV
Calories 90		**Cholesterol** 5mg	2%	**Total Carbohydrate** 16g	5%
Total Fat 0g	0%	**Sodium** 80mg	3%	Dietary Fiber 0g	0%
Saturated Fat 0g	0%	**Protein** 5g		Sugars 10g	
Polyunsaturated Fat 0g					
Monounsaturated Fat 0g		Vitamin A 15% Vitamin C 0%		Calcium 20% Iron 0%	

Yoplait, Light White Chocolate Strawberry Yogurt

1 container / 6oz / 170g

Amount per serving	%DV	Amount per serving	%DV	Amount per serving	%DV
Calories 90		**Cholesterol** 5mg	2%	**Total Carbohydrate** 16g	5%
Total Fat 0g	0%	**Sodium** 80mg	3%	Dietary Fiber 0g	0%
Saturated Fat 0g	0%	**Protein** 5g		Sugars 10g	
Polyunsaturated Fat 0g					
Monounsaturated Fat 0g		Vitamin A 15% Vitamin C 0%		Calcium 20% Iron 0%	

Cheeses

Borden, Fat Free American Flavor Singles

1 slice / 21g

Amount per serving	%DV	Amount per serving	%DV	Amount per serving	%DV
Calories 30		**Cholesterol** 0mg	0%	**Total Carbohydrate** 2g	1%
Total Fat 0g	0%	**Sodium** 320mg	13%	Dietary Fiber 0g	0%
Saturated Fat 0g	0%	**Protein** 5g		Sugars 1g	
Polyunsaturated Fat 0g					
Monounsaturated Fat 0g		Vitamin A 4% Vitamin C 0%		Calcium 15% Iron 0%	

Kraft, American Fat Free Singles

19g

Amount per serving	%DV	Amount per serving	%DV	Amount per serving	%DV
Calories 25		**Cholesterol** 0mg	0%	**Total Carbohydrate** 2g	1%
Total Fat 0g	0%	**Sodium** 250mg	10%	Dietary Fiber 0g	0%
Saturated Fat 0g	0%	**Protein** 4g		Sugars 1g	
Polyunsaturated Fat 0g					
Monounsaturated Fat 0g		Vitamin A 6% Vitamin C 0%		Calcium 15% Iron 0%	

Kraft, Natural Shredded Fat-Free Mozzarella

1 oz

Amount per serving	%DV	Amount per serving	%DV	Amount per serving	%DV
Calories 45		**Cholesterol** 0mg	0%	**Total Carbohydrate** 2g	1%
Total Fat 0g	0%	**Sodium** 280mg	12%	Dietary Fiber 0g	0%
Saturated Fat 0g	0%	**Protein** 9g		Sugars 0g	
Polyunsaturated Fat 0g					
Monounsaturated Fat 0g		Vitamin A 10% Vitamin C 0%		Calcium 25% Iron 0%	

Lifeway Kefir Farmer Cheese, Fat-Free

2 tbsp / 32g

Amount per serving	%DV	Amount per serving	%DV	Amount per serving	%DV
Calories 25		**Cholesterol** 5mg	0%	**Total Carbohydrate** 1g	1%
Total Fat 0g	0%	**Sodium** 15mg	0%	Dietary Fiber 0g	0%
Saturated Fat 0g	0%	**Protein** 5g		Sugars 1g	
Polyunsaturated Fat 0g					
Monounsaturated Fat 0g		Vitamin A 0%	Vitamin C 0%	Calcium 4%	Iron 0%

Lifeway Kefir Farmer, Lite Cheese

2 tbsp / 32g

Amount per serving	%DV	Amount per serving	%DV	Amount per serving	%DV
Calories 30		**Cholesterol** 5mg	2%	**Total Carbohydrate** 1g	0%
Total Fat 1g	2%	**Sodium** 15mg	1%	Dietary Fiber 0g	0%
Saturated Fat 0.5.g	3%	**Protein** 4g		Sugars 1g	
Polyunsaturated Fat 0g					
Monounsaturated Fat 0g		Vitamin A 0%	Vitamin C 0%	Calcium 4%	Iron 0%

Lifeway, Kefir Farmer Cheese

2 tbsp / 32g

Amount per serving	%DV	Amount per serving	%DV	Amount per serving	%DV
Calories 30		**Cholesterol** 5mg	2%	**Total Carbohydrate** 1g	0%
Total Fat 1g	2%	**Sodium** 15mg	1%	Dietary Fiber 0g	0%
Saturated Fat 0.5g	3%	**Protein** 4g		Sugars 1g	
Polyunsaturated Fat 0g					
Monounsaturated Fat 0g		Vitamin A 0%	Vitamin C 0%	Calcium 4%	Iron 0%

Polly-O, Mozzarella Fat-Free

1 oz

Amount per serving	%DV	Amount per serving	%DV	Amount per serving	%DV
Calories 35		**Cholesterol** 0mg	0%	**Total Carbohydrate** 1g	0%
Total Fat 0g	0%	**Sodium** 220mg	9%	Dietary Fiber 0g	0%
Saturated Fat 0g	0%	**Protein** 7g		Sugars 0g	
Polyunsaturated Fat 0g					
Monounsaturated Fat 0g		Vitamin A 4%	Vitamin C 0%	Calcium 15%	Iron 0%

Dairy Alternatives

8th Continent, Fat Free Original Soymilk

1 cup / 8 fl oz / 240ml

Amount per serving	%DV	Amount per serving	%DV	Amount per serving	%DV
Calories 60		**Cholesterol** 0mg	0%	**Total Carbohydrate** 8g	3%
Total Fat 0g	0%	**Sodium** 100mg	4%	Dietary Fiber 0g	0%
Saturated Fat 0g	0%	**Protein** 6g		Sugars 7g	
Polyunsaturated Fat 0g					
Monounsaturated Fat 0g		Vitamin A 10%	Vitamin C 0%	Calcium 30%	Iron 6%

8th Continent, Fat Free Vanilla Soymilk

1 cup / 8 fl oz / 240ml

Amount per serving	%DV	Amount per serving	%DV	Amount per serving	%DV
Calories 70		**Cholesterol** 0mg	0%	**Total Carbohydrate** 11g	4%
Total Fat 0g	0%	**Sodium** 100mg	4%	Dietary Fiber 0g	0%
Saturated Fat 0g	0%	**Protein** 6g		Sugars 10g	
Polyunsaturated Fat 0g					
Monounsaturated Fat 0g		Vitamin A 10% Vitamin C 0%		Calcium 30% Iron 6%	

8th Continent, Light Original Soymilk

1 cup / 8 fl oz / 240ml

Amount per serving	%DV	Amount per serving	%DV	Amount per serving	%DV
Calories 50		**Cholesterol** 0mg	0%	**Total Carbohydrate** 2g	1%
Total Fat 2g	3%	**Sodium** 115mg	5%	Dietary Fiber 0g	0%
Saturated Fat 0g	0%	**Protein** 6g		Sugars 2g	
Polyunsaturated Fat 1.5g					
Monounsaturated Fat 0g		Vitamin A 10% Vitamin C 0%		Calcium 30% Iron 6%	

8th Continent, Original Soymilk

1 cup / 8 fl oz / 240ml

Amount per serving	%DV	Amount per serving	%DV	Amount per serving	%DV
Calories 80		**Cholesterol** 0mg	0%	**Total Carbohydrate** 7g	2%
Total Fat 2.5g	4%	**Sodium** 95mg	4%	Dietary Fiber 0g	0%
Saturated Fat 0g	0%	**Protein** 8g		Sugars 7g	
Polyunsaturated Fat 1.5g					
Monounsaturated Fat 0.5g		Vitamin A 10% Vitamin C 0%		Calcium 30% Iron 6%	

8th Continent, Vanilla Soymilk

1 cup / 8 fl oz / 240ml

Amount per serving	%DV	Amount per serving	%DV	Amount per serving	%DV
Calories 100		**Cholesterol** 0mg	0%	**Total Carbohydrate** 11g	4%
Total Fat 2.5g	4%	**Sodium** 85mg	4%	Dietary Fiber 0g	0%
Saturated Fat 0g	0%	**Protein** 8g		Sugars 11g	
Polyunsaturated Fat 0g					
Monounsaturated Fat 0g		Vitamin A 10% Vitamin C 0%		Calcium 30% Iron 8%	

Blue Diamond, Almond Breeze, Refrigerated Almond Milk, Original

1 cup / 240 ml

Amount per serving	%DV	Amount per serving	%DV	Amount per serving	%DV
Calories 60		**Cholesterol** 0mg	0%	**Total Carbohydrate** 8g	3%
Total Fat 2.5g	4%	**Sodium** 150mg	6%	Dietary Fiber 1g	4%
Saturated Fat 0g	0%	**Protein** 1g		Sugars 7g	
Polyunsaturated Fat 0g					
Monounsaturated Fat 0g		Vitamin A 10% Vitamin C 0%		Calcium 45% Iron 4%	

Blue Diamond, Almond Breeze, Refrigerated Almond Milk, Original, Unsweetened

8 fl oz / 240 ml

Amount per serving	%DV	Amount per serving	%DV	Amount per serving	%DV
Calories 30		**Cholesterol** 0mg	0%	**Total Carbohydrate** 1g	0%
Total Fat 2.5g	4%	**Sodium** 180mg	* 8%	Dietary Fiber 1g	4%
Saturated Fat 0g	0%	**Protein** 1g		Sugars 0g	
Polyunsaturated Fat 0g					
Monounsaturated Fat 0g		Vitamin A 10% Vitamin C 0%		Calcium 45% Iron 4%	

Blue Diamond, Almond Breeze, Refrigerated, Chocolate Flavored Almond Milk

1 cup / 240 ml

Amount per serving	%DV	Amount per serving	%DV	Amount per serving	%DV
Calories 120		**Cholesterol** 0mg	0%	**Total Carbohydrate** 22g	7%
Total Fat 3g	5%	**Sodium** 150mg	6%	Dietary Fiber 1g	4%
Saturated Fat 0g	0%	**Protein** 1g		Sugars 20g	
Polyunsaturated Fat 0g					
Monounsaturated Fat 0g		Vitamin A 10% Vitamin C 0%		Calcium 45% Iron 6%	

Blue Diamond, Almond Breeze, Refrigerated, Vanilla Flavored Almond Milk

1 cup / 240 ml

Amount per serving	%DV	Amount per serving	%DV	Amount per serving	%DV
Calories 80		**Cholesterol** 0mg	0%	**Total Carbohydrate** 14g	5%
Total Fat 2.5g	4%	**Sodium** 150mg	6%	Dietary Fiber 1g	4%
Saturated Fat 0g	0%	**Protein** 1g		Sugars 13g	
Polyunsaturated Fat 0g					
Monounsaturated Fat 0g		Vitamin A 10% Vitamin C 0%		Calcium 45% Iron 40%	

Blue Diamond, Almond Breeze, Shelf Stable, Sweetened, Chocolate Almond Milk

1 cup / 240 ml

Amount per serving	%DV	Amount per serving	%DV	Amount per serving	%DV
Calories 120		**Cholesterol** 0mg	0%	**Total Carbohydrate** 22g	7%
Total Fat 3g	5%	**Sodium** 150mg	6%	Dietary Fiber 1g	4%
Saturated Fat 0g	0%	**Protein** 1g		Sugars 20g	
Polyunsaturated Fat 0g					
Monounsaturated Fat 0g		Vitamin A 10% Vitamin C 0%		Calcium 45% Iron 6%	

Blue Diamond, Almond Breeze, Shelf Stable, Vanilla Almond Milk

1 cup / 240 ml

Amount per serving	%DV	Amount per serving	%DV	Amount per serving	%DV
Calories 90		**Cholesterol** 0mg	0%	**Total Carbohydrate** 16g	5%
Total Fat 2.5g	4%	**Sodium** 150mg	6%	Dietary Fiber 1g	4%
Saturated Fat 0g	0%	**Protein** 1g		Sugars 15g	
Polyunsaturated Fat 0g					
Monounsaturated Fat 0g		Vitamin A 10% Vitamin C 0%		Calcium 45% Iron 4%	

Blue Diamond, Refrigerated, Original Almondmilk Coconutmilk Blend

1 cup / 240 ml

Amount per serving	%DV	Amount per serving	%DV	Amount per serving	%DV
Calories 60		**Cholesterol** 0mg	0%	**Total Carbohydrate** 7g	2%
Total Fat 3g	5%	**Sodium** 125mg	5%	Dietary Fiber 1g	4%
Saturated Fat 1g	5%	**Protein** 1g		Sugars 6g	
Polyunsaturated Fat 0g					
Monounsaturated Fat 0g		Vitamin A 10% Vitamin C 0%		Calcium 45% Iron 4%	

Blue Diamond, Shelf Stable, Vanilla Almondmilk Coconutmilk Blend

1 cup / 240 ml

Amount per serving	%DV	Amount per serving	%DV	Amount per serving	%DV
Calories 70		**Cholesterol** 0mg	0%	**Total Carbohydrate** 10g	3%
Total Fat 3g	5%	**Sodium** 130mg	5%	Dietary Fiber 1g	4%
Saturated Fat 1g	5%	**Protein** 1g		Sugars 9g	
Polyunsaturated Fat 0g					
Monounsaturated Fat 0g		Vitamin A 10% Vitamin C 0%		Calcium 45% Iron 4%	

Blue Diamond, Vanilla Almondmilk Coconutmilk Blend, Unsweetened

1 cup / 240 ml

Amount per serving	%DV	Amount per serving	%DV	Amount per serving	%DV
Calories 70		**Cholesterol** 0mg	0%	**Total Carbohydrate** 10g	3%
Total Fat 3g	5%	**Sodium** 130mg	5%	Dietary Fiber 1g	4%
Saturated Fat 1g	5%	**Protein** 1g		Sugars 9g	
Polyunsaturated Fat 0g					
Monounsaturated Fat 0g		Vitamin A 10% Vitamin C 0%		Calcium 45% Iron 4%	

Earth Balance, Chocolate Soymilk

1 cup / 240 ml

Amount per serving	%DV	Amount per serving	%DV	Amount per serving	%DV
Calories 130		**Cholesterol** 0mg	0%	**Total Carbohydrate** 21g	7%
Total Fat 3g	5%	**Sodium** 100mg	4%	Dietary Fiber 2g	8%
Saturated Fat 0.5g	3%	**Protein** 5g		Sugars 19g	
Polyunsaturated Fat 1.6g					
Monounsaturated Fat 0.5g		Vitamin A 10% Vitamin C 0%		Calcium 30% Iron 8%	

Galaxy, Rice Slices, Cheese Alternative American Flavor

1 slice / 17g

Amount per serving	%DV	Amount per serving	%DV	Amount per serving	%DV
Calories 40		**Cholesterol** 0mg	0%	**Total Carbohydrate** 1g	0%
Total Fat 2.5g	4%	**Sodium** 240mg	10%	Dietary Fiber 0g	0%
Saturated Fat 0g	0%	**Protein** 3g		Sugars 0g	
Polyunsaturated Fat 1g					
Monounsaturated Fat 1g		Vitamin A 10% Vitamin C 0%		Calcium 20% Iron 0%	

Galaxy, Rice Vegan Slices, American Flavor

1 slice / 17g

Amount per serving	%DV	Amount per serving	%DV	Amount per serving	%DV
Calories 40		Cholesterol 0mg	0%	Total Carbohydrate 5g	2%
Total Fat 2g	3%	Sodium 180mg	8%	Dietary Fiber 0g	0%
Saturated Fat 0g	0%	Protein 1g		Sugars 0g	
Polyunsaturated Fat 0.5g					
Monounsaturated Fat 1g		Vitamin A 0% Vitamin C 0%		Calcium 20% Iron 0%	

Galaxy, Veggie Slices, Cheese Alternative American Flavor

1 slice / 17g

Amount per serving	%DV	Amount per serving	%DV	Amount per serving	%DV
Calories 40		Cholesterol 0mg	0%	Total Carbohydrate 1g	0%
Total Fat 2.5g	4%	Sodium 220mg	9%	Dietary Fiber 0g	0%
Saturated Fat 0g	0%	Protein 3g		Sugars 0g	
Polyunsaturated Fat 1g					
Monounsaturated Fat 1.5g		Vitamin A 10% Vitamin C 0%		Calcium 25% Iron 2%	

Good Karma, Original Flax Milk

1 cup / 8 fl oz

Amount per serving	%DV	Amount per serving	%DV	Amount per serving	%DV
Calories 50		Cholesterol 0mg	0%	Total Carbohydrate 7g	2%
Total Fat 2.5g	4%	Sodium 80mg	3%	Dietary Fiber 0g	0%
Saturated Fat 0g	0%	Protein 0g		Sugars 7g	
Polyunsaturated Fat 1.5g					
Monounsaturated Fat 0g		Vitamin A 10% Vitamin C 0%		Calcium 30% Iron 2%	

Good Karma, Unsweetened Flax Milk

1 cup / 8 fl oz

Amount per serving	%DV	Amount per serving	%DV	Amount per serving	%DV
Calories 25		Cholesterol 0mg	0%	Total Carbohydrate 1g	0%
Total Fat 2.5g	4%	Sodium 80mg	3%	Dietary Fiber 0g	0%
Saturated Fat 0g	0%	Protein 0g		Sugars 0g	
Polyunsaturated Fat 1.5g					
Monounsaturated Fat 0g		Vitamin A 10% Vitamin C 0%		Calcium 30% Iron 2%	

Good Karma, Vanilla Flax Milk

1 cup / 8 fl oz

Amount per serving	%DV	Amount per serving	%DV	Amount per serving	%DV
Calories 60		Cholesterol 0mg	0%	Total Carbohydrate 11g	4%
Total Fat 2.5g	4%	Sodium 80mg	3%	Dietary Fiber 0g	0%
Saturated Fat 0g	0%	Protein 0g		Sugars 11g	
Polyunsaturated Fat 1.5g					
Monounsaturated Fat 0g		Vitamin A 10% Vitamin C 0%		Calcium 30% Iron 2%	

Pacific All Natural, Organic Almond Non-Dairy Chocolate Beverage

1 cup, 8 fl oz / 240 ml

Amount per serving	%DV	Amount per serving	%DV	Amount per serving	%DV
Calories 100		**Cholesterol** 0mg	0%	**Total Carbohydrate** 19g	6%
Total Fat 3g	5%	**Sodium** 140mg	6%	Dietary Fiber 1g	4%
Saturated Fat 0g	0%	**Protein** 1g		Sugars 16g	
Polyunsaturated Fat 0g					
Monounsaturated Fat 0g		Vitamin A 10% Vitamin C 0%		Calcium 0% Iron 0%	

Pacific All Natural, Rice Non-Dairy Beverage

1 cup, 8 fl oz / 240 ml

Amount per serving	%DV	Amount per serving	%DV	Amount per serving	%DV
Calories 130		**Cholesterol** 0mg	0%	**Total Carbohydrate** 27g	9%
Total Fat 2g	3%	**Sodium** 60mg	3%	Dietary Fiber 0g	0%
Saturated Fat 0g	0%	**Protein** 1g		Sugars 14g	
Polyunsaturated Fat 0g					
Monounsaturated Fat 0g		Vitamin A 10% Vitamin C 0%		Calcium 30% Iron 6%	

Pacific All Natural, Select Soy Orginal Non-Dairy Soy Beverage

1 cup, 8 fl oz / 240 ml

Amount per serving	%DV	Amount per serving	%DV	Amount per serving	%DV
Calories 70		**Cholesterol** 0mg	0%	**Total Carbohydrate** 9g	3%
Total Fat 2.5g	4%	**Sodium** 115mg	5%	Dietary Fiber 1g	4%
Saturated Fat 0g	0%	**Protein** 5g		Sugars 6g	
Polyunsaturated Fat 0g					
Monounsaturated Fat 0g		Vitamin A 0% Vitamin C 0%		Calcium 2% Iron 4%	

Pacific All Natural, Select Soy Vanilla Non-Dairy Soy Beverage

1 cup, 8 fl oz / 240 ml

Amount per serving	%DV	Amount per serving	%DV	Amount per serving	%DV
Calories 80		**Cholesterol** 0mg	0%	**Total Carbohydrate** 11g	4%
Total Fat 2.5g	4%	**Sodium** 115mg	5%	Dietary Fiber 1g	4%
Saturated Fat 0g	0%	**Protein** 5g		Sugars 9g	
Polyunsaturated Fat 0g					
Monounsaturated Fat 0g		Vitamin A 0% Vitamin C 0%		Calcium 2% Iron 4%	

Pacific All Natural, Vanilla Rice Non-Dairy Beverage

1 cup, 8 fl oz / 240 ml

Amount per serving	%DV	Amount per serving	%DV	Amount per serving	%DV
Calories 130		**Cholesterol** 0mg	0%	**Total Carbohydrate** 27g	9%
Total Fat 2g	3%	**Sodium** 60mg	3%	Dietary Fiber 0g	0%
Saturated Fat 0g	0%	**Protein** 1g		Sugars 14g	
Polyunsaturated Fat 0g					
Monounsaturated Fat 0g		Vitamin A 10% Vitamin C 0%		Calcium 30% Iron 6%	

Pacific Organic, Almond Original Non-Dairy Beverage

1 cup, 8 fl oz / 240 ml

Amount per serving	%DV	Amount per serving	%DV	Amount per serving	%DV
Calories 60		**Cholesterol** 0mg	0%	**Total Carbohydrate** 8g	3%
Total Fat 2.5g	4%	**Sodium** 150mg	6%	Dietary Fiber 0g	0%
Saturated Fat 0g	0%	**Protein** 1g		Sugars 7g	
Polyunsaturated Fat 0g					
Monounsaturated Fat 0g		Vitamin A 10% Vitamin C 0%		Calcium 2% Iron 2%	

Pacific Organic, Almond Vanilla Non-Dairy Beverage

1 cup, 8 fl oz / 240 ml

Amount per serving	%DV	Amount per serving	%DV	Amount per serving	%DV
Calories 70		**Cholesterol** 0mg	0%	**Total Carbohydrate** 11g	4%
Total Fat 2.5g	4%	**Sodium** 150mg	6%	Dietary Fiber 1g	4%
Saturated Fat 0g	0%	**Protein** 1g		Sugars 10g	
Polyunsaturated Fat 0g					
Monounsaturated Fat 0g		Vitamin A 10% Vitamin C 0%		Calcium 2% Iron 2%	

Pacific Organic, Unsweetened Almond Original Non-Dairy Beverage

1 cup, 8 fl oz / 240 ml

Amount per serving	%DV	Amount per serving	%DV	Amount per serving	%DV
Calories 35		**Cholesterol** 0mg	0%	**Total Carbohydrate** 2g	1%
Total Fat 2.5g	4%	**Sodium** 190mg	8%	Dietary Fiber 0g	0%
Saturated Fat 0g	0%	**Protein** 1g		Sugars 0g	
Polyunsaturated Fat 0g					
Monounsaturated Fat 0g		Vitamin A 10% Vitamin C 0%		Calcium 2% Iron 2%	

Pacific Organic, Unsweetened Almond Vanilla Non-Dairy Beverage

1 cup, 8 fl oz / 240 ml

Amount per serving	%DV	Amount per serving	%DV	Amount per serving	%DV
Calories 35		**Cholesterol** 0mg	0%	**Total Carbohydrate** 3g	1%
Total Fat 2.5g	4%	**Sodium** 190mg	8%	Dietary Fiber 0g	0%
Saturated Fat 0g	0%	**Protein** 1g		Sugars 0g	
Polyunsaturated Fat 0g					
Monounsaturated Fat 0g		Vitamin A 10% Vitamin C 0%		Calcium 2% Iron 2%	

Rice Dream, Shelf Stable, Enriched Original Rice Drink

1 cup / 8 fl oz

Amount per serving	%DV	Amount per serving	%DV	Amount per serving	%DV
Calories 120		**Cholesterol** 0mg	0%	**Total Carbohydrate** 23g	8%
Total Fat 2.5g	4%	**Sodium** 100mg	4%	Dietary Fiber 0g	0%
Saturated Fat 0g	0%	**Protein** 1g		Sugars 10g	
Polyunsaturated Fat 0g					
Monounsaturated Fat 0g		Vitamin A 10% Vitamin C 0%		Calcium 30% Iron 4%	

Silk Light Soymilk, Chocolate

1 cup / 240 ml

Amount per serving	%DV	Amount per serving	%DV	Amount per serving	%DV
Calories 90		**Cholesterol** 0mg	0%	**Total Carbohydrate** 16g	5%
Total Fat 1.5g	2%	**Sodium** 85mg	4%	Dietary Fiber 1g	4%
Saturated Fat 0g	0%	**Protein** 3g		Sugars 14g	
Polyunsaturated Fat 1g					
Monounsaturated Fat 0.5g		Vitamin A 10% Vitamin C 0%		Calcium 45% Iron 10%	

Silk Light, Soymilk, Original

1 cup / 240 ml

Amount per serving	%DV	Amount per serving	%DV	Amount per serving	%DV
Calories 60		**Cholesterol** 0mg	0%	**Total Carbohydrate** 5g	2%
Total Fat 1.5g	2%	**Sodium** 135mg	6%	Dietary Fiber 1g	4%
Saturated Fat 0g	0%	**Protein** 6g		Sugars 3g	
Polyunsaturated Fat 1g					
Monounsaturated Fat 0.5g		Vitamin A 10% Vitamin C 0%		Calcium 45% Iron 6%	

Silk Light, Soymilk, Vanilla

1 cup / 240 ml

Amount per serving	%DV	Amount per serving	%DV	Amount per serving	%DV
Calories 70		**Cholesterol** 0mg	0%	**Total Carbohydrate** 7g	2%
Total Fat 1.5g	2%	**Sodium** 110mg	5%	Dietary Fiber 1g	4%
Saturated Fat 0g	0%	**Protein** 6g		Sugars 5g	
Polyunsaturated Fat 1g					
Monounsaturated Fat 0.5g		Vitamin A 10% Vitamin C 0%		Calcium 45% Iron 6%	

Silk, Chocolate, Soy Milk

1 cup / 240 ml

Amount per serving	%DV	Amount per serving	%DV	Amount per serving	%DV
Calories 120		**Cholesterol** 0mg	0%	**Total Carbohydrate** 19g	6%
Total Fat 3g	5%	**Sodium** 95mg	4%	Dietary Fiber 2g	8%
Saturated Fat 0.5g	2%	**Protein** 5g		Sugars 17g	
Polyunsaturated Fat 1.5g					
Monounsaturated Fat 0.5g		Vitamin A 10% Vitamin C 0%		Calcium 45% Iron 15%	

Silk, French Vanilla Creamer

1 tbsp / 15g

Amount per serving	%DV	Amount per serving	%DV	Amount per serving	%DV
Calories 20		**Cholesterol** 0mg	0%	**Total Carbohydrate** 3g	1%
Total Fat 1g	2%	**Sodium** 10mg	0%	Dietary Fiber 0g	0%
Saturated Fat 0g	0%	**Protein** 0g		Sugars 3g	
Polyunsaturated Fat 0g					
Monounsaturated Fat 0g		Vitamin A 0% Vitamin C 0%		Calcium 0% Iron 0%	

Soymilk (All Flavors), Low Fat, with Added Calcium and Vitamins A and D

1 cup / 240 ml

Amount per serving	%DV	Amount per serving	%DV	Amount per serving	%DV
Calories 100		**Cholesterol** 0mg	0%	**Total Carbohydrate** 17g	6%
Total Fat 2g	3%	**Sodium** 90mg	4%	Dietary Fiber 2g	8%
Saturated Fat 0g	0%	**Protein** 4g		Sugars 9g	
Polyunsaturated Fat 0.4g					
Monounsaturated Fat 0.2g		Vitamin A 10% Vitamin C 0%		Calcium 20% Iron 6%	

Soymilk (All Flavors), Non-fat, with Added Calcium and Vitamins A and D

1 cup / 240 ml

Amount per serving	%DV	Amount per serving	%DV	Amount per serving	%DV
Calories 66		**Cholesterol** 0mg	0%	**Total Carbohydrate** 10g	3%
Total Fat 0g	0%	**Sodium** 139mg	6%	Dietary Fiber 0g	0%
Saturated Fat 0g	0%	**Protein** 6g		Sugars 9g	
Polyunsaturated Fat 0.1g					
Monounsaturated Fat 0g		Vitamin A 10% Vitamin C 0%		Calcium 28% Iron 5%	

Soymilk, Chocolate & Other Flavors, Light with Added Calcium & Vitamins A and D

1 cup / 240 ml

Amount per serving	%DV	Amount per serving	%DV	Amount per serving	%DV
Calories 114		**Cholesterol** 0mg	0%	**Total Carbohydrate** 20g	7%
Total Fat 2g	3%	**Sodium** 112mg	5%	Dietary Fiber 2g	8%
Saturated Fat 0g	0%	**Protein** 5g		Sugars 17g	
Polyunsaturated Fat 1g					
Monounsaturated Fat 0.1g		Vitamin A 10% Vitamin C 0%		Calcium 30% Iron 8%	

Soymilk, Original & Vanilla, Light with Added Calcium and Vitamins A and D

1 cup / 240 ml

Amount per serving	%DV	Amount per serving	%DV	Amount per serving	%DV
Calories 73		**Cholesterol** 0mg	0%	**Total Carbohydrate** 9g	3%
Total Fat 2g	3%	**Sodium** 117mg	5%	Dietary Fiber 1g	4%
Saturated Fat 0g	0%	**Protein** 6g		Sugars 6g	
Polyunsaturated Fat 1g					
Monounsaturated Fat 0.5g		Vitamin A 10% Vitamin C 0%		Calcium 30% Iron 6%	

Soymilk, Original & Vanilla, Light, Unsweetened, with Calcium & Vitamins A & D

1 cup / 240 ml

Amount per serving	%DV	Amount per serving	%DV	Amount per serving	%DV
Calories 83		**Cholesterol** 0mg	0%	**Total Carbohydrate** 9g	3%
Total Fat 2g	3%	**Sodium** 153mg	6%	Dietary Fiber 1g	4%
Saturated Fat 0g	0%	**Protein** 6g		Sugars 1g	
Polyunsaturated Fat 1.4g					
Monounsaturated Fat 0.6g		Vitamin A 10% Vitamin C 0%		Calcium 30% Iron 6%	

VitaSoy USA, Vitasoy Light Vanilla Soymilk

1 cup / 250 ml

Amount per serving	%DV	Amount per serving	%DV	Amount per serving	%DV
Calories 70		**Cholesterol** 0mg	0%	**Total Carbohydrate** 10g	3%
Total Fat 2g	3%	**Sodium** 120mg	5%	Dietary Fiber 0g	0%
Saturated Fat 0.5g	3%	**Protein** 4.1g		Sugars 7g	
Polyunsaturated Fat 0g					
Monounsaturated Fat 0g		Vitamin A 6% Vitamin C 0%		Calcium 30% Iron 4%	

WestSoy, Low Fat Plain Soymilk

1 cup / 8 fl oz / 240 ml

Amount per serving	%DV	Amount per serving	%DV	Amount per serving	%DV
Calories 90		**Cholesterol** 0mg	0%	**Total Carbohydrate** 15g	5%
Total Fat 2g	3%	**Sodium** 80mg	3%	Dietary Fiber 1g	4%
Saturated Fat 0g	0%	**Protein** 4g		Sugars 5g	
Polyunsaturated Fat 1g					
Monounsaturated Fat 0.5g		Vitamin A 10% Vitamin C 0%		Calcium 20% Iron 4%	

WestSoy, Low Fat Vanilla Soymilk

1 cup / 8 fl oz

Amount per serving	%DV	Amount per serving	%DV	Amount per serving	%DV
Calories 120		**Cholesterol** 0mg	0%	**Total Carbohydrate** 23g	8%
Total Fat 2g	3%	**Sodium** 65mg	3%	Dietary Fiber 1g	4%
Saturated Fat 0g	0%	**Protein** 4g		Sugars 8g	
Polyunsaturated Fat 1g					
Monounsaturated Fat 0.5g		Vitamin A 10% Vitamin C 0%		Calcium 25% Iron 4%	

WestSoy, Non Fat Plain Soymilk

1 cup / 8 fl oz

Amount per serving	%DV	Amount per serving	%DV	Amount per serving	%DV
Calories 70		**Cholesterol** 0mg	0%	**Total Carbohydrate** 10g	3%
Total Fat 0g	0%	**Sodium** 105mg	4%	Dietary Fiber 1g	4%
Saturated Fat 0g	0%	**Protein** 6g		Sugars 9g	
Polyunsaturated Fat 0g					
Monounsaturated Fat 0g		Vitamin A 10% Vitamin C 0%		Calcium 25% Iron 10%	

WestSoy, Non Fat Vanilla Soymilk

1 cup / 8 fl oz

Amount per serving	%DV	Amount per serving	%DV	Amount per serving	%DV
Calories 80		**Cholesterol** 0mg	0%	**Total Carbohydrate** 12g	4%
Total Fat 0g	0%	**Sodium** 105mg	4%	Dietary Fiber 1g	4%
Saturated Fat 0g	0%	**Protein** 6g		Sugars 10g	
Polyunsaturated Fat 0g					
Monounsaturated Fat 0g		Vitamin A 10% Vitamin C 0%		Calcium 30% Iron 10%	

Fats and Oils

Why Eat Fats and Oils?

Fats and oils provide essential nutrients. Most of the fats you eat should be polyun-saturated (PUFA) or monounsaturated (MUFA). PUFAs contain some fatty acids that are necessary for health—called "essential fatty acids." MUFAs and PUFAs found in fish, nuts, and vegetable oils do not raise LDL ("bad") cholesterol levels in the blood and therefore are good for your heart. Oils are the major source of vitamin E, a potent antioxidant.

Daily Goal

Six teaspoons for an adult on a 2,000-calorie diet.

1 teaspoon equivalents:
1 Tbsp. oil = 2.5 teaspoons
1 Tbsp. mayonnaise = 2.5 teaspoons
1 Tbsp. Italian dressing = 2 teaspoons
4 large olives = ½ teaspoon
1 oz. nuts = 3 teaspoons
2 Tbsp. peanut butter = 4 teaspoons

Heart-Healthy Nutrients in Fats, Oils, and Nuts

Omega-3 fatty acids benefit the heart of healthy people and those at high risk for cardiovascular disease. Research has shown that omega-3 fatty acids decrease the risk of arrhythmias (abnormal heartbeats), which can lead to sud-den death. Omega-3 fatty acids also decrease triglyceride levels, slow growth rate of atherosclerotic plaque, and lower blood pressure (slightly). Flaxseeds, chia seeds, walnuts, olive, and canola oil are good plant sources of omega-3s. Animal sources of omega-3s are fatty fish such as salmon, mackerel, trout, sea bass, and halibut.

Check out the FDA-approved Qualified Health Claim for omega-3 fats and risk of heart disease on page 29.

Polyunsaturated fats (PUFAs) promote lower total blood cholesterol as well as lower LDL cholesterol. Unfortunately, they also lower the good (HDL) cholesterol. Corn oil, safflower oil, soybean oil, sunflower oils, and sesame oils are good sources of polyunsaturated fats. Use less corn oil and soy oil because they are a higher source of omega-6 fatty acids.

Monounsaturated fats (MUFAs) are the best fat for lowering blood cholesterol levels—both total and LDL. They also have been shown to increase HDL cholesterol. Monounsaturated fats are found in nuts and vegetable oils such as canola oil, olive oil, high oleic safflower oil, and sunflower oil.

Check out the FDA-approved Qualified Health Claim for monounsaturated fats and risk of heart disease on page 29.

Antioxidants can help prevent artery damage by fighting products produced in the process of oxidation. The major antioxidant found in fats and oils is vitamin E, which is found in sunflower seeds, sunflower oil, safflower oil, almonds, hazelnuts, and peanuts.

Plant sterols and stanols (collectively called phytosterols) are the plant equivalent to the animal cholesterol found naturally in small amounts in a wide variety of foods. Foods can be fortified with phytosterols in much higher amounts. The main benefit of adding phytosterols to your diet is to help reduce your risk for heart attack and stroke by lowering your LDL cholesterol. Because the structure of phytosterols is similar to that of cholesterol, phytosterols block the absorption of cholesterol in your intestines and lower the amount of cholesterol in your blood. Phytosterols are added to spreads such as Benecol and Smart Balance.

See the FDA-approved Health Claim for phytosterols and risk of heart disease on page 27.

Shopping Tips for Fats and Oils

- **Look for these FDA-approved Heart Health Claims on Fats and Oils:**

  Saturated Fat, Cholesterol, and Trans Fat, and Reduced Risk of Heart Disease
  "Diets low in saturated fat and cholesterol, and as low as possible in trans fat, may reduce the risk of heart disease."

  Foods that display this claim must be low in saturated fat (1 gram or less) and cholesterol (20 mg or less) and contain less than 0.5 g trans fat per serving and less than 6.5 g total fat.

  Dietary Saturated Fat and Cholesterol, and risk of Coronary Heart Disease
  "While many factors affect heart disease, diets low in saturated fat and cholesterol may reduce the risk of this disease."

  Foods that make this claim must be low in total fat, saturated fat, and cholesterol.

Plant Sterol/Stanol Esters and Risk of Coronary Heart Disease

(1) Foods containing at least 0.65 grams per serving of vegetable oil sterol esters, eaten twice a day with meals for a daily total intake of least 1.3 grams, as part of a diet low in saturated fat and cholesterol, may reduce the risk of heart disease. A serving of [name of food] supplies __ grams of vegetable oil sterol esters.

(2) Diets low in saturated fat and cholesterol that include two servings of foods that provide a daily total of at least 3.4 grams of plant stanol esters in two meals may reduce the risk of heart disease. A serving of [name of food] supplies __ grams of plant stanol esters.

Eligible products that make this claim must have at least 0.65 grams plant sterol esters or at least 1.7 grams plant stanol esters per serving. They must also be low in saturated fat and cholesterol.

- **Look for these FDA-approved Qualified Health Claims on Fats, Oils, and Nuts:**

Nuts and Heart Disease
"Scientific evidence suggests but does not prove that eating 1.5 ounces per day of most nuts [such as name of specific nut] as part of a diet low in saturated fat and cholesterol may reduce the risk of heart disease [See nutrition information for fat content.]"

Types of nuts eligible for this claim are restricted to almonds, hazelnuts, peanuts, pecans, some pine nuts, pistachio nuts, and walnuts. Nuts must not exceed 4 g saturated fat per 50 g of nuts. Nut-containing products that contain at least 11 g of one or more of these nuts are also eligible for this claim.

Walnuts and Heart Disease
"Supportive but not conclusive research shows that eating 1.5 ounces per day of walnuts, as part of a low-saturated fat and low-cholesterol diet and not resulting in increased caloric intake, may reduce the risk of coronary heart disease. See nutrition information for fat [and calorie] content."

Find this claim on whole or chopped walnuts.

Omega-3 Fatty Acids and Coronary Heart Disease
"Supportive but not conclusive research shows that consumption of EPA and DHA omega-3 fatty acids may reduce the risk of coronary heart disease. One serving of [Name of the food] provides [ ] gram of EPA and DHA omega-3 fatty acids. [See nutrition information for total fat, saturated fat, and cholesterol content.]"

This claim can be made on all foods that contain EPA and DHA omega-3 fatty acids.

Monounsaturated Fatty Acids from Olive Oil and Coronary Heart Disease

"Limited and not conclusive scientific evidence suggests that eating about 2 table-spoons (23 grams) of olive oil daily may reduce the risk of coronary heart disease due to the monounsaturated fat in olive oil. To achieve this possible benefit, olive oil is to replace a similar amount of saturated fat and not increase the total number of calories you eat in a day. One serving of this product contains ___ grams of olive oil."

This claim can be made by all products that are essentially pure olive oil and labeled as such. Also, olive oil–containing foods that contain 6 grams or more of olive oil per serving are low in cholesterol; contain at least 10% of either vitamin A, vitamin C, iron, calcium, protein, or dietary fiber; and do not contain more than 4 grams of saturated fat per 50 grams. Meal products or main dish products are not eligible for the claim.

- Look for the American Heart Association's Heart-Check mark on nut food labels that meet the Heart Check criteria. For more information on the Heart-Check mark go to *www.heartcheckmark.org*.

- When you must use oils for cooking, baking or in dressings or spreads, choose the ones lowest in saturated fats, trans fats, and cholesterol—including canola oil, corn oil, olive oil, safflower oil, sesame oil, soybean oil, and sunflower oil.

- Buy and use fats and oils in limited amounts. Although many of them are heart healthy, they are high in total calories.

- Stay away from palm oil, palm kernel oil, coconut oil, and cocoa butter. Even though they are vegetable oils and have no cholesterol, they are high in saturated fats.

- Use a nonstick pan or use nonstick vegetable spray when cooking.

- Choose reduced-fat, low-fat, light, or fat-free salad dressings to use with salads, for dips, or as marinades.

- Limit solid fats such as butter, stick margarine, shortening, and animal fats.

- Choose fats high in omega-3s such as olive oil, canola oil, walnuts, and flaxseeds.

- While consuming some oil is needed for health, oils still contain calories. In fact, oils and solid fats both contain about 120 calories per tablespoon. Therefore, the amount of oil consumed needs to be limited to balance total calorie intake.

Shopping List Essentials

Olive oil
Canola oil
Tub margarine
Walnuts
Hazelnuts
Peanuts
Pistachios
Nut butters made without hydrogenated oils

Criteria for Fats and Oils

Using the FDA guidelines for Heart Health Claims, the foods listed meet the following criteria per serving:

- Total fat–no limit
- Saturated fat–4 grams or less
- Trans fat–0.5 grams or less (Trans Fat is not listed in the charts because all items report 0 grams Trans Fat. Since foods with less than 0.5 grams of trans fat can list 0 grams in the Nutrition Facts, be sure to check the ingredients for partially hydrogenated fats to determine if a product contains any trans fats.)
- Sodium–salad dressings and olives: 480mg or less; butters/margarine and nuts: 140 mg or less. Look for lower sodium levels to help reduce high blood pressure.

These products do not meet the Beneficial Nutrients criteria that requires 10% Daily Value or higher of one beneficial nutrient (vitamin A, vitamin C, iron, calcium, protein, or dietary fiber). The emphasis is on reduced saturated fat and sodium.

Products that don't meet these nutritional criteria are regular butter and stick margarine, most salad dressings, and solid shortenings that are high in saturated fats. This does not mean that they are bad foods. Eat them occasionally and in small portions.

Oils

Eden Foods, Hot Pepper Sesame Oil, Imported

1 tbsp

Amount per serving	%DV	Amount per serving	%DV	Amount per serving	%DV
Calories 120		**Cholesterol** 0mg	0%	**Total Carbohydrate** 0g	0%
Total Fat 14g	22%	**Sodium** 0mg	0%	Dietary Fiber 0g	0%
Saturated Fat 2g	10%	**Protein** 0g		Sugars 0g	
Polyunsaturated Fat 0g					
Monounsaturated Fat 0g		Vitamin A 0%	Vitamin C 0%	Calcium 0%	Iron 0%

Eden Foods, Olive Oil, Extra Virgin, Spanish

1 tbsp

Amount per serving	%DV	Amount per serving	%DV	Amount per serving	%DV
Calories 120		**Cholesterol** 0mg	0%	**Total Carbohydrate** 0g	0%
Total Fat 14g	22%	**Sodium** 0mg	0%	Dietary Fiber 0g	0%
Saturated Fat 1.5g	8%	**Protein** 0g		Sugars 0g	
Polyunsaturated Fat 0g					
Monounsaturated Fat 0g		Vitamin A 0%	Vitamin C 0%	Calcium 0%	Iron 0%

Eden Foods, Safflower Oil, High Oleic, Organic

1 tbsp

Amount per serving	%DV	Amount per serving	%DV	Amount per serving	%DV
Calories 120		**Cholesterol** 0mg	0%	**Total Carbohydrate** 0g	0%
Total Fat 14g	22%	**Sodium** 0mg	0%	Dietary Fiber 0g	0%
Saturated Fat 1g	5%	**Protein** 0g		Sugars 0g	
Polyunsaturated Fat 0g					
Monounsaturated Fat 0g		Vitamin A 0%	Vitamin C 0%	Calcium 0%	Iron 0%

Eden Foods, Sesame Oil, Extra Virgin, Organic

1 tbsp

Amount per serving	%DV	Amount per serving	%DV	Amount per serving	%DV
Calories 120		**Cholesterol** 0mg	0%	**Total Carbohydrate** 0g	0%
Total Fat 14g	22%	**Sodium** 0mg	0%	Dietary Fiber 0g	0%
Saturated Fat 2g	10%	**Protein** 0g		Sugars 0g	
Polyunsaturated Fat 0g					
Monounsaturated Fat 0g		Vitamin A 0%	Vitamin C 0%	Calcium 0%	Iron 0%

Eden Foods, Toasted Sesame Oil

1 tbsp

Amount per serving	%DV	Amount per serving	%DV	Amount per serving	%DV
Calories 120		**Cholesterol** 0mg	0%	**Total Carbohydrate** 0g	0%
Total Fat 14g	22%	**Sodium** 0mg	0%	Dietary Fiber 0g	0%
Saturated Fat 2g	10%	**Protein** 0g		Sugars 0g	
Polyunsaturated Fat 0g					
Monounsaturated Fat 0g		Vitamin A 0%	Vitamin C 0%	Calcium 0%	Iron 0%

Lucini, Delicate Lemon, Extra Virgin Olive Oil

1 tbsp

Amount per serving	%DV	Amount per serving	%DV	Amount per serving	%DV
Calories 120		**Cholesterol** 0mg	0%	**Total Carbohydrate** 0g	0%
Total Fat 14g	22%	**Sodium** 0mg	0%	Dietary Fiber 0g	0%
Saturated Fat 2g	10%	**Protein** 0g		Sugars 0g	
Polyunsaturated Fat 1.5g					
Monounsaturated Fat 10g		Vitamin A 0% Vitamin C 0%		Calcium 0% Iron 0%	

Lucini, Estate Select, Extra Virgin Olive Oil

1 tbsp

Amount per serving	%DV	Amount per serving	%DV	Amount per serving	%DV
Calories 120		**Cholesterol** 0mg	0%	**Total Carbohydrate** 0g	0%
Total Fat 14g	22%	**Sodium** 0mg	0%	Dietary Fiber 0g	0%
Saturated Fat 2g	10%	**Protein** 0g		Sugars 0g	
Polyunsaturated Fat 1.5g					
Monounsaturated Fat 10g		Vitamin A 0% Vitamin C 0%		Calcium 0% Iron 0%	

Lucini, Fiery Chili, Extra Virgin Olive Oil

1 tbsp

Amount per serving	%DV	Amount per serving	%DV	Amount per serving	%DV
Calories 120		**Cholesterol** 0mg	0%	**Total Carbohydrate** 0g	0%
Total Fat 14g	22%	**Sodium** 0mg	0%	Dietary Fiber 0g	0%
Saturated Fat 2g	10%	**Protein** 0g		Sugars 0g	
Polyunsaturated Fat 1.5g					
Monounsaturated Fat 10g		Vitamin A 0% Vitamin C 0%		Calcium 0% Iron 0%	

Lucini, Limited Reserve, Premium Select Extra Virgin Olive Oil, 100% Organic

1 tbsp

Amount per serving	%DV	Amount per serving	%DV	Amount per serving	%DV
Calories 120		**Cholesterol** 0mg	0%	**Total Carbohydrate** 0g	0%
Total Fat 14g	22%	**Sodium** 0mg	0%	Dietary Fiber 0g	0%
Saturated Fat 2g	10%	**Protein** 0g		Sugars 0g	
Polyunsaturated Fat 1.5g					
Monounsaturated Fat 10g		Vitamin A 0% Vitamin C 0%		Calcium 0% Iron 0%	

Lucini, Premium Select Extra Virgin Olive Oil

1 tbsp

Amount per serving	%DV	Amount per serving	%DV	Amount per serving	%DV
Calories 120		**Cholesterol** 0mg	0%	**Total Carbohydrate** 0g	0%
Total Fat 14g	22%	**Sodium** 0mg	0%	Dietary Fiber 0g	0%
Saturated Fat 2g	10%	**Protein** 0g		Sugars 0g	
Polyunsaturated Fat 1.5g					
Monounsaturated Fat 10g		Vitamin A 0% Vitamin C 0%		Calcium 0% Iron 0%	

Lucini, Robust Garlic, Extra Virgin Olive Oil

1 tbsp

Amount per serving	%DV	Amount per serving	%DV	Amount per serving	%DV
Calories 120		**Cholesterol** 0mg	0%	**Total Carbohydrate** 0g	0%
Total Fat 14g	22%	**Sodium** 0mg	0%	Dietary Fiber 0g	0%
Saturated Fat 2g	10%	**Protein** 0g		Sugars 0g	
Polyunsaturated Fat 1.5g					
Monounsaturated Fat 10g		Vitamin A 0% Vitamin C 0%		Calcium 0% Iron 0%	

Lucini, Tuscan Basil, Extra Virgin Olive Oil

1 tbsp

Amount per serving	%DV	Amount per serving	%DV	Amount per serving	%DV
Calories 120		**Cholesterol** 0mg	0%	**Total Carbohydrate** 0g	0%
Total Fat 14g	22%	**Sodium** 0mg	0%	Dietary Fiber 0g	0%
Saturated Fat 2g	10%	**Protein** 0g		Sugars 0g	
Polyunsaturated Fat 1.5g					
Monounsaturated Fat 10g		Vitamin A 0% Vitamin C 0%		Calcium 0% Iron 0%	

Mezzetta, Extra Virgin Olive Oil

1 tbsp

Amount per serving	%DV	Amount per serving	%DV	Amount per serving	%DV
Calories 120		**Cholesterol** 0mg	0%	**Total Carbohydrate** 0g	0%
Total Fat 14g	22%	**Sodium** 0mg	0%	Dietary Fiber 0g	0%
Saturated Fat 2g	10%	**Protein** 0g		Sugars 0g	
Polyunsaturated Fat 0g					
Monounsaturated Fat 0g		Vitamin A 0% Vitamin C 0%		Calcium 0% Iron 0%	

Smart Balance, Cooking Oil

1 tbsp

Amount per serving	%DV	Amount per serving	%DV	Amount per serving	%DV
Calories 120		**Cholesterol** 0mg	0%	**Total Carbohydrate** 0g	0%
Total Fat 14g	22%	**Sodium** 0mg	0%	Dietary Fiber 0g	0%
Saturated Fat 1.5g	8%	**Protein** 0g		Sugars 0g	
Polyunsaturated Fat 6g					
Monounsaturated Fat 5g		Vitamin A 0% Vitamin C 0%		Calcium 0% Iron 0%	

Smart Balance, Omega Non-Stick Cooking Spray

1 second spray

Amount per serving	%DV	Amount per serving	%DV	Amount per serving	%DV
Calories 0		**Cholesterol** 0mg	0%	**Total Carbohydrate** 0g	0%
Total Fat 0g	0%	**Sodium** 0mg	0%	Dietary Fiber 0g	0%
Saturated Fat 0g	0%	**Protein** 0g		Sugars 0g	
Polyunsaturated Fat 0g					
Monounsaturated Fat 0g		Vitamin A 0% Vitamin C 0%		Calcium 0% Iron 0%	

Soybean Oil

1 tbsp / 14g

Amount per serving	%DV	Amount per serving	%DV	Amount per serving	%DV
Calories 119		**Cholesterol** 0mg	0%	**Total Carbohydrate** 0g	0%
Total Fat 14g	2%	**Sodium** 0mg	0%	Dietary Fiber 0g	2%
Saturated Fat 2g	0%	**Protein** 0g		Sugars 0g	
Polyunsaturated Fat NA					
Monounsaturated Fat NA		Vitamin A 0% Vitamin C 0%		Calcium 0% Iron 0%	

Margarine/Butter

Benecol, Light Spread

1 tbsp / 14g

Amount per serving	%DV	Amount per serving	%DV	Amount per serving	%DV
Calories 50		**Cholesterol** 0mg	0%	**Total Carbohydrate** 0g	0%
Total Fat 0g	0%	**Sodium** 110mg	5%	Dietary Fiber 0g	0%
Saturated Fat 0.5g	3%	**Protein** 0g		Sugars 0g	
Polyunsaturated Fat 2g					
Monounsaturated Fat 2.5g		Vitamin A 10% Vitamin C 0%		Calcium 0% Iron 0%	

Earth Balance, Olive Oil Spread

1 tbsp

Amount per serving	%DV	Amount per serving	%DV	Amount per serving	%DV
Calories 80		**Cholesterol** 0mg	0%	**Total Carbohydrate** 0g	0%
Total Fat 9g	14%	**Sodium** 75mg	3%	Dietary Fiber 0g	0%
Saturated Fat 2.5g	13%	**Protein** 0g		Sugars 0g	
Polyunsaturated Fat 2.5g					
Monounsaturated Fat 4g		Vitamin A 0% Vitamin C 0%		Calcium 0% Iron 0%	

Earth Balance, Original Buttery Spread

1 tbsp (14g)

Amount per serving	%DV	Amount per serving	%DV	Amount per serving	%DV
Calories 100		**Cholesterol** 0mg	0%	**Total Carbohydrate** 0g	0%
Total Fat 11g	17%	**Sodium** 100mg	4%	Dietary Fiber 0g	0%
Saturated Fat 3g	15%	**Protein** 0g		Sugars 0g	
Polyunsaturated Fat 3g					
Monounsaturated Fat 5g		Vitamin A 0% Vitamin C 0%		Calcium 0% Iron 0%	

Earth Balance, Original Spread

1 tbsp

Amount per serving	%DV	Amount per serving	%DV	Amount per serving	%DV
Calories 100		**Cholesterol** 0mg	0%	**Total Carbohydrate** 0g	0%
Total Fat 11g	17%	**Sodium** 100mg	4%	Dietary Fiber 0g	0%
Saturated Fat 3g	15%	**Protein** 0g		Sugars 0g	
Polyunsaturated Fat 3g					
Monounsaturated Fat 5g		Vitamin A 0% Vitamin C 0%		Calcium 0% Iron 0%	

Earth Balance, Vegan Buttery Baking Sticks

1 tbsp

Amount per serving	%DV	Amount per serving	%DV	Amount per serving	%DV
Calories 100		**Cholesterol** 0mg	0%	**Total Carbohydrate** 0g	0%
Total Fat 11g	17%	**Sodium** 120mg	5%	Dietary Fiber 0g	0%
Saturated Fat 4g	20%	**Protein** 0g		Sugars 0g	
Polyunsaturated Fat 2.5g					
Monounsaturated Fat 4.5g		Vitamin A 0% Vitamin C 0%		Calcium 0% Iron 0%	

Earth Balance, Whipped Spread

1 tbsp

Amount per serving	%DV	Amount per serving	%DV	Amount per serving	%DV
Calories 80		**Cholesterol** 0mg	0%	**Total Carbohydrate** 0g	0%
Total Fat 9g	14%	**Sodium** 100mg	4%	Dietary Fiber 0g	0%
Saturated Fat 2.5g	13%	**Protein** 0g		Sugars 0g	
Polyunsaturated Fat 3g					
Monounsaturated Fat 2.5g		Vitamin A 0% Vitamin C 0%		Calcium 0% Iron 0%	

Fleischmann's, Light Whipped Tub

1 tbsp / 14g

Amount per serving	%DV	Amount per serving	%DV	Amount per serving	%DV
Calories 40		**Cholesterol** 0mg	0%	**Total Carbohydrate** 0g	0%
Total Fat 4.5g	7%	**Sodium** 65mg	3%	Dietary Fiber 0g	0%
Saturated Fat 0.5g	3%	**Protein** 0g		Sugars 0g	
Polyunsaturated Fat 2g					
Monounsaturated Fat 1g		Vitamin A 6% Vitamin C 0%		Calcium 0% Iron 0%	

Olivio, Light Premium Spread

1 tbsp / 14g

Amount per serving	%DV	Amount per serving	%DV	Amount per serving	%DV
Calories 50		**Cholesterol** 0mg	0%	**Total Carbohydrate** 0g	0%
Total Fat 5g	8%	**Sodium** 90mg	4%	Dietary Fiber 0g	0%
Saturated Fat 1g	5%	**Protein** 0g		Sugars 0g	
Polyunsaturated Fat 1g					
Monounsaturated Fat 3g		Vitamin A 10% Vitamin C 0%		Calcium 0% Iron 0%	

Promise, Activ Spread

1 tbsp / 14g

Amount per serving	%DV	Amount per serving	%DV	Amount per serving	%DV
Calories 45		**Cholesterol** 0mg	0%	**Total Carbohydrate** 0g	0%
Total Fat 5g	8%	**Sodium** 85mg	4%	Dietary Fiber 0g	0%
Saturated Fat 0.5g	2%	**Protein** 0g		Sugars 0g	
Polyunsaturated Fat 1.5g					
Monounsaturated Fat 2.5g		Vitamin A 10% Vitamin C 0%		Calcium 0% Iron 0%	

Promise, Light Spread

1 tbsp / 14g

Amount per serving	%DV	Amount per serving	%DV	Amount per serving	%DV
Calories 45		**Cholesterol** 0mg	0%	**Total Carbohydrate** 0g	0%
Total Fat 5g	8%	**Sodium** 85mg	4%	Dietary Fiber 0g	0%
Saturated Fat 1g	5%	**Protein** 0g		Sugars 0g	
Polyunsaturated Fat 2.5g					
Monounsaturated Fat 1.5g		Vitamin A 10% Vitamin C 0%		Calcium 0% Iron 0%	

Smart Balance, Butter & Canola and Extra Virgin Olive Oil Blend, Spreadable Butter

1 tbsp

Amount per serving	%DV	Amount per serving	%DV	Amount per serving	%DV
Calories 100		**Cholesterol** 15mg	5%	**Total Carbohydrate** 0g	0%
Total Fat 11g	17%	**Sodium** 85mg	4%	Dietary Fiber 0g	0%
Saturated Fat 4g	20%	**Protein** 0g		Sugars 0g	
Polyunsaturated Fat 1.5g					
Monounsaturated Fat 5g		Vitamin A 6% Vitamin C 0%		Calcium 0% Iron 0%	

Smart Balance, Butter & Canola Oil Blend, Spreadable Butter

1 tbsp

Amount per serving	%DV	Amount per serving	%DV	Amount per serving	%DV
Calories 100		**Cholesterol** 15mg	5%	**Total Carbohydrate** 0g	0%
Total Fat 11g	17%	**Sodium** 85mg	4%	Dietary Fiber 0g	0%
Saturated Fat 4g	20%	**Protein** 0g		Sugars 0g	
Polyunsaturated Fat 1.5g					
Monounsaturated Fat 4.5g		Vitamin A 6% Vitamin C 0%		Calcium 0% Iron 0%	

Smart Balance, Buttery Burst Spray

1/4 sec spray / 0.25g

Amount per serving	%DV	Amount per serving	%DV	Amount per serving	%DV
Calories 0		**Cholesterol** 0mg	0%	**Total Carbohydrate** 0g	0%
Total Fat 0g	0%	**Sodium** 0mg	0%	Dietary Fiber 0g	0%
Saturated Fat 0g	0%	**Protein** 0g		Sugars 0g	
Polyunsaturated Fat 0g					
Monounsaturated Fat 0g		Vitamin A 0% Vitamin C 0%		Calcium 0% Iron 0%	

Smart Balance, Buttery Spread with Calcium

1 tbsp

Amount per serving	%DV	Amount per serving	%DV	Amount per serving	%DV
Calories 80		**Cholesterol** 0mg	0%	**Total Carbohydrate** 0g	0%
Total Fat 9g	14%	**Sodium** 90mg	4%	Dietary Fiber 0g	0%
Saturated Fat 2.5g	13%	**Protein** 0g		Sugars 0g	
Polyunsaturated Fat 3g					
Monounsaturated Fat 3g		Vitamin A 10% Vitamin C 0%		Calcium 10% Iron 0%	

Smart Balance, Buttery Spread with Extra Virgin Olive Oil

1 tbsp

Amount per serving	%DV	Amount per serving	%DV	Amount per serving	%DV
Calories 60		**Cholesterol** 0mg	0%	**Total Carbohydrate** 0g	0%
Total Fat 7g	11%	**Sodium** 70mg	3%	Dietary Fiber 0g	0%
Saturated Fat 2g	10%	**Protein** 0g		Sugars 0g	
Polyunsaturated Fat 2.5g					
Monounsaturated Fat 2g		Vitamin A 10% Vitamin C 0%		Calcium 0% Iron 0%	

Smart Balance, HeartRight, Light Buttery Spread

1 tbsp

Amount per serving	%DV	Amount per serving	%DV	Amount per serving	%DV
Calories 50		**Cholesterol** 0mg	0%	**Total Carbohydrate** 0g	0%
Total Fat 5g	8%	**Sodium** 80mg	3%	Dietary Fiber 0g	0%
Saturated Fat 1g	5%	**Protein** 0g		Sugars 0g	
Polyunsaturated Fat 1g					
Monounsaturated Fat 2.5g		Vitamin A 10% Vitamin C 0%		Calcium 0% Iron 0%	

Smart Balance, Light Buttery Spread with Flax Oil

1 tbsp

Amount per serving	%DV	Amount per serving	%DV	Amount per serving	%DV
Calories 50		**Cholesterol** 0mg	0%	**Total Carbohydrate** 0g	0%
Total Fat 5g	8%	**Sodium** 90mg	4%	Dietary Fiber 0g	0%
Saturated Fat 1.5g	8%	**Protein** 0g		Sugars 0g	
Polyunsaturated Fat 2g					
Monounsaturated Fat 1.5g		Vitamin A 10% Vitamin C 0%		Calcium 0% Iron 0%	

Smart Balance, Light Original Buttery Spread

1 tbsp

Amount per serving	%DV	Amount per serving	%DV	Amount per serving	%DV
Calories 50		**Cholesterol** 0mg	0%	**Total Carbohydrate** 0g	0%
Total Fat 5g	8%	**Sodium** 85mg	4%	Dietary Fiber 0g	0%
Saturated Fat 1.5g	8%	**Protein** 0g		Sugars 0g	
Polyunsaturated Fat 2g					
Monounsaturated Fat 1.5g		Vitamin A 10% Vitamin C 0%		Calcium 0% Iron 0%	

Smart Balance, Omega-3 Buttery Spread

1 tbsp

Amount per serving	%DV	Amount per serving	%DV	Amount per serving	%DV
Calories 80		**Cholesterol** 0mg	0%	**Total Carbohydrate** 0g	0%
Total Fat 8g	12%	**Sodium** 85mg	4%	Dietary Fiber 0g	0%
Saturated Fat 2.5g	13%	**Protein** 0g		Sugars 0g	
Polyunsaturated Fat 3g					
Monounsaturated Fat 2.5g		Vitamin A 10% Vitamin C 0%		Calcium 0% Iron 0%	

Smart Balance, Omega-3 Light Buttery Spread

1 tbsp

Amount per serving	%DV	Amount per serving	%DV	Amount per serving	%DV
Calories 50		**Cholesterol** 0mg	0%	**Total Carbohydrate** 0g	0%
Total Fat 5g	8%	**Sodium** 80mg	3%	Dietary Fiber 0g	0%
Saturated Fat 1.5g	8%	**Protein** 0g		Sugars 0g	
Polyunsaturated Fat 2g					
Monounsaturated Fat 1.5g		Vitamin A 10% Vitamin C 0%		Calcium 0% Iron 0%	

Smart Balance, Organic Whipped Buttery Spread

1 tbsp

Amount per serving	%DV	Amount per serving	%DV	Amount per serving	%DV
Calories 80		**Cholesterol** 0mg	0%	**Total Carbohydrate** 0g	0%
Total Fat 9g	14%	**Sodium** 100mg	4%	Dietary Fiber 0g	0%
Saturated Fat 2.5g	13%	**Protein** 0g		Sugars 0g	
Polyunsaturated Fat 3g					
Monounsaturated Fat 2.5g		Vitamin A 0% Vitamin C 0%		Calcium 0% Iron 0%	

Smart Balance, Original Buttery Spread

1 tbsp

Amount per serving	%DV	Amount per serving	%DV	Amount per serving	%DV
Calories 80		**Cholesterol** 0mg	0%	**Total Carbohydrate** 0g	0%
Total Fat 9g	14%	**Sodium** 90mg	4%	Dietary Fiber 0g	0%
Saturated Fat 2.5g	13%	**Protein** 0g		Sugars 0g	
Polyunsaturated Fat 3.5g					
Monounsaturated Fat 3g		Vitamin A 10% Vitamin C 0%		Calcium 0% Iron 0%	

Smart Balance, Whipped Low Sodium Buttery Spread

1 tbsp

Amount per serving	%DV	Amount per serving	%DV	Amount per serving	%DV
Calories 60		**Cholesterol** 0mg	0%	**Total Carbohydrate** 0g	0%
Total Fat 7g	11%	**Sodium** 30mg	1%	Dietary Fiber 0g	0%
Saturated Fat 2g	10%	**Protein** 0g		Sugars 0g	
Polyunsaturated Fat 2g					
Monounsaturated Fat 2.5g		Vitamin A 10% Vitamin C 0%		Calcium 0% Iron 0%	

Nuts & Seeds

Almonds, Raw

1 oz / 23 whole kernels / 28 g

Amount per serving	%DV	Amount per serving	%DV	Amount per serving	%DV
Calories 162		**Cholesterol** 0mg	0%	**Total Carbohydrate** 6g	2%
Total Fat 14g	22%	**Sodium** 0mg	0%	Dietary Fiber 3g	12%
Saturated Fat 1g	5%	**Protein** 6g		Sugars 1g	
Polyunsaturated Fat 0g					
Monounsaturated Fat 0g		Vitamin A 0% Vitamin C 0%		Calcium 7% Iron 6%	

Cashew Nuts, Dry Roasted, without Salt Added

1 tbsp / 8g

Amount per serving	%DV	Amount per serving	%DV	Amount per serving	%DV
Calories 49		**Cholesterol** 0mg	0%	**Total Carbohydrate** 3g	1%
Total Fat 4g	6%	**Sodium** 1mg	0%	Dietary Fiber 0g	0%
Saturated Fat 1g	5%	**Protein** 1g		Sugars 0g	
Polyunsaturated Fat 0g					
Monounsaturated Fat 0g		Vitamin A 0% Vitamin C 0%		Calcium 0% Iron 3%	

prevent cancer

Chestnuts, European, Raw, Unpeeled

1 oz / 28g

Amount per serving	%DV	Amount per serving	%DV	Amount per serving	%DV
Calories 60		**Cholesterol** 0mg	0%	**Total Carbohydrate** 13g	4%
Total Fat 1g	2%	**Sodium** 1mg	0%	Dietary Fiber 2g	8%
Saturated Fat 0g	0%	**Protein** 1g		Sugars 0g	
Polyunsaturated Fat 0g					
Monounsaturated Fat 0g		Vitamin A 0% Vitamin C 20%		Calcium 1% Iron 2%	

Chestnuts, European, Roasted

1 oz / 3 kernels / 28g

Amount per serving	%DV	Amount per serving	%DV	Amount per serving	%DV
Calories 69		**Cholesterol** 0mg	0%	**Total Carbohydrate** 15g	5%
Total Fat 1g	2%	**Sodium** 1mg	0%	Dietary Fiber 1g	4%
Saturated Fat 0g	0%	**Protein** 1g		Sugars 3g	
Polyunsaturated Fat 0g					
Monounsaturated Fat 0g		Vitamin A 0% Vitamin C 12%		Calcium 1% Iron 1%	

Chestnuts, Japanese, Dried

1 oz / 28g

Amount per serving	%DV	Amount per serving	%DV	Amount per serving	%DV
Calories 101		**Cholesterol** 0mg	0%	**Total Carbohydrate** 23g	8%
Total Fat 0g	0%	**Sodium** 10mg	0%	Dietary Fiber 0g	0%
Saturated Fat 0g	0%	**Protein** 1g		Sugars 0g	
Polyunsaturated Fat 0g					
Monounsaturated Fat 0g		Vitamin A 0% Vitamin C 29%		Calcium 2% Iron 5%	

Ginkgo Nuts, Canned

1 oz / 28g

Amount per serving	%DV	Amount per serving	%DV	Amount per serving	%DV
Calories 31		**Cholesterol** 0mg	0%	**Total Carbohydrate** 6g	2%
Total Fat 0g	0%	**Sodium** 86mg	4%	Dietary Fiber 3g	12%
Saturated Fat 0g	0%	**Protein** 1g		Sugars 0g	
Polyunsaturated Fat 0g					
Monounsaturated Fat 0g		Vitamin A 2% Vitamin C 4%		Calcium 0% Iron 0%	

Ginkgo Nuts, Dried

1 oz / 28g

Amount per serving	%DV	Amount per serving	%DV	Amount per serving	%DV
Calories 97		**Cholesterol** 0mg	0%	**Total Carbohydrate** 20g	7%
Total Fat 1g	2%	**Sodium** 4mg	0%	Dietary Fiber 0g	0%
Saturated Fat 0g	0%	**Protein** 3g		Sugars 0g	
Polyunsaturated Fat 0g					
Monounsaturated Fat 0g		Vitamin A 6% Vitamin C 14%		Calcium 1% Iron 2%	

Ginkgo Nuts, Raw

1 oz / 28g

Amount per serving	%DV	Amount per serving	%DV	Amount per serving	%DV
Calories 51		**Cholesterol** 0mg	0%	**Total Carbohydrate** 11g	4%
Total Fat 0g	0%	**Sodium** 2mg	0%	Dietary Fiber 0g	0%
Saturated Fat 0g	0%	**Protein** 1g		Sugars 0g	
Polyunsaturated Fat 0g					
Monounsaturated Fat 0g		Vitamin A 3% Vitamin C 7%		Calcium 0% Iron 2%	

Hazelnuts, Raw, Plain

1 oz / 28g

Amount per serving	%DV	Amount per serving	%DV	Amount per serving	%DV
Calories 190		**Cholesterol** 0mg	0%	**Total Carbohydrate** 5g	2%
Total Fat 17g	26%	**Sodium** 0mg	0%	Dietary Fiber 3g	12%
Saturated Fat 1g	5%	**Protein** 4g		Sugars 1g	
Polyunsaturated Fat 0g					
Monounsaturated Fat 0g		Vitamin A 0% Vitamin C 4%		Calcium 4% Iron 8%	

Lotus Seeds, Dried

1 oz / 28g

Amount per serving	%DV	Amount per serving	%DV	Amount per serving	%DV
Calories 94		**Cholesterol** 0mg	0%	**Total Carbohydrate** 18g	6%
Total Fat 1g	2%	**Sodium** 1mg	0%	Dietary Fiber 0g	0%
Saturated Fat 0g	0%	**Protein** 4g		Sugars 0g	
Polyunsaturated Fat 0g					
Monounsaturated Fat 0g		Vitamin A 0% Vitamin C 0%		Calcium 5% Iron 5%	

Lotus Seeds, Raw

1 oz / 28g

Amount per serving	%DV	Amount per serving	%DV	Amount per serving	%DV
Calories 25		**Cholesterol** 0mg	0%	**Total Carbohydrate** 5g	2%
Total Fat 0g	0%	**Sodium** 0mg	0%	Dietary Fiber 0g	0%
Saturated Fat 0g	0%	**Protein** 1g		Sugars 0g	
Polyunsaturated Fat 0g					
Monounsaturated Fat 0g		Vitamin A 0% Vitamin C 0%		Calcium 1% Iron 1%	

Peanuts, All Types, Dry-Roasted, with Salt

1 peanut / 1g

Amount per serving	%DV	Amount per serving	%DV	Amount per serving	%DV
Calories 6		**Cholesterol** 0mg	0%	**Total Carbohydrate** 0g	0%
Total Fat 0g	0%	**Sodium** 8mg	0%	Dietary Fiber 0g	0%
Saturated Fat 0g	0%	**Protein** 0g		Sugars 0g	
Polyunsaturated Fat 0g					
Monounsaturated Fat 0g		Vitamin A 0% Vitamin C 0%		Calcium 0% Iron 0%	

Pecans, Raw

1 oz / 19 halves / 28 g

Amount per serving	%DV	Amount per serving	%DV	Amount per serving	%DV
Calories 195		**Cholesterol** 0mg	0%	**Total Carbohydrate** 4g	1%
Total Fat 20g	31%	**Sodium** 0mg	0%	Dietary Fiber 3g	12%
Saturated Fat 2g	10%	**Protein** 3g		Sugars 1g	
Polyunsaturated Fat 0g					
Monounsaturated Fat 0g		Vitamin A 0% Vitamin C 1%		Calcium 2% Iron 4%	

Pine Nuts, Pinyon, Dried

10 nuts / 1g

Amount per serving	%DV	Amount per serving	%DV	Amount per serving	%DV
Calories 6		**Cholesterol** 0mg	0%	**Total Carbohydrate** 0g	0%
Total Fat 1g	2%	**Sodium** 1mg	0%	Dietary Fiber 0g	0%
Saturated Fat 0g	0%	**Protein** 0g		Sugars 0g	
Polyunsaturated Fat 0g					
Monounsaturated Fat 0g		Vitamin A 0% Vitamin C 0%		Calcium 0% Iron 0%	

Pistachios, Raw

1 oz / 49 kernels / 28 g

Amount per serving	%DV	Amount per serving	%DV	Amount per serving	%DV
Calories 157		**Cholesterol** 0mg	0%	**Total Carbohydrate** 8g	3%
Total Fat 13g	20%	**Sodium** 0mg	0%	Dietary Fiber 3g	12%
Saturated Fat 2g	10%	**Protein** 6g		Sugars 2g	
Polyunsaturated Fat 0g					
Monounsaturated Fat 0g		Vitamin A 3% Vitamin C 2%		Calcium 3% Iron 7%	

Seeds, Lotus Seeds, Dried

1 oz / 28g

Amount per serving	%DV	Amount per serving	%DV	Amount per serving	%DV
Calories 93		**Cholesterol** 0mg	0%	**Total Carbohydrate** 18g	6%
Total Fat 1g	2%	**Sodium** 1mg	0%	Dietary Fiber 0g	0%
Saturated Fat 0g	0%	**Protein** 4g		Sugars 0g	
Polyunsaturated Fat 0g					
Monounsaturated Fat 0g		Vitamin A 0% Vitamin C 0%		Calcium 5% Iron 5%	

Seeds, Breadnut Tree Seeds, Dried

1 oz / 28g

Amount per serving	%DV	Amount per serving	%DV	Amount per serving	%DV
Calories 104		**Cholesterol** 0mg	0%	**Total Carbohydrate** 23g	8%
Total Fat 0.5g	1%	**Sodium** 15mg	1%	Dietary Fiber 4g	16%
Saturated Fat 0g	0%	**Protein** 2.4g		Sugars 0g	
Polyunsaturated Fat 0.5g					
Monounsaturated Fat 0g		Vitamin A 0% Vitamin C 22%		Calcium 3% Iron 7%	

Seeds, Pumpkin and Squash Seeds, Whole, Roasted, without Salt

1 oz / 28g

Amount per serving	%DV	Amount per serving	%DV	Amount per serving	%DV
Calories 125		**Cholesterol** 0mg	0%	**Total Carbohydrate** 15g	5%
Total Fat 5g	8%	**Sodium** 5mg	0%	Dietary Fiber 5g	20%
Saturated Fat 1g	5%	**Protein** 5g		Sugars 0g	
Polyunsaturated Fat 0g					
Monounsaturated Fat 0g		Vitamin A 0% Vitamin C 0%		Calcium 2% Iron 5%	

Seeds, Sisymbrium Seeds, Whole, Dried

1 oz / 28g

Amount per serving	%DV	Amount per serving	%DV	Amount per serving	%DV
Calories 89		**Cholesterol** 0mg	0%	**Total Carbohydrate** 16g	5%
Total Fat 1g	2%	**Sodium** 26mg	1%	Dietary Fiber 0g	0%
Saturated Fat 0g	0%	**Protein** 3g		Sugars 0g	
Polyunsaturated Fat 0g					
Monounsaturated Fat 0g		Vitamin A 0% Vitamin C 14%		Calcium 46% Iron 0%	

Sesame Seeds, Whole, Dried

1 oz / 28g

Amount per serving	%DV	Amount per serving	%DV	Amount per serving	%DV
Calories 160		**Cholesterol** 0mg	0%	**Total Carbohydrate** 7g	2%
Total Fat 4g	6%	**Sodium** 3mg	0%	Dietary Fiber 3g	12%
Saturated Fat 2g	10%	**Protein** 5g		Sugars 0g	
Polyunsaturated Fat 0g					
Monounsaturated Fat 0g		Vitamin A 0% Vitamin C 0%		Calcium 27% Iron 23%	

Walnuts, Black, Dried

1 tbsp / 7g

Amount per serving	%DV	Amount per serving	%DV	Amount per serving	%DV
Calories 48		**Cholesterol** 0mg	0%	**Total Carbohydrate** 1g	0%
Total Fat 5g	8%	**Sodium** 0mg	0%	Dietary Fiber 1g	4%
Saturated Fat 0g	0%	**Protein** 2g		Sugars 0g	
Polyunsaturated Fat 0g					
Monounsaturated Fat 0g		Vitamin A 0% Vitamin C 0%		Calcium 0% Iron 1%	

Salad Dressings

Annie's, Artichoke Parmesan Dressing

2 tbsp

Amount per serving	%DV	Amount per serving	%DV	Amount per serving	%DV
Calories 90		**Cholesterol** 5mg	2%	**Total Carbohydrate** 1g	0%
Total Fat 9g	14%	**Sodium** 290mg	12%	Dietary Fiber 0g	0%
Saturated Fat 1.5g	8%	**Protein** 1g		Sugars 0g	
Polyunsaturated Fat 0g					
Monounsaturated Fat 0g		Vitamin A 0% Vitamin C 2%		Calcium 0% Iron 0%	

Annie's, Balsamic Vinaigrette

2 tbsp

Amount per serving	%DV	Amount per serving	%DV	Amount per serving	%DV
Calories 100		**Cholesterol** 0mg	0%	**Total Carbohydrate** 2g	1%
Total Fat 10g	15%	**Sodium** 55mg	2%	Dietary Fiber 0g	0%
Saturated Fat 1g	5%	**Protein** 0g		Sugars 2g	
Polyunsaturated Fat 0g					
Monounsaturated Fat 0g		Vitamin A 0% Vitamin C 0%		Calcium 0% Iron 0%	

Annie's, Cowgirl Ranch Dressing

2 tbsp

Amount per serving	%DV	Amount per serving	%DV	Amount per serving	%DV
Calories 110		**Cholesterol** 10mg	3%	**Total Carbohydrate** 3g	1%
Total Fat 11g	17%	**Sodium** 250mg	10%	Dietary Fiber 0g	0%
Saturated Fat 1g	5%	**Protein** 1g		Sugars 2g	
Polyunsaturated Fat 0g					
Monounsaturated Fat 0g		Vitamin A 0% Vitamin C 0%		Calcium 2% Iron 0%	

Annie's, Fat Free Raspberry Balsamic Vinaigrette

2 tbsp

Amount per serving	%DV	Amount per serving	%DV	Amount per serving	%DV
Calories 30		**Cholesterol** 0mg	0%	**Total Carbohydrate** 7g	2%
Total Fat 0g	0%	**Sodium** 10mg	0%	Dietary Fiber 0g	0%
Saturated Fat 0g	0%	**Protein** 0g		Sugars 7g	
Polyunsaturated Fat 0g					
Monounsaturated Fat 0g		Vitamin A 0% Vitamin C 0%		Calcium 0% Iron 2%	

Annie's, Lemon & Chive Dressing

2 tbsp

Amount per serving	%DV	Amount per serving	%DV	Amount per serving	%DV
Calories 110		**Cholesterol** 0mg	0%	**Total Carbohydrate** 1g	0%
Total Fat 12g	18%	**Sodium** 170mg	7%	Dietary Fiber 0g	0%
Saturated Fat 1g	5%	**Protein** 0g		Sugars 0g	
Polyunsaturated Fat 0g					
Monounsaturated Fat 0g		Vitamin A 0% Vitamin C 0%		Calcium 0% Iron 2%	

Annie's, Lite Goddess Dressing

2 tbsp

Amount per serving	%DV	Amount per serving	%DV	Amount per serving	%DV
Calories 60		**Cholesterol** 0mg	0%	**Total Carbohydrate** 2g	1%
Total Fat 6g	9%	**Sodium** 240mg	10%	Dietary Fiber 0g	0%
Saturated Fat 0.5g	3%	**Protein** 1g		Sugars 0g	
Polyunsaturated Fat 0g					
Monounsaturated Fat 0g		Vitamin A 0% Vitamin C 4%		Calcium 0% Iron 0%	

Annie's, Lite Herb Balsamic

2 tbsp

Amount per serving	%DV	Amount per serving	%DV	Amount per serving	%DV
Calories 50		**Cholesterol** 0mg	0%	**Total Carbohydrate** 2g	1%
Total Fat 5g	8%	**Sodium** 230mg	10%	Dietary Fiber 0g	0%
Saturated Fat 0g	0%	**Protein** 0g		Sugars 2g	
Polyunsaturated Fat 0g					
Monounsaturated Fat 0g		Vitamin A 0% Vitamin C 0%		Calcium 0% Iron 0%	

Annie's, Lite Honey Mustard Vinaigrette

2 tbsp

Amount per serving	%DV	Amount per serving	%DV	Amount per serving	%DV
Calories 40		**Cholesterol** 0mg	0%	**Total Carbohydrate** 4g	1%
Total Fat 3g	5%	**Sodium** 125mg	5%	Dietary Fiber 0g	0%
Saturated Fat 0g	0%	**Protein** 0g		Sugars 3g	
Polyunsaturated Fat 0g					
Monounsaturated Fat 0g		Vitamin A 0% Vitamin C 0%		Calcium 0% Iron 0%	

Annie's, Lite Poppy Seed Dressing

2 tbsp

Amount per serving	%DV	Amount per serving	%DV	Amount per serving	%DV
Calories 70		**Cholesterol** 5mg	2%	**Total Carbohydrate** 10g	3%
Total Fat 4g	6%	**Sodium** 210mg	9%	Dietary Fiber 0g	0%
Saturated Fat 1g	5%	**Protein** 0g		Sugars 9g	
Polyunsaturated Fat 0g					
Monounsaturated Fat 0g		Vitamin A 0% Vitamin C 0%		Calcium 0% Iron 0%	

Annie's, Lite Raspberry Vinaigrette

2 tbsp

Amount per serving	%DV	Amount per serving	%DV	Amount per serving	%DV
Calories 40		**Cholesterol** 0mg	0%	**Total Carbohydrate** 4g	1%
Total Fat 3g	5%	**Sodium** 55mg	2%	Dietary Fiber 0g	0%
Saturated Fat 0g	0%	**Protein** 0g		Sugars 4g	
Polyunsaturated Fat 0g					
Monounsaturated Fat 0g		Vitamin A 0% Vitamin C 0%		Calcium 0% Iron 0%	

Annie's, Naturals Fat Free Mango Vinaigrette

2 tbsp

Amount per serving	%DV	Amount per serving	%DV	Amount per serving	%DV
Calories 20		**Cholesterol** 0mg	0%	**Total Carbohydrate** 5g	2%
Total Fat 0g	0%	**Sodium** 5mg	0%	Dietary Fiber 0g	0%
Saturated Fat 0g	0%	**Protein** 0g		Sugars 5g	
Polyunsaturated Fat 0g					
Monounsaturated Fat 0g		Vitamin A 6%	Vitamin C 4%	Calcium 0%	Iron 0%

Annie's, Organic Balsamic Vinaigrette

2 tbsp

Amount per serving	%DV	Amount per serving	%DV	Amount per serving	%DV
Calories 100		**Cholesterol** 0mg	0%	**Total Carbohydrate** 1g	0%
Total Fat 10g	15%	**Sodium** 55mg	2%	Dietary Fiber 0g	0%
Saturated Fat 1g	5%	**Protein** 0g		Sugars 1g	
Polyunsaturated Fat 0g					
Monounsaturated Fat 0g		Vitamin A 0%	Vitamin C 0%	Calcium 0%	Iron 0%

Annie's, Organic Buttermilk Dressing

2 tbsp

Amount per serving	%DV	Amount per serving	%DV	Amount per serving	%DV
Calories 70		**Cholesterol** 250mg	83%	**Total Carbohydrate** 1g	0%
Total Fat 6g	9%	**Sodium** 250mg	10%	Dietary Fiber 0g	0%
Saturated Fat 1g	5%	**Protein** 1g		Sugars 1g	
Polyunsaturated Fat 0g					
Monounsaturated Fat 0g		Vitamin A 0%	Vitamin C 0%	Calcium 2%	Iron 0%

Annie's, Organic Caesar Dressing

2 tbsp

Amount per serving	%DV	Amount per serving	%DV	Amount per serving	%DV
Calories 110		**Cholesterol** 10mg	3%	**Total Carbohydrate** 3g	1%
Total Fat 11g	17%	**Sodium** 240mg	10%	Dietary Fiber 0g	0%
Saturated Fat 1g	5%	**Protein** 1g		Sugars 2g	
Polyunsaturated Fat 0g					
Monounsaturated Fat 0g		Vitamin A 0%	Vitamin C 0%	Calcium 2%	Iron 0%

Annie's, Organic Cowgirl Ranch Dressing

2 tbsp

Amount per serving	%DV	Amount per serving	%DV	Amount per serving	%DV
Calories 110		**Cholesterol** 10mg	3%	**Total Carbohydrate** 3g	1%
Total Fat 11g	17%	**Sodium** 240mg	10%	Dietary Fiber 0g	0%
Saturated Fat 1g	5%	**Protein** 1g		Sugars 2g	
Polyunsaturated Fat 0g					
Monounsaturated Fat 0g		Vitamin A 0%	Vitamin C 0%	Calcium 0%	Iron 0%

Annie's, Organic Creamy Asiago Cheese Dressing

2 tbsp

Amount per serving	%DV	Amount per serving	%DV	Amount per serving	%DV
Calories 80		**Cholesterol** 5mg	2%	**Total Carbohydrate** 1g	0%
Total Fat 8g	12%	**Sodium** 320mg	13%	Dietary Fiber 0g	0%
Saturated Fat 1g	5%	**Protein** 1g		Sugars 0g	
Polyunsaturated Fat 0g					
Monounsaturated Fat 0g		Vitamin A 0% Vitamin C 0%		Calcium 0% Iron 0%	

Annie's, Organic French Dressing

2 tbsp

Amount per serving	%DV	Amount per serving	%DV	Amount per serving	%DV
Calories 110		**Cholesterol** 0mg	0%	**Total Carbohydrate** 3g	1%
Total Fat 11g	17%	**Sodium** 200mg	8%	Dietary Fiber 0g	0%
Saturated Fat 1g	5%	**Protein** 0g		Sugars 3g	
Polyunsaturated Fat 0g					
Monounsaturated Fat 0g		Vitamin A 0% Vitamin C 0%		Calcium 0% Iron 0%	

Annie's, Organic Green Garlic Dressing

2 tbsp

Amount per serving	%DV	Amount per serving	%DV	Amount per serving	%DV
Calories 80		**Cholesterol** 0mg	0%	**Total Carbohydrate** 2g	1%
Total Fat 8g	12%	**Sodium** 170mg	7%	Dietary Fiber 0g	0%
Saturated Fat 0.5g	3%	**Protein** 0g		Sugars 1g	
Polyunsaturated Fat 0g					
Monounsaturated Fat 0g		Vitamin A 0% Vitamin C 6%		Calcium 0% Iron 0%	

Annie's, Organic Green Goddess Dressing

2 tbsp

Amount per serving	%DV	Amount per serving	%DV	Amount per serving	%DV
Calories 110		**Cholesterol** 5mg	2%	**Total Carbohydrate** 1g	0%
Total Fat 11g	17%	**Sodium** 260mg	11%	Dietary Fiber 0g	0%
Saturated Fat 1.5g	8%	**Protein** 0g		Sugars 1g	
Polyunsaturated Fat 0g					
Monounsaturated Fat 0g		Vitamin A 0% Vitamin C 0%		Calcium 0% Iron 0%	

Annie's, Organic Oil & Vinegar

2 tbsp

Amount per serving	%DV	Amount per serving	%DV	Amount per serving	%DV
Calories 120		**Cholesterol** 0mg	0%	**Total Carbohydrate** 1g	0%
Total Fat 13g	20%	**Sodium** 220mg	9%	Dietary Fiber 0g	0%
Saturated Fat 1g	5%	**Protein** 0g		Sugars 0g	
Polyunsaturated Fat 0g					
Monounsaturated Fat 0g		Vitamin A 0% Vitamin C 0%		Calcium 0% Iron 0%	

Annie's, Organic Papaya Poppy Seed Dressing

2 tbsp

Amount per serving	%DV	Amount per serving	%DV	Amount per serving	%DV
Calories 90		**Cholesterol** 0mg	0%	**Total Carbohydrate** 5g	2%
Total Fat 8g	12%	**Sodium** 180mg	8%	Dietary Fiber 0g	0%
Saturated Fat 1g	5%	**Protein** 0g		Sugars 4g	
Polyunsaturated Fat 0g					
Monounsaturated Fat 0g		Vitamin A 0% Vitamin C 0%		Calcium 0% Iron 0%	

Annie's, Organic Pomegranate Vinaigrette Dressing

2 tbsp

Amount per serving	%DV	Amount per serving	%DV	Amount per serving	%DV
Calories 70		**Cholesterol** 0mg	0%	**Total Carbohydrate** 2g	1%
Total Fat 7g	11%	**Sodium** 220mg	9%	Dietary Fiber 0g	0%
Saturated Fat 0.5g	3%	**Protein** 0g		Sugars 1g	
Polyunsaturated Fat 0g					
Monounsaturated Fat 0g		Vitamin A 0% Vitamin C 0%		Calcium 0% Iron 0%	

Annie's, Organic Red Wine & Olive Oil Vinaigrette

2 tbsp

Amount per serving	%DV	Amount per serving	%DV	Amount per serving	%DV
Calories 130		**Cholesterol** 0mg	0%	**Total Carbohydrate** 0g	0%
Total Fat 14g	22%	**Sodium** 190mg	8%	Dietary Fiber 0g	0%
Saturated Fat 2g	10%	**Protein** 0g		Sugars 0g	
Polyunsaturated Fat 0g					
Monounsaturated Fat 0g		Vitamin A 0% Vitamin C 0%		Calcium 0% Iron 0%	

Annie's, Organic Roasted Garlic Vinaigrette

2 tbsp

Amount per serving	%DV	Amount per serving	%DV	Amount per serving	%DV
Calories 110		**Cholesterol** 0mg	0%	**Total Carbohydrate** 3g	1%
Total Fat 11g	17%	**Sodium** 220mg	9%	Dietary Fiber 0g	0%
Saturated Fat 1g	5%	**Protein** 0g		Sugars 2g	
Polyunsaturated Fat 0g					
Monounsaturated Fat 0g		Vitamin A 0% Vitamin C 0%		Calcium 0% Iron 0%	

Annie's, Organic Sesame Ginger Vinaigrette

2 tbsp

Amount per serving	%DV	Amount per serving	%DV	Amount per serving	%DV
Calories 90		**Cholesterol** 0mg	0%	**Total Carbohydrate** 4g	1%
Total Fat 8g	12%	**Sodium** 250mg	10%	Dietary Fiber 0g	0%
Saturated Fat 1g	5%	**Protein** 1g		Sugars 3g	
Polyunsaturated Fat 0g					
Monounsaturated Fat 0g		Vitamin A 0% Vitamin C 0%		Calcium 0% Iron 0%	

Annie's, Organic Thousand Island Dressing

2 tbsp

Amount per serving	%DV	Amount per serving	%DV	Amount per serving	%DV
Calories 90		**Cholesterol** 0mg	0%	**Total Carbohydrate** 5g	2%
Total Fat 8g	12%	**Sodium** 360mg	15%	Dietary Fiber 0g	0%
Saturated Fat 1g	5%	**Protein** 0g		Sugars 5g	
Polyunsaturated Fat 0g					
Monounsaturated Fat 0g		Vitamin A 0% Vitamin C 0%		Calcium 0% Iron 2%	

Annie's, Roasted Red Pepper Vinaigrette

2 tbsp

Amount per serving	%DV	Amount per serving	%DV	Amount per serving	%DV
Calories 60		**Cholesterol** 0mg	0%	**Total Carbohydrate** 3g	1%
Total Fat 6g	9%	**Sodium** 240mg	10%	Dietary Fiber 0g	0%
Saturated Fat 0g	0%	**Protein** 0g		Sugars 2g	
Polyunsaturated Fat 0g					
Monounsaturated Fat 0g		Vitamin A 2% Vitamin C 15%		Calcium 0% Iron 0%	

Annie's, Tuscany Italian Dressing

2 tbsp

Amount per serving	%DV	Amount per serving	%DV	Amount per serving	%DV
Calories 100		**Cholesterol** 0mg	0%	**Total Carbohydrate** 3g	1%
Total Fat 9g	14%	**Sodium** 250mg	10%	Dietary Fiber 0g	0%
Saturated Fat 0.5g	3%	**Protein** 0g		Sugars 2g	
Polyunsaturated Fat 0g					
Monounsaturated Fat 0g		Vitamin A 0% Vitamin C 0%		Calcium 0% Iron 0%	

Boar's Head, Deli Dressing

1 tbsp

Amount per serving	%DV	Amount per serving	%DV	Amount per serving	%DV
Calories 100		**Cholesterol** 50mg	17%	**Total Carbohydrate** 0g	0%
Total Fat 11g	17%	**Sodium** 50mg	2%	Dietary Fiber 0g	0%
Saturated Fat 1g	5%	**Protein** 0g		Sugars 0g	
Polyunsaturated Fat 0g					
Monounsaturated Fat 0g		Vitamin A 0% Vitamin C 0%		Calcium 0% Iron 0%	

Cardini's, Light Balsamic Vinaigrette Dressing

2 tbsp / 32g

Amount per serving	%DV	Amount per serving	%DV	Amount per serving	%DV
Calories 50		**Cholesterol** 0mg	0%	**Total Carbohydrate** 5g	2%
Total Fat 1g	2%	**Sodium** 210mg	9%	Dietary Fiber 0g	0%
Saturated Fat 0g	0%	**Protein** 0g		Sugars 5g	
Polyunsaturated Fat 0g					
Monounsaturated Fat 0g		Vitamin A 0% Vitamin C 0%		Calcium 0% Iron 0%	

Cardini's, Light Greek Vinaigrette Dressing

2 tbsp / 30g

Amount per serving	%DV	Amount per serving	%DV	Amount per serving	%DV
Calories 50		**Cholesterol** 0mg	0%	**Total Carbohydrate** 2g	1%
Total Fat 5g	8%	**Sodium** 270mg	11%	Dietary Fiber 0g	0%
Saturated Fat 1g	5%	**Protein** 0g		Sugars 2g	
Polyunsaturated Fat 0g					
Monounsaturated Fat 0g		Vitamin A 0% Vitamin C 0%		Calcium 0% Iron 0%	

Earth Balance, Olive Oil Dressing

1 tbsp

Amount per serving	%DV	Amount per serving	%DV	Amount per serving	%DV
Calories 90		**Cholesterol** 0mg	0%	**Total Carbohydrate** 0g	0%
Total Fat 9g	14%	**Sodium** 70mg	3%	Dietary Fiber 0g	0%
Saturated Fat 0.5g	3%	**Protein** 0g		Sugars 0g	
Polyunsaturated Fat 2.5g					
Monounsaturated Fat 6g		Vitamin A 0% Vitamin C 0%		Calcium 0% Iron 0%	

Earth Balance, Organic Dressing

1 tbsp

Amount per serving	%DV	Amount per serving	%DV	Amount per serving	%DV
Calories 90		**Cholesterol** 0mg	0%	**Total Carbohydrate** 0g	0%
Total Fat 9g	14%	**Sodium** 65mg	3%	Dietary Fiber 0g	0%
Saturated Fat 0.5g	2%	**Protein** 0g		Sugars 0g	
Polyunsaturated Fat 2.5g					
Monounsaturated Fat 6g		Vitamin A 0% Vitamin C 0%		Calcium 0% Iron 0%	

Earth Balance, Original Dressing

1 tbsp

Amount per serving	%DV	Amount per serving	%DV	Amount per serving	%DV
Calories 90		**Cholesterol** 0mg	0%	**Total Carbohydrate** 0g	0%
Total Fat 9g	14%	**Sodium** 70mg	3%	Dietary Fiber 0g	0%
Saturated Fat 0.5g	3%	**Protein** 0g		Sugars 0g	
Polyunsaturated Fat 2.5g					
Monounsaturated Fat 6g		Vitamin A 0% Vitamin C 0%		Calcium 0% Iron 0%	

Girard's, Light Caesar Dressing

2 tbsp / 31g

Amount per serving	%DV	Amount per serving	%DV	Amount per serving	%DV
Calories 80		**Cholesterol** 10mg	3%	**Total Carbohydrate** 5g	2%
Total Fat 7g	11%	**Sodium** 370mg	15%	Dietary Fiber 0g	0%
Saturated Fat 2g	10%	**Protein** 0g		Sugars 2g	
Polyunsaturated Fat 0g					
Monounsaturated Fat 0g		Vitamin A 0% Vitamin C 0%		Calcium 0% Iron 0%	

Girard's, Light Creamy Balsamic Vinaigrette

2 tbsp / 32g

Amount per serving	%DV	Amount per serving	%DV	Amount per serving	%DV
Calories 45		**Cholesterol** 0mg	0%	**Total Carbohydrate** 4g	1%
Total Fat 3g	5%	**Sodium** 250mg	10%	Dietary Fiber 0g	0%
Saturated Fat 0g	0%	**Protein** 0g		Sugars 3g	
Polyunsaturated Fat 0g					
Monounsaturated Fat 0g		Vitamin A 0% Vitamin C 0%		Calcium 0% Iron 0%	

Ken's, Fat Free Sun-Dried Tomato Vinaigrette

2 tbsp / 34g

Amount per serving	%DV	Amount per serving	%DV	Amount per serving	%DV
Calories 70		**Cholesterol** 0mg	0%	**Total Carbohydrate** 16g	5%
Total Fat 0g	0%	**Sodium** 260mg	11%	Dietary Fiber 0g	0%
Saturated Fat 0g	0%	**Protein** 0g		Sugars 12g	
Polyunsaturated Fat 0g					
Monounsaturated Fat 0g		Vitamin A 2% Vitamin C 2%		Calcium 0% Iron 0%	

Ken's, Light Options Balsamic Dressing

2 tbsp / 30g

Amount per serving	%DV	Amount per serving	%DV	Amount per serving	%DV
Calories 60		**Cholesterol** 0mg	0%	**Total Carbohydrate** 4g	1%
Total Fat 4.5g	7%	**Sodium** 210mg	9%	Dietary Fiber 0g	0%
Saturated Fat 0.5g	3%	**Protein** 0g		Sugars 4g	
Polyunsaturated Fat 3g					
Monounsaturated Fat 1.5g		Vitamin A 0% Vitamin C 4%		Calcium 0% Iron 0%	

Ken's, Light Options Honey Dijon

2 tbsp / 30g

Amount per serving	%DV	Amount per serving	%DV	Amount per serving	%DV
Calories 70		**Cholesterol** 10mg	3%	**Total Carbohydrate** 7g	2%
Total Fat 4g	6%	**Sodium** 230mg	10%	Dietary Fiber 0g	0%
Saturated Fat 0g	0%	**Protein** 0g		Sugars 7g	
Polyunsaturated Fat 1.5g					
Monounsaturated Fat 1.5g		Vitamin A 0% Vitamin C 2%		Calcium 0% Iron 0%	

Ken's, Light Options Honey French

2 tbsp / 30g

Amount per serving	%DV	Amount per serving	%DV	Amount per serving	%DV
Calories 70		**Cholesterol** 0mg	0%	**Total Carbohydrate** 8g	3%
Total Fat 4g	6%	**Sodium** 230mg	10%	Dietary Fiber 0g	0%
Saturated Fat 0.5g	3%	**Protein** 0g		Sugars 2g	
Polyunsaturated Fat 2g					
Monounsaturated Fat 1g		Vitamin A 2% Vitamin C 4%		Calcium 0% Iron 2%	

Ken's, Light Options Italian Dressing

2 tbsp / 30g

Amount per serving	%DV	Amount per serving	%DV	Amount per serving	%DV
Calories 45		**Cholesterol** 0mg	0%	**Total Carbohydrate** 2g	1%
Total Fat 1g	2%	**Sodium** 230mg	10%	Dietary Fiber 0g	0%
Saturated Fat 0g	0%	**Protein** 0g		Sugars 1g	
Polyunsaturated Fat 0g					
Monounsaturated Fat 1g		Vitamin A 2% Vitamin C 6%		Calcium 2% Iron 0%	

Ken's, Light Options Olive Oil & Vinegar Dressing

2 tbsp / 30g

Amount per serving	%DV	Amount per serving	%DV	Amount per serving	%DV
Calories 50		**Cholesterol** 0mg	0%	**Total Carbohydrate** 3g	1%
Total Fat 4g	6%	**Sodium** 240mg	10%	Dietary Fiber 0g	0%
Saturated Fat 0.5g	3%	**Protein** 0g		Sugars 3g	
Polyunsaturated Fat 1.5g					
Monounsaturated Fat 2g		Vitamin A 0% Vitamin C 4%		Calcium 0% Iron 0%	

Ken's, Light Options Ranch

2 tbsp / 30g

Amount per serving	%DV	Amount per serving	%DV	Amount per serving	%DV
Calories 80		**Cholesterol** 5mg	2%	**Total Carbohydrate** 3g	1%
Total Fat 2g	3%	**Sodium** 310mg	13%	Dietary Fiber 0g	0%
Saturated Fat 1g	5%	**Protein** 0g		Sugars 2g	
Polyunsaturated Fat 4g					
Monounsaturated Fat 2g		Vitamin A 0% Vitamin C 2%		Calcium 0% Iron 0%	

Ken's, Light Options Raspberry Walnut Dressing

2 tbsp / 30g

Amount per serving	%DV	Amount per serving	%DV	Amount per serving	%DV
Calories 60		**Cholesterol** 0mg	0%	**Total Carbohydrate** 6g	2%
Total Fat 3.5g	5%	**Sodium** 180mg	8%	Dietary Fiber 0g	0%
Saturated Fat 0.5g	3%	**Protein** 0g		Sugars 6g	
Polyunsaturated Fat 0g					
Monounsaturated Fat 1g		Vitamin A 0% Vitamin C 2%		Calcium 0% Iron 0%	

Ken's, Light Options Sweet Vidalia Onion Dressing

2 tbsp / 30g

Amount per serving	%DV	Amount per serving	%DV	Amount per serving	%DV
Calories 60		**Cholesterol** 0mg	0%	**Total Carbohydrate** 7g	2%
Total Fat 4g	6%	**Sodium** 210mg	9%	Dietary Fiber 0g	0%
Saturated Fat 0.5g	3%	**Protein** 0g		Sugars 210g	
Polyunsaturated Fat 2g					
Monounsaturated Fat 1g		Vitamin A 0% Vitamin C 2%		Calcium 2% Iron 0%	

Kraft, Fat Free Mayonnaise

1 tbsp / 16g

Amount per serving	%DV	Amount per serving	%DV	Amount per serving	%DV
Calories 11		**Cholesterol** 2mg	1%	**Total Carbohydrate** 2g	1%
Total Fat 1g	2%	**Sodium** 120mg	5%	Dietary Fiber 0g	0%
Saturated Fat 0g	0%	**Protein** 0g		Sugars 1g	
Polyunsaturated Fat 0g					
Monounsaturated Fat 0g		Vitamin A 0% Vitamin C 0%		Calcium 0% Iron 0%	

Kraft, Light Mayonnaise

1 tbsp / 15g

Amount per serving	%DV	Amount per serving	%DV	Amount per serving	%DV
Calories 50		**Cholesterol** 5mg	2%	**Total Carbohydrate** 1g	0%
Total Fat 5g	8%	**Sodium** 120mg	5%	Dietary Fiber 0g	0%
Saturated Fat 1g	5%	**Protein** 0g		Sugars 1g	
Polyunsaturated Fat 0g					
Monounsaturated Fat 0g		Vitamin A 1% Vitamin C 0%		Calcium 0% Iron 0%	

Kraft, Miracle Whip Free Non-Fat Dressing

1 tbsp / 16g

Amount per serving	%DV	Amount per serving	%DV	Amount per serving	%DV
Calories 13		**Cholesterol** 1mg	0%	**Total Carbohydrate** 2g	1%
Total Fat 0g	0%	**Sodium** 126mg	5%	Dietary Fiber 0g	0%
Saturated Fat 0g	0%	**Protein** 0g		Sugars 2g	
Polyunsaturated Fat 0g					
Monounsaturated Fat 1g		Vitamin A 0% Vitamin C 0%		Calcium 0% Iron 0%	

Kraft, Miracle Whip Light Dressing

1 tbsp / 16g

Amount per serving	%DV	Amount per serving	%DV	Amount per serving	%DV
Calories 37		**Cholesterol** 4mg	1%	**Total Carbohydrate** 2g	1%
Total Fat 3g	5%	**Sodium** 131mg	5%	Dietary Fiber 0g	0%
Saturated Fat 0g	0%	**Protein** 0g		Sugars 2g	
Polyunsaturated Fat 0g					
Monounsaturated Fat 0g		Vitamin A 0% Vitamin C 0%		Calcium 0% Iron 0%	

Litehouse, Lite 1000 Island Dressing

2 tbsp / 30ml

Amount per serving	%DV	Amount per serving	%DV	Amount per serving	%DV
Calories 70		**Cholesterol** 5mg	2%	**Total Carbohydrate** 4g	1%
Total Fat 7g	11%	**Sodium** 240mg	10%	Dietary Fiber 0g	0%
Saturated Fat 0g	0%	**Protein** 0g		Sugars 2g	
Polyunsaturated Fat 2g					
Monounsaturated Fat 4g		Vitamin A 2% Vitamin C 2%		Calcium 0% Iron 0%	

Litehouse, Lite Bleu Cheese Dressing

2 tbsp / 30ml

Amount per serving	%DV	Amount per serving	%DV	Amount per serving	%DV
Calories 80		**Cholesterol** 10mg	3%	**Total Carbohydrate** 3g	1%
Total Fat 8g	12%	**Sodium** 260mg	11%	Dietary Fiber 2g	8%
Saturated Fat 1g	5%	**Protein** 1g		Sugars 1g	
Polyunsaturated Fat 2.5g					
Monounsaturated Fat 4.5g		Vitamin A 0% Vitamin C 0%		Calcium 2% Iron 0%	

Litehouse, Lite Caesar

2 tbsp / 30ml

Amount per serving	%DV	Amount per serving	%DV	Amount per serving	%DV
Calories 70		**Cholesterol** 5mg	2%	**Total Carbohydrate** 2g	1%
Total Fat 7g	11%	**Sodium** 220mg	9%	Dietary Fiber 0g	0%
Saturated Fat 0.5g	3%	**Protein** 0g		Sugars 1g	
Polyunsaturated Fat 2g					
Monounsaturated Fat 4g		Vitamin A 0% Vitamin C 2%		Calcium 2% Iron 2%	

Litehouse, Lite Coleslaw

2 tbsp / 30ml

Amount per serving	%DV	Amount per serving	%DV	Amount per serving	%DV
Calories 70		**Cholesterol** 5mg	2%	**Total Carbohydrate** 9g	3%
Total Fat 3g	5%	**Sodium** 240mg	10%	Dietary Fiber 0g	0%
Saturated Fat 0g	0%	**Protein** 0g		Sugars 8g	
Polyunsaturated Fat 1g					
Monounsaturated Fat 2g		Vitamin A 0% Vitamin C 0%		Calcium 0% Iron 0%	

Litehouse, Lite Jalapeno Ranch

2 tbsp / 30ml

Amount per serving	%DV	Amount per serving	%DV	Amount per serving	%DV
Calories 70		**Cholesterol** 15mg	5%	**Total Carbohydrate** 3g	1%
Total Fat 6g	9%	**Sodium** 270mg	11%	Dietary Fiber 0g	0%
Saturated Fat 1g	5%	**Protein** 1g		Sugars 2g	
Polyunsaturated Fat 1.5g					
Monounsaturated Fat 3.5g		Vitamin A 2% Vitamin C 2%		Calcium 2% Iron 2%	

Lucini, Bold Parmesan & Garlic Vinaigrette

2 tbsp

Amount per serving	%DV	Amount per serving	%DV	Amount per serving	%DV
Calories 130		**Cholesterol** 5mg	2%	**Total Carbohydrate** 2g	1%
Total Fat 13g	20%	**Sodium** 240mg	10%	Dietary Fiber 0g	0%
Saturated Fat 1.5g	8%	**Protein** 0g		Sugars 1g	
Polyunsaturated Fat 0g					
Monounsaturated Fat 0g		Vitamin A 0% Vitamin C 0%		Calcium 2% Iron 0%	

Lucini, Charma Vi Balsamico Artisan Vinegar

1 tbsp / 15ml

Amount per serving	%DV	Amount per serving	%DV	Amount per serving	%DV
Calories 30		**Cholesterol** 0mg	0%	**Total Carbohydrate** 7g	2%
Total Fat 0g	0%	**Sodium** 3mg	0%	Dietary Fiber 0g	0%
Saturated Fat 0g	0%	**Protein** 0g		Sugars 7g	
Polyunsaturated Fat 0g					
Monounsaturated Fat 0g		Vitamin A 0% Vitamin C 0%		Calcium 0% Iron 0%	

Lucini, Cherry Balsamic & Rosemary Vinaigrette

2 tbsp

Amount per serving	%DV	Amount per serving	%DV	Amount per serving	%DV
Calories 120		**Cholesterol** 0mg	0%	**Total Carbohydrate** 3g	1%
Total Fat 12g	18%	**Sodium** 105mg	4%	Dietary Fiber 0g	0%
Saturated Fat 1g	5%	**Protein** 1g		Sugars 3g	
Polyunsaturated Fat 0g					
Monounsaturated Fat 0g		Vitamin A 0% Vitamin C 0%		Calcium 0% Iron 0%	

Lucini, Dark Cherry Balsamico Artisan Vinegar

1 tbsp / 15ml

Amount per serving	%DV	Amount per serving	%DV	Amount per serving	%DV
Calories 30		**Cholesterol** 0mg	0%	**Total Carbohydrate** 7g	2%
Total Fat 0g	0%	**Sodium** 3mg	0%	Dietary Fiber 0g	0%
Saturated Fat 0g	0%	**Protein** 0g		Sugars 7g	
Polyunsaturated Fat 0g					
Monounsaturated Fat 0g		Vitamin A 0% Vitamin C 0%		Calcium 0% Iron 0%	

Lucini, Delicate Cucumber & Shallot Vinaigrette

2 tbsp

Amount per serving	%DV	Amount per serving	%DV	Amount per serving	%DV
Calories 120		**Cholesterol** 0mg	0%	**Total Carbohydrate** 2g	1%
Total Fat 12g	18%	**Sodium** 170mg	7%	Dietary Fiber 0g	0%
Saturated Fat 1g	5%	**Protein** 0g		Sugars 1g	
Polyunsaturated Fat 0g					
Monounsaturated Fat 0g		Vitamin A 0% Vitamin C 0%		Calcium 0% Iron 2%	

Lucini, Fig & Walnut Savory Balsamic Vinaigrette

2 tbsp

Amount per serving	%DV	Amount per serving	%DV	Amount per serving	%DV
Calories 110		**Cholesterol** 0mg	0%	**Total Carbohydrate** 4g	1%
Total Fat 10g	15%	**Sodium** 180mg	8%	Dietary Fiber 0g	0%
Saturated Fat 1g	5%	**Protein** 0g		Sugars 3g	
Polyunsaturated Fat 0g					
Monounsaturated Fat 0g		Vitamin A 0% Vitamin C 0%		Calcium 0% Iron 4%	

Lucini, Roasted Hazelnut & Extra Virgin Vinaigrette

2 tbsp

Amount per serving	%DV	Amount per serving	%DV	Amount per serving	%DV
Calories 120		**Cholesterol** 0mg	0%	**Total Carbohydrate** 3g	1%
Total Fat 11g	17%	**Sodium** 190mg	8%	Dietary Fiber 0g	0%
Saturated Fat 1g	5%	**Protein** 1g		Sugars 2g	
Polyunsaturated Fat 0g					
Monounsaturated Fat 0g		Vitamin A 0% Vitamin C 0%		Calcium 0% Iron 2%	

Lucini, Tuscan Balsamic & Extra Virgin Vinaigrette

2 tbsp

Amount per serving	%DV	Amount per serving	%DV	Amount per serving	%DV
Calories 120		**Cholesterol** 0mg	0%	**Total Carbohydrate** 3g	1%
Total Fat 12g	18%	**Sodium** 180mg	8%	Dietary Fiber 0g	0%
Saturated Fat 1.5g	8%	**Protein** 0g		Sugars 3g	
Polyunsaturated Fat 0g					
Monounsaturated Fat 0g		Vitamin A 0% Vitamin C 0%		Calcium 0% Iron 0%	

Maple Grove Farms, All Natural Dressing, Aged Parmesan Peppercorn

2 tbsp

Amount per serving	%DV	Amount per serving	%DV	Amount per serving	%DV
Calories 110		**Cholesterol** 0mg	0%	**Total Carbohydrate** 3g	1%
Total Fat 11g	17%	**Sodium** 390mg	16%	Dietary Fiber 0g	0%
Saturated Fat 1g	5%	**Protein** 0g		Sugars 3g	
Polyunsaturated Fat 0g					
Monounsaturated Fat 0g		Vitamin A 0% Vitamin C 0%		Calcium 0% Iron 0%	

Maple Grove Farms, All Natural Dressing, Champagne Vinaigrette

2 tbsp

Amount per serving	%DV	Amount per serving	%DV	Amount per serving	%DV
Calories 100		**Cholesterol** 0mg	0%	**Total Carbohydrate** 2g	1%
Total Fat 11g	17%	**Sodium** 130mg	5%	Dietary Fiber 0g	0%
Saturated Fat 1g	5%	**Protein** 0g		Sugars 1g	
Polyunsaturated Fat 0g					
Monounsaturated Fat 0g		Vitamin A 0% Vitamin C 0%		Calcium 0% Iron 0%	

Maple Grove Farms, All Natural Dressing, Creamy Balsamic

2 tbsp

Amount per serving	%DV	Amount per serving	%DV	Amount per serving	%DV
Calories 120		**Cholesterol** 0mg	0%	**Total Carbohydrate** 5g	2%
Total Fat 12g	18%	**Sodium** 230mg	10%	Dietary Fiber 0g	0%
Saturated Fat 1g	5%	**Protein** 0g		Sugars 4g	
Polyunsaturated Fat 0g					
Monounsaturated Fat 0g		Vitamin A 0% Vitamin C 2%		Calcium 0% Iron 0%	

Maple Grove Farms, Original Dressing, Honey Mustard

2 tbsp

Amount per serving	%DV	Amount per serving	%DV	Amount per serving	%DV
Calories 100		**Cholesterol** 0mg	0%	**Total Carbohydrate** 8g	3%
Total Fat 8g	12%	**Sodium** 260mg	11%	Dietary Fiber 0g	0%
Saturated Fat 0.5g	3%	**Protein** 1g		Sugars 7g	
Polyunsaturated Fat 0g					
Monounsaturated Fat 0g		Vitamin A 0% Vitamin C 0%		Calcium 2% Iron 0%	

Maple Grove Farms, Sugar Free Dressing, Italian White Balsamic

2 tbsp

Amount per serving	%DV	Amount per serving	%DV	Amount per serving	%DV
Calories 100		**Cholesterol** 0mg	0%	**Total Carbohydrate** 1g	0%
Total Fat 11g	17%	**Sodium** 70mg	3%	Dietary Fiber 0g	0%
Saturated Fat 1g	5%	**Protein** 0g		Sugars 0g	
Polyunsaturated Fat 0g					
Monounsaturated Fat 0g		Vitamin A 0% Vitamin C 0%		Calcium 0% Iron 0%	

Marie's, Balsamic Vinaigrette Dressing

2 tbsp / 30g

Amount per serving	%DV	Amount per serving	%DV	Amount per serving	%DV
Calories 50		**Cholesterol** 0mg	0%	**Total Carbohydrate** 3g	1%
Total Fat 4.5g	7%	**Sodium** 210mg	9%	Dietary Fiber 0g	0%
Saturated Fat 0.5g	3%	**Protein** 0g		Sugars 2g	
Polyunsaturated Fat 0g					
Monounsaturated Fat 0g		Vitamin A 0% Vitamin C 0%		Calcium 0% Iron 0%	

Marie's, Lite Creamy Ranch Dressing

2 tbsp / 30g

Amount per serving	%DV	Amount per serving	%DV	Amount per serving	%DV
Calories 60		**Cholesterol** 5mg	2%	**Total Carbohydrate** 2g	1%
Total Fat 6g	9%	**Sodium** 200mg	8%	Dietary Fiber 0g	0%
Saturated Fat 1g	5%	**Protein** 1g		Sugars 1g	
Polyunsaturated Fat 0g					
Monounsaturated Fat 0g		Vitamin A 0% Vitamin C 0%		Calcium 2% Iron 0%	

Marie's, Red Wine Vinaigrette Dressing

2 tbsp / 30g

Amount per serving	%DV	Amount per serving	%DV	Amount per serving	%DV
Calories 60		**Cholesterol** 0mg	0%	**Total Carbohydrate** 6g	2%
Total Fat 4g	6%	**Sodium** 200mg	8%	Dietary Fiber 0g	0%
Saturated Fat 0.5g	3%	**Protein** 0g		Sugars 5g	
Polyunsaturated Fat 0g					
Monounsaturated Fat 0g		Vitamin A 0% Vitamin C 0%		Calcium 0% Iron 0%	

Marie's, Yogurt Parmesan Caesar Dressing

2 tbsp / 28g

Amount per serving	%DV	Amount per serving	%DV	Amount per serving	%DV
Calories 50		**Cholesterol** 10mg	3%	**Total Carbohydrate** 2g	1%
Total Fat 5g	8%	**Sodium** 200mg	8%	Dietary Fiber 0g	0%
Saturated Fat 1g	5%	**Protein** 1g		Sugars 1g	
Polyunsaturated Fat 0g					
Monounsaturated Fat 0g		Vitamin A 0% Vitamin C 0%		Calcium 2% Iron 0%	

Marzetti, Fat Free Honey Dijon Dressing

2 tbsp / 35g

Amount per serving	%DV	Amount per serving	%DV	Amount per serving	%DV
Calories 50		**Cholesterol** 0mg	0%	**Total Carbohydrate** 12g	4%
Total Fat 0g	0%	**Sodium** 290mg	12%	Dietary Fiber 0g	0%
Saturated Fat 0g	0%	**Protein** 0g		Sugars 11g	
Polyunsaturated Fat 0g					
Monounsaturated Fat 0g		Vitamin A 0% Vitamin C 0%		Calcium 0% Iron 0%	

Marzetti, Fat Free Italian Dressing

2 tbsp / 32g

Amount per serving	%DV	Amount per serving	%DV	Amount per serving	%DV
Calories 15		**Cholesterol** 0mg	0%	**Total Carbohydrate** 4g	1%
Total Fat 0g	0%	**Sodium** 290mg	12%	Dietary Fiber 0g	0%
Saturated Fat 0g	0%	**Protein** 0g		Sugars 3g	
Polyunsaturated Fat 0g					
Monounsaturated Fat 0g		Vitamin A 0% Vitamin C 0%		Calcium 0% Iron 0%	

Marzetti, Fat Free Sweet & Sour Dressing

2 tbsp / 35g

Amount per serving	%DV	Amount per serving	%DV	Amount per serving	%DV
Calories 45		**Cholesterol** 0mg	0%	**Total Carbohydrate** 12g	4%
Total Fat 0g	0%	**Sodium** 290mg	12%	Dietary Fiber 0g	0%
Saturated Fat 0g	0%	**Protein** 0g		Sugars 10g	
Polyunsaturated Fat 0g					
Monounsaturated Fat 0g		Vitamin A 0% Vitamin C 0%		Calcium 0% Iron 0%	

Marzetti, Light Balsamic Vinaigrette Dressing

2 tbsp / 32g

Amount per serving	%DV	Amount per serving	%DV	Amount per serving	%DV
Calories 50		**Cholesterol** 0mg	0%	**Total Carbohydrate** 5g	2%
Total Fat 3g	5%	**Sodium** 350mg	15%	Dietary Fiber 0g	0%
Saturated Fat 0g	0%	**Protein** 0g		Sugars 5g	
Polyunsaturated Fat 0g					
Monounsaturated Fat 0g		Vitamin A 0% Vitamin C 0%		Calcium 0% Iron 0%	

Marzetti, Light Classic Ranch Dressing

2 tbsp / 30g

Amount per serving	%DV	Amount per serving	%DV	Amount per serving	%DV
Calories 80		**Cholesterol** 10mg	3%	**Total Carbohydrate** 2g	1%
Total Fat 8g	12%	**Sodium** 250mg	10%	Dietary Fiber 0g	0%
Saturated Fat 1g	5%	**Protein** 1g		Sugars 1g	
Polyunsaturated Fat 0g					
Monounsaturated Fat 0g		Vitamin A 0% Vitamin C 0%		Calcium 0% Iron 0%	

Marzetti, Light Honey French Dressing

2 tbsp / 34g

Amount per serving	%DV	Amount per serving	%DV	Amount per serving	%DV
Calories 80		**Cholesterol** 0mg	0%	**Total Carbohydrate** 12g	4%
Total Fat 3.5g	5%	**Sodium** 270mg	11%	Dietary Fiber 0g	0%
Saturated Fat 1g	5%	**Protein** 0g		Sugars 11g	
Polyunsaturated Fat 0g					
Monounsaturated Fat 0g		Vitamin A 0% Vitamin C 0%		Calcium 0% Iron 0%	

Marzetti, Olive Oil & Vinegar Vinaigrette

2 tbsp / 30g

Amount per serving	%DV	Amount per serving	%DV	Amount per serving	%DV
Calories 100		**Cholesterol** 0mg	0%	**Total Carbohydrate** 1g	0%
Total Fat 10g	15%	**Sodium** 190mg	8%	Dietary Fiber 0g	0%
Saturated Fat 2g	10%	**Protein** 0g		Sugars 1g	
Polyunsaturated Fat 0g					
Monounsaturated Fat 0g		Vitamin A 0% Vitamin C 0%		Calcium 0% Iron 0%	

Mayonnaise, Imitation, Soybean

1 tbsp / 15 g

Amount per serving	%DV	Amount per serving	%DV	Amount per serving	%DV
Calories 35		**Cholesterol** 4mg	1%	**Total Carbohydrate** 2g	1%
Total Fat 3g	5%	**Sodium** 75mg	3%	Dietary Fiber 0g	0%
Saturated Fat 0g	0%	**Protein** 0g		Sugars 1g	
Polyunsaturated Fat 1.5g					
Monounsaturated Fat 0.5g		Vitamin A 0% Vitamin C 0%		Calcium 0% Iron 0%	

Mayonnaise, Light

1 tbsp / 15g

Amount per serving	%DV	Amount per serving	%DV	Amount per serving	%DV
Calories 49		**Cholesterol** 5mg	2%	**Total Carbohydrate** 1g	0%
Total Fat 5g	8%	**Sodium** 101mg	4%	Dietary Fiber 0g	0%
Saturated Fat 1g	5%	**Protein** 0g		Sugars 1g	
Polyunsaturated Fat 2g					
Monounsaturated Fat 1g		Vitamin A 1% Vitamin C 0%		Calcium 0% Iron 0%	

Newman's Own, Balsamic Vinaigrette Salad Dressing

2 tbsp

Amount per serving	%DV	Amount per serving	%DV	Amount per serving	%DV
Calories 90		**Cholesterol** 0mg	0%	**Total Carbohydrate** 3g	1%
Total Fat 9g	14%	**Sodium** 290mg	12%	Dietary Fiber 0g	0%
Saturated Fat 1g	5%	**Protein** 0g		Sugars 1g	
Polyunsaturated Fat 0g					
Monounsaturated Fat 0g		Vitamin A 0% Vitamin C 0%		Calcium 0% Iron 0%	

Newman's Own, Caesar Salad Dressing

2 tbsp

Amount per serving	%DV	Amount per serving	%DV	Amount per serving	%DV
Calories 150		**Cholesterol** 0mg	0%	**Total Carbohydrate** 1g	0%
Total Fat 16g	25%	**Sodium** 420mg	18%	Dietary Fiber 0g	0%
Saturated Fat 2.5g	13%	**Protein** 1g		Sugars 1g	
Polyunsaturated Fat 0g					
Monounsaturated Fat 0g		Vitamin A 0% Vitamin C 0%		Calcium 2% Iron 0%	

Newman's Own, Creamy Balsamic Salad Dressing

2 tbsp

Amount per serving	%DV	Amount per serving	%DV	Amount per serving	%DV
Calories 110		**Cholesterol** 0mg	0%	**Total Carbohydrate** 6g	2%
Total Fat 10g	15%	**Sodium** 200mg	8%	Dietary Fiber 0g	0%
Saturated Fat 1.5g	8%	**Protein** 0g		Sugars 5g	
Polyunsaturated Fat 0g					
Monounsaturated Fat 0g		Vitamin A 0% Vitamin C 0%		Calcium 0% Iron 0%	

Newman's Own, Creamy Caesar Salad Dressing

2 tbsp

Amount per serving	%DV	Amount per serving	%DV	Amount per serving	%DV
Calories 150		**Cholesterol** 20mg	7%	**Total Carbohydrate** 1g	0%
Total Fat 16g	25%	**Sodium** 420mg	18%	Dietary Fiber 0g	0%
Saturated Fat 2.5g	13%	**Protein** 1g		Sugars 1g	
Polyunsaturated Fat 0g					
Monounsaturated Fat 0g		Vitamin A 0% Vitamin C 0%		Calcium 0% Iron 0%	

Newman's Own, Greek Vinaigrette Salad Dressing

2 tbsp

Amount per serving	%DV	Amount per serving	%DV	Amount per serving	%DV
Calories 100		**Cholesterol** 0mg	0%	**Total Carbohydrate** 2g	1%
Total Fat 10g	15%	**Sodium** 270mg	11%	Dietary Fiber 0g	0%
Saturated Fat 1.5g	8%	**Protein** 0g		Sugars 1g	
Polyunsaturated Fat 0g					
Monounsaturated Fat 0g		Vitamin A 0% Vitamin C 2%		Calcium 2% Iron 0%	

Newman's Own, Honey French Salad Dressing

2 tbsp

Amount per serving	%DV	Amount per serving	%DV	Amount per serving	%DV
Calories 130		**Cholesterol** 0mg	0%	**Total Carbohydrate** 6g	2%
Total Fat 11g	17%	**Sodium** 170mg	7%	Dietary Fiber 0g	0%
Saturated Fat 1.5g	8%	**Protein** 0g		Sugars 5g	
Polyunsaturated Fat 0g					
Monounsaturated Fat 0g		Vitamin A 2%	Vitamin C 4%	Calcium 0%	Iron 0%

Newman's Own, Lite Balsamic Vinaigrette Salad Dressing

2 tbsp / 30g

Amount per serving	%DV	Amount per serving	%DV	Amount per serving	%DV
Calories 45		**Cholesterol** 0mg	0%	**Total Carbohydrate** 2g	1%
Total Fat 4g	6%	**Sodium** 350mg	15%	Dietary Fiber 0g	0%
Saturated Fat 0.5g	3%	**Protein** 0g		Sugars 2g	
Polyunsaturated Fat 0g					
Monounsaturated Fat 0g		Vitamin A 0%	Vitamin C 0%	Calcium 0%	Iron 0%

Newman's Own, Lite Caesar Salad Dressing

2 tbsp

Amount per serving	%DV	Amount per serving	%DV	Amount per serving	%DV
Calories 70		**Cholesterol** 5mg	2%	**Total Carbohydrate** 3g	1%
Total Fat 6g	9%	**Sodium** 420mg	18%	Dietary Fiber 0g	0%
Saturated Fat 1g	5%	**Protein** 1g		Sugars 2g	
Polyunsaturated Fat 0g					
Monounsaturated Fat 0g		Vitamin A 0%	Vitamin C 0%	Calcium 4%	Iron 0%

Newman's Own, Lite Cranberry Walnut Salad Dressing

2 tbsp

Amount per serving	%DV	Amount per serving	%DV	Amount per serving	%DV
Calories 70		**Cholesterol** 0mg	0%	**Total Carbohydrate** 8g	3%
Total Fat 4g	6%	**Sodium** 230mg	10%	Dietary Fiber 0g	0%
Saturated Fat 0.5g	3%	**Protein** 1g		Sugars 7g	
Polyunsaturated Fat 0g					
Monounsaturated Fat 0g		Vitamin A 0%	Vitamin C 4%	Calcium 4%	Iron 0%

Newman's Own, Lite Honey Mustard Salad Dressing

2 tbsp

Amount per serving	%DV	Amount per serving	%DV	Amount per serving	%DV
Calories 70		**Cholesterol** 0mg	0%	**Total Carbohydrate** 7g	2%
Total Fat 4g	6%	**Sodium** 280mg	12%	Dietary Fiber 0g	0%
Saturated Fat 0.5g	3%	**Protein** 0g		Sugars 5g	
Polyunsaturated Fat 0g					
Monounsaturated Fat 0g		Vitamin A 0%	Vitamin C 0%	Calcium 4%	Iron 0%

Newman's Own, Lite Italian Salad Dressing

2 tbsp

Amount per serving	%DV	Amount per serving	%DV	Amount per serving	%DV
Calories 60		**Cholesterol** 0mg	0%	**Total Carbohydrate** 1g	0%
Total Fat 6g	9%	**Sodium** 260mg	11%	Dietary Fiber 0g	0%
Saturated Fat 1g	5%	**Protein** 0g		Sugars 0g	
Polyunsaturated Fat 0g					
Monounsaturated Fat 0g		Vitamin A 0% Vitamin C 0%		Calcium 0% Iron 0%	

Newman's Own, Lite Lime Vinaigrette Salad Dressing

2 tbsp

Amount per serving	%DV	Amount per serving	%DV	Amount per serving	%DV
Calories 60		**Cholesterol** 0mg	0%	**Total Carbohydrate** 4g	1%
Total Fat 5g	8%	**Sodium** 320mg	13%	Dietary Fiber 0g	0%
Saturated Fat 1g	5%	**Protein** 0g		Sugars 4g	
Polyunsaturated Fat g					
Monounsaturated Fat g		Vitamin A 0% Vitamin C 2%		Calcium 0% Iron 0%	

Newman's Own, Lite Red Wine Vinegar & Olive Oil Salad Dressing

2 tbsp

Amount per serving	%DV	Amount per serving	%DV	Amount per serving	%DV
Calories 50		**Cholesterol** 0mg	0%	**Total Carbohydrate** 3g	1%
Total Fat 4g	6%	**Sodium** 420mg	18%	Dietary Fiber 0g	0%
Saturated Fat 0.5g	3%	**Protein** 0g		Sugars 3g	
Polyunsaturated Fat 0g					
Monounsaturated Fat 0g		Vitamin A 0% Vitamin C 0%		Calcium 0% Iron 0%	

Newman's Own, Lite Roasted Garlic Balsamic Salad Dressing

2 tbsp

Amount per serving	%DV	Amount per serving	%DV	Amount per serving	%DV
Calories 50		**Cholesterol** 0mg	0%	**Total Carbohydrate** 3g	1%
Total Fat 4g	6%	**Sodium** 420mg	18%	Dietary Fiber 0g	0%
Saturated Fat 0.5g	3%	**Protein** 0g		Sugars 3g	
Polyunsaturated Fat 0g					
Monounsaturated Fat 0g		Vitamin A 0% Vitamin C 2%		Calcium 0% Iron 0%	

Newman's Own, Lite Sun Dried Tomato Salad Dressing

2 tbsp

Amount per serving	%DV	Amount per serving	%DV	Amount per serving	%DV
Calories 60		**Cholesterol** 0mg	0%	**Total Carbohydrate** 5g	2%
Total Fat 4g	6%	**Sodium** 380mg	16%	Dietary Fiber 0g	0%
Saturated Fat 0.5g	3%	**Protein** 0g		Sugars 3g	
Polyunsaturated Fat 0g					
Monounsaturated Fat 0g		Vitamin A 0% Vitamin C 4%		Calcium 0% Iron 0%	

Newman's Own, Olive Oil & Vinegar Salad Dressing

2 tbsp

Amount per serving	%DV	Amount per serving	%DV	Amount per serving	%DV
Calories 150		**Cholesterol** 0mg	0%	**Total Carbohydrate** 1g	0%
Total Fat 16g	25%	**Sodium** 150mg	6%	Dietary Fiber 0g	0%
Saturated Fat 2.5g	13%	**Protein** 0g		Sugars 1g	
Polyunsaturated Fat 0g					
Monounsaturated Fat 0g		Vitamin A 0%	Vitamin C 0%	Calcium 0%	Iron 0%

Newman's Own, Organic Lite Balsamic Salad Dressing

2 tbsp

Amount per serving	%DV	Amount per serving	%DV	Amount per serving	%DV
Calories 45		**Cholesterol** 0mg	0%	**Total Carbohydrate** 3g	1%
Total Fat 4g	6%	**Sodium** 450mg	19%	Dietary Fiber 0g	0%
Saturated Fat 0.5g	3%	**Protein** 0g		Sugars 2g	
Polyunsaturated Fat 0g					
Monounsaturated Fat 0g		Vitamin A 0%	Vitamin C 0%	Calcium 0%	Iron 0%

Newman's Own, Organic Tuscan Italian Salad Dressing

2 tbsp

Amount per serving	%DV	Amount per serving	%DV	Amount per serving	%DV
Calories 100		**Cholesterol** 0mg	0%	**Total Carbohydrate** 2g	1%
Total Fat 11g	17%	**Sodium** 380mg	16%	Dietary Fiber 0g	0%
Saturated Fat 1.5g	8%	**Protein** 0g		Sugars 1g	
Polyunsaturated Fat 0g					
Monounsaturated Fat 0g		Vitamin A 0%	Vitamin C 0%	Calcium 0%	Iron 0%

Newman's Own, Parmesan & Roasted Garlic Salad Dressing

2 tbsp

Amount per serving	%DV	Amount per serving	%DV	Amount per serving	%DV
Calories 110		**Cholesterol** 0mg	0%	**Total Carbohydrate** 2g	1%
Total Fat 11g	17%	**Sodium** 340mg	14%	Dietary Fiber 0g	0%
Saturated Fat 2g	10%	**Protein** 1g		Sugars 1g	
Polyunsaturated Fat 0g					
Monounsaturated Fat 0g		Vitamin A 0%	Vitamin C 0%	Calcium 2%	Iron 0%

Newman's Own, Poppy Seed Salad Dressing

2 tbsp

Amount per serving	%DV	Amount per serving	%DV	Amount per serving	%DV
Calories 140		**Cholesterol** 0mg	0%	**Total Carbohydrate** 5g	2%
Total Fat 13g	20%	**Sodium** 220mg	9%	Dietary Fiber 0g	0%
Saturated Fat 2g	10%	**Protein** 0g		Sugars 5g	
Polyunsaturated Fat 0g					
Monounsaturated Fat 0g		Vitamin A 0%	Vitamin C 0%	Calcium 2%	Iron 0%

Newman's Own, Ranch Salad Dressing

2 tbsp

Amount per serving	%DV	Amount per serving	%DV	Amount per serving	%DV
Calories 150		**Cholesterol** 10mg	3%	**Total Carbohydrate** 2g	1%
Total Fat 16g	25%	**Sodium** 310mg	13%	Dietary Fiber 0g	0%
Saturated Fat 2.5g	13%	**Protein** 0g		Sugars 1g	
Polyunsaturated Fat 0g					
Monounsaturated Fat 0g		Vitamin A 0% Vitamin C 0%		Calcium 0% Iron 0%	

Newman's Own, Three Cheese Balsamic Vinaigrette Salad Dressing

2 tbsp

Amount per serving	%DV	Amount per serving	%DV	Amount per serving	%DV
Calories 110		**Cholesterol** 0mg	0%	**Total Carbohydrate** 2g	1%
Total Fat 11g	17%	**Sodium** 380mg	16%	Dietary Fiber 0g	0%
Saturated Fat 1.5g	8%	**Protein** 0g		Sugars 2g	
Polyunsaturated Fat 0g					
Monounsaturated Fat 0g		Vitamin A 0% Vitamin C 2%		Calcium 2% Iron 0%	

Salad Dressing, Honey Mustard Dressing, Reduced Calorie

2 tbsp / 1 serving / 30g

Amount per serving	%DV	Amount per serving	%DV	Amount per serving	%DV
Calories 62		**Cholesterol** 0mg	0%	**Total Carbohydrate** 9g	3%
Total Fat 3g	5%	**Sodium** 270mg	11%	Dietary Fiber 0g	0%
Saturated Fat 0g	0%	**Protein** 0g		Sugars 5g	
Polyunsaturated Fat 0g					
Monounsaturated Fat 0g		Vitamin A 0% Vitamin C 0%		Calcium 2% Iron 1%	

Seeds of Change, Balsamic Vinaigrette Salad Dressing

2 tbsp

Amount per serving	%DV	Amount per serving	%DV	Amount per serving	%DV
Calories 60		**Cholesterol** 0mg	0%	**Total Carbohydrate** 6g	2%
Total Fat 4g	6%	**Sodium** 105mg	4%	Dietary Fiber 0g	0%
Saturated Fat 0g	0%	**Protein** 0g		Sugars 3g	
Polyunsaturated Fat 0g					
Monounsaturated Fat 0g		Vitamin A 0% Vitamin C 0%		Calcium 0% Iron 0%	

Seeds of Change, French Tomato Salad Dressing

2 tbsp

Amount per serving	%DV	Amount per serving	%DV	Amount per serving	%DV
Calories 60		**Cholesterol** 0mg	0%	**Total Carbohydrate** 8g	3%
Total Fat 3g	5%	**Sodium** 210mg	9%	Dietary Fiber 0g	0%
Saturated Fat 0g	0%	**Protein** 0g		Sugars 6g	
Polyunsaturated Fat 0g					
Monounsaturated Fat 3g		Vitamin A 0% Vitamin C 0%		Calcium 0% Iron 0%	

Seeds of Change, Greek Feta Vinaigrette Salad Dressing

2 tbsp

Amount per serving	%DV	Amount per serving	%DV	Amount per serving	%DV
Calories 60		**Cholesterol** 0mg	0%	**Total Carbohydrate** 5g	2%
Total Fat 4.5g	7%	**Sodium** 270mg	11%	Dietary Fiber 0g	0%
Saturated Fat 0.5g	3%	**Protein** 1g		Sugars 2g	
Polyunsaturated Fat 0g					
Monounsaturated Fat 0g		Vitamin A 0% Vitamin C 0%		Calcium 0% Iron 0%	

Seeds of Change, Italian Herb Vinaigrette Salad Dressing

2 tbsp

Amount per serving	%DV	Amount per serving	%DV	Amount per serving	%DV
Calories 60		**Cholesterol** 0mg	0%	**Total Carbohydrate** 5g	2%
Total Fat 4.5g	7%	**Sodium** 260mg	11%	Dietary Fiber 0g	0%
Saturated Fat 0g	0%	**Protein** 0g		Sugars 3g	
Polyunsaturated Fat 0g					
Monounsaturated Fat 0g		Vitamin A 0% Vitamin C 0%		Calcium 0% Iron 0%	

Seeds of Change, Roasted Red Pepper Vinaigrette Salad Dressing

2 tbsp

Amount per serving	%DV	Amount per serving	%DV	Amount per serving	%DV
Calories 50		**Cholesterol** 0mg	0%	**Total Carbohydrate** 5g	2%
Total Fat 3.5g	5%	**Sodium** 240mg	10%	Dietary Fiber 0g	0%
Saturated Fat 0g	0%	**Protein** 0g		Sugars 3g	
Polyunsaturated Fat 0g					
Monounsaturated Fat 0g		Vitamin A 0% Vitamin C 0%		Calcium 0% Iron 0%	

Smart Balance, Omega -3 & Plant Sterols, Light Mayonnaise Dressing

1 tbsp

Amount per serving	%DV	Amount per serving	%DV	Amount per serving	%DV
Calories 50		**Cholesterol** 10mg	3%	**Total Carbohydrate** 1g	0%
Total Fat 5g	8%	**Sodium** 125mg	5%	Dietary Fiber 0g	0%
Saturated Fat 0g	0%	**Protein** 0g		Sugars 1g	
Polyunsaturated Fat 1.5g					
Monounsaturated Fat 2.5g		Vitamin A 0% Vitamin C 0%		Calcium 0% Iron 0%	

The Silver Palate, Fat Free Really Raspberry Salad Splash

2 tbsp / 30ml

Amount per serving	%DV	Amount per serving	%DV	Amount per serving	%DV
Calories 25		**Cholesterol** 0mg	0%	**Total Carbohydrate** 6g	2%
Total Fat 0g	0%	**Sodium** 65mg	3%	Dietary Fiber 0g	0%
Saturated Fat 0g	0%	**Protein** 0g		Sugars 4g	
Polyunsaturated Fat 0g					
Monounsaturated Fat 0g		Vitamin A 0% Vitamin C 2%		Calcium 0% Iron 0%	

The Silver Palate, Lemon Garlic Herb Salad Splash

2 tbsp / 30ml

Amount per serving	%DV	Amount per serving	%DV	Amount per serving	%DV
Calories 25		**Cholesterol** 0mg	0%	**Total Carbohydrate** 6g	2%
Total Fat 0g	0%	**Sodium** 70mg	3%	Dietary Fiber 0g	0%
Saturated Fat 0g	0%	**Protein** 0g		Sugars 4g	
Polyunsaturated Fat 0g					
Monounsaturated Fat 0g		Vitamin A 0% Vitamin C 2%		Calcium 0% Iron 0%	

The Silver Palate, Raspberry Vinegar

2 tbsp / 30ml

Amount per serving	%DV	Amount per serving	%DV	Amount per serving	%DV
Calories 10		**Cholesterol** 0mg	0%	**Total Carbohydrate** 3g	1%
Total Fat 0g	0%	**Sodium** 0mg	0%	Dietary Fiber 0g	0%
Saturated Fat 0g	0%	**Protein** 0g		Sugars 2g	
Polyunsaturated Fat 0g					
Monounsaturated Fat 0g		Vitamin A 0% Vitamin C 0%		Calcium 0% Iron 0%	

Wish-Bone, Balsamic Vinaigrette

2 tbsp / 30ml

Amount per serving	%DV	Amount per serving	%DV	Amount per serving	%DV
Calories 60		**Cholesterol** 0mg	0%	**Total Carbohydrate** 3g	1%
Total Fat 5g	8%	**Sodium** 280mg	12%	Dietary Fiber 0g	0%
Saturated Fat 0.5g	3%	**Protein** 0g		Sugars 3g	
Polyunsaturated Fat 2.5g					
Monounsaturated Fat 1.5g		Vitamin A 0% Vitamin C 0%		Calcium 0% Iron 0%	

Wish-Bone, Fat Free Chunky Blue Cheese

2 tbsp / 30 ml

Amount per serving	%DV	Amount per serving	%DV	Amount per serving	%DV
Calories 30		**Cholesterol** 0mg	0%	**Total Carbohydrate** 7g	2%
Total Fat 0g	0%	**Sodium** 280mg	12%	Dietary Fiber 0g	0%
Saturated Fat 0g	0%	**Protein** 1g		Sugars 2g	
Polyunsaturated Fat 0g					
Monounsaturated Fat 0g		Vitamin A 0% Vitamin C 0%		Calcium 0% Iron 0%	

Wish-Bone, Fat Free Ranch

2 tbsp / 30ml

Amount per serving	%DV	Amount per serving	%DV	Amount per serving	%DV
Calories 30		**Cholesterol** 0mg	0%	**Total Carbohydrate** 6g	2%
Total Fat 0g	0%	**Sodium** 280mg	12%	Dietary Fiber 0g	0%
Saturated Fat 0g	0%	**Protein** 0g		Sugars 3g	
Polyunsaturated Fat 0g					
Monounsaturated Fat 0g		Vitamin A 0% Vitamin C 0%		Calcium 0% Iron 0%	

Wish-Bone, Light Country Italian

2 tbsp / 30ml

Amount per serving	%DV	Amount per serving	%DV	Amount per serving	%DV
Calories 15		**Cholesterol** 0mg	0%	**Total Carbohydrate** 3g	1%
Total Fat 0g	0%	**Sodium** 340mg	14%	Dietary Fiber 0g	0%
Saturated Fat 0g	0%	**Protein** 0g		Sugars 2g	
Polyunsaturated Fat 0g					
Monounsaturated Fat 0g		Vitamin A 0%	Vitamin C 4%	Calcium 0%	Iron 0%

Wish-Bone, Light Deluxe French Style

2 tbsp / 30ml

Amount per serving	%DV	Amount per serving	%DV	Amount per serving	%DV
Calories 70		**Cholesterol** 0mg	0%	**Total Carbohydrate** 2g	1%
Total Fat 5g	8%	**Sodium** 220mg	9%	Dietary Fiber 0g	0%
Saturated Fat 0.5g	3%	**Protein** 0g		Sugars 4g	
Polyunsaturated Fat 3g					
Monounsaturated Fat 1g		Vitamin A 20%	Vitamin C 0%	Calcium 0%	Iron 0%

Wish-Bone, Light Honey Dijon

2 tbsp / 30ml

Amount per serving	%DV	Amount per serving	%DV	Amount per serving	%DV
Calories 70		**Cholesterol** 5mg	2%	**Total Carbohydrate** 6g	2%
Total Fat 5g	8%	**Sodium** 240mg	10%	Dietary Fiber 0g	0%
Saturated Fat 1g	5%	**Protein** 0g		Sugars 4g	
Polyunsaturated Fat 3g					
Monounsaturated Fat 1g		Vitamin A 8%	Vitamin C 0%	Calcium 0%	Iron 0%

Wish-Bone, Light Ranch

2 tbsp / 30ml

Amount per serving	%DV	Amount per serving	%DV	Amount per serving	%DV
Calories 70		**Cholesterol** 0mg	0%	**Total Carbohydrate** 4g	1%
Total Fat 5g	8%	**Sodium** 280mg	12%	Dietary Fiber 0g	0%
Saturated Fat 1g	5%	**Protein** 0g		Sugars 2g	
Polyunsaturated Fat 3g					
Monounsaturated Fat 1g		Vitamin A 0%	Vitamin C 0%	Calcium 0%	Iron 0%

Wish-Bone, Light Thousand Island

2 tbsp / 30ml

Amount per serving	%DV	Amount per serving	%DV	Amount per serving	%DV
Calories 60		**Cholesterol** 0mg	0%	**Total Carbohydrate** 4g	1%
Total Fat 5g	8%	**Sodium** 270mg	11%	Dietary Fiber 0g	0%
Saturated Fat 1g	5%	**Protein** 0g		Sugars 3g	
Polyunsaturated Fat 3g					
Monounsaturated Fat 1g		Vitamin A 0%	Vitamin C 0%	Calcium 0%	Iron 0%

Olives

Mezzetta, Anchovy Stuffed Olives

4 olives

Amount per serving	%DV	Amount per serving	%DV	Amount per serving	%DV
Calories 40		**Cholesterol** 0mg	0%	**Total Carbohydrate** 0g	0%
Total Fat 4g	6%	**Sodium** 240mg	10%	Dietary Fiber 0g	0%
Saturated Fat 0g	0%	**Protein** 0g		Sugars 0g	
Polyunsaturated Fat 0g					
Monounsaturated Fat 0g		Vitamin A 0%	Vitamin C 0%	Calcium 0%	Iron 0%

Mezzetta, Garlic Stuffed Olives

1 serving / 15g

Amount per serving	%DV	Amount per serving	%DV	Amount per serving	%DV
Calories 10		**Cholesterol** 0mg	0%	**Total Carbohydrate** 2g	1%
Total Fat 1g	2%	**Sodium** 125mg	5%	Dietary Fiber 1g	4%
Saturated Fat 0g	0%	**Protein** 1g		Sugars 0g	
Polyunsaturated Fat 1g					
Monounsaturated Fat 0g		Vitamin A 0%	Vitamin C 2%	Calcium 2%	Iron 0%

Mezzetta, Jalapeno Stuffed Olives

1 olive

Amount per serving	%DV	Amount per serving	%DV	Amount per serving	%DV
Calories 10		**Cholesterol** 0mg	0%	**Total Carbohydrate** 1g	0%
Total Fat 1g	2%	**Sodium** 140mg	6%	Dietary Fiber 0g	0%
Saturated Fat 0g	0%	**Protein** 0g		Sugars 0g	
Polyunsaturated Fat 0g					
Monounsaturated Fat 0g		Vitamin A 0%	Vitamin C 0%	Calcium 2%	Iron 0%

Mezzetta, Kalamata Olives

9 pieces

Amount per serving	%DV	Amount per serving	%DV	Amount per serving	%DV
Calories 40		**Cholesterol** 0mg	0%	**Total Carbohydrate** 1g	0%
Total Fat 4g	6%	**Sodium** 240mg	10%	Dietary Fiber 0g	0%
Saturated Fat 0g	0%	**Protein** 0g		Sugars 0g	
Polyunsaturated Fat 0g					
Monounsaturated Fat 0g		Vitamin A 0%	Vitamin C 0%	Calcium 0%	Iron 0%

Mezzetta, Martini Olives

1 olive

Amount per serving	%DV	Amount per serving	%DV	Amount per serving	%DV
Calories 10		**Cholesterol** 0mg	0%	**Total Carbohydrate** 1g	0%
Total Fat 1g	2%	**Sodium** 170mg	7%	Dietary Fiber 0g	0%
Saturated Fat 0g	0%	**Protein** 0g		Sugars 0g	
Polyunsaturated Fat 0g					
Monounsaturated Fat 0g		Vitamin A 0%	Vitamin C 0%	Calcium 0%	Iron 0%

Mezzetta, Salad Olives

5 olives

Amount per serving	%DV	Amount per serving	%DV	Amount per serving	%DV
Calories 20		**Cholesterol** 0mg	0%	**Total Carbohydrate** 0g	0%
Total Fat 2.5g	4%	**Sodium** 270mg	11%	Dietary Fiber 1g	4%
Saturated Fat 0.5g	3%	**Protein** 0g		Sugars 0g	
Polyunsaturated Fat 0g					
Monounsaturated Fat 0g		Vitamin A 2%	Vitamin C 0%	Calcium 0%	Iron 0%

Olives, Pickled, Canned or Bottled, Green

1 olive / 2g

Amount per serving	%DV	Amount per serving	%DV	Amount per serving	%DV
Calories 4		**Cholesterol** 0mg	0%	**Total Carbohydrate** 0g	0%
Total Fat 0g	0%	**Sodium** 39mg	2%	Dietary Fiber 0g	0%
Saturated Fat 0g	0%	**Protein** 0g		Sugars 0g	
Polyunsaturated Fat g					
Monounsaturated Fat g		Vitamin A 0%	Vitamin C 0%	Calcium 0%	Iron 0%

Olives, Ripe, Canned (Jumbo-Super Colossal)

1 super colossal / 15g

Amount per serving	%DV	Amount per serving	%DV	Amount per serving	%DV
Calories 12		**Cholesterol** 0mg	0%	**Total Carbohydrate** 1g	0%
Total Fat 1g	2%	**Sodium** 110.5mg	5%	Dietary Fiber 0.5g	2%
Saturated Fat 0g	0%	**Protein** 0g		Sugars 0g	
Polyunsaturated Fat 0g					
Monounsaturated Fat 1g		Vitamin A 52%	Vitamin C 0%	Calcium 14%	Iron 0.5%

Olives, Ripe, Canned (Small-Extra Large)

1 large / 4.4g

Amount per serving	%DV	Amount per serving	%DV	Amount per serving	%DV
Calories 5		**Cholesterol** 0mg	0%	**Total Carbohydrate** 0.5g	0%
Total Fat 0.5g	1%	**Sodium** 32.5mg	1%	Dietary Fiber 0g	0%
Saturated Fat 0g	0%	**Protein** 0g		Sugars 0g	
Polyunsaturated Fat 0g					
Monounsaturated Fat 0.5g		Vitamin A 17.5%	Vitamin C 0%	Calcium 4%	Iron 0%

Fruits

Why Eat Fruit?

Fruits provide nutrients vital for heart health and body maintenance. Most fruits are naturally low in fat, sodium, and calories. None have cholesterol. Fruits are sources of many essential nutrients that are underconsumed, including potassium, dietary fiber, vitamin C, and folate (folic acid). Diets rich in potassium may help to maintain healthy blood pressure. Dietary fiber from fruits, as part of an overall healthy diet, helps reduce blood cholesterol levels and may lower the risk of heart disease. Vitamin C is important for growth and repair of all body tissues, helps heal cuts and wounds, and keeps teeth and gums healthy.

Daily Goal

Two cups for an adult on a 2,000-calorie diet.

1 cup equivalents:
    2.5" whole fruit
    1 cup chopped or sliced fruit
    ½ cup dried fruit
    8 oz. fruit juice (100%)
    32 seedless grapes
    8 large strawberries

Heart-Healthy Nutrients in Fruit

Potassium helps your heart beat as it squeezes blood through your body. If you have high blood pressure, heart failure, or heart rhythm problems, getting enough potassium is especially important. Although potassium and cholesterol aren't directly related, eating a potassium-rich diet might lower your cholesterol, too.

Good fruit sources of potassium are bananas, oranges, strawberries, raisins, prunes, apricots, cantaloupes, grapefruit juice, honeydew, kiwi, mangoes, papaya, pomegranate, and dates.

Check out the FDA-approved Health Claim for potassium and high blood pressure and stroke on page 27.

Dietary fiber is the term for several materials that make up fruits that your body can't digest. Fiber is classified as soluble or insoluble.

Soluble fiber, when eaten regularly as part of a diet low in saturated fat, trans fat, and cholesterol, can decrease your risk of cardiovascular disease. Soluble fibers modestly reduce LDL ("bad") cholesterol. Fruits high in soluble fiber include apples, oranges, pears, strawberries, and blueberries.

Check out the FDA-approved Health Claim for soluble fiber and risk of heart disease on page 26.

Insoluble fiber has been associated with decreased risk of heart disease. Fruits high in insoluble fiber include raisins and grapes.

Antioxidants can help prevent artery damage by fighting substances produced in the process of oxidation. Some of the major antioxidants found in fruits are:

Antioxidant	Food Sources
Lycopene	Pink/red grapefruit, watermelon, papaya, guava, apricot, tomato
Vitamin E	Kiwi, mango
Resveratrol	Red grape skins, grape juice, berries
Phenolic acids	Apples, pears, dates, citrus fruits
Catechins	Blackberries, apples, pears, grapes
Procyanidins/ Proanthocyanides	Cranberries, strawberries, grapes, black currants
Beta carotene	Brightly colored orange and yellow foods such as cantaloupe, mangoes, apricots, and persimmons
Vitamin C	Berries, broccoli, Brussels sprouts, cantaloupe, cauliflower, grapefruit, honeydew, kale, kiwi, mangoes, nectarines, orange, papaya, red, green or yellow peppers, snow peas, sweet potato, strawberries, and tomatoes

Heart-Healthy Shopping Tips for Fruit

• **Look for these FDA-Approved Heart Health Claims on Fruits:**

Potassium and the Risk of High Blood Pressure and Stroke
"Diets containing foods that are a good source of potassium and that are low in sodium may reduce the risk of high blood pressure and stroke."

Products carrying this claim must be low in sodium, total fat, saturated fat, and cholesterol and contain a good source of potassium (350 mg/10% Daily Value or higher).

Fruits, Vegetables, and Grain Products that Contain Fiber, Particularly Soluble Fiber, and Risk of Coronary Heart Disease
"Diets low in saturated fat and cholesterol and rich in fruits, vegetables, and grain products that contain some types of dietary fiber, particularly soluble fiber, may reduce the risk of heart disease, a disease associated with many factors."

A vegetable that contains this claim must be low in total fat, saturated fat, and cholesterol and contain at least 0.6 grams of soluble fiber per serving (without fortification). The soluble fiber content must be provided on the food label.

- Look for the American Heart Association's Heart-Check mark on fresh, canned, and frozen fruit products and fruit juices. For more information on the Heart-Check mark go to *www.heartcheckmark.org*.

- Eat a variety of fruits. Different fruits have different nutrients.

- Eat the skin of fruit when possible. Many nutrients are concentrated in the skin.

- Choose fresh, in-season fruits and purchase locally grown fruits when available.

- When fresh fruits aren't available, choose frozen or canned fruits in water without added sugars.

- Refrigerate or freeze cut-up fruit to store for use later.

- Fruits that are deeply colored throughout—such as peaches and berries—tend to be higher in vitamins and minerals.

- Stock up on fresh fruits for snacks such as apples, grapes, pears, berries, and bananas.

- Keep fruit visible to encourage eating. Place a few washed pieces on the counter each day for a quick snack.

- Cut up fruit for snacking. Rinse the cut-up fruit in tap water to prevent browning.

- For desserts, buy fresh or canned fruits (in water without added sugars), dried fruit (without added sugars), and gelatin that contains fruit instead of baked goods and sweets.

- Consume 100% fruit juice in moderation. Fruit juice concentrates calories and sugar and eliminates fiber. Eat the whole fruit for all the nutrients.

- Make sure that fruit drinks are 100% fruit and not sugar water with a little fruit juice.

- **Caution:** Some cholesterol-lowering medications may interact with grapefruit, grapefruit juice, pomegranate, and pomegranate juice. Please talk to your health care provider about any potential risks.

Shopping List Essentials

Apples	Berries	Grapes	Grapefruits (red)
Bananas	Melon	Oranges	

Criteria for Fruit

Using the FDA guidelines for Heart Health Claims, the foods listed meet the following criteria:

- Total fat–3 grams or less

- Saturated fat–1 gram or less

- Trans fat–0.5 grams or less (Trans Fat is not listed in the charts because all items report 0 grams Trans Fat.) Since foods with less than 0.5 grams of trans fats can list 0 grams in the Nutrition Facts, be sure to check the ingredients for partially hydrogenated fats to determine if a product contains any trans fats.

- Cholesterol–20 mg or less

- Beneficial Nutrients–10% Daily Value or higher of one beneficial nutrient (vitamin A, vitamin C, iron, calcium, protein, or dietary fiber). Raw, canned, or frozen fruits do not necessarily need to meet these criteria and can be labeled "healthy" if they do not contain ingredients that change the nutritional profile and do not contain more than 360 mg of sodium.

- Sodium–140 mg or less for fresh, frozen, and canned fruit products and fruit juice. Look for lower sodium levels to help reduce high blood pressure.

- Fruit juices must be 100% juice

- No heavy syrup or added sugar allowed for processed fruits

Foods that are not included in this list are canned, frozen, and processed fruits with added sugar and fruit juice beverages that are not 100% juice. It is recommended that we cut down on added sugar. This does not mean that these foods are bad. Eat them occasionally, but focus on fresh fruits when possible.

Fruit Juices

Apricot Nectar, Canned, with Vitamin C

1 cup / 251 g

Amount per serving	%DV	Amount per serving	%DV	Amount per serving	%DV
Calories 141		Cholesterol 0mg	0%	Total Carbohydrate 36g	12%
Total Fat 0g	0%	Sodium 8mg	0%	Dietary Fiber 2g	8%
Saturated Fat 0g	0%	Protein 1g		Sugars 35g	
Polyunsaturated Fat 0g					
Monounsaturated Fat 0g		Vitamin A 66%	Vitamin C 228%	Calcium 2%	Iron 5%

Bolthouse Farms, 100% Pomegranate Juice

8 fl oz / 240 ml

Amount per serving	%DV	Amount per serving	%DV	Amount per serving	%DV
Calories 150		Cholesterol 0mg	0%	Total Carbohydrate 38g	13%
Total Fat 0g	0%	Sodium 50mg	2%	Dietary Fiber 0g	0%
Saturated Fat 0g	0%	Protein 0g		Sugars 31g	
Polyunsaturated Fat 0g					
Monounsaturated Fat 0g		Vitamin A 0%	Vitamin C 0%	Calcium 4%	Iron 0%

Bolthouse Farms, Acai + 10 Superblend Juice

8 fl oz / 240 ml

Amount per serving	%DV	Amount per serving	%DV	Amount per serving	%DV
Calories 120		Cholesterol 0mg	0%	Total Carbohydrate 31g	10%
Total Fat 0g	0%	Sodium 15mg	1%	Dietary Fiber 3g	12%
Saturated Fat 0g	0%	Protein 0g		Sugars 25g	
Polyunsaturated Fat 0g					
Monounsaturated Fat 0g		Vitamin A 0%	Vitamin C 20%	Calcium 2%	Iron 2%

Bolthouse Farms, Berries + Carrot Juice

8 fl oz / 240 ml

Amount per serving	%DV	Amount per serving	%DV	Amount per serving	%DV
Calories 120		Cholesterol 0mg	0%	Total Carbohydrate 30g	10%
Total Fat 0g	0%	Sodium 50mg	2%	Dietary Fiber 2g	8%
Saturated Fat 0g	0%	Protein 1g		Sugars 27g	
Polyunsaturated Fat 0g					
Monounsaturated Fat 0g		Vitamin A 0%	Vitamin C 6%	Calcium 4%	Iron 2%

Bolthouse Farms, Mango Coconut Splash Juice

8 fl oz / 240 ml

Amount per serving	%DV	Amount per serving	%DV	Amount per serving	%DV
Calories 60		Cholesterol 0mg	0%	Total Carbohydrate 15g	5%
Total Fat 0g	0%	Sodium 65mg	3%	Dietary Fiber 0g	0%
Saturated Fat 0g	0%	Protein 0g		Sugars 13g	
Polyunsaturated Fat 0g					
Monounsaturated Fat 0g		Vitamin A 0%	Vitamin C 2%	Calcium 2%	Iron 0%

Bolthouse Farms, Mango Ginger + Carrot Juice

8 fl oz / 240 ml

Amount per serving	%DV	Amount per serving	%DV	Amount per serving	%DV
Calories 110		**Cholesterol** 0mg	0%	**Total Carbohydrate** 27g	9%
Total Fat 0.5g	1%	**Sodium** 65mg	3%	Dietary Fiber 3g	12%
Saturated Fat 0g	0%	**Protein** 1g		Sugars 23g	
Polyunsaturated Fat 0g					
Monounsaturated Fat 0g		Vitamin A 220% Vitamin C 80%		Calcium 2% Iron 2%	

Bolthouse Farms, Mango Lemonade Juice

8 fl oz / 240 ml

Amount per serving	%DV	Amount per serving	%DV	Amount per serving	%DV
Calories 130		**Cholesterol** 0mg	0%	**Total Carbohydrate** 33g	11%
Total Fat 0g	0%	**Sodium** 5mg	0%	Dietary Fiber 0g	0%
Saturated Fat 0g	0%	**Protein** 0g		Sugars 32g	
Polyunsaturated Fat 0g					
Monounsaturated Fat 0g		Vitamin A 10% Vitamin C 10%		Calcium 0% Iron 0%	

Bolthouse Farms, Orange + Carrot Juice

8 fl oz / 240 ml

Amount per serving	%DV	Amount per serving	%DV	Amount per serving	%DV
Calories 120		**Cholesterol** 0mg	0%	**Total Carbohydrate** 27g	9%
Total Fat 0g	0%	**Sodium** 95mg	4%	Dietary Fiber 2g	8%
Saturated Fat 0g	0%	**Protein** 2g		Sugars 23g	
Polyunsaturated Fat 0g					
Monounsaturated Fat 0g		Vitamin A 300% Vitamin C 100%		Calcium 6% Iron 2%	

Bolthouse Farms, Passion Orange Guava Juice

8 fl oz / 240 ml

Amount per serving	%DV	Amount per serving	%DV	Amount per serving	%DV
Calories 170		**Cholesterol** 0mg	0%	**Total Carbohydrate** 41g	14%
Total Fat 1g	2%	**Sodium** 20mg	1%	Dietary Fiber 2g	8%
Saturated Fat 0g	0%	**Protein** 1g		Sugars 33g	
Polyunsaturated Fat 0g					
Monounsaturated Fat 0g		Vitamin A 100% Vitamin C 100%		Calcium 2% Iron 2%	

Bolthouse Farms, Tropical + Carrot Juice

8 fl oz / 240 ml

Amount per serving	%DV	Amount per serving	%DV	Amount per serving	%DV
Calories 140		**Cholesterol** 0mg	0%	**Total Carbohydrate** 32g	11%
Total Fat 0g	0%	**Sodium** 130mg	5%	Dietary Fiber 5g	20%
Saturated Fat 0g	0%	**Protein** 1g		Sugars 25g	
Polyunsaturated Fat 0g					
Monounsaturated Fat 0g		Vitamin A 250% Vitamin C 15%		Calcium 4% Iron 2%	

Campbell's V8 V-Fusion Juices, Strawberry Banana

1 serving / 8 oz / 246g

Amount per serving	%DV	Amount per serving	%DV	Amount per serving	%DV
Calories 110		**Cholesterol** 0mg	0%	**Total Carbohydrate** 28g	9%
Total Fat 0g	0%	**Sodium** 70mg	3%	Dietary Fiber 0g	0%
Saturated Fat 0g	0%	**Protein** 0g		Sugars 24g	
Polyunsaturated Fat 0g					
Monounsaturated Fat 0g		Vitamin A 50% Vitamin C 100% Calcium 2% Iron 15%			

Campbell's V8 V-Fusion Juices, Tropical Orange

1 serving / 8 oz / 246g

Amount per serving	%DV	Amount per serving	%DV	Amount per serving	%DV
Calories 120		**Cholesterol** 0mg	0%	**Total Carbohydrate** 28g	9%
Total Fat 0g	0%	**Sodium** 80mg	3%	Dietary Fiber 0g	0%
Saturated Fat 0g	0%	**Protein** 1g		Sugars 25g	
Polyunsaturated Fat 0g					
Monounsaturated Fat 0g		Vitamin A 80% Vitamin C 100% Calcium 2% Iron 2%			

Campbell's, V8 Diet Splash Berry Blend

8 fl oz / 240 ml

Amount per serving	%DV	Amount per serving	%DV	Amount per serving	%DV
Calories 10		**Cholesterol** 0mg	0%	**Total Carbohydrate** 3g	1%
Total Fat 0g	0%	**Sodium** 30mg	1%	Dietary Fiber 0g	0%
Saturated Fat 0g	0%	**Protein** 0g		Sugars 2g	
Polyunsaturated Fat 0g					
Monounsaturated Fat 0g		Vitamin A 10% Vitamin C 0% Calcium 2% Iron 0%			

Campbell's, V8 Diet Splash Tropical Blend

8 fl oz / 240 ml

Amount per serving	%DV	Amount per serving	%DV	Amount per serving	%DV
Calories 10		**Cholesterol** 0mg	0%	**Total Carbohydrate** 3g	1%
Total Fat 0g	0%	**Sodium** 30mg	1%	Dietary Fiber 0g	0%
Saturated Fat 0g	0%	**Protein** 0g		Sugars 2g	
Polyunsaturated Fat 0g					
Monounsaturated Fat 0g		Vitamin A 10% Vitamin C 0% Calcium 2% Iron 0%			

Campbell's, V8 Splash Berry Blend

8 fl oz / 240 ml

Amount per serving	%DV	Amount per serving	%DV	Amount per serving	%DV
Calories 70		**Cholesterol** 0mg	0%	**Total Carbohydrate** 18g	6%
Total Fat 0g	0%	**Sodium** 50mg	2%	Dietary Fiber 0g	0%
Saturated Fat 0g	0%	**Protein** 0g		Sugars 16g	
Polyunsaturated Fat 0g					
Monounsaturated Fat 0g		Vitamin A 20% Vitamin C 0% Calcium 0% Iron 0%			

Campbell's, V8 Splash Cherry Pomegranate

8 fl oz / 240 ml

Amount per serving	%DV	Amount per serving	%DV	Amount per serving	%DV
Calories 70		**Cholesterol** 0mg	0%	**Total Carbohydrate** 18g	6%
Total Fat 0g	0%	**Sodium** 50mg	2%	Dietary Fiber 0g	0%
Saturated Fat 0g	0%	**Protein** 0g		Sugars 16g	
Polyunsaturated Fat 0g					
Monounsaturated Fat 0g		Vitamin A 50% Vitamin C 0%		Calcium 0% Iron 0%	

Campbell's, V8 Splash Fruit Medley

8 fl oz / 240 ml

Amount per serving	%DV	Amount per serving	%DV	Amount per serving	%DV
Calories 70		**Cholesterol** 0mg	0%	**Total Carbohydrate** 18g	6%
Total Fat 0g	0%	**Sodium** 50mg	2%	Dietary Fiber 0g	0%
Saturated Fat 0g	0%	**Protein** 0g		Sugars 17g	
Polyunsaturated Fat 0g					
Monounsaturated Fat 0g		Vitamin A 20% Vitamin C 0%		Calcium 0% Iron 0%	

Campbell's, V8 Splash Mango Peach

8 fl oz / 240 ml

Amount per serving	%DV	Amount per serving	%DV	Amount per serving	%DV
Calories 80		**Cholesterol** 0mg	0%	**Total Carbohydrate** 20g	7%
Total Fat 0g	0%	**Sodium** 35mg	1%	Dietary Fiber 0g	0%
Saturated Fat 0g	0%	**Protein** 0g		Sugars 18g	
Polyunsaturated Fat 0g					
Monounsaturated Fat 0g		Vitamin A 20% Vitamin C 0%		Calcium 0% Iron 0%	

Campbell's, V8 Splash Strawberry Kiwi

8 fl oz / 240 ml

Amount per serving	%DV	Amount per serving	%DV	Amount per serving	%DV
Calories 70		**Cholesterol** 0mg	0%	**Total Carbohydrate** 18g	6%
Total Fat 0g	0%	**Sodium** 30mg	1%	Dietary Fiber 0g	0%
Saturated Fat 0g	0%	**Protein** 0g		Sugars 16g	
Polyunsaturated Fat 0g					
Monounsaturated Fat 0g		Vitamin A 20% Vitamin C 0%		Calcium 2% Iron 0%	

Campbell's, V8 Splash Tropical Blend

8 fl oz / 240 ml

Amount per serving	%DV	Amount per serving	%DV	Amount per serving	%DV
Calories 70		**Cholesterol** 0mg	0%	**Total Carbohydrate** 18g	6%
Total Fat 0g	0%	**Sodium** 50mg	2%	Dietary Fiber 0g	0%
Saturated Fat 0g	0%	**Protein** 0g		Sugars 16g	
Polyunsaturated Fat 0g					
Monounsaturated Fat 0g		Vitamin A 20% Vitamin C 0%		Calcium 2% Iron 0%	

Campbell's, V8 V-Fusion Smoothie, Wild Berry

8 fl oz / 240 ml

Amount per serving	%DV	Amount per serving	%DV	Amount per serving	%DV
Calories 120		**Cholesterol** 0mg	0%	**Total Carbohydrate** 29g	10%
Total Fat 0g	0%	**Sodium** 80mg	3%	Dietary Fiber 2g	8%
Saturated Fat 0g	0%	**Protein** 1g		Sugars 20g	
Polyunsaturated Fat 0g					
Monounsaturated Fat 0g		Vitamin A 15% Vitamin C 100%		Calcium 2% Iron 2%	

Campbell's, V8 V-Fusion Strawberry Banana

8 fl oz / 240 ml

Amount per serving	%DV	Amount per serving	%DV	Amount per serving	%DV
Calories 110		**Cholesterol** 0mg	0%	**Total Carbohydrate** 28g	9%
Total Fat 0g	0%	**Sodium** 70mg	3%	Dietary Fiber 0g	0%
Saturated Fat 0g	0%	**Protein** 0g		Sugars 24g	
Polyunsaturated Fat 0g					
Monounsaturated Fat 0g		Vitamin A 50% Vitamin C 100%		Calcium 2% Iron 0%	

Campbell's, V8 V-Fusion, Acai Mixed Berry

8 fl oz / 240 ml

Amount per serving	%DV	Amount per serving	%DV	Amount per serving	%DV
Calories 110		**Cholesterol** 0mg	0%	**Total Carbohydrate** 27g	9%
Total Fat 0g	0%	**Sodium** 90mg	4%	Dietary Fiber 0g	0%
Saturated Fat 0g	0%	**Protein** 0g		Sugars 24g	
Polyunsaturated Fat 0g					
Monounsaturated Fat 0g		Vitamin A 10% Vitamin C 0%		Calcium 2% Iron 0%	

Campbell's, V8 V-Fusion, Concord Grape Raspberry

8 fl oz / 240 ml

Amount per serving	%DV	Amount per serving	%DV	Amount per serving	%DV
Calories 140		**Cholesterol** 0mg	0%	**Total Carbohydrate** 33g	11%
Total Fat 0g	0%	**Sodium** 105mg	4%	Dietary Fiber 0g	0%
Saturated Fat 0g	0%	**Protein** 1g		Sugars 31g	
Polyunsaturated Fat 0g					
Monounsaturated Fat 0g		Vitamin A 10% Vitamin C 0%		Calcium 2% Iron 0%	

Campbell's, V8 V-Fusion, Cranberry Blackberry

8 fl oz / 240 ml

Amount per serving	%DV	Amount per serving	%DV	Amount per serving	%DV
Calories 100		**Cholesterol** 0mg	0%	**Total Carbohydrate** 26g	9%
Total Fat 0g	0%	**Sodium** 90mg	4%	Dietary Fiber 0g	0%
Saturated Fat 0g	0%	**Protein** 0g		Sugars 21g	
Polyunsaturated Fat 0g					
Monounsaturated Fat 0g		Vitamin A 15% Vitamin C 0%		Calcium 2% Iron 0%	

Campbell's, V8 V-Fusion, Goji Raspberry

8 fl oz / 240 ml

Amount per serving	%DV	Amount per serving	%DV	Amount per serving	%DV
Calories 110		**Cholesterol** 0mg	0%	**Total Carbohydrate** 27g	9%
Total Fat 0g	0%	**Sodium** 120mg	5%	Dietary Fiber 0g	0%
Saturated Fat 0g	0%	**Protein** 0g		Sugars 24g	
Polyunsaturated Fat 0g					
Monounsaturated Fat 0g		Vitamin A 50% Vitamin C 0%		Calcium 2% Iron 0%	

Campbell's, V8 V-Fusion, Light Acai Mixed Berry

8 fl oz / 240 ml

Amount per serving	%DV	Amount per serving	%DV	Amount per serving	%DV
Calories 110		**Cholesterol** 0mg	0%	**Total Carbohydrate** 27g	9%
Total Fat 0g	0%	**Sodium** 90mg	4%	Dietary Fiber 0g	0%
Saturated Fat 0g	0%	**Protein** 0g		Sugars 24g	
Polyunsaturated Fat 0g					
Monounsaturated Fat 0g		Vitamin A 10% Vitamin C 0%		Calcium 0% Iron 0%	

Campbell's, V8 V-Fusion, Light Concord Grape Raspberry

8 fl oz / 240 ml

Amount per serving	%DV	Amount per serving	%DV	Amount per serving	%DV
Calories 50		**Cholesterol** 0mg	0%	**Total Carbohydrate** 13g	4%
Total Fat 0g	0%	**Sodium** 65mg	3%	Dietary Fiber 0g	0%
Saturated Fat 0g	0%	**Protein** 0g		Sugars 11g	
Polyunsaturated Fat 0g					
Monounsaturated Fat 0g		Vitamin A 10% Vitamin C 0%		Calcium 2% Iron 0%	

Campbell's, V8 V-Fusion, Light Cranberry Blackberry

8 fl oz / 240 ml

Amount per serving	%DV	Amount per serving	%DV	Amount per serving	%DV
Calories 50		**Cholesterol** 0mg	0%	**Total Carbohydrate** 12g	4%
Total Fat 0g	0%	**Sodium** 70mg	3%	Dietary Fiber 0g	0%
Saturated Fat 0g	0%	**Protein** 0g		Sugars 10g	
Polyunsaturated Fat 0g					
Monounsaturated Fat 0g		Vitamin A 15% Vitamin C 0%		Calcium 2% Iron 0%	

Campbell's, V8 V-Fusion, Light Peach Mango

8 fl oz / 240 ml

Amount per serving	%DV	Amount per serving	%DV	Amount per serving	%DV
Calories 50		**Cholesterol** 0mg	0%	**Total Carbohydrate** 12g	4%
Total Fat 0g	0%	**Sodium** 60mg	2%	Dietary Fiber 0g	0%
Saturated Fat 0g	0%	**Protein** 0g		Sugars 10g	
Polyunsaturated Fat 0g					
Monounsaturated Fat 0g		Vitamin A 15% Vitamin C 0%		Calcium 2% Iron 0%	

Campbell's, V8 V-Fusion, Light Pomegranate Blueberry

8 fl oz / 240 ml

Amount per serving	%DV	Amount per serving	%DV	Amount per serving	%DV
Calories 50		**Cholesterol** 0mg	0%	**Total Carbohydrate** 13g	4%
Total Fat 0g	0%	**Sodium** 115mg	5%	Dietary Fiber 0g	0%
Saturated Fat 0g	0%	**Protein** 0g		Sugars 10g	
Polyunsaturated Fat 0g					
Monounsaturated Fat 0g		Vitamin A 15% Vitamin C 0%		Calcium 2% Iron 0%	

Campbell's, V8 V-Fusion, Light Strawberry Banana

8 fl oz / 240 ml

Amount per serving	%DV	Amount per serving	%DV	Amount per serving	%DV
Calories 50		**Cholesterol** 0mg	0%	**Total Carbohydrate** 12g	4%
Total Fat 0g	0%	**Sodium** 60mg	2%	Dietary Fiber 0g	0%
Saturated Fat 0g	0%	**Protein** 0g		Sugars 10g	
Polyunsaturated Fat 0g					
Monounsaturated Fat 0g		Vitamin A 30% Vitamin C 0%		Calcium 2% Iron 0%	

Campbell's, V8 V-Fusion, Peach Mango

8 fl oz / 240 ml

Amount per serving	%DV	Amount per serving	%DV	Amount per serving	%DV
Calories 120		**Cholesterol** 0mg	0%	**Total Carbohydrate** 28g	9%
Total Fat 0g	0%	**Sodium** 70mg	3%	Dietary Fiber 0g	0%
Saturated Fat 0g	0%	**Protein** 1g		Sugars 26g	
Polyunsaturated Fat 0g					
Monounsaturated Fat 0g		Vitamin A 20% Vitamin C 0%		Calcium 2% Iron 0%	

Campbell's, V8 V-Fusion, Pomegranate Blueberry

8 fl oz / 240 ml

Amount per serving	%DV	Amount per serving	%DV	Amount per serving	%DV
Calories 100		**Cholesterol** 0mg	0%	**Total Carbohydrate** 25g	8%
Total Fat 0g	0%	**Sodium** 95mg	4%	Dietary Fiber 0g	0%
Saturated Fat 0g	0%	**Protein** 0g		Sugars 22g	
Polyunsaturated Fat 0g					
Monounsaturated Fat 0g		Vitamin A 10% Vitamin C 0%		Calcium 2% Iron 0%	

Campbell's, V8 V-Fusion, Smoothie Mango

8 fl oz / 240 ml

Amount per serving	%DV	Amount per serving	%DV	Amount per serving	%DV
Calories 120		**Cholesterol** 0mg	0%	**Total Carbohydrate** 30g	10%
Total Fat 0g	0%	**Sodium** 70mg	3%	Dietary Fiber 2g	8%
Saturated Fat 0g	0%	**Protein** 1g		Sugars 23g	
Polyunsaturated Fat 0g					
Monounsaturated Fat 0g		Vitamin A 50% Vitamin C 100%		Calcium 2% Iron 2%	

Campbell's, V8 V-Fusion, Smoothie Strawberry Banana

8 fl oz / 240 ml

Amount per serving	%DV	Amount per serving	%DV	Amount per serving	%DV
Calories 130		**Cholesterol** 0mg	0%	**Total Carbohydrate** 32g	11%
Total Fat 0g	0%	**Sodium** 70mg	3%	Dietary Fiber 2g	8%
Saturated Fat 0g	0%	**Protein** 1g		Sugars 24g	
Polyunsaturated Fat 0g					
Monounsaturated Fat 0g		Vitamin A 50% Vitamin C 100% Calcium 2% Iron 2%			

Campbell's, V8 V-Fusion, Tropical Orange

8 fl oz / 240 ml

Amount per serving	%DV	Amount per serving	%DV	Amount per serving	%DV
Calories 120		**Cholesterol** 0mg	0%	**Total Carbohydrate** 28g	9%
Total Fat 0g	0%	**Sodium** 80mg	3%	Dietary Fiber 0g	0%
Saturated Fat 0g	0%	**Protein** 1g		Sugars 25g	
Polyunsaturated Fat 0g					
Monounsaturated Fat 0g		Vitamin A 80% Vitamin C 0% Calcium 2% Iron 2%			

Campbell's V8 Splash Juice Drinks, Berry Blend

1 serving / 8 oz / 243g

Amount per serving	%DV	Amount per serving	%DV	Amount per serving	%DV
Calories 70		**Cholesterol** 0mg	0%	**Total Carbohydrate** 18g	6%
Total Fat 0g	0%	**Sodium** 50mg	2%	Dietary Fiber 0g	0%
Saturated Fat 0g	0%	**Protein** 0g		Sugars 16g	
Polyunsaturated Fat 0g					
Monounsaturated Fat 0g		Vitamin A 20% Vitamin C 50% Calcium 0% Iron 0%			

Campbell's V8 Splash Juice Drinks, Fruit Medley

1 serving, 8 oz (243g)

Amount per serving	%DV	Amount per serving	%DV	Amount per serving	%DV
Calories 90		**Cholesterol** 0mg	0%	**Total Carbohydrate** 20g	7%
Total Fat 0g	0%	**Sodium** 70mg	3%	Dietary Fiber 0g	0%
Saturated Fat 0g	0%	**Protein** 3g		Sugars 18g	
Polyunsaturated Fat g					
Monounsaturated Fat g		Vitamin A 20% Vitamin C 100% Calcium 0% Iron 0%			

Campbell's V8 Splash Juice Drinks, Strawberry Kiwi

1 serving / 8 oz / 243g

Amount per serving	%DV	Amount per serving	%DV	Amount per serving	%DV
Calories 80		**Cholesterol** 0mg	0%	**Total Carbohydrate** 20g	7%
Total Fat 0g	0%	**Sodium** 35mg	1%	Dietary Fiber 0g	0%
Saturated Fat 0g	0%	**Protein** 0g		Sugars 18g	
Polyunsaturated Fat 0g					
Monounsaturated Fat 0g		Vitamin A 20% Vitamin C 50% Calcium 0% Iron 0%			

Cranberry Juice, Unsweetened

8 fl oz

Amount per serving	%DV	Amount per serving	%DV	Amount per serving	%DV
Calories 104		**Cholesterol** 0mg	0%	**Total Carbohydrate** 27g	9%
Total Fat 0g	0%	**Sodium** 5mg	0%	Dietary Fiber 0g	0%
Saturated Fat 0g	0%	**Protein** 0g		Sugars 27g	
Polyunsaturated Fat 0g					
Monounsaturated Fat 0g		Vitamin A 2% Vitamin C 35%		Calcium 2% Iron 3%	

Eden Foods, Apple Juice, Organic

8 oz / 240 ml

Amount per serving	%DV	Amount per serving	%DV	Amount per serving	%DV
Calories 90		**Cholesterol** 0mg	0%	**Total Carbohydrate** 24g	8%
Total Fat 0g	0%	**Sodium** 0mg	0%	Dietary Fiber 0g	0%
Saturated Fat 0g	0%	**Protein** 0g		Sugars 12g	
Polyunsaturated Fat 0g					
Monounsaturated Fat 0g		Vitamin A 0% Vitamin C 0%		Calcium 0% Iron 0%	

Eden Foods, Concord Grape Juice, Organic

8 oz / 240 ml

Amount per serving	%DV	Amount per serving	%DV	Amount per serving	%DV
Calories 150		**Cholesterol** 0mg	0%	**Total Carbohydrate** 37g	12%
Total Fat 0g	0%	**Sodium** 35mg	1%	Dietary Fiber 1g	4%
Saturated Fat 0g	0%	**Protein** 1g		Sugars 32g	
Polyunsaturated Fat 0g					
Monounsaturated Fat 0g		Vitamin A 0% Vitamin C 0%		Calcium 2% Iron 4%	

Eden Foods, Montmorency Tart Cherry Juice, Organic

8 oz / 240 ml

Amount per serving	%DV	Amount per serving	%DV	Amount per serving	%DV
Calories 140		**Cholesterol** 0mg	0%	**Total Carbohydrate** 33g	11%
Total Fat 0g	0%	**Sodium** 30mg	1%	Dietary Fiber 0g	0%
Saturated Fat 0g	0%	**Protein** 1g		Sugars 25g	
Polyunsaturated Fat 0g					
Monounsaturated Fat 0g		Vitamin A 4% Vitamin C 0%		Calcium 2% Iron 8%	

Florida's Natural Most Pulp Orange Juice

8 fl oz / 240 ml

Amount per serving	%DV	Amount per serving	%DV	Amount per serving	%DV
Calories 110		**Cholesterol** 0mg	0%	**Total Carbohydrate** 26g	9%
Total Fat 0g	0%	**Sodium** 0mg	0%	Dietary Fiber 0g	0%
Saturated Fat 0g	0%	**Protein** 2g		Sugars 22g	
Polyunsaturated Fat 0g					
Monounsaturated Fat 0g		Vitamin A 0% Vitamin C 120%		Calcium 0% Iron 0%	

Florida's Natural No Pulp Orange Juice

8 fl oz / 240 ml

Amount per serving	%DV	Amount per serving	%DV	Amount per serving	%DV
Calories 110		**Cholesterol** 0mg	0%	**Total Carbohydrate** 26g	9%
Total Fat 0g	0%	**Sodium** 0mg	0%	Dietary Fiber 0g	0%
Saturated Fat 0g	0%	**Protein** 2g		Sugars 22g	
Polyunsaturated Fat 0g					
Monounsaturated Fat 0g		Vitamin A 0% Vitamin C 120% Calcium 0% Iron 0%			

Florida's Natural with Pulp Orange Juice

8 fl oz / 240 ml

Amount per serving	%DV	Amount per serving	%DV	Amount per serving	%DV
Calories 110		**Cholesterol** 0mg	0%	**Total Carbohydrate** 26g	9%
Total Fat 0g	0%	**Sodium** 0mg	0%	Dietary Fiber 0g	0%
Saturated Fat 0g	0%	**Protein** 2g		Sugars 22g	
Polyunsaturated Fat 0g					
Monounsaturated Fat 0g		Vitamin A 0% Vitamin C 120% Calcium 0% Iron 0%			

Florida's Natural, Calcium & Vitamin D No Pulp Orange Juice

8 fl oz / 240 ml

Amount per serving	%DV	Amount per serving	%DV	Amount per serving	%DV
Calories 110		**Cholesterol** 0mg	0%	**Total Carbohydrate** 26g	9%
Total Fat 0g	0%	**Sodium** 0mg	0%	Dietary Fiber 0g	0%
Saturated Fat 0g	0%	**Protein** 2g		Sugars 22g	
Polyunsaturated Fat 0g					
Monounsaturated Fat 0g		Vitamin A 0% Vitamin C 120% Calcium 35% Iron 0%			

Florida's Natural, Calcium & Vitamin D with Pulp Orange Juice

8 fl oz / 240 ml

Amount per serving	%DV	Amount per serving	%DV	Amount per serving	%DV
Calories 110		**Cholesterol** 0mg	0%	**Total Carbohydrate** 26g	9%
Total Fat 0g	0%	**Sodium** 0mg	0%	Dietary Fiber 0g	0%
Saturated Fat 0g	0%	**Protein** 2g		Sugars 22g	
Polyunsaturated Fat 0g					
Monounsaturated Fat 0g		Vitamin A 0% Vitamin C 120% Calcium 35% Iron 0%			

Grapefruit Juice, Pink, Raw

1 cup / 247g

Amount per serving	%DV	Amount per serving	%DV	Amount per serving	%DV
Calories 96		**Cholesterol** 0mg	0%	**Total Carbohydrate** 18g	6%
Total Fat 0g	0%	**Sodium** 2mg	0%	Dietary Fiber 0g	0%
Saturated Fat 0g	0%	**Protein** 1g		Sugars 0g	
Polyunsaturated Fat 0g					
Monounsaturated Fat 0g		Vitamin A 22% Vitamin C 156% Calcium 2% Iron 3%			

Hansen's Natural, Aguas Frescas Juice, Jamaica

8 fl oz / 237 ml

Amount per serving	%DV	Amount per serving	%DV	Amount per serving	%DV
Calories 70		**Cholesterol** 0mg	0%	**Total Carbohydrate** 18g	6%
Total Fat 0g	0%	**Sodium** 0mg	0%	Dietary Fiber 0g	0%
Saturated Fat 0g	0%	**Protein** 0g		Sugars 18g	
Polyunsaturated Fat 0g					
Monounsaturated Fat 0g		Vitamin A 0% Vitamin C 0%		Calcium 0% Iron 0%	

Hansen's Natural, Aguas Frescas Juice, Tamarindo

8 fl oz / 237 ml

Amount per serving	%DV	Amount per serving	%DV	Amount per serving	%DV
Calories 90		**Cholesterol** 0mg	0%	**Total Carbohydrate** 23g	8%
Total Fat 0g	0%	**Sodium** 75mg	3%	Dietary Fiber 0g	0%
Saturated Fat 0g	0%	**Protein** 0g		Sugars 22g	
Polyunsaturated Fat 0g					
Monounsaturated Fat 0g		Vitamin A 0% Vitamin C 0%		Calcium 0% Iron 0%	

Hansen's Natural, Junior Juice, Apple

1 package / 125 ml

Amount per serving	%DV	Amount per serving	%DV	Amount per serving	%DV
Calories 60		**Cholesterol** 0mg	0%	**Total Carbohydrate** 15g	5%
Total Fat 0g	0%	**Sodium** 5mg	0%	Dietary Fiber 0g	0%
Saturated Fat 0g	0%	**Protein** 0g		Sugars 14g	
Polyunsaturated Fat 0g					
Monounsaturated Fat 0g		Vitamin A 0% Vitamin C 100%		Calcium 10% Iron 0%	

Hansen's Natural, Junior Juice, Apple Grape

1 package / 125 ml

Amount per serving	%DV	Amount per serving	%DV	Amount per serving	%DV
Calories 60		**Cholesterol** 0mg	0%	**Total Carbohydrate** 16g	5%
Total Fat 0g	0%	**Sodium** 5mg	0%	Dietary Fiber 0g	0%
Saturated Fat 0g	0%	**Protein** 0g		Sugars 16g	
Polyunsaturated Fat 0g					
Monounsaturated Fat 0g		Vitamin A 0% Vitamin C 100%		Calcium 10% Iron 0%	

Hansen's Natural, Junior Juice, Fruit Punch

1 package / 125 ml

Amount per serving	%DV	Amount per serving	%DV	Amount per serving	%DV
Calories 60		**Cholesterol** 0mg	0%	**Total Carbohydrate** 15g	5%
Total Fat 0g	0%	**Sodium** 5mg	0%	Dietary Fiber 0g	0%
Saturated Fat 0g	0%	**Protein** 0g		Sugars 14g	
Polyunsaturated Fat 0g					
Monounsaturated Fat 0g		Vitamin A 0% Vitamin C 100%		Calcium 10% Iron 0%	

Hansen's Natural, Junior Juice, Island Splash

8 fl oz / 240 ml

Amount per serving	%DV	Amount per serving	%DV	Amount per serving	%DV
Calories 110		Cholesterol 0mg	0%	Total Carbohydrate 29g	10%
Total Fat 0g	0%	Sodium 5mg	0%	Dietary Fiber 0g	0%
Saturated Fat 0g	0%	Protein 0g		Sugars 29g	
Polyunsaturated Fat 0g					
Monounsaturated Fat 0g		Vitamin A 0%	Vitamin C 100%	Calcium 18%	Iron 4%

Hansen's Natural, Junior Juice, Mixed Fruit

1 package / 125 ml

Amount per serving	%DV	Amount per serving	%DV	Amount per serving	%DV
Calories 60		Cholesterol 0mg	0%	Total Carbohydrate 15g	5%
Total Fat 0g	0%	Sodium 5mg	0%	Dietary Fiber 0g	0%
Saturated Fat 0g	0%	Protein 0g		Sugars 14g	
Polyunsaturated Fat 0g					
Monounsaturated Fat 0g		Vitamin A 0%	Vitamin C 100%	Calcium 10%	Iron 0%

Hansen's Natural, Organic Junior Juice, Apple

1 package / 125 ml

Amount per serving	%DV	Amount per serving	%DV	Amount per serving	%DV
Calories 60		Cholesterol 0mg	0%	Total Carbohydrate 15g	5%
Total Fat 0g	0%	Sodium 10mg	0%	Dietary Fiber 0g	0%
Saturated Fat 0g	0%	Protein 0g		Sugars 15g	
Polyunsaturated Fat 0g					
Monounsaturated Fat 0g		Vitamin A 0%	Vitamin C 100%	Calcium 0%	Iron 2%

Hansen's Natural, Organic Junior Juice, Berry Medley

1 package / 125 ml

Amount per serving	%DV	Amount per serving	%DV	Amount per serving	%DV
Calories 60		Cholesterol 0mg	0%	Total Carbohydrate 15g	5%
Total Fat 0g	0%	Sodium 10mg	0%	Dietary Fiber 0g	0%
Saturated Fat 0g	0%	Protein 0g		Sugars 15g	
Polyunsaturated Fat 0g					
Monounsaturated Fat 0g		Vitamin A 0%	Vitamin C 100%	Calcium 0%	Iron 2%

Kedem Concord Grape Juice - 100% Juice - No Sugar Added

8 fl oz

Amount per serving	%DV	Amount per serving	%DV	Amount per serving	%DV
Calories 150		Cholesterol 0mg	0%	Total Carbohydrate 37g	12%
Total Fat 0g	0%	Sodium 20mg	1%	Dietary Fiber 0g	0%
Saturated Fat 0g	0%	Protein 0g		Sugars 37g	
Polyunsaturated Fat 0g					
Monounsaturated Fat 0g		Vitamin A 0%	Vitamin C 20%	Calcium 0%	Iron 0%

Lime Juice, Canned or Bottled, Unsweetened

1 cup / 246g

Amount per serving	%DV	Amount per serving	%DV	Amount per serving	%DV
Calories 52		**Cholesterol** 0mg	0%	**Total Carbohydrate** 16g	5%
Total Fat 1g	2%	**Sodium** 39mg	2%	Dietary Fiber 1g	4%
Saturated Fat 0g	0%	**Protein** 1g		Sugars 3g	
Polyunsaturated Fat 0g					
Monounsaturated Fat 0g		Vitamin A 1% Vitamin C 26%		Calcium 3% Iron 3%	

Minute Maid Premium Country Style Orange Juice

8 fl oz / 240 ml

Amount per serving	%DV	Amount per serving	%DV	Amount per serving	%DV
Calories 110		**Cholesterol** 0mg	0%	**Total Carbohydrate** 27g	9%
Total Fat 0g	0%	**Sodium** 15mg	1%	Dietary Fiber 0g	0%
Saturated Fat 0g	0%	**Protein** 2g		Sugars 24g	
Polyunsaturated Fat 0g					
Monounsaturated Fat 0g		Vitamin A 0% Vitamin C 120%		Calcium 2% Iron 0%	

Minute Maid Premium Home Squeezed Style Calcium + Vitamin D Orange Juice

8 fl oz / 240 ml

Amount per serving	%DV	Amount per serving	%DV	Amount per serving	%DV
Calories 110		**Cholesterol** 0mg	0%	**Total Carbohydrate** 27g	9%
Total Fat 0g	0%	**Sodium** 15mg	1%	Dietary Fiber 0g	0%
Saturated Fat 0g	0%	**Protein** 2g		Sugars 24g	
Polyunsaturated Fat 0g					
Monounsaturated Fat 0g		Vitamin A 0% Vitamin C 120%		Calcium 35% Iron 0%	

Minute Maid, Heart Wise Orange Juice

8 fl oz / 240 ml

Amount per serving	%DV	Amount per serving	%DV	Amount per serving	%DV
Calories 110		**Cholesterol** 0mg	0%	**Total Carbohydrate** 27g	9%
Total Fat 0g	0%	**Sodium** 20mg	1%	Dietary Fiber 0g	0%
Saturated Fat 0g	0%	**Protein** 2g		Sugars 24g	
Polyunsaturated Fat 0g					
Monounsaturated Fat 0g		Vitamin A 0% Vitamin C 120%		Calcium 2% Iron 0%	

Minute Maid, Premium Low Acid Orange Juice

8 fl oz / 240 ml

Amount per serving	%DV	Amount per serving	%DV	Amount per serving	%DV
Calories 110		**Cholesterol** 0mg	0%	**Total Carbohydrate** 27g	9%
Total Fat 0g	0%	**Sodium** 20mg	1%	Dietary Fiber 0g	0%
Saturated Fat 0g	0%	**Protein** 2g		Sugars 24g	
Polyunsaturated Fat 0g					
Monounsaturated Fat 0g		Vitamin A 0% Vitamin C 120%		Calcium 2% Iron 0%	

Minute Maid, Premium Pulp Free Orange Juice

8 fl oz / 240 ml

Amount per serving	%DV	Amount per serving	%DV	Amount per serving	%DV
Calories 110		**Cholesterol** 0mg	0%	**Total Carbohydrate** 27g	9%
Total Fat 0g	0%	**Sodium** 15mg	1%	Dietary Fiber 0g	0%
Saturated Fat 0g	0%	**Protein** 2g		Sugars 24g	
Polyunsaturated Fat 0g					
Monounsaturated Fat 0g		Vitamin A 0% Vitamin C 130% Calcium 2% Iron 0%			

Minute Maid, Pure Squeezed No Pulp

8 fl oz / 240 ml

Amount per serving	%DV	Amount per serving	%DV	Amount per serving	%DV
Calories 110		**Cholesterol** 0mg	0%	**Total Carbohydrate** 26g	9%
Total Fat 0g	0%	**Sodium** 0mg	0%	Dietary Fiber 0g	0%
Saturated Fat 0g	0%	**Protein** 2g		Sugars 22g	
Polyunsaturated Fat 0g					
Monounsaturated Fat 0g		Vitamin A 0% Vitamin C 100% Calcium 2% Iron 0%			

Minute Maid, Pure Squeezed No Pulp with Calcium & Vitamin D

8 fl oz / 240 ml

Amount per serving	%DV	Amount per serving	%DV	Amount per serving	%DV
Calories 110		**Cholesterol** 0mg	0%	**Total Carbohydrate** 26g	9%
Total Fat 0g	0%	**Sodium** 0mg	0%	Dietary Fiber 0g	0%
Saturated Fat 0g	0%	**Protein** 2g		Sugars 22g	
Polyunsaturated Fat 0g					
Monounsaturated Fat 0g		Vitamin A 0% Vitamin C 100% Calcium 35% Iron 0%			

Minute Maid, Pure Squeezed Some Pulp

8 fl oz / 240 ml

Amount per serving	%DV	Amount per serving	%DV	Amount per serving	%DV
Calories 110		**Cholesterol** 0mg	0%	**Total Carbohydrate** 26g	9%
Total Fat 0g	0%	**Sodium** 0mg	0%	Dietary Fiber 0g	0%
Saturated Fat 0g	0%	**Protein** 2g		Sugars 22g	
Polyunsaturated Fat 0g					
Monounsaturated Fat 0g		Vitamin A 0% Vitamin C 100% Calcium 2% Iron 0%			

Old Orchard 100% Grape Juice

8 fl oz

Amount per serving	%DV	Amount per serving	%DV	Amount per serving	%DV
Calories 160		**Cholesterol** 0mg	0%	**Total Carbohydrate** 41g	14%
Total Fat 0g	0%	**Sodium** 30mg	1%	Dietary Fiber 0g	0%
Saturated Fat 0g	0%	**Protein** 0g		Sugars 39g	
Polyunsaturated Fat 0g					
Monounsaturated Fat 0g		Vitamin A 0% Vitamin C 120% Calcium 0% Iron 0%			

Old Orchard 100% Grape Juice - Frozen Concentrate

8 fl oz

Amount per serving	%DV	Amount per serving	%DV	Amount per serving	%DV
Calories 160		**Cholesterol** 0mg	0%	**Total Carbohydrate** 42g	14%
Total Fat 0g	0%	**Sodium** 30mg	1%	Dietary Fiber 0g	0%
Saturated Fat 0g	0%	**Protein** 0g		Sugars 40g	
Polyunsaturated Fat 0g					
Monounsaturated Fat 0g		Vitamin A 0%	Vitamin C 120%	Calcium 0%	Iron 0%

Pom Wonderful, Pomegrante 100% Juice

8 fl oz

Amount per serving	%DV	Amount per serving	%DV	Amount per serving	%DV
Calories 150		**Cholesterol** 0mg	0%	**Total Carbohydrate** 36g	12%
Total Fat 0g	0%	**Sodium** 0mg	0%	Dietary Fiber 0g	0%
Saturated Fat 0g	0%	**Protein** 0g		Sugars 32g	
Polyunsaturated Fat 0g					
Monounsaturated Fat 0g		Vitamin A 1%	Vitamin C 1%	Calcium 1%	Iron 0%

Sambazon, Acai Berry + Yerba Mate + Guarana

8 fl oz / 240 ml

Amount per serving	%DV	Amount per serving	%DV	Amount per serving	%DV
Calories 150		**Cholesterol** 0mg	0%	**Total Carbohydrate** 32g	11%
Total Fat 2g	3%	**Sodium** 20mg	1%	Dietary Fiber 1g	4%
Saturated Fat 0.5g	2%	**Protein** 1g		Sugars 28g	
Polyunsaturated Fat 0g					
Monounsaturated Fat 0g		Vitamin A 6%	Vitamin C 0%	Calcium 4%	Iron 2%

Sambazon, Acai with Blueberry + Pomegranate

8 fl oz / 240 ml

Amount per serving	%DV	Amount per serving	%DV	Amount per serving	%DV
Calories 130		**Cholesterol** 0mg	0%	**Total Carbohydrate** 28g	9%
Total Fat 2g	3%	**Sodium** 25mg	1%	Dietary Fiber 1g	4%
Saturated Fat 0.5g	2%	**Protein** 1g		Sugars 22g	
Polyunsaturated Fat 0g					
Monounsaturated Fat 0g		Vitamin A 6%	Vitamin C 100%	Calcium 2%	Iron 2%

Sambazon, Original Acai Juice

8 fl oz / 240 ml

Amount per serving	%DV	Amount per serving	%DV	Amount per serving	%DV
Calories 140		**Cholesterol** 0mg	0%	**Total Carbohydrate** 28g	9%
Total Fat 3g	5%	**Sodium** 65mg	3%	Dietary Fiber 1g	4%
Saturated Fat 1g	5%	**Protein** 1g		Sugars 24g	
Polyunsaturated Fat 0g					
Monounsaturated Fat 0g		Vitamin A 6%	Vitamin C 0%	Calcium 6%	Iron 4%

Simply Orange Original Pulp Free 100% Orange Juice

8 fl oz / 240 mL

Amount per serving	%DV	Amount per serving	%DV	Amount per serving	%DV
Calories 110		**Cholesterol** 0mg	0%	**Total Carbohydrate** 26g	9%
Total Fat 0g	0%	**Sodium** 0mg	0%	Dietary Fiber 0g	0%
Saturated Fat 0g	0%	**Protein** 2g		Sugars 23g	
Polyunsaturated Fat 0g					
Monounsaturated Fat 0g		Vitamin A 0% Vitamin C 100% Calcium 2% Iron 0%			

Snapple, 100% Juiced Fruit Punch

11.5 fl oz

Amount per serving	%DV	Amount per serving	%DV	Amount per serving	%DV
Calories 170		**Cholesterol** 0mg	0%	**Total Carbohydrate** 42g	14%
Total Fat 0g	0%	**Sodium** 30mg	1%	Dietary Fiber 0g	0%
Saturated Fat 0g	0%	**Protein** 0g		Sugars 40g	
Polyunsaturated Fat 0g					
Monounsaturated Fat 0g		Vitamin A 15% Vitamin C 100% Calcium 15% Iron 6%			

Snapple, 100% Juiced Grape

11.5 fl oz

Amount per serving	%DV	Amount per serving	%DV	Amount per serving	%DV
Calories 170		**Cholesterol** 0mg	0%	**Total Carbohydrate** 42g	14%
Total Fat 0g	0%	**Sodium** 30mg	1%	Dietary Fiber 0g	0%
Saturated Fat 0g	0%	**Protein** 0g		Sugars 41g	
Polyunsaturated Fat 0g					
Monounsaturated Fat 0g		Vitamin A 15% Vitamin C 100% Calcium 15% Iron 6%			

Snapple, 100% Juiced Green Apple

11.5 fl oz

Amount per serving	%DV	Amount per serving	%DV	Amount per serving	%DV
Calories 170		**Cholesterol** 0mg	0%	**Total Carbohydrate** 41g	14%
Total Fat 0g	0%	**Sodium** 30mg	1%	Dietary Fiber 0g	0%
Saturated Fat 0g	0%	**Protein** 0g		Sugars 39g	
Polyunsaturated Fat 0g					
Monounsaturated Fat 0g		Vitamin A 15% Vitamin C 100% Calcium 15% Iron 6%			

Tropicana Pure Premium, 100% Florida Orange Juice, Lots Pulp, Calc & Vit D

8 fl oz / 240 ml

Amount per serving	%DV	Amount per serving	%DV	Amount per serving	%DV
Calories 110		**Cholesterol** 0mg	0%	**Total Carbohydrate** 26g	9%
Total Fat 0g	0%	**Sodium** 0mg	0%	Dietary Fiber 0g	0%
Saturated Fat 0g	0%	**Protein** 2g		Sugars 22g	
Polyunsaturated Fat 0g					
Monounsaturated Fat 0g		Vitamin A 0% Vitamin C 120% Calcium 35% Iron 0%			

Tropicana Pure Premium, 100% Florida Orange Juice, No Pulp, Calc + Vit D

8 fl oz / 240 ml

Amount per serving	%DV	Amount per serving	%DV	Amount per serving	%DV
Calories 110		**Cholesterol** 0mg	0%	**Total Carbohydrate** 25g	8%
Total Fat 0g	0%	**Sodium** 0mg	0%	Dietary Fiber g	%
Saturated Fat 0g	0%	**Protein** 2g		Sugars 22g	
Polyunsaturated Fat 0g					
Monounsaturated Fat 0g		Vitamin A 0% Vitamin C 120% Calcium 35% Iron 0%			

Tropicana Pure Premium, 100% Pure Florida Orange Juice

8 fl oz / 240 ml

Amount per serving	%DV	Amount per serving	%DV	Amount per serving	%DV
Calories 110		**Cholesterol** 0mg	0%	**Total Carbohydrate** 26g	9%
Total Fat 0g	0%	**Sodium** 0mg	0%	Dietary Fiber 0g	0%
Saturated Fat 0g	0%	**Protein** 2g		Sugars 22g	
Polyunsaturated Fat 0g					
Monounsaturated Fat 0g		Vitamin A 0% Vitamin C 120% Calcium 2% Iron 0%			

Tropicana Pure Premium, 100% Pure Florida Orange Juice, Grovestand, Lots of Pulp

8 fl oz / 240 ml

Amount per serving	%DV	Amount per serving	%DV	Amount per serving	%DV
Calories 110		**Cholesterol** 0mg	0%	**Total Carbohydrate** 26g	9%
Total Fat 0g	0%	**Sodium** 0mg	0%	Dietary Fiber 0g	0%
Saturated Fat 0g	0%	**Protein** 2g		Sugars 22g	
Polyunsaturated Fat 0g					
Monounsaturated Fat 0g		Vitamin A 0% Vitamin C 120% Calcium 2% Iron 0%			

Tropicana Pure Premium, 100% Pure Florida Orange Juice, Healthy Kids

8 fl oz / 240 ml

Amount per serving	%DV	Amount per serving	%DV	Amount per serving	%DV
Calories 110		**Cholesterol** 0mg	0%	**Total Carbohydrate** 26g	9%
Total Fat 0g	0%	**Sodium** 0mg	0%	Dietary Fiber 0g	0%
Saturated Fat 0g	0%	**Protein** 2g		Sugars 22g	
Polyunsaturated Ful 0g					
Monounsaturated Fat 0g		Vitamin A 20% Vitamin C 120% Calcium 35% Iron 0%			

Tropicana Pure Premium, 100% Pure Florida Orange Juice, Some Pulp

8 fl oz / 240 ml

Amount per serving	%DV	Amount per serving	%DV	Amount per serving	%DV
Calories 110		**Cholesterol** 0mg	0%	**Total Carbohydrate** 26g	9%
Total Fat 0g	0%	**Sodium** 0mg	0%	Dietary Fiber 0g	0%
Saturated Fat 0g	0%	**Protein** 2g		Sugars 22g	
Polyunsaturated Fat 0g					
Monounsaturated Fat 0g		Vitamin A 0% Vitamin C 120% Calcium 2% Iron 0%			

Tropicana Tropics, 100% Juice Orange Pineapple

8 fl oz / 240 ml

Amount per serving	%DV	Amount per serving	%DV	Amount per serving	%DV
Calories 120		**Cholesterol** 0mg	0%	**Total Carbohydrate** 30g	10%
Total Fat 0g	0%	**Sodium** 10mg	0%	Dietary Fiber 0g	0%
Saturated Fat 0g	0%	**Protein** 1g		Sugars 26g	
Polyunsaturated Fat 0g					
Monounsaturated Fat 0g		Vitamin A 0%	Vitamin C 100%	Calcium 2%	Iron 0%

Tropicana Tropics, 100% Juice Orange Strawberry Banana

8 fl oz / 240 ml

Amount per serving	%DV	Amount per serving	%DV	Amount per serving	%DV
Calories 120		**Cholesterol** 0mg	0%	**Total Carbohydrate** 29g	10%
Total Fat 0g	0%	**Sodium** 10mg	0%	Dietary Fiber 0g	0%
Saturated Fat 0g	0%	**Protein** 1g		Sugars 27g	
Polyunsaturated Fat 0g					
Monounsaturated Fat 0g		Vitamin A 0%	Vitamin C 100%	Calcium 0%	Iron 0%

Welch's, 100% Black Cherry Concord Grape Juice

8 fl oz

Amount per serving	%DV	Amount per serving	%DV	Amount per serving	%DV
Calories 170		**Cholesterol** 0mg	0%	**Total Carbohydrate** 42g	14%
Total Fat 0g	0%	**Sodium** 20mg	1%	Dietary Fiber 0g	0%
Saturated Fat 0g	0%	**Protein** 0g		Sugars 41g	
Polyunsaturated Fat 0g					
Monounsaturated Fat 0g		Vitamin A 0%	Vitamin C 100%	Calcium 0%	Iron 0%

Welch's, 100% Grape Juice

8 fl oz

Amount per serving	%DV	Amount per serving	%DV	Amount per serving	%DV
Calories 140		**Cholesterol** 0mg	0%	**Total Carbohydrate** 38g	13%
Total Fat 0g	0%	**Sodium** 15mg	1%	Dietary Fiber 0g	0%
Saturated Fat 0g	0%	**Protein** 1g		Sugars 36g	
Polyunsaturated Fat 0g					
Monounsaturated Fat 0g		Vitamin A 120%	Vitamin C 0%	Calcium 2%	Iron 0%

Welch's, 100% Grape Juice with Calcium

8 fl oz

Amount per serving	%DV	Amount per serving	%DV	Amount per serving	%DV
Calories 140		**Cholesterol** 0mg	0%	**Total Carbohydrate** 38g	13%
Total Fat 0g	0%	**Sodium** 15mg	1%	Dietary Fiber 0g	0%
Saturated Fat 0g	0%	**Protein** 1g		Sugars 36g	
Polyunsaturated Fat 0g					
Monounsaturated Fat 0g		Vitamin A 0%	Vitamin C 100%	Calcium 10%	Iron 0%

Welch's, 100% Grape Juice with Fiber

8 fl oz

Amount per serving	%DV	Amount per serving	%DV	Amount per serving	%DV
Calories 150		**Cholesterol** 0mg	0%	**Total Carbohydrate** 41g	14%
Total Fat 0g	0%	**Sodium** 15mg	1%	Dietary Fiber 3g	12%
Saturated Fat 0g	0%	**Protein** 1g		Sugars 36g	
Polyunsaturated Fat 0g					
Monounsaturated Fat 0g		Vitamin A 0% Vitamin C 100% Calcium 2% Iron 0%			

Welch's, 100% White Grape Cherry Juice

8 fl oz

Amount per serving	%DV	Amount per serving	%DV	Amount per serving	%DV
Calories 140		**Cholesterol** 0mg	0%	**Total Carbohydrate** 35g	12%
Total Fat 0g	0%	**Sodium** 15mg	1%	Dietary Fiber 0g	0%
Saturated Fat 0g	0%	**Protein** 0g		Sugars 33g	
Polyunsaturated Fat 0g					
Monounsaturated Fat 0g		Vitamin A 0% Vitamin C 100% Calcium 0% Iron 0%			

Welch's, 100% White Grape Juice

8 fl oz

Amount per serving	%DV	Amount per serving	%DV	Amount per serving	%DV
Calories 160		**Cholesterol** 0mg	0%	**Total Carbohydrate** 39g	13%
Total Fat 0g	0%	**Sodium** 20mg	1%	Dietary Fiber 0g	0%
Saturated Fat 0g	0%	**Protein** 0g		Sugars 38g	
Polyunsaturated Fat 0g					
Monounsaturated Fat 0g		Vitamin A 0% Vitamin C 120% Calcium 0% Iron 0%			

Welch's, 100% White Grape Peach Juice

8 fl oz

Amount per serving	%DV	Amount per serving	%DV	Amount per serving	%DV
Calories 160		**Cholesterol** 0mg	0%	**Total Carbohydrate** 39g	13%
Total Fat 0g	0%	**Sodium** 15mg	1%	Dietary Fiber 0g	0%
Saturated Fat 0g	0%	**Protein** 0g		Sugars 37g	
Polyunsaturated Fat 0g					
Monounsaturated Fat 0g		Vitamin A 0% Vitamin C 100% Calcium 0% Iron 0%			

Fruits

Apples, Raw, with Skin

1 cup, slices / 109g

Amount per serving	%DV	Amount per serving	%DV	Amount per serving	%DV
Calories 57		**Cholesterol** 0mg	0%	**Total Carbohydrate** 15g	5%
Total Fat 0g	0%	**Sodium** 1mg	0%	Dietary Fiber 3g	12%
Saturated Fat 0g	0%	**Protein** 0g		Sugars 11g	
Polyunsaturated Fat 0g					
Monounsaturated Fat 0g		Vitamin A 1% Vitamin C 8% Calcium 1% Iron 1%			

Apples, Raw, without Skin

1 large / 3-1/4" diameter / 216g

Amount per serving	%DV	Amount per serving	%DV	Amount per serving	%DV
Calories 104		**Cholesterol** 0mg	0%	**Total Carbohydrate** 28g	9%
Total Fat 0g	0%	**Sodium** 0mg	0%	Dietary Fiber 3g	12%
Saturated Fat 0g	0%	**Protein** 1g		Sugars 22g	
Polyunsaturated Fat 0g					
Monounsaturated Fat 0g		Vitamin A 2%	Vitamin C 14%	Calcium 1% · Iron 1%	

Apricots, Raw

1 cup, sliced / 165g

Amount per serving	%DV	Amount per serving	%DV	Amount per serving	%DV
Calories 79		**Cholesterol** 0mg	0%	**Total Carbohydrate** 18.5g	6%
Total Fat 0.5g	1%	**Sodium** 1.5mg	0%	Dietary Fiber 3.5g	14%
Saturated Fat 0g	0%	**Protein** 2.5g		Sugars 15g	
Polyunsaturated Fat 0g					
Monounsaturated Fat 0.5g		Vitamin A 64%	Vitamin C 27%	Calcium 2%	Iron 4%

Bananas, Raw

1 cup, sliced / 150g

Amount per serving	%DV	Amount per serving	%DV	Amount per serving	%DV
Calories 133.5		**Cholesterol** 0mg	0%	**Total Carbohydrate** 34.5g	12%
Total Fat 0.5g	1%	**Sodium** 1.5mg	0%	Dietary Fiber 4g	16%
Saturated Fat 0g	0%	**Protein** 1.5g		Sugars 18.5g	
Polyunsaturated Fat 0g					
Monounsaturated Fat 0g		Vitamin A 96%	Vitamin C 13%	Calcium 7.5%	Iron 0.5%

Blackberries, Frozen, Unsweetened

1 cup, unthawed / 151g

Amount per serving	%DV	Amount per serving	%DV	Amount per serving	%DV
Calories 97		**Cholesterol** 0mg	0%	**Total Carbohydrate** 23.7g	8%
Total Fat 0.6g	1%	**Sodium** 2mg	0%	Dietary Fiber 7.5g	30%
Saturated Fat 0g	0%	**Protein** 1.8g		Sugars 16.1g	
Polyunsaturated Fat 0.4g					
Monounsaturated Fat 0.1g		Vitamin A 3%	Vitamin C 8%	Calcium 4%	Iron 7%

Blackberries, Raw

1 cup / 144g

Amount per serving	%DV	Amount per serving	%DV	Amount per serving	%DV
Calories 62		**Cholesterol** 0mg	0%	**Total Carbohydrate** 15g	5%
Total Fat 1g	2%	**Sodium** 1mg	0%	Dietary Fiber 8g	31%
Saturated Fat 0g	0%	**Protein** 2g		Sugars 7g	
Polyunsaturated Fat 0g					
Monounsaturated Fat 0g		Vitamin A 6%	Vitamin C 50%	Calcium 4%	Iron 5%

Blueberries, Raw

50 berries / 68g

Amount per serving	%DV	Amount per serving	%DV	Amount per serving	%DV
Calories 39		**Cholesterol** 0mg	0%	**Total Carbohydrate** 10g	3%
Total Fat 0g	0%	**Sodium** 0.5mg	0%	Dietary Fiber 1.5g	6%
Saturated Fat 0g	0%	**Protein** 0.5g		Sugars 7g	
Polyunsaturated Fat 0g					
Monounsaturated Fat 0g		Vitamin A 36.5%	Vitamin C 6.5%	Calcium 4%	Iron 0%

Boysenberries, Frozen, Unsweetened

1 package, 10 oz / 284g

Amount per serving	%DV	Amount per serving	%DV	Amount per serving	%DV
Calories 142		**Cholesterol** 0mg	0%	**Total Carbohydrate** 35g	12%
Total Fat 1g	1%	**Sodium** 3mg	0%	Dietary Fiber 15g	60%
Saturated Fat 0g	0%	**Protein** 3g		Sugars 20g	
Polyunsaturated Fat 0.5g					
Monounsaturated Fat 0g		Vitamin A 4%	Vitamin C 15%	Calcium 8%	Iron 13%

California Dates - Deglet Noor Variety

5-6 dates / 40g

Amount per serving	%DV	Amount per serving	%DV	Amount per serving	%DV
Calories 120		**Cholesterol** 0mg	0%	**Total Carbohydrate** 30g	10%
Total Fat 0g	0%	**Sodium** 0mg	0%	Dietary Fiber 3g	12%
Saturated Fat 0g	0%	**Protein** 1g		Sugars 25g	
Polyunsaturated Fat 0g					
Monounsaturated Fat 0g		Vitamin A 0%	Vitamin C 0%	Calcium 0%	Iron 2%

Chayote, Fruit, Cooked, Boiled, Drained, without Salt

1 cup, 1″ pieces / 160g

Amount per serving	%DV	Amount per serving	%DV	Amount per serving	%DV
Calories 38		**Cholesterol** 0mg	0%	**Total Carbohydrate** 8g	3%
Total Fat 1g	2%	**Sodium** 2mg	0%	Dietary Fiber 4g	16%
Saturated Fat 0g	0%	**Protein** 1g		Sugars 0g	
Polyunsaturated Fat 0g					
Monounsaturated Fat 0g		Vitamin A 2%	Vitamin C 21%	Calcium 2%	Iron 2%

Cherimoya, Raw

1 cup, pieces / 160g

Amount per serving	%DV	Amount per serving	%DV	Amount per serving	%DV
Calories 120		**Cholesterol** 0mg	0%	**Total Carbohydrate** 28.5g	10%
Total Fat 1g	2%	**Sodium** 11mg	0%	Dietary Fiber 5g	20%
Saturated Fat 0.5g	3%	**Protein** 2.5g		Sugars 20.5g	
Polyunsaturated Fat 0.5g					
Monounsaturated Fat 0g		Vitamin A 8%	Vitamin C 20%	Calcium 16%	Iron 0.5%

Cherries, Sour, Red, Frozen, Unsweetened

1 cup, unthawed (155g)

Amount per serving	%DV	Amount per serving	%DV	Amount per serving	%DV
Calories 71		**Cholesterol** 0mg	0%	**Total Carbohydrate** 17g	6%
Total Fat 1g	2%	**Sodium** 2mg	0%	Dietary Fiber 2g	10%
Saturated Fat 0g	0%	**Protein** 1g		Sugars 14g	
Polyunsaturated Fat 0g					
Monounsaturated Fat 0g		Vitamin A 27% Vitamin C 4%		Calcium 2% Iron 5%	

Cherries, Sour, Red, Raw

1 cup, without pits (155g)

Amount per serving	%DV	Amount per serving	%DV	Amount per serving	%DV
Calories 77		**Cholesterol** 0mg	0%	**Total Carbohydrate** 19g	6%
Total Fat 0g	0%	**Sodium** 5mg	0%	Dietary Fiber 2g	10%
Saturated Fat 0g	0%	**Protein** 2g		Sugars 13g	
Polyunsaturated Fat 0g					
Monounsaturated Fat 0g		Vitamin A 40% Vitamin C 26%		Calcium 2% Iron 3%	

Cherries, Sweet, Raw

1 cup, without pits / 154g

Amount per serving	%DV	Amount per serving	%DV	Amount per serving	%DV
Calories 97		**Cholesterol** 0mg	0%	**Total Carbohydrate** 25g	8%
Total Fat 0g	0%	**Sodium** 0mg	0%	Dietary Fiber 3g	12%
Saturated Fat 0g	0%	**Protein** 2g		Sugars 20g	
Polyunsaturated Fat 0g					
Monounsaturated Fat 0g		Vitamin A 2% Vitamin C 18%		Calcium 2% Iron 3%	

Clementines, Raw

1 fruit / 74g

Amount per serving	%DV	Amount per serving	%DV	Amount per serving	%DV
Calories 35		**Cholesterol** 0mg	0%	**Total Carbohydrate** 9g	3%
Total Fat 0g	0%	**Sodium** 1mg	0%	Dietary Fiber 1g	4%
Saturated Fat 0g	0%	**Protein** 1g		Sugars 7g	
Polyunsaturated Fat 0g					
Monounsaturated Fat 0g		Vitamin A 0% Vitamin C 60%		Calcium 2% Iron 1%	

Cranberries, Raw

1 cup, whole / 100g

Amount per serving	%DV	Amount per serving	%DV	Amount per serving	%DV
Calories 46		**Cholesterol** 0mg	0%	**Total Carbohydrate** 12g	4%
Total Fat 0g	0%	**Sodium** 2mg	0%	Dietary Fiber 5g	20%
Saturated Fat 0g	0%	**Protein** 0g		Sugars 4g	
Polyunsaturated Fat 0g					
Monounsaturated Fat 0g		Vitamin A 1% Vitamin C 22%		Calcium 1% Iron 1%	

Currants, European Black, Raw

1 cup / 112g

Amount per serving	%DV	Amount per serving	%DV	Amount per serving	%DV
Calories 71		**Cholesterol** 0mg	0%	**Total Carbohydrate** 17g	6%
Total Fat 0g	0%	**Sodium** 2mg	0%	Dietary Fiber 0g	0%
Saturated Fat 0g	0%	**Protein** 2g		Sugars 0g	
Polyunsaturated Fat 0g					
Monounsaturated Fat 0g		Vitamin A 5%	Vitamin C 338%	Calcium 6%	Iron 10%

Currants, Red and White, Raw

1 cup / 112g

Amount per serving	%DV	Amount per serving	%DV	Amount per serving	%DV
Calories 63		**Cholesterol** 0mg	0%	**Total Carbohydrate** 15g	5%
Total Fat 0g	0%	**Sodium** 1mg	0%	Dietary Fiber 5g	20%
Saturated Fat 0g	0%	**Protein** 2g		Sugars 8g	
Polyunsaturated Fat 0g					
Monounsaturated Fat 0g		Vitamin A 1%	Vitamin C 77%	Calcium 4%	Iron 6%

Dates, Deglet Noor

1 date, pitted / 7.1g

Amount per serving	%DV	Amount per serving	%DV	Amount per serving	%DV
Calories 20		**Cholesterol** 0mg	0%	**Total Carbohydrate** 5.5g	2%
Total Fat 0g	0%	**Sodium** 0mg	0%	Dietary Fiber 0.5g	2%
Saturated Fat 0g	0%	**Protein** 0g		Sugars 4.5g	
Polyunsaturated Fat 0g					
Monounsaturated Fat 0g		Vitamin A 0.5%	Vitamin C 0%	Calcium 3%	Iron 0%

Elderberries, Raw

1 cup / 145g

Amount per serving	%DV	Amount per serving	%DV	Amount per serving	%DV
Calories 106		**Cholesterol** 0mg	0%	**Total Carbohydrate** 27g	9%
Total Fat 1g	2%	**Sodium** 9mg	0%	Dietary Fiber 10g	40%
Saturated Fat 0g	0%	**Protein** 1g		Sugars 0g	
Polyunsaturated Fat 0g					
Monounsaturated Fat 0g		Vitamin A 17%	Vitamin C 87%	Calcium 6%	Iron 13%

Figs, Raw

1 medium, 2-1/4" diameter / 50g

Amount per serving	%DV	Amount per serving	%DV	Amount per serving	%DV
Calories 37		**Cholesterol** 0mg	0%	**Total Carbohydrate** 10g	3%
Total Fat 0g	0%	**Sodium** 1mg	0%	Dietary Fiber 1g	4%
Saturated Fat 0g	0%	**Protein** 0g		Sugars 8g	
Polyunsaturated Fat 0g					
Monounsaturated Fat 0g		Vitamin A 1%	Vitamin C 2%	Calcium 2%	Iron 1%

Grapefruit, Raw, Pink and Red and White, All Areas

1/2 large (approx 4-1/2″ diameter) (166g)

Amount per serving	%DV	Amount per serving	%DV	Amount per serving	%DV
Calories 53		**Cholesterol** 0mg	0%	**Total Carbohydrate** 13g	4%
Total Fat 0g	0%	**Sodium** 0mg	0%	Dietary Fiber 2g	7%
Saturated Fat 0g	0%	**Protein** 1g		Sugars 12g	
Polyunsaturated Fat 0g					
Monounsaturated Fat 0g		Vitamin A 31% Vitamin C 95%		Calcium 2% Iron 1%	

Grapefruit, Raw, Pink and Red, All Areas

1/2 fruit, 3-3/4″ diameter / 123g

Amount per serving	%DV	Amount per serving	%DV	Amount per serving	%DV
Calories 52		**Cholesterol** 0mg	0%	**Total Carbohydrate** 13g	4%
Total Fat 0g	0%	**Sodium** 0mg	0%	Dietary Fiber 2g	8%
Saturated Fat 0g	0%	**Protein** 1g		Sugars 8g	
Polyunsaturated Fat 0g					
Monounsaturated Fat 0g		Vitamin A 28% Vitamin C 64%		Calcium 3% Iron1%	

Grapefruit, Raw, Pink and Red, California and Arizona

1/2 fruit, 3-3/4″ diameter / 123g

Amount per serving	%DV	Amount per serving	%DV	Amount per serving	%DV
Calories 45.5		**Cholesterol** 0mg	0%	**Total Carbohydrate** 12g	4%
Total Fat 0g	0%	**Sodium** 1mg	0%	Dietary Fiber 0g	0%
Saturated Fat 0g	0%	**Protein** 1g		Sugars 0g	
Polyunsaturated Fat 0g					
Monounsaturated Fat 0g		Vitamin A 6% Vitamin C 78%		Calcium 1% Iron 1%	

Grapefruit, Raw, Pink and Red, Florida

1/2 fruit, 3-3/4″ diameter / 123g

Amount per serving	%DV	Amount per serving	%DV	Amount per serving	%DV
Calories 37		**Cholesterol** 0mg	0%	**Total Carbohydrate** 9g	3%
Total Fat 0g	0%	**Sodium** 0mg	0%	Dietary Fiber 1g	6%
Saturated Fat 0g	0%	**Protein** 1g		Sugars 0g	
Polyunsaturated Fat 0g					
Monounsaturated Fat 0g		Vitamin A 6% Vitamin C 76%		Calcium 2% Iron 1%	

Grapefruit, Raw, White, All Areas

1/2 fruit, 3-3/4″ diameter / 118g

Amount per serving	%DV	Amount per serving	%DV	Amount per serving	%DV
Calories 39		**Cholesterol** 0mg	0%	**Total Carbohydrate** 10g	3%
Total Fat 0g	0%	**Sodium** 0mg	0%	Dietary Fiber 1.5g	6%
Saturated Fat 0g	0%	**Protein** 1g		Sugars 8.5g	
Polyunsaturated Fat 0g					
Monounsaturated Fat 0g		Vitamin A 39% Vitamin C 39.5%		Calcium 14% Iron 0%	

Grapefruit, Raw, White, California

1/2 fruit, 3-3/4″ diameter / 118g

Amount per serving	%DV	Amount per serving	%DV	Amount per serving	%DV
Calories 43.5		**Cholesterol** 0mg	0%	**Total Carbohydrate** 10.5g	4%
Total Fat 0g	0%	**Sodium** 0mg	0%	Dietary Fiber 0g	0%
Saturated Fat 0g	0%	**Protein** 1g		Sugars 0g	
Polyunsaturated Fat 0g					
Monounsaturated Fat 0g		Vitamin A 12% Vitamin C 39.5% Calcium 14% Iron 0%			

Grapefruit, Raw, White, Florida

1/2 fruit, 3-3/4″ diameter / 118g

Amount per serving	%DV	Amount per serving	%DV	Amount per serving	%DV
Calories 38		**Cholesterol** 0mg	0%	**Total Carbohydrate** 9.5g	3%
Total Fat 0g	0%	**Sodium** 0mg	0%	Dietary Fiber 0g	0%
Saturated Fat 0g	0%	**Protein** 0.5g		Sugars 0g	
Polyunsaturated Fat 0g					
Monounsaturated Fat 0g		Vitamin A 0% Vitamin C 73% Calcium 2% Iron 0%			

Grapes, American Type (Slip Skin), Raw

1 grape / 2.4g

Amount per serving	%DV	Amount per serving	%DV	Amount per serving	%DV
Calories 1.5		**Cholesterol** 0mg	0%	**Total Carbohydrate** 0.5g	0%
Total Fat 0g	0%	**Sodium** 0mg	0%	Dietary Fiber 0g	0%
Saturated Fat 0g	0%	**Protein** 0g		Sugars 0.5g	
Polyunsaturated Fat 0g					
Monounsaturated Fat 0g		Vitamin A 2.5% Vitamin C 0% Calcium 0.5% Iron 0%			

Grapes, Red or Green (European Type, Such as Thompson Seedless), Raw

10 grapes / 49g

Amount per serving	%DV	Amount per serving	%DV	Amount per serving	%DV
Calories 34		**Cholesterol** 0mg	0%	**Total Carbohydrate** 9g	3%
Total Fat 0g	0%	**Sodium** 1mg	0%	Dietary Fiber 0.5g	2%
Saturated Fat 0g	0%	**Protein** 0.5g		Sugars 7.5g	
Polyunsaturated Fat 0g					
Monounsaturated Fat 0g		Vitamin A 32.5% Vitamin C 1.5% Calcium 5% Iron 0%			

Guavas, Common, Raw

1 fruit, without refuse/ 55g

Amount per serving	%DV	Amount per serving	%DV	Amount per serving	%DV
Calories 37.5		**Cholesterol** 0mg	0%	**Total Carbohydrate** 8g	3%
Total Fat 0.5g	1%	**Sodium** 1mg	0%	Dietary Fiber 3g	12%
Saturated Fat 0g	0%	**Protein** 1.5g		Sugars 5g	
Polyunsaturated Fat 0g					
Monounsaturated Fat 0g		Vitamin A 343% Vitamin C 125.5% Calcium 10% Iron 0%			

Guavas, Strawberry, Raw

1 fruit, without refuse / 6g

Amount per serving	%DV	Amount per serving	%DV	Amount per serving	%DV
Calories 4		**Cholesterol** 0mg	0%	**Total Carbohydrate** 1g	0%
Total Fat 0g	0%	**Sodium** 2mg	0%	Dietary Fiber 0.5g	2%
Saturated Fat 0g	0%	**Protein** 0g		Sugars 0g	
Polyunsaturated Fat 0g					
Monounsaturated Fat 0g		Vitamin A 5.5% Vitamin C 2%		Calcium 1.5% Iron 0%	

Horned Melon (Kiwano)

1 fruit, 4-2/3″ long x 2-3/4″ diameter / 209g

Amount per serving	%DV	Amount per serving	%DV	Amount per serving	%DV
Calories 92		**Cholesterol** 0mg	0%	**Total Carbohydrate** 16g	5%
Total Fat 2.5g	4%	**Sodium** 4mg	0%	Dietary Fiber 0g	0%
Saturated Fat 0g	0%	**Protein** 3.5g		Sugars 0g	
Polyunsaturated Fat 0g					
Monounsaturated Fat 0g		Vitamin A 307% Vitamin C 11%		Calcium 27% Iron 2.5%	

Java-plum, (Jambolan), Raw

3 fruit / 9g

Amount per serving	%DV	Amount per serving	%DV	Amount per serving	%DV
Calories 5.5		**Cholesterol** 0mg	0%	**Total Carbohydrate** 1.5g	0%
Total Fat 0g	0%	**Sodium** 1.5mg	0%	Dietary Fiber 0g	0%
Saturated Fat 0g	0%	**Protein** 0g		Sugars 0g	
Polyunsaturated Fat 0g					
Monounsaturated Fat 0g		Vitamin A 0.5% Vitamin C 1.5%		Calcium 1.5% Iron 0%	

Kiwifruit, Gold, Raw

1 fruit / 86g

Amount per serving	%DV	Amount per serving	%DV	Amount per serving	%DV
Calories 51.5		**Cholesterol** 0mg	0%	**Total Carbohydrate** 12g	4%
Total Fat 0.5g	1%	**Sodium** 2.5mg	0%	Dietary Fiber 1.5g	6%
Saturated Fat 0g	0%	**Protein** 1g		Sugars 9.5g	
Polyunsaturated Fat 0g					
Monounsaturated Fat 0g		Vitamin A 62% Vitamin C 90.5% Calcium 17% Iron 0%			

Kiwifruit, Green, Raw

1 fruit, 2″ diameter / 69g

Amount per serving	%DV	Amount per serving	%DV	Amount per serving	%DV
Calories 42		**Cholesterol** 0mg	0%	**Total Carbohydrate** 10g	3%
Total Fat 0.5g	1%	**Sodium** 2mg	0%	Dietary Fiber 2g	8%
Saturated Fat 0g	0%	**Protein** 1g		Sugars 6g	
Polyunsaturated Fat 0g					
Monounsaturated Fat 0g		Vitamin A 60% Vitamin C 64%		Calcium 23.5% Iron 0%	

Kumquats, Raw

1 fruit, without refuse / 19g

Amount per serving	%DV	Amount per serving	%DV	Amount per serving	%DV
Calories 13		**Cholesterol** 0mg	0%	**Total Carbohydrate** 3g	1%
Total Fat 0g	0%	**Sodium** 2mg	0%	Dietary Fiber 1g	4%
Saturated Fat 0g	0%	**Protein** 0g		Sugars 2g	
Polyunsaturated Fat 0g					
Monounsaturated Fat 0g		Vitamin A 1% Vitamin C 14%		Calcium 1% Iron 1%	

Lemons, Raw, without Peel

1 fruit, 2-1/8″ diameter / 58g

Amount per serving	%DV	Amount per serving	%DV	Amount per serving	%DV
Calories 17		**Cholesterol** 0mg	0%	**Total Carbohydrate** 5.5g	2%
Total Fat 0g	0%	**Sodium** 1mg	0%	Dietary Fiber 1.5g	6%
Saturated Fat 0g	0%	**Protein** 0.5g		Sugars 1.5g	
Polyunsaturated Fat 0g					
Monounsaturated Fat 0g		Vitamin A 13% Vitamin C 30.5%		Calcium 15% Iron 0.5%	

Limes, Raw

1 fruit / 67g

Amount per serving	%DV	Amount per serving	%DV	Amount per serving	%DV
Calories 20		**Cholesterol** 0mg	0%	**Total Carbohydrate** 7g	2%
Total Fat 0g	0%	**Sodium** 1mg	0%	Dietary Fiber 2g	8%
Saturated Fat 0g	0%	**Protein** 0g		Sugars 1g	
Polyunsaturated Fat 0g					
Monounsaturated Fat 0g		Vitamin A 1% Vitamin C 32%		Calcium 2% Iron 2%	

Litchis, Raw

1 fruit, without refuse / 9.6g

Amount per serving	%DV	Amount per serving	%DV	Amount per serving	%DV
Calories 6.5		**Cholesterol** 0mg	0%	**Total Carbohydrate** 1.5g	0%
Total Fat 0g	0%	**Sodium** 0mg	0%	Dietary Fiber 0g	0%
Saturated Fat 0g	0%	**Protein** 0g		Sugars 1.5g	
Polyunsaturated Fat 0g					
Monounsaturated Fat 0g		Vitamin A 0% Vitamin C 7%		Calcium 0.5% Iron 0%	

Loganberries, Frozen

1 cup, unthawed / 147g

Amount per serving	%DV	Amount per serving	%DV	Amount per serving	%DV
Calories 81		**Cholesterol** 0mg	0%	**Total Carbohydrate** 19g	6%
Total Fat 0g	0%	**Sodium** 1mg	0%	Dietary Fiber 8g	32%
Saturated Fat 0g	0%	**Protein** 2g		Sugars 11g	
Polyunsaturated Fat 0g					
Monounsaturated Fat 0g		Vitamin A 1% Vitamin C 37%		Calcium 4% Iron 5%	

Loquats, Raw

1 large / 20g

Amount per serving	%DV	Amount per serving	%DV	Amount per serving	%DV
Calories 9		**Cholesterol** 0mg	0%	**Total Carbohydrate** 2g	1%
Total Fat 0g	0%	**Sodium** 0mg	0%	Dietary Fiber 0g	2%
Saturated Fat 0g	0%	**Protein** 0g		Sugars 0g	
Polyunsaturated Fat 0g					
Monounsaturated Fat 0g		Vitamin A 6%	Vitamin C 0%	Calcium 0%	Iron 0%

Mangos, Raw

1 fruit, without refuse / 207g

Amount per serving	%DV	Amount per serving	%DV	Amount per serving	%DV
Calories 135		**Cholesterol** 0mg	0%	**Total Carbohydrate** 35g	12%
Total Fat 1g	2%	**Sodium** 4mg	0%	Dietary Fiber 4g	16%
Saturated Fat 0g	0%	**Protein** 1g		Sugars 31g	
Polyunsaturated Fat 0g					
Monounsaturated Fat 0g		Vitamin A 32%	Vitamin C 96%	Calcium 2%	Iron 1%

Melon, Cantaloupe, Raw

1 cup, cubes / 160g

Amount per serving	%DV	Amount per serving	%DV	Amount per serving	%DV
Calories 54.5		**Cholesterol** 0mg	0%	**Total Carbohydrate** 13g	4%
Total Fat 0.5g	1%	**Sodium** 25.5mg	1%	Dietary Fiber 1.5g	6%
Saturated Fat 0g	0%	**Protein** 1.5g		Sugars 12.5g	
Polyunsaturated Fat 0g					
Monounsaturated Fat 0g		Vitamin A 108%	Vitamin C 98%	Calcium 1%	Iron 2%

Melon, Casaba, Raw

1 cup, cubes / 170g

Amount per serving	%DV	Amount per serving	%DV	Amount per serving	%DV
Calories 48		**Cholesterol** 0mg	0%	**Total Carbohydrate** 11g	36%
Total Fat 0g	2%	**Sodium** 15mg	6%	Dietary Fiber 2g	60%
Saturated Fat 0g	2%	**Protein** 2g		Sugars 10g	
Polyunsaturated Fat 0g					
Monounsaturated Fat 0g		Vitamin A 0%	Vitamin C 62%	Calcium 2%	Iron 3%

Melon, Honeydew, Raw

1 cup, diced / approx 20 pieces per cup / 170g

Amount per serving	%DV	Amount per serving	%DV	Amount per serving	%DV
Calories 61		**Cholesterol** 0mg	0%	**Total Carbohydrate** 15.5g	5%
Total Fat 0g	0%	**Sodium** 30.5mg	1%	Dietary Fiber 1.5g	6%
Saturated Fat 0g	0%	**Protein** 1g		Sugars 14g	
Polyunsaturated Fat 0g					
Monounsaturated Fat 0g		Vitamin A 85%	Vitamin C 30.5%	Calcium 10%	Iron 0.5%

Mulberries, Raw

10 fruit / 15g

Amount per serving	%DV	Amount per serving	%DV	Amount per serving	%DV
Calories 6.5		**Cholesterol** 0mg	0%	**Total Carbohydrate** 1.5g	0%
Total Fat 0g	0%	**Sodium** 1.5mg	0%	Dietary Fiber 0.5g	2%
Saturated Fat 0g	0%	**Protein** 0g		Sugars 1g	
Polyunsaturated Fat 0g					
Monounsaturated Fat 0g		Vitamin A 4%	Vitamin C 5.5%	Calcium 6%	Iron 0.5%

Nance, Frozen, Unsweetened

3 fruit, without pits thawed / 9.8g

Amount per serving	%DV	Amount per serving	%DV	Amount per serving	%DV
Calories 7		**Cholesterol** 0mg	0%	**Total Carbohydrate** 1.5g	0%
Total Fat 0g	0%	**Sodium** 0.5mg	0%	Dietary Fiber 0.5g	2%
Saturated Fat 0g	0%	**Protein** 0g		Sugars 1g	
Polyunsaturated Fat 0g					
Monounsaturated Fat 0g		Vitamin A 7.5%	Vitamin C 9%	Calcium 4.5%	Iron 0%

Nectarines, Raw

1 small, 2-1/3" diameter / 129g

Amount per serving	%DV	Amount per serving	%DV	Amount per serving	%DV
Calories 57		**Cholesterol** 0mg	0%	**Total Carbohydrate** 14g	4%
Total Fat 0g	1%	**Sodium** 0mg	0%	Dietary Fiber 2g	8%
Saturated Fat 0g	0%	**Protein** 1g		Sugars 10g	
Polyunsaturated Fat 0g					
Monounsaturated Fat 0g		Vitamin A 9%	Vitamin C 12%	Calcium 1%	Iron 2%

Oheloberries, Raw

10 fruit / 11g

Amount per serving	%DV	Amount per serving	%DV	Amount per serving	%DV
Calories 3		**Cholesterol** 0mg	0%	**Total Carbohydrate** 1g	0%
Total Fat 0g	0%	**Sodium** 0mg	0%	Dietary Fiber 0g	0%
Saturated Fat 0g	0%	**Protein** 0g		Sugars 0g	
Polyunsaturated Fat 0g					
Monounsaturated Fat 0g		Vitamin A 91.5%	Vitamin C 0.5%	Calcium 1%	Iron 0%

Oranges, Raw, All Commercial Varieties

1 large, 3-1/16" diameter / 184g

Amount per serving	%DV	Amount per serving	%DV	Amount per serving	%DV
Calories 86.5		**Cholesterol** 0mg	0%	**Total Carbohydrate** 21.5g	7%
Total Fat 0g	0%	**Sodium** 0mg	0%	Dietary Fiber 4.5g	18%
Saturated Fat 0g	0%	**Protein** 1.5g		Sugars 17g	
Polyunsaturated Fat 0g					
Monounsaturated Fat 0g		Vitamin A 414%	Vitamin C 98%	Calcium 73.5%	Iron 0%

Oranges, Raw, California, Valencias

1 fruit, 2-5/8″ diameter / 121g

Amount per serving	%DV	Amount per serving	%DV	Amount per serving	%DV
Calories 59.5		**Cholesterol** 0mg	0%	**Total Carbohydrate** 14.5g	5%
Total Fat 0.5g	1%	**Sodium** 0mg	0%	Dietary Fiber 3g	12%
Saturated Fat 0g	0%	**Protein** 1.5g		Sugars 14g	
Polyunsaturated Fat 0g					
Monounsaturated Fat 0g		Vitamin A 6%	Vitamin C 98%	Calcium 5%	Iron 1%

Oranges, Raw, Florida

1 fruit, 2-5/8″ diameter / 141g

Amount per serving	%DV	Amount per serving	%DV	Amount per serving	%DV
Calories 65		**Cholesterol** 0mg	0%	**Total Carbohydrate** 16g	5%
Total Fat 0g	0%	**Sodium** 0mg	0%	Dietary Fiber 3g	14%
Saturated Fat 0g	0%	**Protein** 1g		Sugars 13g	
Polyunsaturated Fat 0g					
Monounsaturated Fat 0g		Vitamin A 6%	Vitamin C 106%	Calcium 6%	Iron 1%

Oranges, Raw, Navels

1 fruit, 2-7/8″ diameter / 140g

Amount per serving	%DV	Amount per serving	%DV	Amount per serving	%DV
Calories 69		**Cholesterol** 0mg	0%	**Total Carbohydrate** 18g	6%
Total Fat 0g	0%	**Sodium** 1mg	0%	Dietary Fiber 3g	12%
Saturated Fat 0g	0%	**Protein** 1g		Sugars 12g	
Polyunsaturated Fat 0g					
Monounsaturated Fat 0g		Vitamin A 7%	Vitamin C 138%	Calcium 6%	Iron 1%

Papayas, Raw

1 cup, mashed / 230g

Amount per serving	%DV	Amount per serving	%DV	Amount per serving	%DV
Calories 90		**Cholesterol** 0mg	0%	**Total Carbohydrate** 23g	8%
Total Fat 0g	0%	**Sodium** 7mg	0%	Dietary Fiber 4g	17%
Saturated Fat 0g	0%	**Protein** 1g		Sugars 14g	
Polyunsaturated Fat 0g					
Monounsaturated Fat 0g		Vitamin A 50%	Vitamin C 237%	Calcium 6%	Iron 1%

Passion-Fruit (Granadilla), Purple, Raw

1 fruit, without refuse / 18g

Amount per serving	%DV	Amount per serving	%DV	Amount per serving	%DV
Calories 17.5		**Cholesterol** 0mg	0%	**Total Carbohydrate** 4g	1%
Total Fat 0g	0%	**Sodium** 5mg	0%	Dietary Fiber 2g	8%
Saturated Fat 0g	0%	**Protein** 0.5g		Sugars 2g	
Polyunsaturated Fat 0g					
Monounsaturated Fat 0g		Vitamin A 229%	Vitamin C 5.5%	Calcium 2%	Iron 0.5%

Peaches, Raw

1 small, 2-1/2″ diameter / 130g

Amount per serving	%DV	Amount per serving	%DV	Amount per serving	%DV
Calories 50.5		**Cholesterol** 0mg	0%	**Total Carbohydrate** 12.5g	4%
Total Fat 0.5g	1%	**Sodium** 0mg	0%	Dietary Fiber 2g	8%
Saturated Fat 0g	0%	**Protein** 1g		Sugars 11g	
Polyunsaturated Fat 0g					
Monounsaturated Fat 0g		Vitamin A 424%	Vitamin C 8.5%	Calcium 8%	Iron 0.5%

Pears, Asian, Raw

1 fruit, 3-3/8″ high x 3″ diameter / 275g

Amount per serving	%DV	Amount per serving	%DV	Amount per serving	%DV
Calories 115.5		**Cholesterol** 0mg	0%	**Total Carbohydrate** 29.5g	10%
Total Fat 0.5g	1%	**Sodium** 0mg	0%	Dietary Fiber 10g	40%
Saturated Fat 0g	0%	**Protein** 1.5g		Sugars 19.5g	
Polyunsaturated Fat 0g					
Monounsaturated Fat 0g		Vitamin A 0%	Vitamin C 10.5%	Calcium 11%	Iron 0%

Pears, Raw

1 medium / 178g

Amount per serving	%DV	Amount per serving	%DV	Amount per serving	%DV
Calories 101.5		**Cholesterol** 0mg	0%	**Total Carbohydrate** 27g	9%
Total Fat 0g	0%	**Sodium** 2mg	0%	Dietary Fiber 5.5g	22%
Saturated Fat 0g	0%	**Protein** 0.5g		Sugars 17.5g	
Polyunsaturated Fat 0g					
Monounsaturated Fat 0g		Vitamin A 44.5%	Vitamin C 7.5%	Calcium 16%	Iron 0.5%

Pears, Raw, Bartlett

1 medium / 177g

Amount per serving	%DV	Amount per serving	%DV	Amount per serving	%DV
Calories 111.5		**Cholesterol** 0mg	0%	**Total Carbohydrate** 26.5g	9%
Total Fat 0.5g	1%	**Sodium** 2mg	0%	Dietary Fiber 5.5g	22%
Saturated Fat 0g	0%	**Protein** 0.5g		Sugars 17g	
Polyunsaturated Fat 0g					
Monounsaturated Fat 0g		Vitamin A 49.5%	Vitamin C 8%	Calcium 16%	Iron 0.5%

Pineapple, Raw, All Varieties

1 slice, thin (3-1/2″ diameter x 1/2″ thick) (56g)

Amount per serving	%DV	Amount per serving	%DV	Amount per serving	%DV
Calories 28		**Cholesterol** 0mg	0%	**Total Carbohydrate** 7g	2%
Total Fat 0g	0%	**Sodium** 1mg	0%	Dietary Fiber 1g	4%
Saturated Fat 0g	0%	**Protein** 0g		Sugars 6g	
Polyunsaturated Fat 0g					
Monounsaturated Fat 0g		Vitamin A 1%	Vitamin C 45%	Calcium 1%	Iron 1%

Pineapple, Raw, Extra Sweet Variety

1 slice, 4-2/3″ diameter x 3/4″ thick / 166g

Amount per serving	%DV	Amount per serving	%DV	Amount per serving	%DV
Calories 84.5		**Cholesterol** 0mg	0%	**Total Carbohydrate** 22.5g	8%
Total Fat 0g	0%	**Sodium** 1.5mg	0%	Dietary Fiber 2.5g	10%
Saturated Fat 0g	0%	**Protein** 1g		Sugars 17g	
Polyunsaturated Fat 0g					
Monounsaturated Fat 0g		Vitamin A 94.5%	Vitamin C 93.5%	Calcium 21.5%	Iron 0.5%

Pineapple, Raw, Traditional Variety

1 slice, 4-2/3″ diameter x 3/4″ thick / 175g

Amount per serving	%DV	Amount per serving	%DV	Amount per serving	%DV
Calories 79		**Cholesterol** 0mg	0%	**Total Carbohydrate** 20.5g	7%
Total Fat 0g	0%	**Sodium** 2mg	0%	Dietary Fiber 0g	0%
Saturated Fat 0g	0%	**Protein** 1g		Sugars 14.5g	
Polyunsaturated Fat 0g					
Monounsaturated Fat 0g		Vitamin A 91%	Vitamin C 29.5%	Calcium 23%	Iron 0.5%

Pitanga, (Surinam-Cherry), Raw

1 fruit, without refuse / 7g

Amount per serving	%DV	Amount per serving	%DV	Amount per serving	%DV
Calories 2.5		**Cholesterol** 0mg	0%	**Total Carbohydrate** 0.5g	0%
Total Fat 0g	0%	**Sodium** 0mg	0%	Dietary Fiber 0g	0%
Saturated Fat 0g	0%	**Protein** 0g		Sugars 0g	
Polyunsaturated Fat 0g					
Monounsaturated Fat 0g		Vitamin A 105%	Vitamin C 2%	Calcium 0.5%	Iron 0%

Plains Pricklypear, Raw (Northern Plains Indians)

1 pad / 61g

Amount per serving	%DV	Amount per serving	%DV	Amount per serving	%DV
Calories 25.5		**Cholesterol** 0mg	0%	**Total Carbohydrate** 6g	2%
Total Fat 0g	0%	**Sodium** 2.5mg	0%	Dietary Fiber 3g	12%
Saturated Fat 0g	0%	**Protein** 0g		Sugars 0.5g	
Polyunsaturated Fat 0g					
Monounsaturated Fat 0g		Vitamin A 0%	Vitamin C 6.5%	Calcium 110%	Iron 0%

Plantains, Cooked

1 cup, slices / 154g

Amount per serving	%DV	Amount per serving	%DV	Amount per serving	%DV
Calories 179		**Cholesterol** 0mg	0%	**Total Carbohydrate** 48g	16%
Total Fat 0g	0%	**Sodium** 8mg	0%	Dietary Fiber 4g	14%
Saturated Fat 0g	0%	**Protein** 1g		Sugars 22g	
Polyunsaturated Fat 0g					
Monounsaturated Fat 0g		Vitamin A 28%	Vitamin C 28%	Calcium 0%	Iron 5%

Plantains, Raw

1 medium / 179g

Amount per serving	%DV	Amount per serving	%DV	Amount per serving	%DV
Calories 218		**Cholesterol** 0mg	0%	**Total Carbohydrate** 57g	19%
Total Fat 1g	1%	**Sodium** 7mg	0%	Dietary Fiber 4g	16%
Saturated Fat 0g	1%	**Protein** 2g		Sugars 27g	
Polyunsaturated Fat 0g					
Monounsaturated Fat 0g		Vitamin A 40% Vitamin C 55%		Calcium 1% Iron 6%	

Plums, Dried (Prunes), Uncooked

1 prune, pitted / 9.5g

Amount per serving	%DV	Amount per serving	%DV	Amount per serving	%DV
Calories 23		**Cholesterol** 0mg	0%	**Total Carbohydrate** 6g	2%
Total Fat 0g	0%	**Sodium** 0mg	0%	Dietary Fiber 0.5g	2%
Saturated Fat 0g	0%	**Protein** 0g		Sugars 3.5g	
Polyunsaturated Fat 0g					
Monounsaturated Fat 0g		Vitamin A 74% Vitamin C 0%		Calcium 4% Iron 0%	

Plums, Raw

1 plum, 2-1/8″ diameter/ 66g

Amount per serving	%DV	Amount per serving	%DV	Amount per serving	%DV
Calories 30.5		**Cholesterol** 0mg	0%	**Total Carbohydrate** 7.5g	2%
Total Fat 0g	0%	**Sodium** 0mg	0%	Dietary Fiber 1g	4%
Saturated Fat 0g	0%	**Protein** 0.5g		Sugars 6.5g	
Polyunsaturated Fat 0g					
Monounsaturated Fat 0g		Vitamin A 5% Vitamin C 10%		Calcium 0% Iron 1%	

Pomegranates, Raw

.5 cup, arils, seed / juice sacs / 87g

Amount per serving	%DV	Amount per serving	%DV	Amount per serving	%DV
Calories 72		**Cholesterol** 0mg	0%	**Total Carbohydrate** 16.5g	6%
Total Fat 1g	2%	**Sodium** 2.5mg	0%	Dietary Fiber 3.5g	14%
Saturated Fat 0g	0%	**Protein** 1.5g		Sugars 12g	
Polyunsaturated Fat 0g					
Monounsaturated Fat 0g		Vitamin A 0% Vitamin C 9%		Calcium 8.5% Iron 0.5%	

Prickly Pears, Raw

1 fruit, without refuse / 103g

Amount per serving	%DV	Amount per serving	%DV	Amount per serving	%DV
Calories 42		**Cholesterol** 0mg	0%	**Total Carbohydrate** 10g	3%
Total Fat 0.5g	1%	**Sodium** 5mg	0%	Dietary Fiber 3.5g	14%
Saturated Fat 0g	0%	**Protein** 1g		Sugars 0g	
Polyunsaturated Fat 0g					
Monounsaturated Fat 0g		Vitamin A 44.5% Vitamin C 14.5%		Calcium 57.5% Iron 0.5%	

Pummelo, Raw

1 fruit, without refuse / 609g

Amount per serving	%DV	Amount per serving	%DV	Amount per serving	%DV
Calories 231.5		**Cholesterol** 0mg	0%	**Total Carbohydrate** 58.5g	20%
Total Fat 0g	0%	**Sodium** 6mg	0%	Dietary Fiber 6g	24%
Saturated Fat 0g	0%	**Protein** 4.5g		Sugars NA	
Polyunsaturated Fat 0g					
Monounsaturated Fat 0g		Vitamin A 48.5% Vitamin C 371.5% Calcium 24.5% Iron 0.5%			

Quinces, Raw

1 fruit, without refuse / 92g

Amount per serving	%DV	Amount per serving	%DV	Amount per serving	%DV
Calories 52		**Cholesterol** 0mg	0%	**Total Carbohydrate** 14g	5%
Total Fat 0g	0%	**Sodium** 4mg	0%	Dietary Fiber 2g	8%
Saturated Fat 0g	0%	**Protein** 0g		Sugars 0g	
Polyunsaturated Fat 0g					
Monounsaturated Fat 0g		Vitamin A 1% Vitamin C 23% Calcium 1% Iron 4%			

Raisins, Seeded

1 oz / 28g

Amount per serving	%DV	Amount per serving	%DV	Amount per serving	%DV
Calories 83		**Cholesterol** 0mg	0%	**Total Carbohydrate** 22g	7%
Total Fat 0g	0%	**Sodium** 8mg	0%	Dietary Fiber 2g	8%
Saturated Fat 0g	0%	**Protein** 1g		Sugars 95g	
Polyunsaturated Fat 0g					
Monounsaturated Fat 0g		Vitamin A 0% Vitamin C 3% Calcium 1% Iron 4%			

Raspberries, Raw

1 pint, as purchased, yields / 312g

Amount per serving	%DV	Amount per serving	%DV	Amount per serving	%DV
Calories 162		**Cholesterol** 0mg	0%	**Total Carbohydrate** 37.5g	12%
Total Fat 2g	3%	**Sodium** 3mg	0%	Dietary Fiber 20.5g	82%
Saturated Fat 0g	0%	**Protein** 3.5g		Sugars 14g	
Polyunsaturated Fat 1g					
Monounsaturated Fat 0g		Vitamin A 103% Vitamin C 81.5% Calcium 78% Iron 2%			

Rhubarb, Raw

1 stalk / 51g

Amount per serving	%DV	Amount per serving	%DV	Amount per serving	%DV
Calories 10.5		**Cholesterol** 0mg	0%	**Total Carbohydrate** 2.5g	1%
Total Fat 0g	0%	**Sodium** 2mg	0%	Dietary Fiber 1g	4%
Saturated Fat 0g	0%	**Protein** 0.5g		Sugars 0.5g	
Polyunsaturated Fat 0g					
Monounsaturated Fat 0g		Vitamin A 52% Vitamin C 4% Calcium 44% Iron 0%			

Sapodilla, Raw

1 sapodilla / 170g

Amount per serving	%DV	Amount per serving	%DV	Amount per serving	%DV
Calories 141		**Cholesterol** 0mg	0%	**Total Carbohydrate** 34g	11%
Total Fat 2g	3%	**Sodium** 20.5mg	1%	Dietary Fiber 9g	36%
Saturated Fat 0.5g	2%	**Protein** 0.5g		Sugars 0g	
Polyunsaturated Fat 0g					
Monounsaturated Fat 1g		Vitamin A 102% Vitamin C 25%		Calcium 35.5% Iron 1.5%	

Strawberries, Frozen, Unsweetened

1 cup, unthawed / 149g

Amount per serving	%DV	Amount per serving	%DV	Amount per serving	%DV
Calories 52		**Cholesterol** 0mg	0%	**Total Carbohydrate** 13.5g	5%
Total Fat 0g	0%	**Sodium** 3mg	0%	Dietary Fiber 3g	12%
Saturated Fat 0g	0%	**Protein** 0.5g		Sugars 7g	
Polyunsaturated Fat 0g					
Monounsaturated Fat 0g		Vitamin A 67% Vitamin C 61.5% Calcium 24% Iron 1%			

Strawberries, Raw

1 cup, pureed / 232g

Amount per serving	%DV	Amount per serving	%DV	Amount per serving	%DV
Calories 74		**Cholesterol** 0mg	0%	**Total Carbohydrate** 18g	6%
Total Fat 0.5g	1%	**Sodium** 2.5mg	0%	Dietary Fiber 4.5g	18%
Saturated Fat 0g	0%	**Protein** 1.5g		Sugars 11.5g	
Polyunsaturated Fat 0.5g					
Monounsaturated Fat 0g		Vitamin A 28% Vitamin C 136.5% Calcium 37% Iron 1%			

Tamarinds, Raw

1 fruit, 3″ x 1″ / 2g

Amount per serving	%DV	Amount per serving	%DV	Amount per serving	%DV
Calories 5		**Cholesterol** 0mg	0%	**Total Carbohydrate** 1.5g	0%
Total Fat 0g	0%	**Sodium** 0.5mg	0%	Dietary Fiber 0g	0%
Saturated Fat 0g	0%	**Protein** 0g		Sugars 1g	
Polyunsaturated Fat 0g					
Monounsaturated Fat 0g		Vitamin A 0.5% Vitamin C 0%		Calcium 1.5% Iron 0%	

Tangerines (Mandarin Oranges), Raw

1 small, 2-1/4″ diameter / 76g

Amount per serving	%DV	Amount per serving	%DV	Amount per serving	%DV
Calories 40		**Cholesterol** 0mg	0%	**Total Carbohydrate** 10g	3%
Total Fat 0g	0%	**Sodium** 2mg	0%	Dietary Fiber 1g	6%
Saturated Fat 0g	0%	**Protein** 1g		Sugars 8g	
Polyunsaturated Fat 0g					
Monounsaturated Fat 0g		Vitamin A 10% Vitamin C 34%		Calcium 3% Iron 1%	

Watermelon

1 cup, diced

Amount per serving	%DV	Amount per serving	%DV	Amount per serving	%DV
Calories 46		**Cholesterol** 0mg	0%	**Total Carbohydrate** 11g	4%
Total Fat 0g	0%	**Sodium** 2mg	0%	Dietary Fiber 1g	4%
Saturated Fat 0g	0%	**Protein** 1g		Sugars 9g	
Polyunsaturated Fat 0g					
Monounsaturated Fat 0g		Vitamin A 17% Vitamin C 21%		Calcium 1% Iron 2%	

Fruit Products

Applesauce, Canned, Unsweetened, with Vitamin C

1 cup / 244g

Amount per serving	%DV	Amount per serving	%DV	Amount per serving	%DV
Calories 102		**Cholesterol** 0mg	0%	**Total Carbohydrate** 27g	9%
Total Fat 0g	0%	**Sodium** 5mg	0%	Dietary Fiber 3g	12%
Saturated Fat 0g	0%	**Protein** 0g		Sugars 23g	
Polyunsaturated Fat 0g					
Monounsaturated Fat 0g		Vitamin A 1% Vitamin C 86%		Calcium 1% Iron 3%	

Brummel & Brown, Simply Strawberry Creamy Fruit Spread

1 tbsp / 12g

Amount per serving	%DV	Amount per serving	%DV	Amount per serving	%DV
Calories 50		**Cholesterol** 0mg	0%	**Total Carbohydrate** 3g	1%
Total Fat 4g	6%	**Sodium** 45mg	2%	Dietary Fiber 0g	0%
Saturated Fat 1g	5%	**Protein** 0g		Sugars 2g	
Polyunsaturated Fat 2g					
Monounsaturated Fat 1g		Vitamin A 8% Vitamin C 0%		Calcium 0% Iron 0%	

Cherries, Sour, Red, Canned, Water Packed, Solids and Liquids

1 cup / 244g

Amount per serving	%DV	Amount per serving	%DV	Amount per serving	%DV
Calories 88		**Cholesterol** 0mg	0%	**Total Carbohydrate** 22g	7%
Total Fat 0g	0%	**Sodium** 17mg	1%	Dietary Fiber 3g	12%
Saturated Fat 0g	0%	**Protein** 2g		Sugars 19g	
Polyunsaturated Fat 0g					
Monounsaturated Fat 0g		Vitamin A 37% Vitamin C 9%		Calcium 3% Iron 19%	

Daily Chef, Dried Montmorency Tart Cherries

1/4 cup / 40g

Amount per serving	%DV	Amount per serving	%DV	Amount per serving	%DV
Calories 130		**Cholesterol** 0mg	0%	**Total Carbohydrate** 32g	11%
Total Fat 0g	0%	**Sodium** 10mg	0%	Dietary Fiber 1g	4%
Saturated Fat 0g	0%	**Protein** 1g		Sugars 25g	
Polyunsaturated Fat 0g					
Monounsaturated Fat 0g		Vitamin A 35% Vitamin C 0%		Calcium 0% Iron 2%	

Del Monte, Crushed Pineapple in 100% Juice

1/2 cup / 122g

Amount per serving	%DV	Amount per serving	%DV	Amount per serving	%DV
Calories 70		**Cholesterol** 0mg	0%	**Total Carbohydrate** 17g	6%
Total Fat 0g	0%	**Sodium** 10mg	0%	Dietary Fiber 1g	4%
Saturated Fat 0g	0%	**Protein** 0g		Sugars 15g	
Polyunsaturated Fat 0g					
Monounsaturated Fat 0g		Vitamin A 0% Vitamin C 20%		Calcium 0% Iron 0%	

Del Monte, Diced Peaches, No Sugar Added

1 cup

Amount per serving	%DV	Amount per serving	%DV	Amount per serving	%DV
Calories 25		**Cholesterol** 0mg	0%	**Total Carbohydrate** 6g	2%
Total Fat 0g	0%	**Sodium** 10mg	0%	Dietary Fiber 4g	16%
Saturated Fat 0g	0%	**Protein** 0g		Sugars 5g	
Polyunsaturated Fat 0g					
Monounsaturated Fat 0g		Vitamin A 4% Vitamin C 100%		Calcium 0% Iron %	

Del Monte, Diced Pears, No Sugar Added

1/2 cup / 125g

Amount per serving	%DV	Amount per serving	%DV	Amount per serving	%DV
Calories 40		**Cholesterol** 0mg	0%	**Total Carbohydrate** 10g	3%
Total Fat 0g	0%	**Sodium** 10mg	0%	Dietary Fiber 0g	0%
Saturated Fat 0g	0%	**Protein** 0g		Sugars 5g	
Polyunsaturated Fat 0g					
Monounsaturated Fat 0g		Vitamin A 0% Vitamin C 100%		Calcium 0% Iron 0%	

Del Monte, Fruit in 100% Juice

1/2 cup 122g

Amount per serving	%DV	Amount per serving	%DV	Amount per serving	%DV
Calories 70		**Cholesterol** 0mg	0%	**Total Carbohydrate** 17g	6%
Total Fat 0g	0%	**Sodium** 10mg	0%	Dietary Fiber 1g	4%
Saturated Fat 0g	0%	**Protein** 0g		Sugars 15g	
Polyunsaturated Fat 0g					
Monounsaturated Fat 0g		Vitamin A 0% Vitamin C 20%		Calcium 0% Iron 2%	

Del Monte, Pineapple Slices in 100% Juice

2 slices / 114g

Amount per serving	%DV	Amount per serving	%DV	Amount per serving	%DV
Calories 60		**Cholesterol** 0mg	0%	**Total Carbohydrate** 16g	5%
Total Fat 0g	0%	**Sodium** 10mg	0%	Dietary Fiber 1g	4%
Saturated Fat 0g	0%	**Protein** 0g		Sugars 14g	
Polyunsaturated Fat 0g					
Monounsaturated Fat 0g		Vitamin A 0% Vitamin C 20%		Calcium 0% Iron 2%	

Del Monte, Pineapple Tidbits in 100% Juice

1 cup / 113g

Amount per serving	%DV	Amount per serving	%DV	Amount per serving	%DV
Calories 50		**Cholesterol** 0mg	0%	**Total Carbohydrate** 15g	5%
Total Fat 0g	0%	**Sodium** 10mg	0%	Dietary Fiber 1g	4%
Saturated Fat 0g	0%	**Protein** 0g		Sugars 15g	
Polyunsaturated Fat 0g					
Monounsaturated Fat 0g		Vitamin A 0%	Vitamin C 20%	Calcium 0%	Iron 2%

Del Monte, Tropical Fruit Salad in 100% Juice

1/2 cup / 126g

Amount per serving	%DV	Amount per serving	%DV	Amount per serving	%DV
Calories 60		**Cholesterol** 0mg	0%	**Total Carbohydrate** 21g	7%
Total Fat 0g	0%	**Sodium** 10mg	0%	Dietary Fiber 1g	4%
Saturated Fat 0g	0%	**Protein** 0g		Sugars 20g	
Polyunsaturated Fat 0g					
Monounsaturated Fat 0g		Vitamin A 4%	Vitamin C 80%	Calcium 0%	Iron 2%

Dole, Fresh Fruits, Apple

1 medium apple / 154g

Amount per serving	%DV	Amount per serving	%DV	Amount per serving	%DV
Calories 80		**Cholesterol** 0mg	0%	**Total Carbohydrate** 22g	7%
Total Fat 0g	0%	**Sodium** 0mg	0%	Dietary Fiber 4g	16%
Saturated Fat 0g	0%	**Protein** 0g		Sugars 16g	
Polyunsaturated Fat 0g					
Monounsaturated Fat 0g		Vitamin A 2%	Vitamin C 10%	Calcium 0%	Iron 2%

Dole, Fresh Fruits, Apricots

3 apricots / 114g

Amount per serving	%DV	Amount per serving	%DV	Amount per serving	%DV
Calories 60		**Cholesterol** 0mg	0%	**Total Carbohydrate** 11g	4%
Total Fat 1g	2%	**Sodium** 0mg	0%	Dietary Fiber 1g	4%
Saturated Fat 0g	0%	**Protein** 0g		Sugars 11g	
Polyunsaturated Fat 0g					
Monounsaturated Fat 0g		Vitamin A 39%	Vitamin C 17%	Calcium 2%	Iron 2%

Dole, Fresh Fruits, Avocados

1/5 medium / 30g

Amount per serving	%DV	Amount per serving	%DV	Amount per serving	%DV
Calories 50		**Cholesterol** 0mg	0%	**Total Carbohydrate** 3g	1%
Total Fat 5g	8%	**Sodium** 0mg	0%	Dietary Fiber 2g	8%
Saturated Fat 1g	5%	**Protein** 1g		Sugars 0g	
Polyunsaturated Fat 0g					
Monounsaturated Fat 0g		Vitamin A 0%	Vitamin C 4%	Calcium 0%	Iron 2%

Dole, Fresh Fruits, Baby Bananas

81g

Amount per serving	%DV	Amount per serving	%DV	Amount per serving	%DV
Calories 72		**Cholesterol** 0mg	0%	**Total Carbohydrate** 19g	6%
Total Fat 0g	0%	**Sodium** 1mg	0%	Dietary Fiber 2g	8%
Saturated Fat 0g	0%	**Protein** 1g		Sugars 10g	
Polyunsaturated Fat 0g					
Monounsaturated Fat 0g		Vitamin A 1% Vitamin C 12%		Calcium 0% Iron 1%	

Dole, Fresh Fruits, Bananas

1 medium banana / 126g

Amount per serving	%DV	Amount per serving	%DV	Amount per serving	%DV
Calories 110		**Cholesterol** 0mg	0%	**Total Carbohydrate** 29g	10%
Total Fat 0g	0%	**Sodium** 0mg	0%	Dietary Fiber 3g	12%
Saturated Fat 0g	0%	**Protein** 1g		Sugars 15g	
Polyunsaturated Fat 0g					
Monounsaturated Fat 0g		Vitamin A 2% Vitamin C 20%		Calcium 0% Iron 2%	

Dole, Fresh Fruits, Blackberries

1 cup / 144g

Amount per serving	%DV	Amount per serving	%DV	Amount per serving	%DV
Calories 60		**Cholesterol** 0mg	0%	**Total Carbohydrate** 14g	5%
Total Fat 1g	2%	**Sodium** 0mg	0%	Dietary Fiber 8g	32%
Saturated Fat 0g	0%	**Protein** 2g		Sugars 7g	
Polyunsaturated Fat 0g					
Monounsaturated Fat 0g		Vitamin A 6% Vitamin C 50%		Calcium 4% Iron 4%	

Dole, Fresh Fruits, Chayote

1/2 cup / cooked / 80g

Amount per serving	%DV	Amount per serving	%DV	Amount per serving	%DV
Calories 17		**Cholesterol** 0mg	0%	**Total Carbohydrate** 4g	1%
Total Fat 0g	0%	**Sodium** 3mg	0%	Dietary Fiber 2g	8%
Saturated Fat 0g	0%	**Protein** 1g		Sugars 0g	
Polyunsaturated Fat 0g					
Monounsaturated Fat 0g		Vitamin A 0% Vitamin C 13%		Calcium 0% Iron 0%	

Dole, Fresh Fruits, Cherries

1 cup / 140g

Amount per serving	%DV	Amount per serving	%DV	Amount per serving	%DV
Calories 90		**Cholesterol** 0mg	0%	**Total Carbohydrate** 22g	7%
Total Fat 0g	0%	**Sodium** 0mg	0%	Dietary Fiber 3g	12%
Saturated Fat 0g	0%	**Protein** 1g		Sugars 18g	
Polyunsaturated Fat 0g					
Monounsaturated Fat 0g		Vitamin A 2% Vitamin C 15%		Calcium 2% Iron 2%	

Dole, Fresh Fruits, Cranberries

1 cup / 95g

Amount per serving	%DV	Amount per serving	%DV	Amount per serving	%DV
Calories 45		**Cholesterol** 0mg	0%	**Total Carbohydrate** 12g	4%
Total Fat 0g	0%	**Sodium** 0mg	0%	Dietary Fiber 4g	16%
Saturated Fat 0g	0%	**Protein** 0g		Sugars 4g	
Polyunsaturated Fat 0g					
Monounsaturated Fat 0g		Vitamin A 2% Vitamin C 20%		Calcium 0% Iron 2%	

Dole, Fresh Fruits, Grapes

26 grapes / about 3/4 cup / 126g

Amount per serving	%DV	Amount per serving	%DV	Amount per serving	%DV
Calories 90		**Cholesterol** 0mg	0%	**Total Carbohydrate** 23g	8%
Total Fat 0g	0%	**Sodium** 0mg	0%	Dietary Fiber 1g	4%
Saturated Fat 0g	0%	**Protein** 1g		Sugars 20g	
Polyunsaturated Fat 0g					
Monounsaturated Fat 0g		Vitamin A 2% Vitamin C 25%		Calcium 2% Iron 2%	

Dole, Fresh Fruits, Nectarines

1 medium nectarine / 140g

Amount per serving	%DV	Amount per serving	%DV	Amount per serving	%DV
Calories 60		**Cholesterol** 0mg	0%	**Total Carbohydrate** 15g	5%
Total Fat 0g	0%	**Sodium** 0mg	0%	Dietary Fiber 2g	8%
Saturated Fat 0g	0%	**Protein** 1g		Sugars 11g	
Polyunsaturated Fat 0g					
Monounsaturated Fat 0g		Vitamin A 10% Vitamin C 15%		Calcium 0% Iron 2%	

Dole, Fresh Fruits, Oranges

1 medium orange / 121g

Amount per serving	%DV	Amount per serving	%DV	Amount per serving	%DV
Calories 60		**Cholesterol** 0mg	0%	**Total Carbohydrate** 14g	5%
Total Fat 0g	0%	**Sodium** 0mg	0%	Dietary Fiber 3g	12%
Saturated Fat 0g	0%	**Protein** 1g		Sugars 13g	
Polyunsaturated Fat 0g					
Monounsaturated Fat 0g		Vitamin A 6% Vitamin C 100%		Calcium 4% Iron 0%	

Dole, Fresh Fruits, Organic Bananas

1 medium banana / 126g

Amount per serving	%DV	Amount per serving	%DV	Amount per serving	%DV
Calories 110		**Cholesterol** 0mg	0%	**Total Carbohydrate** 29g	10%
Total Fat 0g	0%	**Sodium** 0mg	0%	Dietary Fiber 3g	12%
Saturated Fat 0g	0%	**Protein** 0g		Sugars 15g	
Polyunsaturated Fat 0g					
Monounsaturated Fat 0g		Vitamin A 0% Vitamin C 18%		Calcium 0% Iron 2%	

Dole, Fresh Fruits, Organic Pineapple

3 slices

Amount per serving	%DV	Amount per serving	%DV	Amount per serving	%DV
Calories 60		**Cholesterol** 0mg	0%	**Total Carbohydrate** 15g	5%
Total Fat 0g	0%	**Sodium** 0mg	0%	Dietary Fiber 2g	8%
Saturated Fat 0g	0%	**Protein** 1g		Sugars 12g	
Polyunsaturated Fat 0g					
Monounsaturated Fat 0g		Vitamin A 2% Vitamin C 110%		Calcium 2% Iron 2%	

Dole, Fresh Fruits, Peaches

1 large peach / 147g

Amount per serving	%DV	Amount per serving	%DV	Amount per serving	%DV
Calories 60		**Cholesterol** 0mg	0%	**Total Carbohydrate** 14g	5%
Total Fat 0g	0%	**Sodium** 0mg	0%	Dietary Fiber 2g	8%
Saturated Fat 0g	0%	**Protein** 1g		Sugars 12g	
Polyunsaturated Fat 0g					
Monounsaturated Fat 0g		Vitamin A 10% Vitamin C 15%		Calcium 0% Iron 2%	

Dole, Fresh Fruits, Pears

1 medium pear / 166g

Amount per serving	%DV	Amount per serving	%DV	Amount per serving	%DV
Calories 100		**Cholesterol** 0mg	0%	**Total Carbohydrate** 26g	9%
Total Fat 0g	0%	**Sodium** 0mg	0%	Dietary Fiber 5g	20%
Saturated Fat 0g	0%	**Protein** 1g		Sugars 16g	
Polyunsaturated Fat 0g					
Monounsaturated Fat 0g		Vitamin A 0% Vitamin C 10%		Calcium 2% Iron 2%	

Dole, Fresh Fruits, Pineapples

2 slices / 3 inch diameter / 3/4 inch thick / 112g

Amount per serving	%DV	Amount per serving	%DV	Amount per serving	%DV
Calories 60		**Cholesterol** 0mg	0%	**Total Carbohydrate** 15g	5%
Total Fat 0g	0%	**Sodium** 0mg	0%	Dietary Fiber 2g	8%
Saturated Fat 0g	0%	**Protein** 1g		Sugars 12g	
Polyunsaturated Fat 0g					
Monounsaturated Fat 0g		Vitamin A 2% Vitamin C 110%		Calcium 2% Iron 2%	

Dole, Fresh Fruits, Plantains

1/2 medium / cooked / 90g

Amount per serving	%DV	Amount per serving	%DV	Amount per serving	%DV
Calories 100		**Cholesterol** 0mg	0%	**Total Carbohydrate** 28g	9%
Total Fat 0g	0%	**Sodium** 0mg	0%	Dietary Fiber 2g	8%
Saturated Fat 0g	0%	**Protein** 1g		Sugars 13g	
Polyunsaturated Fat 0g					
Monounsaturated Fat 0g		Vitamin A 15% Vitamin C 15%		Calcium 0% Iron 2%	

Dole, Fresh Fruits, Plums

2 medium / 151g

Amount per serving	%DV	Amount per serving	%DV	Amount per serving	%DV
Calories 70		**Cholesterol** 0mg	0%	**Total Carbohydrate** 17g	6%
Total Fat 0g	0%	**Sodium** 0mg	0%	Dietary Fiber 2g	8%
Saturated Fat 0g	0%	**Protein** 1g		Sugars 15g	
Polyunsaturated Fat 0g					
Monounsaturated Fat 0g		Vitamin A 10% Vitamin C 25%		Calcium 0% Iron 25%	

Dole, Fresh Fruits, Red Raspberries

1 cup / 123g

Amount per serving	%DV	Amount per serving	%DV	Amount per serving	%DV
Calories 60		**Cholesterol** 0mg	0%	**Total Carbohydrate** 15g	5%
Total Fat 1g	2%	**Sodium** 0mg	0%	Dietary Fiber 8g	32%
Saturated Fat 0g	0%	**Protein** 1g		Sugars 5g	
Polyunsaturated Fat 0g					
Monounsaturated Fat 0g		Vitamin A 0% Vitamin C 50%		Calcium 4% Iron 6%	

Dole, Fresh Fruits, Strawberries

1 cup whole / 147g

Amount per serving	%DV	Amount per serving	%DV	Amount per serving	%DV
Calories 45		**Cholesterol** 0mg	0%	**Total Carbohydrate** 11g	4%
Total Fat 0g	0%	**Sodium** 0mg	0%	Dietary Fiber 3g	12%
Saturated Fat 0g	0%	**Protein** 1g		Sugars 7g	
Polyunsaturated Fat 0g					
Monounsaturated Fat 0g		Vitamin A 0% Vitamin C 140%		Calcium 2% Iron 4%	

Driscoll's Raspberries

1 cup / 123g

Amount per serving	%DV	Amount per serving	%DV	Amount per serving	%DV
Calories 52		**Cholesterol** 0mg	0%	**Total Carbohydrate** 12g	4%
Total Fat 0.7g	1%	**Sodium** 1mg	0%	Dietary Fiber 7g	28%
Saturated Fat 0g	0%	**Protein** 1g		Sugars 4g	
Polyunsaturated Fat 0g					
Monounsaturated Fat 0g		Vitamin A 0% Vitamin C 0%		Calcium 3% Iron 44%	

Eden Foods, Apple Butter, Organic

1 tbsp / 15g

Amount per serving	%DV	Amount per serving	%DV	Amount per serving	%DV
Calories 20		**Cholesterol** 0mg	0%	**Total Carbohydrate** 4g	1%
Total Fat 0g	0%	**Sodium** 0mg	0%	Dietary Fiber 1g	4%
Saturated Fat 0g	0%	**Protein** 0g		Sugars 4g	
Polyunsaturated Fat 0g					
Monounsaturated Fat 0g		Vitamin A 0% Vitamin C 0%		Calcium 0% Iron 0%	

Eden Foods, Apple Cherry Butter, Organic

1 tbsp / 15g

Amount per serving	%DV	Amount per serving	%DV	Amount per serving	%DV
Calories 25		**Cholesterol** 0mg	0%	**Total Carbohydrate** 6g	2%
Total Fat 0g	0%	**Sodium** 0mg	0%	Dietary Fiber 1g	4%
Saturated Fat 0g	0%	**Protein** 0g		Sugars 5g	
Polyunsaturated Fat 0g					
Monounsaturated Fat 0g		Vitamin A 0% Vitamin C 0%		Calcium 0% Iron 0%	

Eden Foods, Apple Cherry Sauce, Organic

1/2 cup / 124g

Amount per serving	%DV	Amount per serving	%DV	Amount per serving	%DV
Calories 70		**Cholesterol** 0mg	0%	**Total Carbohydrate** 17g	6%
Total Fat 0g	0%	**Sodium** 10mg	0%	Dietary Fiber 3g	12%
Saturated Fat 0g	0%	**Protein** 0g		Sugars 12g	
Polyunsaturated Fat 0g					
Monounsaturated Fat 0g		Vitamin A 0% Vitamin C 0%		Calcium 0% Iron 0%	

Eden Foods, Apple Cinnamon Sauce, Organic

1/2 cup / 122g

Amount per serving	%DV	Amount per serving	%DV	Amount per serving	%DV
Calories 60		**Cholesterol** 0mg	0%	**Total Carbohydrate** 14g	5%
Total Fat 0g	0%	**Sodium** 10mg	0%	Dietary Fiber 2g	8%
Saturated Fat 0g	0%	**Protein** 0g		Sugars 12g	
Polyunsaturated Fat 0g					
Monounsaturated Fat 0g		Vitamin A 0% Vitamin C 0%		Calcium 0% Iron 0%	

Eden Foods, Apple Sauce, Organic

1/2 cup / 122g

Amount per serving	%DV	Amount per serving	%DV	Amount per serving	%DV
Calories 60		**Cholesterol** 0mg	0%	**Total Carbohydrate** 13g	4%
Total Fat 0g	0%	**Sodium** 10mg	0%	Dietary Fiber 2g	8%
Saturated Fat 0g	0%	**Protein** 0g		Sugars 10g	
Polyunsaturated Fat 0g					
Monounsaturated Fat 0g		Vitamin A 0% Vitamin C 0%		Calcium 0% Iron 0%	

Eden Foods, Apple Strawberry Sauce, Organic

1/2 cup / 122g

Amount per serving	%DV	Amount per serving	%DV	Amount per serving	%DV
Calories 60		**Cholesterol** 0mg	0%	**Total Carbohydrate** 13g	4%
Total Fat 0g	0%	**Sodium** 10mg	0%	Dietary Fiber 2g	8%
Saturated Fat 0g	0%	**Protein** 0g		Sugars 10g	
Polyunsaturated Fat 0g					
Monounsaturated Fat 0g		Vitamin A 0% Vitamin C 0%		Calcium 0% Iron 0%	

Eden Foods, Thompson Raisins, Organic

1/4 cup / 40g

Amount per serving	%DV	Amount per serving	%DV	Amount per serving	%DV
Calories 130		**Cholesterol** 0mg	0%	**Total Carbohydrate** 32g	11%
Total Fat 0g	0%	**Sodium** 0mg	0%	Dietary Fiber 1.5g	6%
Saturated Fat 0g	0%	**Protein** 1g		Sugars 24g	
Polyunsaturated Fat 0g					
Monounsaturated Fat 0g		Vitamin A 0% Vitamin C 0%		Calcium 2% Iron 4%	

Figs, Canned, Water Packed, Solids and Liquids

1 fig, with liquid / 27g

Amount per serving	%DV	Amount per serving	%DV	Amount per serving	%DV
Calories 14.5		**Cholesterol** 0mg	0%	**Total Carbohydrate** 4g	1%
Total Fat 0g	0%	**Sodium** 0.5mg	0%	Dietary Fiber 0.5g	2%
Saturated Fat 0g	0%	**Protein** 0g		Sugars 3g	
Polyunsaturated Fat 0g					
Monounsaturated Fat 0g		Vitamin A 10.5% Vitamin C 0.5%		Calcium 7.5% Iron 0%	

Figs, Dried, Uncooked

1 fig / 8.4g

Amount per serving	%DV	Amount per serving	%DV	Amount per serving	%DV
Calories 21		**Cholesterol** 0mg	0%	**Total Carbohydrate** 5.5g	2%
Total Fat 0g	0%	**Sodium** 1mg	0%	Dietary Fiber 1g	4%
Saturated Fat 0g	0%	**Protein** 0.5g		Sugars 4g	
Polyunsaturated Fat 0g					
Monounsaturated Fat 0g		Vitamin A 1% Vitamin C 0%		Calcium 13.5% Iron 0%	

Fruit Cocktail, Canned, Juice Packed, Solids and Liquids

1 cup / 237g

Amount per serving	%DV	Amount per serving	%DV	Amount per serving	%DV
Calories 109		**Cholesterol** 0mg	0%	**Total Carbohydrate** 28g	9%
Total Fat 0g	0%	**Sodium** 9mg	0%	Dietary Fiber 2g	8%
Saturated Fat 0g	0%	**Protein** 1g		Sugars 26g	
Polyunsaturated Fat 0g					
Monounsaturated Fat 0g		Vitamin A 14% Vitamin C 11%		Calcium 2% Iron 3%	

Fruit Cocktail, Canned, Water Packed, Solids and Liquids

1 cup / 237g

Amount per serving	%DV	Amount per serving	%DV	Amount per serving	%DV
Calories 76		**Cholesterol** 0mg	0%	**Total Carbohydrate** 20g	7%
Total Fat 0g	0%	**Sodium** 9mg	0%	Dietary Fiber 2g	8%
Saturated Fat 0g	0%	**Protein** 1g		Sugars 18g	
Polyunsaturated Fat 0g					
Monounsaturated Fat 0g		Vitamin A 12% Vitamin C 8%		Calcium 1% Iron 3%	

Fruit Salad, Canned, Juice Packed, Solids and Liquids

1 cup / 249g

Amount per serving	%DV	Amount per serving	%DV	Amount per serving	%DV
Calories 124		**Cholesterol** 0mg	0%	**Total Carbohydrate** 32g	11%
Total Fat 0g	0%	**Sodium** 12mg	0%	Dietary Fiber 2g	8%
Saturated Fat 0g	0%	**Protein** 1g		Sugars NA	
Polyunsaturated Fat 0g					
Monounsaturated Fat 0g		Vitamin A 30% Vitamin C 14%		Calcium 3% Iron 3%	

Fruit Salad, Canned, Water Packed, Solids and Liquids

1 cup / 245g

Amount per serving	%DV	Amount per serving	%DV	Amount per serving	%DV
Calories 74		**Cholesterol** 0mg	0%	**Total Carbohydrate** 19g	6%
Total Fat 0g	0%	**Sodium** 7mg	0%	Dietary Fiber 2g	8%
Saturated Fat 0g	0%	**Protein** 1g		Sugars NA	
Polyunsaturated Fat 0g					
Monounsaturated Fat 0g		Vitamin A 22% Vitamin C 8%		Calcium 2% Iron 4%	

Fruit, Mixed (Prune and Apricot and Pear), Dried

1/4 cup

Amount per serving	%DV	Amount per serving	%DV	Amount per serving	%DV
Calories 68		**Cholesterol** 0mg	0%	**Total Carbohydrate** 18g	6%
Total Fat 0g	0%	**Sodium** 5mg	0%	Dietary Fiber 2g	8%
Saturated Fat 0g	0%	**Protein** 1g		Sugars 150g	
Polyunsaturated Fat 0g					
Monounsaturated Fat 0g		Vitamin A 14% Vitamin C 2%		Calcium 1% Iron 4%	

Hadley Dates, Whole Deglet Noor

5 dates / 41.3g

Amount per serving	%DV	Amount per serving	%DV	Amount per serving	%DV
Calories 120		**Cholesterol** 0mg	0%	**Total Carbohydrate** 31g	10%
Total Fat 0g	0%	**Sodium** 0mg	0%	Dietary Fiber 3g	12%
Saturated Fat 0g	0%	**Protein** 1g		Sugars 29g	
Polyunsulurated Fat 0g					
Monounsaturated Fat 0g		Vitamin A 0% Vitamin C 0%		Calcium 2% Iron 2%	

Hadley Dates, Whole Fancy Medjool

1 - 2 dates / 40g

Amount per serving	%DV	Amount per serving	%DV	Amount per serving	%DV
Calories 120		**Cholesterol** 0mg	0%	**Total Carbohydrate** 31g	10%
Total Fat 0g	0%	**Sodium** 10mg	0%	Dietary Fiber 3g	12%
Saturated Fat 0g	0%	**Protein** 1g		Sugars 25g	
Polyunsaturated Fat 0g					
Monounsaturated Fat 0g		Vitamin A 0% Vitamin C 0%		Calcium 0% Iron 2%	

Litchis, Dried

1 fruit / 2.5g

Amount per serving	%DV	Amount per serving	%DV	Amount per serving	%DV
Calories 7		**Cholesterol** 0mg	0%	**Total Carbohydrate** 2g	1%
Total Fat 0g	0%	**Sodium** 0mg	0%	Dietary Fiber 0g	0%
Saturated Fat 0g	0%	**Protein** 0g		Sugars 2g	
Polyunsaturated Fat 0g					
Monounsaturated Fat 0g		Vitamin A 0% Vitamin C 8%		Calcium 0% Iron 0%	

Mariani Premium Fruit, Berries 'N Cherries

1/3 cup / 40g

Amount per serving	%DV	Amount per serving	%DV	Amount per serving	%DV
Calories 140		**Cholesterol** 0mg	0%	**Total Carbohydrate** 33g	11%
Total Fat 0g	0%	**Sodium** 15mg	1%	Dietary Fiber 2g	8%
Saturated Fat 0g	0%	**Protein** 1g		Sugars 28g	
Polyunsaturated Fat 0g					
Monounsaturated Fat 0g		Vitamin A 15% Vitamin C 2%		Calcium 2% Iron 2%	

Mariani Premium Fruit, Cherries

1/4 cup / 40g

Amount per serving	%DV	Amount per serving	%DV	Amount per serving	%DV
Calories 140		**Cholesterol** 0mg	0%	**Total Carbohydrate** 33g	11%
Total Fat 0g	0%	**Sodium** 0mg	0%	Dietary Fiber 1g	4%
Saturated Fat 0g	0%	**Protein** 1g		Sugars 27g	
Polyunsaturated Fat 0g					
Monounsaturated Fat 0g		Vitamin A 35% Vitamin C 0%		Calcium 2% Iron 0%	

Mariani Premium Fruit, Cherry Pie Cherries

1/4 cup / 40g

Amount per serving	%DV	Amount per serving	%DV	Amount per serving	%DV
Calories 130		**Cholesterol** 0mg	0%	**Total Carbohydrate** 31g	10%
Total Fat 0g	0%	**Sodium** 15mg	1%	Dietary Fiber 2g	8%
Saturated Fat 0g	0%	**Protein** 1g		Sugars 27g	
Polyunsaturated Fat 0g					
Monounsaturated Fat 0g		Vitamin A 10% Vitamin C 0%		Calcium 6% Iron 4%	

Mariani Premium Fruit, Chopped Dates

1/3 cup / 40g

Amount per serving	%DV	Amount per serving	%DV	Amount per serving	%DV
Calories 130		**Cholesterol** 0mg	0%	**Total Carbohydrate** 33g	11%
Total Fat 0g	0%	**Sodium** 0mg	0%	Dietary Fiber 3g	12%
Saturated Fat 0g	0%	**Protein** 0g		Sugars 26g	
Polyunsaturated Fat 0g					
Monounsaturated Fat 0g		Vitamin A 0% Vitamin C 0%		Calcium 2% Iron 6%	

Mariani Premium Fruit, Cranberries

1/3 cup

Amount per serving	%DV	Amount per serving	%DV	Amount per serving	%DV
Calories 130		**Cholesterol** 0mg	0%	**Total Carbohydrate** 33g	11%
Total Fat 0g	0%	**Sodium** 0mg	0%	Dietary Fiber 2g	8%
Saturated Fat 0g	0%	**Protein** 0g		Sugars 27g	
Polyunsaturated Fat 0g					
Monounsaturated Fat 0g		Vitamin A 0%	Vitamin C 0%	Calcium 0%	Iron 0%

Mariani Premium Fruit, Cranberries (Snack Box)

1 box / 43g

Amount per serving	%DV	Amount per serving	%DV	Amount per serving	%DV
Calories 140		**Cholesterol** 0mg	0%	**Total Carbohydrate** 35g	12%
Total Fat 0g	0%	**Sodium** 30mg	1%	Dietary Fiber 2g	8%
Saturated Fat 0g	0%	**Protein** 0g		Sugars 29g	
Polyunsaturated Fat 0g					
Monounsaturated Fat 0g		Vitamin A 0%	Vitamin C 0%	Calcium 0%	Iron 0%

Mariani Premium Fruit, Orchard Fruit, California Apricots

1/4 cup / 40g

Amount per serving	%DV	Amount per serving	%DV	Amount per serving	%DV
Calories 110		**Cholesterol** 0mg	0%	**Total Carbohydrate** 25g	8%
Total Fat 0g	0%	**Sodium** 15mg	1%	Dietary Fiber 4g	16%
Saturated Fat 0g	0%	**Protein** 1g		Sugars 20g	
Polyunsaturated Fat 0g					
Monounsaturated Fat 0g		Vitamin A 60%	Vitamin C 2%	Calcium 2%	Iron 8%

Mariani Premium Fruit, Orchard Fruit, Mediterranean Apricots

1/4 cup / 40g

Amount per serving	%DV	Amount per serving	%DV	Amount per serving	%DV
Calories 110		**Cholesterol** 0mg	0%	**Total Carbohydrate** 25g	8%
Total Fat 0g	0%	**Sodium** 10mg	0%	Dietary Fiber 2g	8%
Saturated Fat 0g	0%	**Protein** 1g		Sugars 15g	
Polyunsaturated Fat 0g					
Monounsaturated Fat 0g		Vitamin A 10%	Vitamin C 0%	Calcium 2%	Iron 4%

Mariani Premium Fruit, Orchard Fruit, Mixed Fruit

1/4 cup / 40g

Amount per serving	%DV	Amount per serving	%DV	Amount per serving	%DV
Calories 110		**Cholesterol** 0mg	0%	**Total Carbohydrate** 25g	8%
Total Fat 0g	0%	**Sodium** 20mg	1%	Dietary Fiber 4g	16%
Saturated Fat 0g	0%	**Protein** 1g		Sugars 17g	
Polyunsaturated Fat 0g					
Monounsaturated Fat 0g		Vitamin A 15%	Vitamin C 0%	Calcium 2%	Iron 4%

Mariani Premium Fruit, Orchard Fruit, Plum Support with Glucosamine

1/4 cup

Amount per serving	%DV	Amount per serving	%DV	Amount per serving	%DV
Calories 110		Cholesterol 0mg	0%	Total Carbohydrate 25g	8%
Total Fat 0g	0%	Sodium 0.5mg	0%	Dietary Fiber 3g	12%
Saturated Fat 0g	0%	Protein 1g		Sugars 17g	
Polyunsaturated Fat 0g					
Monounsaturated Fat 0g		Vitamin A 15% Vitamin C 2%		Calcium 0% Iron 20%	

Mariani Premium Fruit, Orchard Fruit, Sliced Apples

1/3 cup / 40g

Amount per serving	%DV	Amount per serving	%DV	Amount per serving	%DV
Calories 100		Cholesterol 0mg	0%	Total Carbohydrate 25g	8%
Total Fat 0g	0%	Sodium 130mg	5%	Dietary Fiber 3g	12%
Saturated Fat 0g	0%	Protein 1g		Sugars 13g	
Polyunsaturated Fat 0g					
Monounsaturated Fat 0g		Vitamin A 2% Vitamin C 20%		Calcium 0% Iron 20%	

Mariani Premium Fruit, Orchard Fruit, Ultimate Apricots

1/4 cup / 40g

Amount per serving	%DV	Amount per serving	%DV	Amount per serving	%DV
Calories 100		Cholesterol 0mg	0%	Total Carbohydrate 24g	8%
Total Fat 0g	0%	Sodium 15mg	1%	Dietary Fiber 2g	8%
Saturated Fat 0g	0%	Protein 1g		Sugars 13g	
Polyunsaturated Fat 0g					
Monounsaturated Fat 0g		Vitamin A 6% Vitamin C 0%		Calcium 2% Iron 2%	

Mariani Premium Fruit, Pitted Dates

6-7 dates / 40g

Amount per serving	%DV	Amount per serving	%DV	Amount per serving	%DV
Calories 120		Cholesterol 0mg	0%	Total Carbohydrate 30g	10%
Total Fat 0g	0%	Sodium 0mg	0%	Dietary Fiber 3g	12%
Saturated Fat 0g	0%	Protein 1g		Sugars 25g	
Polyunsaturated Fat 0g					
Monounsaturated Fat 0g		Vitamin A 0% Vitamin C 0%		Calcium 2% Iron 2%	

Mariani Premium Fruit, Raisins

1/4 cup / 40g

Amount per serving	%DV	Amount per serving	%DV	Amount per serving	%DV
Calories 120		Cholesterol 0mg	0%	Total Carbohydrate 32g	11%
Total Fat 0g	0%	Sodium 0mg	0%	Dietary Fiber 1g	4%
Saturated Fat 0g	0%	Protein 1g		Sugars 24g	
Polyunsaturated Fat 0g					
Monounsaturated Fat 0g		Vitamin A 0% Vitamin C 2%		Calcium 2% Iron 4%	

Mariani Premium Fruit, Strawberries

1/4 cup / 40g

Amount per serving	%DV	Amount per serving	%DV	Amount per serving	%DV
Calories 140		**Cholesterol** 0mg	0%	**Total Carbohydrate** 32g	11%
Total Fat 0g	0%	**Sodium** 15mg	1%	Dietary Fiber 2g	8%
Saturated Fat 0g	0%	**Protein** 0g		Sugars 28g	
Polyunsaturated Fat 0g					
Monounsaturated Fat 0g		Vitamin A 0% Vitamin C 10%		Calcium 4% Iron 2%	

Mariani Premium Fruit, Tropical Fruit, Island Fruits

1/4 cup / 40g

Amount per serving	%DV	Amount per serving	%DV	Amount per serving	%DV
Calories 140		**Cholesterol** 0mg	0%	**Total Carbohydrate** 34g	11%
Total Fat 0g	0%	**Sodium** 120mg	5%	Dietary Fiber 1g	4%
Saturated Fat 0g	0%	**Protein** 0g		Sugars 30g	
Polyunsaturated Fat 0g					
Monounsaturated Fat 0g		Vitamin A 4% Vitamin C 0%		Calcium 4% Iron 0%	

Mariani Premium Fruit, Tropical Fruit, Mango

5 slices / 40g

Amount per serving	%DV	Amount per serving	%DV	Amount per serving	%DV
Calories 140		**Cholesterol** 0mg	0%	**Total Carbohydrate** 36g	12%
Total Fat 0g	0%	**Sodium** 15mg	1%	Dietary Fiber 1g	4%
Saturated Fat 0g	0%	**Protein** 0g		Sugars 28g	
Polyunsaturated Fat 0g					
Monounsaturated Fat 0g		Vitamin A 4% Vitamin C 0%		Calcium 6% Iron 0%	

Mariani Premium Fruit, Tropical Fruit, Philippine Mango

6 slices / 40g

Amount per serving	%DV	Amount per serving	%DV	Amount per serving	%DV
Calories 130		**Cholesterol** 0mg	0%	**Total Carbohydrate** 32g	11%
Total Fat 0g	0%	**Sodium** 60mg	3%	Dietary Fiber 1g	4%
Saturated Fat 0g	0%	**Protein** 1g		Sugars 27g	
Polyunsaturated Fat 0g					
Monounsaturated Fat 0g		Vitamin A 35% Vitamin C 25%		Calcium 0% Iron 0%	

Mariani Premium Fruit, Tropical Fruit, Tropical Medley

1/3 cup / 40g

Amount per serving	%DV	Amount per serving	%DV	Amount per serving	%DV
Calories 130		**Cholesterol** 0mg	0%	**Total Carbohydrate** 31g	10%
Total Fat 0g	0%	**Sodium** 40mg	2%	Dietary Fiber 3g	12%
Saturated Fat 0g	0%	**Protein** 1g		Sugars 22g	
Polyunsaturated Fat 0g					
Monounsaturated Fat 0g		Vitamin A 15% Vitamin C 0%		Calcium 2% Iron 4%	

Mariani Premium Fruit, Tropical Fruit, Tropical Pineapple

1/3 cup / 40g

Amount per serving	%DV	Amount per serving	%DV	Amount per serving	%DV
Calories 140		**Cholesterol** 0mg	0%	**Total Carbohydrate** 35g	12%
Total Fat 0g	0%	**Sodium** 85mg	4%	Dietary Fiber 1g	4%
Saturated Fat 0g	0%	**Protein** 0g		Sugars 31g	
Polyunsaturated Fat 0g					
Monounsaturated Fat 0g		Vitamin A 0%	Vitamin C 0%	Calcium 2%	Iron 0%

Mariani Premium Fruit, Wild Blueberries

1/4 cup / 40g

Amount per serving	%DV	Amount per serving	%DV	Amount per serving	%DV
Calories 140		**Cholesterol** 0mg	0%	**Total Carbohydrate** 35g	12%
Total Fat 0g	0%	**Sodium** 0mg	0%	Dietary Fiber 2g	8%
Saturated Fat 0g	0%	**Protein** 0g		Sugars 30g	
Polyunsaturated Fat 0g					
Monounsaturated Fat 0g		Vitamin A 0%	Vitamin C 0%	Calcium 2%	Iron 0%

Mariani Premium Fruit, Yogurt Coated, Cranberry Crunch

1 bag / 43g

Amount per serving	%DV	Amount per serving	%DV	Amount per serving	%DV
Calories 160		**Cholesterol** 0mg	0%	**Total Carbohydrate** 34g	11%
Total Fat 2g	3%	**Sodium** 25mg	1%	Dietary Fiber 2g	8%
Saturated Fat 0.5g	3%	**Protein** 1g		Sugars 28g	
Polyunsaturated Fat 0g					
Monounsaturated Fat 0g		Vitamin A 2%	Vitamin C 0%	Calcium 2%	Iron 6%

Mariani Premium Tropical Fruit, Pineapple Tango

1/3 cup

Amount per serving	%DV	Amount per serving	%DV	Amount per serving	%DV
Calories 130		**Cholesterol** 0mg	0%	**Total Carbohydrate** 33g	11%
Total Fat 0g	0%	**Sodium** 110mg	5%	Dietary Fiber 2g	8%
Saturated Fat 0g	0%	**Protein** 0g		Sugars 25g	
Polyunsaturated Fat 0g					
Monounsaturated Fat 0g		Vitamin A 0%	Vitamin C 0%	Calcium 0%	Iron 4%

Native Forest, Organic Mango Chunks

1/2 cup

Amount per serving	%DV	Amount per serving	%DV	Amount per serving	%DV
Calories 70		**Cholesterol** 0mg	0%	**Total Carbohydrate** 19g	6%
Total Fat 0g	0%	**Sodium** 0mg	0%	Dietary Fiber 2g	8%
Saturated Fat 0g	0%	**Protein** 0g		Sugars 17g	
Polyunsaturated Fat 0g					
Monounsaturated Fat 0g		Vitamin A 10%	Vitamin C 40%	Calcium 0%	Iron 0%

Native Forest, Organic Mangosteen

1/2 cup / 140g including liquid

Amount per serving	%DV	Amount per serving	%DV	Amount per serving	%DV
Calories 90		**Cholesterol** 0mg	0%	**Total Carbohydrate** 23g	8%
Total Fat 0g	0%	**Sodium** 10mg	0%	Dietary Fiber 1g	4%
Saturated Fat 0g	0%	**Protein** 0g		Sugars 22g	
Polyunsaturated Fat 0g					
Monounsaturated Fat 0g		Vitamin A 0% Vitamin C 0%		Calcium 0% Iron 0%	

Native Forest, Organic Papaya Chunks

1/2 cup / 123g

Amount per serving	%DV	Amount per serving	%DV	Amount per serving	%DV
Calories 60		**Cholesterol** 0mg	0%	**Total Carbohydrate** 14g	5%
Total Fat 0g	0%	**Sodium** 0mg	0%	Dietary Fiber 1g	4%
Saturated Fat 0g	0%	**Protein** 1g		Sugars 11g	
Polyunsaturated Fat 0g					
Monounsaturated Fat 0g		Vitamin A 15% Vitamin C 80%		Calcium 2% Iron 0%	

Native Forest, Organic Pineapple Chunks

1/2 cup with juice / 125g

Amount per serving	%DV	Amount per serving	%DV	Amount per serving	%DV
Calories 60		**Cholesterol** 0mg	0%	**Total Carbohydrate** 15g	5%
Total Fat 0g	0%	**Sodium** 10mg	0%	Dietary Fiber 1g	4%
Saturated Fat 0g	0%	**Protein** 0g		Sugars 13g	'
Polyunsaturated Fat 0g					
Monounsaturated Fat 0g		Vitamin A 0% Vitamin C 25%		Calcium 0% Iron 2%	

Native Forest, Organic Pineapple Crushed

1/2 cup with juice / 125g

Amount per serving	%DV	Amount per serving	%DV	Amount per serving	%DV
Calories 60		**Cholesterol** 0mg	0%	**Total Carbohydrate** 15g	5%
Total Fat 0g	0%	**Sodium** 10mg	0%	Dietary Fiber 1g	4%
Saturated Fat 0g	0%	**Protein** 0g		Sugars 13g	
Polyunsaturated Fat 0g					
Monounsaturated Fat 0g		Vitamin A 0% Vitamin C 25%		Calcium 0% Iron 2%	

Native Forest, Organic Pineapple Slices

1/2 cup with juice / 125g

Amount per serving	%DV	Amount per serving	%DV	Amount per serving	%DV
Calories 60		**Cholesterol** 0mg	0%	**Total Carbohydrate** 15g	5%
Total Fat 0g	0%	**Sodium** 10mg	0%	Dietary Fiber 1g	4%
Saturated Fat 0g	0%	**Protein** 0g		Sugars 13g	
Polyunsaturated Fat 0g					
Monounsaturated Fat 0g		Vitamin A 0% Vitamin C 25%		Calcium 0% Iron 2%	

Native Forest, Organic Rambutan

1/2 cup / 137g

Amount per serving	%DV	Amount per serving	%DV	Amount per serving	%DV
Calories 100		**Cholesterol** 0mg	0%	**Total Carbohydrate** 24g	8%
Total Fat 0g	0%	**Sodium** 10mg	0%	Dietary Fiber 1g	4%
Saturated Fat 0g	0%	**Protein** 0g		Sugars 23g	
Polyunsaturated Fat 0g					
Monounsaturated Fat 0g		Vitamin A 0%	Vitamin C 0%	Calcium 0%	Iron 0%

Native Forest, Organic Sliced Asian Pears

1/2 cup / 120g

Amount per serving	%DV	Amount per serving	%DV	Amount per serving	%DV
Calories 45		**Cholesterol** 0mg	0%	**Total Carbohydrate** 11g	4%
Total Fat 0g	0%	**Sodium** 5mg	0%	Dietary Fiber 2g	8%
Saturated Fat 0g	0%	**Protein** 0g		Sugars 8g	
Polyunsaturated Fat 0g					
Monounsaturated Fat 0g		Vitamin A 0%	Vitamin C 0%	Calcium 0%	Iron 0%

Native Forest, Organic Sliced Peaches

1/2 cup / 124g

Amount per serving	%DV	Amount per serving	%DV	Amount per serving	%DV
Calories 60		**Cholesterol** 0mg	0%	**Total Carbohydrate** 14g	5%
Total Fat 0g	0%	**Sodium** 3mg	0%	Dietary Fiber 1g	4%
Saturated Fat 0g	0%	**Protein** 1g		Sugars 13g	
Polyunsaturated Fat 0g					
Monounsaturated Fat 0g		Vitamin A 8%	Vitamin C 8%	Calcium 0%	Iron 4%

Native Forest, Organic Tropical Fruit Salad

1/2 cup / 133g

Amount per serving	%DV	Amount per serving	%DV	Amount per serving	%DV
Calories 70		**Cholesterol** 0mg	0%	**Total Carbohydrate** 16g	5%
Total Fat 0g	0%	**Sodium** 0mg	0%	Dietary Fiber 1g	4%
Saturated Fat 0g	0%	**Protein** 1g		Sugars 14g	
Polyunsaturated Fat 0g					
Monounsaturated Fat 0g		Vitamin A 10%	Vitamin C 70%	Calcium 2%	Iron 0%

Peaches, Canned, Juice Pack, Solids and Liquids

1 cup, halves or slices / 250g

Amount per serving	%DV	Amount per serving	%DV	Amount per serving	%DV
Calories 110		**Cholesterol** 0mg	0%	**Total Carbohydrate** 29g	10%
Total Fat 0g	0%	**Sodium** 10mg	0%	Dietary Fiber 3g	12%
Saturated Fat 0g	0%	**Protein** 2g		Sugars 26g	
Polyunsaturated Fat 0g					
Monounsaturated Fat 0g		Vitamin A 19%	Vitamin C 15%	Calcium 1%	Iron 4%

Peaches, Canned, Water Pack, Solids and Liquids

1 half, with liquid / 98g

Amount per serving	%DV	Amount per serving	%DV	Amount per serving	%DV
Calories 24		Cholesterol 0mg	0%	Total Carbohydrate 6g	2%
Total Fat 0g	0%	Sodium 3mg	0%	Dietary Fiber 1g	6%
Saturated Fat 0g	0%	Protein 0g		Sugars 5g	
Polyunsaturated Fat 0g					
Monounsaturated Fat 0g		Vitamin A 10% Vitamin C 5%		Calcium 0% Iron 2%	

Pears, Canned, Juice Pack, Solids and Liquids

1 half, with liquid / 76g

Amount per serving	%DV	Amount per serving	%DV	Amount per serving	%DV
Calories 38		Cholesterol 0mg	0%	Total Carbohydrate 10g	3%
Total Fat 0g	0%	Sodium 3mg	0%	Dietary Fiber 1g	4%
Saturated Fat 0g	0%	Protein 0.5g		Sugars 7.5g	
Polyunsaturated Fat 0g					
Monounsaturated Fat 0g		Vitamin A 4.5% Vitamin C 1%		Calcium 7% Iron 0%	

Pears, Canned, Water Pack, Solids and Liquids

1 half, with liquid / 76g

Amount per serving	%DV	Amount per serving	%DV	Amount per serving	%DV
Calories 22		Cholesterol 0mg	0%	Total Carbohydrate 6g	2%
Total Fat 0g	0%	Sodium 1.5mg	0%	Dietary Fiber 1g	4%
Saturated Fat 0g	0%	Protein 0g		Sugars 4.5g	
Polyunsaturated Fat 0g					
Monounsaturated Fat 0g		Vitamin A 0% Vitamin C 1%		Calcium 3% Iron 0%	

Peterson Farms Dried Cherries

1/4 cup / 40g

Amount per serving	%DV	Amount per serving	%DV	Amount per serving	%DV
Calories 140		Cholesterol 0mg	0%	Total Carbohydrate 33g	11%
Total Fat 0g	0%	Sodium 15mg	1%	Dietary Fiber 1g	4%
Saturated Fat 0g	0%	Protein 1g		Sugars 26g	
Polyunsaturated Fat 0g					
Monounsaturated Fat 0g		Vitamin A 15% Vitamin C 0%		Calcium 0% Iron 2%	

Pineapple, Canned, Juice Pack, Solids and Liquids

1 slice, or ring, 3″ diameter, with liquid / 47g

Amount per serving	%DV	Amount per serving	%DV	Amount per serving	%DV
Calories 28		Cholesterol 0mg	0%	Total Carbohydrate 7g	2%
Total Fat 0g	0%	Sodium 0mg	0%	Dietary Fiber 0g	0%
Saturated Fat 0g	0%	Protein 0g		Sugars 7g	
Polyunsaturated Fat 0g					
Monounsaturated Fat 0g		Vitamin A 0% Vitamin C 7%		Calcium 1% Iron 1%	

Pineapple, Canned, Water Pack, Solids and Liquids

1 slice, or ring / 3″ diameter with liquid / 47g

Amount per serving	%DV	Amount per serving	%DV	Amount per serving	%DV
Calories 15		**Cholesterol** 0mg	0%	**Total Carbohydrate** 4g	1%
Total Fat 0g	0%	**Sodium** 0.5mg	0%	Dietary Fiber 0.5g	2%
Saturated Fat 0g	0%	**Protein** 0g		Sugars 3.5g	
Polyunsaturated Fat 0g					
Monounsaturated Fat 0g		Vitamin A 18%	Vitamin C 3.5%	Calcium 7%	Iron 0%

Plums, Canned, Purple, Juice Pack, Solids and Liquids

1 plum, with liquid / 46g

Amount per serving	%DV	Amount per serving	%DV	Amount per serving	%DV
Calories 26.5		**Cholesterol** 0mg	0%	**Total Carbohydrate** 7g	2%
Total Fat 0g	0%	**Sodium** 0.5mg	0%	Dietary Fiber 0.5g	2%
Saturated Fat 0g	0%	**Protein** 0g		Sugars 6.5g	
Polyunsaturated Fat 0g					
Monounsaturated Fat 0g		Vitamin A 464%	Vitamin C 1.5%	Calcium 4.5%	Iron 0%

Plums, Canned, Purple, Water Pack, Solids and Liquids

1 plum, with liquid / 46g

Amount per serving	%DV	Amount per serving	%DV	Amount per serving	%DV
Calories 19		**Cholesterol** 0mg	0%	**Total Carbohydrate** 5g	2%
Total Fat 0g	0%	**Sodium** 0.5mg	0%	Dietary Fiber 0.5g	2%
Saturated Fat 0g	0%	**Protein** 0g		Sugars 4.5g	
Polyunsaturated Fat 0g					
Monounsaturated Fat 0g		Vitamin A 46%	Vitamin C 11%	Calcium 2%	Iron 2%

Rader Farms Tripleberry - Blueberries, Blackberries, Raspberries

1/4 cup

Amount per serving	%DV	Amount per serving	%DV	Amount per serving	%DV
Calories 17		**Cholesterol** 0mg	0%	**Total Carbohydrate** 4g	1%
Total Fat 0g	0%	**Sodium** 0mg	0%	Dietary Fiber 1g	4%
Saturated Fat 0g	0%	**Protein** 1g		Sugars 3g	
Polyunsaturated Fat 0g					
Monounsaturated Fat 0g		Vitamin A 0%	Vitamin C 0%	Calcium 25%	Iron 1%

Strawberries, Well-Pict, Sliced, Frozen

1 cup

Amount per serving	%DV	Amount per serving	%DV	Amount per serving	%DV
Calories 50		**Cholesterol** 0mg	0%	**Total Carbohydrate** 13g	4%
Total Fat 0g	0%	**Sodium** 0mg	0%	Dietary Fiber 3g	12%
Saturated Fat 0g	0%	**Protein** 0g		Sugars 6g	
Polyunsaturated Fat 0g					
Monounsaturated Fat 0g		Vitamin A 0%	Vitamin C 0%	Calcium 0%	Iron 4%

SunDate, California Fancy Medjool Dates

2-3 dates / 40g

Amount per serving	%DV	Amount per serving	%DV	Amount per serving	%DV
Calories 120		**Cholesterol** 0mg	0%	**Total Carbohydrate** 31g	10%
Total Fat 0g	0%	**Sodium** 0mg	0%	Dietary Fiber 3g	12%
Saturated Fat 0g	0%	**Protein** 1g		Sugars 25g	
Polyunsaturated Fat 0g					
Monounsaturated Fat 0g		Vitamin A 0% Vitamin C 0%		Calcium 2% Iron 2%	

SunDate, California Pitted Deglet Noor Dates

5-6 dates / 40g

Amount per serving	%DV	Amount per serving	%DV	Amount per serving	%DV
Calories 120		**Cholesterol** 0mg	0%	**Total Carbohydrate** 31g	10%
Total Fat 0g	0%	**Sodium** 0mg	0%	Dietary Fiber 3g	12%
Saturated Fat 0g	0%	**Protein** 1g		Sugars 25g	
Polyunsaturated Fat 0g					
Monounsaturated Fat 0g		Vitamin A 0% Vitamin C 0%		Calcium 4% Iron 2%	

Sunsweet Prunes

1 1/2 oz / about 6 prunes

Amount per serving	%DV	Amount per serving	%DV	Amount per serving	%DV
Calories 100		**Cholesterol** 0mg	0%	**Total Carbohydrate** 24g	8%
Total Fat 0g	0%	**Sodium** 5mg	0%	Dietary Fiber 3g	12%
Saturated Fat 0g	0%	**Protein** 1g		Sugars 12g	
Polyunsaturated Fat 0g					
Monounsaturated Fat 0g		Vitamin A 10% Vitamin C 0%		Calcium 2% Iron 2%	

Tangerines (Mandarin Oranges), Canned, Juice Packed, Drained

1 cup / 189g

Amount per serving	%DV	Amount per serving	%DV	Amount per serving	%DV
Calories 72		**Cholesterol** 0mg	0%	**Total Carbohydrate** 18g	6%
Total Fat 0g	0%	**Sodium** 9mg	0%	Dietary Fiber 2g	8%
Saturated Fat 0g	0%	**Protein** 1g		Sugars 16g	
Polyunsaturated Fat 0g					
Monounsaturated Fat 0g		Vitamin A 50% Vitamin C 107%		Calcium 2% Iron 3%	

Whole Grains

Why Eat Whole Grains?

Grains are important sources of many nutrients, including dietary fiber, several B vitamins (thiamin, riboflavin, niacin, and folate), and minerals (iron, magnesium, and selenium). Eating whole grains as part of a healthy diet may reduce the risk of heart disease and help with weight management. Additionally, consuming foods containing fiber, such as whole grains, may reduce constipation and diverticulitis. B vitamins play a role in metabolism and are essential for a healthy nervous system. Folate (folic acid), a B vitamin, is important before and during pregnancy because it helps prevent birth defects.

Daily Goal

The amount of grains you need to eat depends on your age, sex, and level of physical activity.

Children: 3 to 6 ounces
Adults: 6 to 8 ounces

1 ounce equivalents:
  1 slice of bread
  1 cup cereal
  ½ cup rice or pasta
  ½ cup cooked cereal
  1 6" tortilla

Grains are divided into two subgroups, whole grains and refined grains.

Whole grains contain the entire grain kernel—the bran, germ, and endosperm.

Examples of whole grains are:
- whole-wheat flour
- bulgur (cracked wheat)
- oatmeal
- quinoa
- farro
- brown rice

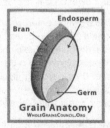

211

Refined grains have been milled, a process that removes the bran and germ. This is done to give grains a finer texture and improve their shelf life, but it also removes dietary fiber, iron, and many B vitamins.

Examples of refined grain products are:
- white flour ✗
- de-germed cornmeal ✗
- white bread ✗
- white rice ✗

Most refined grains are enriched. This means certain B vitamins (thiamin, riboflavin, niacin, folic acid) and iron are added back after processing. Fiber is not added back to enriched grains. Check the ingredient list on refined grain products to make sure that the word "enriched" is included in the grain name. Some food products are made from mixtures of whole grains and refined grains.

Half your grains should be whole grains (48 grams per day, or three 16 oz. servings).

Examples of servings of whole grains:
- 1/2 cup cooked brown rice or other cooked grain
- 1/2 cup cooked 100% whole-grain pasta
- 1/2 cup cooked hot cereal, such as oatmeal
- 1 ounce uncooked whole-grain pasta, brown rice, or other grain
- 1 slice 100% whole-grain bread
- 1 very small (1 oz.) 100% whole grain muffin
- 1 cup 100% whole-grain ready-to-eat cereal

Check out the FDA-approved Health Claim for whole grains and heart disease on page 28.

Heart-Healthy Nutrients in Whole Grains

Dietary fiber is the term for several materials that make up the parts of plants your body can't digest. Fiber is classified as soluble or insoluble.

Soluble fiber, when eaten regularly as part of a diet low in saturated fat, trans fat, and cholesterol, has been associated with a decreased risk of cardiovascular disease. Soluble fibers modestly reduce LDL ("bad") cholesterol beyond levels achieved by a diet low in saturated and trans fats and cholesterol alone. Oats have the highest proportion of soluble fiber of any grain. Foods high in soluble fiber include oat bran, oatmeal, beans, peas, rice bran, barley, citrus fruits, strawberries, and apple pulp.

There are two FDA-approved Health Claims for soluble fiber and heart disease on pages 25 and 26.

Insoluble fiber has been associated with decreased cardiovascular risk and slower progression of cardiovascular disease in high-risk individuals. Foods high in insoluble fiber include whole-wheat breads, wheat cereals, wheat bran, rye, rice, barley, most other grains, cabbage, beets, carrots, Brussels sprouts, turnips, cauliflower, and apple skin.

Many commercial oat bran and wheat bran products (muffins, chips, waffles) contain very little bran. They also may be high in sodium, total fat, and saturated fat. Read labels carefully.

Antioxidants can help prevent artery damage by fighting free radicals produced in the process of oxidation. The major antioxidants found in grains are phenolic acids, which are found in whole-wheat products, brown rice, and oats.

Heart-Healthy Shopping Tips for Whole Grains

• **Look for these FDA-approved Heart Health Claims on Whole Grains:**

Grain Products that contain Fiber, Particularly Soluble Fiber, and Risk of Coronary Heart Disease
"Diets low in saturated fat and cholesterol and rich in fruits, vegetables, and grain products that contain some types of dietary fiber, particularly soluble fiber, may reduce the risk of heart disease, a disease associated with many factors."

Products carrying this claim must be low in total fat, saturated fat, and cholesterol and naturally contain at least 0.6 grams of soluble fiber per serving. The amount of soluble fiber must be provided on the label.

Soluble Fiber from Certain Foods and Risk of Coronary Heart Disease
"Soluble fiber from foods such as [name of soluble fiber source, and, if desired, name of food product], as part of a diet low in saturated fat and cholesterol, may reduce the risk of heart disease. A serving of [name of food product] supplies __ grams of the [necessary daily dietary intake for the benefit] soluble fiber from [name of soluble fiber source] necessary per day to have this effect."

Besides being low in total fat, saturated fat, and cholesterol, a product that makes this claim must include one or more of the following whole oat or barley foods: oat bran, rolled oats, whole oat flour, whole grain barley or dry milled barley; the whole oat or barley food must contain at least 0.75 grams of soluble fiber per serving. The amount of soluble fiber must be declared on the nutrition label.

Whole-Grain Foods and Risk of Heart Disease and Certain Cancers

"Diets rich in whole-grain foods and other plant foods and low in total fat, saturated fat, and cholesterol may reduce the risk of heart disease and some cancers."

Foods with this claim must contain 51% or more whole-grain ingredients by weight per serving and be low in total fat, saturated fat, and cholesterol and contain a good source of total fiber (2.5 grams/10% Daily Value or more per serving).

- Look for the American Heart Association's Heart Check mark on grain-based products including breads, biscuits, cereals (ready-to-eat and cooked), crackers, pancakes, French toast, waffles, muffins, and sweet quick-type breads. The American Heart Association does not certify cereal bars or grain-based desserts. For more information on the Heart-Check mark, go to *www.heartcheckmark.org*.

- Choose foods that name one of the following whole-grain ingredients first on the label's ingredient list:

brown rice	oatmeal	whole-grain corn	whole oats
buckwheat	quinoa	whole-grain	whole rye
bulgur	rolled oats	sorghum	whole wheat
millet	whole-grain barley	whole-grain triticale	wild rice

- Color is not an indication of a whole grain. Bread can be brown because of molasses or other added ingredients. Read the ingredient list to see if it is a whole grain.

- Foods labeled with the words "multi-grain," "stone-ground," "100% wheat," "cracked wheat," "seven-grain," or "bran" are usually not whole-grain products.

- Select whole-grain products that are good sources of total fiber. Use the Nutrition Facts label and choose whole grain products with at least 10% Daily Value or higher. Many, but not all, whole-grain products are good or excellent sources of fiber.

- Look for the Whole Grain Stamp when you purchase grain products. Each "stamped" product guarantees at least half a serving of whole grains. The stamp makes it easy to get your recommended three servings or more of whole grains each day. Eating three whole grain food products labeled "100% whole grain" does the trick—or six products bearing ANY Whole Grain stamp.

- Read the food label's ingredient list. Look for terms that indicate added sugars (such as sucrose, high-fructose corn syrup, honey, malt syrup, maple syrup, molasses, or raw sugar) that add extra calories. Choose foods with fewer added sugars.

- Check the sodium and choose products with lower sodium levels. Use the Nutrition Facts label to find foods with 10% Daily Value or less. Foods with less than 140 mg of sodium per serving can be labeled as low-sodium foods. Claims such as "low in sodium" or "very low in sodium" on the front of the food label can help you identify foods that contain less salt (or sodium).

- Limit the amount of bakery products you purchase, including donuts, pies, cakes, and cookies. Look instead for fat-free or low-fat and low-sodium varieties of whole-grain crackers, snack chips, cookies, and cakes.

- Remember that most store-baked goods are made with egg yolks, saturated fats, and/or trans fats. (Read the Nutrition Facts label to determine the saturated fat, trans fat, and cholesterol content.) Check for store-baked goods that are made with polyunsaturated or monounsaturated oils, skim or reduced-fat milk, and egg whites—or make your own.

- Instead of buying a raisin bran muffin, buy a loaf of raisin bread and enjoy a slice for breakfast or lunch.

Shopping List Essentials

100% whole-grain bread	Whole-wheat pasta
Whole-grain breakfast cereals	Corn, barley, bulgur
Oatmeal	Quinoa
Brown or wild rice	Farro

Criteria for Whole Grains

Using the FDA guidelines for Heart Health Claims, the grain foods listed meet the following criteria:

- Total Fat–Less than 3 grams

- Saturated Fat–1 gram or less

- Trans Fat–Less than 0.5 gram (Trans Fat is not listed in the charts because all items report 0 grams Trans Fat. Since foods with less than 0.5 grams of trans fat can list 0 grams in the Nutrition Facts, be sure to check the ingredients for partially hydrogenated fats to determine if a product contains any trans fats.)

- Cholesterol–20 mg or less

- Sodium: 480 mg or less. Look for lower sodium levels to reduce high blood pressure.

- Beneficial Nutrients: 10% or more of the Daily Value of one of six nutrients (vitamin A, vitamin C, iron, calcium, protein, or dietary fiber). Certain cereal-grain products do not necessarily need to meet these criteria and can be labeled "healthy" if they do not contain ingredients that change the nutritional profile and they conform to the standards of identity

- Whole-Grain Content: 51% or more by weight. Since the weight of whole grains in a product is not always reported on a product label, we were not able to determine this in all cases. Products listed do claim "Whole Grain" or "Whole Wheat."

- Good source of dietary fiber–10% Daily Value or higher (2.5 grams of fiber or higher)

Grain products not included in this list are those that are made with refined grains (not whole grains) such as crackers, breads, cereals, pasta, etc. White rice is excluded for the same reason. Most snacks, even those made with whole grains, are excluded because their fat and sodium levels are too high. This does not mean that these are bad foods. Eat them occasionally and moderate the portion.

Grains

Ancient Harvest, Inca Red Original Quinoa, Dry

1/4 cup / 48g

Amount per serving	%DV	Amount per serving	%DV	Amount per serving	%DV
Calories 180		Cholesterol 0mg	0%	Total Carbohydrate 33g	11%
Total Fat 3g	5%	Sodium 2mg	0%	Dietary Fiber 6g	24%
Saturated Fat 0g	0%	Protein 6g		Sugars 3g	
Polyunsaturated Fat 0g					
Monounsaturated Fat 0g		Vitamin A 0% Vitamin C 0%		Calcium 0% Iron 12%	

Ancient Harvest, Traditional Original Quinoa, Dry

1/4 cup

Amount per serving	%DV	Amount per serving	%DV	Amount per serving	%DV
Calories 172		Cholesterol 0mg	0%	Total Carbohydrate 31g	10%
Total Fat 2.8g	4%	Sodium 1mg	0%	Dietary Fiber 3g	12%
Saturated Fat 0g	0%	Protein 5g		Sugars 0g	
Polyunsaturated Fat 0g					
Monounsaturated Fat 0g		Vitamin A 0% Vitamin C 0%		Calcium 0% Iron 12%	

Arrowhead Mills, Amaranth

1/4 cup / 47g

Amount per serving	%DV	Amount per serving	%DV	Amount per serving	%DV
Calories 180		Cholesterol 0mg	0%	Total Carbohydrate 31g	10%
Total Fat 3g	5%	Sodium 10mg	0%	Dietary Fiber 7g	28%
Saturated Fat 1g	5%	Protein 7g		Sugars 1g	
Polyunsaturated Fat 0g					
Monounsaturated Fat 0g		Vitamin A 0% Vitamin C 4%		Calcium 8% Iron 20%	

Arrowhead Mills, Quinoa

1/3 cup / 43g

Amount per serving	%DV	Amount per serving	%DV	Amount per serving	%DV
Calories 160		Cholesterol 0mg	0%	Total Carbohydrate 30g	10%
Total Fat 2.5g	4%	Sodium 10mg	0%	Dietary Fiber 3g	12%
Saturated Fat 0g	0%	Protein 6g		Sugars 0g	
Polyunsaturated Fat 0g					
Monounsaturated Fat 0g		Vitamin A 0% Vitamin C 0%		Calcium 2% Iron 20%	

Buckwheat

1/4 cup

Amount per serving	%DV	Amount per serving	%DV	Amount per serving	%DV
Calories 145.7		Cholesterol 0mg	0%	Total Carbohydrate 30.3g	10%
Total Fat 1.4g	2%	Sodium 0.4mg	0%	Dietary Fiber 4g	16%
Saturated Fat 0.3g	2%	Protein 5.6g		Sugars 0g	
Polyunsaturated Fat 0.4g					
Monounsaturated Fat 0.4g		Vitamin A 0% Vitamin C 0%		Calcium 7.6% Iron 0.9%	

Bulgur Wheat, Cooked

1 cup

Amount per serving	%DV	Amount per serving	%DV	Amount per serving	%DV
Calories 151		**Cholesterol** 0mg	0%	**Total Carbohydrate** 33.8g	11%
Total Fat 0.4g	1%	**Sodium** 9.1mg	0%	Dietary Fiber 8.1g	32%
Saturated Fat 0g	0%	**Protein** 5.6g		Sugars 0.1g	
Polyunsaturated Fat 0.1g					
Monounsaturated Fat 0g		Vitamin A 3.6% Vitamin C 0%		Calcium 18.2% Iron 1.7%	

Bulgur Wheat, Dry

1/4 cup

Amount per serving	%DV	Amount per serving	%DV	Amount per serving	%DV
Calories 119.7		**Cholesterol** 0mg	0%	**Total Carbohydrate** 26.5g	9%
Total Fat 0.4g	1%	**Sodium** 5.9mg	0%	Dietary Fiber 6.5g	26%
Saturated Fat 0g	0%	**Protein** 4.3g		Sugars 0.1g	
Polyunsaturated Fat 0.1g					
Monounsaturated Fat 0g		Vitamin A 3.1% Vitamin C 0%		Calcium 12.2% Iron 0.8%	

Eden Foods, Millet, 100% Whole Grain, Organic, Uncooked

1/4 cup uncooked / 45g

Amount per serving	%DV	Amount per serving	%DV	Amount per serving	%DV
Calories 160		**Cholesterol** 0mg	0%	**Total Carbohydrate** 30g	10%
Total Fat 2g	3%	**Sodium** 5mg	0%	Dietary Fiber 4g	16%
Saturated Fat 0g	0%	**Protein** 5g		Sugars 0g	
Polyunsaturated Fat 0g					
Monounsaturated Fat 0g		Vitamin A 0% Vitamin C 0%		Calcium 0% Iron 6%	

Eden Foods, Quinoa, 100% Whole Grain, Organic

1/4 cup / 45g

Amount per serving	%DV	Amount per serving	%DV	Amount per serving	%DV
Calories 170		**Cholesterol** 0mg	0%	**Total Carbohydrate** 31g	10%
Total Fat 2.5g	4%	**Sodium** 0mg	0%	Dietary Fiber 4g	16%
Saturated Fat 0g	0%	**Protein** 5g		Sugars 1g	
Polyunsaturated Fat 0g					
Monounsaturated Fat 0g		Vitamin A 0% Vitamin C 0%		Calcium 0% Iron 10%	

Eden Foods, Red Quinoa, 100% Whole Grain, Organic, Uncooked

1/4 cup / 45g

Amount per serving	%DV	Amount per serving	%DV	Amount per serving	%DV
Calories 170		**Cholesterol** 0mg	0%	**Total Carbohydrate** 32g	11%
Total Fat 2g	3%	**Sodium** 5mg	0%	Dietary Fiber 5g	20%
Saturated Fat 0g	0%	**Protein** 6g		Sugars 2g	
Polyunsaturated Fat 0g					
Monounsaturated Fat 0g		Vitamin A 0% Vitamin C 0%		Calcium 0% Iron 10%	

Hominy, Canned, White

1 cup / 165g

Amount per serving	%DV	Amount per serving	%DV	Amount per serving	%DV
Calories 119		**Cholesterol** 0mg	0%	**Total Carbohydrate** 24g	8%
Total Fat 1g	2%	**Sodium** 346mg	14%	Dietary Fiber 4g	16%
Saturated Fat 0g	0%	**Protein** 2g		Sugars 3g	
Polyunsaturated Fat 0g					
Monounsaturated Fat 0g		Vitamin A 0% Vitamin C 0%		Calcium 2% Iron 6%	

Hominy, Canned, Yellow

1 cup / 160g

Amount per serving	%DV	Amount per serving	%DV	Amount per serving	%DV
Calories 115		**Cholesterol** 0mg	0%	**Total Carbohydrate** 23g	8%
Total Fat 1g	2%	**Sodium** 336mg	14%	Dietary Fiber 4g	16%
Saturated Fat 0g	0%	**Protein** 2g		Sugars 0g	
Polyunsaturated Fat 0g					
Monounsaturated Fat 0g		Vitamin A 4% Vitamin C 0%		Calcium 2% Iron 6%	

Medium Rye Flour

1/4 cup

Amount per serving	%DV	Amount per serving	%DV	Amount per serving	%DV
Calories 90.2		**Cholesterol** 0mg	0%	**Total Carbohydrate** 19.7g	7%
Total Fat 0.4g	1%	**Sodium** 0mg	0%	Dietary Fiber 3.7g	15%
Saturated Fat 0g	0%	**Protein** 2.3g		Sugars 0.2g	
Polyunsaturated Fat 0.2g					
Monounsaturated Fat 0g		Vitamin A 0% Vitamin C 0%		Calcium 6.1% Iron 0.5%	

Millet, Cooked

1 cup

Amount per serving	%DV	Amount per serving	%DV	Amount per serving	%DV
Calories 207		**Cholesterol** 0mg	0%	**Total Carbohydrate** 41.1g	14%
Total Fat 1.7g	3%	**Sodium** 3.4mg	0%	Dietary Fiber 2.5g	10%
Saturated Fat 0.3g	2%	**Protein** 6.1g		Sugars 0.2g	
Polyunsaturated Fat 0.8g					
Monounsaturated Fat 0.3g		Vitamin A 5.2% Vitamin C 0%		Calcium 5.2% Iron 1.1%	

Millet, Dry

1/4 cup

Amount per serving	%DV	Amount per serving	%DV	Amount per serving	%DV
Calories 189		**Cholesterol** 0mg	0%	**Total Carbohydrate** 36.4g	12%
Total Fat 2.1g	3%	**Sodium** 2.5mg	0%	Dietary Fiber 4g	16%
Saturated Fat 0.3g	2%	**Protein** 5.5g		Sugars 0.7g	
Polyunsaturated Fat 1g					
Monounsaturated Fat 0.3g		Vitamin A 0% Vitamin C 0%		Calcium 4% Iron 1.5%	

Quinoa, Dry

1/4 cup

Amount per serving	%DV	Amount per serving	%DV	Amount per serving	%DV
Calories 158.9		**Cholesterol** 0mg	0%	**Total Carbohydrate** 29.2g	10%
Total Fat 2.4g	4%	**Sodium** 8.9mg	0%	Dietary Fiber 2.5g	10%
Saturated Fat 0.2g	1%	**Protein** 5.5g		Sugars 0g	
Polyunsaturated Fat 1g					
Monounsaturated Fat 0.6g		Vitamin A 0%　Vitamin C 0%		Calcium 25.5% Iron 3.9%	

Spelt, Cooked

1 cup / 194g

Amount per serving	%DV	Amount per serving	%DV	Amount per serving	%DV
Calories 246		**Cholesterol** 0mg	0%	**Total Carbohydrate** 51g	17%
Total Fat 2g	3%	**Sodium** 10mg	0%	Dietary Fiber 7.5g	30%
Saturated Fat 0g	0%	**Protein** 11g		Sugars 0g	
Polyunsaturated Fat 0g					
Monounsaturated Fat 0g		Vitamin A 0%　Vitamin C 0%		Calcium 2%　　Iron 18%	

Tasty Bite, Meal Inspirations Barley Medley

1/2 pack / 4 oz / 114g

Amount per serving	%DV	Amount per serving	%DV	Amount per serving	%DV
Calories 210		**Cholesterol** 0mg	0%	**Total Carbohydrate** 41g	14%
Total Fat 2g	3%	**Sodium** 350mg	15%	Dietary Fiber 9g	36%
Saturated Fat 0g	0%	**Protein** 9g		Sugars 6g	
Polyunsaturated Fat 0g					
Monounsaturated Fat 0g		Vitamin A 2%　Vitamin C 0%		Calcium 4%　　Iron 15%	

Teff, Cooked

1 cup / 252g

Amount per serving	%DV	Amount per serving	%DV	Amount per serving	%DV
Calories 255		**Cholesterol** 0mg	0%	**Total Carbohydrate** 50g	17%
Total Fat 2g	3%	**Sodium** 20mg	1%	Dietary Fiber 7g	28%
Saturated Fat 0g	0%	**Protein** 10g		Sugars 0g	
Polyunsaturated Fat 0g					
Monounsaturated Fat 0g		Vitamin A 0%　Vitamin C 0%		Calcium 0%　　Iron 0%	

Whole Barley, Cooked

1 cup

Amount per serving	%DV	Amount per serving	%DV	Amount per serving	%DV
Calories 270		**Cholesterol** 0mg	0%	**Total Carbohydrate** 59.4g	20%
Total Fat 2.1g	3%	**Sodium** 8.9mg	0%	Dietary Fiber 13.5g	54%
Saturated Fat 0.4g	2%	**Protein** 7.4g		Sugars 0g	
Polyunsaturated Fat 1.2g					
Monounsaturated Fat 0.2g		Vitamin A 0%　Vitamin C 0%		Calcium 25.6% Iron 2%	

Breads

Arnold, 100% Whole Wheat Bread

1 slice / 43g

Amount per serving	%DV	Amount per serving	%DV	Amount per serving	%DV
Calories 110		**Cholesterol** 0mg	0%	**Total Carbohydrate** 20g	7%
Total Fat 1g	2%	**Sodium** 150mg	6%	Dietary Fiber 3g	12%
Saturated Fat 0g	0%	**Protein** 5g		Sugars 4g	
Polyunsaturated Fat 0.5g					
Monounsaturated Fat 0g		Vitamin A 0% Vitamin C 0%		Calcium 4% Iron 6%	

Arnold, 12 Grain Bread

1 slice / 43g

Amount per serving	%DV	Amount per serving	%DV	Amount per serving	%DV
Calories 110		**Cholesterol** 0mg	0%	**Total Carbohydrate** 21g	7%
Total Fat 1.5g	2%	**Sodium** 170mg	7%	Dietary Fiber 3g	12%
Saturated Fat 0g	0%	**Protein** 5g		Sugars 3g	
Polyunsaturated Fat 1g					
Monounsaturated Fat 0g		Vitamin A 0% Vitamin C 0%		Calcium 4% Iron 6%	

Arnold, Double Fiber Bread

1 slice / 43g

Amount per serving	%DV	Amount per serving	%DV	Amount per serving	%DV
Calories 100		**Cholesterol** 0mg	0%	**Total Carbohydrate** 21g	7%
Total Fat 1.5g	2%	**Sodium** 170mg	7%	Dietary Fiber 6g	24%
Saturated Fat 0g	0%	**Protein** 4g		Sugars 2g	
Polyunsaturated Fat 0.5g					
Monounsaturated Fat 0g		Vitamin A 0% Vitamin C 0%		Calcium 2% Iron 6%	

Arnold, Dutch Country 100% Whole Wheat Bread

1 slice / 38g

Amount per serving	%DV	Amount per serving	%DV	Amount per serving	%DV
Calories 100		**Cholesterol** 0mg	0%	**Total Carbohydrate** 18g	6%
Total Fat 1.5g	2%	**Sodium** 200mg	8%	Dietary Fiber 3g	12%
Saturated Fat 0g	0%	**Protein** 4g		Sugars 3g	
Polyunsaturated Fat 1g					
Monounsaturated Fat 0g		Vitamin A 15% Vitamin C 0%		Calcium 10% Iron 4%	

Arnold, Dutch Country Extra Fiber Bread

1 slice / 38g

Amount per serving	%DV	Amount per serving	%DV	Amount per serving	%DV
Calories 90		**Cholesterol** 0mg	0%	**Total Carbohydrate** 18g	6%
Total Fat 1.5g	2%	**Sodium** 190mg	8%	Dietary Fiber 4g	16%
Saturated Fat 0g	0%	**Protein** 4g		Sugars 3g	
Polyunsaturated Fat 0.5g					
Monounsaturated Fat 0g		Vitamin A 10% Vitamin C 0%		Calcium 10% Iron 6%	

Arnold, Healthy Multi-Grain Bread

1 slice / 43g

Amount per serving	%DV	Amount per serving	%DV	Amount per serving	%DV
Calories 100		**Cholesterol** 0mg	0%	**Total Carbohydrate** 20g	7%
Total Fat 1.5g	2%	**Sodium** 150mg	6%	Dietary Fiber 4g	16%
Saturated Fat 0g	0%	**Protein** 5g		Sugars 4g	
Polyunsaturated Fat 1g					
Monounsaturated Fat 0g		Vitamin A 0% Vitamin C 0%		Calcium 4% Iron 6%	

Arnold, Stone Ground 100% Whole Wheat Bread

2 slices / 50g

Amount per serving	%DV	Amount per serving	%DV	Amount per serving	%DV
Calories 130		**Cholesterol** 0mg	0%	**Total Carbohydrate** 22g	7%
Total Fat 2g	3%	**Sodium** 260mg	11%	Dietary Fiber 3g	12%
Saturated Fat 0g	0%	**Protein** 6g		Sugars 4g	
Polyunsaturated Fat 1g					
Monounsaturated Fat 0g		Vitamin A 0% Vitamin C 0%		Calcium 6% Iron 6%	

Arnold, Whole Grains Honey Whole Wheat Bread

1 slice / 43g

Amount per serving	%DV	Amount per serving	%DV	Amount per serving	%DV
Calories 100		**Cholesterol** 0mg	0%	**Total Carbohydrate** 20g	7%
Total Fat 1g	2%	**Sodium** 150mg	6%	Dietary Fiber 3g	12%
Saturated Fat 0g	0%	**Protein** 5g		Sugars 4g	
Polyunsaturated Fat 0.5g					
Monounsaturated Fat 0g		Vitamin A 0% Vitamin C 0%		Calcium 4% Iron 6%	

Brownberry, 100% Whole Wheat Bread

1 slice / 43g

Amount per serving	%DV	Amount per serving	%DV	Amount per serving	%DV
Calories 110		**Cholesterol** 0mg	0%	**Total Carbohydrate** 20g	7%
Total Fat 1g	2%	**Sodium** 150mg	6%	Dietary Fiber 3g	12%
Saturated Fat 0g	0%	**Protein** 5g		Sugars 4g	
Polyunsaturated Fat 0.5g					
Monounsaturated Fat 0g		Vitamin A 0% Vitamin C 0%		Calcium 4% Iron 6%	

Brownberry, 12 Grain Bread

1 slice / 43g

Amount per serving	%DV	Amount per serving	%DV	Amount per serving	%DV
Calories 110		**Cholesterol** 0mg	0%	**Total Carbohydrate** 20g	7%
Total Fat 2g	3%	**Sodium** 150mg	6%	Dietary Fiber 3g	12%
Saturated Fat 0g	0%	**Protein** 5g		Sugars 3g	
Polyunsaturated Fat 1g					
Monounsaturated Fat 0g		Vitamin A 0% Vitamin C 0%		Calcium 4% Iron 6%	

Brownberry, Double Fiber Bread

1 slice / 43g

Amount per serving	%DV	Amount per serving	%DV	Amount per serving	%DV
Calories 100		**Cholesterol** 0mg	0%	**Total Carbohydrate** 21g	7%
Total Fat 1.5g	2%	**Sodium** 150mg	6%	Dietary Fiber 6g	24%
Saturated Fat 0g	0%	**Protein** 4g		Sugars 2g	
Polyunsaturated Fat 0.5g					
Monounsaturated Fat 0g		Vitamin A 0%	Vitamin C 0%	Calcium 4%	Iron 6%

Brownberry, Healthy Multi-Grain Bread

1 slice / 43g

Amount per serving	%DV	Amount per serving	%DV	Amount per serving	%DV
Calories 100		**Cholesterol** 0mg	0%	**Total Carbohydrate** 20g	7%
Total Fat 1.5g	2%	**Sodium** 150mg	6%	Dietary Fiber 4g	16%
Saturated Fat 0g	0%	**Protein** 5g		Sugars 4g	
Polyunsaturated Fat 1g					
Monounsaturated Fat 0g		Vitamin A 0%	Vitamin C 0%	Calcium 4%	Iron 6%

Brownberry, Whole Grains Honey Whole Wheat Bread

1 slice / 43g

Amount per serving	%DV	Amount per serving	%DV	Amount per serving	%DV
Calories 100		**Cholesterol** 0mg	0%	**Total Carbohydrate** 20g	7%
Total Fat 1g	2%	**Sodium** 150mg	6%	Dietary Fiber 3g	12%
Saturated Fat 0g	0%	**Protein** 5g		Sugars 4g	
Polyunsaturated Fat 0.5g					
Monounsaturated Fat 0g		Vitamin A 0%	Vitamin C 0%	Calcium 4%	Iron 6%

Damascus Bakeries, All Natural Flax Roll-Ups

1 roll up / 2 oz / 57g

Amount per serving	%DV	Amount per serving	%DV	Amount per serving	%DV
Calories 110		**Cholesterol** 0mg	0%	**Total Carbohydrate** 15g	5%
Total Fat 3g	5%	**Sodium** 360mg	15%	Dietary Fiber 9g	36%
Saturated Fat 0.5g	2%	**Protein** 12g		Sugars 1g	
Polyunsaturated Fat 0g					
Monounsaturated Fat 0g		Vitamin A 0%	Vitamin C 0%	Calcium 4%	Iron 10%

Damascus Bakeries, All Natural Plain Roll-Ups

1 roll up / 2 oz / 57g

Amount per serving	%DV	Amount per serving	%DV	Amount per serving	%DV
Calories 70		**Cholesterol** 0mg	0%	**Total Carbohydrate** 14g	5%
Total Fat 2g	3%	**Sodium** 180mg	8%	Dietary Fiber 5g	20%
Saturated Fat 0g	0%	**Protein** 6g		Sugars 1g	
Polyunsaturated Fat 0g					
Monounsaturated Fat 0g		Vitamin A 0%	Vitamin C 0%	Calcium 10%	Iron 6%

Damascus Bakeries, All Natural Whole Wheat Roll-Ups

1 roll up / 2 oz / 57g

Amount per serving	%DV	Amount per serving	%DV	Amount per serving	%DV
Calories 70		**Cholesterol** 0mg	0%	**Total Carbohydrate** 13g	4%
Total Fat 2g	3%	**Sodium** 170mg	7%	Dietary Fiber 5g	20%
Saturated Fat 0g	0%	**Protein** 6g		Sugars 0g	
Polyunsaturated Fat 0g					
Monounsaturated Fat 0g		Vitamin A 0% Vitamin C 0%		Calcium 10% Iron 4%	

English Muffins, Whole-Wheat

1 muffin / 66g

Amount per serving	%DV	Amount per serving	%DV	Amount per serving	%DV
Calories 134		**Cholesterol** 0mg	0%	**Total Carbohydrate** 26.5g	9%
Total Fat 1.5g	2%	**Sodium** 240mg	10%	Dietary Fiber 4.5g	18%
Saturated Fat 0g	0%	**Protein** 6g		Sugars 5.5g	
Polyunsaturated Fat 0.5g					
Monounsaturated Fat 0.5g		Vitamin A 3.5% Vitamin C 0%		Calcium 175% Iron 1.5%	

English Muffins, Whole-Wheat, Toasted

1 muffin / 61g

Amount per serving	%DV	Amount per serving	%DV	Amount per serving	%DV
Calories 135		**Cholesterol** 0mg	0%	**Total Carbohydrate** 27g	9%
Total Fat 1.5g	2%	**Sodium** 241.5mg	10%	Dietary Fiber 4.5g	18%
Saturated Fat 0g	0%	**Protein** 6g		Sugars 5.5g	
Polyunsaturated Fat 0.5g					
Monounsaturated Fat 0.5g		Vitamin A 0% Vitamin C 0%		Calcium 175.5% Iron 1.5%	

Milton's Craft Bakers, All Natural Healthy Whole Grain Bread

1 slice / 38g

Amount per serving	%DV	Amount per serving	%DV	Amount per serving	%DV
Calories 80		**Cholesterol** 0mg	0%	**Total Carbohydrate** 17g	6%
Total Fat 1g	2%	**Sodium** 140mg	6%	Dietary Fiber 4g	16%
Saturated Fat 0g	0%	**Protein** 5g		Sugars 5g	
Polyunsaturated Fat 0g					
Monounsaturated Fat 0g		Vitamin A 0% Vitamin C 0%		Calcium 2% Iron 4%	

Milton's Craft Bakers, All Natural Multi-Grain Bread

1 slice / 43g

Amount per serving	%DV	Amount per serving	%DV	Amount per serving	%DV
Calories 110		**Cholesterol** 0mg	0%	**Total Carbohydrate** 22g	7%
Total Fat 1g	2%	**Sodium** 150mg	6%	Dietary Fiber 3g	12%
Saturated Fat 0g	0%	**Protein** 5g		Sugars 5g	
Polyunsaturated Fat 0g					
Monounsaturated Fat 0g		Vitamin A 0% Vitamin C 0%		Calcium 10% Iron 15%	

Milton's Healthy, Multi-Grain English Muffins

1 muffin / 57g

Amount per serving	%DV	Amount per serving	%DV	Amount per serving	%DV
Calories 130		**Cholesterol** 0mg	0%	**Total Carbohydrate** 31g	10%
Total Fat 0.5g	1%	**Sodium** 180mg	8%	Dietary Fiber 3g	12%
Saturated Fat 0g	0%	**Protein** 4g		Sugars 7g	
Polyunsaturated Fat 0g					
Monounsaturated Fat 0g		Vitamin A 0% Vitamin C 0%		Calcium 0% Iron 15%	

Milton's Healthy, Multi-Grain Plus Bread

1 slice / 49g

Amount per serving	%DV	Amount per serving	%DV	Amount per serving	%DV
Calories 120		**Cholesterol** 0mg	0%	**Total Carbohydrate** 25g	8%
Total Fat 1g	2%	**Sodium** 150mg	6%	Dietary Fiber 4g	16%
Saturated Fat 0g	0%	**Protein** 5g		Sugars 7g	
Polyunsaturated Fat 0g					
Monounsaturated Fat 0g		Vitamin A 0% Vitamin C 0%		Calcium 10% Iron 15%	

Oroweat, 100% Whole Wheat English Muffins

1 muffin / 65g

Amount per serving	%DV	Amount per serving	%DV	Amount per serving	%DV
Calories 150		**Cholesterol** 0mg	0%	**Total Carbohydrate** 27g	9%
Total Fat 2g	3%	**Sodium** 250mg	10%	Dietary Fiber 4g	16%
Saturated Fat 0g	0%	**Protein** 6g		Sugars 6g	
Polyunsaturated Fat 1g					
Monounsaturated Fat 0g		Vitamin A 0% Vitamin C 0%		Calcium 6% Iron 8%	

Oroweat, Healthy Whole Grains Healthy Multi-Grain Bread

1 slice / 38g

Amount per serving	%DV	Amount per serving	%DV	Amount per serving	%DV
Calories 90		**Cholesterol** 0mg	0%	**Total Carbohydrate** 18g	6%
Total Fat 1.5g	2%	**Sodium** 135mg	6%	Dietary Fiber 3g	12%
Saturated Fat 0g	0%	**Protein** 4g		Sugars 3g	
Polyunsaturated Fat 0.5g					
Monounsaturated Fat 0g		Vitamin A 0% Vitamin C 0%		Calcium 4% Iron 4%	

Oroweat, Whole Grains Double Fiber Bread

1 slice / 38g

Amount per serving	%DV	Amount per serving	%DV	Amount per serving	%DV
Calories 80		**Cholesterol** 0mg	0%	**Total Carbohydrate** 18g	6%
Total Fat 1.5g	2%	**Sodium** 130mg	5%	Dietary Fiber 5g	20%
Saturated Fat 0g	0%	**Protein** 4g		Sugars 3g	
Polyunsaturated Fat 0.5g					
Monounsaturated Fat 0g		Vitamin A 0% Vitamin C 0%		Calcium 4% Iron 4%	

Pepperidge Farm Farmhouse Whole Grain White Bread

1 slice

Amount per serving	%DV	Amount per serving	%DV	Amount per serving	%DV
Calories 110		**Cholesterol** 0mg	0%	**Total Carbohydrate** 21g	7%
Total Fat 2g	3%	**Sodium** 150mg	6%	Dietary Fiber 3g	12%
Saturated Fat 0.5g	3%	**Protein** 4g		Sugars 4g	
Polyunsaturated Fat 1g					
Monounsaturated Fat 0g		Vitamin A 0%	Vitamin C 0%	Calcium 10%	Iron 4%

Pepperidge Farm, 100% Whole Wheat Hearty Texture Whole Grain Bread

1 slice

Amount per serving	%DV	Amount per serving	%DV	Amount per serving	%DV
Calories 100		**Cholesterol** 0mg	0%	**Total Carbohydrate** 20g	7%
Total Fat 1.5g	2%	**Sodium** 105mg	4%	Dietary Fiber 4g	16%
Saturated Fat 0.5g	3%	**Protein** 5g		Sugars 3g	
Polyunsaturated Fat 1g					
Monounsaturated Fat 0g		Vitamin A 0%	Vitamin C 0%	Calcium 4%	Iron 6%

Pepperidge Farm, 15 Grain Hearty Texture Whole Grain Bread

1 slice

Amount per serving	%DV	Amount per serving	%DV	Amount per serving	%DV
Calories 100		**Cholesterol** 0mg	0%	**Total Carbohydrate** 20g	7%
Total Fat 2g	3%	**Sodium** 115mg	5%	Dietary Fiber 4g	16%
Saturated Fat 0.5g	3%	**Protein** 5g		Sugars 3g	
Polyunsaturated Fat 1g					
Monounsaturated Fat 0.5g		Vitamin A 0%	Vitamin C 0%	Calcium 4%	Iron 6%

Pepperidge Farm, Light Style 7 Grain Bread

3 slices

Amount per serving	%DV	Amount per serving	%DV	Amount per serving	%DV
Calories 130		**Cholesterol** 0mg	0%	**Total Carbohydrate** 26g	9%
Total Fat 1g	2%	**Sodium** 220mg	9%	Dietary Fiber 4g	16%
Saturated Fat 0g	0%	**Protein** 7g		Sugars 3g	
Polyunsaturated Fat 0g					
Monounsaturated Fat 0g		Vitamin A 0%	Vitamin C 0%	Calcium 6%	Iron 10%

Pepperidge Farm, Light Style Extra Fiber Bread

3 slices

Amount per serving	%DV	Amount per serving	%DV	Amount per serving	%DV
Calories 120		**Cholesterol** 0mg	0%	**Total Carbohydrate** 26g	9%
Total Fat 1g	2%	**Sodium** 200mg	8%	Dietary Fiber 6g	24%
Saturated Fat 0g	0%	**Protein** 6g		Sugars 3g	
Polyunsaturated Fat 0g					
Monounsaturated Fat 0g		Vitamin A 0%	Vitamin C 0%	Calcium 8%	Iron 10%

Pepperidge Farm, Light Style Soft Wheat Bread

3 slices

Amount per serving	%DV	Amount per serving	%DV	Amount per serving	%DV
Calories 130		**Cholesterol** 0mg	0%	**Total Carbohydrate** 25g	8%
Total Fat 1g	2%	**Sodium** 220mg	9%	Dietary Fiber 4g	16%
Saturated Fat 0g	0%	**Protein** 8g		Sugars 3g	
Polyunsaturated Fat 0.5g					
Monounsaturated Fat 0g		Vitamin A 0%	Vitamin C 0%	Calcium 6%	Iron 10%

Pepperidge Farm, Oatmeal Hearty Texture Whole Grain Bread

1 slice

Amount per serving	%DV	Amount per serving	%DV	Amount per serving	%DV
Calories 100		**Cholesterol** 0mg	0%	**Total Carbohydrate** 20g	7%
Total Fat 1.5g	2%	**Sodium** 110mg	5%	Dietary Fiber 4g	16%
Saturated Fat 0g	0%	**Protein** 4g		Sugars 3g	
Polyunsaturated Fat 1g					
Monounsaturated Fat 0g		Vitamin A 0%	Vitamin C 0%	Calcium 4%	Iron 6%

Pepperidge Farm, Small Slice 15 Grain Hearty Texture Whole Grain Bread

1 slice

Amount per serving	%DV	Amount per serving	%DV	Amount per serving	%DV
Calories 70		**Cholesterol** 0mg	0%	**Total Carbohydrate** 13g	4%
Total Fat 1.5g	2%	**Sodium** 75mg	3%	Dietary Fiber 3g	12%
Saturated Fat 0g	0%	**Protein** 3g		Sugars 2g	
Polyunsaturated Fat 1g					
Monounsaturated Fat 0g		Vitamin A 0%	Vitamin C 0%	Calcium 2%	Iron 4%

Pepperidge Farm, Very Thin 100% Whole Wheat Bread

3 slices

Amount per serving	%DV	Amount per serving	%DV	Amount per serving	%DV
Calories 110		**Cholesterol** 0mg	0%	**Total Carbohydrate** 20g	7%
Total Fat 2g	3%	**Sodium** 160mg	7%	Dietary Fiber 3g	12%
Saturated Fat 0.5g	3%	**Protein** 4g		Sugars 3g	
Polyunsaturated Fat 1g					
Monounsaturated Fat 0g		Vitamin A 0%	Vitamin C 0%	Calcium 6%	Iron 6%

Pepperidge Farm, Whole Grain 100% Natural German Dark Wheat Bread

1 slice

Amount per serving	%DV	Amount per serving	%DV	Amount per serving	%DV
Calories 100		**Cholesterol** 0mg	0%	**Total Carbohydrate** 17g	6%
Total Fat 1.5g	2%	**Sodium** 130mg	5%	Dietary Fiber 3g	12%
Saturated Fat 0g	0%	**Protein** 3g		Sugars 2g	
Polyunsaturated Fat 0.5g					
Monounsaturated Fat 0.5g		Vitamin A 0%	Vitamin C 0%	Calcium 4%	Iron 6%

Pepperidge Farm, Whole Grain Ancient Grains Bread

1 slice

Amount per serving	%DV	Amount per serving	%DV	Amount per serving	%DV
Calories 100		**Cholesterol** 0mg	0%	**Total Carbohydrate** 20g	7%
Total Fat 2g	3%	**Sodium** 120mg	5%	Dietary Fiber 4g	16%
Saturated Fat 0g	0%	**Protein** 5g		Sugars 3g	
Polyunsaturated Fat 1g					
Monounsaturated Fat 0g		Vitamin A 0%	Vitamin C 0%	Calcium 4%	Iron 6%

Pepperidge Farm, Whole Grain Double Fiber Soft 100% Whole Wheat Bread

1 slice

Amount per serving	%DV	Amount per serving	%DV	Amount per serving	%DV
Calories 100		**Cholesterol** 0mg	0%	**Total Carbohydrate** 21g	7%
Total Fat 1g	2%	**Sodium** 115mg	5%	Dietary Fiber 6g	24%
Saturated Fat 0.5g	3%	**Protein** 4g		Sugars 2g	
Polyunsaturated Fat 0.5g					
Monounsaturated Fat 0g		Vitamin A 0%	Vitamin C 0%	Calcium 4%	Iron 6%

Pepperidge Farm, Whole Grain Stone Ground 100% Natural Whole Wheat Bread

1 slice

Amount per serving	%DV	Amount per serving	%DV	Amount per serving	%DV
Calories 100		**Cholesterol** 0mg	0%	**Total Carbohydrate** 20g	7%
Total Fat 2g	3%	**Sodium** 130mg	5%	Dietary Fiber 3g	12%
Saturated Fat 0g	0%	**Protein** 4g		Sugars 3g	
Polyunsaturated Fat 0.5g					
Monounsaturated Fat 1g		Vitamin A 0%	Vitamin C 0%	Calcium 2%	Iron 6%

Pepperidge Farm, Whole Grain Swirled Dark & Honey 100% Whole Wheat Bread

1 slice

Amount per serving	%DV	Amount per serving	%DV	Amount per serving	%DV
Calories 100		**Cholesterol** 0mg	0%	**Total Carbohydrate** 20g	7%
Total Fat 1.5g	2%	**Sodium** 115mg	5%	Dietary Fiber 4g	16%
Saturated Fat 0g	0%	**Protein** 5g		Sugars 4g	
Polyunsaturated Fat 0.5g					
Monounsaturated Fat 0g		Vitamin A 0%	Vitamin C 0%	Calcium 2%	Iron 6%

Rolls, Dinner, Whole-Wheat

1 roll, hamburger, frankfurter roll / 43g

Amount per serving	%DV	Amount per serving	%DV	Amount per serving	%DV
Calories 114.5		**Cholesterol** 0mg	0%	**Total Carbohydrate** 22g	7%
Total Fat 2g	3%	**Sodium** 224mg	9%	Dietary Fiber 3g	12%
Saturated Fat 0.5g	3%	**Protein** 3.5g		Sugars 3.5g	
Polyunsaturated Fat 1g					
Monounsaturated Fat 0.5g		Vitamin A 0%	Vitamin C 0%	Calcium 45.5%	Iron 1%

St-Methode Campagnolo, 100% Whole Grain Multigrain Loaf

2 slices / 64g

Amount per serving	%DV	Amount per serving	%DV	Amount per serving	%DV
Calories 160		**Cholesterol** 0mg	0%	**Total Carbohydrate** 27g	9%
Total Fat 2g	3%	**Sodium** 210mg	9%	Dietary Fiber 6g	24%
Saturated Fat 0.3g	2%	**Protein** 8g		Sugars 1g	
Polyunsaturated Fat 0.5g					
Monounsaturated Fat 0.8g		Vitamin A 0% Vitamin C 8%		Calcium 6% Iron 10%	

Thomas', 100% Whole Wheat Bagel Thins

1 bagel / 46g

Amount per serving	%DV	Amount per serving	%DV	Amount per serving	%DV
Calories 110		**Cholesterol** 0mg	0%	**Total Carbohydrate** 24g	8%
Total Fat 1g	2%	**Sodium** 190mg	8%	Dietary Fiber 5g	20%
Saturated Fat 0g	0%	**Protein** 6g		Sugars 3g	
Polyunsaturated Fat 0g					
Monounsaturated Fat 0g		Vitamin A 0% Vitamin C 0%		Calcium 4% Iron 6%	

Toufayan Whole Wheat Pita

1 pita

Amount per serving	%DV	Amount per serving	%DV	Amount per serving	%DV
Calories 150		**Cholesterol** 0mg	0%	**Total Carbohydrate** 30g	10%
Total Fat 1g	2%	**Sodium** 225mg	9%	Dietary Fiber 3g	12%
Saturated Fat 0g	0%	**Protein** 6g		Sugars 2g	
Polyunsaturated Fat 0g					
Monounsaturated Fat 0g		Vitamin A 0% Vitamin C 0%		Calcium 0% Iron 6%	

Cold Cereals

Ancient Harvest, Original Quinoa Flakes

1/3 cup dry

Amount per serving	%DV	Amount per serving	%DV	Amount per serving	%DV
Calories 131		**Cholesterol** 0mg	0%	**Total Carbohydrate** 23g	8%
Total Fat 2g	3%	**Sodium** 2mg	0%	Dietary Fiber 2.5g	10%
Saturated Fat 0g	0%	**Protein** 4.3g		Sugars 2g	
Polyunsaturated Fat 0g					
Monounsaturated Fat 0g		Vitamin A 0% Vitamin C 0%		Calcium 0% Iron 8%	

Back to Nature, Apple-Blueberry

50g

Amount per serving	%DV	Amount per serving	%DV	Amount per serving	%DV
Calories 200		**Cholesterol** 0mg	0%	**Total Carbohydrate** 39g	13%
Total Fat 2.5g	4%	**Sodium** 10mg	0%	Dietary Fiber 4g	16%
Saturated Fat 0g	0%	**Protein** 6g		Sugars 13g	
Polyunsaturated Fat 0g					
Monounsaturated Fat 1g		Vitamin A 0% Vitamin C 0%		Calcium 2% Iron 15%	

Back to Nature, Classic Granola

51g

Amount per serving	%DV	Amount per serving	%DV	Amount per serving	%DV
Calories 200		**Cholesterol** 0mg	0%	**Total Carbohydrate** 39g	13%
Total Fat 3g	5%	**Sodium** 0mg	0%	Dietary Fiber 4g	16%
Saturated Fat 0.5g	3%	**Protein** 6g		Sugars 11g	
Polyunsaturated Fat 0g					
Monounsaturated Fat 1g		Vitamin A 0% Vitamin C 8%		Calcium 2% Iron 10%	

Barbara's Bakery, Puffins Honey Rice Cereal

3/4 cup

Amount per serving	%DV	Amount per serving	%DV	Amount per serving	%DV
Calories 120		**Cholesterol** 0mg	0%	**Total Carbohydrate** 25g	8%
Total Fat 1g	2%	**Sodium** 80mg	3%	Dietary Fiber 3g	12%
Saturated Fat 0g	0%	**Protein** 2g		Sugars 6g	
Polyunsaturated Fat 0g					
Monounsaturated Fat 0g		Vitamin A 0% Vitamin C 0%		Calcium 10% Iron 4%	

Barbara's Bakery, Puffins Multigrain Cereal

3/4 cup

Amount per serving	%DV	Amount per serving	%DV	Amount per serving	%DV
Calories 110		**Cholesterol** 0mg	0%	**Total Carbohydrate** 25g	8%
Total Fat 0g	0%	**Sodium** 80mg	3%	Dietary Fiber 3g	12%
Saturated Fat 0g	0%	**Protein** 2g		Sugars 6g	
Polyunsaturated Fat 0g					
Monounsaturated Fat 0g		Vitamin A 0% Vitamin C 25%		Calcium 25% Iron 25%	

Barbara's Shredded Wheat

2 biscuits / 40g

Amount per serving	%DV	Amount per serving	%DV	Amount per serving	%DV
Calories 140		**Cholesterol** 0mg	0%	**Total Carbohydrate** 31g	10%
Total Fat 1g	2%	**Sodium** 0mg	0%	Dietary Fiber 5g	20%
Saturated Fat 0g	0%	**Protein** 4g		Sugars 0g	
Polyunsaturated Fat 0g					
Monounsaturated Fat 0g		Vitamin A 0% Vitamin C 0%		Calcium 2% Iron 6%	

Bob's Red Mill, Apple Cinnamon Granola

1/2 cup / 45g

Amount per serving	%DV	Amount per serving	%DV	Amount per serving	%DV
Calories 170		**Cholesterol** 0mg	0%	**Total Carbohydrate** 33g	11%
Total Fat 2g	3%	**Sodium** 5mg	0%	Dietary Fiber 3g	12%
Saturated Fat 0g	0%	**Protein** 5g		Sugars 11g	
Polyunsaturated Fat 0g					
Monounsaturated Fat 0g		Vitamin A 0% Vitamin C 0%		Calcium 2% Iron 8%	

Bob's Red Mill, Apple Strawberry Granola

1/2 cup / 45g

Amount per serving	%DV	Amount per serving	%DV	Amount per serving	%DV
Calories 170		**Cholesterol** 0mg	0%	**Total Carbohydrate** 33g	11%
Total Fat 2g	3%	**Sodium** 5mg	0%	Dietary Fiber 3g	12%
Saturated Fat 0g	0%	**Protein** 5g		Sugars 11g	
Polyunsaturated Fat 0g					
Monounsaturated Fat 0g		Vitamin A 0%	Vitamin C 2%	Calcium 2%	Iron 8%

Cheerios

1 cup / with 1/2 cup skim milk / 28g

Amount per serving	%DV	Amount per serving	%DV	Amount per serving	%DV
Calories 140		**Cholesterol** 0mg	0%	**Total Carbohydrate** 20g	7%
Total Fat 2g	3%	**Sodium** 160mg	7%	Dietary Fiber 3g	12%
Saturated Fat 0g	0%	**Protein** 3g		Sugars 1g	
Polyunsaturated Fat 0.5g					
Monounsaturated Fat 0.5g		Vitamin A 15%	Vitamin C 10%	Calcium 25%	Iron 45%

Enjoy Life Foods, Crunchy Flax Cereal

3/4 cup

Amount per serving	%DV	Amount per serving	%DV	Amount per serving	%DV
Calories 200		**Cholesterol** 0mg	0%	**Total Carbohydrate** 42g	14%
Total Fat 3g	5%	**Sodium** 115mg	5%	Dietary Fiber 6g	24%
Saturated Fat 0g	0%	**Protein** 7g		Sugars 2g	
Polyunsaturated Fat 0g					
Monounsaturated Fat 0g		Vitamin A 0%	Vitamin C 0%	Calcium 2%	Iron 15%

Erewhon, Raisin Bran

1 cup / 52g

Amount per serving	%DV	Amount per serving	%DV	Amount per serving	%DV
Calories 180		**Cholesterol** 0mg	0%	**Total Carbohydrate** 40g	13%
Total Fat 1g	2%	**Sodium** 115mg	5%	Dietary Fiber 6g	24%
Saturated Fat 0g	0%	**Protein** 6g		Sugars 8g	
Polyunsaturated Fat 0g					
Monounsaturated Fat 0g		Vitamin A 0%	Vitamin C 0%	Calcium 2%	Iron 10%

Food for Life, Ezekiel 4:9 Sprouted Whole Grain Cereal

1/2 cup / 57g

Amount per serving	%DV	Amount per serving	%DV	Amount per serving	%DV
Calories 190		**Cholesterol** 0mg	0%	**Total Carbohydrate** 40g	13%
Total Fat 1g	2%	**Sodium** 200mg	8%	Dietary Fiber 6g	24%
Saturated Fat 0g	0%	**Protein** 8g		Sugars 0g	
Polyunsaturated Fat 0g					
Monounsaturated Fat 0g		Vitamin A 0%	Vitamin C 0%	Calcium 0%	Iron 10%

General Mills, Wheat Chex Cereal

3/4 cup / 47g

Amount per serving	%DV	Amount per serving	%DV	Amount per serving	%DV
Calories 160		**Cholesterol** 0mg	0%	**Total Carbohydrate** 39g	13%
Total Fat 1g	2%	**Sodium** 270mg	11%	Dietary Fiber 6g	24%
Saturated Fat 0g	0%	**Protein** 5g		Sugars 5g	
Polyunsaturated Fat 0.5g					
Monounsaturated Fat 0g		Vitamin A 10% Vitamin C 10%		Calcium 10% Iron 80%	

General Mills, Wheaties

3/4 cup / skim milk / 27g

Amount per serving	%DV	Amount per serving	%DV	Amount per serving	%DV
Calories 140		**Cholesterol** 0mg	0%	**Total Carbohydrate** 22g	7%
Total Fat 0.5g	1%	**Sodium** 190mg	8%	Dietary Fiber 3g	12%
Saturated Fat 0g	0%	**Protein** 2g		Sugars 4g	
Polyunsaturated Fat 0g					
Monounsaturated Fat 0g		Vitamin A 15% Vitamin C 10%		Calcium 15% Iron 45%	

General Mills, Whole Grain Total

3/4 cup / skim milk / 30g

Amount per serving	%DV	Amount per serving	%DV	Amount per serving	%DV
Calories 140		**Cholesterol** 0mg	0%	**Total Carbohydrate** 22g	7%
Total Fat 0.5g	1%	**Sodium** 140mg	6%	Dietary Fiber 3g	12%
Saturated Fat 0g	0%	**Protein** 2g		Sugars 5g	
Polyunsaturated Fat 0g					
Monounsaturated Fat 0g		Vitamin A 15% Vitamin C 100%		Calcium 100% Iron 100%	

Kashi, 7 Whole Grain Nuggets

1/2 cup / 2 oz / 56g

Amount per serving	%DV	Amount per serving	%DV	Amount per serving	%DV
Calories 210		**Cholesterol** 0mg	0%	**Total Carbohydrate** 47g	16%
Total Fat 1.5g	2%	**Sodium** 260mg	11%	Dietary Fiber 7g	28%
Saturated Fat 0g	0%	**Protein** 7g		Sugars 3g	
Polyunsaturated Fat 1g					
Monounsaturated Fat 0.5g		Vitamin A 0% Vitamin C 0%		Calcium 2% Iron 8%	

Kashi, Autumn Wheat

29 biscuits / 54g

Amount per serving	%DV	Amount per serving	%DV	Amount per serving	%DV
Calories 180		**Cholesterol** 0mg	0%	**Total Carbohydrate** 43g	14%
Total Fat 1g	2%	**Sodium** 0mg	0%	Dietary Fiber 6g	24%
Saturated Fat 0g	0%	**Protein** 6g		Sugars 7g	
Polyunsaturated Fat 0.5g					
Monounsaturated Fat 0g		Vitamin A 0% Vitamin C 0%		Calcium 0% Iron 8%	

Kashi, Cinnamon Harvest

28 biscuits / 1.9 oz / 55g

Amount per serving	%DV	Amount per serving	%DV	Amount per serving	%DV
Calories 180		**Cholesterol** 0mg	0%	**Total Carbohydrate** 43g	14%
Total Fat 1g	2%	**Sodium** 0mg	0%	Dietary Fiber 5g	20%
Saturated Fat 0g	0%	**Protein** 6g		Sugars 9g	
Polyunsaturated Fat 0.5g					
Monounsaturated Fat 0g		Vitamin A 0% Vitamin C 0%		Calcium 0% Iron 8%	

Kashi, GoLean Cereal

1 cup / 1.8 oz / 52g

Amount per serving	%DV	Amount per serving	%DV	Amount per serving	%DV
Calories 160		**Cholesterol** 0mg	0%	**Total Carbohydrate** 35g	12%
Total Fat 1g	2%	**Sodium** 90mg	4%	Dietary Fiber 10g	40%
Saturated Fat 0g	0%	**Protein** 13g		Sugars 9g	
Polyunsaturated Fat 0g					
Monounsaturated Fat 0g		Vitamin A 0% Vitamin C 0%		Calcium 6% Iron 15%	

Kashi, Heart to Heart Honey Toasted Oat

3/4 cup / 1.2 oz / 33g

Amount per serving	%DV	Amount per serving	%DV	Amount per serving	%DV
Calories 120		**Cholesterol** 0mg	0%	**Total Carbohydrate** 26g	9%
Total Fat 1.5g	2%	**Sodium** 85mg	4%	Dietary Fiber 5g	20%
Saturated Fat 0g	0%	**Protein** 3g		Sugars 5g	
Polyunsaturated Fat 0.5g					
Monounsaturated Fat 0.5g		Vitamin A 25% Vitamin C 50%		Calcium 2% Iron 10%	

Kashi, Heart to Heart Oat Flakes & Blueberry Clusters

1 cup / 1.9 oz / 55g

Amount per serving	%DV	Amount per serving	%DV	Amount per serving	%DV
Calories 200		**Cholesterol** 0mg	0%	**Total Carbohydrate** 44g	15%
Total Fat 2g	3%	**Sodium** 135mg	6%	Dietary Fiber 4g	16%
Saturated Fat 0g	0%	**Protein** 6g		Sugars 12g	
Polyunsaturated Fat 0.5g					
Monounsaturated Fat 0.5g		Vitamin A 25% Vitamin C 50%		Calcium 0% Iron 10%	

Kashi, Heart to Heart Warm Cinnamon Oat Cereal

3/4 cup / 1.2 oz / 33g

Amount per serving	%DV	Amount per serving	%DV	Amount per serving	%DV
Calories 120		**Cholesterol** 0mg	0%	**Total Carbohydrate** 25g	8%
Total Fat 1.5g	2%	**Sodium** 80mg	3%	Dietary Fiber 5g	20%
Saturated Fat 0g	0%	**Protein** 4g		Sugars 5g	
Polyunsaturated Fat 0.5g					
Monounsaturated Fat 0.5g		Vitamin A 25% Vitamin C 50%		Calcium 0% Iron 15%	

Kashi, Island Vanilla

27 biscuits / 55g

Amount per serving	%DV	Amount per serving	%DV	Amount per serving	%DV
Calories 190		**Cholesterol** 0mg	0%	**Total Carbohydrate** 44g	15%
Total Fat 1g	2%	**Sodium** 5mg	0%	Dietary Fiber 6g	24%
Saturated Fat 0g	0%	**Protein** 6g		Sugars 9g	
Polyunsaturated Fat 0.5g					
Monounsaturated Fat 0g		Vitamin A 0% Vitamin C 0%		Calcium 0% Iron 8%	

Kellogg's, Frosted Mini-Wheats Big Bite

7 biscuits / 58g

Amount per serving	%DV	Amount per serving	%DV	Amount per serving	%DV
Calories 200		**Cholesterol** 0mg	0%	**Total Carbohydrate** 49g	16%
Total Fat 1g	2%	**Sodium** 0mg	0%	Dietary Fiber 6g	24%
Saturated Fat 0g	0%	**Protein** 5g		Sugars 12g	
Polyunsaturated Fat 0.5g					
Monounsaturated Fat 0g		Vitamin A 0% Vitamin C 0%		Calcium 0% Iron 90%	

Kellogg's, Mini-Wheats Unfrosted Bite Size

30 biscuits / 55g

Amount per serving	%DV	Amount per serving	%DV	Amount per serving	%DV
Calories 190		**Cholesterol** 0mg	0%	**Total Carbohydrate** 45g	15%
Total Fat 1g	2%	**Sodium** 0mg	0%	Dietary Fiber 8g	32%
Saturated Fat 0g	0%	**Protein** 6g		Sugars 0g	
Polyunsaturated Fat 0.5g					
Monounsaturated Fat 0g		Vitamin A 0% Vitamin C 0%		Calcium 0% Iron 90%	

Kellogg's, Raisin Bran

1 cup / with 1/2 cup skim milk / 59g

Amount per serving	%DV	Amount per serving	%DV	Amount per serving	%DV
Calories 230		**Cholesterol** 0mg	0%	**Total Carbohydrate** 46g	15%
Total Fat 1g	2%	**Sodium** 210mg	9%	Dietary Fiber 7g	28%
Saturated Fat 0g	0%	**Protein** 5g		Sugars 18g	
Polyunsaturated Fat 0g					
Monounsaturated Fat 0g		Vitamin A 15% Vitamin C 0%		Calcium 15% Iron 25%	

Kellogg's, Raisin Bran Cinnamon Almond

1 1/4 cups / with 1/2 cup skim milk / 59g

Amount per serving	%DV	Amount per serving	%DV	Amount per serving	%DV
Calories 240		**Cholesterol** 0mg	0%	**Total Carbohydrate** 47g	16%
Total Fat 1.5g	2%	**Sodium** 220mg	9%	Dietary Fiber 5g	20%
Saturated Fat 0g	0%	**Protein** 4g		Sugars 18g	
Polyunsaturated Fat 0.5g					
Monounsaturated Fat 0.5g		Vitamin A 15% Vitamin C 4%		Calcium 15% Iron 25%	

Kellogg's, Raisin Bran Omega-3 from Flaxseed

1 cup / with 1/2 cup skim milk / 59g

Amount per serving	%DV	Amount per serving	%DV	Amount per serving	%DV
Calories 220		**Cholesterol** 0mg	0%	**Total Carbohydrate** 44g	15%
Total Fat 1.5g	2%	**Sodium** 190mg	8%	Dietary Fiber 5g	20%
Saturated Fat 0g	0%	**Protein** 4g		Sugars 17g	
Polyunsaturated Fat 1g					
Monounsaturated Fat 0g		Vitamin A 15% Vitamin C 4%		Calcium 15% Iron 25%	

Malt-O-Meal, Frosted Mini Spooners

1 cup / with skim milk / 55g

Amount per serving	%DV	Amount per serving	%DV	Amount per serving	%DV
Calories 230		**Cholesterol** 0mg	0%	**Total Carbohydrate** 45g	15%
Total Fat 1g	2%	**Sodium** 10mg	0%	Dietary Fiber 6g	24%
Saturated Fat 0g	0%	**Protein** 5g		Sugars 11g	
Polyunsaturated Fat 0.5g					
Monounsaturated Fat 0g		Vitamin A 6% Vitamin C 2%		Calcium 15% Iron 90%	

Multi Grain Cheerios

1 cup / with 1/2 cup skim milk /29g

Amount per serving	%DV	Amount per serving	%DV	Amount per serving	%DV
Calories 150		**Cholesterol** 0mg	0%	**Total Carbohydrate** 24g	8%
Total Fat 1g	2%	**Sodium** 120mg	5%	Dietary Fiber 3g	12%
Saturated Fat 0g	0%	**Protein** 2g		Sugars 6g	
Polyunsaturated Fat 0g					
Monounsaturated Fat 0g		Vitamin A 15% Vitamin C 10%		Calcium 25% Iron 45%	

Post, Shredded Wheat

2 biscuits / 47g

Amount per serving	%DV	Amount per serving	%DV	Amount per serving	%DV
Calories 160		**Cholesterol** 0mg	0%	**Total Carbohydrate** 37g	12%
Total Fat 1g	2%	**Sodium** 0mg	0%	Dietary Fiber 6g	24%
Saturated Fat 0g	0%	**Protein** 5g		Sugars 0g	
Polyunsaturated Fat 0.5g					
Monounsaturated Fat 0g		Vitamin A 0% Vitamin C 0%		Calcium 2% Iron 6%	

Quaker, Oatmeal Squares Brown Sugar

1 cup / with 1/2 cup Vit A & D skim milk / 56g

Amount per serving	%DV	Amount per serving	%DV	Amount per serving	%DV
Calories 250		**Cholesterol** 0mg	0%	**Total Carbohydrate** 44g	15%
Total Fat 2.5g	4%	**Sodium** 190mg	8%	Dietary Fiber 5g	20%
Saturated Fat 0.5g	3%	**Protein** 6g		Sugars 9g	
Polyunsaturated Fat 1g					
Monounsaturated Fat 1g		Vitamin A 15% Vitamin C 10%		Calcium 25% Iron 90%	

Quaker, Oatmeal Squares Cinnamon

1 cup / with 1/2 cup Vit A & D skim milk / 56g

Amount per serving	%DV	Amount per serving	%DV	Amount per serving	%DV
Calories 250		**Cholesterol** 0mg	0%	**Total Carbohydrate** 44g	15%
Total Fat 2.5g	4%	**Sodium** 190mg	8%	Dietary Fiber 5g	20%
Saturated Fat 0.5g	3%	**Protein** 6g		Sugars 9g	
Polyunsaturated Fat 1g					
Monounsaturated Fat 1g		Vitamin A 15% Vitamin C 10%		Calcium 25% Iron 90%	

Quaker, Oatmeal Squares Golden Maple

1 cup / with 1/2 cup Vit A & D skim milk / 56g

Amount per serving	%DV	Amount per serving	%DV	Amount per serving	%DV
Calories 250		**Cholesterol** 0mg	0%	**Total Carbohydrate** 44g	15%
Total Fat 3g	5%	**Sodium** 190mg	8%	Dietary Fiber 5g	20%
Saturated Fat 0.5g	3%	**Protein** 6g		Sugars 9g	
Polyunsaturated Fat 1g					
Monounsaturated Fat 1g		Vitamin A 15% Vitamin C 10%		Calcium 25% Iron 90%	

Quaker, Oatmeal Squares Honey Nut

1 package / 56g

Amount per serving	%DV	Amount per serving	%DV	Amount per serving	%DV
Calories 210		**Cholesterol** 0mg	0%	**Total Carbohydrate** 44g	15%
Total Fat 2.5g	4%	**Sodium** 190mg	8%	Dietary Fiber 5g	20%
Saturated Fat 0.5g	3%	**Protein** 6g		Sugars 9g	
Polyunsaturated Fat 1g					
Monounsaturated Fat 1g		Vitamin A 10% Vitamin C 15%		Calcium 8% Iron 90%	

Quaker, Toasted Multigrain Crisps

1/4 cup / with 1/2 cup Vit A & D skim milk / 57g

Amount per serving	%DV	Amount per serving	%DV	Amount per serving	%DV
Calories 250		**Cholesterol** 0mg	0%	**Total Carbohydrate** 43g	14%
Total Fat 3g	5%	**Sodium** 210mg	9%	Dietary Fiber 6g	24%
Saturated Fat 0.5g	3%	**Protein** 7g		Sugars 9g	
Polyunsaturated Fat 1g					
Monounsaturated Fat 1g		Vitamin A 15% Vitamin C 10%		Calcium 25% Iron 90%	

Quaker, Whole Hearts

3/4 cup / 28g

Amount per serving	%DV	Amount per serving	%DV	Amount per serving	%DV
Calories 110		**Cholesterol** 0mg	0%	**Total Carbohydrate** 23g	8%
Total Fat 1.5g	2%	**Sodium** 160mg	7%	Dietary Fiber 3g	12%
Saturated Fat 0g	0%	**Protein** 2g		Sugars 6g	
Polyunsaturated Fat 0.5g					
Monounsaturated Fat 1g		Vitamin A 0% Vitamin C 0%		Calcium 0% Iron 45%	

Skinner's Raisin Bran

1 cup / 55g

Amount per serving	%DV	Amount per serving	%DV	Amount per serving	%DV
Calories 170		**Cholesterol** 0mg	0%	**Total Carbohydrate** 41g	14%
Total Fat 1g	2%	**Sodium** 85mg	4%	Dietary Fiber 7g	28%
Saturated Fat 0g	0%	**Protein** 6g		Sugars 13g	
Polyunsaturated Fat 0g					
Monounsaturated Fat 0g		Vitamin A 0% Vitamin C 0%		Calcium 0% Iron 6%	

Weetabix, Organic

2 biscuits / 35g

Amount per serving	%DV	Amount per serving	%DV	Amount per serving	%DV
Calories 120		**Cholesterol** 0mg	0%	**Total Carbohydrate** 28g	9%
Total Fat 1g	2%	**Sodium** 130mg	5%	Dietary Fiber 4g	16%
Saturated Fat 0g	0%	**Protein** 4g		Sugars 2g	
Polyunsaturated Fat 0g					
Monounsaturated Fat 0g		Vitamin A 0% Vitamin C 25%		Calcium 0% Iron 25%	

Hot Cereals

Arrowhead Mills, 4 Grain Plus Flax Hot Cereal

1/4 cup / 39g

Amount per serving	%DV	Amount per serving	%DV	Amount per serving	%DV
Calories 140		**Cholesterol** 0mg	0%	**Total Carbohydrate** 28g	9%
Total Fat 1.5g	2%	**Sodium** 0mg	0%	Dietary Fiber 9g	36%
Saturated Fat 0g	0%	**Protein** 5g		Sugars 0g	
Polyunsaturated Fat 0.5g					
Monounsaturated Fat 0.5g		Vitamin A 0% Vitamin C 0%		Calcium 2% Iron 6%	

Bob's Red Mill, 5 Grain Rolled Cereal

1/3 cup dry / 35g

Amount per serving	%DV	Amount per serving	%DV	Amount per serving	%DV
Calories 120		**Cholesterol** 0mg	0%	**Total Carbohydrate** 24g	8%
Total Fat 1.5g	2%	**Sodium** 0mg	0%	Dietary Fiber 5g	20%
Saturated Fat 0g	0%	**Protein** 5g		Sugars 0g	
Polyunsaturated Fat 0g					
Monounsaturated Fat 0g		Vitamin A 0% Vitamin C 0%		Calcium 2% Iron 6%	

Bob's Red Mill, Gluten Free Quick Rolled Oats

1/2 cup dry / 45g

Amount per serving	%DV	Amount per serving	%DV	Amount per serving	%DV
Calories 180		**Cholesterol** 0mg	0%	**Total Carbohydrate** 29g	10%
Total Fat 3g	5%	**Sodium** 0mg	0%	Dietary Fiber 5g	20%
Saturated Fat 0.5g	3%	**Protein** 7g		Sugars 1g	
Polyunsaturated Fat 0g					
Monounsaturated Fat 0g		Vitamin A 0% Vitamin C 0%		Calcium 2% Iron 10%	

Bob's Red Mill, Mighty Tasty Hot Cereal

1/4 cup / 42g

Amount per serving	%DV	Amount per serving	%DV	Amount per serving	%DV
Calories 150		**Cholesterol** 0mg	0%	**Total Carbohydrate** 31g	10%
Total Fat 1.5g	2%	**Sodium** 5mg	0%	Dietary Fiber 4g	16%
Saturated Fat 0g	0%	**Protein** 4g		Sugars 0g	
Polyunsaturated Fat 0g					
Monounsaturated Fat 0g		Vitamin A 2%	Vitamin C 0%	Calcium 0%	Iron 6%

Bob's Red Mill, Oat Bran Cereal

1/3 cup / 40g

Amount per serving	%DV	Amount per serving	%DV	Amount per serving	%DV
Calories 150		**Cholesterol** 0mg	0%	**Total Carbohydrate** 27g	9%
Total Fat 2g	3%	**Sodium** 0mg	0%	Dietary Fiber 7g	28%
Saturated Fat 0.5g	3%	**Protein** 7g		Sugars 0g	
Polyunsaturated Fat 0g					
Monounsaturated Fat 0g		Vitamin A 0%	Vitamin C 0%	Calcium 2%	Iron 10%

Bob's Red Mill, Regular Rolled Oats

1/2 cup dry / 41g

Amount per serving	%DV	Amount per serving	%DV	Amount per serving	%DV
Calories 150		**Cholesterol** 0mg	0%	**Total Carbohydrate** 27g	9%
Total Fat 2.5g	4%	**Sodium** 0mg	0%	Dietary Fiber 4g	16%
Saturated Fat 0.5g	3%	**Protein** 7g		Sugars 1g	
Polyunsaturated Fat 0g					
Monounsaturated Fat 0g		Vitamin A 0%	Vitamin C 0%	Calcium 2%	Iron 10%

Bob's Red Mill, Thick Rolled Oats

1/2 cup dry / 41g

Amount per serving	%DV	Amount per serving	%DV	Amount per serving	%DV
Calories 160		**Cholesterol** 0mg	0%	**Total Carbohydrate** 27g	9%
Total Fat 2.5g	4%	**Sodium** 0mg	0%	Dietary Fiber 4g	16%
Saturated Fat 0.5g	3%	**Protein** 7g		Sugars 1g	
Polyunsaturated Fat 0g					
Monounsaturated Fat 0g		Vitamin A 0%	Vitamin C 0%	Calcium 2%	Iron 10%

Country Choice, Multigrain

1/2 cup dry / 40g

Amount per serving	%DV	Amount per serving	%DV	Amount per serving	%DV
Calories 130		**Cholesterol** 0mg	0%	**Total Carbohydrate** 29g	10%
Total Fat 1g	2%	**Sodium** 0mg	0%	Dietary Fiber 5g	20%
Saturated Fat 0g	0%	**Protein** 5g		Sugars 0g	
Polyunsaturated Fat 0.5g					
Monounsaturated Fat 0g		Vitamin A 0%	Vitamin C 0%	Calcium 0%	Iron 8%

Country Choice, Organics Steel Cut Oats

1/4 cup dry / 40g

Amount per serving	%DV	Amount per serving	%DV	Amount per serving	%DV
Calories 150		**Cholesterol** 0mg	0%	**Total Carbohydrate** 27g	9%
Total Fat 3g	5%	**Sodium** 0mg	0%	Dietary Fiber 4g	16%
Saturated Fat 0g	0%	**Protein** 5g		Sugars 1g	
Polyunsaturated Fat 1g					
Monounsaturated Fat 1g		Vitamin A 0%	Vitamin C 0%	Calcium 0%	Iron 10%

Cream of Wheat, 1 Minute, Cooked with Water, Microwaved, without Salt

1 cup / 237g

Amount per serving	%DV	Amount per serving	%DV	Amount per serving	%DV
Calories 130		**Cholesterol** 0mg	0%	**Total Carbohydrate** 25g	8%
Total Fat 1g	2%	**Sodium** 9mg	0%	Dietary Fiber 3.5g	14%
Saturated Fat 0g	0%	**Protein** 5g		Sugars 7g	
Polyunsaturated Fat 0g					
Monounsaturated Fat 0g		Vitamin A 37%	Vitamin C 0%	Calcium 15%	Iron 66%

Cream of Wheat, Healthy Grain

1 package / 45g

Amount per serving	%DV	Amount per serving	%DV	Amount per serving	%DV
Calories 150		**Cholesterol** 0mg	0%	**Total Carbohydrate** 30g	10%
Total Fat 1g	2%	**Sodium** 170mg	7%	Dietary Fiber 6g	24%
Saturated Fat 0g	0%	**Protein** 7g		Sugars 0g	
Polyunsaturated Fat 0g					
Monounsaturated Fat 0g		Vitamin A 30%	Vitamin C 0%	Calcium 20%	Iron 70%

Earth's Best, Yummy Tummy Instant Oatmeal, Maple & Brown Sugar

1 pouch / 43g

Amount per serving	%DV	Amount per serving	%DV	Amount per serving	%DV
Calories 160		**Cholesterol** 0mg	0%	**Total Carbohydrate** 31g	10%
Total Fat 2.5g	4%	**Sodium** 85mg	4%	Dietary Fiber 5g	20%
Saturated Fat 0g	0%	**Protein** 5g		Sugars 8g	
Polyunsaturated Ful 0g					
Monounsaturated Fat 0g		Vitamin A 0%	Vitamin C 0%	Calcium 0%	Iron 0%

Eden Foods, Buckwheat, 100% Whole Grain, Organic

1/4 cup uncooked

Amount per serving	%DV	Amount per serving	%DV	Amount per serving	%DV
Calories 160		**Cholesterol** 0mg	0%	**Total Carbohydrate** 31g	10%
Total Fat 1g	2%	**Sodium** 0mg	0%	Dietary Fiber 5g	20%
Saturated Fat 0g	0%	**Protein** 5g		Sugars 0g	
Polyunsaturated Fat 0g					
Monounsaturated Fat 0g		Vitamin A 0%	Vitamin C 0%	Calcium 0%	Iron 6%

Kashi, GoLean Instant Hot Cereal, Honey & Cinnamon

1 packet / 40g

Amount per serving	%DV	Amount per serving	%DV	Amount per serving	%DV
Calories 150		**Cholesterol** 0mg	0%	**Total Carbohydrate** 26g	9%
Total Fat 2g	3%	**Sodium** 100mg	4%	Dietary Fiber 5g	20%
Saturated Fat 0g	0%	**Protein** 8g		Sugars 7g	
Polyunsaturated Fat 1g					
Monounsaturated Fat 0.5g		Vitamin A 0% Vitamin C 0%		Calcium 0% Iron 8%	

Kashi, Heart to Heart Apple Cinnamon Instant Oatmeal

1 packet / 1.5 oz / 43g

Amount per serving	%DV	Amount per serving	%DV	Amount per serving	%DV
Calories 160		**Cholesterol** 0mg	0%	**Total Carbohydrate** 33g	11%
Total Fat 2g	3%	**Sodium** 110mg	5%	Dietary Fiber 5g	20%
Saturated Fat 0g	0%	**Protein** 4g		Sugars 12g	
Polyunsaturated Fat 1g					
Monounsaturated Fat 1g		Vitamin A 25% Vitamin C 5%		Calcium 10% Iron 10%	

Kashi, Heart to Heart Golden Maple Instant Oatmeal

1 packet / 1.5 oz / 43g

Amount per serving	%DV	Amount per serving	%DV	Amount per serving	%DV
Calories 160		**Cholesterol** 0mg	0%	**Total Carbohydrate** 33g	11%
Total Fat 2g	3%	**Sodium** 100mg	4%	Dietary Fiber 5g	20%
Saturated Fat 0g	0%	**Protein** 4g		Sugars 12g	
Polyunsaturated Fat 1g					
Monounsaturated Fat 1g		Vitamin A 25% Vitamin C 50%		Calcium 10% Iron 10%	

Kashi, Heart to Heart Instant Oatmeal, Golden Maple

1 package / 43g

Amount per serving	%DV	Amount per serving	%DV	Amount per serving	%DV
Calories 160		**Cholesterol** 0mg	0%	**Total Carbohydrate** 33g	11%
Total Fat 2g	3%	**Sodium** 100mg	4%	Dietary Fiber 5g	20%
Saturated Fat 0g	0%	**Protein** 4g		Sugars 12g	
Polyunsaturated Fat 1g					
Monounsaturated Fat 1g		Vitamin A 25% Vitamin C 50%		Calcium 10% Iron 10%	

Nature's Path, Organic Flax Plus Instant Hot Oatmeal

1 package / 50g

Amount per serving	%DV	Amount per serving	%DV	Amount per serving	%DV
Calories 210		**Cholesterol** 0mg	0%	**Total Carbohydrate** 38g	13%
Total Fat 3g	5%	**Sodium** 140mg	6%	Dietary Fiber 5g	20%
Saturated Fat 0.5g	3%	**Protein** 6g		Sugars 10g	
Polyunsaturated Fat 0g					
Monounsaturated Fat 0g		Vitamin A 0% Vitamin C 0%		Calcium 2% Iron 10%	

Nature's Path, Organic Instant Hot Oatmeal Original

1 package / 50g

Amount per serving	%DV	Amount per serving	%DV	Amount per serving	%DV
Calories 190		**Cholesterol** 0mg	0%	**Total Carbohydrate** 34g	11%
Total Fat 3g	5%	**Sodium** 0mg	0%	Dietary Fiber 6g	24%
Saturated Fat 1g	5%	**Protein** 8g		Sugars 1g	
Polyunsaturated Fat 0g					
Monounsaturated Fat 0g		Vitamin A 0% Vitamin C 0%		Calcium 2% Iron 10%	

Nature's Path, Organic Instant Hot Oatmeal, Multigrain Raisin Spice

1 package / 50g

Amount per serving	%DV	Amount per serving	%DV	Amount per serving	%DV
Calories 180		**Cholesterol** 0mg	0%	**Total Carbohydrate** 39g	13%
Total Fat 1g	2%	**Sodium** 100mg	4%	Dietary Fiber 4g	16%
Saturated Fat 0g	0%	**Protein** 4g		Sugars 18g	
Polyunsaturated Fat 0g					
Monounsaturated Fat 0g		Vitamin A 0% Vitamin C 0%		Calcium 0% Iron 8%	

Quaker Oats Old-Fashioned

1/2 cup dry / 40g

Amount per serving	%DV	Amount per serving	%DV	Amount per serving	%DV
Calories 150		**Cholesterol** 0mg	0%	**Total Carbohydrate** 27g	9%
Total Fat 3g	5%	**Sodium** 0mg	0%	Dietary Fiber 4g	16%
Saturated Fat 0.5g	3%	**Protein** 5g		Sugars 1g	
Polyunsaturated Fat 1g					
Monounsaturated Fat 1g		Vitamin A 0% Vitamin C 0%		Calcium 0% Iron 10%	

Quaker Oats Quick 1-Minute

1/2 cup / with 1/2 cup Vit A & D skim milk / 40g

Amount per serving	%DV	Amount per serving	%DV	Amount per serving	%DV
Calories 190		**Cholesterol** 0mg	0%	**Total Carbohydrate** 27g	9%
Total Fat 3g	5%	**Sodium** 0mg	0%	Dietary Fiber 4g	16%
Saturated Fat 0.5g	3%	**Protein** 5g		Sugars 1g	
Polyunsaturated Fat 1g					
Monounsaturated Fat 1g		Vitamin A 4% Vitamin C 0%		Calcium 15% Iron 10%	

Quaker Oats, Lower Sugar Instant Oatmeal, Maple & Brown Sugar

1 packet / 34g

Amount per serving	%DV	Amount per serving	%DV	Amount per serving	%DV
Calories 120		**Cholesterol** 0mg	0%	**Total Carbohydrate** 24g	8%
Total Fat 2g	3%	**Sodium** 290mg	12%	Dietary Fiber 3g	12%
Saturated Fat 0g	0%	**Protein** 4g		Sugars 4g	
Polyunsaturated Fat 0.5g					
Monounsaturated Fat 0.5g		Vitamin A 20% Vitamin C 0%		Calcium 10% Iron 20%	

Quaker Oats, Quaker High Fiber Instant Oatmeal

1 packet / 45g

Amount per serving	%DV	Amount per serving	%DV	Amount per serving	%DV
Calories 160		**Cholesterol** 0mg	0%	**Total Carbohydrate** 34g	11%
Total Fat 2g	3%	**Sodium** 210mg	9%	Dietary Fiber 10g	40%
Saturated Fat 0.5g	3%	**Protein** 4g		Sugars 7g	
Polyunsaturated Fat 0.5g					
Monounsaturated Fat 1g		Vitamin A 25%　Vitamin C 0%		Calcium 10%　Iron 20%	

Quaker Oats, Weight Control Instant Oatmeal, Maple & Brown Sugar

1 packet / 45g

Amount per serving	%DV	Amount per serving	%DV	Amount per serving	%DV
Calories 160		**Cholesterol** 0mg	0%	**Total Carbohydrate** 29g	10%
Total Fat 3g	5%	**Sodium** 290mg	12%	Dietary Fiber 6g	24%
Saturated Fat 0.5g	3%	**Protein** 7g		Sugars 1g	
Polyunsaturated Fat 1g					
Monounsaturated Fat 1g		Vitamin A 20%　Vitamin C 0%		Calcium 10%　Iron 20%	

Quaker, Instant Oatmeal Apples & Cinnamon

1 packet / 43g

Amount per serving	%DV	Amount per serving	%DV	Amount per serving	%DV
Calories 160		**Cholesterol** 0mg	0%	**Total Carbohydrate** 33g	11%
Total Fat 2g	3%	**Sodium** 200mg	8%	Dietary Fiber 4g	16%
Saturated Fat 0g	0%	**Protein** 4g		Sugars 12g	
Polyunsaturated Fat 0.5g					
Monounsaturated Fat 0.5g		Vitamin A 30%　Vitamin C 0%		Calcium 10%　Iron 20%	

Quaker, Instant Oatmeal Cinnamon & Spice

1 packet / 43g

Amount per serving	%DV	Amount per serving	%DV	Amount per serving	%DV
Calories 160		**Cholesterol** 0mg	0%	**Total Carbohydrate** 32g	11%
Total Fat 2g	3%	**Sodium** 210mg	9%	Dietary Fiber 3g	12%
Saturated Fat 0.5g	3%	**Protein** 4g		Sugars 11g	
Polyunsaturated Fat 0.5g					
Monounsaturated Fat 1g		Vitamin A 15%　Vitamin C 0%		Calcium 10%　Iron 20%	

Quaker, Instant Oatmeal Cinnamon Roll

1 packet / 43g

Amount per serving	%DV	Amount per serving	%DV	Amount per serving	%DV
Calories 160		**Cholesterol** 0mg	0%	**Total Carbohydrate** 32g	11%
Total Fat 2.5g	4%	**Sodium** 220mg	9%	Dietary Fiber 3g	12%
Saturated Fat 0.5g	3%	**Protein** 4g		Sugars 9g	
Polyunsaturated Fat 0.5g					
Monounsaturated Fat 41g		Vitamin A 15%　Vitamin C 0%		Calcium 10%　Iron 20%	

Quaker, Instant Oatmeal High Fiber Cinnamon Swirl

1 packet / 43g

Amount per serving	%DV	Amount per serving	%DV	Amount per serving	%DV
Calories 160		**Cholesterol** 0mg	0%	**Total Carbohydrate** 34g	11%
Total Fat 2g	3%	**Sodium** 210mg	9%	Dietary Fiber 10g	40%
Saturated Fat 0.5g	3%	**Protein** 4g		Sugars 7g	
Polyunsaturated Fat 0.5g					
Monounsaturated Fat 1g		Vitamin A 25% Vitamin C 0%		Calcium 10% Iron 20%	

Quaker, Instant Oatmeal High Fiber, Maple & Brown Sugar

1 packet / 45g

Amount per serving	%DV	Amount per serving	%DV	Amount per serving	%DV
Calories 160		**Cholesterol** 0mg	0%	**Total Carbohydrate** 34g	11%
Total Fat 2g	3%	**Sodium** 260mg	11%	Dietary Fiber 10g	40%
Saturated Fat 0g	0%	**Protein** 4g		Sugars 7g	
Polyunsaturated Fat 0.5g					
Monounsaturated Fat 0.5g		Vitamin A 25% Vitamin C 0%		Calcium 10% Iron 20%	

Quaker, Instant Oatmeal Maple & Brown Sugar

1 packet / 43g

Amount per serving	%DV	Amount per serving	%DV	Amount per serving	%DV
Calories 160		**Cholesterol** 0mg	0%	**Total Carbohydrate** 32g	11%
Total Fat 2g	3%	**Sodium** 260mg	11%	Dietary Fiber 3g	12%
Saturated Fat 0.5g	3%	**Protein** 4g		Sugars 12g	
Polyunsaturated Fat 0.5g					
Monounsaturated Fat 1g		Vitamin A 20% Vitamin C 0%		Calcium 8% Iron 10%	

Quaker, Instant Oatmeal Original

1 packet / 28g

Amount per serving	%DV	Amount per serving	%DV	Amount per serving	%DV
Calories 100		**Cholesterol** 0mg	0%	**Total Carbohydrate** 19g	6%
Total Fat 2g	3%	**Sodium** 75mg	3%	Dietary Fiber 3g	12%
Saturated Fat 0g	0%	**Protein** 4g		Sugars 0g	
Polyunsaturated Fat 0.5g					
Monounsaturated Fat 0.5g		Vitamin A 25% Vitamin C 0%		Calcium 10% Iron 40%	

Quaker, Instant Oatmeal Raisins & Spice

1 packet / 43g

Amount per serving	%DV	Amount per serving	%DV	Amount per serving	%DV
Calories 150		**Cholesterol** 0mg	0%	**Total Carbohydrate** 32g	11%
Total Fat 2g	3%	**Sodium** 210mg	9%	Dietary Fiber 3g	12%
Saturated Fat 0g	0%	**Protein** 4g		Sugars 14g	
Polyunsaturated Fat 0.5g					
Monounsaturated Fat 1g		Vitamin A 15% Vitamin C 0%		Calcium 10% Iron 20%	

Quaker, Lower Sugar Instant Oatmeal, Apples & Cinnamon

1 packet / 31g

Amount per serving	%DV	Amount per serving	%DV	Amount per serving	%DV
Calories 110		**Cholesterol** 0mg	0%	**Total Carbohydrate** 22g	7%
Total Fat 1.5g	2%	**Sodium** 170mg	7%	Dietary Fiber 3g	12%
Saturated Fat 0g	0%	**Protein** 3g		Sugars 6g	
Polyunsaturated Fat 0.5g					
Monounsaturated Fat 0.5g		Vitamin A 20%	Vitamin C 0%	Calcium 10%	Iron 20%

Quaker, Multigrain Hot Cereal

1/2 cup / with 1/2 cup Vit A & D skim milk / 40g

Amount per serving	%DV	Amount per serving	%DV	Amount per serving	%DV
Calories 170		**Cholesterol** 0mg	0%	**Total Carbohydrate** 29g	10%
Total Fat 1g	2%	**Sodium** 0mg	0%	Dietary Fiber 5g	20%
Saturated Fat 0g	0%	**Protein** 5g		Sugars 0g	
Polyunsaturated Fat 0.5g					
Monounsaturated Fat 0g		Vitamin A 4%	Vitamin C 0%	Calcium 15%	Iron 6%

Quaker, Oat Bran Hot Cereal

1/2 cup / with 1/2 cup Vit A & D skim milk / 40g

Amount per serving	%DV	Amount per serving	%DV	Amount per serving	%DV
Calories 190		**Cholesterol** 0mg	0%	**Total Carbohydrate** 25g	8%
Total Fat 3g	5%	**Sodium** 0mg	0%	Dietary Fiber 6g	24%
Saturated Fat 0.5g	3%	**Protein** 7g		Sugars 1g	
Polyunsaturated Fat 1g					
Monounsaturated Fat 1g		Vitamin A 4%	Vitamin C 0%	Calcium 15%	Iron 15%

Quaker, Steel Cut Oats

1/4 cup / 40g

Amount per serving	%DV	Amount per serving	%DV	Amount per serving	%DV
Calories 150		**Cholesterol** 0mg	0%	**Total Carbohydrate** 27g	9%
Total Fat 2.5g	4%	**Sodium** 0mg	0%	Dietary Fiber 4g	16%
Saturated Fat 0.5g	3%	**Protein** 5g		Sugars 1g	
Polyunsaturated Fat 1g					
Monounsaturated Fat 1g		Vitamin A 0%	Vitamin C 0%	Calcium 0%	Iron 10%

Pastas

Ancient Harvest Quinoa, Gluten-Free Linguine Pasta

2 oz dry / 57g

Amount per serving	%DV	Amount per serving	%DV	Amount per serving	%DV
Calories 205		**Cholesterol** 0mg	0%	**Total Carbohydrate** 46g	15%
Total Fat 1g	2%	**Sodium** 4mg	0%	Dietary Fiber 4g	16%
Saturated Fat 0g	0%	**Protein** 4g		Sugars 1g	
Polyunsaturated Fat 0g					
Monounsaturated Fat 0g		Vitamin A 0%	Vitamin C 0%	Calcium 0%	Iron 9%

Ancient Harvest Quinoa, Gluten-Free Pasta Elbows

2 oz dry / 57g

Amount per serving	%DV	Amount per serving	%DV	Amount per serving	%DV
Calories 205		**Cholesterol** 0mg	0%	**Total Carbohydrate** 46g	15%
Total Fat 1g	2%	**Sodium** 4mg	0%	Dietary Fiber 4g	16%
Saturated Fat 0g	0%	**Protein** 4g		Sugars 1g	
Polyunsaturated Fat 0g					
Monounsaturated Fat 0g		Vitamin A 0% Vitamin C 0%		Calcium 0% Iron 9%	

Ancient Harvest Quinoa, Gluten-Free Pasta Shells

2 oz dry

Amount per serving	%DV	Amount per serving	%DV	Amount per serving	%DV
Calories 205		**Cholesterol** 0mg	0%	**Total Carbohydrate** 46g	15%
Total Fat 1g	2%	**Sodium** 4mg	0%	Dietary Fiber 4g	16%
Saturated Fat 0g	0%	**Protein** 4g		Sugars 1g	
Polyunsaturated Fat 0g					
Monounsaturated Fat 0g		Vitamin A 0% Vitamin C 0%		Calcium 0% Iron 2%	

Ancient Harvest Quinoa, Gluten-Free Spaghetti Pasta

2 oz dry

Amount per serving	%DV	Amount per serving	%DV	Amount per serving	%DV
Calories 205		**Cholesterol** 0mg	0%	**Total Carbohydrate** 46g	15%
Total Fat 1g	2%	**Sodium** 4mg	0%	Dietary Fiber 4g	16%
Saturated Fat 0g	0%	**Protein** 4g		Sugars 1g	
Polyunsaturated Fat 0g					
Monounsaturated Fat 0g		Vitamin A 0% Vitamin C 0%		Calcium 0% Iron 9%	

Ancient Harvest, Garden Pagodas

2 oz dry / 56.8g

Amount per serving	%DV	Amount per serving	%DV	Amount per serving	%DV
Calories 205		**Cholesterol** 0mg	0%	**Total Carbohydrate** 46g	15%
Total Fat 1g	2%	**Sodium** 4mg	0%	Dietary Fiber 4g	16%
Saturated Fat 0g	0%	**Protein** 4g		Sugars 1g	
Polyunsaturated Fat 0g					
Monounsaturated Fat 0g		Vitamin A 0% Vitamin C 0%		Calcium 0% Iron 9%	

Andean Dream, Quinoa Fusilli

2 oz / 56g

Amount per serving	%DV	Amount per serving	%DV	Amount per serving	%DV
Calories 207		**Cholesterol** 0mg	0%	**Total Carbohydrate** 42g	14%
Total Fat 1g	2%	**Sodium** 0mg	0%	Dietary Fiber 3g	12%
Saturated Fat 0g	0%	**Protein** 6g		Sugars 3g	
Polyunsaturated Fat 0g					
Monounsaturated Fat 0g		Vitamin A 0% Vitamin C 0%		Calcium 6% Iron 12%	

Andean Dream, Quinoa Macaroni

2 oz / 56g

Amount per serving	%DV	Amount per serving	%DV	Amount per serving	%DV
Calories 207		**Cholesterol** 0mg	0%	**Total Carbohydrate** 42g	14%
Total Fat 1g	2%	**Sodium** 0mg	0%	Dietary Fiber 3g	12%
Saturated Fat 0g	0%	**Protein** 6g		Sugars 3g	
Polyunsaturated Fat 0g					
Monounsaturated Fat 0g		Vitamin A 0% Vitamin C 0%		Calcium 6% Iron 12%	

Andean Dream, Quinoa Shells

2 oz / 56g

Amount per serving	%DV	Amount per serving	%DV	Amount per serving	%DV
Calories 207		**Cholesterol** 0mg	0%	**Total Carbohydrate** 42g	14%
Total Fat 1g	2%	**Sodium** 0mg	0%	Dietary Fiber 3g	12%
Saturated Fat 0g	0%	**Protein** 6g		Sugars 3g	
Polyunsaturated Fat 0g					
Monounsaturated Fat 0g		Vitamin A 0% Vitamin C 0%		Calcium 6% Iron 12%	

Andean Dream, Quinoa Spaghetti

2 oz / 56g

Amount per serving	%DV	Amount per serving	%DV	Amount per serving	%DV
Calories 207		**Cholesterol** 0mg	0%	**Total Carbohydrate** 42g	14%
Total Fat 1g	2%	**Sodium** 0mg	0%	Dietary Fiber 3g	12%
Saturated Fat 0g	0%	**Protein** 6g		Sugars 3g	
Polyunsaturated Fat 0g					
Monounsaturated Fat 0g		Vitamin A 0% Vitamin C 0%		Calcium 6% Iron 12%	

Anthony's, 100% Whole Grain Angel Hair

2 oz

Amount per serving	%DV	Amount per serving	%DV	Amount per serving	%DV
Calories 190		**Cholesterol** 0mg	0%	**Total Carbohydrate** 40g	13%
Total Fat 1.5g	2%	**Sodium** 0mg	0%	Dietary Fiber 5g	20%
Saturated Fat 0g	0%	**Protein** 7g		Sugars 2g	
Polyunsaturated Fat 0g					
Monounsaturated Fat 0g		Vitamin A 0% Vitamin C 0%		Calcium 0% Iron 0%	

Anthony's, 100% Whole Grain Elbows

2 oz

Amount per serving	%DV	Amount per serving	%DV	Amount per serving	%DV
Calories 190		**Cholesterol** 0mg	0%	**Total Carbohydrate** 40g	13%
Total Fat 1.5g	2%	**Sodium** 0mg	0%	Dietary Fiber 5g	20%
Saturated Fat 0g	0%	**Protein** 7g		Sugars 2g	
Polyunsaturated Fat 0g					
Monounsaturated Fat 0g		Vitamin A 0% Vitamin C 0%		Calcium 0% Iron 0%	

Anthony's, 100% Whole Grain Penne Rigate

2 oz

Amount per serving	%DV	Amount per serving	%DV	Amount per serving	%DV
Calories 190		**Cholesterol** 0mg	0%	**Total Carbohydrate** 40g	13%
Total Fat 1.5g	2%	**Sodium** 0mg	0%	Dietary Fiber 5g	20%
Saturated Fat 0g	0%	**Protein** 7g		Sugars 2g	
Polyunsaturated Fat 0g					
Monounsaturated Fat 0g		Vitamin A 0% Vitamin C 0%		Calcium 0% Iron 0%	

Anthony's, 100% Whole Grain Spaghetti

2 oz

Amount per serving	%DV	Amount per serving	%DV	Amount per serving	%DV
Calories 190		**Cholesterol** 0mg	0%	**Total Carbohydrate** 40g	13%
Total Fat 1.5g	2%	**Sodium** 0mg	0%	Dietary Fiber 5g	20%
Saturated Fat 0g	0%	**Protein** 7g		Sugars 2g	
Polyunsaturated Fat 0g					
Monounsaturated Fat 0g		Vitamin A 0% Vitamin C 0%		Calcium 0% Iron 0%	

DeBoles, Organic Whole Wheat Penne Pasta

2 oz / about 3/4 cup / 56g

Amount per serving	%DV	Amount per serving	%DV	Amount per serving	%DV
Calories 210		**Cholesterol** 0mg	0%	**Total Carbohydrate** 42g	14%
Total Fat 1.5g	2%	**Sodium** 10mg	0%	Dietary Fiber 5g	20%
Saturated Fat 0g	0%	**Protein** 7g		Sugars 2g	
Polyunsaturated Fat 0g					
Monounsaturated Fat 0g		Vitamin A 0% Vitamin C 0%		Calcium 2% Iron 10%	

DeBoles, Organic Whole Wheat Spaghetti Style Pasta

2 oz / 1/4 of package / 56g

Amount per serving	%DV	Amount per serving	%DV	Amount per serving	%DV
Calories 210		**Cholesterol** 0mg	0%	**Total Carbohydrate** 42g	14%
Total Fat 1.5g	2%	**Sodium** 10mg	0%	Dietary Fiber 5g	20%
Saturated Fat 0g	0%	**Protein** 7g		Sugars 2g	
Polyunsaturated Fat 0g					
Monounsaturated Fat 0g		Vitamin A 0% Vitamin C 0%		Calcium 2% Iron 10%	

Golden Grain, 100% Whole Grain Angel Hair

2 oz

Amount per serving	%DV	Amount per serving	%DV	Amount per serving	%DV
Calories 190		**Cholesterol** 0mg	0%	**Total Carbohydrate** 40g	13%
Total Fat 1.5g	2%	**Sodium** 0mg	0%	Dietary Fiber 5g	20%
Saturated Fat 0g	0%	**Protein** 7g		Sugars 2g	
Polyunsaturated Fat 0g					
Monounsaturated Fat 0g		Vitamin A 0% Vitamin C 0%		Calcium 0% Iron 0%	

Golden Grain, 100% Whole Grain Elbows

2 oz

Amount per serving	%DV	Amount per serving	%DV	Amount per serving	%DV
Calories 190		**Cholesterol** 0mg	0%	**Total Carbohydrate** 40g	13%
Total Fat 1.5g	2%	**Sodium** 0mg	0%	Dietary Fiber 5g	20%
Saturated Fat 0g	0%	**Protein** 7g		Sugars 2g	
Polyunsaturated Fat 0g					
Monounsaturated Fat 0g		Vitamin A 0%	Vitamin C 0%	Calcium 0%	Iron 0%

Golden Grain, 100% Whole Grain Penne Rigate

2 oz

Amount per serving	%DV	Amount per serving	%DV	Amount per serving	%DV
Calories 190		**Cholesterol** 0mg	0%	**Total Carbohydrate** 40g	13%
Total Fat 1.5g	2%	**Sodium** 0mg	0%	Dietary Fiber 5g	20%
Saturated Fat 0g	0%	**Protein** 7g		Sugars 2g	
Polyunsaturated Fat 0g					
Monounsaturated Fat 0g		Vitamin A 0%	Vitamin C 0%	Calcium 0%	Iron 0%

Golden Grain, 100% Whole Grain Spaghetti

2 oz

Amount per serving	%DV	Amount per serving	%DV	Amount per serving	%DV
Calories 190		**Cholesterol** 0mg	0%	**Total Carbohydrate** 40g	13%
Total Fat 1.5g	2%	**Sodium** 0mg	0%	Dietary Fiber 5g	20%
Saturated Fat 0g	0%	**Protein** 7g		Sugars 2g	
Polyunsaturated Fat 0g					
Monounsaturated Fat 0g		Vitamin A 0%	Vitamin C 0%	Calcium 0%	Iron 0%

Heartland, 100% Whole Grain Angel Hair

2 oz

Amount per serving	%DV	Amount per serving	%DV	Amount per serving	%DV
Calories 190		**Cholesterol** 0mg	0%	**Total Carbohydrate** 40g	13%
Total Fat 1.5g	2%	**Sodium** 0mg	0%	Dietary Fiber 5g	20%
Saturated Fat 0g	0%	**Protein** 7g		Sugars 2g	
Polyunsaturated Fat 0g					
Monounsaturated Fat 0g		Vitamin A 0%	Vitamin C 0%	Calcium 0%	Iron 0%

Heartland, 100% Whole Grain Elbows

2 oz

Amount per serving	%DV	Amount per serving	%DV	Amount per serving	%DV
Calories 190		**Cholesterol** 0mg	0%	**Total Carbohydrate** 40g	13%
Total Fat 1.5g	2%	**Sodium** 0mg	0%	Dietary Fiber 5g	20%
Saturated Fat 0g	0%	**Protein** 7g		Sugars 2g	
Polyunsaturated Fat 0g					
Monounsaturated Fat 0g		Vitamin A 0%	Vitamin C 0%	Calcium 0%	Iron 0%

Heartland, 100% Whole Grain Penne

2 oz

Amount per serving	%DV	Amount per serving	%DV	Amount per serving	%DV
Calories 190		**Cholesterol** 0mg	0%	**Total Carbohydrate** 40g	13%
Total Fat 1.5g	2%	**Sodium** 0mg	0%	Dietary Fiber 5g	20%
Saturated Fat 0g	0%	**Protein** 7g		Sugars 2g	
Polyunsaturated Fat 0g					
Monounsaturated Fat 0g		Vitamin A 0%	Vitamin C 0%	Calcium 0%	Iron 0%

Heartland, 100% Whole Grain Rotini

2 oz

Amount per serving	%DV	Amount per serving	%DV	Amount per serving	%DV
Calories 190		**Cholesterol** 0mg	0%	**Total Carbohydrate** 40g	13%
Total Fat 1.5g	2%	**Sodium** 0mg	0%	Dietary Fiber 5g	20%
Saturated Fat 0g	0%	**Protein** 7g		Sugars 2g	
Polyunsaturated Fat 0g					
Monounsaturated Fat 0g		Vitamin A 0%	Vitamin C 0%	Calcium 0%	Iron 0%

Heartland, 100% Whole Grain Spaghetti

2 oz

Amount per serving	%DV	Amount per serving	%DV	Amount per serving	%DV
Calories 190		**Cholesterol** 0mg	0%	**Total Carbohydrate** 40g	13%
Total Fat 1.5g	2%	**Sodium** 0mg	0%	Dietary Fiber 5g	20%
Saturated Fat 0g	0%	**Protein** 7g		Sugars 2g	
Polyunsaturated Fat 0g					
Monounsaturated Fat 0g		Vitamin A 0%	Vitamin C 0%	Calcium 0%	Iron 0%

Lundberg Family Farms, Elbow Pasta, Dry

55g dry

Amount per serving	%DV	Amount per serving	%DV	Amount per serving	%DV
Calories 190		**Cholesterol** 0mg	0%	**Total Carbohydrate** 40g	13%
Total Fat 3g	5%	**Sodium** 0mg	0%	Dietary Fiber 4g	16%
Saturated Fat 0.5g	3%	**Protein** 4g		Sugars 1g	
Polyunsaturated Fat 0g					
Monounsaturated Fat 0g		Vitamin A 0%	Vitamin C 0%	Calcium 0%	Iron 8%

Lundberg Family Farms, Penne Pasta

55g dry

Amount per serving	%DV	Amount per serving	%DV	Amount per serving	%DV
Calories 190		**Cholesterol** 0mg	0%	**Total Carbohydrate** 40g	13%
Total Fat 3g	5%	**Sodium** 0mg	0%	Dietary Fiber 4g	16%
Saturated Fat 0.5g	3%	**Protein** 4g		Sugars 1g	
Polyunsaturated Fat 0g					
Monounsaturated Fat 0g		Vitamin A 0%	Vitamin C 0%	Calcium 0%	Iron 8%

Lundberg Family Farms, Roasted Organic Plain Original Brown Rice Couscous, Dry

45g / 1/4 cup dry / 1 cup prepared

Amount per serving	%DV	Amount per serving	%DV	Amount per serving	%DV
Calories 160		**Cholesterol** 0mg	0%	**Total Carbohydrate** 37g	12%
Total Fat 1.5g	2%	**Sodium** 0mg	0%	Dietary Fiber 3g	12%
Saturated Fat 0g	0%	**Protein** 3g		Sugars 1g	
Polyunsaturated Fat 0g					
Monounsaturated Fat 0g		Vitamin A 0% Vitamin C 0%		Calcium 0% Iron 2%	

Lundberg Family Farms, Rotini Brown Rice Pasta

55g dry

Amount per serving	%DV	Amount per serving	%DV	Amount per serving	%DV
Calories 190		**Cholesterol** 0mg	0%	**Total Carbohydrate** 40g	13%
Total Fat 3g	5%	**Sodium** 0mg	0%	Dietary Fiber 4g	16%
Saturated Fat 0.5g	3%	**Protein** 4g		Sugars 1g	
Polyunsaturated Fat 0g					
Monounsaturated Fat 0g		Vitamin A 0% Vitamin C 0%		Calcium 0% Iron 8%	

Lundberg Family Farms, Spaghetti Pasta

55g dry

Amount per serving	%DV	Amount per serving	%DV	Amount per serving	%DV
Calories 190		**Cholesterol** 0mg	0%	**Total Carbohydrate** 40g	13%
Total Fat 3g	5%	**Sodium** 0mg	0%	Dietary Fiber 4g	16%
Saturated Fat 0.5g	3%	**Protein** 4g		Sugars 1g	
Polyunsaturated Fat 0g					
Monounsaturated Fat 0g		Vitamin A 0% Vitamin C 0%		Calcium 0% Iron 8%	

Luxury, 100% Whole Grain Angel Hair

2 oz

Amount per serving	%DV	Amount per serving	%DV	Amount per serving	%DV
Calories 190		**Cholesterol** 0mg	0%	**Total Carbohydrate** 40g	13%
Total Fat 1.5g	2%	**Sodium** 0mg	0%	Dietary Fiber 5g	20%
Saturated Fat 0g	0%	**Protein** 7g		Sugars 2g	
Polyunsaturated Fat 0g					
Monounsaturated Fat 0g		Vitamin A 0% Vitamin C 0%		Calcium 0% Iron 0%	

Luxury, 100% Whole Grain Elbows

2 oz

Amount per serving	%DV	Amount per serving	%DV	Amount per serving	%DV
Calories 190		**Cholesterol** 0mg	0%	**Total Carbohydrate** 40g	13%
Total Fat 1.5g	2%	**Sodium** 0mg	0%	Dietary Fiber 5g	20%
Saturated Fat 0g	0%	**Protein** 7g		Sugars 2g	
Polyunsaturated Fat 0g					
Monounsaturated Fat 0g		Vitamin A 0% Vitamin C 0%		Calcium 0% Iron 0%	

Luxury, 100% Whole Grain Penne

2 oz

Amount per serving	%DV	Amount per serving	%DV	Amount per serving	%DV
Calories 190		**Cholesterol** 0mg	0%	**Total Carbohydrate** 40g	13%
Total Fat 1.5g	2%	**Sodium** 0mg	0%	Dietary Fiber 5g	20%
Saturated Fat 0g	0%	**Protein** 7g		Sugars 2g	
Polyunsaturated Fat 0g					
Monounsaturated Fat 0g		Vitamin A 0% Vitamin C 0%		Calcium 0% Iron 0%	

Luxury, 100% Whole Grain Spaghetti

2 oz

Amount per serving	%DV	Amount per serving	%DV	Amount per serving	%DV
Calories 190		**Cholesterol** 0mg	0%	**Total Carbohydrate** 40g	13%
Total Fat 1.5g	2%	**Sodium** 0mg	0%	Dietary Fiber 5g	20%
Saturated Fat 0g	0%	**Protein** 7g		Sugars 2g	
Polyunsaturated Fat 0g					
Monounsaturated Fat 0g		Vitamin A 0% Vitamin C 0%		Calcium 0% Iron 0%	

Macaroni, Whole-Wheat, Dry

2 oz / 57g

Amount per serving	%DV	Amount per serving	%DV	Amount per serving	%DV
Calories 198.5		**Cholesterol** 0mg	0%	**Total Carbohydrate** 43g	14%
Total Fat 1g	2%	**Sodium** 4.5mg	0%	Dietary Fiber 4.5g	18%
Saturated Fat 0g	0%	**Protein** 8.5g		Sugars 0g	
Polyunsaturated Fat 0.5g					
Monounsaturated Fat 0g		Vitamin A 0% Vitamin C 0%		Calcium 23% Iron 2%	

Mueller's, 100% Whole Grain Angel Hair

2 oz

Amount per serving	%DV	Amount per serving	%DV	Amount per serving	%DV
Calories 190		**Cholesterol** 0mg	0%	**Total Carbohydrate** 40g	13%
Total Fat 1.5g	2%	**Sodium** 0mg	0%	Dietary Fiber 5g	20%
Saturated Fat 0g	0%	**Protein** 7g		Sugars 2g	
Polyunsaturated Fat 0g					
Monounsaturated Fat 0g		Vitamin A 0% Vitamin C 0%		Calcium 0% Iron 0%	

Mueller's, 100% Whole Grain Elbows

2 oz

Amount per serving	%DV	Amount per serving	%DV	Amount per serving	%DV
Calories 190		**Cholesterol** 0mg	0%	**Total Carbohydrate** 40g	13%
Total Fat 1.5g	2%	**Sodium** 0mg	0%	Dietary Fiber 5g	20%
Saturated Fat 0g	0%	**Protein** 7g		Sugars 2g	
Polyunsaturated Fat 0g					
Monounsaturated Fat 0g		Vitamin A 0% Vitamin C 0%		Calcium 0% Iron 0%	

Mueller's, 100% Whole Grain Penne

2 oz

Amount per serving	%DV	Amount per serving	%DV	Amount per serving	%DV
Calories 190		**Cholesterol** 0mg	0%	**Total Carbohydrate** 40g	13%
Total Fat 1.5g	2%	**Sodium** 0mg	0%	Dietary Fiber 5g	20%
Saturated Fat 0g	0%	**Protein** 7g		Sugars 2g	
Polyunsaturated Fat 0g					
Monounsaturated Fat 0g		Vitamin A 0% Vitamin C 0%		Calcium 0% Iron 0%	

Mueller's, 100% Whole Grain Spaghetti

2 oz

Amount per serving	%DV	Amount per serving	%DV	Amount per serving	%DV
Calories 190		**Cholesterol** 0mg	0%	**Total Carbohydrate** 40g	13%
Total Fat 1.5g	2%	**Sodium** 0mg	0%	Dietary Fiber 5g	20%
Saturated Fat 0g	0%	**Protein** 7g		Sugars 2g	
Polyunsaturated Fat 0g					
Monounsaturated Fat 0g		Vitamin A 0% Vitamin C 0%		Calcium 0% Iron 0%	

Pastariso, Organic Brown Rice Gluten-Free Pasta (Elb, Las, Pen, Spag, Ling, Fett)

2 oz

Amount per serving	%DV	Amount per serving	%DV	Amount per serving	%DV
Calories 190		**Cholesterol** 0mg	0%	**Total Carbohydrate** 42g	14%
Total Fat 0.6g	1%	**Sodium** 5mg	0%	Dietary Fiber 3g	12%
Saturated Fat 0g	0%	**Protein** 4g		Sugars 3g	
Polyunsaturated Fat 0g					
Monounsaturated Fat 0g		Vitamin A 0% Vitamin C 0%		Calcium 2% Iron 6%	

Ronco, 100% Whole Grain Angel Hair

2 oz

Amount per serving	%DV	Amount per serving	%DV	Amount per serving	%DV
Calories 190		**Cholesterol** 0mg	0%	**Total Carbohydrate** 40g	13%
Total Fat 1.5g	2%	**Sodium** 0mg	0%	Dietary Fiber 5g	20%
Saturated Fat 0g	0%	**Protein** 7g		Sugars 2g	
Polyunsaturated Fat 0g					
Monounsaturated Fat 0g		Vitamin A 0% Vitamin C 0%		Calcium 0% Iron 0%	

Ronco, 100% Whole Grain Elbows

2 oz

Amount per serving	%DV	Amount per serving	%DV	Amount per serving	%DV
Calories 190		**Cholesterol** 0mg	0%	**Total Carbohydrate** 40g	13%
Total Fat 1.5g	2%	**Sodium** 0mg	0%	Dietary Fiber 5g	20%
Saturated Fat 0g	0%	**Protein** 7g		Sugars 2g	
Polyunsaturated Fat 0g					
Monounsaturated Fat 0g		Vitamin A 0% Vitamin C 0%		Calcium 0% Iron 0%	

Ronco, 100% Whole Grain Penne

2 oz

Amount per serving	%DV	Amount per serving	%DV	Amount per serving	%DV
Calories 190		**Cholesterol** 0mg	0%	**Total Carbohydrate** 40g	13%
Total Fat 1.5g	2%	**Sodium** 0mg	0%	Dietary Fiber 5g	20%
Saturated Fat 0g	0%	**Protein** 7g		Sugars 2g	
Polyunsaturated Fat 0g					
Monounsaturated Fat 0g		Vitamin A 0%	Vitamin C 0%	Calcium 4%	Iron 0%

Ronco, 100% Whole Grain Spaghetti

2 oz

Amount per serving	%DV	Amount per serving	%DV	Amount per serving	%DV
Calories 190		**Cholesterol** 0mg	0%	**Total Carbohydrate** 40g	13%
Total Fat 1.5g	2%	**Sodium** 0mg	0%	Dietary Fiber 5g	20%
Saturated Fat 0g	0%	**Protein** 7g		Sugars 2g	
Polyunsaturated Fat 0g					
Monounsaturated Fat 0g		Vitamin A 0%	Vitamin C 0%	Calcium 4%	Iron 0%

Spaghetti, Whole Wheat, Cooked

1 cup / 140g

Amount per serving	%DV	Amount per serving	%DV	Amount per serving	%DV
Calories 174		**Cholesterol** 0mg	0%	**Total Carbohydrate** 37g	12%
Total Fat 1g	2%	**Sodium** 4mg	0%	Dietary Fiber 6.5g	26%
Saturated Fat 0g	0%	**Protein** 7g		Sugars 1g	
Polyunsaturated Fat 0g					
Monounsaturated Fat 0g		Vitamin A 0%	Vitamin C 0%	Calcium 2%	Iron 8%

Rice

Eden Foods, Short Grain Brown Rice, 100% Whole Grain, Organic

1/4 cup / 45g

Amount per serving	%DV	Amount per serving	%DV	Amount per serving	%DV
Calories 150		**Cholesterol** 0mg	0%	**Total Carbohydrate** 35g	12%
Total Fat 1.5g	2%	**Sodium** 0mg	0%	Dietary Fiber 3g	12%
Saturated Fat 0g	0%	**Protein** 3g		Sugars 1g	
Polyunsaturated Fat 0g					
Monounsaturated Fat 0g		Vitamin A 0%	Vitamin C 0%	Calcium 0%	Iron 2%

Lundberg Family Farms, Eco-Farmed Long Grain Brown Rice

1/4 cup dry /45g

Amount per serving	%DV	Amount per serving	%DV	Amount per serving	%DV
Calories 170		**Cholesterol** 0mg	0%	**Total Carbohydrate** 37g	12%
Total Fat 2g	3%	**Sodium** 0mg	0%	Dietary Fiber 3g	12%
Saturated Fat 0g	0%	**Protein** 3g		Sugars 0g	
Polyunsaturated Fat 0g					
Monounsaturated Fat 0g		Vitamin A 0%	Vitamin C 0%	Calcium 0%	Iron 2%

Lundberg Family Farms, Eco-Farmed Short Grain Brown Rice

1/4 cup dry / 51g

Amount per serving	%DV	Amount per serving	%DV	Amount per serving	%DV
Calories 170		**Cholesterol** 0mg	0%	**Total Carbohydrate** 40g	13%
Total Fat 1.5g	2%	**Sodium** 0mg	0%	Dietary Fiber 3g	12%
Saturated Fat 0g	0%	**Protein** 3g		Sugars 0g	
Polyunsaturated Fat 0g					
Monounsaturated Fat 0g		Vitamin A 0% Vitamin C 0%		Calcium 0% Iron 4%	

Lundberg Family Farms, Heat & Eat, Organic Countrywild, Brown Rice Bowl

210g

Amount per serving	%DV	Amount per serving	%DV	Amount per serving	%DV
Calories 280		**Cholesterol** 0mg	0%	**Total Carbohydrate** 65g	22%
Total Fat 3g	5%	**Sodium** 0mg	0%	Dietary Fiber 6g	24%
Saturated Fat 0g	0%	**Protein** 6g		Sugars 0g	
Polyunsaturated Fat 0g					
Monounsaturated Fat 0g		Vitamin A 0% Vitamin C 0%		Calcium 0% Iron 4%	

Lundberg Family Farms, Heat & Eat, Organic Long Grain Brown Rice Bowl

210g

Amount per serving	%DV	Amount per serving	%DV	Amount per serving	%DV
Calories 290		**Cholesterol** 0mg	0%	**Total Carbohydrate** 65g	22%
Total Fat 3g	5%	**Sodium** 5mg	0%	Dietary Fiber 6g	24%
Saturated Fat 0.5g	2%	**Protein** 6g		Sugars 1g	
Polyunsaturated Fat 0g					
Monounsaturated Fat 0g		Vitamin A 0% Vitamin C 0%		Calcium 0% Iron 4%	

Lundberg Family Farms, Organic Long Grain Brown Rice

45g

Amount per serving	%DV	Amount per serving	%DV	Amount per serving	%DV
Calories 150		**Cholesterol** 0mg	0%	**Total Carbohydrate** 35g	12%
Total Fat 1.5g	2%	**Sodium** 0mg	0%	Dietary Fiber 3g	12%
Saturated Fat 0g	0%	**Protein** 3g		Sugars 0g	
Polyunsaturated Fat 0g					
Monounsaturated Fat 0g		Vitamin A 0% Vitamin C 0%		Calcium 0% Iron 2%	

Lundberg Family Farms, Organic Short Grain Brown Rice

1/4 cup dry / 45g

Amount per serving	%DV	Amount per serving	%DV	Amount per serving	%DV
Calories 150		**Cholesterol** 0mg	0%	**Total Carbohydrate** 35g	12%
Total Fat 1.5g	2%	**Sodium** 0mg	0%	Dietary Fiber 3g	12%
Saturated Fat 0g	0%	**Protein** 3g		Sugars 1g	
Polyunsaturated Fat 0g					
Monounsaturated Fat 0g		Vitamin A 0% Vitamin C 0%		Calcium 0% Iron 2%	

Rice, Brown, Long-Grain, Cooked

1 cup / 195g

Amount per serving	%DV	Amount per serving	%DV	Amount per serving	%DV
Calories 216		**Cholesterol** 0mg	0%	**Total Carbohydrate** 45g	15%
Total Fat 2g	3%	**Sodium** 10mg	0%	Dietary Fiber 4g	16%
Saturated Fat 0g	0%	**Protein** 5g		Sugars 1g	
Polyunsaturated Fat 0g					
Monounsaturated Fat 0g		Vitamin A 0% Vitamin C 0%		Calcium 2% Iron 5%	

Rice, Brown, Medium-Grain, Cooked

1 cup / 195g

Amount per serving	%DV	Amount per serving	%DV	Amount per serving	%DV
Calories 218		**Cholesterol** 0mg	0%	**Total Carbohydrate** 46g	15%
Total Fat 2g	3%	**Sodium** 2mg	0%	Dietary Fiber 4g	16%
Saturated Fat 0g	0%	**Protein** 5g		Sugars 0g	
Polyunsaturated Fat 0g					
Monounsaturated Fat 0g		Vitamin A 0% Vitamin C 0%		Calcium 2% Iron 6%	

Wild Rice, Cooked

1 cup / 164g

Amount per serving	%DV	Amount per serving	%DV	Amount per serving	%DV
Calories 166		**Cholesterol** 0mg	0%	**Total Carbohydrate** 35g	12%
Total Fat 1g	1%	**Sodium** 5mg	0%	Dietary Fiber 3g	12%
Saturated Fat 0g	0%	**Protein** 7g		Sugars 1g	
Polyunsaturated Fat 0g					
Monounsaturated Fat 0g		Vitamin A 0% Vitamin C 0%		Calcium 0% Iron 5%	

Snacks/Crackers

Crackers, Matzo, Whole-Wheat

1 matzo / 28g

Amount per serving	%DV	Amount per serving	%DV	Amount per serving	%DV
Calories 98.5		**Cholesterol** 0mg	0%	**Total Carbohydrate** 22g	7%
Total Fat 0.5g	1%	**Sodium** 0.5mg	0%	Dietary Fiber 3.5g	14%
Saturated Fat 0g	0%	**Protein** 3.5g		Sugars 0g	
Polyunsaturated Fat 0g					
Monounsaturated Fat 0g		Vitamin A 0% Vitamin C 0%		Calcium 6.5% Iron 1.5%	

Crunchmaster, Gluten-Free Multi-Grain, Roasted Vegetable Crackers

15 crackers / 30g

Amount per serving	%DV	Amount per serving	%DV	Amount per serving	%DV
Calories 130		**Cholesterol** 0mg	0%	**Total Carbohydrate** 23g	8%
Total Fat 3g	5%	**Sodium** 100mg	4%	Dietary Fiber 3g	12%
Saturated Fat 0g	0%	**Protein** 2g		Sugars 2g	
Polyunsaturated Fat 0g					
Monounsaturated Fat 0g		Vitamin A 0% Vitamin C 0%		Calcium 2% Iron 4%	

Crunchmaster, Gluten-Free Multi-Grain, Sea Salt Crackers

16 crackers / 30g

Amount per serving	%DV	Amount per serving	%DV	Amount per serving	%DV
Calories 130		Cholesterol 0mg	0%	Total Carbohydrate 23g	8%
Total Fat 3g	5%	Sodium 135mg	6%	Dietary Fiber 3g	12%
Saturated Fat 0g	0%	Protein 2g		Sugars 2g	
Polyunsaturated Fat 0g					
Monounsaturated Fat 0g		Vitamin A 0% Vitamin C 0%		Calcium 2% Iron 4%	

Crunchmaster, Gluten-Free Multi-Grain, White Cheddar Crackers

15 crackers / 30g

Amount per serving	%DV	Amount per serving	%DV	Amount per serving	%DV
Calories 130		Cholesterol 0mg	0%	Total Carbohydrate 23g	8%
Total Fat 3g	5%	Sodium 125mg	5%	Dietary Fiber 3g	12%
Saturated Fat 0g	0%	Protein 2g		Sugars 2g	
Polyunsaturated Fat 0g					
Monounsaturated Fat 0g		Vitamin A 0% Vitamin C 0%		Calcium 2% Iron 4%	

Eden Foods, Popcorn, 100% Whole Grain, Organic

2 tbsp / 28g

Amount per serving	%DV	Amount per serving	%DV	Amount per serving	%DV
Calories 80		Cholesterol 0mg	0%	Total Carbohydrate 20g	7%
Total Fat 1g	2%	Sodium 0mg	0%	Dietary Fiber 5g	20%
Saturated Fat 0g	0%	Protein 2g		Sugars 0g	
Polyunsaturated Fat 0g					
Monounsaturated Fat 0g		Vitamin A 0% Vitamin C 0%		Calcium 0% Iron 4%	

Newman's Own, 94% Fat Free Butter Flavor Microwave Popcorn

3.5 cup / 30g

Amount per serving	%DV	Amount per serving	%DV	Amount per serving	%DV
Calories 110		Cholesterol 0mg	0%	Total Carbohydrate 20g	7%
Total Fat 1.5g	2%	Sodium 250mg	10%	Dietary Fiber 4g	16%
Saturated Fat 0g	0%	Protein 3g		Sugars 0g	
Polyunsaturated Fat 0g					
Monounsaturated Fat 0g		Vitamin A 0% Vitamin C 0%		Calcium 0% Iron 4%	

Newman's Own, Natural 100 Calorie Mini-Bags Microwave Popcorn

3.5 cup

Amount per serving	%DV	Amount per serving	%DV	Amount per serving	%DV
Calories 100		Cholesterol 0mg	0%	Total Carbohydrate 18g	6%
Total Fat 2.5g	4%	Sodium 210mg	9%	Dietary Fiber 4g	16%
Saturated Fat 1g	5%	Protein 2g		Sugars 0g	
Polyunsaturated Fat 0g					
Monounsaturated Fat 0g		Vitamin A 0% Vitamin C 0%		Calcium 0% Iron 4%	

Smart Balance, Smart 'N Healthy Deluxe Microwave Popcorn

3 tbsp / 1 cup popped

Amount per serving	%DV	Amount per serving	%DV	Amount per serving	%DV
Calories 20		**Cholesterol** 0mg	0%	**Total Carbohydrate** 24g	8%
Total Fat 2g	3%	**Sodium** 85mg	4%	Dietary Fiber 5g	20%
Saturated Fat 0g	0%	**Protein** 4g		Sugars 0g	
Polyunsaturated Fat 0g					
Monounsaturated Fat 0.5g		Vitamin A 0% Vitamin C 0%		Calcium 0% Iron 0%	

Mixed Dishes

Why Eat Mixed Dishes?

Mixed dishes are convenient and enjoyable to eat, but they don't fit neatly into one food group. For example, a cheese pizza counts in several groups—the crust in the grains group, the tomato sauce in the vegetable group, and the cheese in the dairy group. For the nutrient benefits of mixed foods, you need to look at each food component. Frozen and shelf-stable partially prepared foods are convenient and can be healthy if you follow some basic techniques to limit total fat, saturated fat, cholesterol, and sodium.

Daily Goal

There is no daily goal for mixed dishes. Compare each component of the mixed food with the daily goal for that food.

A prepared entrée should have:
> 300 to 500 calories
> 10 g or more protein
> 30% or less fat calories (10 to 28 grams total fat)
> 10% or less saturated fat (1 to 2 grams)
> 480 mg or less sodium

Heart-Healthy Nutrients in Mixed Dishes

See the heart-healthy nutrients for each individual food ingredient found in each mixed dish.

Nutrients of Concern for Heart Health

Sodium—Eating less sodium can lower some people's blood pressure, which can result in a lower risk of heart disease. The basic recommendation for adults is 2,300 mg of sodium per day (about one teaspoon of salt). But for nearly half of all Americans and almost all adults, the recommendation was cut to just 1,500 mg of sodium per day. Count yourself in this group if you are older than 51; are African-American; or have high blood pressure, diabetes, or chronic kidney disease.

Find tips on trimming salt in meals on page 35. Check out the FDA approved Health Claim on sodium and hypertension on page 25.

Heart-Healthy Shopping Tips for Mixed Dishes

- Look for this FDA-Approved Heart-Health Claim for Sodium:

  Sodium and Hypertension
  Diets low in sodium may reduce the risk of high blood pressure, a disease associated with many factors.

  Foods with this claim must be low sodium—600 mg or less, except for soups (480 mg or less).

- Look for products that claim to be "healthy." These have limits on fat, saturated fat, and sodium and must contain a good source of at least one positive nutrient. See the guidelines for "healthy" on page 6.

- Look for the American Heart Association's Heart-Check mark on food labels on entrees/meals/soup/side dishes food labels that meet the Heart Check criteria. For more information on the Heart-Check mark, go to *www.heartcheckmark.org*.

- Most prepared entrees don't include a serving of dairy. If the calcium level is below 10% Daily Value, plan to add a glass of milk.

- Fresh fruits and vegetables are usually lacking in prepared meals. Plan a side salad or vegetable.

- Choose mixed dishes with sauces in separate packets so that you can decide how much to use.

- Look for low-sodium soups.

- Use and prepare foods that contain little or no salt.

- Avoid using prepackaged seasoning mixes because they often contain a lot of salt.

- Use fresh herbs whenever possible. Grind herbs with a mortar and pestle for the freshest and fullest flavor.

- Add dried herbs such as thyme, rosemary, and marjoram to dishes for a more pungent flavor.

- Use vinegar or citrus juice as flavor enhancers.

- To add a little "bite" to your dishes, add some fresh hot peppers.

- Some mixed dishes can contain a lot of fat or sugar, which adds empty calories. Mixed dishes are also usually high in sodium.

Shopping List Essentials

Healthy frozen dinners and prepackaged entrees
Low-sodium soups
Whole-grain-based entrees—brown rice, quinoa, whole-grain pasta

Criteria for Mixed Dishes

Using the FDA guidelines for Heart Health Claims, the foods listed meet the following criteria per serving:

- Total fat–3 grams or less per 100 grams (30% or less calories from fat)

- Saturated fat–1 gram or less per 100 grams (10% or less calories from fat)

- Trans fat–0.5 grams or less (Trans Fat is not listed in the charts because all items report 0 grams Trans Fat. Since foods with less than 0.5 grams of trans fat can list 0 grams in the Nutrition Facts, be sure to check the ingredients for partially hydrogenated fats to determine if a product contains any trans fats.)

- Cholesterol–20 mg or less per 100 grams

- Beneficial Nutrients–10% Daily Value or higher of one beneficial nutrient (vitamin A, vitamin C, iron, calcium, protein, or dietary fiber). We waived the 10% rule for condiments.

- Sodium–Entrees/meals: 600 mg or less; soups/sauces/side dishes/condiments: 480 mg or less. Look for lower sodium levels to help reduce high blood pressure.

Foods not included in this list are entrees and meals with high levels of total fat, saturated fat, and sodium. The high amount of sodium in soups also keeps many off our list. This does not mean that these foods are bad foods. Eat them occasionally and balance them with low-fat and low-sodium choices.

Entrées

Amy's, Baked Ziti Bowl

9.5 oz

Amount per serving	%DV	Amount per serving	%DV	Amount per serving	%DV
Calories 390		**Cholesterol** 0mg	0%	**Total Carbohydrate** 62g	21%
Total Fat 12g	18%	**Sodium** 590mg	25%	Dietary Fiber 6g	24%
Saturated Fat 2g	10%	**Protein** 9g		Sugars 8g	
Polyunsaturated Fat 0g					
Monounsaturated Fat 0g		Vitamin A 10% Vitamin C 20%		Calcium 10% Iron 15%	

Amy's, Kids Baked Ziti Meal

8 oz

Amount per serving	%DV	Amount per serving	%DV	Amount per serving	%DV
Calories 360		**Cholesterol** 0mg	0%	**Total Carbohydrate** 57g	19%
Total Fat 12g	18%	**Sodium** 460mg	19%	Dietary Fiber 4g	16%
Saturated Fat 1.5g	8%	**Protein** 7g		Sugars 15g	
Polyunsaturated Fat 0g					
Monounsaturated Fat 0g		Vitamin A 10% Vitamin C 30%		Calcium 6% Iron 10%	

Amy's, Shepherd's Pie

8 oz

Amount per serving	%DV	Amount per serving	%DV	Amount per serving	%DV
Calories 160		**Cholesterol** 0mg	0%	**Total Carbohydrate** 27g	9%
Total Fat 4g	6%	**Sodium** 590mg	25%	Dietary Fiber 5g	20%
Saturated Fat 0g	0%	**Protein** 5g		Sugars 5g	
Polyunsaturated Fat 0g					
Monounsaturated Fat 0g		Vitamin A 50% Vitamin C 30%		Calcium 10% Iron 15%	

Annie's, Gluten-Free Microwaveable Mac & Cheese

1 packet

Amount per serving	%DV	Amount per serving	%DV	Amount per serving	%DV
Calories 240		**Cholesterol** 10mg	3%	**Total Carbohydrate** 43g	14%
Total Fat 4.5g	7%	**Sodium** 540mg	22%	Dietary Fiber 1g	4%
Saturated Fat 2.5g	12%	**Protein** 6g		Sugars 4g	
Polyunsaturated Fat 0g					
Monounsaturated Fat 0g		Vitamin A 2% Vitamin C 0%		Calcium 10% Iron 2%	

Annie's, Gluten-Free Rice Pasta & Cheddar

2.5 oz

Amount per serving	%DV	Amount per serving	%DV	Amount per serving	%DV
Calories 270		**Cholesterol** 10mg	3%	**Total Carbohydrate** 51g	17%
Total Fat 4g	6%	**Sodium** 390mg	16%	Dietary Fiber 1g	4%
Saturated Fat 2g	10%	**Protein** 6g		Sugars 4g	
Polyunsaturated Fat 0g					
Monounsaturated Fat 0g		Vitamin A 2% Vitamin C 0%		Calcium 15% Iron 2%	

Annie's, Gluten-Free Rice Shells with Creamy White Cheddar

3 oz

Amount per serving	%DV	Amount per serving	%DV	Amount per serving	%DV
Calories 330		**Cholesterol** 10mg	3%	**Total Carbohydrate** 62g	21%
Total Fat 4.5g	7%	**Sodium** 490mg	20%	Dietary Fiber 2g	8%
Saturated Fat 2.5g	13%	**Protein** 7g		Sugars 4g	
Polyunsaturated Fat 0g					
Monounsaturated Fat 0g		Vitamin A 2% Vitamin C 0%		Calcium 10% Iron 2%	

Earth's Best Organic, Frozen Whole Grain Cheese Pizza

1 pizza / 87g

Amount per serving	%DV	Amount per serving	%DV	Amount per serving	%DV
Calories 190		**Cholesterol** 15mg	5%	**Total Carbohydrate** 26g	9%
Total Fat 6g	9%	**Sodium** 380mg	16%	Dietary Fiber 4g	16%
Saturated Fat 3g	15%	**Protein** 9g		Sugars 1g	
Polyunsaturated Fat 0g					
Monounsaturated Fat 0g		Vitamin A 2% Vitamin C 0%		Calcium 10% Iron 25%	

Eden Foods, Brown Rice & Chick Peas, Organic

1/2 cup / 130g

Amount per serving	%DV	Amount per serving	%DV	Amount per serving	%DV
Calories 110		**Cholesterol** 0mg	0%	**Total Carbohydrate** 23g	8%
Total Fat 1g	2%	**Sodium** 135mg	6%	Dietary Fiber 2g	8%
Saturated Fat 0g	0%	**Protein** 3g		Sugars 0g	
Polyunsaturated Fat 0.5g					
Monounsaturated Fat 0g		Vitamin A 0% Vitamin C 0%		Calcium 2% Iron 4%	

Eden Foods, Mexican Rice & Black Beans, Organic

1/2 cup / 130g

Amount per serving	%DV	Amount per serving	%DV	Amount per serving	%DV
Calories 110		**Cholesterol** 0mg	0%	**Total Carbohydrate** 22g	7%
Total Fat 1g	2%	**Sodium** 270mg	11%	Dietary Fiber 3g	12%
Saturated Fat 0g	0%	**Protein** 5g		Sugars 1g	
Polyunsaturated Fat 0g					
Monounsaturated Fat 0g		Vitamin A 0% Vitamin C 0%		Calcium 4% Iron 10%	

Eden Foods, Moroccan Rice & Garbanzo Beans, Organic

1/2 cup / 130g

Amount per serving	%DV	Amount per serving	%DV	Amount per serving	%DV
Calories 110		**Cholesterol** 0mg	0%	**Total Carbohydrate** 22g	7%
Total Fat 1g	2%	**Sodium** 230mg	10%	Dietary Fiber 3g	12%
Saturated Fat 0g	0%	**Protein** 4g		Sugars 1g	
Polyunsaturated Fat 0g					
Monounsaturated Fat 0g		Vitamin A 0% Vitamin C 0%		Calcium 4% Iron 10%	

Healthy Choice Complete Meals Golden Roasted Turkey Breast

1 meal

Amount per serving	%DV	Amount per serving	%DV	Amount per serving	%DV
Calories 270		**Cholesterol** 30mg	10%	**Total Carbohydrate** 38g	13%
Total Fat 4g	6%	**Sodium** 520mg	22%	Dietary Fiber 7g	28%
Saturated Fat 1g	5%	**Protein** 19g		Sugars 13g	
Polyunsaturated Fat 1.5g					
Monounsaturated Fat 1.5g		Vitamin A 8% Vitamin C 0%		Calcium 4% Iron 10%	

Healthy Choice Complete Meals Lemon Pepper Fish

1 meal

Amount per serving	%DV	Amount per serving	%DV	Amount per serving	%DV
Calories 330		**Cholesterol** 30mg	10%	**Total Carbohydrate** 58g	19%
Total Fat 4g	6%	**Sodium** 530mg	22%	Dietary Fiber 4g	16%
Saturated Fat 1g	5%	**Protein** 14g		Sugars 18g	
Polyunsaturated Fat 1g					
Monounsaturated Fat 2g		Vitamin A 8% Vitamin C 0%		Calcium 15% Iron 6%	

Healthy Choice Modern Classics Beef and Broccoli

1 meal

Amount per serving	%DV	Amount per serving	%DV	Amount per serving	%DV
Calories 280		**Cholesterol** 45mg	15%	**Total Carbohydrate** 37g	12%
Total Fat 6g	9%	**Sodium** 520mg	22%	Dietary Fiber 4g	16%
Saturated Fat 2g	10%	**Protein** 19g		Sugars 4g	
Polyunsaturated Fat 1g					
Monounsaturated Fat 2.5g		Vitamin A 8% Vitamin C 0%		Calcium 4% Iron 10%	

Healthy Choice Modern Classics Chicken Pesto Alfredo

1 meal

Amount per serving	%DV	Amount per serving	%DV	Amount per serving	%DV
Calories 310		**Cholesterol** 40mg	13%	**Total Carbohydrate** 36g	12%
Total Fat 7g	11%	**Sodium** 500mg	21%	Dietary Fiber 7g	28%
Saturated Fat 2.5g	13%	**Protein** 24g		Sugars 4g	
Polyunsaturated Fat 1g					
Monounsaturated Fat 3g		Vitamin A 90% Vitamin C 0%		Calcium 4% Iron 10%	

Healthy Choice Traditional Classics Beef Pot Roast

1 meal

Amount per serving	%DV	Amount per serving	%DV	Amount per serving	%DV
Calories 250		**Cholesterol** 40mg	13%	**Total Carbohydrate** 32g	11%
Total Fat 6g	9%	**Sodium** 500mg	21%	Dietary Fiber 5g	20%
Saturated Fat 2g	10%	**Protein** 17g		Sugars 14g	
Polyunsaturated Fat 1g					
Monounsaturated Fat 3g		Vitamin A 20% Vitamin C 0%		Calcium 4% Iron 10%	

Healthy Choice Traditional Classics Classic Meat Loaf

1 meal

Amount per serving	%DV	Amount per serving	%DV	Amount per serving	%DV
Calories 330		**Cholesterol** 30mg	10%	**Total Carbohydrate** 51g	17%
Total Fat 7g	11%	**Sodium** 550mg	23%	Dietary Fiber 7g	28%
Saturated Fat 2.5g	13%	**Protein** 15g		Sugars 16g	
Polyunsaturated Fat 1.5g					
Monounsaturated Fat 2.5g		Vitamin A 0% Vitamin C 0%		Calcium 4% Iron 10%	

Healthy Choice Traditional Classics Country Herb Chicken

1 meal

Amount per serving	%DV	Amount per serving	%DV	Amount per serving	%DV
Calories 250		**Cholesterol** 40mg	13%	**Total Carbohydrate** 34g	11%
Total Fat 5g	8%	**Sodium** 500mg	21%	Dietary Fiber 6g	24%
Saturated Fat 1.5g	8%	**Protein** 16g		Sugars 12g	
Polyunsaturated Fat 1.5g					
Monounsaturated Fat 2g		Vitamin A 20% Vitamin C 0%		Calcium 0% Iron 6%	

Healthy Choice Traditional Classics Oven Roasted Chicken

1 meal

Amount per serving	%DV	Amount per serving	%DV	Amount per serving	%DV
Calories 240		**Cholesterol** 35mg	12%	**Total Carbohydrate** 33g	11%
Total Fat 5g	8%	**Sodium** 530mg	22%	Dietary Fiber 4g	16%
Saturated Fat 1.5g	8%	**Protein** 15g		Sugars 12g	
Polyunsaturated Fat 1g					
Monounsaturated Fat 2.5g		Vitamin A 20% Vitamin C 0%		Calcium 0% Iron 4%	

Ian's Natural Foods, Mac & No Cheese Sauce

1 bowl

Amount per serving	%DV	Amount per serving	%DV	Amount per serving	%DV
Calories 230		**Cholesterol** 0mg	0%	**Total Carbohydrate** 36g	12%
Total Fat 7g	11%	**Sodium** 320mg	13%	Dietary Fiber 2g	8%
Saturated Fat 0g	0%	**Protein** 4g		Sugars 1g	
Polyunsaturated Fat 0g					
Monounsaturated Fat 0g		Vitamin A 2% Vitamin C 0%		Calcium 10% Iron 15%	

Lean Cuisine, Deep Dish Spinach & Mushroom Pizza

1 package

Amount per serving	%DV	Amount per serving	%DV	Amount per serving	%DV
Calories 340		**Cholesterol** 10mg	3%	**Total Carbohydrate** 52g	17%
Total Fat 7g	11%	**Sodium** 430mg	18%	Dietary Fiber 2g	8%
Saturated Fat 3g	15%	**Protein** 18g		Sugars 5g	
Polyunsaturated Fat 0g					
Monounsaturated Fat 0g		Vitamin A 0% Vitamin C 3%		Calcium 3% Iron 111%

Lean Cuisine, Lemon Pepper Fish

1 package / 9.0 ounces

Amount per serving	%DV	Amount per serving	%DV	Amount per serving	%DV
Calories 300		Cholesterol 25mg	8%	Total Carbohydrate 40g	13%
Total Fat 8g	12%	Sodium 530mg	22%	Dietary Fiber 2g	8%
Saturated Fat 2g	10%	Protein 13g		Sugars 4g	
Polyunsaturated Fat 3.5g					
Monounsaturated Fat 2g		Vitamin A 10% Vitamin C 30%		Calcium 6% Iron 6%	

Lean Cuisine, Salmon with Basil

1 package / 10.0 ounces

Amount per serving	%DV	Amount per serving	%DV	Amount per serving	%DV
Calories 250		Cholesterol 20mg	7%	Total Carbohydrate 38g	13%
Total Fat 2.5g	4%	Sodium 500mg	21%	Dietary Fiber 4g	16%
Saturated Fat 0.5g	3%	Protein 19g		Sugars 6g	
Polyunsaturated Fat 1.5g					
Monounsaturated Fat 0.5g		Vitamin A 90% Vitamin C 0%		Calcium 15% Iron 20%	

Lundberg Family Farms, Heat & Eat, Organic Short Grain Brown Rice Bowl

210g

Amount per serving	%DV	Amount per serving	%DV	Amount per serving	%DV
Calories 290		Cholesterol 0mg	0%	Total Carbohydrate 65g	22%
Total Fat 2.5g	4%	Sodium 10mg	0%	Dietary Fiber 5g	20%
Saturated Fat 0.5g	2%	Protein 5g		Sugars 1g	
Polyunsaturated Fat 0g					
Monounsaturated Fat 0g		Vitamin A 0% Vitamin C 0%		Calcium 0% Iron 4%	

Morningstar Farms Italian Herb Chik Patties, Frozen, Unprepared

1 patty / 71g

Amount per serving	%DV	Amount per serving	%DV	Amount per serving	%DV
Calories 170		Cholesterol 0mg	0%	Total Carbohydrate 22g	7%
Total Fat 5g	8%	Sodium 480mg	20%	Dietary Fiber 2g	8%
Saturated Fat 0.5g	3%	Protein 10g		Sugars 1g	
Polyunsaturated Fat 3.5g					
Monounsaturated Fat 1g		Vitamin A 0% Vitamin C 0%		Calcium 2% Iron 15%	

Morningstar Farms Lasagna with Veggie Sausage, Frozen, Unprepared

1 serving / 284g

Amount per serving	%DV	Amount per serving	%DV	Amount per serving	%DV
Calories 270		Cholesterol 10mg	3%	Total Carbohydrate 41g	14%
Total Fat 6g	9%	Sodium 590mg	25%	Dietary Fiber 6g	24%
Saturated Fat 2.5g	13%	Protein 20g		Sugars 5g	
Polyunsaturated Fat 0g					
Monounsaturated Fat 0g		Vitamin A 20% Vitamin C 6%		Calcium 25% Iron 20%	

Organic Bistro, Ginger Chicken Meals

1 entrée / 284 g

Amount per serving	%DV	Amount per serving	%DV	Amount per serving	%DV
Calories 350		**Cholesterol** 35mg	12%	**Total Carbohydrate** 39g	13%
Total Fat 11g	17%	**Sodium** 450mg	19%	Dietary Fiber 6g	24%
Saturated Fat 1.5g	8%	**Protein** 22g		Sugars 8g	
Polyunsaturated Fat 0g					
Monounsaturated Fat 0g		Vitamin A 80%	Vitamin C 30%	Calcium 10%	Iron 15%

Organic Bistro, Savory Turkey Meals

1 entrée / 284 g

Amount per serving	%DV	Amount per serving	%DV	Amount per serving	%DV
Calories 330		**Cholesterol** 40mg	13%	**Total Carbohydrate** 35g	12%
Total Fat 10g	15%	**Sodium** 450mg	19%	Dietary Fiber 8g	32%
Saturated Fat 1g	5%	**Protein** 24g		Sugars 5g	
Polyunsaturated Fat 0g					
Monounsaturated Fat 0g		Vitamin A 6%	Vitamin C 20%	Calcium 8%	Iron 30%

Organic Bistro, Sesame Ginger Wild Salmon Organic Bistro Bowl

1 entrée / 284 g

Amount per serving	%DV	Amount per serving	%DV	Amount per serving	%DV
Calories 270		**Cholesterol** 30mg	10%	**Total Carbohydrate** 39g	13%
Total Fat 6g	9%	**Sodium** 480mg	20%	Dietary Fiber 3g	12%
Saturated Fat 1g	5%	**Protein** 15g		Sugars 19g	
Polyunsaturated Fat 0g					
Monounsaturated Fat 0g		Vitamin A 25%	Vitamin C 45%	Calcium 15%	Iron 10%

Organic Bistro, Spiced Chicken Morocco Meal

1 entrée / 284 g

Amount per serving	%DV	Amount per serving	%DV	Amount per serving	%DV
Calories 270		**Cholesterol** 30mg	10%	**Total Carbohydrate** 31g	10%
Total Fat 8g	12%	**Sodium** 360mg	15%	Dietary Fiber 5g	20%
Saturated Fat 1g	5%	**Protein** 17g		Sugars 7g	
Polyunsaturated Fat 0g					
Monounsaturated Fat 0g		Vitamin A 100%	Vitamin C 15%	Calcium 8%	Iron 10%

Organic Bistro, Wild Alaskan Salmon Organic Bistro Bake

1 bake

Amount per serving	%DV	Amount per serving	%DV	Amount per serving	%DV
Calories 240		**Cholesterol** 35mg	12%	**Total Carbohydrate** 30g	10%
Total Fat 7g	11%	**Sodium** 280mg	12%	Dietary Fiber 1g	4%
Saturated Fat 2g	10%	**Protein** 16g		Sugars 1g	
Polyunsaturated Fat 0g					
Monounsaturated Fat 0g		Vitamin A 6%	Vitamin C 8%	Calcium 10%	Iron 4%

Worthington Vegetable Steaks, Canned, Unprepared

2 slices / 72g

Amount per serving	%DV	Amount per serving	%DV	Amount per serving	%DV
Calories 81		Cholesterol 0mg	0%	Total Carbohydrate 4g	1%
Total Fat 1g	2%	Sodium 300mg	12%	Dietary Fiber 1.5g	6%
Saturated Fat 0g	0%	Protein 15g		Sugars 0g	
Polyunsaturated Fat 0g					
Monounsaturated Fat 0g		Vitamin A 0% Vitamin C 0%		Calcium 0% Iron 15%	

Soups

Amy's, Organic Light in Sodium, Chunky Tomato Bisque

1 cup

Amount per serving	%DV	Amount per serving	%DV	Amount per serving	%DV
Calories 130		Cholesterol 10mg	3%	Total Carbohydrate 21g	7%
Total Fat 3.5g	5%	Sodium 340mg	14%	Dietary Fiber 3g	12%
Saturated Fat 2g	10%	Protein 3g		Sugars 14g	
Polyunsaturated Fat 0g					
Monounsaturated Fat 0g		Vitamin A 20% Vitamin C 40%		Calcium 8% Iron 6%	

Amy's, Organic Light in Sodium, Cream of Tomato Soup

1 cup

Amount per serving	%DV	Amount per serving	%DV	Amount per serving	%DV
Calories 110		Cholesterol 10mg	3%	Total Carbohydrate 19g	6%
Total Fat 2.5g	4%	Sodium 340mg	14%	Dietary Fiber 3g	12%
Saturated Fat 1.5g	8%	Protein 3g		Sugars 13g	
Polyunsaturated Fat 0g					
Monounsaturated Fat 0g		Vitamin A 20% Vitamin C 15%		Calcium 4% Iron 10%	

Campbell's Healthy Request Chicken with Whole-Grain Pasta

1 cup / 240 ml

Amount per serving	%DV	Amount per serving	%DV	Amount per serving	%DV
Calories 100		Cholesterol 10mg	3%	Total Carbohydrate 13g	4%
Total Fat 2g	3%	Sodium 410mg	17%	Dietary Fiber 1g	4%
Saturated Fat 0.5g	3%	Protein 7g		Sugars 3g	
Polyunsaturated Fat 0g					
Monounsaturated Fat 0.5g		Vitamin A 20% Vitamin C 0%		Calcium 2% Iron 0%	

Campbell's Healthy Request Condensed Vegetable Soup

1/2 cup / 120 ml

Amount per serving	%DV	Amount per serving	%DV	Amount per serving	%DV
Calories 100		Cholesterol 0mg	0%	Total Carbohydrate 19g	6%
Total Fat 1g	2%	Sodium 410mg	17%	Dietary Fiber 3g	12%
Saturated Fat 0g	0%	Protein 3g		Sugars 5g	
Polyunsaturated Fat 1g					
Monounsaturated Fat 0g		Vitamin A 35% Vitamin C 0%		Calcium 2% Iron 4%	

Campbell's Healthy Request Italian-Style Wedding Microwavable Bowl

1 cup / 240 ml

Amount per serving	%DV	Amount per serving	%DV	Amount per serving	%DV
Calories 100		**Cholesterol** 10mg	3%	**Total Carbohydrate** 13g	4%
Total Fat 2.5g	4%	**Sodium** 410mg	17%	Dietary Fiber 2g	8%
Saturated Fat 1g	5%	**Protein** 6g		Sugars 4g	
Polyunsaturated Fat 0g					
Monounsaturated Fat 0.5g		Vitamin A 20% Vitamin C 0%		Calcium 4% Iron 4%	

Campbell's Healthy Request Savory Chicken and Brown Rice Microwaveable Bowl

1 cup / 240 ml

Amount per serving	%DV	Amount per serving	%DV	Amount per serving	%DV
Calories 110		**Cholesterol** 15mg	5%	**Total Carbohydrate** 16g	5%
Total Fat 2.5g	4%	**Sodium** 410mg	17%	Dietary Fiber 1g	4%
Saturated Fat 0.5g	2%	**Protein** 5g		Sugars 4g	
Polyunsaturated Fat 0.5g					
Monounsaturated Fat 1g		Vitamin A 20% Vitamin C 0%		Calcium 2% Iron 2%	

Campbell's Healthy Request Whole-Grain Pasta Fagioli

1 cup / 240 ml

Amount per serving	%DV	Amount per serving	%DV	Amount per serving	%DV
Calories 90		**Cholesterol** 0mg	0%	**Total Carbohydrate** 18g	6%
Total Fat 0.5g	1%	**Sodium** 410mg	17%	Dietary Fiber 3g	12%
Saturated Fat 0g	0%	**Protein** 4g		Sugars 6g	
Polyunsaturated Fat 0g					
Monounsaturated Fat 0g		Vitamin A 20% Vitamin C 0%		Calcium 6% Iron 6%	

Campbell's Low Sodium Soups, Chicken with Noodle Soup

1 serving, 1 container / 305g

Amount per serving	%DV	Amount per serving	%DV	Amount per serving	%DV
Calories 160		**Cholesterol** 30mg	10%	**Total Carbohydrate** 17g	6%
Total Fat 4.5g	7%	**Sodium** 140mg	6%	Dietary Fiber 2g	8%
Saturated Fat 1.5g	8%	**Protein** 12g		Sugars 4g	
Polyunsaturated Fat 1g					
Monounsaturated Fat 2g		Vitamin A 30% Vitamin C 0%		Calcium 2% Iron 6%	

Campbell's Select, Bowls, Microwavable Healthy Request, Italian Style Wedding Soup

1 cup / 240 ml

Amount per serving	%DV	Amount per serving	%DV	Amount per serving	%DV
Calories 100		**Cholesterol** 10mg	3%	**Total Carbohydrate** 13g	4%
Total Fat 2.5g	4%	**Sodium** 410mg	17%	Dietary Fiber 2g	8%
Saturated Fat 1g	5%	**Protein** 6g		Sugars 4g	
Polyunsaturated Fat 0g					
Monounsaturated Fat 0.5g		Vitamin A 20% Vitamin C 0%		Calcium 4% Iron 4%	

Campbell's Select, Microwavable Bowls, Healthy Request, Mexican Style Tortilla

1 cup / 240 ml

Amount per serving	%DV	Amount per serving	%DV	Amount per serving	%DV
Calories 130		Cholesterol 10mg	3%	Total Carbohydrate 19g	6%
Total Fat 2.5g	4%	Sodium 410mg	17%	Dietary Fiber 3g	12%
Saturated Fat 0.5g	2%	Protein 7g		Sugars 3g	
Polyunsaturated Fat 0g					
Monounsaturated Fat 0.5g		Vitamin A 6% Vitamin C 2%		Calcium 4% Iron 6%	

Campbell's, 100% Natural Healthy Request Mexican-Style Chicken Tortilla

1 cup / 240 ml

Amount per serving	%DV	Amount per serving	%DV	Amount per serving	%DV
Calories 140		Cholesterol 10mg	3%	Total Carbohydrate 22g	7%
Total Fat 2.5g	4%	Sodium 410mg	17%	Dietary Fiber 3g	12%
Saturated Fat 0.5g	3%	Protein 7g		Sugars 3g	
Polyunsaturated Fat 0g					
Monounsaturated Fat 0.5g		Vitamin A 8% Vitamin C 0%		Calcium 4% Iron 6%	

Campbell's, Chunky Healthy Request Beef with Country Vegetables

1 cup / 240 ml

Amount per serving	%DV	Amount per serving	%DV	Amount per serving	%DV
Calories 110		Cholesterol 10mg	3%	Total Carbohydrate 17g	6%
Total Fat 1.5g	2%	Sodium 410mg	17%	Dietary Fiber 3g	12%
Saturated Fat 0.5g	3%	Protein 6g		Sugars 4g	
Polyunsaturated Fat 0g					
Monounsaturated Fat 0g		Vitamin A 20% Vitamin C 2%		Calcium 2% Iron 6%	

Campbell's, Chunky Healthy Request Chicken Corn Chowder

1 cup / 240 ml

Amount per serving	%DV	Amount per serving	%DV	Amount per serving	%DV
Calories 140		Cholesterol 10mg	3%	Total Carbohydrate 22g	7%
Total Fat 3g	5%	Sodium 410mg	17%	Dietary Fiber 3g	12%
Saturated Fat 1g	5%	Protein 6g		Sugars 5g	
Polyunsaturated Fat 1g					
Monounsaturated Fat 1g		Vitamin A 20% Vitamin C 0%		Calcium 2% Iron 4%	

Campbell's, Chunky Healthy Request Chicken Noodle

1 cup / 240 ml

Amount per serving	%DV	Amount per serving	%DV	Amount per serving	%DV
Calories 120		Cholesterol 20mg	7%	Total Carbohydrate 17g	6%
Total Fat 3g	5%	Sodium 410mg	17%	Dietary Fiber 1g	4%
Saturated Fat 1g	5%	Protein 7g		Sugars 2g	
Polyunsaturated Fat 0g					
Monounsaturated Fat 0g		Vitamin A 20% Vitamin C 2%		Calcium 2% Iron 4%	

Campbell's, Chunky Healthy Request Classic Chicken Noodle Microwaveable Bowl

1 cup / 240 ml

Amount per serving	%DV	Amount per serving	%DV	Amount per serving	%DV
Calories 120		Cholesterol 20mg	7%	Total Carbohydrate 17g	6%
Total Fat 3g	5%	Sodium 410mg	17%	Dietary Fiber 1g	4%
Saturated Fat 1g	5%	Protein 7g		Sugars 2g	
Polyunsaturated Fat 0g					
Monounsaturated Fat 0g		Vitamin A 20% Vitamin C 2%		Calcium 2% Iron 4%	

Campbell's, Chunky Healthy Request Grilled Chicken & Sausage Gumbo

1 cup / 240 ml

Amount per serving	%DV	Amount per serving	%DV	Amount per serving	%DV
Calories 130		Cholesterol 10mg	3%	Total Carbohydrate 18g	6%
Total Fat 3g	5%	Sodium 410mg	17%	Dietary Fiber 2g	8%
Saturated Fat 1g	5%	Protein 7g		Sugars 4g	
Polyunsaturated Fat 0g					
Monounsaturated Fat 0g		Vitamin A 10% Vitamin C 2%		Calcium 4% Iron 2%	

Campbell's, Chunky Healthy Request Hearty Italian-Style Wedding Soup

1 cup / 240 ml

Amount per serving	%DV	Amount per serving	%DV	Amount per serving	%DV
Calories 130		Cholesterol 10mg	3%	Total Carbohydrate 20g	7%
Total Fat 2.5g	4%	Sodium 410mg	17%	Dietary Fiber 3g	12%
Saturated Fat 1g	5%	Protein 7g		Sugars 7g	
Polyunsaturated Fat 0g					
Monounsaturated Fat 0.5g		Vitamin A 20% Vitamin C 0%		Calcium 4% Iron 6%	

Campbell's, Chunky Healthy Request New England Clam Chowder

1 cup / 240 ml

Amount per serving	%DV	Amount per serving	%DV	Amount per serving	%DV
Calories 130		Cholesterol 10mg	3%	Total Carbohydrate 20g	7%
Total Fat 3g	5%	Sodium 410mg	17%	Dietary Fiber 2g	8%
Saturated Fat 1g	6%	Protein 5g		Sugars 2g	
Polyunsaturated Fat 1g					
Monounsaturated Fat 0.5g		Vitamin A 0% Vitamin C 0%		Calcium 10% Iron 8%	

Campbell's, Chunky Healthy Request Old Fashioned Vegetable Beef

1 cup / 240 ml

Amount per serving	%DV	Amount per serving	%DV	Amount per serving	%DV
Calories 120		Cholesterol 10mg	3%	Total Carbohydrate 19g	6%
Total Fat 2.5g	4%	Sodium 410mg	17%	Dietary Fiber 3g	12%
Saturated Fat 0.5g	3%	Protein 6g		Sugars 4g	
Polyunsaturated Fat 0g					
Monounsaturated Fat 1g		Vitamin A 25% Vitamin C 2%		Calcium 4% Iron 6%	

Campbell's, Chunky Healthy Request Roasted Chicken with Country Vegetables

1 cup / 240 ml

Amount per serving	%DV	Amount per serving	%DV	Amount per serving	%DV
Calories 100		**Cholesterol** 10mg	3%	**Total Carbohydrate** 16g	5%
Total Fat 1g	2%	**Sodium** 410mg	17%	Dietary Fiber 3g	12%
Saturated Fat 0.5g	2%	**Protein** 6g		Sugars 4g	
Polyunsaturated Fat 0g					
Monounsaturated Fat 0.5g		Vitamin A 30% Vitamin C 0%		Calcium 4% Iron 4%	

Campbell's, Chunky Healthy Request Sirloin Burger with Country Vegetables

1 cup / 240 ml

Amount per serving	%DV	Amount per serving	%DV	Amount per serving	%DV
Calories 130		**Cholesterol** 15mg	5%	**Total Carbohydrate** 19g	6%
Total Fat 2g	3%	**Sodium** 410mg	17%	Dietary Fiber 3g	12%
Saturated Fat 1g	5%	**Protein** 8g		Sugars 4g	
Polyunsaturated Fat 0g					
Monounsaturated Fat 1g		Vitamin A 40% Vitamin C 0%		Calcium 2% Iron 8%	

Campbell's, Chunky Healthy Request Split Pea & Ham with Natural Smoke Flavor

1 cup / 240 ml

Amount per serving	%DV	Amount per serving	%DV	Amount per serving	%DV
Calories 160		**Cholesterol** 10mg	3%	**Total Carbohydrate** 22g	7%
Total Fat 2.5g	4%	**Sodium** 410mg	17%	Dietary Fiber 5g	20%
Saturated Fat 1g	5%	**Protein** 12g		Sugars 4g	
Polyunsaturated Fat 0.5g					
Monounsaturated Fat 1g		Vitamin A 20% Vitamin C 2%		Calcium 2% Iron 8%	

Campbell's, Healthy Request Condensed Bean with Bacon

1/2 cup / 120 ml

Amount per serving	%DV	Amount per serving	%DV	Amount per serving	%DV
Calories 160		**Cholesterol** 5mg	2%	**Total Carbohydrate** 25g	8%
Total Fat 2.5g	4%	**Sodium** 410mg	17%	Dietary Fiber 9g	36%
Saturated Fat 0.5g	2%	**Protein** 9g		Sugars 5g	
Polyunsaturated Fat 1g					
Monounsaturated Fat 1g		Vitamin A 6% Vitamin C 2%		Calcium 6% Iron 10%	

Campbell's, Healthy Request Condensed Cheddar Cheese

1/2 cup / 120 ml

Amount per serving	%DV	Amount per serving	%DV	Amount per serving	%DV
Calories 70		**Cholesterol** 5mg	2%	**Total Carbohydrate** 12g	4%
Total Fat 1.5g	2%	**Sodium** 410mg	17%	Dietary Fiber 1g	4%
Saturated Fat 1g	5%	**Protein** 1g		Sugars 2g	
Polyunsaturated Fat 0g					
Monounsaturated Fat 0.5g		Vitamin A 10% Vitamin C 0%		Calcium 4% Iron 0%	

Campbell's, Healthy Request Condensed Chicken Noodle Soup

1/2 cup / 120 ml

Amount per serving	%DV	Amount per serving	%DV	Amount per serving	%DV
Calories 60		**Cholesterol** 10mg	3%	**Total Carbohydrate** 8g	3%
Total Fat 2g	3%	**Sodium** 410mg	17%	Dietary Fiber 1g	4%
Saturated Fat 0.5g	3%	**Protein** 3g		Sugars 1g	
Polyunsaturated Fat 0.5g					
Monounsaturated Fat 0.5g		Vitamin A 10% Vitamin C 0%		Calcium 0% Iron 0%	

Campbell's, Healthy Request Condensed Chicken with Rice Soup

1/2 cup / 120 ml

Amount per serving	%DV	Amount per serving	%DV	Amount per serving	%DV
Calories 70		**Cholesterol** 5mg	2%	**Total Carbohydrate** 13g	4%
Total Fat 1.5g	2%	**Sodium** 410mg	17%	Dietary Fiber 1g	4%
Saturated Fat 0.5g	2%	**Protein** 2g		Sugars 1g	
Polyunsaturated Fat 0g					
Monounsaturated Fat 0.5g		Vitamin A 10% Vitamin C 2%		Calcium 0% Iron 0%	

Campbell's, Healthy Request Condensed Cream of Celery Soup

1/2 cup / 120 ml

Amount per serving	%DV	Amount per serving	%DV	Amount per serving	%DV
Calories 60		**Cholesterol** 5mg	2%	**Total Carbohydrate** 10g	3%
Total Fat 2g	3%	**Sodium** 410mg	17%	Dietary Fiber 1g	4%
Saturated Fat 0.5g	2%	**Protein** 1g		Sugars 2g	
Polyunsaturated Fat 1g					
Monounsaturated Fat 0.5g		Vitamin A 6% Vitamin C 0%		Calcium 10% Iron 2%	

Campbell's, Healthy Request Condensed Cream of Chicken Soup

1/2 cup / 120 ml

Amount per serving	%DV	Amount per serving	%DV	Amount per serving	%DV
Calories 60		**Cholesterol** 5mg	2%	**Total Carbohydrate** 9g	3%
Total Fat 2g	3%	**Sodium** 410mg	17%	Dietary Fiber 0g	0%
Saturated Fat 0.5g	2%	**Protein** 1g		Sugars 1g	
Polyunsaturated Fat 1g					
Monounsaturated Fat 0.5g		Vitamin A 10% Vitamin C 0%		Calcium 0% Iron 0%	

Campbell's, Healthy Request Condensed Cream of Mushroom Soup

1/2 cup / 120 ml

Amount per serving	%DV	Amount per serving	%DV	Amount per serving	%DV
Calories 60		**Cholesterol** 5mg	2%	**Total Carbohydrate** 10g	3%
Total Fat 2g	3%	**Sodium** 410mg	17%	Dietary Fiber 1g	4%
Saturated Fat 0.5g	3%	**Protein** 1g		Sugars 2g	
Polyunsaturated Fat 1g					
Monounsaturated Fat 0.5g		Vitamin A 0% Vitamin C 0%		Calcium 10% Iron 0%	

Campbell's, Healthy Request Condensed Homestyle Chicken Noodle

1/2 cup / 120 ml

Amount per serving	%DV	Amount per serving	%DV	Amount per serving	%DV
Calories 60		Cholesterol 10mg	3%	Total Carbohydrate 10g	3%
Total Fat 1.5g	2%	Sodium 410mg	17%	Dietary Fiber 1g	4%
Saturated Fat 0.5g	3%	Protein 3g		Sugars 1g	
Polyunsaturated Fat 0.5g					
Monounsaturated Fat 0.5g		Vitamin A 10% Vitamin C 0%		Calcium 0% Iron 2%	

Campbell's, Healthy Request Condensed Minestrone Soup

1/2 cup / 120 ml

Amount per serving	%DV	Amount per serving	%DV	Amount per serving	%DV
Calories 80		Cholesterol 0mg	0%	Total Carbohydrate 15g	5%
Total Fat 0.5g	1%	Sodium 410mg	17%	Dietary Fiber 3g	12%
Saturated Fat 0g	0%	Protein 3g		Sugars 4g	
Polyunsaturated Fat 0g					
Monounsaturated Fat 0g		Vitamin A 20% Vitamin C 0%		Calcium 4% Iron 6%	

Campbell's, Healthy Request Condensed Tomato Soup

1/2 cup / 120 ml

Amount per serving	%DV	Amount per serving	%DV	Amount per serving	%DV
Calories 90		Cholesterol 0mg	0%	Total Carbohydrate 17g	6%
Total Fat 1.5g	2%	Sodium 410mg	17%	Dietary Fiber 1g	4%
Saturated Fat 0.5g	3%	Protein 2g		Sugars 10g	
Polyunsaturated Fat 0.5g					
Monounsaturated Fat 0g		Vitamin A 8% Vitamin C 10%		Calcium 0% Iron 0%	

Campbell's, Healthy Request Condensed Vegetable Beef Soup

1/2 cup / 120 ml

Amount per serving	%DV	Amount per serving	%DV	Amount per serving	%DV
Calories 90		Cholesterol 5mg	2%	Total Carbohydrate 15g	5%
Total Fat 1g	2%	Sodium 410mg	17%	Dietary Fiber 3g	12%
Saturated Fat 0.5g	3%	Protein 4g		Sugars 2g	
Polyunsaturated Fat 0.5g					
Monounsaturated Fat 0g		Vitamin A 30% Vitamin C 0%		Calcium 2% Iron 4%	

Campbell's, Red and White, Healthy Kids Chicken Alphabet Soup, Condensed

1/2 cup / 120 ml

Amount per serving	%DV	Amount per serving	%DV	Amount per serving	%DV
Calories 70		Cholesterol 5mg	2%	Total Carbohydrate 12g	4%
Total Fat 2g	3%	Sodium 480mg	20%	Dietary Fiber 1g	4%
Saturated Fat 0.5g	2%	Protein 2g		Sugars 1g	
Polyunsaturated Fat 0.5g					
Monounsaturated Fat 1g		Vitamin A 10% Vitamin C 0%		Calcium 0% Iron 2%	

Campbell's, Red and White, Healthy Kids Chicken Noodleo's Soup, Condensed

1/2 cup / 120 ml

Amount per serving	%DV	Amount per serving	%DV	Amount per serving	%DV
Calories 90		**Cholesterol** 20mg	7%	**Total Carbohydrate** 15g	5%
Total Fat 2.5g	4%	**Sodium** 480mg	20%	Dietary Fiber 1g	4%
Saturated Fat 1g	5%	**Protein** 3g		Sugars 1g	
Polyunsaturated Fat 0.5g					
Monounsaturated Fat 1g		Vitamin A 10% Vitamin C 0%		Calcium 0% Iron 4%	

Campbell's, Red and White, Healthy Kids Goldfish Pasta with Chicken Soup

1/2 cup / 120 ml

Amount per serving	%DV	Amount per serving	%DV	Amount per serving	%DV
Calories 80		**Cholesterol** 5mg	2%	**Total Carbohydrate** 12g	4%
Total Fat 2g	3%	**Sodium** 480mg	20%	Dietary Fiber 1g	4%
Saturated Fat 0.5g	3%	**Protein** 3g		Sugars 1g	
Polyunsaturated Fat 0.5g					
Monounsaturated Fat 1g		Vitamin A 10% Vitamin C 0%		Calcium 0% Iron 2%	

Campbell's, Red and White, Tomato Soup, Condensed

1/2 cup / 120 ml

Amount per serving	%DV	Amount per serving	%DV	Amount per serving	%DV
Calories 90		**Cholesterol** 0mg	0%	**Total Carbohydrate** 20g	7%
Total Fat 0g	0%	**Sodium** 480mg	20%	Dietary Fiber 1g	4%
Saturated Fat 0g	0%	**Protein** 2g		Sugars 12g	
Polyunsaturated Fat 0g					
Monounsaturated Fat 0g		Vitamin A 8% Vitamin C 10%		Calcium 0% Iron 4%	

Dr. McDougall's Right Foods, Lentil Cousous Soup

1 container / 62g

Amount per serving	%DV	Amount per serving	%DV	Amount per serving	%DV
Calories 190		**Cholesterol** 0mg	0%	**Total Carbohydrate** 37g	12%
Total Fat 1g	2%	**Sodium** 330mg	14%	Dietary Fiber 9g	36%
Saturated Fat 0g	0%	**Protein** 12g		Sugars 3g	
Polyunsaturated Fat 0g					
Monounsaturated Fat 0g		Vitamin A 26% Vitamin C 6%		Calcium 2% Iron 12%	

Dr. McDougall's Right Foods, Light Sodium Tomato Basil Pasta Soup

1 package / 39g

Amount per serving	%DV	Amount per serving	%DV	Amount per serving	%DV
Calories 100		**Cholesterol** 0mg	0%	**Total Carbohydrate** 21g	7%
Total Fat 0.5g	1%	**Sodium** 360mg	15%	Dietary Fiber 3g	12%
Saturated Fat 0g	0%	**Protein** 4g		Sugars 1g	
Polyunsaturated Fat 0g					
Monounsaturated Fat 0g		Vitamin A 0% Vitamin C 0%		Calcium 0% Iron 0%	

Dr. McDougall's Right Foods, Light Sodium Vegan Gluten-Free Split Pea Soup

1 container

Amount per serving	%DV	Amount per serving	%DV	Amount per serving	%DV
Calories 200		**Cholesterol** 0mg	0%	**Total Carbohydrate** 35g	12%
Total Fat 1g	2%	**Sodium** 360mg	15%	Dietary Fiber 9g	36%
Saturated Fat 0g	0%	**Protein** 13g		Sugars 2g	
Polyunsaturated Fat 0g					
Monounsaturated Fat 0g		Vitamin A 0%	Vitamin C 0%	Calcium 0%	Iron 0%

Dr. McDougall's Right Foods, Tamale Soup

1/2 package

Amount per serving	%DV	Amount per serving	%DV	Amount per serving	%DV
Calories 100		**Cholesterol** 0mg	0%	**Total Carbohydrate** 18g	6%
Total Fat 1g	2%	**Sodium** 320mg	13%	Dietary Fiber 3g	12%
Saturated Fat 0g	0%	**Protein** 4g		Sugars 1g	
Polyunsaturated Fat 0g					
Monounsaturated Fat 0g		Vitamin A 5%	Vitamin C 15%	Calcium 1%	Iron 5%

Dr. McDougall's Right Foods, Vegan Black Bean & Lime Soup

1/2 container / 47g

Amount per serving	%DV	Amount per serving	%DV	Amount per serving	%DV
Calories 170		**Cholesterol** 0mg	0%	**Total Carbohydrate** 30g	10%
Total Fat 1g	2%	**Sodium** 330mg	14%	Dietary Fiber 14g	56%
Saturated Fat 0g	0%	**Protein** 10g		Sugars 2g	
Polyunsaturated Fat 0g					
Monounsaturated Fat 0g		Vitamin A 2%	Vitamin C 4%	Calcium 5%	Iron 14%

Dr. McDougall's Right Foods, Vegan Chicken Noodle Soup

1 container / 40g

Amount per serving	%DV	Amount per serving	%DV	Amount per serving	%DV
Calories 140		**Cholesterol** 0mg	0%	**Total Carbohydrate** 28g	9%
Total Fat 0.5g	1%	**Sodium** 360mg	15%	Dietary Fiber 2g	8%
Saturated Fat 0g	0%	**Protein** 3g		Sugars 2g	
Polyunsaturated Fat 0g					
Monounsaturated Fat 0g		Vitamin A 30%	Vitamin C 2%	Calcium 2%	Iron 3%

Dr. McDougall's Right Foods, Vegan Split Pea with Barley

1/2 package / 35g

Amount per serving	%DV	Amount per serving	%DV	Amount per serving	%DV
Calories 120		**Cholesterol** 0mg	0%	**Total Carbohydrate** 21g	7%
Total Fat 0.5g	1%	**Sodium** 300mg	12%	Dietary Fiber 5g	20%
Saturated Fat 0g	0%	**Protein** 8g		Sugars 1g	
Polyunsaturated Fat 0g					
Monounsaturated Fat 0g		Vitamin A 0%	Vitamin C 0%	Calcium 0%	Iron 0%

Dr. McDougall's Right Foods, Vegan White Bean & Pasta Soup

1 container / 52g

Amount per serving	%DV	Amount per serving	%DV	Amount per serving	%DV
Calories 170		**Cholesterol** 0mg	0%	**Total Carbohydrate** 34g	11%
Total Fat 1g	2%	**Sodium** 360mg	15%	Dietary Fiber 8g	32%
Saturated Fat 0g	0%	**Protein** 7g		Sugars 2g	
Polyunsaturated Fat 0g					
Monounsaturated Fat 0g		Vitamin A 30% Vitamin C 6%		Calcium 4% Iron 10%	

Eden Foods, Black Bean & Quinoa Chili

1 cup / 240g

Amount per serving	%DV	Amount per serving	%DV	Amount per serving	%DV
Calories 190		**Cholesterol** 0mg	0%	**Total Carbohydrate** 35g	12%
Total Fat 1.5g	2%	**Sodium** 460mg	19%	Dietary Fiber 6g	24%
Saturated Fat 0g	0%	**Protein** 10g		Sugars 3g	
Polyunsaturated Fat 0g					
Monounsaturated Fat 0g		Vitamin A 2% Vitamin C 0%		Calcium 8% Iron 30%	

Health Valley Organic, No Salt Added Black Bean Soup

1 cup / 240g

Amount per serving	%DV	Amount per serving	%DV	Amount per serving	%DV
Calories 140		**Cholesterol** 0mg	0%	**Total Carbohydrate** 29g	10%
Total Fat 1.5g	2%	**Sodium** 30mg	1%	Dietary Fiber 6g	24%
Saturated Fat 0g	0%	**Protein** 7g		Sugars 4g	
Polyunsaturated Fat 0g					
Monounsaturated Fat 0g		Vitamin A 10% Vitamin C 25%		Calcium 6% Iron 15%	

Health Valley Organic, No Salt Added Lentil Soup

1 cup / 240g

Amount per serving	%DV	Amount per serving	%DV	Amount per serving	%DV
Calories 140		**Cholesterol** 0mg	0%	**Total Carbohydrate** 27g	9%
Total Fat 1.5g	2%	**Sodium** 30mg	1%	Dietary Fiber 8g	32%
Saturated Fat 0g	0%	**Protein** 9g		Sugars 5g	
Polyunsaturated Fat 0g					
Monounsaturated Fat 0g		Vitamin A 25% Vitamin C 10%		Calcium 4% Iron 20%	

Health Valley Organic, No Salt Added Minestrone Soup

1 cup / 240g

Amount per serving	%DV	Amount per serving	%DV	Amount per serving	%DV
Calories 90		**Cholesterol** 0mg	0%	**Total Carbohydrate** 16g	5%
Total Fat 2g	3%	**Sodium** 50mg	2%	Dietary Fiber 3g	12%
Saturated Fat 0g	0%	**Protein** 4g		Sugars 5g	
Polyunsaturated Fat 0g					
Monounsaturated Fat 0g		Vitamin A 40% Vitamin C 15%		Calcium 4% Iron 8%	

Health Valley Organic, No Salt Added Mushroom Barley Soup

1 cup / 240g

Amount per serving	%DV	Amount per serving	%DV	Amount per serving	%DV
Calories 90		**Cholesterol** 0mg	0%	**Total Carbohydrate** 15g	5%
Total Fat 2.5g	4%	**Sodium** 60mg	3%	Dietary Fiber 3g	12%
Saturated Fat 0g	0%	**Protein** 2g		Sugars 2g	
Polyunsaturated Fat 0g					
Monounsaturated Fat 0g		Vitamin A 30% Vitamin C 6%		Calcium 0% Iron 4%	

Health Valley Organic, No Salt Added Potato Leek Soup

1 cup / 240g

Amount per serving	%DV	Amount per serving	%DV	Amount per serving	%DV
Calories 100		**Cholesterol** 0mg	0%	**Total Carbohydrate** 20g	7%
Total Fat 2g	3%	**Sodium** 30mg	1%	Dietary Fiber 3g	12%
Saturated Fat 0g	0%	**Protein** 2g		Sugars 2g	
Polyunsaturated Fat 0g					
Monounsaturated Fat 0g		Vitamin A 30% Vitamin C 10%		Calcium 4% Iron 6%	

Health Valley Organic, No Salt Added Split Pea Soup

1 cup / 240g

Amount per serving	%DV	Amount per serving	%DV	Amount per serving	%DV
Calories 140		**Cholesterol** 0mg	0%	**Total Carbohydrate** 26g	9%
Total Fat 2.5g	4%	**Sodium** 85mg	4%	Dietary Fiber 8g	32%
Saturated Fat 1g	5%	**Protein** 8g		Sugars 4g	
Polyunsaturated Fat 0g					
Monounsaturated Fat 0g		Vitamin A 30% Vitamin C 2%		Calcium 2% Iron 8%	

Health Valley Organic, No Salt Added Tomato Soup

1 cup / 240g

Amount per serving	%DV	Amount per serving	%DV	Amount per serving	%DV
Calories 100		**Cholesterol** 5mg	2%	**Total Carbohydrate** 19g	6%
Total Fat 2.5g	4%	**Sodium** 60mg	2%	Dietary Fiber 3g	12%
Saturated Fat 1g	5%	**Protein** 1g		Sugars 13g	
Polyunsaturated Fat 0g					
Monounsaturated Fat 0g		Vitamin A 8% Vitamin C 25%		Calcium 6% Iron 2%	

Health Valley Organic, No Salt Added Vegetable Soup

1 cup / 240g

Amount per serving	%DV	Amount per serving	%DV	Amount per serving	%DV
Calories 100		**Cholesterol** 0mg	0%	**Total Carbohydrate** 18g	6%
Total Fat 2.5g	4%	**Sodium** 50mg	2%	Dietary Fiber 4g	16%
Saturated Fat 0g	0%	**Protein** 3g		Sugars 4g	
Polyunsaturated Fat 0g					
Monounsaturated Fat 0g		Vitamin A 45% Vitamin C 20%		Calcium 4% Iron 8%	

Kettle Cuisine, Three Bean Chili

1 cup / 240g

Amount per serving	%DV	Amount per serving	%DV	Amount per serving	%DV
Calories 190		**Cholesterol** 0mg	0%	**Total Carbohydrate** 31g	10%
Total Fat 3g	5%	**Sodium** 380mg	16%	Dietary Fiber 11g	44%
Saturated Fat 0.5g	2%	**Protein** 9g		Sugars 10g	
Polyunsaturated Fat 0g					
Monounsaturated Fat 0g		Vitamin A 15% Vitamin C 8%		Calcium 8% Iron 10%	

Kitchen Basics, Original Beef Stock

1 cup / 240 ml

Amount per serving	%DV	Amount per serving	%DV	Amount per serving	%DV
Calories 20		**Cholesterol** 0mg	0%	**Total Carbohydrate** 1g	0%
Total Fat 0g	0%	**Sodium** 430mg	18%	Dietary Fiber 0g	0%
Saturated Fat 0g	0%	**Protein** 5g		Sugars 0g	
Polyunsaturated Fat 0g					
Monounsaturated Fat 0g		Vitamin A 0% Vitamin C 0%		Calcium 0% Iron 0%	

Kitchen Basics, Original Chicken Cooking Stock

1 cup / 245g

Amount per serving	%DV	Amount per serving	%DV	Amount per serving	%DV
Calories 20		**Cholesterol** 0mg	0%	**Total Carbohydrate** 1g	0%
Total Fat 0g	0%	**Sodium** 430mg	18%	Dietary Fiber 0g	0%
Saturated Fat 0g	0%	**Protein** 5g		Sugars 0g	
Polyunsaturated Fat 0g					
Monounsaturated Fat 0g		Vitamin A 0% Vitamin C 0%		Calcium 0% Iron 0%	

Kitchen Basics, Original Seafood Cooking Stock

1 cup / 245g

Amount per serving	%DV	Amount per serving	%DV	Amount per serving	%DV
Calories 10		**Cholesterol** 0mg	0%	**Total Carbohydrate** 0g	0%
Total Fat 0g	0%	**Sodium** 420mg	18%	Dietary Fiber 0g	0%
Saturated Fat 0g	0%	**Protein** 3g		Sugars 0g	
Polyunsaturated Fat 0g					
Monounsaturated Fat 0g		Vitamin A 0% Vitamin C 0%		Calcium 0% Iron 0%	

Kitchen Basics, Unsalted Beef Stock

1 cup / 240 ml

Amount per serving	%DV	Amount per serving	%DV	Amount per serving	%DV
Calories 30		**Cholesterol** 0mg	0%	**Total Carbohydrate** 2g	1%
Total Fat 0g	0%	**Sodium** 200mg	8%	Dietary Fiber 0g	0%
Saturated Fat 0g	0%	**Protein** 5g		Sugars 0g	
Polyunsaturated Fat 0g					
Monounsaturated Fat 0g		Vitamin A 0% Vitamin C 0%		Calcium 0% Iron 0%	

Kitchen Basics, Unsalted Chicken Stock

1 cup / 240 ml

Amount per serving	%DV	Amount per serving	%DV	Amount per serving	%DV
Calories 20		**Cholesterol** 0mg	0%	**Total Carbohydrate** 1g	0%
Total Fat 0g	0%	**Sodium** 150mg	6%	Dietary Fiber 0g	0%
Saturated Fat 0g	0%	**Protein** 5g		Sugars 0g	
Polyunsaturated Fat 0g					
Monounsaturated Fat 0g		Vitamin A 0% Vitamin C 0%		Calcium 0% Iron 0%	

Pacific Foods, Organic Free Range Low Sodium Chicken Broth

1 cup / 8 fl oz / 240 ml

Amount per serving	%DV	Amount per serving	%DV	Amount per serving	%DV
Calories 10		**Cholesterol** 0mg	0%	**Total Carbohydrate** 1g	0%
Total Fat 0g	0%	**Sodium** 70mg	3%	Dietary Fiber 0g	0%
Saturated Fat 0g	0%	**Protein** 2g		Sugars 0g	
Polyunsaturated Fat 0g					
Monounsaturated Fat 0g		Vitamin A 0% Vitamin C 0%		Calcium 0% Iron 2%	

Pacific Foods, Organic Light Sodium Creamy Butternut Squash Soup

1 cup / 8 fl oz / 240 ml

Amount per serving	%DV	Amount per serving	%DV	Amount per serving	%DV
Calories 90		**Cholesterol** 0mg	0%	**Total Carbohydrate** 17g	6%
Total Fat 2g	3%	**Sodium** 280mg	12%	Dietary Fiber 3g	12%
Saturated Fat 0g	0%	**Protein** 2g		Sugars 4g	
Polyunsaturated Fat 0g					
Monounsaturated Fat 0g		Vitamin A 50% Vitamin C 4%		Calcium 4% Iron 4%	

Pacific Natural Foods, Organic Light Sodium Creamy Tomato Soup

8 fl oz

Amount per serving	%DV	Amount per serving	%DV	Amount per serving	%DV
Calories 100		**Cholesterol** 10mg	3%	**Total Carbohydrate** 16g	5%
Total Fat 2g	3%	**Sodium** 380mg	16%	Dietary Fiber 1g	4%
Saturated Fat 1.5g	8%	**Protein** 5g		Sugars 12g	
Polyunsaturated Fat 0g					
Monounsaturated Fat 0g		Vitamin A 15% Vitamin C 8%		Calcium 15% Iron 2%	

Pacific Natural Foods, Organic Light Sodium Roasted Red Pepper & Tomato Soup

8 fl oz

Amount per serving	%DV	Amount per serving	%DV	Amount per serving	%DV
Calories 110		**Cholesterol** 10mg	3%	**Total Carbohydrate** 16g	5%
Total Fat 0g	0%	**Sodium** 360mg	15%	Dietary Fiber 1g	4%
Saturated Fat 1.5g	8%	**Protein** 5g		Sugars 12g	
Polyunsaturated Fat 0g					
Monounsaturated Fat 0g		Vitamin A 10% Vitamin C 4%		Calcium 15% Iron 2%	

Progresso, Reduced Sodium Beef & Vegetable

1 cup

Amount per serving	%DV	Amount per serving	%DV	Amount per serving	%DV
Calories 130		**Cholesterol** 15mg	5%	**Total Carbohydrate** 23g	8%
Total Fat 1g	2%	**Sodium** 480mg	20%	Dietary Fiber 3g	12%
Saturated Fat 0.5g	2%	**Protein** 9g		Sugars 5g	
Polyunsaturated Fat 0g					
Monounsaturated Fat 0g		Vitamin A 70% Vitamin C 0%		Calcium 2% Iron 8%	

Progresso, Reduced Sodium Chicken Gumbo

1 cup

Amount per serving	%DV	Amount per serving	%DV	Amount per serving	%DV
Calories 110		**Cholesterol** 10mg	3%	**Total Carbohydrate** 18g	6%
Total Fat 2g	3%	**Sodium** 480mg	20%	Dietary Fiber 4g	16%
Saturated Fat 0.5g	3%	**Protein** 7g		Sugars 3g	
Polyunsaturated Fat 0.5g					
Monounsaturated Fat 1g		Vitamin A 20% Vitamin C 0%		Calcium 4% Iron 8%	

Progresso, Reduced Sodium Chicken Gumbo Soup

1 cup

Amount per serving	%DV	Amount per serving	%DV	Amount per serving	%DV
Calories 110		**Cholesterol** 10mg	3%	**Total Carbohydrate** 18g	6%
Total Fat 2g	3%	**Sodium** 480mg	20%	Dietary Fiber 4g	16%
Saturated Fat 0.5g	3%	**Protein** 7g		Sugars 3g	
Polyunsaturated Fat 0.5g					
Monounsaturated Fat 1g		Vitamin A 20% Vitamin C 0%		Calcium 4% Iron 8%	

Progresso, Reduced Sodium Chicken Noodle Soup

1 cup

Amount per serving	%DV	Amount per serving	%DV	Amount per serving	%DV
Calories 90		**Cholesterol** 20mg	7%	**Total Carbohydrate** 13g	4%
Total Fat 2g	3%	**Sodium** 470mg	20%	Dietary Fiber 1g	4%
Saturated Fat 0.5g	3%	**Protein** 6g		Sugars 1g	
Polyunsaturated Fat 0g					
Monounsaturated Fat 0.5g		Vitamin A 25% Vitamin C 0%		Calcium 0% Iron 4%	

Progresso, Reduced Sodium Garden Vegetable

1 cup

Amount per serving	%DV	Amount per serving	%DV	Amount per serving	%DV
Calories 100		**Cholesterol** 0mg	0%	**Total Carbohydrate** 22g	7%
Total Fat 0g	0%	**Sodium** 450mg	19%	Dietary Fiber 3g	12%
Saturated Fat 0g	0%	**Protein** 3g		Sugars 4g	
Polyunsaturated Fat 0g					
Monounsaturated Fat 0g		Vitamin A 20% Vitamin C 0%		Calcium 2% Iron 4%	

Progresso, Reduced Sodium Garden Vegetable Soup

1 cup

Amount per serving	%DV	Amount per serving	%DV	Amount per serving	%DV
Calories 100		**Cholesterol** 0mg	0%	**Total Carbohydrate** 22g	7%
Total Fat 0g	0%	**Sodium** 450mg	19%	Dietary Fiber 3g	12%
Saturated Fat 0g	0%	**Protein** 3g		Sugars 4g	
Polyunsaturated Fat 0g					
Monounsaturated Fat 0g		Vitamin A 20% Vitamin C 0%		Calcium 2% Iron 4%	

Progresso, Reduced Sodium Italian-Style Wedding

1 cup

Amount per serving	%DV	Amount per serving	%DV	Amount per serving	%DV
Calories 110		**Cholesterol** 5mg	2%	**Total Carbohydrate** 18g	6%
Total Fat 3g	5%	**Sodium** 480mg	20%	Dietary Fiber 4g	16%
Saturated Fat 1g	5%	**Protein** 6g		Sugars 1g	
Polyunsaturated Fat 0.5g					
Monounsaturated Fat 1g		Vitamin A 30% Vitamin C 0%		Calcium 2% Iron 6%	

Progresso, Reduced Sodium Minestrone

1 cup

Amount per serving	%DV	Amount per serving	%DV	Amount per serving	%DV
Calories 120		**Cholesterol** 0mg	0%	**Total Carbohydrate** 22g	7%
Total Fat 2g	3%	**Sodium** 470mg	20%	Dietary Fiber 4g	16%
Saturated Fat 0.5g	3%	**Protein** 5g		Sugars 4g	
Polyunsaturated Fat 1g					
Monounsaturated Fat 0.5g		Vitamin A 20% Vitamin C 0%		Calcium 2% Iron 10%	

Progresso, Reduced Sodium Minestrone Soup

1 serving

Amount per serving	%DV	Amount per serving	%DV	Amount per serving	%DV
Calories 120		**Cholesterol** 0mg	0%	**Total Carbohydrate** 22g	7%
Total Fat 2g	3%	**Sodium** 470mg	20%	Dietary Fiber 4g	16%
Saturated Fat 0.5g	3%	**Protein** 5g		Sugars 4g	
Polyunsaturated Fat 1g					
Monounsaturated Fat 0.5g		Vitamin A 20% Vitamin C 0%		Calcium 2% Iron 10%	

Progresso, Reduced Sodium Tomato Parmesan

1 cup

Amount per serving	%DV	Amount per serving	%DV	Amount per serving	%DV
Calories 100		**Cholesterol** 5mg	2%	**Total Carbohydrate** 17g	6%
Total Fat 1.5g	2%	**Sodium** 480mg	20%	Dietary Fiber 3g	12%
Saturated Fat 1g	5%	**Protein** 5g		Sugars 9g	
Polyunsaturated Fat 0g					
Monounsaturated Fat 0.5g		Vitamin A 15% Vitamin C 0%		Calcium 10% Iron 6%	

Sauces

505 Southwestern, Green Chile Sauce

2 tbsp / 30 ml

Amount per serving	%DV	Amount per serving	%DV	Amount per serving	%DV
Calories 5		**Cholesterol** 0mg	0%	**Total Carbohydrate** 2g	1%
Total Fat 0g	0%	**Sodium** 95mg	4%	Dietary Fiber 0g	0%
Saturated Fat 0g	0%	**Protein** 0g		Sugars 1g	
Polyunsaturated Fat 0g					
Monounsaturated Fat 0g		Vitamin A 2%	Vitamin C 30%	Calcium 0%	Iron 0%

Annie's, Organic Annie's, Original BBQ Sauce

2 tbsp / 34g

Amount per serving	%DV	Amount per serving	%DV	Amount per serving	%DV
Calories 45		**Cholesterol** 0mg	0%	**Total Carbohydrate** 9g	3%
Total Fat 1g	2%	**Sodium** 240mg	10%	Dietary Fiber 0g	0%
Saturated Fat 0g	0%	**Protein** 0g		Sugars 5g	
Polyunsaturated Fat 0g					
Monounsaturated Fat 0g		Vitamin A 2%	Vitamin C 0%	Calcium 0%	Iron 0%

Annie's, Organic Hot Chipotle BBQ Sauce

2 tbsp / 34g

Amount per serving	%DV	Amount per serving	%DV	Amount per serving	%DV
Calories 45		**Cholesterol** 0mg	0%	**Total Carbohydrate** 9g	3%
Total Fat 1g	2%	**Sodium** 250mg	10%	Dietary Fiber 1g	4%
Saturated Fat 0g	0%	**Protein** 0g		Sugars 5g	
Polyunsaturated Fat 0g					
Monounsaturated Fat 0g		Vitamin A 4%	Vitamin C 0%	Calcium 0%	Iron 2%

Campbell's, Pace, Enchilada Sauce

1 serving (60g)

Amount per serving	%DV	Amount per serving	%DV	Amount per serving	%DV
Calories 24		**Cholesterol** 0mg	0%	**Total Carbohydrate** 5g	2%
Total Fat 0g	0%	**Sodium** 520mg	22%	Dietary Fiber 1g	4%
Saturated Fat 0g	0%	**Protein** 1g		Sugars 4g	
Polyunsaturated Fat 0g					
Monounsaturated Fat 0g		Vitamin A 4%	Vitamin C 0%	Calcium 0%	Iron 0%

Campbell's, Pace, Organic Picante Sauce

2 tbsp / 32g

Amount per serving	%DV	Amount per serving	%DV	Amount per serving	%DV
Calories 10		**Cholesterol** 0mg	0%	**Total Carbohydrate** 2g	1%
Total Fat 0g	0%	**Sodium** 220mg	9%	Dietary Fiber 1g	4%
Saturated Fat 0g	0%	**Protein** 0g		Sugars 2g	
Polyunsaturated Fat 0g					
Monounsaturated Fat 0g		Vitamin A 4%	Vitamin C 0%	Calcium 0%	Iron 0%

Campbell's, Pace, Picante Sauce

2 tbsp / 32g

Amount per serving	%DV	Amount per serving	%DV	Amount per serving	%DV
Calories 8		**Cholesterol** 0mg	0%	**Total Carbohydrate** 2g	1%
Total Fat 0g	0%	**Sodium** 250mg	10%	Dietary Fiber 1g	4%
Saturated Fat 0g	0%	**Protein** 0g		Sugars 2g	
Polyunsaturated Fat 0g					
Monounsaturated Fat 0g		Vitamin A 2% Vitamin C 0%		Calcium 0% Iron 0%	

Campbell's, Prego sauce, Chunky Garden Tomato, Onion and Garlic, Ready-to-serve

1 serving, 1/2 cup / 130g

Amount per serving	%DV	Amount per serving	%DV	Amount per serving	%DV
Calories 90		**Cholesterol** 0mg	0%	**Total Carbohydrate** 14g	5%
Total Fat 3g	5%	**Sodium** 470mg	20%	Dietary Fiber 3g	12%
Saturated Fat 0g	0%	**Protein** 2g		Sugars 10g	
Polyunsaturated Fat 0g					
Monounsaturated Fat 0g		Vitamin A 10% Vitamin C 6%		Calcium 2% Iron 4%	

Campbell's, Prego sauce, Fresh Mushroom, Ready-to-serve

1 serving / 1/2 cup / 130g

Amount per serving	%DV	Amount per serving	%DV	Amount per serving	%DV
Calories 70		**Cholesterol** 0mg	0%	**Total Carbohydrate** 13g	4%
Total Fat 1.5g	2%	**Sodium** 480mg	20%	Dietary Fiber 3g	12%
Saturated Fat 0g	0%	**Protein** 2g		Sugars 11g	
Polyunsaturated Fat 0g					
Monounsaturated Fat 0g		Vitamin A 10% Vitamin C 6%		Calcium 2% Iron 4%	

Campbell's, Prego sauce, Italian Sausage and Garlic, Ready-to-serve

1 serving / 1/2 cup / 130g

Amount per serving	%DV	Amount per serving	%DV	Amount per serving	%DV
Calories 90		**Cholesterol** 5mg	2%	**Total Carbohydrate** 13g	4%
Total Fat 3g	5%	**Sodium** 480mg	20%	Dietary Fiber 3g	12%
Saturated Fat 1g	5%	**Protein** 3g		Sugars 10g	
Polyunsaturated Fat 0g					
Monounsaturated Fat 0g		Vitamin A 10% Vitamin C 2%		Calcium 2% Iron 4%	

Campbell's, Prego, Heart Smart - Traditional Sauce

1/2 cup / 120ml

Amount per serving	%DV	Amount per serving	%DV	Amount per serving	%DV
Calories 70		**Cholesterol** 0mg	0%	**Total Carbohydrate** 13g	4%
Total Fat 1.5g	2%	**Sodium** 470mg	20%	Dietary Fiber 3g	12%
Saturated Fat 0g	0%	**Protein** 2g		Sugars 10g	
Polyunsaturated Fat 0.5g					
Monounsaturated Fat 1g		Vitamin A 10% Vitamin C 4%		Calcium 2% Iron 4%	

Classico, Red Sauce, Cabernet Marinara with Herbs

1/2 cup / 125g

Amount per serving	%DV	Amount per serving	%DV	Amount per serving	%DV
Calories 60		**Cholesterol** 0mg	0%	**Total Carbohydrate** 10g	3%
Total Fat 1.5g	2%	**Sodium** 380mg	16%	Dietary Fiber 2g	8%
Saturated Fat 0g	0%	**Protein** 2g		Sugars 6g	
Polyunsaturated Fat 0g					
Monounsaturated Fat 0g		Vitamin A 15% Vitamin C 2%		Calcium 4% Iron 8%	

Classico, Red Sauce, Carmelized Onion and Roasted Garlic

1/2 cup / 125g

Amount per serving	%DV	Amount per serving	%DV	Amount per serving	%DV
Calories 70		**Cholesterol** 0mg	0%	**Total Carbohydrate** 12g	4%
Total Fat 1.5g	2%	**Sodium** 470mg	20%	Dietary Fiber 2g	8%
Saturated Fat 0g	0%	**Protein** 2g		Sugars 7g	
Polyunsaturated Fat 0g					
Monounsaturated Fat 0g		Vitamin A 6% Vitamin C 7%		Calcium 4% Iron 4%	

Classico, Red Sauce, Fire-Roasted Tomato and Garlic

1/2 cup / 125g

Amount per serving	%DV	Amount per serving	%DV	Amount per serving	%DV
Calories 60		**Cholesterol** 0mg	0%	**Total Carbohydrate** 10g	3%
Total Fat 1.5g	2%	**Sodium** 380mg	16%	Dietary Fiber 3g	12%
Saturated Fat 0g	0%	**Protein** 2g		Sugars 6g	
Polyunsaturated Fat 0g					
Monounsaturated Fat 0g		Vitamin A 8% Vitamin C 6%		Calcium 4% Iron 4%	

Classico, Red Sauce, Marinara with Plum Tomatoes

1/2 cup / 125g

Amount per serving	%DV	Amount per serving	%DV	Amount per serving	%DV
Calories 70		**Cholesterol** 0mg	0%	**Total Carbohydrate** 10g	3%
Total Fat 2g	3%	**Sodium** 460mg	19%	Dietary Fiber 2g	8%
Saturated Fat 0g	0%	**Protein** 2g		Sugars 6g	
Polyunsaturated Fat 0g					
Monounsaturated Fat 0g		Vitamin A 8% Vitamin C 2%		Calcium 6% Iron 4%	

Classico, Red Sauce, Mushroom and Ripe Olives

1/2 cup / 125g

Amount per serving	%DV	Amount per serving	%DV	Amount per serving	%DV
Calories 60		**Cholesterol** 0mg	0%	**Total Carbohydrate** 10g	3%
Total Fat 1g	2%	**Sodium** 450mg	19%	Dietary Fiber 2g	8%
Saturated Fat 0g	0%	**Protein** 2g		Sugars 6g	
Polyunsaturated Fat 0g					
Monounsaturated Fat 0g		Vitamin A 15% Vitamin C 4%		Calcium 4% Iron 8%	

Classico, Red Sauce, Organic Spinach and Garlic

1/2 cup / 125g

Amount per serving	%DV	Amount per serving	%DV	Amount per serving	%DV
Calories 70		**Cholesterol** 0mg	0%	**Total Carbohydrate** 11g	4%
Total Fat 1.5g	2%	**Sodium** 330mg	14%	Dietary Fiber 2g	8%
Saturated Fat 0g	0%	**Protein** 2g		Sugars 7g	
Polyunsaturated Fat 0g					
Monounsaturated Fat 0g		Vitamin A 16% Vitamin C 0%		Calcium 4% Iron 4%	

Classico, Red Sauce, Organic Tomato, Herbs and Spices

1/2 cup / 125g

Amount per serving	%DV	Amount per serving	%DV	Amount per serving	%DV
Calories 70		**Cholesterol** 0mg	0%	**Total Carbohydrate** 12g	4%
Total Fat 1g	2%	**Sodium** 400mg	17%	Dietary Fiber 2g	8%
Saturated Fat 0g	0%	**Protein** 2g		Sugars 7g	
Polyunsaturated Fat 0g					
Monounsaturated Fat 0g		Vitamin A 14% Vitamin C 2%		Calcium 6% Iron 4%	

Classico, Red Sauce, Portobello, Crimini & Champignon Mushroom

1/2 cup / 125g

Amount per serving	%DV	Amount per serving	%DV	Amount per serving	%DV
Calories 70		**Cholesterol** 0mg	0%	**Total Carbohydrate** 11g	4%
Total Fat 2g	3%	**Sodium** 390mg	16%	Dietary Fiber 3g	12%
Saturated Fat 0g	0%	**Protein** 2g		Sugars 6g	
Polyunsaturated Fat 0g					
Monounsaturated Fat 0g		Vitamin A 10% Vitamin C 20%		Calcium 4% Iron 4%	

Classico, Red Sauce, Roasted Garlic

1/2 cup / 125g

Amount per serving	%DV	Amount per serving	%DV	Amount per serving	%DV
Calories 50		**Cholesterol** 0mg	0%	**Total Carbohydrate** 8g	3%
Total Fat 1g	2%	**Sodium** 320mg	13%	Dietary Fiber 2g	8%
Saturated Fat 0g	0%	**Protein** 2g		Sugars 5g	
Polyunsaturated Fat 0g					
Monounsaturated Fat 0g		Vitamin A 10% Vitamin C 2%		Calcium 6% Iron 6%	

Classico, Red Sauce, Spicy Red Pepper

1/2 cup / 125g

Amount per serving	%DV	Amount per serving	%DV	Amount per serving	%DV
Calories 50		**Cholesterol** 0mg	0%	**Total Carbohydrate** 8g	3%
Total Fat 1.5g	2%	**Sodium** 310mg	13%	Dietary Fiber 2g	8%
Saturated Fat 0g	0%	**Protein** 2g		Sugars 4g	
Polyunsaturated Fat 0g					
Monounsaturated Fat 0g		Vitamin A 6% Vitamin C 6%		Calcium 4% Iron 4%	

Classico, Red Sauce, Spicy Tomato and Basil

1/2 cup / 125g

Amount per serving	%DV	Amount per serving	%DV	Amount per serving	%DV
Calories 50		**Cholesterol** 0mg	0%	**Total Carbohydrate** 10g	3%
Total Fat 1g	2%	**Sodium** 480mg	20%	Dietary Fiber 2g	8%
Saturated Fat 0g	0%	**Protein** 2g		Sugars 6g	
Polyunsaturated Fat 0g					
Monounsaturated Fat 0g		Vitamin A 15% Vitamin C 4%		Calcium 4% Iron 6%	

Classico, Red Sauce, Tomato and Basil

1/2 cup / 125g

Amount per serving	%DV	Amount per serving	%DV	Amount per serving	%DV
Calories 45		**Cholesterol** 0mg	0%	**Total Carbohydrate** 8g	3%
Total Fat 0.5g	1%	**Sodium** 400mg	17%	Dietary Fiber 2g	8%
Saturated Fat 0g	0%	**Protein** 2g		Sugars 5g	
Polyunsaturated Fat 0g					
Monounsaturated Fat 0g		Vitamin A 15% Vitamin C 4%		Calcium 6% Iron 8%	

Classico, Red Sauce, Traditional Sweet Basil

1/2 cup / 125g

Amount per serving	%DV	Amount per serving	%DV	Amount per serving	%DV
Calories 70		**Cholesterol** 0mg	0%	**Total Carbohydrate** 13g	4%
Total Fat 1g	2%	**Sodium** 480mg	20%	Dietary Fiber 3g	12%
Saturated Fat 0g	0%	**Protein** 2g		Sugars 9g	
Polyunsaturated Fat 0g					
Monounsaturated Fat 0g		Vitamin A 6% Vitamin C 4%		Calcium 4% Iron 4%	

Classico, Red Sauce, Tuscan Olive and Garlic

1/2 cup / 125g

Amount per serving	%DV	Amount per serving	%DV	Amount per serving	%DV
Calories 60		**Cholesterol** 0mg	0%	**Total Carbohydrate** 10g	3%
Total Fat 2g	3%	**Sodium** 440mg	18%	Dietary Fiber 2g	8%
Saturated Fat 0g	0%	**Protein** 2g		Sugars 6g	
Polyunsaturated Fat 0g					
Monounsaturated Fat 0g		Vitamin A 15% Vitamin C 4%		Calcium 4% Iron 8%	

Classico, Traditional Pizza Sauce

1/4 cup / 60g

Amount per serving	%DV	Amount per serving	%DV	Amount per serving	%DV
Calories 40		**Cholesterol** 0mg	0%	**Total Carbohydrate** 7g	2%
Total Fat 1g	2%	**Sodium** 320mg	13%	Dietary Fiber 1g	4%
Saturated Fat 0g	0%	**Protein** 1g		Sugars 5g	
Polyunsaturated Fat 0g					
Monounsaturated Fat 0g		Vitamin A 4% Vitamin C 20%		Calcium 2% Iron 2%	

Del Monte, Green Peppers & Mushrooms Spaghetti Sauce

1/2 cup / 125g

Amount per serving	%DV	Amount per serving	%DV	Amount per serving	%DV
Calories 80		**Cholesterol** 0mg	0%	**Total Carbohydrate** 14g	5%
Total Fat 1g	2%	**Sodium** 450mg	19%	Dietary Fiber 2g	8%
Saturated Fat 0g	0%	**Protein** 2g		Sugars 10g	
Polyunsaturated Fat 0g					
Monounsaturated Fat 0g		Vitamin A 10% Vitamin C 15%		Calcium 2% Iron 6%	

Eden Foods, Pizza-Pasta Sauce, Organic

1/4 cup / 60g

Amount per serving	%DV	Amount per serving	%DV	Amount per serving	%DV
Calories 35		**Cholesterol** 0mg	0%	**Total Carbohydrate** 4g	1%
Total Fat 1g	2%	**Sodium** 150mg	6%	Dietary Fiber 2g	8%
Saturated Fat 0g	0%	**Protein** 1g		Sugars 2g	
Polyunsaturated Fat 0g					
Monounsaturated Fat 0g		Vitamin A 10% Vitamin C 10%		Calcium 2% Iron 5%	

Francesco Rinaldi, ToBe Healthy Garlic & Onion Pasta Sauce

1/2 cup / 123g

Amount per serving	%DV	Amount per serving	%DV	Amount per serving	%DV
Calories 60		**Cholesterol** 0mg	0%	**Total Carbohydrate** 10g	3%
Total Fat 2g	3%	**Sodium** 310mg	13%	Dietary Fiber 2g	8%
Saturated Fat 0g	0%	**Protein** 2g		Sugars 5g	
Polyunsaturated Fat 0g					
Monounsaturated Fat 0g		Vitamin A 25% Vitamin C 0%		Calcium 2% Iron 4%	

Lucini, Savory Tomato Parmigiano Sauce

1/2 cup

Amount per serving	%DV	Amount per serving	%DV	Amount per serving	%DV
Calories 80		**Cholesterol** 5mg	2%	**Total Carbohydrate** 10g	3%
Total Fat 2.5g	4%	**Sodium** 340mg	14%	Dietary Fiber 2g	8%
Saturated Fat 1.5g	8%	**Protein** 5g		Sugars 5g	
Polyunsaturated Fat 0g					
Monounsaturated Fat 0g		Vitamin A 20% Vitamin C 6%		Calcium 15% Iron 2%	

Lucini, Sicilian Olive & Wild Caper Tomato Sauce

1/2 cup / 125g

Amount per serving	%DV	Amount per serving	%DV	Amount per serving	%DV
Calories 50		**Cholesterol** 0mg	0%	**Total Carbohydrate** 8g	3%
Total Fat 1.5g	2%	**Sodium** 290mg	12%	Dietary Fiber 2g	8%
Saturated Fat 0g	0%	**Protein** 1g		Sugars 2g	
Polyunsaturated Fat 0g					
Monounsaturated Fat 0g		Vitamin A 2% Vitamin C 10%		Calcium 2% Iron 2%	

Newman's Own, Garden Peppers Pasta Sauce

1/2 cup / 125g

Amount per serving	%DV	Amount per serving	%DV	Amount per serving	%DV
Calories 60		**Cholesterol** 0mg	0%	**Total Carbohydrate** 9g	3%
Total Fat 1g	2%	**Sodium** 440mg	18%	Dietary Fiber 0g	0%
Saturated Fat 0g	0%	**Protein** 2g		Sugars 5g	
Polyunsaturated Fat 0g					
Monounsaturated Fat 0g		Vitamin A 20% Vitamin C 0%		Calcium 6% Iron 6%	

Newman's Own, Lemon Pepper Marinade

1 tbsp / 15 ml

Amount per serving	%DV	Amount per serving	%DV	Amount per serving	%DV
Calories 15		**Cholesterol** 0mg	0%	**Total Carbohydrate** 3g	1%
Total Fat 0g	0%	**Sodium** 300mg	12%	Dietary Fiber 0g	0%
Saturated Fat 0g	0%	**Protein** 0g		Sugars 2g	
Polyunsaturated Fat 0g					
Monounsaturated Fat 0g		Vitamin A 0% Vitamin C 0%		Calcium 0% Iron 0%	

Newman's Own, Marinara Pasta Sauce

1/2 cup / 125g

Amount per serving	%DV	Amount per serving	%DV	Amount per serving	%DV
Calories 70		**Cholesterol** 0mg	0%	**Total Carbohydrate** 12g	4%
Total Fat 2g	3%	**Sodium** 460mg	19%	Dietary Fiber 3g	12%
Saturated Fat 0g	0%	**Protein** 2g		Sugars 8g	
Polyunsaturated Fat 0g					
Monounsaturated Fat 0g		Vitamin A 30% Vitamin C 0%		Calcium 4% Iron 10%	

Newman's Own, Sockarooni Pasta Sauce

1/2 cup / 125g

Amount per serving	%DV	Amount per serving	%DV	Amount per serving	%DV
Calories 70		**Cholesterol** 0mg	0%	**Total Carbohydrate** 12g	4%
Total Fat 2g	3%	**Sodium** 460mg	19%	Dietary Fiber 3g	12%
Saturated Fat 0g	0%	**Protein** 2g		Sugars 8g	
Polyunsaturated Fat 0g					
Monounsaturated Fat 0g		Vitamin A 25% Vitamin C 0%		Calcium 4% Iron 8%	

Prego, Chunky Garden Combo Italian Sauce

1/2 cup / 120 ml

Amount per serving	%DV	Amount per serving	%DV	Amount per serving	%DV
Calories 70		**Cholesterol** 0mg	0%	**Total Carbohydrate** 13g	4%
Total Fat 1g	2%	**Sodium** 470mg	20%	Dietary Fiber 3g	12%
Saturated Fat 0g	0%	**Protein** 2g		Sugars 10g	
Polyunsaturated Fat 0.5g					
Monounsaturated Fat 1g		Vitamin A 10% Vitamin C 6%		Calcium 2% Iron 4%	

Prego, Heart Smart Italian Mushroom Sauce

1/2 cup / 120 ml

Amount per serving	%DV	Amount per serving	%DV	Amount per serving	%DV
Calories 70		**Cholesterol** 0mg	0%	**Total Carbohydrate** 13g	4%
Total Fat 1.5g	2%	**Sodium** 360mg	15%	Dietary Fiber 3g	12%
Saturated Fat 0g	0%	**Protein** 2g		Sugars 9g	
Polyunsaturated Fat 0g					
Monounsaturated Fat 0g		Vitamin A 10% Vitamin C 4%		Calcium 2% Iron 4%	

Prego, Heart Smart Italian Ricotta Parmesan Sauce

1/2 cup

Amount per serving	%DV	Amount per serving	%DV	Amount per serving	%DV
Calories 90		**Cholesterol** 5mg	2%	**Total Carbohydrate** 13g	4%
Total Fat 2.5g	4%	**Sodium** 360mg	15%	Dietary Fiber 3g	12%
Saturated Fat 1g	5%	**Protein** 3g		Sugars 10g	
Polyunsaturated Fat 0g					
Monounsaturated Fat 0g		Vitamin A 10% Vitamin C 6%		Calcium 6% Iron 4%	

Prego, Heart Smart Roasted Red Pepper & Garlic Italian Sauce

1/2 cup / 120 ml

Amount per serving	%DV	Amount per serving	%DV	Amount per serving	%DV
Calories 70		**Cholesterol** 0mg	0%	**Total Carbohydrate** 13g	4%
Total Fat 1.5g	2%	**Sodium** 360mg	15%	Dietary Fiber 3g	12%
Saturated Fat 0g	0%	**Protein** 2g		Sugars 9g	
Polyunsaturated Fat 0.5g					
Monounsaturated Fat 1g		Vitamin A 15% Vitamin C 4%		Calcium 2% Iron 4%	

Prego, Heart Smart Traditional Italian Sauce

1/2 cup / 120 ml

Amount per serving	%DV	Amount per serving	%DV	Amount per serving	%DV
Calories 70		**Cholesterol** 0mg	0%	**Total Carbohydrate** 13g	4%
Total Fat 1.5g	2%	**Sodium** 360mg	15%	Dietary Fiber 3g	12%
Saturated Fat 0g	0%	**Protein** 2g		Sugars 10g	
Polyunsaturated Fat 0.5g					
Monounsaturated Fat 1g		Vitamin A 10% Vitamin C 4%		Calcium 2% Iron 4%	

Prego, Italian Sauage & Garlic Sauce

1/2 cup / 120 ml

Amount per serving	%DV	Amount per serving	%DV	Amount per serving	%DV
Calories 90		**Cholesterol** 5mg	2%	**Total Carbohydrate** 13g	4%
Total Fat 3g	5%	**Sodium** 480mg	20%	Dietary Fiber 3g	12%
Saturated Fat 1g	5%	**Protein** 3g		Sugars 10g	
Polyunsaturated Fat 0.5g					
Monounsaturated Fat 1.5g		Vitamin A 10% Vitamin C 2%		Calcium 2% Iron 4%	

Prego, Mini Meatballs Meat Sauce

1/2 cup / 120 ml

Amount per serving	%DV	Amount per serving	%DV	Amount per serving	%DV
Calories 100		**Cholesterol** 5mg	2%	**Total Carbohydrate** 13g	4%
Total Fat 3g	5%	**Sodium** 480mg	20%	Dietary Fiber 3g	12%
Saturated Fat 1g	5%	**Protein** 4g		Sugars 10g	
Polyunsaturated Fat 0.5g					
Monounsaturated Fat 1.5g		Vitamin A 10% Vitamin C 4%		Calcium 0% Iron 6%	

Prego, Mushroom Supreme with Baby Portobello

1/2 cup / 120 ml

Amount per serving	%DV	Amount per serving	%DV	Amount per serving	%DV
Calories 90		**Cholesterol** 0mg	0%	**Total Carbohydrate** 13g	4%
Total Fat 3g	5%	**Sodium** 460mg	19%	Dietary Fiber 3g	12%
Saturated Fat 0g	0%	**Protein** 2g		Sugars 10g	
Polyunsaturated Fat 1g					
Monounsaturated Fat 1.5g		Vitamin A 10% Vitamin C 8%		Calcium 4% Iron 8%	

Prego, Pizzeria Style Pizza Sauce

1/4 cup / 60 ml

Amount per serving	%DV	Amount per serving	%DV	Amount per serving	%DV
Calories 35		**Cholesterol** 0mg	0%	**Total Carbohydrate** 6g	2%
Total Fat 1g	2%	**Sodium** 200mg	8%	Dietary Fiber 2g	8%
Saturated Fat 0g	0%	**Protein** 1g		Sugars 4g	
Polyunsaturated Fat 0g					
Monounsaturated Fat 0g		Vitamin A 6% Vitamin C 4%		Calcium 0% Iron 2%	

Prego, Tomato Onion & Garlic

1/2 cup / 120 ml

Amount per serving	%DV	Amount per serving	%DV	Amount per serving	%DV
Calories 90		**Cholesterol** 0mg	0%	**Total Carbohydrate** 13g	4%
Total Fat 3g	5%	**Sodium** 470mg	20%	Dietary Fiber 3g	12%
Saturated Fat 0g	0%	**Protein** 2g		Sugars 10g	
Polyunsaturated Fat 1g					
Monounsaturated Fat 1.5g		Vitamin A 10% Vitamin C 6%		Calcium 2% Iron 4%	

Prego, Veggie Smart Pizza Sauce

1/4 cup / 60 ml

Amount per serving	%DV	Amount per serving	%DV	Amount per serving	%DV
Calories 45		**Cholesterol** 0mg	0%	**Total Carbohydrate** 8g	3%
Total Fat 1g	2%	**Sodium** 220mg	9%	Dietary Fiber 2g	8%
Saturated Fat 0g	0%	**Protein** 1g		Sugars 6g	
Polyunsaturated Fat 0g					
Monounsaturated Fat 0g		Vitamin A 15% Vitamin C 4%		Calcium 0% Iron 2%	

Ragu Light, No Sugar Added Tomato & Basil Pasta Sauce

125g

Amount per serving	%DV	Amount per serving	%DV	Amount per serving	%DV
Calories 60		**Cholesterol** 0mg	0%	**Total Carbohydrate** 10g	3%
Total Fat 1g	2%	**Sodium** 320mg	13%	Dietary Fiber 2g	8%
Saturated Fat 0g	0%	**Protein** 2g		Sugars 6g	
Polyunsaturated Fat 0g					
Monounsaturated Fat 0g		Vitamin A 15% Vitamin C 15%		Calcium 4% Iron 6%	

Ragu Light, Tomato & Basil Pasta Sauce

125g

Amount per serving	%DV	Amount per serving	%DV	Amount per serving	%DV
Calories 60		**Cholesterol** 0mg	0%	**Total Carbohydrate** 13g	4%
Total Fat 0g	0%	**Sodium** 330mg	14%	Dietary Fiber 2g	8%
Saturated Fat 0g	0%	**Protein** 2g		Sugars 9g	
Polyunsaturated Fat 0g					
Monounsaturated Fat 0g		Vitamin A 15% Vitamin C 15%		Calcium 2% Iron 6%	

Sauce, Barbecue

1 oz / 28g

Amount per serving	%DV	Amount per serving	%DV	Amount per serving	%DV
Calories 42		**Cholesterol** 0mg	0%	**Total Carbohydrate** 10g	3%
Total Fat 0g	0%	**Sodium** 313mg	13%	Dietary Fiber 0g	0%
Saturated Fat 0g	0%	**Protein** 0g		Sugars 7g	
Polyunsaturated Fat 0g					
Monounsaturated Fat 0g		Vitamin A 1% Vitamin C 0%		Calcium 0% Iron 0%	

Sauce, Chili, Peppers, Hot, Immature Green, Canned

1 tbsp / 15g

Amount per serving	%DV	Amount per serving	%DV	Amount per serving	%DV
Calories 3		**Cholesterol** 0mg	0%	**Total Carbohydrate** 1g	0%
Total Fat 0g	0%	**Sodium** 4mg	0%	Dietary Fiber 0g	0%
Saturated Fat 0g	0%	**Protein** 0g		Sugars 0g	
Polyunsaturated Fat 0g					
Monounsaturated Fat 0g		Vitamin A 2% Vitamin C 17%		Calcium 0% Iron 0%	

Sauce, Hoisin, Ready-to-Serve

1 tbsp / 16g

Amount per serving	%DV	Amount per serving	%DV	Amount per serving	%DV
Calories 35		**Cholesterol** 0mg	0%	**Total Carbohydrate** 7g	2%
Total Fat 1g	2%	**Sodium** 258mg	11%	Dietary Fiber 0g	0%
Saturated Fat 0g	0%	**Protein** 1g		Sugars 4g	
Polyunsaturated Fat 0g					
Monounsaturated Fat 0g		Vitamin A 0% Vitamin C 0%		Calcium 1% Iron 1%	

Sauce, Peppers, Hot, Chili, Mature Red, Canned

1 cup / 245g

Amount per serving	%DV	Amount per serving	%DV	Amount per serving	%DV
Calories 51		**Cholesterol** 0mg	0%	**Total Carbohydrate** 10g	3%
Total Fat 1g	2%	**Sodium** 61mg	3%	Dietary Fiber 2g	8%
Saturated Fat 0g	0%	**Protein** 2g		Sugars 6g	
Polyunsaturated Fat 0g					
Monounsaturated Fat 0g		Vitamin A 22% Vitamin C 123%		Calcium 2% Iron 7%	

Sauce, Pizza, Canned, Ready-to-Serve

1/4 cup / 63g

Amount per serving	%DV	Amount per serving	%DV	Amount per serving	%DV
Calories 34		**Cholesterol** 2mg	1%	**Total Carbohydrate** 5g	2%
Total Fat 1g	2%	**Sodium** 117mg	5%	Dietary Fiber 1g	4%
Saturated Fat 0g	0%	**Protein** 1g		Sugars 1g	
Polyunsaturated Fat 0g					
Monounsaturated Fat 0g		Vitamin A 8% Vitamin C 12%		Calcium 3% Iron 3%	

Sauce, Plum, Ready-to-Serve

1 oz / 28g

Amount per serving	%DV	Amount per serving	%DV	Amount per serving	%DV
Calories 52		**Cholesterol** 0mg	0%	**Total Carbohydrate** 12g	4%
Total Fat 0g	0%	**Sodium** 151mg	6%	Dietary Fiber 0g	0%
Saturated Fat 0g	0%	**Protein** 0g		Sugars 0g	
Polyunsaturated Fat 0g					
Monounsaturated Fat 0g		Vitamin A 0% Vitamin C 0%		Calcium 0% Iron 2%	

Sauce, Ready-to-Serve, Pepper or Hot

1 tsp / 4g

Amount per serving	%DV	Amount per serving	%DV	Amount per serving	%DV
Calories 0.1		**Cholesterol** 0mg	0%	**Total Carbohydrate** 0g	0%
Total Fat 0g	0%	**Sodium** 119mg	5%	Dietary Fiber 0g	0%
Saturated Fat 0g	0%	**Protein** 0g		Sugars 0g	
Polyunsaturated Fat 0g					
Monounsaturated Fat 0g		Vitamin A 0% Vitamin C 6%		Calcium 0% Iron 0%	

Sauce, Ready-to-Serve, Pepper, Tabasco

1 tsp / 4g

Amount per serving	%DV	Amount per serving	%DV	Amount per serving	%DV
Calories 1		**Cholesterol** 0mg	0%	**Total Carbohydrate** 0g	0%
Total Fat 0g	0%	**Sodium** 28mg	1%	Dietary Fiber 0g	0%
Saturated Fat 0g	0%	**Protein** 0g		Sugars 0g	
Polyunsaturated Fat 0g					
Monounsaturated Fat 0g		Vitamin A 1% Vitamin C 0%		Calcium 0% Iron 0%	

Sauce, Tomato Chili Sauce, Bottled, No Salt, Low Sodium

1 tbsp / 17g

Amount per serving	%DV	Amount per serving	%DV	Amount per serving	%DV
Calories 18		**Cholesterol** 0mg	0%	**Total Carbohydrate** 5g	2%
Total Fat 0g	0%	**Sodium** 3mg	0%	Dietary Fiber 0g	0%
Saturated Fat 0g	0%	**Protein** 0g		Sugars 2g	
Polyunsaturated Fat 0g					
Monounsaturated Fat 0g		Vitamin A 1%	Vitamin C 5%	Calcium 0%	Iron 1%

Sauce, Tomato Chili Sauce, Bottled, with Salt

1 packet / 6g

Amount per serving	%DV	Amount per serving	%DV	Amount per serving	%DV
Calories 6		**Cholesterol** 0mg	0%	**Total Carbohydrate** 1g	0%
Total Fat 0g	0%	**Sodium** 80mg	3%	Dietary Fiber 0g	0%
Saturated Fat 0g	0%	**Protein** 0g		Sugars 1g	
Polyunsaturated Fat 0g					
Monounsaturated Fat 0g		Vitamin A 1%	Vitamin C 2%	Calcium 0%	Iron 0%

Hispanic Cuisine

Amy's, Gluten-Free Cheddar Burrito

1 burrito

Amount per serving	%DV	Amount per serving	%DV	Amount per serving	%DV
Calories 260		**Cholesterol** 5mg	2%	**Total Carbohydrate** 37g	12%
Total Fat 8g	12%	**Sodium** 430mg	18%	Dietary Fiber 5g	20%
Saturated Fat 2g	10%	**Protein** 9g		Sugars 3g	
Polyunsaturated Fat 0g					
Monounsaturated Fat 0g		Vitamin A 4%	Vitamin C 6%	Calcium 10%	Iron 10%

Amy's, Light & Lean Black Bean & Cheese Enchilada

1 enchilada

Amount per serving	%DV	Amount per serving	%DV	Amount per serving	%DV
Calories 240		**Cholesterol** 5mg	2%	**Total Carbohydrate** 44g	15%
Total Fat 4.5g	7%	**Sodium** 480mg	20%	Dietary Fiber 4g	16%
Saturated Fat 2g	10%	**Protein** 8g		Sugars 5g	
Polyunsaturated Fat 0g					
Monounsaturated Fat 0g		Vitamin A 20%	Vitamin C 8%	Calcium 10%	Iron 10%

Amy's, Light & Lean Soft Taco Fiesta

1 taco

Amount per serving	%DV	Amount per serving	%DV	Amount per serving	%DV
Calories 220		**Cholesterol** 5mg	2%	**Total Carbohydrate** 40g	13%
Total Fat 4.5g	7%	**Sodium** 560mg	23%	Dietary Fiber 5g	20%
Saturated Fat 1.5g	8%	**Protein** 7g		Sugars 6g	
Polyunsaturated Fat 0g					
Monounsaturated Fat 0g		Vitamin A 20%	Vitamin C 25%	Calcium 10%	Iron 10%

Amy's, Mexican Tamale Pie

8 oz

Amount per serving	%DV	Amount per serving	%DV	Amount per serving	%DV
Calories 150		**Cholesterol** 0mg	0%	**Total Carbohydrate** 27g	9%
Total Fat 3g	5%	**Sodium** 590mg	25%	Dietary Fiber 4g	16%
Saturated Fat 0g	0%	**Protein** 5g		Sugars 2g	
Polyunsaturated Fat 0g					
Monounsaturated Fat 0g		Vitamin A 15% Vitamin C 10%		Calcium 4% Iron 10%	

Healthy Choice Café Steamers Chicken Margherita

1 meal

Amount per serving	%DV	Amount per serving	%DV	Amount per serving	%DV
Calories 310		**Cholesterol** 35mg	12%	**Total Carbohydrate** 40g	13%
Total Fat 8g	12%	**Sodium** 600mg	25%	Dietary Fiber 4g	16%
Saturated Fat 1.5g	8%	**Protein** 19g		Sugars 10g	
Polyunsaturated Fat 1.5g					
Monounsaturated Fat 5g		Vitamin A 6% Vitamin C 0%		Calcium 10% Iron 10%	

Indian Cuisine

Amy's, Gluten-Free Indian Aloo Mattar Wrap

5.5 oz

Amount per serving	%DV	Amount per serving	%DV	Amount per serving	%DV
Calories 270		**Cholesterol** 0mg	0%	**Total Carbohydrate** 32g	11%
Total Fat 9g	14%	**Sodium** 590mg	25%	Dietary Fiber 6g	24%
Saturated Fat 0.5g	3%	**Protein** 9g		Sugars 5g	
Polyunsaturated Fat 0g					
Monounsaturated Fat 0g		Vitamin A 4% Vitamin C 10%		Calcium 4% Iron 10%	

Amy's, Light in Sodium, Indian Mattar Paneer

10 oz

Amount per serving	%DV	Amount per serving	%DV	Amount per serving	%DV
Calories 370		**Cholesterol** 20mg	7%	**Total Carbohydrate** 54g	18%
Total Fat 11g	17%	**Sodium** 390mg	16%	Dietary Fiber 6g	24%
Saturated Fat 4g	20%	**Protein** 13g		Sugars 8g	
Polyunsaturated Fat 0g					
Monounsaturated Fat 0g		Vitamin A 10% Vitamin C 15%		Calcium 10% Iron 15%	

Tasty Bite, Aloo Palak

1/2 pack / 5 oz / 142.5g

Amount per serving	%DV	Amount per serving	%DV	Amount per serving	%DV
Calories 100		**Cholesterol** 0mg	0%	**Total Carbohydrate** 13g	4%
Total Fat 3g	5%	**Sodium** 400mg	17%	Dietary Fiber 3g	12%
Saturated Fat 0g	0%	**Protein** 3g		Sugars 3g	
Polyunsaturated Fat 0g					
Monounsaturated Fat 0g		Vitamin A 24% Vitamin C 4%		Calcium 6% Iron 10%	

Tasty Bite, Jodhpur Lentils

1/2 pack / 5 oz / 142.5g

Amount per serving	%DV	Amount per serving	%DV	Amount per serving	%DV
Calories 110		**Cholesterol** 0mg	0%	**Total Carbohydrate** 16g	5%
Total Fat 2.5g	4%	**Sodium** 460mg	19%	Dietary Fiber 4g	16%
Saturated Fat 0g	0%	**Protein** 6g		Sugars 1g	
Polyunsaturated Fat 0g					
Monounsaturated Fat 0g		Vitamin A 2%	Vitamin C 0%	Calcium 4%	Iron 10%

Asian Cuisine

Amy's, Gluten-Free Teriyaki Wrap

5.5 oz

Amount per serving	%DV	Amount per serving	%DV	Amount per serving	%DV
Calories 250		**Cholesterol** 0mg	0%	**Total Carbohydrate** 38g	13%
Total Fat 6g	9%	**Sodium** 540mg	22%	Dietary Fiber 3g	12%
Saturated Fat 0.5g	2%	**Protein** 9g		Sugars 7g	
Polyunsaturated Fat 0g					
Monounsaturated Fat 0g		Vitamin A 15%	Vitamin C 25%	Calcium 8%	Iron 4%

Annie Chun's, Organic Chow Mein, Asian Meal Starter

1/3 box

Amount per serving	%DV	Amount per serving	%DV	Amount per serving	%DV
Calories 220		**Cholesterol** 0mg	0%	**Total Carbohydrate** 42g	14%
Total Fat 1.5g	2%	**Sodium** 570mg	24%	Dietary Fiber 1g	4%
Saturated Fat 0g	0%	**Protein** 8g		Sugars 6g	
Polyunsaturated Fat 0g					
Monounsaturated Fat 0g		Vitamin A 0%	Vitamin C 0%	Calcium 0%	Iron 0%

Annie Chun's, Organic Soy Ginger, Asian Meal Starter

1/3 box

Amount per serving	%DV	Amount per serving	%DV	Amount per serving	%DV
Calories 220		**Cholesterol** 0mg	0%	**Total Carbohydrate** 41g	14%
Total Fat 1.5g	2%	**Sodium** 600mg	25%	Dietary Fiber 1g	4%
Saturated Fat 0g	0%	**Protein** 8g		Sugars 5g	
Polyunsaturated Fat 0g					
Monounsaturated Fat 0g		Vitamin A 0%	Vitamin C 0%	Calcium 0%	Iron 0%

Annie Chun's, Organic Teriyaki, Asian Meal Starter

1/3 box

Amount per serving	%DV	Amount per serving	%DV	Amount per serving	%DV
Calories 220		**Cholesterol** 0mg	0%	**Total Carbohydrate** 43g	14%
Total Fat 1.5g	2%	**Sodium** 590mg	25%	Dietary Fiber 1g	4%
Saturated Fat 0g	0%	**Protein** 8g		Sugars 7g	
Polyunsaturated Fat 0g					
Monounsaturated Fat 0g		Vitamin A 0%	Vitamin C 0%	Calcium 0%	Iron 0%

Dr. McDougall's Right Foods, Masala Lentil Pilaf

1 container / 76g

Amount per serving	%DV	Amount per serving	%DV	Amount per serving	%DV
Calories 280		**Cholesterol** 0mg	0%	**Total Carbohydrate** 56g	19%
Total Fat 2g	3%	**Sodium** 460mg	19%	Dietary Fiber 6g	24%
Saturated Fat 0g	0%	**Protein** 8g		Sugars 8g	
Polyunsaturated Fat 0g					
Monounsaturated Fat 0g		Vitamin A 8% Vitamin C 4%		Calcium 4% Iron 4%	

Feel Good Foods, Chicken and Vegetable Egg Rolls

3 oz / 84g

Amount per serving	%DV	Amount per serving	%DV	Amount per serving	%DV
Calories 130		**Cholesterol** 25mg	8%	**Total Carbohydrate** 15g	5%
Total Fat 3.5g	5%	**Sodium** 380mg	16%	Dietary Fiber 2g	8%
Saturated Fat 1g	5%	**Protein** 9g		Sugars 1g	
Polyunsaturated Fat 0g					
Monounsaturated Fat 0g		Vitamin A 30% Vitamin C 15%		Calcium 4% Iron 4%	

Feel Good Foods, Shrimp and Vegetable Egg Rolls

3 oz / 84g

Amount per serving	%DV	Amount per serving	%DV	Amount per serving	%DV
Calories 100		**Cholesterol** 45mg	15%	**Total Carbohydrate** 14g	5%
Total Fat 1.5g	2%	**Sodium** 420mg	18%	Dietary Fiber 2g	8%
Saturated Fat 0g	0%	**Protein** 7g		Sugars 1g	
Polyunsaturated Fat 0g					
Monounsaturated Fat 0g		Vitamin A 30% Vitamin C 15%		Calcium 4% Iron 6%	

Feel Good Foods, Vegetable Dumplings, including sauce

4 dumplings / 136g

Amount per serving	%DV	Amount per serving	%DV	Amount per serving	%DV
Calories 335		**Cholesterol** 0mg	0%	**Total Carbohydrate** 48g	16%
Total Fat 9g	14%	**Sodium** 430mg	18%	Dietary Fiber 2g	8%
Saturated Fat 1.5g	8%	**Protein** 3g		Sugars 3g	
Polyunsaturated Fat 0g					
Monounsaturated Fat 0g		Vitamin A 8% Vitamin C 15%		Calcium 4% Iron 2%	

Feel Good Foods, Vegetable Egg Rolls

1 egg roll / 92g

Amount per serving	%DV	Amount per serving	%DV	Amount per serving	%DV
Calories 90		**Cholesterol** 0mg	0%	**Total Carbohydrate** 14g	5%
Total Fat 2.5g	4%	**Sodium** 420mg	18%	Dietary Fiber 1g	4%
Saturated Fat 0g	0%	**Protein** 2g		Sugars 3g	
Polyunsaturated Fat 0g					
Monounsaturated Fat 0g		Vitamin A 20% Vitamin C 20%		Calcium 4% Iron 2%	

Healthy Choice Café Steamers Asian Inspired General Tso's Spicy Chicken

1 meal

Amount per serving	%DV	Amount per serving	%DV	Amount per serving	%DV
Calories 300		**Cholesterol** 30mg	10%	**Total Carbohydrate** 53g	18%
Total Fat 3g	5%	**Sodium** 500mg	21%	Dietary Fiber 4g	16%
Saturated Fat 1g	5%	**Protein** 15g		Sugars 12g	
Polyunsaturated Fat 0.5g					
Monounsaturated Fat 1.5g		Vitamin A 50%　Vitamin C 0%		Calcium 10%　Iron 4%	

Italian Cuisine

Amy's, Light & Lean Roasted Polenta

8 oz

Amount per serving	%DV	Amount per serving	%DV	Amount per serving	%DV
Calories 140		**Cholesterol** 10mg	3%	**Total Carbohydrate** 20g	7%
Total Fat 4g	6%	**Sodium** 540mg	22%	Dietary Fiber 4g	16%
Saturated Fat 1.5g	8%	**Protein** 6g		Sugars 7g	
Polyunsaturated Fat 0g					
Monounsaturated Fat 0g		Vitamin A 30%　Vitamin C 25%		Calcium 15%　Iron 15%	

Conte's, Pierogies (Potato/Cheese/Onion)

4 pierogies / 12 oz

Amount per serving	%DV	Amount per serving	%DV	Amount per serving	%DV
Calories 220		**Cholesterol** 55mg	18%	**Total Carbohydrate** 39g	13%
Total Fat 5g	8%	**Sodium** 330mg	14%	Dietary Fiber 2g	8%
Saturated Fat 2g	10%	**Protein** 6g		Sugars 2g	
Polyunsaturated Fat 0g					
Monounsaturated Fat 0g		Vitamin A 4%　Vitamin C 6%		Calcium 8%　Iron 2%	

Conte's, Pierogies (Potato/Onion)

4 pierogies / 12 oz

Amount per serving	%DV	Amount per serving	%DV	Amount per serving	%DV
Calories 180		**Cholesterol** 45mg	15%	**Total Carbohydrate** 39g	13%
Total Fat 1.5g	2%	**Sodium** 110mg	5%	Dietary Fiber 3g	12%
Saturated Fat 0g	0%	**Protein** 3g		Sugars 1g	
Polyunsaturated Fat 0g					
Monounsaturated Fat 0g		Vitamin A 2%　Vitamin C 8%		Calcium 2%　Iron 2%	

Healthy Choice Café Steamers Grilled Chicken Marinara with Parmesan

1 meal

Amount per serving	%DV	Amount per serving	%DV	Amount per serving	%DV
Calories 280		**Cholesterol** 35mg	12%	**Total Carbohydrate** 38g	13%
Total Fat 4.5g	7%	**Sodium** 570mg	24%	Dietary Fiber 6g	24%
Saturated Fat 1.5g	8%	**Protein** 20g		Sugars 7g	
Polyunsaturated Fat 1g					
Monounsaturated Fat 2g		Vitamin A 15%　Vitamin C 0%		Calcium 6%　Iron 10%	

Healthy Choice Café Steamers Grilled Chicken Pesto with Vegetables

1 meal

Amount per serving	%DV	Amount per serving	%DV	Amount per serving	%DV
Calories 310		**Cholesterol** 40mg	13%	**Total Carbohydrate** 37g	12%
Total Fat 9g	14%	**Sodium** 550mg	23%	Dietary Fiber 3g	12%
Saturated Fat 2.5g	12%	**Protein** 21g		Sugars 3g	
Polyunsaturated Fat 1g					
Monounsaturated Fat 5g		Vitamin A 10% Vitamin C 0%		Calcium 4% Iron 10%	

Healthy Choice Café Steamers Mediterranean Inspired Grilled Basil Chicken

1 meal

Amount per serving	%DV	Amount per serving	%DV	Amount per serving	%DV
Calories 270		**Cholesterol** 25mg	8%	**Total Carbohydrate** 35g	12%
Total Fat 6g	9%	**Sodium** 500mg	21%	Dietary Fiber 6g	24%
Saturated Fat 1.5g	8%	**Protein** 18g		Sugars 4g	
Polyunsaturated Fat 1.5g					
Monounsaturated Fat 2.5g		Vitamin A 10% Vitamin C 0%		Calcium 4% Iron 10%	

Mrs. Leepers, Gluten-Free Chicken Alfredo

1 cup

Amount per serving	%DV	Amount per serving	%DV	Amount per serving	%DV
Calories 330		**Cholesterol** 10mg	3%	**Total Carbohydrate** 27g	9%
Total Fat 3.5g	5%	**Sodium** 590mg	25%	Dietary Fiber 1g	4%
Saturated Fat 2g	10%	**Protein** 3g		Sugars 2g	
Polyunsaturated Fat 0g					
Monounsaturated Fat 0g		Vitamin A 4% Vitamin C 2%		Calcium 10% Iron 10%	

Condiments

Annie's, Organic Dijon Mustard

1 tsp / 5g

Amount per serving	%DV	Amount per serving	%DV	Amount per serving	%DV
Calories 5		**Cholesterol** 0mg	0%	**Total Carbohydrate** 1g	0%
Total Fat 0g	0%	**Sodium** 120mg	5%	Dietary Fiber 0g	0%
Saturated Fat 0g	0%	**Protein** 0g		Sugars 0g	
Polyunsaturated Fat 0g					
Monounsaturated Fat 0g		Vitamin A 0% Vitamin C 0%		Calcium 0% Iron 0%	

Annie's, Organic Honey Mustard

1 tsp / 5g

Amount per serving	%DV	Amount per serving	%DV	Amount per serving	%DV
Calories 10		**Cholesterol** 0mg	0%	**Total Carbohydrate** 2g	1%
Total Fat 0g	0%	**Sodium** 45mg	2%	Dietary Fiber 0g	0%
Saturated Fat 0g	0%	**Protein** 0g		Sugars 2g	
Polyunsaturated Fat 0g					
Monounsaturated Fat 0g		Vitamin A 0% Vitamin C 0%		Calcium 0% Iron 0%	

Annie's, Organic Horseradish Mustard

1 tsp / 5g

Amount per serving	%DV	Amount per serving	%DV	Amount per serving	%DV
Calories 5		**Cholesterol** 0mg	0%	**Total Carbohydrate** 1g	0%
Total Fat 0g	0%	**Sodium** 60mg	3%	Dietary Fiber 0g	0%
Saturated Fat 0g	0%	**Protein** 0g		Sugars 0g	
Polyunsaturated Fat 0g					
Monounsaturated Fat 0g		Vitamin A 0% Vitamin C 0%		Calcium 0% Iron 0%	

Annie's, Organic Ketchup

1 tbsp / 17g

Amount per serving	%DV	Amount per serving	%DV	Amount per serving	%DV
Calories 15		**Cholesterol** 0mg	0%	**Total Carbohydrate** 5g	2%
Total Fat 0g	0%	**Sodium** 170mg	7%	Dietary Fiber 0g	0%
Saturated Fat 0g	0%	**Protein** 0g		Sugars 4g	
Polyunsaturated Fat 0g					
Monounsaturated Fat 0g		Vitamin A 2% Vitamin C 0%		Calcium 0% Iron 0%	

Annie's, Organic Yellow Mustard

1 tsp / 5g

Amount per serving	%DV	Amount per serving	%DV	Amount per serving	%DV
Calories 5		**Cholesterol** 0mg	0%	**Total Carbohydrate** 1g	0%
Total Fat 0g	0%	**Sodium** 50mg	2%	Dietary Fiber 0g	0%
Saturated Fat 0g	0%	**Protein** 0g		Sugars 0g	
Polyunsaturated Fat 0g					
Monounsaturated Fat 0g		Vitamin A 0% Vitamin C 0%		Calcium 0% Iron 0%	

Boar's Head, Delicatessen Style Mustard

1 tsp / 5g

Amount per serving	%DV	Amount per serving	%DV	Amount per serving	%DV
Calories 0.1		**Cholesterol** 0mg	0%	**Total Carbohydrate** 0g	0%
Total Fat 0g	0%	**Sodium** 40mg	2%	Dietary Fiber 0g	0%
Saturated Fat 0g	0%	**Protein** 0g		Sugars 0g	
Polyunsaturated Fat 0g					
Monounsaturated Fat 0g		Vitamin A 0% Vitamin C 0%		Calcium 0% Iron 0%	

Boar's Head, Honey Mustard

1 tsp / 5g

Amount per serving	%DV	Amount per serving	%DV	Amount per serving	%DV
Calories 10		**Cholesterol** 0mg	0%	**Total Carbohydrate** 2g	1%
Total Fat 0g	0%	**Sodium** 25mg	1%	Dietary Fiber 0g	0%
Saturated Fat 0g	0%	**Protein** 0g		Sugars 1g	
Polyunsaturated Fat 0g					
Monounsaturated Fat 0g		Vitamin A 0% Vitamin C 0%		Calcium 0% Iron 0%	

Boar's Head, Horseradish

1 tsp / 5g

Amount per serving	%DV	Amount per serving	%DV	Amount per serving	%DV
Calories 0.1		**Cholesterol** 0mg	0%	**Total Carbohydrate** 0g	0%
Total Fat 0g	0%	**Sodium** 30mg	1%	Dietary Fiber 0g	0%
Saturated Fat 0g	0%	**Protein** 0g		Sugars 0g	
Polyunsaturated Fat 0g					
Monounsaturated Fat 0g		Vitamin A 0% Vitamin C 0%		Calcium 0% Iron 0%	

Eden Foods, Brown Mustard, Organic Jar

1 tsp / 5.2g

Amount per serving	%DV	Amount per serving	%DV	Amount per serving	%DV
Calories 0.1		**Cholesterol** 0mg	0%	**Total Carbohydrate** 1g	0%
Total Fat 0g	0%	**Sodium** 80mg	3%	Dietary Fiber 0g	0%
Saturated Fat 0g	0%	**Protein** 0g		Sugars 0g	
Polyunsaturated Fat 0g					
Monounsaturated Fat 0g		Vitamin A 0% Vitamin C 0%		Calcium 0% Iron 0%	

Eden Foods, Brown Mustard, Organic, Squeeze Bottle

1 tsp / 5.2g

Amount per serving	%DV	Amount per serving	%DV	Amount per serving	%DV
Calories 0.1		**Cholesterol** 0mg	0%	**Total Carbohydrate** 1g	0%
Total Fat 0g	0%	**Sodium** 80mg	3%	Dietary Fiber 0g	0%
Saturated Fat 0g	0%	**Protein** 0g		Sugars 0g	
Polyunsaturated Fat 0g					
Monounsaturated Fat 0g		Vitamin A 0% Vitamin C 0%		Calcium 0% Iron 0%	

Eden Foods, Brown Rice Vinegar, Organic, Imported

1 tbsp / 14g

Amount per serving	%DV	Amount per serving	%DV	Amount per serving	%DV
Calories 2		**Cholesterol** 0mg	0%	**Total Carbohydrate** 0g	0%
Total Fat 0g	0%	**Sodium** 0mg	0%	Dietary Fiber 0g	0%
Saturated Fat 0g	0%	**Protein** 0g		Sugars 0g	
Polyunsaturated Fat 0g					
Monounsaturated Fat 0g		Vitamin A 0% Vitamin C 0%		Calcium 0% Iron 0%	

Eden Foods, Mirin (Rice Cooking Wine)

1 tbsp / 17g

Amount per serving	%DV	Amount per serving	%DV	Amount per serving	%DV
Calories 25		**Cholesterol** 0mg	0%	**Total Carbohydrate** 7g	2%
Total Fat 0g	0%	**Sodium** 130mg	5%	Dietary Fiber 0g	0%
Saturated Fat 0g	0%	**Protein** 0g		Sugars 4g	
Polyunsaturated Fat 0g					
Monounsaturated Fat 0g		Vitamin A 0% Vitamin C 0%		Calcium 0% Iron 0%	

Eden Foods, Organic Shiro Miso (Aged and Fermented Rice and Soybeans)

1 tbsp / 17g

Amount per serving	%DV	Amount per serving	%DV	Amount per serving	%DV
Calories 30		Cholesterol 0mg	0%	Total Carbohydrate 6g	2%
Total Fat 0.5g	1%	Sodium 330mg	14%	Dietary Fiber 1g	4%
Saturated Fat 0g	0%	Protein 1g		Sugars 4g	
Polyunsaturated Fat 0g					
Monounsaturated Fat 0g		Vitamin A 0% Vitamin C 0%		Calcium 0% Iron 0%	

Eden Foods, Red Wine Vinegar

1 tbsp / 14g

Amount per serving	%DV	Amount per serving	%DV	Amount per serving	%DV
Calories 0.1		Cholesterol 0mg	0%	Total Carbohydrate 0g	0%
Total Fat 0g	0%	Sodium 0mg	0%	Dietary Fiber 0g	0%
Saturated Fat 0g	0%	Protein 0g		Sugars 0g	
Polyunsaturated Fat 0g					
Monounsaturated Fat 0g		Vitamin A 0% Vitamin C 0%		Calcium 0% Iron 0%	

Eden Foods, Red Wine Vinegar, Raw, Unpasteurized

1 tbsp / 14g

Amount per serving	%DV	Amount per serving	%DV	Amount per serving	%DV
Calories 0.1		Cholesterol 0mg	0%	Total Carbohydrate 0g	0%
Total Fat 0g	0%	Sodium 0mg	0%	Dietary Fiber 0g	0%
Saturated Fat 0g	0%	Protein 0g		Sugars 0g	
Polyunsaturated Fat 0g					
Monounsaturated Fat 0g		Vitamin A 0% Vitamin C 0%		Calcium 0% Iron 0%	

Eden Foods, Tekka (Miso Condiment)

1 tsp / 1.3g

Amount per serving	%DV	Amount per serving	%DV	Amount per serving	%DV
Calories 5		Cholesterol 0mg	0%	Total Carbohydrate 1g	0%
Total Fat 0g	0%	Sodium 70mg	3%	Dietary Fiber 0g	0%
Saturated Fat 0g	0%	Protein 1g		Sugars 0g	
Polyunsaturated Fat 0g					
Monounsaturated Fat 0g		Vitamin A 0% Vitamin C 0%		Calcium 0% Iron 2%	

Eden Foods, Yellow Mustard, Organic, Jar

1 tsp / 5.2g

Amount per serving	%DV	Amount per serving	%DV	Amount per serving	%DV
Calories 0.1		Cholesterol 0mg	0%	Total Carbohydrate 0g	0%
Total Fat 0g	0%	Sodium 80mg	3%	Dietary Fiber 0g	0%
Saturated Fat 0g	0%	Protein 0g		Sugars 0g	
Polyunsaturated Fat 0g					
Monounsaturated Fat 0g		Vitamin A 0% Vitamin C 0%		Calcium 0% Iron 0%	

Eden Foods, Yellow Mustard, Organic, Squeeze Bottle

1 tsp / 5.2g

Amount per serving	%DV	Amount per serving	%DV	Amount per serving	%DV
Calories 0.1		**Cholesterol** 0mg	0%	**Total Carbohydrate** 0g	0%
Total Fat 0g	0%	**Sodium** 80mg	3%	Dietary Fiber 0g	0%
Saturated Fat 0g	0%	**Protein** 0g		Sugars 0g	
Polyunsaturated Fat 0g					
Monounsaturated Fat 0g		Vitamin A 0% Vitamin C 0%		Calcium 0% Iron 0%	

Lucini, 10-Year Gran Riserva Balsamico Vinegar

1 tbsp / 15 ml

Amount per serving	%DV	Amount per serving	%DV	Amount per serving	%DV
Calories 20		**Cholesterol** 0mg	0%	**Total Carbohydrate** 4g	1%
Total Fat 0g	0%	**Sodium** 0mg	0%	Dietary Fiber 0g	0%
Saturated Fat 0g	0%	**Protein** 0g		Sugars 4g	
Polyunsaturated Fat 0g					
Monounsaturated Fat 0g		Vitamin A 0% Vitamin C 0%		Calcium 0% Iron 0%	

Lucini, Estate Select Balsamic Vinegar

1 tbsp / 15 ml

Amount per serving	%DV	Amount per serving	%DV	Amount per serving	%DV
Calories 20		**Cholesterol** 0mg	0%	**Total Carbohydrate** 4g	1%
Total Fat 0g	0%	**Sodium** 0mg	0%	Dietary Fiber 0g	0%
Saturated Fat 0g	0%	**Protein** 0g		Sugars 4g	
Polyunsaturated Fat 0g					
Monounsaturated Fat 0g		Vitamin A 0% Vitamin C 0%		Calcium 0% Iron 0%	

Lucini, Pinot Grigio Italian Wine Vinegar

1 tbsp / 15 ml

Amount per serving	%DV	Amount per serving	%DV	Amount per serving	%DV
Calories 0.1		**Cholesterol** 0mg	0%	**Total Carbohydrate** 0g	0%
Total Fat 0g	0%	**Sodium** 2mg	0%	Dietary Fiber 0g	0%
Saturated Fat 0g	0%	**Protein** 0g		Sugars 0g	
Polyunsaturated Fat 0g					
Monounsaturated Fat 0g		Vitamin A 0% Vitamin C 0%		Calcium 0% Iron 0%	

Lucini, Pinot Noir Italian Wine Vinegar

1 tbsp / 15 ml

Amount per serving	%DV	Amount per serving	%DV	Amount per serving	%DV
Calories 1		**Cholesterol** 0mg	0%	**Total Carbohydrate** 0g	0%
Total Fat 0g	0%	**Sodium** 2mg	0%	Dietary Fiber 0g	0%
Saturated Fat 0g	0%	**Protein** 0g		Sugars 0g	
Polyunsaturated Fat 0g					
Monounsaturated Fat 0g		Vitamin A 0% Vitamin C 0%		Calcium 0% Iron 0%	

Lucini, Savory Fig Balsamico Artisan Vinegar

1 tbsp / 15 ml

Amount per serving	%DV	Amount per serving	%DV	Amount per serving	%DV
Calories 30		**Cholesterol** 0mg	0%	**Total Carbohydrate** 7g	2%
Total Fat 0g	0%	**Sodium** 3mg	0%	Dietary Fiber 0g	0%
Saturated Fat 0g	0%	**Protein** 0g		Sugars 7g	
Polyunsaturated Fat 0g					
Monounsaturated Fat 0g		Vitamin A 0%	Vitamin C 0%	Calcium 0%	Iron 0%

Mezzetta, Crushed Garlic

2 tsp / 15g

Amount per serving	%DV	Amount per serving	%DV	Amount per serving	%DV
Calories 20		**Cholesterol** 0mg	0%	**Total Carbohydrate** 4g	1%
Total Fat 0g	0%	**Sodium** 0mg	0%	Dietary Fiber 0g	0%
Saturated Fat 0g	0%	**Protein** 1g		Sugars 0g	
Polyunsaturated Fat 0g					
Monounsaturated Fat 0g		Vitamin A 0%	Vitamin C 0%	Calcium 0%	Iron 0%

Pace, Green Taco Sauce

1 tbsp

Amount per serving	%DV	Amount per serving	%DV	Amount per serving	%DV
Calories 10		**Cholesterol** 0mg	0%	**Total Carbohydrate** 2g	1%
Total Fat 0g	0%	**Sodium** 130mg	5%	Dietary Fiber 0g	0%
Saturated Fat 0g	0%	**Protein** 0g		Sugars 1g	
Polyunsaturated Fat 0g					
Monounsaturated Fat 0g		Vitamin A 2%	Vitamin C 0%	Calcium 0%	Iron 0%

Pace, Picante Sauce

2 tbsp / 30ml

Amount per serving	%DV	Amount per serving	%DV	Amount per serving	%DV
Calories 10		**Cholesterol** 0mg	0%	**Total Carbohydrate** 3g	1%
Total Fat 0g	0%	**Sodium** 250mg	10%	Dietary Fiber 1g	4%
Saturated Fat 0g	0%	**Protein** 0g		Sugars 2g	
Polyunsaturated Fat 0g					
Monounsaturated Fat 0g		Vitamin A 2%	Vitamin C 0%	Calcium 0%	Iron 0%

Pace, Picante Sauce, Hot

2 tbsp / 30ml

Amount per serving	%DV	Amount per serving	%DV	Amount per serving	%DV
Calories 10		**Cholesterol** 0mg	0%	**Total Carbohydrate** 3g	1%
Total Fat 0g	0%	**Sodium** 250mg	10%	Dietary Fiber 1g	4%
Saturated Fat 0g	0%	**Protein** 0g		Sugars 2g	
Polyunsaturated Fat 0g					
Monounsaturated Fat 0g		Vitamin A 2%	Vitamin C 0%	Calcium 0%	Iron 0%

Pace, Picante Sauce, Medium

2 tbsp

Amount per serving	%DV	Amount per serving	%DV	Amount per serving	%DV
Calories 10		**Cholesterol** 0mg	0%	**Total Carbohydrate** 3g	1%
Total Fat 0g	0%	**Sodium** 250mg	10%	Dietary Fiber 1g	4%
Saturated Fat 0g	0%	**Protein** 0g		Sugars 2g	
Polyunsaturated Fat 0g					
Monounsaturated Fat 0g		Vitamin A 2%	Vitamin C 0%	Calcium 0%	Iron 0%

Pace, Picante Sauce, Mild

2 tbsp

Amount per serving	%DV	Amount per serving	%DV	Amount per serving	%DV
Calories 10		**Cholesterol** 0mg	0%	**Total Carbohydrate** 3g	1%
Total Fat 0g	0%	**Sodium** 250mg	10%	Dietary Fiber 1g	4%
Saturated Fat 0g	0%	**Protein** 0g		Sugars 2g	
Polyunsaturated Fat 0g					
Monounsaturated Fat 0g		Vitamin A 2%	Vitamin C 0%	Calcium 0%	Iron 0%

Pace, Red Taco Sauce

1 tbsp

Amount per serving	%DV	Amount per serving	%DV	Amount per serving	%DV
Calories 10		**Cholesterol** 0mg	0%	**Total Carbohydrate** 2g	1%
Total Fat 0g	0%	**Sodium** 130mg	5%	Dietary Fiber 0g	0%
Saturated Fat 0g	0%	**Protein** 0g		Sugars 1g	
Polyunsaturated Fat 0g					
Monounsaturated Fat 0g		Vitamin A 2%	Vitamin C 0%	Calcium 0%	Iron 0%

Thumann's, Dusseldorf Mustard

1 tsp / 5g

Amount per serving	%DV	Amount per serving	%DV	Amount per serving	%DV
Calories 3.7		**Cholesterol** 0mg	0%	**Total Carbohydrate** 0g	0%
Total Fat 0g	0%	**Sodium** 63mg	3%	Dietary Fiber 0g	0%
Saturated Fat 0g	0%	**Protein** 0g		Sugars 0g	
Polyunsaturated Fat 0g					
Monounsaturated Fat 0g		Vitamin A 0%	Vitamin C 0%	Calcium 0%	Iron 0%

Thumann's, Gourmet Onions in Sauce

1 tsp / 16g

Amount per serving	%DV	Amount per serving	%DV	Amount per serving	%DV
Calories 10		**Cholesterol** 0mg	0%	**Total Carbohydrate** 3g	1%
Total Fat 0g	0%	**Sodium** 105mg	4%	Dietary Fiber 0g	0%
Saturated Fat 0g	0%	**Protein** 0g		Sugars 2g	
Polyunsaturated Fat 0g					
Monounsaturated Fat 0g		Vitamin A 0%	Vitamin C 0%	Calcium 0%	Iron 0%

Vinegar, Balsamic

1 tbsp / 16g

Amount per serving	%DV	Amount per serving	%DV	Amount per serving	%DV
Calories 14		Cholesterol 0mg	0%	Total Carbohydrate 3g	1%
Total Fat 0g	0%	Sodium 4mg	0%	Dietary Fiber 0g	0%
Saturated Fat 0g	0%	Protein 0g		Sugars 2g	
Polyunsaturated Fat 0g					
Monounsaturated Fat 0g		Vitamin A 0% Vitamin C 0%		Calcium 0% Iron 1%	

Vinegar, Cider

1 tbsp / 15g

Amount per serving	%DV	Amount per serving	%DV	Amount per serving	%DV
Calories 3		Cholesterol 0mg	0%	Total Carbohydrate 0g	0%
Total Fat 0g	0%	Sodium 1mg	0%	Dietary Fiber 0g	0%
Saturated Fat 0g	0%	Protein 0g		Sugars 0g	
Polyunsaturated Fat 0g					
Monounsaturated Fat 0g		Vitamin A 0% Vitamin C 0%		Calcium 0% Iron 0%	

Vinegar, Distilled

1 tbsp / 15g

Amount per serving	%DV	Amount per serving	%DV	Amount per serving	%DV
Calories 3		Cholesterol 0mg	0%	Total Carbohydrate 0g	0%
Total Fat 0g	0%	Sodium 0mg	0%	Dietary Fiber 0g	0%
Saturated Fat 0g	0%	Protein 0g		Sugars 0g	
Polyunsaturated Fat 0g					
Monounsaturated Fat 0g		Vitamin A 0% Vitamin C 0%		Calcium 0% Iron 0%	

Vinegar, Red Wine

1 tbsp / 15g

Amount per serving	%DV	Amount per serving	%DV	Amount per serving	%DV
Calories 3		Cholesterol 0mg	0%	Total Carbohydrate 0g	0%
Total Fat 0g	0%	Sodium 1mg	0%	Dietary Fiber 0g	0%
Saturated Fat 0g	0%	Protein 0g		Sugars 0g	
Polyunsaturated Fat 0g					
Monounsaturated Fat 0g		Vitamin A 0% Vitamin C 0%		Calcium 0% Iron 0%	

Souffles

Garden Lites, Frozen, Low Calorie Broccoli Souffle

7 oz container / 1 souffle

Amount per serving	%DV	Amount per serving	%DV	Amount per serving	%DV
Calories 140		Cholesterol 0mg	0%	Total Carbohydrate 27g	9%
Total Fat 1.5g	2%	Sodium 490mg	20%	Dietary Fiber 4g	16%
Saturated Fat 0g	0%	Protein 11g		Sugars 5g	
Polyunsaturated Fat 0g					
Monounsaturated Fat 0g		Vitamin A 45% Vitamin C 90%		Calcium 8% Iron 6%	

Garden Lites, Frozen, Low Calorie Butternut Squash Souffle

7 oz container / 1 souffle

Amount per serving	%DV	Amount per serving	%DV	Amount per serving	%DV
Calories 180		**Cholesterol** 55mg	18%	**Total Carbohydrate** 35g	12%
Total Fat 2g	3%	**Sodium** 135mg	6%	Dietary Fiber 3g	12%
Saturated Fat 0.5g	2%	**Protein** 8g		Sugars 18g	
Polyunsaturated Fat 0g					
Monounsaturated Fat 0g		Vitamin A 120% Vitamin C 15%		Calcium 2% Iron 4%	

Garden Lites, Frozen, Low Calorie Cauliflower Souffle

7 oz container / 1 souffle

Amount per serving	%DV	Amount per serving	%DV	Amount per serving	%DV
Calories 140		**Cholesterol** 0mg	0%	**Total Carbohydrate** 27g	9%
Total Fat 1.5g	2%	**Sodium** 490mg	20%	Dietary Fiber 4g	16%
Saturated Fat 0g	0%	**Protein** 9g		Sugars 7g	
Polyunsaturated Fat 0g					
Monounsaturated Fat 0g		Vitamin A 30% Vitamin C 90%		Calcium 4% Iron 4%	

Garden Lites, Frozen, Low Calorie Roasted Vegetable Souffle

7 oz container / 1 souffle

Amount per serving	%DV	Amount per serving	%DV	Amount per serving	%DV
Calories 140		**Cholesterol** 0mg	0%	**Total Carbohydrate** 28g	9%
Total Fat 1.5g	2%	**Sodium** 490mg	20%	Dietary Fiber 4g	16%
Saturated Fat 0g	0%	**Protein** 9g		Sugars 8g	
Polyunsaturated Fat 0g					
Monounsaturated Fat 0g		Vitamin A 170% Vitamin C 60%		Calcium 8% Iron 6%	

Garden Lites, Frozen, Low Calorie Spinach Souffle

7 oz container / 1 souffle

Amount per serving	%DV	Amount per serving	%DV	Amount per serving	%DV
Calories 140		**Cholesterol** 0mg	0%	**Total Carbohydrate** 26g	9%
Total Fat 1.5g	2%	**Sodium** 490mg	20%	Dietary Fiber 4g	16%
Saturated Fat 0g	0%	**Protein** 10g		Sugars 6g	
Polyunsaturated Fat 0g					
Monounsaturated Fat 0g		Vitamin A 6% Vitamin C 40%		Calcium 2% Iron 4%	

Garden Lites, Frozen, Low Calorie Zucchini Souffle

7 oz container / 1 souffle

Amount per serving	%DV	Amount per serving	%DV	Amount per serving	%DV
Calories 140		**Cholesterol** 0mg	0%	**Total Carbohydrate** 30g	10%
Total Fat 1.5g	2%	**Sodium** 490mg	20%	Dietary Fiber 3g	12%
Saturated Fat 0g	0%	**Protein** 9g		Sugars 6g	
Polyunsaturated Fat 0g					
Monounsaturated Fat 0g		Vitamin A 6% Vitamin C 40%		Calcium 2% Iron 4%	

Thai Cuisine

Thai Kitchen, Green Curry Kit

84g

Amount per serving	%DV	Amount per serving	%DV	Amount per serving	%DV
Calories 210		**Cholesterol** 0mg	0%	**Total Carbohydrate** 35g	12%
Total Fat 6g	9%	**Sodium** 310mg	13%	Dietary Fiber 1g	4%
Saturated Fat 5g	25%	**Protein** 3g		Sugars 4g	
Polyunsaturated Fat 0g					
Monounsaturated Fat 0g		Vitamin A 0% Vitamin C 0%		Calcium 2% Iron 4%	

Protein

Why Eat Protein?

Protein foods include both animal and plant proteins—meat, poultry, fish, eggs, beans, nuts, and seeds. These foods provide nutrients that are vital for health and maintenance of your body. Nutrients include B vitamins (niacin, thiamin, riboflavin, and B6), vitamin E, iron, zinc, and magnesium. Proteins function as building blocks for bones, muscles, cartilage, skin, and blood. B vitamins help the body release energy, play a vital role in the function of the nervous system, aid in the formation of red blood cells, and help build tissues. Iron is used to carry oxygen in the blood.

Seafood contains a range of nutrients, notably the omega-3 fatty acids: EPA and DHA. Eating about 8 ounces per week of a variety of seafood contributes to the prevention of heart disease.

Daily Goal

5½ ounces for an adult on a 2,000-calorie diet
8 ounces per week of fish

> 1 ounce equivalents: 1 ounce lean meat, poultry, or fish
> ½ oz. nuts or seeds (listed in Fats/Oils)
> 1 Tbsp. peanut butter (listed in Fats/Oils)
> ¼ cup cooked dried beans or peas
> ¼ cup tofu/roasted soybeans

Heart-Healthy Nutrients in Protein

Soy Protein–Soy is beneficial to overall cardiovascular health because it is high in polyunsaturated (good) fats, low in saturated fat and naturally cholesterol-free. When you substitute animal protein with soy proteins, you're replacing saturated fats and cholesterol with a much healthier protein for your heart. In addition, soy has been shown to improve blood vessel elasticity—a measure of how "hardened" your blood vessels are. Meat alternatives are often made with soy protein.

Check out the FDA-approved Health Claim for soy protein and risk of heart disease on page 26.

Omega-3 fatty acids benefit the hearts of healthy people and those at high risk for cardiovascular disease. Research has shown that omega-3 fatty acids decrease the risk of arrhythmias (abnormal heartbeats), which can lead to sudden death. Omega-3 fatty acids also decrease triglyceride levels, slow growth rate of atherosclerotic plaque, and lower blood pressure (slightly). The American Heart Association recommends eating fish, particularly fatty fish that is high in omega-3s, at least two times (two servings) a week. Each serving is 3.5 oz. cooked, or about ¾ cup of flaked fish. Fatty fish like salmon, mackerel, herring, rainbow trout, sardines, and albacore tuna are high in omega-3 fatty acids. You can also find omega-3 fats in 100% grass fed beef. Some eggs contain omega-3 fats as well.

Check out the FDA-approved Qualified Health Claim for omega-3 Fats and risk of heart disease on page 29.

Heart-Healthy Shopping Tips for Protein

- **Look for these FDA-Approved Heart Health Claims on Protein Foods:**

Saturated Fat, Cholesterol, and Trans Fat, and Reduced Risk of Heart Disease
"Diets low in saturated fat and cholesterol, and as low as possible in trans fat, may reduce the risk of heart disease."

Foods that display this claim must be low in saturated fat (1 gram or less) low cholesterol (20 mg or less) and contain less than 0.5 g trans fat per serving and contain less than 6.5 g total fat.

Dietary Saturated Fat and Cholesterol, and Risk of Coronary Heart Disease
"While many factors affect heart disease, diets low in saturated fat and cholesterol may reduce the risk of this disease."

Foods that make this claim must be low in total fat, saturated fat, and cholesterol.

Soy Protein and Risk of Coronary Heart Disease

(1) 25 grams of soy protein a day, as part of a diet low in saturated fat and cholesterol, may reduce the risk of heart disease. A serving of [name of food] supplies __ grams of soy protein.

(2) Diets low in saturated fat and cholesterol that include 25 grams of soy protein a day may reduce the risk of heart disease. One serving of [name of food] provides __ grams of soy protein.

Soy foods that carry this claim must contain at least 6.25 g soy protein per serving and be low in total fat, saturated fat, and cholesterol. Foods made from whole soybeans that contain no fat in addition to that inherent in the whole soybean are exempt from the "low fat" requirement.

Omega-3 Fatty Acids and Coronary Heart Disease
Supportive but not conclusive research shows that consumption of EPA and DHA omega-3 fatty acids may reduce the risk of coronary heart disease. One serving of [name of the food] provides ___ grams of EPA and DHA omega-3 fatty acids. [See nutrition information for total fat, saturated fat, and cholesterol content.]

Find this claim on conventional foods that contain EPA and DHA omega-3 fatty acids, including fish.

- Look for the American Heart Association's Heart-Check mark on protein food labels. You will find the AHA Heart-Check mark on meats (beef, lamb, pork, and game); poultry; seafood (fish and shellfish); deli meats; protein alternatives (soy, vegetables); legume and bean products; and liquid egg products. For more information on the Heart-Check mark, go to *www.heartcheckmark.org*.

- When choosing protein, look for low-fat options, such as lean meats, fish, or other foods with high levels of protein. Legumes, for example, can pack about 16 grams of protein per cup and are a low-fat and inexpensive alternative to meat.

- Use low-fat cooking methods for meats—bake, broil, or grill.

- Trim visible fat and skin from meat before cooking.

- Buy and prepare more fish. You should eat one serving of grilled or baked fish at least twice a week. (A serving is roughly the size of a checkbook.)

- Select fish rich in omega-3 fats—salmon, trout, or herring.

- Season fish with lemon juice and spices. Don't add cream sauces.

- Stay away from fried fish. It's very high in fat—often trans fat.

- Choose cuts of red meat and pork labeled "loin" and "round"; they usually have the least fat. • Stay away from fried fish. It's very high in fat—often trans fat.

- Look for 100% grass fed beef, which is lower in total fat and contains a good source of omega-3 fatty acids.

- Buy "choice" or "select" grades of beef rather than "prime," and be sure to trim off the fat before cooking.

- When buying or eating poultry, choose the leaner light meat (breasts) rather than the fattier dark meat (legs and thighs). Try the skinless version or remove the skin yourself.

- Select more meat substitutes such as dried beans, peas, lentils, or tofu (soybean curd) and use them as entrees or in salads and soups. A one-cup serving of cooked beans, peas, lentils, or tofu can replace a two-ounce serving of meat, poultry, or fish.

- Pick up nuts and seeds, which are good sources of protein and polyunsaturated and monounsaturated fats, but remember: they tend to be high in calories, so eat them in moderation.

- Choose main dishes that combine meat and vegetables together, such as low-fat soups or a stir-fry that emphasizes veggies.

- Vary your meals with more fish, beans, peas, nuts, and seeds.

- Watch portion size. Aim for a 2-to 3-ounce serving. MyPlate recommends that only ¼ of your plate should be a protein.

- Use egg whites or egg substitutes instead of egg yolks. (Substitute two egg-whites for each egg yolk in recipes that call for eggs.) Egg yolks are high in cholesterol. A medium-size egg yolk contains 185 mg cholesterol, and a large egg yolk has 210 mg cholesterol. The recommendation on cholesterol is 300 mg per day for general health and 200 mg a day for people at risk for heart disease.

- Look for whole eggs containing omega-3 fats and limit them to 4 whole eggs per week.

Shopping List Essentials

Lean or grass fed beef	Fish
Omega-3 eggs	Egg substitutes
Chicken	Almonds (listed in Fats/Oils)
Turkey	Beans and legumes

Criteria for Protein

Using the FDA guidelines for Heart Health Claims, the foods listed meet the following criteria per serving:

Meats (beef, lamb, pork, game, and organ) including poultry; lunch meats, sausage, protein alternatives (soy, nuts, vegetables), and legume and bean products.

- Total fat–5 grams or less
- Saturated fat–2 grams or less

- Trans fat–0.5 grams or less (Trans Fat is not listed in the charts because all items report 0 grams Trans Fat.)
- Cholesterol–95 mg or less
- Beneficial Nutrients–10% Daily Value or higher of one beneficial nutrient (vitamin A, vitamin C, iron, calcium, protein, or dietary fiber)
- Sodium–480 mg or less

Seafood (fish and shellfish)
- Total fat–16 grams or less
- Saturated fat–4 gram or lessl
- Trans fat–0.5 grams or less (Trans Fat is not listed in the charts because all items report 0 grams Trans Fat. Since foods with less than 0.5 grams of trans fat can list 0 grams in the Nutrition Facts, be sure to check the ingredients for partially hydrogenated fats to determine if a product contains any trans fats.)
- Cholesterol–95 mg or less
- Beneficial Nutrients–10% Daily Value or higher of one beneficial nutrient (vitamin A, vitamin C, iron, calcium, protein, or dietary fiber)
- Sodium–480 mg or less. Look for lower sodium levels to help reduce high blood pressure.

Fish that contains 500 mg or more of EPA and DHA omega-3s per 85 grams (3 ounces cooked) is recommended for heart health. Fish high in omega-3s are salmon, tuna, mackerel, rainbow trout, sea bass, swordfish, and sardines. Wild ocean caught fish may have a higher amount of omega-3 fats than farm raised fish.

High-fat cuts of meat do not make this list, and shrimp is low in fat but too high in cholesterol for this list. This does not mean that these are bad foods. Eat them occasionally and balance them with low-fat and low-cholesterol side dishes.

Beans, Peas, and Legumes

Arrowhead Mills, Adzuki Beans

1/4 cup / 41g

Amount per serving	%DV	Amount per serving	%DV	Amount per serving	%DV
Calories 130		**Cholesterol** 0mg	0%	**Total Carbohydrate** 26g	9%
Total Fat 0g	0%	**Sodium** 0mg	0%	Dietary Fiber 5g	20%
Saturated Fat 0g	0%	**Protein** 8g		Sugars 1g	
Polyunsaturated Fat 0g					
Monounsaturated Fat 0g		Vitamin A 0%	Vitamin C 0%	Calcium 2%	Iron 10%

Arrowhead Mills, Chickpeas (Garbanzos)

1/4 cup / 45g

Amount per serving	%DV	Amount per serving	%DV	Amount per serving	%DV
Calories 160		**Cholesterol** 0mg	0%	**Total Carbohydrate** 27g	9%
Total Fat 2.5g	4%	**Sodium** 10mg	0%	Dietary Fiber 8g	32%
Saturated Fat 0g	0%	**Protein** 9g		Sugars 5g	
Polyunsaturated Fat 0g					
Monounsaturated Fat 0g		Vitamin A 0%	Vitamin C 4%	Calcium 4%	Iron 15%

Arrowhead Mills, Green Lentils

1/4 cup / 44g

Amount per serving	%DV	Amount per serving	%DV	Amount per serving	%DV
Calories 150		**Cholesterol** 0mg	0%	**Total Carbohydrate** 27g	9%
Total Fat 1g	2%	**Sodium** 5mg	0%	Dietary Fiber 7g	28%
Saturated Fat 0g	0%	**Protein** 10g		Sugars 1g	
Polyunsaturated Fat 0g					
Monounsaturated Fat 0g		Vitamin A 2%	Vitamin C 0%	Calcium 2%	Iron 15%

Arrowhead Mills, Green Split Peas

1/4 cup / 44g

Amount per serving	%DV	Amount per serving	%DV	Amount per serving	%DV
Calories 160		**Cholesterol** 0mg	0%	**Total Carbohydrate** 24g	8%
Total Fat 1g	2%	**Sodium** 10mg	0%	Dietary Fiber 4g	16%
Saturated Fat 0g	0%	**Protein** 12g		Sugars 1g	
Polyunsaturated Fat 0g					
Monounsaturated Fat 0g		Vitamin A 2%	Vitamin C 2%	Calcium 2%	Iron 15%

Arrowhead Mills, Red Lentils

1/4 cup / 47g

Amount per serving	%DV	Amount per serving	%DV	Amount per serving	%DV
Calories 170		**Cholesterol** 0mg	0%	**Total Carbohydrate** 28g	9%
Total Fat 1g	2%	**Sodium** 5mg	0%	Dietary Fiber 7g	28%
Saturated Fat 0g	0%	**Protein** 13g		Sugars 1g	
Polyunsaturated Fat 0g					
Monounsaturated Fat 0g		Vitamin A 0%	Vitamin C 0%	Calcium 2%	Iron 15%

Arrowhead Mills, Sunflower Seeds

1/4 cup / 30g

Amount per serving	%DV	Amount per serving	%DV	Amount per serving	%DV
Calories 170		**Cholesterol** 0mg	0%	**Total Carbohydrate** 6g	2%
Total Fat 1g	2%	**Sodium** 0mg	0%	Dietary Fiber 3g	12%
Saturated Fat 1.5g	8%	**Protein** 7g		Sugars 1g	
Polyunsaturated Fat 0g					
Monounsaturated Fat 0g		Vitamin A 0% Vitamin C 0%		Calcium 4% Iron 10%	

Beans, Kidney, All Types, Mature Seeds, Raw

1 cup / 184g

Amount per serving	%DV	Amount per serving	%DV	Amount per serving	%DV
Calories 613		**Cholesterol** 0mg	0%	**Total Carbohydrate** 110g	37%
Total Fat 2g	3%	**Sodium** 44mg	2%	Dietary Fiber 46g	184%
Saturated Fat 0g	0%	**Protein** 43g		Sugars 4g	
Polyunsaturated Fat 0g					
Monounsaturated Fat 0g		Vitamin A 0% Vitamin C 14%		Calcium 26% Iron 84%	

Beans, Kidney, California Red, Mature Seeds, Cooked, Boiled, with Salt

1 cup / 177g

Amount per serving	%DV	Amount per serving	%DV	Amount per serving	%DV
Calories 219		**Cholesterol** 0mg	0%	**Total Carbohydrate** 40g	13%
Total Fat 0g	0%	**Sodium** 425mg	18%	Dietary Fiber 16g	64%
Saturated Fat 0g	0%	**Protein** 16g		Sugars 0g	
Polyunsaturated Fat 0g					
Monounsaturated Fat 0g		Vitamin A 0% Vitamin C 4%		Calcium 12% Iron 29%	

Beans, Kidney, California Red, Mature Seeds, Cooked, Boiled, without Salt

1 cup / 177g

Amount per serving	%DV	Amount per serving	%DV	Amount per serving	%DV
Calories 219		**Cholesterol** 0mg	0%	**Total Carbohydrate** 40g	13%
Total Fat 0g	0%	**Sodium** 7mg	0%	Dietary Fiber 16g	64%
Saturated Fat 0g	0%	**Protein** 16g		Sugars 0g	
Polyunsaturated Fat 0g					
Monounsaturated Fat 0g		Vitamin A 0% Vitamin C 4%		Calcium 12% Iron 29%	

Beans, Kidney, California Red, Mature Seeds, Raw

1 cup / 184g

Amount per serving	%DV	Amount per serving	%DV	Amount per serving	%DV
Calories 607		**Cholesterol** 0mg	0%	**Total Carbohydrate** 110g	37%
Total Fat 0g	0%	**Sodium** 20mg	1%	Dietary Fiber 46g	184%
Saturated Fat 0g	0%	**Protein** 45g		Sugars 0g	
Polyunsaturated Fat 0g					
Monounsaturated Fat 0g		Vitamin A 0% Vitamin C 14%		Calcium 36% Iron 96%	

Beans, Kidney, Mature Seeds, Sprouted, Raw

1 cup / 184g

Amount per serving	%DV	Amount per serving	%DV	Amount per serving	%DV
Calories 53		**Cholesterol** 0mg	0%	**Total Carbohydrate** 8g	3%
Total Fat 1g	2%	**Sodium** 11mg	0%	Dietary Fiber 0g	0%
Saturated Fat 0g	0%	**Protein** 8g		Sugars 0g	
Polyunsaturated Fat 0g					
Monounsaturated Fat 0g		Vitamin A 0%	Vitamin C 119%	Calcium 3%	Iron 8%

Beans, Kidney, Red, Mature Seeds, Cooked, Boiled, with Salt

1 cup / 177g

Amount per serving	%DV	Amount per serving	%DV	Amount per serving	%DV
Calories 225		**Cholesterol** 0mg	0%	**Total Carbohydrate** 40g	13%
Total Fat 1g	2%	**Sodium** 421mg	18%	Dietary Fiber 13g	52%
Saturated Fat 0g	0%	**Protein** 15g		Sugars 0.6g	
Polyunsaturated Fat 0g					
Monounsaturated Fat 0g		Vitamin A 0%	Vitamin C 4%	Calcium 5%	Iron 29%

Beans, Kidney, Red, Mature Seeds, Raw

1 cup / 184g

Amount per serving	%DV	Amount per serving	%DV	Amount per serving	%DV
Calories 620		**Cholesterol** 0mg	0%	**Total Carbohydrate** 113g	38%
Total Fat 0g	0%	**Sodium** 22mg	1%	Dietary Fiber 28g	112%
Saturated Fat 0g	0%	**Protein** 41g		Sugars 4g	
Polyunsaturated Fat 0g					
Monounsaturated Fat 0g		Vitamin A 0%	Vitamin C 14%	Calcium 15%	Iron 68%

Beans, Kidney, Royal Red, Mature Seeds, Cooked, Boiled with Salt

1 cup / 177g

Amount per serving	%DV	Amount per serving	%DV	Amount per serving	%DV
Calories 218		**Cholesterol** 0mg	0%	**Total Carbohydrate** 39g	13%
Total Fat 0g	0%	**Sodium** 427mg	18%	Dietary Fiber 16g	64%
Saturated Fat 0g	0%	**Protein** 17g		Sugars 0g	
Polyunsaturated Fat 0g					
Monounsaturated Fat 0g		Vitamin A 0%	Vitamin C 4%	Calcium 8%	Iron 27%

Beans, Kidney, Royal Red, Mature Seeds, Cooked, Boiled, without Salt

1 cup / 177g

Amount per serving	%DV	Amount per serving	%DV	Amount per serving	%DV
Calories 218		**Cholesterol** 0mg	0%	**Total Carbohydrate** 39g	13%
Total Fat 0g	0%	**Sodium** 9mg	0%	Dietary Fiber 16g	64%
Saturated Fat 0g	0%	**Protein** 17g		Sugars 0g	
Polyunsaturated Fat 0g					
Monounsaturated Fat 0g		Vitamin A 0%	Vitamin C 4%	Calcium 8%	Iron 27%

Beans, Kidney, Royal Red, Mature Seeds, Raw

1 cup / 184g

Amount per serving	%DV	Amount per serving	%DV	Amount per serving	%DV
Calories 605		**Cholesterol** 0mg	0%	**Total Carbohydrate** 107g	36%
Total Fat 1g	2%	**Sodium** 24mg	1%	Dietary Fiber 46g	184%
Saturated Fat 0g	0%	**Protein** 47g		Sugars 0g	
Polyunsaturated Fat 0g					
Monounsaturated Fat 0g		Vitamin A 0%	Vitamin C 14%	Calcium 24%	Iron 89%

Beans, Lima, Immature Seeds, Cooked, Boiled, Drained, without Salt

1 cup / 170g

Amount per serving	%DV	Amount per serving	%DV	Amount per serving	%DV
Calories 209		**Cholesterol** 0mg	0%	**Total Carbohydrate** 40g	13%
Total Fat 1g	2%	**Sodium** 29mg	1%	Dietary Fiber 9g	36%
Saturated Fat 0g	0%	**Protein** 12g		Sugars 3g	
Polyunsaturated Fat 0g					
Monounsaturated Fat 0g		Vitamin A 10%	Vitamin C 29%	Calcium 5%	Iron 23%

Beans, Lima, Immature Seeds, Frozen, Baby, Cooked, Boiled, Drained, without Salt

1 cup / 170g

Amount per serving	%DV	Amount per serving	%DV	Amount per serving	%DV
Calories 209		**Cholesterol** 0mg	0%	**Total Carbohydrate** 40g	13%
Total Fat 1g	2%	**Sodium** 430mg	18%	Dietary Fiber 9g	36%
Saturated Fat 0g	0%	**Protein** 12g		Sugars 3g	
Polyunsaturated Fat 0g					
Monounsaturated Fat 0g		Vitamin A 13%	Vitamin C 29%	Calcium 5%	Iron 23%

Beans, Lima, Immature Seeds, Frozen, Fordhook, Unprepared

1/2 cup

Amount per serving	%DV	Amount per serving	%DV	Amount per serving	%DV
Calories 301		**Cholesterol** 0mg	0%	**Total Carbohydrate** 16g	5%
Total Fat 1g	2%	**Sodium** 46mg	2%	Dietary Fiber 4g	16%
Saturated Fat 0g	0%	**Protein** 18g		Sugars 46g	
Polyunsaturated Fat 0g					
Monounsaturated Fat 0g		Vitamin A 4%	Vitamin C 26%	Calcium 2%	Iron 7%

Beans, Lima, Immature Seeds, Raw

1 cup / 156g

Amount per serving	%DV	Amount per serving	%DV	Amount per serving	%DV
Calories 176		**Cholesterol** 0mg	0%	**Total Carbohydrate** 31g	10%
Total Fat 1g	2%	**Sodium** 12mg	0%	Dietary Fiber 8g	32%
Saturated Fat 0g	0%	**Protein** 11g		Sugars 2g	
Polyunsaturated Fat 0g					
Monounsaturated Fat 0g		Vitamin A 7%	Vitamin C 61%	Calcium 5%	Iron 27%

Beans, Navy, Mature Seeds, Sprouted, Raw

1 cup / 104g

Amount per serving	%DV	Amount per serving	%DV	Amount per serving	%DV
Calories 70		**Cholesterol** 0mg	0%	**Total Carbohydrate** 14g	5%
Total Fat 1g	2%	**Sodium** 14mg	1%	Dietary Fiber 0g	0%
Saturated Fat 0g	0%	**Protein** 6g		Sugars 0g	
Polyunsaturated Fat 0g					
Monounsaturated Fat 0g		Vitamin A 0% · Vitamin C 33%		Calcium 2% · Iron 11%	

Beans, Pinto, Immature Seeds, Frozen, Cooked, Boiled, Drained, with Salt

1/3 package, 10 oz yields / 94g

Amount per serving	%DV	Amount per serving	%DV	Amount per serving	%DV
Calories 152		**Cholesterol** 0mg	0%	**Total Carbohydrate** 29g	10%
Total Fat 0g	0%	**Sodium** 300mg	12%	Dietary Fiber 8g	32%
Saturated Fat 0g	0%	**Protein** 9g		Sugars 0g	
Polyunsaturated Fat 0g					
Monounsaturated Fat 0g		Vitamin A 0% · Vitamin C 1%		Calcium 5% · Iron 14%	

Beans, Pinto, Immature Seeds, Frozen, Cooked, Boiled, Drained, without Salt

1/3 package / 10 oz yields / 94g

Amount per serving	%DV	Amount per serving	%DV	Amount per serving	%DV
Calories 152		**Cholesterol** 0mg	0%	**Total Carbohydrate** 29g	10%
Total Fat 0g	0%	**Sodium** 78mg	3%	Dietary Fiber 8g	32%
Saturated Fat 0g	0%	**Protein** 9g		Sugars 0g	
Polyunsaturated Fat 0g					
Monounsaturated Fat 0g		Vitamin A 0% · Vitamin C 1%		Calcium 5% · Iron 14%	

Beans, Pinto, Immature Seeds, Frozen, Unprepared

1/3 package / 10 oz / 94g

Amount per serving	%DV	Amount per serving	%DV	Amount per serving	%DV
Calories 160		**Cholesterol** 0mg	0%	**Total Carbohydrate** 31g	10%
Total Fat 0g	0%	**Sodium** 86mg	4%	Dietary Fiber 5g	20%
Saturated Fat 0g	0%	**Protein** 9g		Sugars 0g	
Polyunsaturated Fat 0g					
Monounsaturated Fat 0g		Vitamin A 0% · Vitamin C 2%		Calcium 5% · Iron 16%	

Beans, Pinto, Mature Seeds, Cooked, Boiled, with Salt

1 cup / 171g

Amount per serving	%DV	Amount per serving	%DV	Amount per serving	%DV
Calories 245		**Cholesterol** 0mg	0%	**Total Carbohydrate** 45g	15%
Total Fat 1g	2%	**Sodium** 407mg	17%	Dietary Fiber 15g	60%
Saturated Fat 0g	0%	**Protein** 15g		Sugars 1g	
Polyunsaturated Fat 0g					
Monounsaturated Fat 0g		Vitamin A 0% · Vitamin C 2%		Calcium 8% · Iron 20%	

Beans, Small White, Mature Seeds, Cooked, Boiled, with Salt

1 cup / 179g

Amount per serving	%DV	Amount per serving	%DV	Amount per serving	%DV
Calories 254		**Cholesterol** 0mg	0%	**Total Carbohydrate** 46g	15%
Total Fat 1g	2%	**Sodium** 426mg	18%	Dietary Fiber 19g	76%
Saturated Fat 0g	0%	**Protein** 16g		Sugars 0g	
Polyunsaturated Fat 0g					
Monounsaturated Fat 0g		Vitamin A 0%	Vitamin C 0%	Calcium 13%	Iron 28%

Beans, Small White, Mature Seeds, Cooked, Boiled, without Salt

1 cup / 179g

Amount per serving	%DV	Amount per serving	%DV	Amount per serving	%DV
Calories 254		**Cholesterol** 0mg	0%	**Total Carbohydrate** 46g	15%
Total Fat 1g	2%	**Sodium** 4mg	0%	Dietary Fiber 19g	76%
Saturated Fat 0g	0%	**Protein** 16g		Sugars 0g	
Polyunsaturated Fat 0g					
Monounsaturated Fat 0g		Vitamin A 0%	Vitamin C 0%	Calcium 13%	Iron 28%

Beans, Small White, Mature Seeds, Raw

1 cup / 215g

Amount per serving	%DV	Amount per serving	%DV	Amount per serving	%DV
Calories 722		**Cholesterol** 0mg	0%	**Total Carbohydrate** 134g	45%
Total Fat 3g	5%	**Sodium** 26mg	1%	Dietary Fiber 54g	216%
Saturated Fat 1g	5%	**Protein** 45g		Sugars 0g	
Polyunsaturated Fat 0g					
Monounsaturated Fat 0g		Vitamin A 0%	Vitamin C 0%	Calcium 37%	Iron 92%

Eden Foods, Aduki Beans, Dry, Organic

3 tbsp / 35g

Amount per serving	%DV	Amount per serving	%DV	Amount per serving	%DV
Calories 120		**Cholesterol** 0mg	0%	**Total Carbohydrate** 22g	7%
Total Fat 0g	0%	**Sodium** 0mg	0%	Dietary Fiber 5g	20%
Saturated Fat 0g	0%	**Protein** 7g		Sugars 0g	
Polyunsaturated Fat 0g					
Monounsaturated Fat 0g		Vitamin A 0%	Vitamin C 0%	Calcium 2%	Iron 10%

Eden Foods, Baked Beans with Sorghum & Mustard, Organic

1/2 cup / 130g

Amount per serving	%DV	Amount per serving	%DV	Amount per serving	%DV
Calories 150		**Cholesterol** 0mg	0%	**Total Carbohydrate** 27g	9%
Total Fat 0g	0%	**Sodium** 130mg	5%	Dietary Fiber 7g	28%
Saturated Fat 0g	0%	**Protein** 8g		Sugars 6g	
Polyunsaturated Fat 0g					
Monounsaturated Fat 0g		Vitamin A 0%	Vitamin C 0%	Calcium 10%	Iron 20%

Eden Foods, Black Beans, Organic

1/2 cup / 30g

Amount per serving	%DV	Amount per serving	%DV	Amount per serving	%DV
Calories 110		**Cholesterol** 0mg	0%	**Total Carbohydrate** 18g	6%
Total Fat 1g	2%	**Sodium** 15mg	1%	Dietary Fiber 6g	24%
Saturated Fat 0g	0%	**Protein** 7g		Sugars 0g	
Polyunsaturated Fat 0g					
Monounsaturated Fat 0g		Vitamin A 0% Vitamin C 0%		Calcium 6% Iron 10%	

Eden Foods, Black Eyed Peas, Organic

1/2 cup / 130g

Amount per serving	%DV	Amount per serving	%DV	Amount per serving	%DV
Calories 90		**Cholesterol** 0mg	0%	**Total Carbohydrate** 16g	5%
Total Fat 1g	2%	**Sodium** 25mg	1%	Dietary Fiber 4g	16%
Saturated Fat 0g	0%	**Protein** 6g		Sugars 1g	
Polyunsaturated Fat 0g					
Monounsaturated Fat 0g		Vitamin A 0% Vitamin C 0%		Calcium 2% Iron 10%	

Eden Foods, Black Turtle Beans, Dry, Organic

3 tbsp / 35g

Amount per serving	%DV	Amount per serving	%DV	Amount per serving	%DV
Calories 110		**Cholesterol** 0mg	0%	**Total Carbohydrate** 18g	6%
Total Fat 1g	2%	**Sodium** 15mg	0%	Dietary Fiber 6g	24%
Saturated Fat 0g	0%	**Protein** 7g		Sugars 1g	
Polyunsaturated Fat 0g					
Monounsaturated Fat 0g		Vitamin A 0% Vitamin C 0%		Calcium 6% Iron 10%	

Eden Foods, Brown Rice & Kidney Beans, Organic

1/2 cup / 130g

Amount per serving	%DV	Amount per serving	%DV	Amount per serving	%DV
Calories 110		**Cholesterol** 0mg	0%	**Total Carbohydrate** 23g	8%
Total Fat 1g	2%	**Sodium** 135mg	6%	Dietary Fiber 3g	12%
Saturated Fat 0g	0%	**Protein** 3g		Sugars 0g	
Polyunsaturated Fat 0g					
Monounsaturated Fat 0g		Vitamin A 0% Vitamin C 0%		Calcium 2% Iron 6%	

Eden Foods, Brown Rice & Lentils, Organic

1/2 cup / 130g

Amount per serving	%DV	Amount per serving	%DV	Amount per serving	%DV
Calories 120		**Cholesterol** 0mg	0%	**Total Carbohydrate** 23g	8%
Total Fat 1g	2%	**Sodium** 120mg	5%	Dietary Fiber 2g	8%
Saturated Fat 0g	0%	**Protein** 4g		Sugars 0g	
Polyunsaturated Fat 0g					
Monounsaturated Fat 0g		Vitamin A 0% Vitamin C 0%		Calcium 2% Iron 8%	

Eden Foods, Brown Rice & Mugwort Mochi, 100% Whole Grain

1 square / 50g

Amount per serving	%DV	Amount per serving	%DV	Amount per serving	%DV
Calories 110		**Cholesterol** 0mg	0%	**Total Carbohydrate** 24g	8%
Total Fat 1g	2%	**Sodium** 10mg	0%	Dietary Fiber 2g	8%
Saturated Fat 0g	0%	**Protein** 2g		Sugars 0g	
Polyunsaturated Fat 0g					
Monounsaturated Fat 0g		Vitamin A 0% Vitamin C 0%		Calcium 0% Iron 2%	

Eden Foods, Brown Rice & Pinto Beans, Organic

1/2 cup / 130g

Amount per serving	%DV	Amount per serving	%DV	Amount per serving	%DV
Calories 120		**Cholesterol** 0mg	0%	**Total Carbohydrate** 24g	8%
Total Fat 1g	2%	**Sodium** 140mg	6%	Dietary Fiber 3g	12%
Saturated Fat 0g	0%	**Protein** 4g		Sugars 1g	
Polyunsaturated Fat 0g					
Monounsaturated Fat 0g		Vitamin A 0% Vitamin C 0%		Calcium 2% Iron 6%	

Eden Foods, Butter Beans (Baby Lima), Organic

1/2 cup / 130g

Amount per serving	%DV	Amount per serving	%DV	Amount per serving	%DV
Calories 100		**Cholesterol** 0mg	0%	**Total Carbohydrate** 17g	6%
Total Fat 1g	2%	**Sodium** 35mg	1%	Dietary Fiber 4g	16%
Saturated Fat 0g	0%	**Protein** 5g		Sugars 0g	
Polyunsaturated Fat 0g					
Monounsaturated Fat 0g		Vitamin A 0% Vitamin C 0%		Calcium 2% Iron 10%	

Eden Foods, Cannellini (White Kidney) Beans, Organic

1/2 cup / 130g

Amount per serving	%DV	Amount per serving	%DV	Amount per serving	%DV
Calories 100		**Cholesterol** 0mg	0%	**Total Carbohydrate** 17g	6%
Total Fat 1g	2%	**Sodium** 40mg	2%	Dietary Fiber 5g	20%
Saturated Fat 0g	0%	**Protein** 6g		Sugars 1g	
Polyunsaturated Fat 0g					
Monounsaturated Fat 0g		Vitamin A 0% Vitamin C 0%		Calcium 4% Iron 10%	

Eden Foods, Caribbean Black Beans, Organic

1/2 cup / 130g

Amount per serving	%DV	Amount per serving	%DV	Amount per serving	%DV
Calories 90		**Cholesterol** 0mg	0%	**Total Carbohydrate** 20g	7%
Total Fat 0.5g	1%	**Sodium** 135mg	6%	Dietary Fiber 7g	28%
Saturated Fat 0g	0%	**Protein** 7g		Sugars 1g	
Polyunsaturated Fat 0g					
Monounsaturated Fat 0g		Vitamin A 0% Vitamin C 0%		Calcium 4% Iron 15%	

Eden Foods, Dark Red Kidney Beans, Dry, Organic

1/4 cup / 43g

Amount per serving	%DV	Amount per serving	%DV	Amount per serving	%DV
Calories 150		Cholesterol 0mg	0%	Total Carbohydrate 26g	7%
Total Fat 0g	0%	Sodium 10mg	0%	Dietary Fiber 13g	20%
Saturated Fat 0g	0%	Protein 10g		Sugars 1g	
Polyunsaturated Fat 0g					
Monounsaturated Fat 0g		Vitamin A 0%	Vitamin C 0%	Calcium 2%	Iron 15%

Eden Foods, Garbanzo Beans (Chick Peas), Organic

1/2 cup / 130g

Amount per serving	%DV	Amount per serving	%DV	Amount per serving	%DV
Calories 130		Cholesterol 0mg	0%	Total Carbohydrate 23g	8%
Total Fat 1g	2%	Sodium 30mg	1%	Dietary Fiber 5g	20%
Saturated Fat 0g	0%	Protein 7g		Sugars 1g	
Polyunsaturated Fat 0g					
Monounsaturated Fat 0g		Vitamin A 0%	Vitamin C 0%	Calcium 6%	Iron 8%

Eden Foods, Great Northern Beans, Organic

1/2 cup / 130g

Amount per serving	%DV	Amount per serving	%DV	Amount per serving	%DV
Calories 110		Cholesterol 0mg	0%	Total Carbohydrate 20g	7%
Total Fat 1g	2%	Sodium 45mg	2%	Dietary Fiber 8g	32%
Saturated Fat 0g	0%	Protein 5g		Sugars 1g	
Polyunsaturated Fat 0g					
Monounsaturated Fat 0g		Vitamin A 0%	Vitamin C 0%	Calcium 8%	Iron 8%

Eden Foods, Green Lentils, Dry, Organic

1/4 cup / 48g

Amount per serving	%DV	Amount per serving	%DV	Amount per serving	%DV
Calories 170		Cholesterol 0mg	0%	Total Carbohydrate 30g	7%
Total Fat 1g	2%	Sodium 10mg	0%	Dietary Fiber 12g	44%
Saturated Fat 0g	0%	Protein 11g		Sugars 0g	
Polyunsaturated Fat 0g					
Monounsaturated Fat 0g		Vitamin A 0%	Vitamin C 0%	Calcium 2%	Iron 20%

Eden Foods, Green Split Peas, Dry, Organic

3 tbsp / 35g

Amount per serving	%DV	Amount per serving	%DV	Amount per serving	%DV
Calories 120		Cholesterol 0mg	0%	Total Carbohydrate 21g	7%
Total Fat 0g	0%	Sodium 5mg	0%	Dietary Fiber 9g	36%
Saturated Fat 0g	0%	Protein 9g		Sugars 3g	
Polyunsaturated Fat 0g					
Monounsaturated Fat 0g		Vitamin A 2%	Vitamin C 2%	Calcium 2%	Iron 8%

Eden Foods, Kidney (Dark Red) Beans, Organic

1/2 cup / 130g

Amount per serving	%DV	Amount per serving	%DV	Amount per serving	%DV
Calories 100		**Cholesterol** 0mg	0%	**Total Carbohydrate** 18g	6%
Total Fat 0g	0%	**Sodium** 15mg	1%	Dietary Fiber 10g	40%
Saturated Fat 0g	0%	**Protein** 8g		Sugars 1g	
Polyunsaturated Fat 0g					
Monounsaturated Fat 0g		Vitamin A 0% Vitamin C 0%		Calcium 6% Iron 8%	

Eden Foods, Lentils with Onion & Bay Leaf, Organic

1/2 cup / 130g

Amount per serving	%DV	Amount per serving	%DV	Amount per serving	%DV
Calories 90		**Cholesterol** 0mg	0%	**Total Carbohydrate** 13g	4%
Total Fat 0g	0%	**Sodium** 210mg	9%	Dietary Fiber 4g	16%
Saturated Fat 0g	0%	**Protein** 8g		Sugars 0g	
Polyunsaturated Fat 0g					
Monounsaturated Fat 0g		Vitamin A 0% Vitamin C 0%		Calcium 4% Iron 10%	

Eden Foods, Navy Beans, Dry, Organic

1/4 cup / 48g

Amount per serving	%DV	Amount per serving	%DV	Amount per serving	%DV
Calories 160		**Cholesterol** 0mg	0%	**Total Carbohydrate** 28g	7%
Total Fat 0.5g	1%	**Sodium** 10mg	0%	Dietary Fiber 12g	36%
Saturated Fat 0g	0%	**Protein** 9g		Sugars 1g	
Polyunsaturated Fat 0g					
Monounsaturated Fat 0g		Vitamin A 0% Vitamin C 0%		Calcium 4% Iron 20%	

Eden Foods, Pinto Beans, Dry, Organic

1/4 cup / 43g

Amount per serving	%DV	Amount per serving	%DV	Amount per serving	%DV
Calories 140		**Cholesterol** 0mg	0%	**Total Carbohydrate** 26g	9%
Total Fat 0.5g	0%	**Sodium** 5mg	0%	Dietary Fiber 11g	20%
Saturated Fat 0g	0%	**Protein** 8g		Sugars 1g	
Polyunsaturated Fat 0g					
Monounsaturated Fat 0g		Vitamin A 0% Vitamin C 0%		Calcium 2% Iron 15%	

Eden Foods, Pinto Beans, Organic

1/2 cup / 130g

Amount per serving	%DV	Amount per serving	%DV	Amount per serving	%DV
Calories 110		**Cholesterol** 0mg	0%	**Total Carbohydrate** 18g	6%
Total Fat 1g	2%	**Sodium** 15mg	1%	Dietary Fiber 6g	24%
Saturated Fat 0g	0%	**Protein** 6g		Sugars 1g	
Polyunsaturated Fat 0g					
Monounsaturated Fat 0g		Vitamin A 0% Vitamin C 0%		Calcium 6% Iron 10%	

Eden Foods, Refried Black Beans, Organic

1/2 cup / 130g

Amount per serving	%DV	Amount per serving	%DV	Amount per serving	%DV
Calories 110		**Cholesterol** 0mg	0%	**Total Carbohydrate** 18g	6%
Total Fat 1.5g	2%	**Sodium** 180mg	8%	Dietary Fiber 7g	28%
Saturated Fat 0g	0%	**Protein** 6g		Sugars 0g	
Polyunsaturated Fat 0g					
Monounsaturated Fat 0g		Vitamin A 0%	Vitamin C 0%	Calcium 4%	Iron 15%

Eden Foods, Refried Black Soy & Black Beans, Organic

1/2 cup / 130g

Amount per serving	%DV	Amount per serving	%DV	Amount per serving	%DV
Calories 90		**Cholesterol** 0mg	0%	**Total Carbohydrate** 13g	4%
Total Fat 3g	5%	**Sodium** 170mg	7%	Dietary Fiber 6g	24%
Saturated Fat 0.5g	3%	**Protein** 8g		Sugars 1g	
Polyunsaturated Fat 0g					
Monounsaturated Fat 0g		Vitamin A 0%	Vitamin C 0%	Calcium 4%	Iron 10%

Eden Foods, Refried Kidney Beans, Organic

1/2 cup / 130g

Amount per serving	%DV	Amount per serving	%DV	Amount per serving	%DV
Calories 80		**Cholesterol** 0mg	0%	**Total Carbohydrate** 15g	5%
Total Fat 1g	2%	**Sodium** 180mg	8%	Dietary Fiber 6g	24%
Saturated Fat 0g	0%	**Protein** 7g		Sugars 0g	
Polyunsaturated Fat 0g					
Monounsaturated Fat 0g		Vitamin A 0%	Vitamin C 0%	Calcium 4%	Iron 10%

Eden Foods, Refried Pinto Beans, Organic

1/2 cup / 130g

Amount per serving	%DV	Amount per serving	%DV	Amount per serving	%DV
Calories 90		**Cholesterol** 0mg	0%	**Total Carbohydrate** 19g	6%
Total Fat 1g	2%	**Sodium** 180mg	8%	Dietary Fiber 7g	28%
Saturated Fat 0g	0%	**Protein** 6g		Sugars 1g	
Polyunsaturated Fat 0g					
Monounsaturated Fat 0g		Vitamin A 0%	Vitamin C 0%	Calcium 4%	Iron 8%

Eden Foods, Small Red Beans, Dry, Organic

3 tbsp / 35g

Amount per serving	%DV	Amount per serving	%DV	Amount per serving	%DV
Calories 120		**Cholesterol** 0mg	0%	**Total Carbohydrate** 22g	7%
Total Fat 0g	0%	**Sodium** 5mg	0%	Dietary Fiber 3g	12%
Saturated Fat 0g	0%	**Protein** 8g		Sugars 1g	
Polyunsaturated Fat 0g					
Monounsaturated Fat 0g		Vitamin A 0%	Vitamin C 0%	Calcium 6%	Iron 15%

Eden Foods, Small Red Beans, Organic

1/2 cup / 130g

Amount per serving	%DV	Amount per serving	%DV	Amount per serving	%DV
Calories 100		**Cholesterol** 0mg	0%	**Total Carbohydrate** 17g	6%
Total Fat 0.5g	1%	**Sodium** 25mg	1%	Dietary Fiber 5g	20%
Saturated Fat 0g	0%	**Protein** 6g		Sugars 1g	
Polyunsaturated Fat 0g					
Monounsaturated Fat 0g		Vitamin A 0%	Vitamin C 0%	Calcium 4%	Iron 8%

Eden Foods, Spicy Refried Black Beans, Organic

1/2 cup / 130g

Amount per serving	%DV	Amount per serving	%DV	Amount per serving	%DV
Calories 110		**Cholesterol** 0mg	0%	**Total Carbohydrate** 18g	6%
Total Fat 1.5g	2%	**Sodium** 180mg	8%	Dietary Fiber 7g	28%
Saturated Fat 0g	0%	**Protein** 6g		Sugars 0g	
Polyunsaturated Fat 0g					
Monounsaturated Fat 0g		Vitamin A 0%	Vitamin C 0%	Calcium 4%	Iron 15%

Frieda's, Edamame

1/2 cup / 75g

Amount per serving	%DV	Amount per serving	%DV	Amount per serving	%DV
Calories 100		**Cholesterol** 0mg	0%	**Total Carbohydrate** 10g	3%
Total Fat 3g	5%	**Sodium** 10mg	0%	Dietary Fiber 5g	20%
Saturated Fat 0g	0%	**Protein** 8g		Sugars 2g	
Polyunsaturated Fat 0g					
Monounsaturated Fat 0g		Vitamin A 10%	Vitamin C 10%	Calcium 4%	Iron 8%

Glory Foods, Sensibly Seasoned Lower Sodium Black Beans

1/2 cup / 120g

Amount per serving	%DV	Amount per serving	%DV	Amount per serving	%DV
Calories 100		**Cholesterol** 0mg	0%	**Total Carbohydrate** 18g	6%
Total Fat 0.5g	1%	**Sodium** 210mg	9%	Dietary Fiber 4g	16%
Saturated Fat 0g	0%	**Protein** 6g		Sugars 4g	
Polyunsaturated Fat 0g					
Monounsaturated Fat 0g		Vitamin A 0%	Vitamin C 0%	Calcium 4%	Iron 8%

Glory Foods, Sensibly Seasoned Lower Sodium Blackeye Peas

1/2 cup / 120g

Amount per serving	%DV	Amount per serving	%DV	Amount per serving	%DV
Calories 100		**Cholesterol** 0mg	0%	**Total Carbohydrate** 18g	6%
Total Fat 1g	2%	**Sodium** 250mg	10%	Dietary Fiber 3g	12%
Saturated Fat 0g	0%	**Protein** 7g		Sugars 2g	
Polyunsaturated Fat 0g					
Monounsaturated Fat 0g		Vitamin A 0%	Vitamin C 2%	Calcium 4%	Iron 15%

Glory Foods, Sensibly Seasoned Lower Sodium Red Beans

1/2 cup /120g

Amount per serving	%DV	Amount per serving	%DV	Amount per serving	%DV
Calories 100		**Cholesterol** 0mg	0%	**Total Carbohydrate** 18g	6%
Total Fat 0.5g	1%	**Sodium** 250mg	10%	Dietary Fiber 4g	16%
Saturated Fat 0g	0%	**Protein** 7g		Sugars 2g	
Polyunsaturated Fat 0g					
Monounsaturated Fat 0g		Vitamin A 0%	Vitamin C 2%	Calcium 4%	Iron 10%

Hummus, Commercial

1 tbsp / 15g

Amount per serving	%DV	Amount per serving	%DV	Amount per serving	%DV
Calories 25		**Cholesterol** 0mg	0%	**Total Carbohydrate** 2g	1%
Total Fat 1g	2%	**Sodium** 57mg	2%	Dietary Fiber 1g	4%
Saturated Fat 0g	0%	**Protein** 1g		Sugars 0g	
Polyunsaturated Fat 0g					
Monounsaturated Fat 0g		Vitamin A 0%	Vitamin C 0%	Calcium 1%	Iron 2%

Hummus, Home Prepared

1 tbsp / 15g

Amount per serving	%DV	Amount per serving	%DV	Amount per serving	%DV
Calories 27		**Cholesterol** 0mg	0%	**Total Carbohydrate** 3g	1%
Total Fat 1g	2%	**Sodium** 36mg	2%	Dietary Fiber 1g	4%
Saturated Fat 0g	0%	**Protein** 1g		Sugars 0g	
Polyunsaturated Fat 0.5g					
Monounsaturated Fat 0.5g		Vitamin A 0%	Vitamin C 2%	Calcium 1%	Iron 1%

Hyacinth Beans, Immature Seeds, Cooked, Boiled, Drained, with Salt

1 cup / 87g

Amount per serving	%DV	Amount per serving	%DV	Amount per serving	%DV
Calories 43		**Cholesterol** 0mg	0%	**Total Carbohydrate** 8g	3%
Total Fat 0g	0%	**Sodium** 207mg	9%	Dietary Fiber 0g	0%
Saturated Fat 0g	0%	**Protein** 3g		Sugars 0g	
Polyunsaturated Fat 0g					
Monounsaturated Fat 0g		Vitamin A 2%	Vitamin C 7%	Calcium 4%	Iron 4%

Hyacinth Beans, Immature Seeds, Cooked, Boiled, Drained, without Salt

1 cup / 87g

Amount per serving	%DV	Amount per serving	%DV	Amount per serving	%DV
Calories 43		**Cholesterol** 0mg	0%	**Total Carbohydrate** 8g	3%
Total Fat 0g	0%	**Sodium** 2mg	0%	Dietary Fiber 0g	0%
Saturated Fat 0g	0%	**Protein** 3g		Sugars 0g	
Polyunsaturated Fat 0g					
Monounsaturated Fat 0g		Vitamin A 2%	Vitamin C 7%	Calcium 4%	Iron 4%

Hyacinth Beans, Immature Seeds, Raw

1 cup / 80g

Amount per serving	%DV	Amount per serving	%DV	Amount per serving	%DV
Calories 37		**Cholesterol** 0mg	0%	**Total Carbohydrate** 7g	2%
Total Fat 0g	0%	**Sodium** 2mg	0%	Dietary Fiber 0g	0%
Saturated Fat 0g	0%	**Protein** 2g		Sugars 0g	
Polyunsaturated Fat 0g					
Monounsaturated Fat 0g		Vitamin A 2%	Vitamin C 17%	Calcium 4%	Iron 3%

Lentils, Mature Seeds, Cooked, Boiled, with Salt

1 cup / 198g

Amount per serving	%DV	Amount per serving	%DV	Amount per serving	%DV
Calories 226		**Cholesterol** 0mg	0%	**Total Carbohydrate** 39g	13%
Total Fat 1g	2%	**Sodium** 471mg	20%	Dietary Fiber 16g	64%
Saturated Fat 0g	0%	**Protein** 18g		Sugars 4g	
Polyunsaturated Fat 0g					
Monounsaturated Fat 0g		Vitamin A 0%	Vitamin C 5%	Calcium 4%	Iron 37%

Lentils, Pink, Raw

1 cup / 192g

Amount per serving	%DV	Amount per serving	%DV	Amount per serving	%DV
Calories 662		**Cholesterol** 0mg	0%	**Total Carbohydrate** 113g	38%
Total Fat 4g	6%	**Sodium** 13mg	1%	Dietary Fiber 20.7g	83%
Saturated Fat 1g	5%	**Protein** 47.9g		Sugars 0g	
Polyunsaturated Fat 2.2g					
Monounsaturated Fat 1g		Vitamin A 2%	Vitamin C 5%	Calcium 8%	Iron 81%

Lentils, Sprouted, Raw

1 cup / 77g

Amount per serving	%DV	Amount per serving	%DV	Amount per serving	%DV
Calories 82		**Cholesterol** 0mg	0%	**Total Carbohydrate** 17g	6%
Total Fat 0g	0%	**Sodium** 8mg	0%	Dietary Fiber 0g	0%
Saturated Fat 0g	0%	**Protein** 6.9g		Sugars 0g	
Polyunsaturated Fat 0.2g					
Monounsaturated Fat 0.1g		Vitamin A 1%	Vitamin C 21%	Calcium 2%	Iron 14%

Lima Beans, Large, Mature Seeds, Cooked, Boiled, without Salt

1 cup

Amount per serving	%DV	Amount per serving	%DV	Amount per serving	%DV
Calories 216		**Cholesterol** 0mg	0%	**Total Carbohydrate** 39.3g	13%
Total Fat 0g	0%	**Sodium** 4mg	0%	Dietary Fiber 13.2g	53%
Saturated Fat 0g	0%	**Protein** 14.7g		Sugars 5.5g	
Polyunsaturated Fat 0g					
Monounsaturated Fat 0g		Vitamin A 0%	Vitamin C 0%	Calcium 3%	Iron 25%

Lima Beans, Large, Mature Seeds, Raw

1 cup

Amount per serving	%DV	Amount per serving	%DV	Amount per serving	%DV
Calories 602		**Cholesterol** 0mg	0%	**Total Carbohydrate** 112.8g	38%
Total Fat 1.2g	2%	**Sodium** 32mg	1%	Dietary Fiber 33.8g	135%
Saturated Fat 0g	0%	**Protein** 38.2g		Sugars 15.1g	
Polyunsaturated Fat 0g					
Monounsaturated Fat 0g		Vitamin A 0%	Vitamin C 0%	Calcium 14%	Iron 74%

Lima Beans, Thin Seeded (Baby), Mature Seeds, Cooked, Boiled, with Salt

1 cup / 182g

Amount per serving	%DV	Amount per serving	%DV	Amount per serving	%DV
Calories 229		**Cholesterol** 0mg	0%	**Total Carbohydrate** 42g	14%
Total Fat 0.7g	1%	**Sodium** 435mg	18%	Dietary Fiber 14g	56%
Saturated Fat 0g	0%	**Protein** 14.6g		Sugars 0g	
Polyunsaturated Fat 0g					
Monounsaturated Fat 0g		Vitamin A 0%	Vitamin C 0%	Calcium 5%	Iron 24%

Lima Beans, Thin Seeded (Baby), Mature Seeds, Cooked, Boiled, without Salt

1 cup / 182g

Amount per serving	%DV	Amount per serving	%DV	Amount per serving	%DV
Calories 229		**Cholesterol** 0mg	0%	**Total Carbohydrate** 42g	14%
Total Fat 1g	2%	**Sodium** 5mg	0%	Dietary Fiber 14g	56%
Saturated Fat 0g	0%	**Protein** 14.6g		Sugars 0g	
Polyunsaturated Fat 0g					
Monounsaturated Fat 0g		Vitamin A 0%	Vitamin C 0%	Calcium 5%	Iron 24%

Lima Beans, Thin Seeded (Baby), Mature Seeds, Raw

1 cup / 202g

Amount per serving	%DV	Amount per serving	%DV	Amount per serving	%DV
Calories 677		**Cholesterol** 0mg	0%	**Total Carbohydrate** 126.9g	42%
Total Fat 2g	3%	**Sodium** 26mg	1%	Dietary Fiber 41.6g	166%
Saturated Fat 0g	0%	**Protein** 41.7g		Sugars 16.8g	
Polyunsaturated Fat 0g					
Monounsaturated Fat 0g		Vitamin A 0%	Vitamin C 0%	Calcium 16%	Iron 69%

Mung Beans, Mature Seeds, Cooked, Boiled, without Salt

1 cup / 180g

Amount per serving	%DV	Amount per serving	%DV	Amount per serving	%DV
Calories 189		**Cholesterol** 0mg	0%	**Total Carbohydrate** 3.3g	1%
Total Fat 1g	2%	**Sodium** 13mg	1%	Dietary Fiber 12g	48%
Saturated Fat 0g	0%	**Protein** 14g		Sugars 4g	
Polyunsaturated Fat 0g					
Monounsaturated Fat 0g		Vitamin A 1%	Vitamin C 3%	Calcium 10%	Iron 18%

Mung Beans, Mature Seeds, Raw

1 cup / 104g

Amount per serving	%DV	Amount per serving	%DV	Amount per serving	%DV
Calories 31		**Cholesterol** 0mg	0%	**Total Carbohydrate** 6g	3%
Total Fat 0g	0%	**Sodium** 6mg	0%	Dietary Fiber 4g	16%
Saturated Fat 0g	0%	**Protein** 3g		Sugars 4g	
Polyunsaturated Fat 0g					
Monounsaturated Fat 0g		Vitamin A 0%	Vitamin C 23%	Calcium 1%	Iron 5%

Mung Beans, Mature Seeds, Sprouted, Cooked, Boiled, Drained, with Salt

1 cup / 124g

Amount per serving	%DV	Amount per serving	%DV	Amount per serving	%DV
Calories 26		**Cholesterol** 0mg	0%	**Total Carbohydrate** 5g	2%
Total Fat 0g	0%	**Sodium** 12mg	1%	Dietary Fiber 1g	4%
Saturated Fat 0g	0%	**Protein** 3g		Sugars 4g	
Polyunsaturated Fat 0g					
Monounsaturated Fat 0g		Vitamin A 0%	Vitamin C 24%	Calcium 1%	Iron 4%

Mung Beans, Mature Seeds, Sprouted, Cooked, Boiled, Drained, without Salt

1 cup / 124g

Amount per serving	%DV	Amount per serving	%DV	Amount per serving	%DV
Calories 26		**Cholesterol** 0mg	0%	**Total Carbohydrate** 5g	2%
Total Fat 0g	0%	**Sodium** 12mg	1%	Dietary Fiber 1g	4%
Saturated Fat 0g	0%	**Protein** 3g		Sugars 4g	
Polyunsaturated Fat 0g					
Monounsaturated Fat 0g		Vitamin A 0%	Vitamin C 24%	Calcium 1%	Iron 4%

Mung Beans, Mature Seeds, Sprouted, Cooked, Stir-Fried

1 cup / 124g

Amount per serving	%DV	Amount per serving	%DV	Amount per serving	%DV
Calories 62		**Cholesterol** 0mg	0%	**Total Carbohydrate** 13g	4%
Total Fat 0g	0%	**Sodium** 11mg	0%	Dietary Fiber 2g	8%
Saturated Fat 0g	0%	**Protein** 5g		Sugars 0g	
Polyunsaturated Fat 0g					
Monounsaturated Fat 0g		Vitamin A 1%	Vitamin C 33%	Calcium 2%	Iron 13%

Peas, Mature Seeds, Sprouted, Raw

1 cup / 120g

Amount per serving	%DV	Amount per serving	%DV	Amount per serving	%DV
Calories 154		**Cholesterol** 0mg	0%	**Total Carbohydrate** 33.9g	11%
Total Fat 0.8g	1%	**Sodium** 24mg	1%	Dietary Fiber 0g	0%
Saturated Fat 0g	0%	**Protein** 10.6g		Sugars 0g	
Polyunsaturated Fat 0g					
Monounsaturated Fat 0g		Vitamin A 4%	Vitamin C 21%	Calcium 4%	Iron 15%

Peas, Split, Mature Seeds, Cooked, Boiled, with Salt

1 cup / 196g

Amount per serving	%DV	Amount per serving	%DV	Amount per serving	%DV
Calories 227		**Cholesterol** 0mg	0%	**Total Carbohydrate** 40g	13%
Total Fat 1g	2%	**Sodium** 466mg	19%	Dietary Fiber 16g	64%
Saturated Fat 0g	0%	**Protein** 16g		Sugars 6g	
Polyunsaturated Fat 0g					
Monounsaturated Fat 0g		Vitamin A 0%	Vitamin C 1%	Calcium 3%	Iron 14%

S & W, Premium Black Beans - 50% Less Sodium

1/2 cup / 130g

Amount per serving	%DV	Amount per serving	%DV	Amount per serving	%DV
Calories 110		**Cholesterol** 0mg	0%	**Total Carbohydrate** 22g	7%
Total Fat 0.5g	1%	**Sodium** 180mg	8%	Dietary Fiber 9g	36%
Saturated Fat 0g	0%	**Protein** 7g		Sugars 1g	
Polyunsaturated Fat 0g					
Monounsaturated Fat 0g		Vitamin A 0%	Vitamin C 0%	Calcium 6%	Iron 10%

S & W, Premium Chili Beans - 50% Less Sodium

1/2 cup / 130g

Amount per serving	%DV	Amount per serving	%DV	Amount per serving	%DV
Calories 130		**Cholesterol** 0mg	0%	**Total Carbohydrate** 23g	8%
Total Fat 1.5g	2%	**Sodium** 190mg	8%	Dietary Fiber 7g	28%
Saturated Fat 0g	0%	**Protein** 7g		Sugars 3g	
Polyunsaturated Fat 0g					
Monounsaturated Fat 0g		Vitamin A 2%	Vitamin C 2%	Calcium 6%	Iron 10%

S & W, Premium Garbanzo Beans - 50% Less Sodium

1/2 cup / 130g

Amount per serving	%DV	Amount per serving	%DV	Amount per serving	%DV
Calories 110		**Cholesterol** 0mg	0%	**Total Carbohydrate** 20g	7%
Total Fat 2g	3%	**Sodium** 180mg	8%	Dietary Fiber 6g	24%
Saturated Fat 0g	0%	**Protein** 7g		Sugars 3g	
Polyunsaturated Fat 0g					
Monounsaturated Fat 0g		Vitamin A 0%	Vitamin C 0%	Calcium 4%	Iron 10%

S & W, Premium Kidney Beans - 50% Less Sodium

1/2 cup / 130g

Amount per serving	%DV	Amount per serving	%DV	Amount per serving	%DV
Calories 110		**Cholesterol** 0mg	0%	**Total Carbohydrate** 21g	7%
Total Fat 0g	0%	**Sodium** 180mg	8%	Dietary Fiber 8g	32%
Saturated Fat 0g	0%	**Protein** 7g		Sugars 1g	
Polyunsaturated Fat 0g					
Monounsaturated Fat 0g		Vitamin A 0%	Vitamin C 0%	Calcium 6%	Iron 10%

S & W, Premium Pinto Beans - 50% Less Sodium

1/2 cup / 130g

Amount per serving	%DV	Amount per serving	%DV	Amount per serving	%DV
Calories 100		Cholesterol 0mg	0%	Total Carbohydrate 20g	7%
Total Fat 0g	0%	Sodium 270mg	11%	Dietary Fiber 7g	28%
Saturated Fat 0g	0%	Protein 6g		Sugars 1g	
Polyunsaturated Fat 0g					
Monounsaturated Fat 0g		Vitamin A 0% Vitamin C 0%		Calcium 6% Iron 8%	

S & W, Premium White Beans - 50% Less Sodium

1/2 cup / 130g

Amount per serving	%DV	Amount per serving	%DV	Amount per serving	%DV
Calories 110		Cholesterol 0mg	0%	Total Carbohydrate 21g	7%
Total Fat 0.5g	1%	Sodium 220mg	9%	Dietary Fiber 6g	24%
Saturated Fat 0g	0%	Protein 7g		Sugars 1g	
Polyunsaturated Fat 0g					
Monounsaturated Fat 0g		Vitamin A 0% Vitamin C 0%		Calcium 8% Iron 10%	

Sabra, Asian Fusion Garden Hummus

2 tbsp / 28g / 1oz

Amount per serving	%DV	Amount per serving	%DV	Amount per serving	%DV
Calories 70		Cholesterol 0mg	0%	Total Carbohydrate 5g	2%
Total Fat 5g	0%	Sodium 120mg	5%	Dietary Fiber 2g	8%
Saturated Fat 0.5g	3%	Protein 2g		Sugars 1g	
Polyunsaturated Fat 0g					
Monounsaturated Fat 0g		Vitamin A 2% Vitamin C 0%		Calcium 2% Iron 4%	

Sabra, Chipotle Hummus

2 tbsp / 28g / 1oz

Amount per serving	%DV	Amount per serving	%DV	Amount per serving	%DV
Calories 70		Cholesterol 0mg	0%	Total Carbohydrate 5g	2%
Total Fat 4.5g	7%	Sodium 130mg	5%	Dietary Fiber 2g	8%
Saturated Fat 0.5g	3%	Protein 2g		Sugars 0g	
Polyunsaturated Fat 0g					
Monounsaturated Fat 0g		Vitamin A 2% Vitamin C 0%		Calcium 2% Iron 4%	

Sabra, Classic Hummus

2 tbsp / 28g / 1oz

Amount per serving	%DV	Amount per serving	%DV	Amount per serving	%DV
Calories 70		Cholesterol 0mg	0%	Total Carbohydrate 4g	1%
Total Fat 5g	8%	Sodium 130mg	5%	Dietary Fiber 2g	8%
Saturated Fat 1g	5%	Protein 2g		Sugars 0g	
Polyunsaturated Fat 0g					
Monounsaturated Fat 0g		Vitamin A 0% Vitamin C 0%		Calcium 2% Iron 4%	

Sabra, Greek Olive Hummus

2 tbsp / 28g / 1oz

Amount per serving	%DV	Amount per serving	%DV	Amount per serving	%DV
Calories 70		**Cholesterol** 0mg	0%	**Total Carbohydrate** 2g	1%
Total Fat 5g	8%	**Sodium** 160mg	7%	Dietary Fiber 1g	4%
Saturated Fat 1g	5%	**Protein** 2g		Sugars 0g	
Polyunsaturated Fat 0g					
Monounsaturated Fat 0g		Vitamin A 0%	Vitamin C 0%	Calcium 2%	Iron 4%

Sabra, Jalapeno Hummus

2 tbsp /28g / 1oz

Amount per serving	%DV	Amount per serving	%DV	Amount per serving	%DV
Calories 70		**Cholesterol** 0mg	0%	**Total Carbohydrate** 4g	1%
Total Fat 4.5g	7%	**Sodium** 150mg	6%	Dietary Fiber 2g	8%
Saturated Fat 0.5g	3%	**Protein** 2g		Sugars 0g	
Polyunsaturated Fat 0g					
Monounsaturated Fat 0g		Vitamin A 0%	Vitamin C 0%	Calcium 2%	Iron 4%

Sabra, Roasted Garlic Hummus

2 tbsp / 28g / 1oz

Amount per serving	%DV	Amount per serving	%DV	Amount per serving	%DV
Calories 70		**Cholesterol** 0mg	0%	**Total Carbohydrate** 5g	2%
Total Fat 5g	8%	**Sodium** 130mg	5%	Dietary Fiber 2g	8%
Saturated Fat 1g	5%	**Protein** 2g		Sugars 1g	
Polyunsaturated Fat 0g					
Monounsaturated Fat 0g		Vitamin A 0%	Vitamin C 0%	Calcium 2%	Iron 4%

Sabra, Roasted Red Pepper Hummus

2 tbsp / 28g / 1oz

Amount per serving	%DV	Amount per serving	%DV	Amount per serving	%DV
Calories 70		**Cholesterol** 0mg	0%	**Total Carbohydrate** 4g	1%
Total Fat 5g	8%	**Sodium** 130mg	5%	Dietary Fiber 2g	8%
Saturated Fat 1g	5%	**Protein** 2g		Sugars 0g	
Polyunsaturated Fat 0g					
Monounsaturated Fat 0g		Vitamin A 0%	Vitamin C 0%	Calcium 2%	Iron 4%

Sabra, Southwest Garden Hummus

2 tbsp / 28g / 1oz

Amount per serving	%DV	Amount per serving	%DV	Amount per serving	%DV
Calories 70		**Cholesterol** 0mg	0%	**Total Carbohydrate** 5g	2%
Total Fat 4.5g	7%	**Sodium** 130mg	5%	Dietary Fiber 2g	8%
Saturated Fat 0.5g	3%	**Protein** 2g		Sugars 1g	
Polyunsaturated Fat 0g					
Monounsaturated Fat 0g		Vitamin A 2%	Vitamin C 0%	Calcium 2%	Iron 4%

Sabra, Sun Dried Tomato Hummus

2 tbsp / 28g / 1 oz

Amount per serving	%DV	Amount per serving	%DV	Amount per serving	%DV
Calories 70		**Cholesterol** 0mg	0%	**Total Carbohydrate** 5g	2%
Total Fat 5g	8%	**Sodium** 135mg	6%	Dietary Fiber 2g	8%
Saturated Fat 1g	5%	**Protein** 2g		Sugars 1g	
Polyunsaturated Fat 0g					
Monounsaturated Fat 0g		Vitamin A 0% Vitamin C 0%		Calcium 2% Iron 4%	

Sabra, Supremely Spicy Hummus

2 tbsp / 28g / 1oz

Amount per serving	%DV	Amount per serving	%DV	Amount per serving	%DV
Calories 70		**Cholesterol** 0mg	0%	**Total Carbohydrate** 4g	1%
Total Fat 5g	8%	**Sodium** 130mg	5%	Dietary Fiber 2g	8%
Saturated Fat 1g	5%	**Protein** 2g		Sugars 0g	
Polyunsaturated Fat 0g					
Monounsaturated Fat 0g		Vitamin A 2% Vitamin C 0%		Calcium 2% Iron 4%	

Sabra, Tuscan Garden Hummus

2 tbsp / 28g / 1oz

Amount per serving	%DV	Amount per serving	%DV	Amount per serving	%DV
Calories 70		**Cholesterol** 0mg	0%	**Total Carbohydrate** 5g	2%
Total Fat 5g	8%	**Sodium** 110mg	5%	Dietary Fiber 2g	8%
Saturated Fat 0.5g	3%	**Protein** 2g		Sugars 1g	
Polyunsaturated Fat 0g					
Monounsaturated Fat 0g		Vitamin A 2% Vitamin C 0%		Calcium 2% Iron 4%	

Soybeans, Mature Seeds, Sprouted, Cooked, Steamed

1 cup / 94g

Amount per serving	%DV	Amount per serving	%DV	Amount per serving	%DV
Calories 76		**Cholesterol** 0mg	0%	**Total Carbohydrate** 6g	2%
Total Fat 4g	6%	**Sodium** 9mg	0%	Dietary Fiber 1g	4%
Saturated Fat 1g	5%	**Protein** 8g		Sugars 0g	
Polyunsaturated Fat 0g					
Monounsaturated Fat 0g		Vitamin A 1% Vitamin C 13%		Calcium 6% Iron 7%	

Soybeans, Mature Seeds, Sprouted, Cooked, Steamed, with Salt

1 cup / 94g

Amount per serving	%DV	Amount per serving	%DV	Amount per serving	%DV
Calories 76		**Cholesterol** 0mg	0%	**Total Carbohydrate** 6g	2%
Total Fat 4g	6%	**Sodium** 231mg	10%	Dietary Fiber 1g	4%
Saturated Fat 1g	5%	**Protein** 8g		Sugars 0g	
Polyunsaturated Fat g					
Monounsaturated Fat g		Vitamin A 1% Vitamin C 13%		Calcium 6% Iron 7%	

Soybeans, Mature, Cooked, Boiled, without Salt

1 oz / 28g

Amount per serving	%DV	Amount per serving	%DV	Amount per serving	%DV
Calories 48		**Cholesterol** 0mg	0%	**Total Carbohydrate** 3g	1%
Total Fat 3g	5%	**Sodium** 0mg	0%	Dietary Fiber 2g	8%
Saturated Fat 0g	0%	**Protein** 5g		Sugars 1g	
Polyunsaturated Fat 0g					
Monounsaturated Fat 0g		Vitamin A 0%	Vitamin C 1%	Calcium 3%	Iron 8%

Yardlong Beans, Mature Seeds, Cooked, Boiled, without Salt

1 cup / 171g

Amount per serving	%DV	Amount per serving	%DV	Amount per serving	%DV
Calories 202		**Cholesterol** 0mg	0%	**Total Carbohydrate** 36g	12%
Total Fat 1g	2%	**Sodium** 9mg	0%	Dietary Fiber 6.5g	26%
Saturated Fat 0g	0%	**Protein** 14g		Sugars 0g	
Polyunsaturated Fat 0g					
Monounsaturated Fat 0g		Vitamin A 0%	Vitamin C 1%	Calcium 7%	Iron 25%

Yardlong Beans, Mature Seeds, Raw

1 cup / 167g

Amount per serving	%DV	Amount per serving	%DV	Amount per serving	%DV
Calories 580		**Cholesterol** 0mg	0%	**Total Carbohydrate** 103g	34%
Total Fat 2g	3%	**Sodium** 28mg	1%	Dietary Fiber 18g	72%
Saturated Fat 1g	5%	**Protein** 41g		Sugars 0g	
Polyunsaturated Fat 0g					
Monounsaturated Fat 0g		Vitamin A 2%	Vitamin C 4%	Calcium 23%	Iron 80%

Eggs

Crystal Farms, All Whites - 100% Liquid Egg Whites

3 tbsp / 46g

Amount per serving	%DV	Amount per serving	%DV	Amount per serving	%DV
Calories 25		**Cholesterol** 0mg	0%	**Total Carbohydrate** 0g	0%
Total Fat 0g	0%	**Sodium** 75mg	3%	Dietary Fiber 0g	0%
Saturated Fat 0g	0%	**Protein** 5g		Sugars 0g	
Polyunsaturated Fat 0g					
Monounsaturated Fat 0g		Vitamin A 0%	Vitamin C 0%	Calcium 2%	Iron 0%

Crystal Farms, Better 'n Eggs

1/4 cup / 56g

Amount per serving	%DV	Amount per serving	%DV	Amount per serving	%DV
Calories 30		**Cholesterol** 0mg	0%	**Total Carbohydrate** 1g	0%
Total Fat 0g	0%	**Sodium** 120mg	5%	Dietary Fiber 0g	0%
Saturated Fat 0g	0%	**Protein** 6g		Sugars 0g	
Polyunsaturated Fat 0g					
Monounsaturated Fat 0g		Vitamin A 8%	Vitamin C 0%	Calcium 2%	Iron 4%

Crystal Farms, Better 'n Eggs Plus

1/4 cup / 56g

Amount per serving	%DV	Amount per serving	%DV	Amount per serving	%DV
Calories 35		**Cholesterol** 0mg	0%	**Total Carbohydrate** 1g	0%
Total Fat 0g	0%	**Sodium** 105mg	4%	Dietary Fiber 0g	0%
Saturated Fat 0g	0%	**Protein** 6g		Sugars 0g	
Polyunsaturated Fat 0g					
Monounsaturated Fat 0g		Vitamin A 15% Vitamin C 0%		Calcium 10% Iron 6%	

Egg Beaters

3 tbsp

Amount per serving	%DV	Amount per serving	%DV	Amount per serving	%DV
Calories 25		**Cholesterol** 0mg	0%	**Total Carbohydrate** 1g	0%
Total Fat 0g	0%	**Sodium** 75mg	3%	Dietary Fiber 0g	0%
Saturated Fat 0g	0%	**Protein** 5g		Sugars 0g	
Polyunsaturated Fat 0g					
Monounsaturated Fat 0g		Vitamin A 0% Vitamin C 0%		Calcium 4% Iron 0%	

Eggland's Best, 100% Liquid Egg Whites

3 tbsp

Amount per serving	%DV	Amount per serving	%DV	Amount per serving	%DV
Calories 25		**Cholesterol** 0mg	0%	**Total Carbohydrate** 0g	0%
Total Fat 0g	0%	**Sodium** 75mg	3%	Dietary Fiber 0g	0%
Saturated Fat 0g	0%	**Protein** 5g		Sugars 0g	
Polyunsaturated Fat 0g					
Monounsaturated Fat 0g		Vitamin A 0% Vitamin C 0%		Calcium 6% Iron 0%	

Egg Substitute, Liquid or Frozen, Fat Free

.25 cup / 60g

Amount per serving	%DV	Amount per serving	%DV	Amount per serving	%DV
Calories 29		**Cholesterol** 0mg	0%	**Total Carbohydrate** 1g	0%
Total Fat 0g	0%	**Sodium** 119.5mg	5%	Dietary Fiber 0g	0%
Saturated Fat 0g	0%	**Protein** 6g		Sugars 1g	
Polyunsaturated Fat 0g					
Monounsaturated Fat 0g		Vitamin A 135% Vitamin C 0.5%		Calcium 44% Iron 1%	

Egg, White, Raw, Fresh

1 large / 33g

Amount per serving	%DV	Amount per serving	%DV	Amount per serving	%DV
Calories 17		**Cholesterol** 0mg	0%	**Total Carbohydrate** 0g	0%
Total Fat 0g	0%	**Sodium** 55mg	2%	Dietary Fiber 0g	0%
Saturated Fat 0g	0%	**Protein** 3.5g		Sugars 0g	
Polyunsaturated Fat 0g					
Monounsaturated Fat 0g		Vitamin A 0% Vitamin C 0%		Calcium 2.5% Iron 0%	

Ener-G, Egg Replacer

1-1/2 tsp / 4g

Amount per serving	%DV	Amount per serving	%DV	Amount per serving	%DV
Calories 15		**Cholesterol** 0mg	0%	**Total Carbohydrate** 4g	1%
Total Fat 0g	0%	**Sodium** 5mg	0%	Dietary Fiber 0g	0%
Saturated Fat 0g	0%	**Protein** 0g		Sugars 0g	
Polyunsaturated Fat 0g					
Monounsaturated Fat 0g		Vitamin A 0% Vitamin C 0%		Calcium 10% Iron 0%	

Kirkland Signature, Real Egg Product

1/4 cup / 2 oz

Amount per serving	%DV	Amount per serving	%DV	Amount per serving	%DV
Calories 30		**Cholesterol** 0mg	0%	**Total Carbohydrate** 1g	0%
Total Fat 0g	0%	**Sodium** 120mg	5%	Dietary Fiber 0g	0%
Saturated Fat 0g	0%	**Protein** 6g		Sugars 1g	
Polyunsaturated Fat 0g					
Monounsaturated Fat 0g		Vitamin A 15% Vitamin C 0%		Calcium 15% Iron 6%	

Kirkland Signature Egg Whites

1/4 cup / 2 oz

Amount per serving	%DV	Amount per serving	%DV	Amount per serving	%DV
Calories 30		**Cholesterol** 0mg	0%	**Total Carbohydrate** 1g	0%
Total Fat 0g	0%	**Sodium** 115mg	5%	Dietary Fiber 0g	0%
Saturated Fat 0g	0%	**Protein** 6g		Sugars 1g	
Polyunsaturated Fat 0g					
Monounsaturated Fat 0g		Vitamin A 15% Vitamin C 0%		Calcium 15% Iron 6%	

Kroger, Break-Free Real Egg Product

1/4 cup / 61g

Amount per serving	%DV	Amount per serving	%DV	Amount per serving	%DV
Calories 30		**Cholesterol** 0mg	0%	**Total Carbohydrate** 1g	0%
Total Fat 0g	0%	**Sodium** 115mg	5%	Dietary Fiber 0g	0%
Saturated Fat 0g	0%	**Protein** 6g		Sugars 0.5g	
Polyunsaturated Fat 0g					
Monounsaturated Fat 0g		Vitamin A 15% Vitamin C 0%		Calcium 0% Iron 6%	

Kroger, Break-Free 100% Egg Whites

1/4 cup / 61g

Amount per serving	%DV	Amount per serving	%DV	Amount per serving	%DV
Calories 30		**Cholesterol** 0mg	0%	**Total Carbohydrate** 1g	0%
Total Fat 0g	0%	**Sodium** 115mg	5%	Dietary Fiber 0g	0%
Saturated Fat 0g	0%	**Protein** 6g		Sugars 1g	
Polyunsaturated Fat 0g					
Monounsaturated Fat 0g		Vitamin A 15% Vitamin C 0%		Calcium 0% Iron 6%	

Market Pantry, 100% Egg Whites

3 tbsp / 46g

Amount per serving	%DV	Amount per serving	%DV	Amount per serving	%DV
Calories 25		**Cholesterol** 0mg	0%	**Total Carbohydrate** 0g	0%
Total Fat 0g	0%	**Sodium** 75mg	3%	Dietary Fiber 0g	0%
Saturated Fat 0g	0%	**Protein** 5g		Sugars 0g	
Polyunsaturated Fat 0g					
Monounsaturated Fat 0g		Vitamin A 0% Vitamin C 0%		Calcium 2% Iron 0%	

Second Nature Eggs, 99% Pure Egg Whites

1/4 cup / 60 ml

Amount per serving	%DV	Amount per serving	%DV	Amount per serving	%DV
Calories 35		**Cholesterol** 0mg	0%	**Total Carbohydrate** 1g	0%
Total Fat 0g	0%	**Sodium** 160mg	7%	Dietary Fiber 0g	0%
Saturated Fat 0g	0%	**Protein** 6g		Sugars 1g	
Polyunsaturated Fat 0g					
Monounsaturated Fat 0g		Vitamin A 12% Vitamin C 0%		Calcium 4% Iron 6%	

Meats, Beef

96/4 All Natural Extra Lean Ground Beef

112g

Amount per serving	%DV	Amount per serving	%DV	Amount per serving	%DV
Calories 130		**Cholesterol** 65mg	22%	**Total Carbohydrate** 0g	0%
Total Fat 4g	6%	**Sodium** 50mg	2%	Dietary Fiber 0g	0%
Saturated Fat 1.5g	8%	**Protein** 24g		Sugars 0g	
Polyunsaturated Fat 0g					
Monounsaturated Fat 0g		Vitamin A 0% Vitamin C 0%		Calcium 0% Iron 0%	

96/4 Extra Lean Ground Beef

112g

Amount per serving	%DV	Amount per serving	%DV	Amount per serving	%DV
Calories 150		**Cholesterol** 60mg	20%	**Total Carbohydrate** 0g	0%
Total Fat 4.5g	7%	**Sodium** 65mg	3%	Dietary Fiber 0g	0%
Saturated Fat 1.5g	8%	**Protein** 24g		Sugars 0g	
Polyunsaturated Fat 0g					
Monounsaturated Fat 0g		Vitamin A 0% Vitamin C 0%		Calcium 1% Iron 0%	

Beef, Chuck, Clod, Shoulder Tender, Medium, Lean & Fat, 0" Fat, Select, Grilled

1 serving / 3 oz / 85g

Amount per serving	%DV	Amount per serving	%DV	Amount per serving	%DV
Calories 146		**Cholesterol** 61mg	20%	**Total Carbohydrate** 0g	0%
Total Fat 4.9g	8%	**Sodium** 63mg	3%	Dietary Fiber 0g	0%
Saturated Fat 1.8g	9%	**Protein** 23.9g		Sugars 0g	
Polyunsaturated Fat 0.3g					
Monounsaturated Fat 2.5g		Vitamin A 0% Vitamin C 0%		Calcium 1% Iron 15%	

Beef, Chuck, Tender Steak, Lean, 0" Fat, Choice, Cooked, Broiled

3 oz / 1 serving / 85g

Amount per serving	%DV	Amount per serving	%DV	Amount per serving	%DV
Calories 137		**Cholesterol** 55mg	18%	**Total Carbohydrate** 0g	0%
Total Fat 4.9g	8%	**Sodium** 62mg	3%	Dietary Fiber 0g	0%
Saturated Fat 1.5g	8%	**Protein** 21.9g		Sugars 0g	
Polyunsaturated Fat 0.3g					
Monounsaturated Fat 2.3g		Vitamin A 0% Vitamin C 0%		Calcium 1% Iron 14%	

Beef, Chuck, Tender Steak, Lean, 0" Fat, Select, Cooked, Broiled

3 oz / 1 serving / 85g

Amount per serving	%DV	Amount per serving	%DV	Amount per serving	%DV
Calories 135		**Cholesterol** 51mg	17%	**Total Carbohydrate** 0g	0%
Total Fat 4.5g	7%	**Sodium** 58mg	2%	Dietary Fiber 0g	0%
Saturated Fat 1.8g	9%	**Protein** 22.2g		Sugars 0g	
Polyunsaturated Fat 0.3g					
Monounsaturated Fat 2.2g		Vitamin A 0% Vitamin C 0%		Calcium 1% Iron 13%	

Beef, Grass Feed, Organic Ground

3 oz / 93/7 cooked

Amount per serving	%DV	Amount per serving	%DV	Amount per serving	%DV
Calories 160		**Cholesterol** 70mg	8%	**Total Carbohydrate** 0g	0%
Total Fat 7g	5%	**Sodium** 55mg	1%	Dietary Fiber 0g	0%
Saturated Fat 3g	5%	**Protein** 22g		Sugars 0g	
Polyunsaturated Fat 0g					
Monounsaturated Fat 0g		Vitamin A 0% Vitamin C 0%		Calcium 0% Iron 15%	

Beef, Round, Bottom Round, Steak, Lean & Fat, 0" Fat, Select, Grilled

1 serving / 3 oz / 85g

Amount per serving	%DV	Amount per serving	%DV	Amount per serving	%DV
Calories 128		**Cholesterol** 52mg	17%	**Total Carbohydrate** 0g	0%
Total Fat 5g	8%	**Sodium** 54mg	2%	Dietary Fiber 0g	0%
Saturated Fat 1g	5%	**Protein** 18g		Sugars 0g	
Polyunsaturated Fat 0g					
Monounsaturated Fat 2g		Vitamin A 0% Vitamin C 0%		Calcium 0% Iron 11%	

Beef, Round, Full Cut, Lean, 1/4" Fat, Select, Cooked, Broiled

3 oz / 85g

Amount per serving	%DV	Amount per serving	%DV	Amount per serving	%DV
Calories 146		**Cholesterol** 66mg	22%	**Total Carbohydrate** 0g	0%
Total Fat 4.4g	7%	**Sodium** 54mg	2%	Dietary Fiber 0g	0%
Saturated Fat 1.6g	8%	**Protein** 24.9g		Sugars 0g	
Polyunsaturated Fat 0.2g					
Monounsaturated Fat 1.9g		Vitamin A 0% Vitamin C 0%		Calcium 0% Iron 13%	

Beef, Round, Knuckle, Tip Side, Steak, Lean and Fat, 0" Fat, Choice, Grilled

1 serving / 3 oz / 85g

Amount per serving	%DV	Amount per serving	%DV	Amount per serving	%DV
Calories 148		**Cholesterol** 69.7mg	23%	**Total Carbohydrate** 0g	0%
Total Fat 5g	8%	**Sodium** 46.7mg	2%	Dietary Fiber 0g	0%
Saturated Fat 2g	10%	**Protein** 24g		Sugars 3g	
Polyunsaturated Fat 0g					
Monounsaturated Fat 2g		Vitamin A 0% Vitamin C 0%		Calcium 4% Iron 2.2%	

Beef, Round, Top Round, Lean and Fat, 0" Fat, All Grades, Cooked, Braised

3 oz / 85g

Amount per serving	%DV	Amount per serving	%DV	Amount per serving	%DV
Calories 169		**Cholesterol** 77mg	26%	**Total Carbohydrate** 0g	0%
Total Fat 4.2g	6%	**Sodium** 38mg	2%	Dietary Fiber 0g	0%
Saturated Fat 1.5g	8%	**Protein** 30.7g		Sugars 0g	
Polyunsaturated Fat 0.2g					
Monounsaturated Fat 1.6g		Vitamin A 0% Vitamin C 0%		Calcium 0% Iron 16%	

Beef, Round, Top Round, Lean and Fat, 0" Fat, Select, Cooked, Braised

3 oz / 85g

Amount per serving	%DV	Amount per serving	%DV	Amount per serving	%DV
Calories 162		**Cholesterol** 77mg	26%	**Total Carbohydrate** 0g	0%
Total Fat 3.4g	5%	**Sodium** 38mg	2%	Dietary Fiber 0g	0%
Saturated Fat 1.2g	6%	**Protein** 30.7g		Sugars 0g	
Polyunsaturated Fat 0.2g					
Monounsaturated Fat 1.3g		Vitamin A 0% Vitamin C 0%		Calcium 0% Iron 16%	

Beef, Round, Top Round, Lean, 0" Fat, All Grades, Cooked, Braised

3 oz / 85g

Amount per serving	%DV	Amount per serving	%DV	Amount per serving	%DV
Calories 174		**Cholesterol** 77mg	26%	**Total Carbohydrate** 0g	0%
Total Fat 4.8g	7%	**Sodium** 38mg	2%	Dietary Fiber 0g	0%
Saturated Fat 1.6g	8%	**Protein** 30.7g		Sugars 0g	
Polyunsaturated Fat 0.2g					
Monounsaturated Fat 1.9g		Vitamin A 0% Vitamin C 0%		Calcium 0% Iron 16%	

Beef, Round, Top Round, Lean, 0" Fat, Select, Cooked, Braised

3 oz / 85g

Amount per serving	%DV	Amount per serving	%DV	Amount per serving	%DV
Calories 170		**Cholesterol** 76mg	25%	**Total Carbohydrate** 0g	0%
Total Fat 4.5g	7%	**Sodium** 38mg	2%	Dietary Fiber 0g	0%
Saturated Fat 1.6g	8%	**Protein** 30g		Sugars 0g	
Polyunsaturated Fat 0g					
Monounsaturated Fat 1g		Vitamin A 0% Vitamin C 0%		Calcium 3.4% Iron 2.7%	

Beef, Shoulder Steak, Boneless, Lean Only, 0" Fat, Choice, Cooked, Grilled

3 oz / 1 serving / 85g

Amount per serving	%DV	Amount per serving	%DV	Amount per serving	%DV
Calories 151		**Cholesterol** 68mg	23%	**Total Carbohydrate** 0g	0%
Total Fat 5g	8%	**Sodium** 58mg	2%	Dietary Fiber 0g	0%
Saturated Fat 2g	10%	**Protein** 24g		Sugars 0g	
Polyunsaturated Fat 0g					
Monounsaturated Fat 2g		Vitamin A 3.4% Vitamin C 0%		Calcium 10.2% Iron 25%	

Beef, Top Loin, Steak, Lean, 0" Fat, Select, Cooked, Broiled

3 oz / 85g

Amount per serving	%DV	Amount per serving	%DV	Amount per serving	%DV
Calories 146		**Cholesterol** 43mg	14%	**Total Carbohydrate** 0g	0%
Total Fat 4.3g	7%	**Sodium** 53mg	2%	Dietary Fiber 0g	0%
Saturated Fat 1.7g	9%	**Protein** 25.2g		Sugars 0g	
Polyunsaturated Fat 0.2g					
Monounsaturated Fat 1.7g		Vitamin A 0% Vitamin C 0%		Calcium 2% Iron 9%	

Beef, Top Sirloin, Steak, Lean, 0" Fat, Select, Cooked, Broiled

3 oz / 85g

Amount per serving	%DV	Amount per serving	%DV	Amount per serving	%DV
Calories 150		**Cholesterol** 43mg	14%	**Total Carbohydrate** 0g	0%
Total Fat 4.3g	7%	**Sodium** 56mg	2%	Dietary Fiber 0g	0%
Saturated Fat 1.6g	8%	**Protein** 26.2g		Sugars 0g	
Polyunsaturated Fat 0.2g					
Monounsaturated Fat 1.7g		Vitamin A 0% Vitamin C 0%		Calcium 2% Iron 9%	

Boneless Top Sirloin Petite Roast

100g

Amount per serving	%DV	Amount per serving	%DV	Amount per serving	%DV
Calories 122		**Cholesterol** 69mg	23%	**Total Carbohydrate** 0g	0%
Total Fat 3g	5%	**Sodium** 58mg	2%	Dietary Fiber 0g	0%
Saturated Fat 1g	5%	**Protein** 23g		Sugars 0g	
Polyunsaturated Fat 0g					
Monounsaturated Fat 0g		Vitamin A 0% Vitamin C 0%		Calcium 0% Iron 24%	

California Gourmet Burgers, Beef Patty, 96% lean, 4% fat

4 oz / 1 patty

Amount per serving	%DV	Amount per serving	%DV	Amount per serving	%DV
Calories 130		**Cholesterol** 60mg	20%	**Total Carbohydrate** 0g	0%
Total Fat 4g	6%	**Sodium** 65mg	3%	Dietary Fiber 0g	0%
Saturated Fat 2g	10%	**Protein** 22g		Sugars 0g	
Polyunsaturated Fat 0g					
Monounsaturated Fat 0g		Vitamin A 0% Vitamin C 0%		Calcium 0% Iron 10%	

Kansas City Ground Beef and Vidalia Onion Patty

1 patty

Amount per serving	%DV	Amount per serving	%DV	Amount per serving	%DV
Calories 130		**Cholesterol** 35mg	12%	**Total Carbohydrate** 2g	1%
Total Fat 4g	6%	**Sodium** 420mg	18%	Dietary Fiber 0g	0%
Saturated Fat 1.5g	8%	**Protein** 21g		Sugars 0g	
Polyunsaturated Fat 0g					
Monounsaturated Fat 0g		Vitamin A 0% Vitamin C 0%		Calcium 0% Iron 10%	

Kansas City Ground Beef Patty

4 oz patty

Amount per serving	%DV	Amount per serving	%DV	Amount per serving	%DV
Calories 120		**Cholesterol** 50mg	17%	**Total Carbohydrate** 3g	1%
Total Fat 0.5g	1%	**Sodium** 460mg	19%	Dietary Fiber 0g	0%
Saturated Fat 0g	0%	**Protein** 22g		Sugars 0g	
Polyunsaturated Fat 0g					
Monounsaturated Fat 0g		Vitamin A 4% Vitamin C 0%		Calcium 0% Iron 15%	

Kansas City Seasoned Steaks

1 steak / 140g

Amount per serving	%DV	Amount per serving	%DV	Amount per serving	%DV
Calories 130		**Cholesterol** 55mg	18%	**Total Carbohydrate** 1g	0%
Total Fat 2g	3%	**Sodium** 360mg	15%	Dietary Fiber 0g	0%
Saturated Fat 1g	5%	**Protein** 27g		Sugars 1g	
Polyunsaturated Fat 0g					
Monounsaturated Fat 0g		Vitamin A 0% Vitamin C 0%		Calcium 0% Iron 10%	

Kansas City Top Sirloin Steaks

4.5 oz steak

Amount per serving	%DV	Amount per serving	%DV	Amount per serving	%DV
Calories 120		**Cholesterol** 50mg	17%	**Total Carbohydrate** 1g	0%
Total Fat 1.5g	2%	**Sodium** 180mg	8%	Dietary Fiber 1g	4%
Saturated Fat 0.5g	2%	**Protein** 28g		Sugars 1g	
Polyunsaturated Fat 0g					
Monounsaturated Fat 0g		Vitamin A 2% Vitamin C 0%		Calcium 0% Iron 15%	

Laura's Kitchen Beef Pot Roast Au Jus

3 oz / 85g

Amount per serving	%DV	Amount per serving	%DV	Amount per serving	%DV
Calories 110		**Cholesterol** 45mg	15%	**Total Carbohydrate** 3g	1%
Total Fat 4g	6%	**Sodium** 380mg	16%	Dietary Fiber 0g	0%
Saturated Fat 1.5g	8%	**Protein** 17g		Sugars 0g	
Polyunsaturated Fat 0g					
Monounsaturated Fat 0g		Vitamin A 0% Vitamin C 0%		Calcium 0% Iron 0%	

Laura's Lean Beef 4% Fat Ground Round

4 oz

Amount per serving	%DV	Amount per serving	%DV	Amount per serving	%DV
Calories 140		**Cholesterol** 60mg	20%	**Total Carbohydrate** 0g	0%
Total Fat 4.5g	7%	**Sodium** 85mg	4%	Dietary Fiber 0g	0%
Saturated Fat 2g	10%	**Protein** 24g		Sugars 0g	
Polyunsaturated Fat 0g					
Monounsaturated Fat 0g		Vitamin A 0%	Vitamin C 0%	Calcium 0%	Iron 0%

Laura's Lean Beef 4% Fat Ground Sirloin

4 oz

Amount per serving	%DV	Amount per serving	%DV	Amount per serving	%DV
Calories 140		**Cholesterol** 60mg	20%	**Total Carbohydrate** 0g	0%
Total Fat 4.5g	7%	**Sodium** 85mg	4%	Dietary Fiber 0g	0%
Saturated Fat 2g	10%	**Protein** 24g		Sugars 0g	
Polyunsaturated Fat 0g					
Monounsaturated Fat 0g		Vitamin A 0%	Vitamin C 0%	Calcium 0%	Iron 0%

Laura's Lean Beef Sirloin Steak

4 oz

Amount per serving	%DV	Amount per serving	%DV	Amount per serving	%DV
Calories 145		**Cholesterol** 65mg	22%	**Total Carbohydrate** 0g	0%
Total Fat 5g	8%	**Sodium** 70mg	3%	Dietary Fiber 0g	0%
Saturated Fat 2g	10%	**Protein** 24g		Sugars 0g	
Polyunsaturated Fat 0g					
Monounsaturated Fat 0g		Vitamin A 0%	Vitamin C 0%	Calcium 0%	Iron 0%

Meats, Bison

Bison, Chuck, Shoulder Clod, Lean, 3-5 lb. Roasted, Cooked, Braised

1 serving / 3 oz / 85g

Amount per serving	%DV	Amount per serving	%DV	Amount per serving	%DV
Calories 164		**Cholesterol** 94mg	31%	**Total Carbohydrate** 0g	0%
Total Fat 4.6g	7%	**Sodium** 48mg	2%	Dietary Fiber 0g	0%
Saturated Fat 2g	10%	**Protein** 28.7g		Sugars 0g	
Polyunsaturated Fat 0.2g					
Monounsaturated Fat 1.8g		Vitamin A 0%	Vitamin C 0%	Calcium 1%	Iron 23%

Bison, Lean, Cooked, Roasted

3 oz / 85g

Amount per serving	%DV	Amount per serving	%DV	Amount per serving	%DV
Calories 122		**Cholesterol** 70mg	23%	**Total Carbohydrate** 0g	0%
Total Fat 2.1g	3%	**Sodium** 48mg	2%	Dietary Fiber 0g	0%
Saturated Fat 0.8g	4%	**Protein** 24.2g		Sugars 0g	
Polyunsaturated Fat 0.2g					
Monounsaturated Fat 0.8g		Vitamin A 0%	Vitamin C 0%	Calcium 1%	Iron 16%

Bison, Top Round, Lean, 1" Steak, Cooked, Broiled

1 serving / 3 oz / 85g

Amount per serving	%DV	Amount per serving	%DV	Amount per serving	%DV
Calories 148		**Cholesterol** 72mg	24%	**Total Carbohydrate** 0g	0%
Total Fat 4.2g	6%	**Sodium** 35mg	1%	Dietary Fiber 0g	0%
Saturated Fat 1.7g	8%	**Protein** 25.7g		Sugars 0g	
Polyunsaturated Fat 0.2g					
Monounsaturated Fat 1.5g		Vitamin A 0% Vitamin C 0%		Calcium 0% Iron 17%	

High Plains Bison, Bison Filet Mignon

5 oz

Amount per serving	%DV	Amount per serving	%DV	Amount per serving	%DV
Calories 150		**Cholesterol** 85mg	28%	**Total Carbohydrate** 1g	0%
Total Fat 4g	6%	**Sodium** 60mg	2%	Dietary Fiber 0g	0%
Saturated Fat 2g	10%	**Protein** 29g		Sugars 0g	
Polyunsaturated Fat 0g					
Monounsaturated Fat 0g		Vitamin A 0% Vitamin C 0%		Calcium 2% Iron 20%	

High Plains Bison, Bison Top Sirloin Steak

4 oz / 113g

Amount per serving	%DV	Amount per serving	%DV	Amount per serving	%DV
Calories 110		**Cholesterol** 50mg	17%	**Total Carbohydrate** 0g	0%
Total Fat 3g	5%	**Sodium** 60mg	2%	Dietary Fiber 0g	0%
Saturated Fat 2g	10%	**Protein** 25g		Sugars 0g	
Polyunsaturated Fat 0g					
Monounsaturated Fat 0g		Vitamin A 0% Vitamin C 0%		Calcium 2% Iron 20%	

Meats, Game

Game Meat, Boar, Wild, Cooked, Roasted

3 oz / 85g

Amount per serving	%DV	Amount per serving	%DV	Amount per serving	%DV
Calories 136		**Cholesterol** 65mg	22%	**Total Carbohydrate** 0g	0%
Total Fat 4g	6%	**Sodium** 51mg	2%	Dietary Fiber 0g	0%
Saturated Fat 1g	5%	**Protein** 24g		Sugars 0g	
Polyunsaturated Fat 0g					
Monounsaturated Fat 0g		Vitamin A 0% Vitamin C 0%		Calcium 1% Iron 5%	

Game Meat, Buffalo, Water, Cooked, Roasted

3 oz / 85g

Amount per serving	%DV	Amount per serving	%DV	Amount per serving	%DV
Calories 111		**Cholesterol** 52mg	17%	**Total Carbohydrate** 0g	0%
Total Fat 1.5g	2%	**Sodium** 48mg	2%	Dietary Fiber 0g	0%
Saturated Fat 0.5g	3%	**Protein** 22.8g		Sugars 0g	
Polyunsaturated Fat 0.3g					
Monounsaturated Fat 0.5g		Vitamin A 0% Vitamin C 0%		Calcium 1% Iron 10%	

Game Meat, Caribou, Cooked, Roasted

3 oz / 85g

Amount per serving	%DV	Amount per serving	%DV	Amount per serving	%DV
Calories 142		**Cholesterol** 93mg	31%	**Total Carbohydrate** 0g	0%
Total Fat 3.8g	6%	**Sodium** 51mg	2%	Dietary Fiber 0g	0%
Saturated Fat 1.4g	7%	**Protein** 25.3g		Sugars 0g	
Polyunsaturated Fat 0.5g					
Monounsaturated Fat 1.1g		Vitamin A 0% Vitamin C 0%		Calcium 2% Iron 29%	

Game Meat, Deer, Loin, Lean, 1" Steak, Cooked, Broiled

1 serving /3 oz / 85g

Amount per serving	%DV	Amount per serving	%DV	Amount per serving	%DV
Calories 127		**Cholesterol** 75mg	25%	**Total Carbohydrate** 0g	0%
Total Fat 2g	3%	**Sodium** 48mg	2%	Dietary Fiber 0g	0%
Saturated Fat 1g	5%	**Protein** 25.4g		Sugars 0g	
Polyunsaturated Fat 0.1g					
Monounsaturated Fat 0.5g		Vitamin A 0% Vitamin C 0%		Calcium 0% Iron 20%	

Game Meat, Deer, Tenderloin, Lean, 0.5-1 lb. Roasted, Cooked, Broiled

1 serving / 3 oz / 85g

Amount per serving	%DV	Amount per serving	%DV	Amount per serving	%DV
Calories 127		**Cholesterol** 75mg	25%	**Total Carbohydrate** 0g	0%
Total Fat 2g	3%	**Sodium** 48mg	2%	Dietary Fiber 0g	0%
Saturated Fat 1g	5%	**Protein** 25.4g		Sugars 0g	
Polyunsaturated Fat 0.1g					
Monounsaturated Fat 0.5g		Vitamin A 0% Vitamin C 0%		Calcium 0% Iron 20%	

Game Meat, Deer, Top Round, Lean, 1" Steak, Cooked, Broiled

1 steak / 13.4 g raw meat

Amount per serving	%DV	Amount per serving	%DV	Amount per serving	%DV
Calories 155		**Cholesterol** 87mg	29%	**Total Carbohydrate** 0g	0%
Total Fat 1.9g	3%	**Sodium** 46mg	2%	Dietary Fiber 0g	0%
Saturated Fat 1g	5%	**Protein** 32.1g		Sugars 0g	
Polyunsaturated Fat 0.1g					
Monounsaturated Fat 0.4g		Vitamin A 0% Vitamin C 0%		Calcium 0% Iron 24%	

Game Meat, Elk, Cooked, Roasted

3 oz / 85g

Amount per serving	%DV	Amount per serving	%DV	Amount per serving	%DV
Calories 124		**Cholesterol** 62mg	21%	**Total Carbohydrate** 0g	0%
Total Fat 1.6g	2%	**Sodium** 52mg	2%	Dietary Fiber 0g	0%
Saturated Fat 0.6g	3%	**Protein** 26g		Sugars 0g	
Polyunsaturated Fat 0.3g					
Monounsaturated Fat 0.4g		Vitamin A 0% Vitamin C 0%		Calcium 0% Iron 17%	

Game Meat, Elk, Loin, Lean, Cooked, Broiled

1 serving / 3 oz / 85g

Amount per serving	%DV	Amount per serving	%DV	Amount per serving	%DV
Calories 190		**Cholesterol** 86mg	29%	**Total Carbohydrate** 0g	0%
Total Fat 4.4g	7%	**Sodium** 62mg	3%	Dietary Fiber 0g	0%
Saturated Fat 1.7g	8%	**Protein** 35.3g		Sugars 0g	
Polyunsaturated Fat 0.2g					
Monounsaturated Fat 1.2g		Vitamin A 0% Vitamin C 0%		Calcium 1% Iron 25%	

Game Meat, Elk, Round, Lean, Cooked, Broiled

1 serving / 3 oz / 85g

Amount per serving	%DV	Amount per serving	%DV	Amount per serving	%DV
Calories 133		**Cholesterol** 66mg	22%	**Total Carbohydrate** 0g	0%
Total Fat 2g	3%	**Sodium** 43mg	2%	Dietary Fiber 0g	0%
Saturated Fat 1g	5%	**Protein** 26g		Sugars 0g	
Polyunsaturated Fat 0.1g					
Monounsaturated Fat 0.6g		Vitamin A 0% Vitamin C 0%		Calcium 0% Iron 19%	

Game Meat, Elk, Tenderloin, Lean, Cooked, Broiled

1 steak / 123.5 g raw meat

Amount per serving	%DV	Amount per serving	%DV	Amount per serving	%DV
Calories 149		**Cholesterol** 66mg	22%	**Total Carbohydrate** 0g	0%
Total Fat 3.1g	5%	**Sodium** 46mg	2%	Dietary Fiber 0g	0%
Saturated Fat 1.2g	6%	**Protein** 28.3g		Sugars 0g	
Polyunsaturated Fat 0.1g					
Monounsaturated Fat 0.9g		Vitamin A 0% Vitamin C 0%		Calcium 0% Iron 21%	

Game Meat, Goat, Cooked, Roasted

3 oz / 85g

Amount per serving	%DV	Amount per serving	%DV	Amount per serving	%DV
Calories 122		**Cholesterol** 64mg	21%	**Total Carbohydrate** 0g	0%
Total Fat 2.6g	4%	**Sodium** 73mg	3%	Dietary Fiber 0g	0%
Saturated Fat 0.8g	4%	**Protein** 23g		Sugars 0g	
Polyunsaturated Fat 0.2g					
Monounsaturated Fat 1.2g		Vitamin A 0% Vitamin C 0%		Calcium 1% Iron 18%	

Meats, Lamb

Lamb, New Zealand, Imported, Frozen, Loin, Lean, Cooked, Broiled

1 chop / excluding refuse / yield from 1 raw chop, with refuse / 5g /30g

Amount per serving	%DV	Amount per serving	%DV	Amount per serving	%DV
Calories 60		**Cholesterol** 34mg	11%	**Total Carbohydrate** 0g	0%
Total Fat 2g	3%	**Sodium** 17mg	1%	Dietary Fiber 0g	0%
Saturated Fat 1g	5%	**Protein** 9g		Sugars 0g	
Polyunsaturated Fat 0g					
Monounsaturated Fat 0g		Vitamin A 0% Vitamin C 0%		Calcium 1% Iron 4%	

Meats, Poultry

Applegate Farms, Gluten-Free Chicken Breast Tenders

2 pieces

Amount per serving	%DV	Amount per serving	%DV	Amount per serving	%DV
Calories 130		**Cholesterol** 30mg	10%	**Total Carbohydrate** 10g	3%
Total Fat 4.5g	7%	**Sodium** 350mg	15%	Dietary Fiber 0g	0%
Saturated Fat 1g	5%	**Protein** 11g		Sugars 0g	
Polyunsaturated Fat 0g					
Monounsaturated Fat 0g		Vitamin A 0% Vitamin C 2%		Calcium 0% Iron 2%	

Applegate Farms, Grilled Chicken Breast Strips

3 oz

Amount per serving	%DV	Amount per serving	%DV	Amount per serving	%DV
Calories 100		**Cholesterol** 40mg	13%	**Total Carbohydrate** 0g	0%
Total Fat 1g	2%	**Sodium** 290mg	12%	Dietary Fiber 0g	0%
Saturated Fat 0g	0%	**Protein** 24g		Sugars 0g	
Polyunsaturated Fat 0g					
Monounsaturated Fat 0g		Vitamin A 0% Vitamin C 0%		Calcium 10% Iron 0%	

Applegate Farms, Organic Turkey Bacon

1 pan fried slice

Amount per serving	%DV	Amount per serving	%DV	Amount per serving	%DV
Calories 35		**Cholesterol** 25mg	8%	**Total Carbohydrate** 0g	0%
Total Fat 1.5g	2%	**Sodium** 200mg	8%	Dietary Fiber 0g	0%
Saturated Fat 0g	0%	**Protein** 6g		Sugars 0g	
Polyunsaturated Fat 0g					
Monounsaturated Fat 0g		Vitamin A 0% Vitamin C 0%		Calcium 0% Iron 0%	

Applegate Farms, Southwestern Grilled Chicken Breast Strips

3 oz

Amount per serving	%DV	Amount per serving	%DV	Amount per serving	%DV
Calories 100		**Cholesterol** 45mg	15%	**Total Carbohydrate** 2g	1%
Total Fat 2g	3%	**Sodium** 340mg	14%	Dietary Fiber 0g	0%
Saturated Fat 0g	0%	**Protein** 15g		Sugars 0g	
Polyunsaturated Fat 0g					
Monounsaturated Fat 0g		Vitamin A 0% Vitamin C 0%		Calcium 10% Iron 0%	

Bubba Turkey Burger

1- 4 oz burger / 112g

Amount per serving	%DV	Amount per serving	%DV	Amount per serving	%DV
Calories 160		**Cholesterol** 85mg	28%	**Total Carbohydrate** 1g	0%
Total Fat 5g	8%	**Sodium** 290mg	12%	Dietary Fiber 0g	0%
Saturated Fat 1.5g	8%	**Protein** 25g		Sugars 0g	
Polyunsaturated Fat 0g					
Monounsaturated Fat 0g		Vitamin A 0% Vitamin C 0%		Calcium 0% Iron 6%	

Buddig Fix Quix Grilled Chicken Breast Cubes

1.75 oz / 50g

Amount per serving	%DV	Amount per serving	%DV	Amount per serving	%DV
Calories 60		**Cholesterol** 30mg	10%	**Total Carbohydrate** 1g	0%
Total Fat 1g	2%	**Sodium** 310mg	13%	Dietary Fiber 0g	0%
Saturated Fat 0.5g	2%	**Protein** 11g		Sugars 1g	
Polyunsaturated Fat 0g					
Monounsaturated Fat 0g		Vitamin A 0% Vitamin C 0%		Calcium 0% Iron 1%	

Butterball All Natural Ground Turkey Breast

4 oz / 112g

Amount per serving	%DV	Amount per serving	%DV	Amount per serving	%DV
Calories 120		**Cholesterol** 55mg	18%	**Total Carbohydrate** 0g	0%
Total Fat 1g	2%	**Sodium** 80mg	3%	Dietary Fiber 0g	0%
Saturated Fat 0.5g	3%	**Protein** 27g		Sugars 0g	
Polyunsaturated Fat 0g					
Monounsaturated Fat 0g		Vitamin A 0% Vitamin C 0%		Calcium 0% Iron 4%	

Butterball All Natural Ground White Turkey

4 oz / 112g

Amount per serving	%DV	Amount per serving	%DV	Amount per serving	%DV
Calories 130		**Cholesterol** 75mg	25%	**Total Carbohydrate** 0g	0%
Total Fat 3.5g	5%	**Sodium** 75mg	3%	Dietary Fiber 0g	0%
Saturated Fat 1g	5%	**Protein** 26g		Sugars 0g	
Polyunsaturated Fat 0g					
Monounsaturated Fat 0g		Vitamin A 0% Vitamin C 0%		Calcium 0% Iron 8%	

Butterball All Natural Turkey Breast Filets

4 oz / 112g

Amount per serving	%DV	Amount per serving	%DV	Amount per serving	%DV
Calories 120		**Cholesterol** 70mg	23%	**Total Carbohydrate** 0g	0%
Total Fat 0.5g	1%	**Sodium** 55mg	2%	Dietary Fiber 0g	0%
Saturated Fat 0g	0%	**Protein** 28g		Sugars 0g	
Polyunsaturated Fat 0g					
Monounsaturated Fat 0g		Vitamin A 0% Vitamin C 0%		Calcium 0% Iron 8%	

Butterball All Natural Turkey Breast Tenders

4 oz / 112g

Amount per serving	%DV	Amount per serving	%DV	Amount per serving	%DV
Calories 120		**Cholesterol** 70mg	23%	**Total Carbohydrate** 0g	0%
Total Fat 0.5g	1%	**Sodium** 55mg	2%	Dietary Fiber 0g	0%
Saturated Fat 0g	0%	**Protein** 28g		Sugars 0g	
Polyunsaturated Fat 0g					
Monounsaturated Fat 0g		Vitamin A 0% Vitamin C 0%		Calcium 0% Iron 8%	

Butterball Fresh All Natural Turkey Filets

4 oz / 112g

Amount per serving	%DV	Amount per serving	%DV	Amount per serving	%DV
Calories 120		**Cholesterol** 70mg	23%	**Total Carbohydrate** 0g	0%
Total Fat 0.5g	1%	**Sodium** 55mg	2%	Dietary Fiber 0g	0%
Saturated Fat 0g	0%	**Protein** 28g		Sugars 0g	
Polyunsaturated Fat 0g					
Monounsaturated Fat 0g		Vitamin A 0% Vitamin C 0%		Calcium 0% Iron 8%	

Butterball Fresh All Natural Turkey Tenders

4 oz / 112g

Amount per serving	%DV	Amount per serving	%DV	Amount per serving	%DV
Calories 120		**Cholesterol** 70mg	23%	**Total Carbohydrate** 0g	0%
Total Fat 0.5g	1%	**Sodium** 55mg	2%	Dietary Fiber 0g	0%
Saturated Fat 0g	0%	**Protein** 28g		Sugars 0g	
Polyunsaturated Fat 0g					
Monounsaturated Fat 0g		Vitamin A 0% Vitamin C 0%		Calcium 2% Iron 8%	

Butterball Ready to Roast Classic Turkey Breast

4 oz

Amount per serving	%DV	Amount per serving	%DV	Amount per serving	%DV
Calories 170		**Cholesterol** 17mg	6%	**Total Carbohydrate** 1g	0%
Total Fat 5g	8%	**Sodium** 320mg	13%	Dietary Fiber 0g	0%
Saturated Fat 1.5g	8%	**Protein** 29g		Sugars 0g	
Polyunsaturated Fat 0g					
Monounsaturated Fat 0g		Vitamin A 0% Vitamin C 0%		Calcium 2% Iron 10%	

Chicken Breast, Oven-Roasted, Fat Free, Sliced

1 serving, 2 slices / 42g

Amount per serving	%DV	Amount per serving	%DV	Amount per serving	%DV
Calories 33		**Cholesterol** 15mg	5%	**Total Carbohydrate** 0.9g	0%
Total Fat 0.2g	0%	**Sodium** 457mg	19%	Dietary Fiber 0g	0%
Saturated Fat 0.1g	0%	**Protein** 7g		Sugars 0g	
Polyunsaturated Fat 0g					
Monounsaturated Fat 0g		Vitamin A 0% Vitamin C 0%		Calcium 0% Iron 1%	

Chicken, Broilers or Fryers, Back, Meat Only, Cooked, Stewed

.5 back / bone and skin removed / 42g

Amount per serving	%DV	Amount per serving	%DV	Amount per serving	%DV
Calories 54		**Cholesterol** 22mg	7%	**Total Carbohydrate** 0g	0%
Total Fat 3g	5%	**Sodium** 17mg	1%	Dietary Fiber 0g	0%
Saturated Fat 1g	5%	**Protein** 7g		Sugars 0g	
Polyunsaturated Fat 1g					
Monounsaturated Fat 1g		Vitamin A 0% Vitamin C 0%		Calcium 1% Iron 2%	

Chicken, Broilers or Fryers, Breast, Meat and Skin, Cooked, Roasted

1 unit / yield from 1 lb ready-to-cook chicken /58g

Amount per serving	%DV	Amount per serving	%DV	Amount per serving	%DV
Calories 114		**Cholesterol** 49mg	16%	**Total Carbohydrate** 0g	0%
Total Fat 4.5g	7%	**Sodium** 41mg	2%	Dietary Fiber 0g	0%
Saturated Fat 1.3g	6%	**Protein** 17g		Sugars 0g	
Polyunsaturated Fat 0g					
Monounsaturated Fat 0g		Vitamin A 0% Vitamin C 0%		Calcium 1% Iron 3%	

Chicken, Broilers or Fryers, Breast, Meat Only, Cooked, Fried

.5 breast, bone and skin removed / 86g

Amount per serving	%DV	Amount per serving	%DV	Amount per serving	%DV
Calories 97		**Cholesterol** 47mg	16%	**Total Carbohydrate** 0.2g	0%
Total Fat 2.4g	4%	**Sodium** 41mg	2%	Dietary Fiber 0g	0%
Saturated Fat 0.6g	3%	**Protein** 17.3g		Sugars 0g	
Polyunsaturated Fat 0g					
Monounsaturated Fat 0g		Vitamin A 12% Vitamin C 0%		Calcium 8% Iron 0.5%	

Chicken, Cooked, Boilers or Fryers, Back, Meat Only, Roasted

.5 back / bone and skin removed / 40g

Amount per serving	%DV	Amount per serving	%DV	Amount per serving	%DV
Calories 95.6		**Cholesterol** 36mg	12%	**Total Carbohydrate** 0g	0%
Total Fat 5g	8%	**Sodium** 38mg	2%	Dietary Fiber 0g	0%
Saturated Fat 1g	5%	**Protein** 11g		Sugars 0g	
Polyunsaturated Fat 1g					
Monounsaturated Fat 1g		Vitamin A 0% Vitamin C 0%		Calcium 96% Iron 0%	

Chicken, Roasting, Light Meat, Meat Only, Cooked, Roasted

1 unit / yield from 1 lb ready-to-cook chicken / 78g

Amount per serving	%DV	Amount per serving	%DV	Amount per serving	%DV
Calories 119		**Cholesterol** 58.5mg	20%	**Total Carbohydrate** 0g	0%
Total Fat 3g	5%	**Sodium** 40mg	2%	Dietary Fiber 0g	0%
Saturated Fat 1g	5%	**Protein** 21g		Sugars 0g	
Polyunsaturated Fat 0g					
Monounsaturated Fat 1.1g		Vitamin A 19% Vitamin C 0%		Calcium 10% Iron 0%	

Coleman Organic 99% Fat-Free Boneless & Skinless Organic Chicken Breasts

4 oz / 112g

Amount per serving	%DV	Amount per serving	%DV	Amount per serving	%DV
Calories 120		**Cholesterol** 55mg	18%	**Total Carbohydrate** 0g	0%
Total Fat 1g	2%	**Sodium** 75mg	3%	Dietary Fiber 0g	0%
Saturated Fat 0g	0%	**Protein** 26g		Sugars 0g	
Polyunsaturated Fat 0g					
Monounsaturated Fat 0g		Vitamin A 0% Vitamin C 0%		Calcium 0% Iron 4%	

Duck, Young, Duckling, Dom, White Peking, Breast, Boneless, without Skin, Broiled

1 unit / yield from 1 lb ready-to-cook duck / 44g

Amount per serving	%DV	Amount per serving	%DV	Amount per serving	%DV
Calories 62		**Cholesterol** 63mg	21%	**Total Carbohydrate** 0g	0%
Total Fat 1g	2%	**Sodium** 46mg	2%	Dietary Fiber 0g	0%
Saturated Fat 0g	0%	**Protein** 12g		Sugars 0g	
Polyunsaturated Fat 0g					
Monounsaturated Fat 0g		Vitamin A 0% Vitamin C 3%		Calcium 1% Iron 11%	

Eating Right All Natural White Turkey Burgers

1 burger /113g

Amount per serving	%DV	Amount per serving	%DV	Amount per serving	%DV
Calories 120		**Cholesterol** 75mg	25%	**Total Carbohydrate** 6g	2%
Total Fat 2g	3%	**Sodium** 440mg	18%	Dietary Fiber 0g	0%
Saturated Fat 0.5g	3%	**Protein** 19g		Sugars 1g	
Polyunsaturated Fat 0g					
Monounsaturated Fat 0g		Vitamin A 2% Vitamin C 0%		Calcium 4% Iron 10%	

Fieldale Farms, Tenderized Boneless, Skinless, Chicken Breasts

1/2 cup /cooked

Amount per serving	%DV	Amount per serving	%DV	Amount per serving	%DV
Calories 110		**Cholesterol** 70mg	23%	**Total Carbohydrate** 0g	0%
Total Fat 2g	3%	**Sodium** 90mg	4%	Dietary Fiber 0g	0%
Saturated Fat 0g	0%	**Protein** 26g		Sugars 0g	
Polyunsaturated Fat 0g					
Monounsaturated Fat 0g		Vitamin A 0% Vitamin C 0%		Calcium 35% Iron 6%	

Fieldale Farms, Thin-Sliced Boneless & Skinless Chicken Breasts

1 piece

Amount per serving	%DV	Amount per serving	%DV	Amount per serving	%DV
Calories 140		**Cholesterol** 65mg	22%	**Total Carbohydrate** 0g	0%
Total Fat 1g	2%	**Sodium** 75mg	3%	Dietary Fiber 0g	0%
Saturated Fat 0g	0%	**Protein** 31g		Sugars 0g	
Polyunsaturated Fat 0g					
Monounsaturated Fat 0g		Vitamin A 0% Vitamin C 0%		Calcium 35% Iron 6%	

Foster Farms 100% Natural Chicken 99% Fat-Free Boneless & Skinless Breast Fillets

4 oz /112g

Amount per serving	%DV	Amount per serving	%DV	Amount per serving	%DV
Calories 120		**Cholesterol** 65mg	22%	**Total Carbohydrate** 0g	0%
Total Fat 1.5g	2%	**Sodium** 75mg	3%	Dietary Fiber 0g	0%
Saturated Fat 0g	0%	**Protein** 26g		Sugars 0g	
Polyunsaturated Fat 0g					
Monounsaturated Fat 0g		Vitamin A 0% Vitamin C 0%		Calcium 0% Iron 4%	

Foster Farms 99% Fat-Free Natural Boneless/Skinless Thin-Sliced Chicken Breasts

1 piece / 132g

Amount per serving	%DV	Amount per serving	%DV	Amount per serving	%DV
Calories 140		**Cholesterol** 65mg	22%	**Total Carbohydrate** 0g	0%
Total Fat 1g	2%	**Sodium** 75mg	3%	Dietary Fiber 0g	0%
Saturated Fat 0g	0%	**Protein** 31g		Sugars 0g	
Polyunsaturated Fat 0g					
Monounsaturated Fat 0g		Vitamin A 0% Vitamin C 0%		Calcium 20% Iron 6%	

Ground Turkey, Fat-Free, Pan-Broiled Crumbles

3 oz / 85g

Amount per serving	%DV	Amount per serving	%DV	Amount per serving	%DV
Calories 128		**Cholesterol** 60mg	20%	**Total Carbohydrate** 0g	0%
Total Fat 2g	3%	**Sodium** 51mg	2%	Dietary Fiber 0g	0%
Saturated Fat 0g	0%	**Protein** 26.9g		Sugars 0g	
Polyunsaturated Fat 0.7g					
Monounsaturated Fat 0.6g		Vitamin A 25.5% Vitamin C 0%		Calcium 5.1% Iron 0%	

Ground Turkey, Fat-Free, Patties, Broiled

3 oz / 85g

Amount per serving	%DV	Amount per serving	%DV	Amount per serving	%DV
Calories 117		**Cholesterol** 55mg	18%	**Total Carbohydrate** 0g	0%
Total Fat 2g	3%	**Sodium** 50mg	2%	Dietary Fiber 0g	0%
Saturated Fat 1g	5%	**Protein** 25g		Sugars 0g	
Polyunsaturated Fat 0g					
Monounsaturated Fat 0g		Vitamin A 0% Vitamin C 0%		Calcium 1% Iron 4%	

Member's Mark, Boneless, Skinless Chicken Breast

4 oz / 113g

Amount per serving	%DV	Amount per serving	%DV	Amount per serving	%DV
Calories 130		**Cholesterol** 65mg	22%	**Total Carbohydrate** 1g	0%
Total Fat 2g	3%	**Sodium** 190mg	8%	Dietary Fiber 0g	0%
Saturated Fat 1g	5%	**Protein** 24g		Sugars 0g	
Polyunsaturated Fat 0g					
Monounsaturated Fat 0g		Vitamin A 0% Vitamin C 0%		Calcium 0% Iron 2%	

Member's Mark, Boneless, Skinless Chicken Tenderloins

4 oz / 113g

Amount per serving	%DV	Amount per serving	%DV	Amount per serving	%DV
Calories 90		**Cholesterol** 65mg	22%	**Total Carbohydrate** 1g	0%
Total Fat 1g	2%	**Sodium** 300mg	12%	Dietary Fiber 0g	0%
Saturated Fat 0g	0%	**Protein** 21g		Sugars 0g	
Polyunsaturated Fat 0g					
Monounsaturated Fat 0g		Vitamin A 0% Vitamin C 0%		Calcium 0% Iron 6%	

Member's Mark, 100% All Natural Boneless Skinless Chicken Tenderloins

4 oz / 100g

Amount per serving	%DV	Amount per serving	%DV	Amount per serving	%DV
Calories 100		**Cholesterol** 75mg	25%	**Total Carbohydrate** 0g	0%
Total Fat 1g	2%	**Sodium** 210mg	9%	Dietary Fiber 0g	0%
Saturated Fat 0g	0%	**Protein** 24g		Sugars 0g	
Polyunsaturated Fat 0g					
Monounsaturated Fat 0g		Vitamin A 0% Vitamin C 0%		Calcium 0% Iron 0%	

Member's Mark, 100% All Natural Boneless, Skinless Chicken Breast w/Rib Meat

4 oz / 113g

Amount per serving	%DV	Amount per serving	%DV	Amount per serving	%DV
Calories 100		**Cholesterol** 55mg	18%	**Total Carbohydrate** 0g	0%
Total Fat 2g	3%	**Sodium** 150mg	6%	Dietary Fiber 0g	0%
Saturated Fat 1g	5%	**Protein** 21g		Sugars 0g	
Polyunsaturated Fat 0g					
Monounsaturated Fat 0g		Vitamin A 0% Vitamin C 0%		Calcium 0% Iron 4%	

MorningStar Farms, Grillers California Turkey Burger

1 burger / 64g

Amount per serving	%DV	Amount per serving	%DV	Amount per serving	%DV
Calories 90		**Cholesterol** 0mg	0%	**Total Carbohydrate** 7g	2%
Total Fat 5g	8%	**Sodium** 390mg	16%	Dietary Fiber 5g	20%
Saturated Fat 0.5g	32%	**Protein** 9g		Sugars 1g	
Polyunsaturated Fat 2g					
Monounsaturated Fat 1.5g		Vitamin A 0% Vitamin C 0%		Calcium 4% Iron 15%	

MorningStar Farms, Grillers Chik'n Veggie Patties

1 burger / 67g

Amount per serving	%DV	Amount per serving	%DV	Amount per serving	%DV
Calories 80		**Cholesterol** 0mg	0%	**Total Carbohydrate** 7g	2%
Total Fat 3g	5%	**Sodium** 350mg	15%	Dietary Fiber 5g	20%
Saturated Fat 0g	0%	**Protein** 9g		Sugars 0g	
Polyunsaturated Fat 1g					
Monounsaturated Fat 1.5g		Vitamin A 0% Vitamin C 0%		Calcium 4% Iron 6%	

Murray's All Natural Boneless & Skinless Chicken Breasts

4 oz

Amount per serving	%DV	Amount per serving	%DV	Amount per serving	%DV
Calories 120		**Cholesterol** 70mg	23%	**Total Carbohydrate** 0g	0%
Total Fat 1g	2%	**Sodium** 30mg	1%	Dietary Fiber 0g	0%
Saturated Fat 0g	0%	**Protein** 28g		Sugars 0g	
Polyunsaturated Fat 0g					
Monounsaturated Fat 0g		Vitamin A 0% Vitamin C 0%		Calcium 0% Iron 0%	

Murray's All Natural Boneless & Skinless Chicken Breasts

4 oz / 112g

Amount per serving	%DV	Amount per serving	%DV	Amount per serving	%DV
Calories 110		**Cholesterol** 70mg	23%	**Total Carbohydrate** 0g	0%
Total Fat 1g	2%	**Sodium** 50mg	2%	Dietary Fiber 0g	0%
Saturated Fat 0g	0%	**Protein** 25g		Sugars 0g	
Polyunsaturated Fat 0g					
Monounsaturated Fat 0g		Vitamin A 0% Vitamin C 0%		Calcium 1% Iron 0%	

Randall Farms All Natural Boneless, Skinless Chicken Breast with Rib Meat

4 oz

Amount per serving	%DV	Amount per serving	%DV	Amount per serving	%DV
Calories 120		**Cholesterol** 65mg	22%	**Total Carbohydrate** 0g	0%
Total Fat 2g	3%	**Sodium** 75mg	3%	Dietary Fiber 0g	0%
Saturated Fat 0g	0%	**Protein** 26g		Sugars 0g	
Polyunsaturated Fat 0g					
Monounsaturated Fat 0g		Vitamin A 0% Vitamin C 0%		Calcium 0% Iron 0%	

Sanderson Farms Natural 99% Fat-Free Chicken Breast Tenderloins

4 oz / 112g

Amount per serving	%DV	Amount per serving	%DV	Amount per serving	%DV
Calories 110		**Cholesterol** 65mg	22%	**Total Carbohydrate** 1g	0%
Total Fat 1g	2%	**Sodium** 35mg	1%	Dietary Fiber 0g	0%
Saturated Fat 0g	0%	**Protein** 25g		Sugars 1g	
Polyunsaturated Fat 0g					
Monounsaturated Fat 0g		Vitamin A 0% Vitamin C 0%		Calcium 0% Iron 2%	

Sanderson Farms Natural 99% Fat-Free Skinless Chicken Breast Fillets

4 oz / 112g

Amount per serving	%DV	Amount per serving	%DV	Amount per serving	%DV
Calories 130		**Cholesterol** 75mg	25%	**Total Carbohydrate** 2g	1%
Total Fat 3g	5%	**Sodium** 45mg	2%	Dietary Fiber 0g	0%
Saturated Fat 1g	5%	**Protein** 24g		Sugars 0g	
Polyunsaturated Fat 0g					
Monounsaturated Fat 0g		Vitamin A 0% Vitamin C 0%		Calcium 0% Iron 2%	

Sanderson Farms Natural 99% Fat-Free Thin Sliced Skinless Chicken Breast Fillet

4 oz / 112g

Amount per serving	%DV	Amount per serving	%DV	Amount per serving	%DV
Calories 120		**Cholesterol** 75mg	25%	**Total Carbohydrate** 2g	1%
Total Fat 1g	2%	**Sodium** 45mg	2%	Dietary Fiber 0g	0%
Saturated Fat 0g	0%	**Protein** 25g		Sugars 0g	
Polyunsaturated Fat 0g					
Monounsaturated Fat 0g		Vitamin A 0% Vitamin C 0%		Calcium 2% Iron 4%	

Turkey Roll, Light and Dark Meat

2 slices / 57g

Amount per serving	%DV	Amount per serving	%DV	Amount per serving	%DV
Calories 85		Cholesterol 31mg	10%	Total Carbohydrate 1g	0%
Total Fat 4g	6%	Sodium 334mg	14%	Dietary Fiber 0g	0%
Saturated Fat 1g	5%	Protein 10g		Sugars 0g	
Polyunsaturated Fat 1g					
Monounsaturated Fat 1.3g		Vitamin A 0%	Vitamin C 0%	Calcium 2%	Iron 4%

Turkey, All Classes, Light Meat, Cooked, Roasted

1 unit / yield from 1 lb ready-to-cook turkey / 117g

Amount per serving	%DV	Amount per serving	%DV	Amount per serving	%DV
Calories 184		Cholesterol 81mg	27%	Total Carbohydrate 0g	0%
Total Fat 3.7g	6%	Sodium 75mg	3%	Dietary Fiber 0g	0%
Saturated Fat 1.1g	6%	Protein 35g		Sugars 0g	
Polyunsaturated Fat 1g					
Monounsaturated Fat 0.6g		Vitamin A 0%	Vitamin C 0%	Calcium 3%	Iron 9%

Turkey, Fryer-Roasters, Wing, Meat Only, Cooked, Roasted

1 wing / bone and skin removed / 60g

Amount per serving	%DV	Amount per serving	%DV	Amount per serving	%DV
Calories 98		Cholesterol 61mg	20%	Total Carbohydrate 0g	0%
Total Fat 2.1g	3%	Sodium 47mg	2%	Dietary Fiber 0g	0%
Saturated Fat 0.7g	4%	Protein 18.5g		Sugars 0g	
Polyunsaturated Fat 0.6g					
Monounsaturated Fat 0.4g		Vitamin A 0%	Vitamin C 0%	Calcium 2%	Iron 6%

Turkey, Young Hen, Light Meat, Meat Only, Cooked, Roasted

1 unit / yield from 1 lb ready-to-cook turkey / 119g

Amount per serving	%DV	Amount per serving	%DV	Amount per serving	%DV
Calories 192		Cholesterol 81mg	27%	Total Carbohydrate 0g	0%
Total Fat 4.5g	7%	Sodium 71mg	3%	Dietary Fiber 0g	0%
Saturated Fat 1.4g	7%	Protein 35.6g		Sugars 0g	
Polyunsaturated Fat 1.2g					
Monounsaturated Fat 0.8g		Vitamin A 0%	Vitamin C 0%	Calcium 2%	Iron 9%

Turkey, Young Tom, Light Meat, Meat Only, Cooked, Roasted

1 unit / yield from 1 lb ready-to-cook turkey / 117g

Amount per serving	%DV	Amount per serving	%DV	Amount per serving	%DV
Calories 180		Cholesterol 80mg	27%	Total Carbohydrate 0g	0%
Total Fat 3.4g	5%	Sodium 79.5mg	3%	Dietary Fiber 0g	0%
Saturated Fat 1g	5%	Protein 34.9g		Sugars 0g	
Polyunsaturated Fat 0g					
Monounsaturated Fat 0g		Vitamin A 0%	Vitamin C 0%	Calcium 2%	Iron 1.5%

Meats, Pork

Farmer John California Natural Premium Extra Lean Boneless Pork Tenderloins

4 oz / 112g

Amount per serving	%DV	Amount per serving	%DV	Amount per serving	%DV
Calories 120		**Cholesterol** 75mg	25%	**Total Carbohydrate** 0g	0%
Total Fat 2.5g	4%	**Sodium** 55mg	2%	Dietary Fiber 0g	0%
Saturated Fat 1g	5%	**Protein** 24g		Sugars 0g	
Polyunsaturated Fat 0g					
Monounsaturated Fat 0g		Vitamin A 0% Vitamin C 0%		Calcium 2% Iron 6%	

Hormel Always Tender Extra Lean Boneless Pork Tenderloin

112g

Amount per serving	%DV	Amount per serving	%DV	Amount per serving	%DV
Calories 120		**Cholesterol** 50mg	17%	**Total Carbohydrate** 1g	0%
Total Fat 4g	6%	**Sodium** 250mg	10%	Dietary Fiber 0g	0%
Saturated Fat 1.5g	8%	**Protein** 19g		Sugars 0g	
Polyunsaturated Fat 0g					
Monounsaturated Fat 0g		Vitamin A 0% Vitamin C 0%		Calcium 0% Iron 0%	

Pork, Fresh, Loin, Tenderloin

85g

Amount per serving	%DV	Amount per serving	%DV	Amount per serving	%DV
Calories 122		**Cholesterol** 62mg	21%	**Total Carbohydrate** 0g	0%
Total Fat 3g	5%	**Sodium** 48mg	2%	Dietary Fiber 0g	0%
Saturated Fat 1g	5%	**Protein** 22g		Sugars 0g	
Polyunsaturated Fat 0.4g					
Monounsaturated Fat 0g		Vitamin A 0% Vitamin C 0%		Calcium 0% Iron 5%	

Pork, Fresh, Loin, Tenderloin, Lean, Cooked, Roasted

3 oz / 85g

Amount per serving	%DV	Amount per serving	%DV	Amount per serving	%DV
Calories 122		**Cholesterol** 62mg	21%	**Total Carbohydrate** 0g	0%
Total Fat 3g	5%	**Sodium** 48mg	2%	Dietary Fiber 0g	0%
Saturated Fat 1g	5%	**Protein** 22g		Sugars 0g	
Polyunsaturated Fat 0.4g					
Monounsaturated Fat 1.1g		Vitamin A 0% Vitamin C 0%		Calcium 1% Iron 5%	

Pork, Fresh, Loin, Top Loin (Roasts), Boneless, Lean, Cooked, Roasted

3 oz / 85g

Amount per serving	%DV	Amount per serving	%DV	Amount per serving	%DV
Calories 147		**Cholesterol** 67mg	22%	**Total Carbohydrate** 0g	0%
Total Fat 5g	8%	**Sodium** 40mg	2%	Dietary Fiber 0g	0%
Saturated Fat 0.6g	3%	**Protein** 23g		Sugars 0g	
Polyunsaturated Fat 0.5g					
Monounsaturated Fat 2.1g		Vitamin A 0% Vitamin C 0%		Calcium 1% Iron 3%	

Pork, Shoulder, Petite Tender, Boneless, Lean and Fat, Cooked, Broiled

1 piece / 92g

Amount per serving	%DV	Amount per serving	%DV	Amount per serving	%DV
Calories 143		**Cholesterol** 75mg	25%	**Total Carbohydrate** 0g	0%
Total Fat 4g	6%	**Sodium** 49mg	2%	Dietary Fiber 0g	0%
Saturated Fat 1g	5%	**Protein** 25g		Sugars 0g	
Polyunsaturated Fat 0g					
Monounsaturated Fat 0g		Vitamin A 0% Vitamin C 0%		Calcium 1% Iron 6%	

Swift / Kirkland Signature Pork Sirloin Tip Roast

4 oz / 112g

Amount per serving	%DV	Amount per serving	%DV	Amount per serving	%DV
Calories 100		**Cholesterol** 30mg	10%	**Total Carbohydrate** 0g	0%
Total Fat 1.5g	2%	**Sodium** 290mg	12%	Dietary Fiber 0g	0%
Saturated Fat 0g	0%	**Protein** 22g		Sugars 0g	
Polyunsaturated Fat 0g					
Monounsaturated Fat 0g		Vitamin A 0% Vitamin C 0%		Calcium 0% Iron 0%	

Swift Pork Tenderloin

4 oz

Amount per serving	%DV	Amount per serving	%DV	Amount per serving	%DV
Calories 120		**Cholesterol** 45mg	15%	**Total Carbohydrate** 1g	0%
Total Fat 2.5g	4%	**Sodium** 70mg	3%	Dietary Fiber 0g	0%
Saturated Fat 1g	5%	**Protein** 24g		Sugars 0g	
Polyunsaturated Fat 0g					
Monounsaturated Fat 0g		Vitamin A 0% Vitamin C 0%		Calcium 2% Iron 0%	

Tender Choice, 97% Fat-Free Pork Tenderloins

4 oz / 112g

Amount per serving	%DV	Amount per serving	%DV	Amount per serving	%DV
Calories 120		**Cholesterol** 65mg	22%	**Total Carbohydrate** 2g	1%
Total Fat 2.5g	4%	**Sodium** 230mg	10%	Dietary Fiber 0g	0%
Saturated Fat 1g	5%	**Protein** 21g		Sugars 0g	
Polyunsaturated Fat 0g					
Monounsaturated Fat 0g		Vitamin A 0% Vitamin C 0%		Calcium 0% Iron 6%	

Meats, Veal

Veal, Leg (Top Round), Lean, Cooked, Roasted

3 oz / 85g

Amount per serving	%DV	Amount per serving	%DV	Amount per serving	%DV
Calories 136		**Cholesterol** 88mg	29%	**Total Carbohydrate** 0g	0%
Total Fat 4g	6%	**Sodium** 58mg	2%	Dietary Fiber 0g	0%
Saturated Fat 2g	10%	**Protein** 24g		Sugars 0g	
Polyunsaturated Fat 0g					
Monounsaturated Fat 0g		Vitamin A 0% Vitamin C 0%		Calcium 1% Iron 4%	

Veal, Sirloin, Lean, Cooked, Roasted

3 oz / 85g

Amount per serving	%DV	Amount per serving	%DV	Amount per serving	%DV
Calories 143		**Cholesterol** 88mg	29%	**Total Carbohydrate** 0g	0%
Total Fat 5g	8%	**Sodium** 72mg	3%	Dietary Fiber 0g	0%
Saturated Fat 2g	10%	**Protein** 22g		Sugars 0g	
Polyunsaturated Fat 0g					
Monounsaturated Fat 0g		Vitamin A 0% Vitamin C 0%		Calcium 1% Iron 4%	

Frankfurters/Hot Dogs

Applegate Farms, Great Organic Chicken Hot Dog

1 hot dog

Amount per serving	%DV	Amount per serving	%DV	Amount per serving	%DV
Calories 70		**Cholesterol** 35mg	12%	**Total Carbohydrate** 0g	0%
Total Fat 3.5g	5%	**Sodium** 360mg	15%	Dietary Fiber 0g	0%
Saturated Fat 1g	5%	**Protein** 8g		Sugars 0g	
Polyunsaturated Fat 0g					
Monounsaturated Fat 0g		Vitamin A 0% Vitamin C 0%		Calcium 0% Iron 2%	

Applegate Farms, Great Organic Turkey Hot Dog

1 hot dog

Amount per serving	%DV	Amount per serving	%DV	Amount per serving	%DV
Calories 60		**Cholesterol** 25mg	8%	**Total Carbohydrate** 1g	0%
Total Fat 3.5g	5%	**Sodium** 370mg	15%	Dietary Fiber 0g	0%
Saturated Fat 1g	5%	**Protein** 7g		Sugars 0g	
Polyunsaturated Fat 0g					
Monounsaturated Fat 0g		Vitamin A 2% Vitamin C 0%		Calcium 0% Iron 2%	

Applegate Farms, Super Natural Uncured Chicken Hot Dog

1 hot dog

Amount per serving	%DV	Amount per serving	%DV	Amount per serving	%DV
Calories 60		**Cholesterol** 35mg	12%	**Total Carbohydrate** 0g	0%
Total Fat 3g	5%	**Sodium** 370mg	15%	Dietary Fiber 0g	0%
Saturated Fat 1g	5%	**Protein** 7g		Sugars 0g	
Polyunsaturated Fat 0g					
Monounsaturated Fat 0g		Vitamin A 0% Vitamin C 0%		Calcium 0% Iron 2%	

Applegate Farms, Super Natural Uncured Turkey Hot Dog

1 hot dog

Amount per serving	%DV	Amount per serving	%DV	Amount per serving	%DV
Calories 50		**Cholesterol** 25mg	8%	**Total Carbohydrate** 0g	0%
Total Fat 3.5g	5%	**Sodium** 260mg	11%	Dietary Fiber 0g	0%
Saturated Fat 1g	5%	**Protein** 5g		Sugars 0g	
Polyunsaturated Fat 0g					
Monounsaturated Fat 0g		Vitamin A 2% Vitamin C 0%		Calcium 0% Iron 2%	

Frankfurter, Beef, Pork and Turkey, Fat Free

1 frankfurter / 1 NLEA serving / 57g

Amount per serving	%DV	Amount per serving	%DV	Amount per serving	%DV
Calories 62		**Cholesterol** 23mg	8%	**Total Carbohydrate** 6g	2%
Total Fat 1g	2%	**Sodium** 455mg	19%	Dietary Fiber 0g	0%
Saturated Fat 0g	0%	**Protein** 7g		Sugars 0g	
Polyunsaturated Fat 0g					
Monounsaturated Fat 0g		Vitamin A 0% Vitamin C 23%		Calcium 3% Iron 6%	

Protein Alternatives

Amy's, Bistro Veggie Burger

2.5 oz

Amount per serving	%DV	Amount per serving	%DV	Amount per serving	%DV
Calories 110		**Cholesterol** 0mg	0%	**Total Carbohydrate** 15g	5%
Total Fat 3g	5%	**Sodium** 330mg	14%	Dietary Fiber 2g	8%
Saturated Fat 0g	0%	**Protein** 5g		Sugars 1g	
Polyunsaturated Fat 0g					
Monounsaturated Fat 0g		Vitamin A 10% Vitamin C 4%		Calcium 2% Iron 4%	

Eden Foods, Dried Tofu

1 piece / 10g

Amount per serving	%DV	Amount per serving	%DV	Amount per serving	%DV
Calories 50		**Cholesterol** 0mg	0%	**Total Carbohydrate** 0g	0%
Total Fat 2.5g	4%	**Sodium** 0mg	0%	Dietary Fiber 2g	8%
Saturated Fat 0g	0%	**Protein** 5g		Sugars 0g	
Polyunsaturated Fat 0g					
Monounsaturated Fat 0g		Vitamin A 0% Vitamin C 0%		Calcium 6% Iron 2%	

Frieda's, Soft Tofu

3 oz

Amount per serving	%DV	Amount per serving	%DV	Amount per serving	%DV
Calories 45		**Cholesterol** 0mg	0%	**Total Carbohydrate** 1g	0%
Total Fat 2.5g	4%	**Sodium** 15mg	1%	Dietary Fiber 0g	0%
Saturated Fat 0g	0%	**Protein** 5g		Sugars 0g	
Polyunsaturated Fat 0g					
Monounsaturated Fat 0g		Vitamin A 0% Vitamin C 0%		Calcium 6% Iron 4%	

Gardenburger, Black Bean Chipotle Burger

1 patty / 71g

Amount per serving	%DV	Amount per serving	%DV	Amount per serving	%DV
Calories 90		**Cholesterol** 0mg	0%	**Total Carbohydrate** 16g	5%
Total Fat 3g	5%	**Sodium** 390mg	16%	Dietary Fiber 4g	16%
Saturated Fat 0g	0%	**Protein** 5g		Sugars 3g	
Polyunsaturated Fat 0.5g					
Monounsaturated Fat 1.5g		Vitamin A 0% Vitamin C 0%		Calcium 2% Iron 8%	

Gardenburger, Sun-Dried Tomato Basil Burger

1 patty / 71g

Amount per serving	%DV	Amount per serving	%DV	Amount per serving	%DV
Calories 100		**Cholesterol** 5mg	2%	**Total Carbohydrate** 17g	6%
Total Fat 2.5g	4%	**Sodium** 270mg	11%	Dietary Fiber 4g	16%
Saturated Fat 0.5g	2%	**Protein** 4g		Sugars 2g	
Polyunsaturated Fat 0g					
Monounsaturated Fat 0g		Vitamin A 4%	Vitamin C 4%	Calcium 2%	Iron 4%

Green Giant, Harvest Burger, Original Flavor, All Vegetable Protein Patties, Frozen

1 patty / 90g

Amount per serving	%DV	Amount per serving	%DV	Amount per serving	%DV
Calories 138		**Cholesterol** 0mg	0%	**Total Carbohydrate** 7g	2%
Total Fat 4g	6%	**Sodium** 411mg	17%	Dietary Fiber 5.7g	23%
Saturated Fat 1g	5%	**Protein** 18g		Sugars 0g	
Polyunsaturated Fat 0.3g					
Monounsaturated Fat 2.1g		Vitamin A 0%	Vitamin C 0%	Calcium 10%	Iron 21%

House Foods, Premium Firm Tofu

3 oz / 84g

Amount per serving	%DV	Amount per serving	%DV	Amount per serving	%DV
Calories 70		**Cholesterol** 0mg	0%	**Total Carbohydrate** 2g	1%
Total Fat 4g	6%	**Sodium** 10mg	0%	Dietary Fiber 2g	8%
Saturated Fat 0.5g	2%	**Protein** 7g		Sugars 0g	
Polyunsaturated Fat 0g					
Monounsaturated Fat 0g		Vitamin A 0%	Vitamin C 0%	Calcium 15%	Iron 8%

House Foods, Premium Soft Tofu

3 oz / 85g

Amount per serving	%DV	Amount per serving	%DV	Amount per serving	%DV
Calories 60		**Cholesterol** 0mg	0%	**Total Carbohydrate** 2g	1%
Total Fat 3g	5%	**Sodium** 10mg	0%	Dietary Fiber 1g	4%
Saturated Fat 0g	0%	**Protein** 5g		Sugars 0g	
Polyunsaturated Fat 0g					
Monounsaturated Fat 0g		Vitamin A 0%	Vitamin C 0%	Calcium 6%	Iron 6%

Loma Linda Vege-Burger, Canned, Unprepared

1/4 cup / 55g

Amount per serving	%DV	Amount per serving	%DV	Amount per serving	%DV
Calories 60		**Cholesterol** 0mg	0%	**Total Carbohydrate** 2g	1%
Total Fat 0.5g	1%	**Sodium** 130mg	5%	Dietary Fiber 1.5g	6%
Saturated Fat 0g	0%	**Protein** 12g		Sugars 0g	
Polyunsaturated Fat 0.5g					
Monounsaturated Fat 0g		Vitamin A 0%	Vitamin C 0%	Calcium 0%	Iron 2%

VitaSoy USA, Nasoya Lite Firm Tofu

1/4 pkg / 79g

Amount per serving	%DV	Amount per serving	%DV	Amount per serving	%DV
Calories 40		**Cholesterol** 0mg	0%	**Total Carbohydrate** 1g	0%
Total Fat 1.5g	2%	**Sodium** 25mg	1%	Dietary Fiber 1g	4%
Saturated Fat 0g	0%	**Protein** 7g		Sugars 0g	
Polyunsaturated Fat 1g					
Monounsaturated Fat 0g		Vitamin A 30% Vitamin C 0%		Calcium 15% Iron 8%	

Luncheon Meats

Applegate Farms, Antibiotic-Free Herb Turkey

2 oz

Amount per serving	%DV	Amount per serving	%DV	Amount per serving	%DV
Calories 50		**Cholesterol** 30mg	10%	**Total Carbohydrate** 0g	0%
Total Fat 0g	0%	**Sodium** 360mg	15%	Dietary Fiber 0g	0%
Saturated Fat 0g	0%	**Protein** 12g		Sugars 0g	
Polyunsaturated Fat 0g					
Monounsaturated Fat 0g		Vitamin A 0% Vitamin C 0%		Calcium 0% Iron 4%	

Applegate Farms, Antibiotic-Free Honey & Maple Turkey Breast

2 oz

Amount per serving	%DV	Amount per serving	%DV	Amount per serving	%DV
Calories 60		**Cholesterol** 25mg	8%	**Total Carbohydrate** 2g	1%
Total Fat 0.5g	1%	**Sodium** 450mg	19%	Dietary Fiber 0g	0%
Saturated Fat 0g	0%	**Protein** 11g		Sugars 2g	
Polyunsaturated Fat 0g					
Monounsaturated Fat 0g		Vitamin A 0% Vitamin C 0%		Calcium 0% Iron 2%	

Applegate Farms, Antibiotic-Free Honey Ham

2 oz

Amount per serving	%DV	Amount per serving	%DV	Amount per serving	%DV
Calories 70		**Cholesterol** 30mg	10%	**Total Carbohydrate** 3g	1%
Total Fat 1.5g	2%	**Sodium** 450mg	19%	Dietary Fiber 0g	0%
Saturated Fat 0.5g	3%	**Protein** 10g		Sugars 3g	
Polyunsaturated Fat 0g					
Monounsaturated Fat 0g		Vitamin A 0% Vitamin C 0%		Calcium 0% Iron 2%	

Applegate Farms, Antibiotic-Free Roast Beef

2 oz

Amount per serving	%DV	Amount per serving	%DV	Amount per serving	%DV
Calories 80		**Cholesterol** 35mg	12%	**Total Carbohydrate** 0g	0%
Total Fat 3g	5%	**Sodium** 320mg	13%	Dietary Fiber 0g	0%
Saturated Fat 1g	5%	**Protein** 12g		Sugars 0g	
Polyunsaturated Fat 0g					
Monounsaturated Fat 0g		Vitamin A 0% Vitamin C 0%		Calcium 0% Iron 6%	

Applegate Farms, Antibiotic-Free Roasted Chicken Breast

2 oz

Amount per serving	%DV	Amount per serving	%DV	Amount per serving	%DV
Calories 60		**Cholesterol** 30mg	10%	**Total Carbohydrate** 1g	0%
Total Fat 1.5g	2%	**Sodium** 360mg	15%	Dietary Fiber 0g	0%
Saturated Fat 0.5g	2%	**Protein** 10g		Sugars 1g	
Polyunsaturated Fat 0g					
Monounsaturated Fat 0g		Vitamin A 0% Vitamin C 0%		Calcium 0% Iron 4%	

Applegate Farms, Antibiotic-Free Roasted Turkey Breast

2 oz

Amount per serving	%DV	Amount per serving	%DV	Amount per serving	%DV
Calories 50		**Cholesterol** 30mg	10%	**Total Carbohydrate** 0g	0%
Total Fat 0g	0%	**Sodium** 360mg	15%	Dietary Fiber 0g	0%
Saturated Fat 0g	0%	**Protein** 12g		Sugars 0g	
Polyunsaturated Fat 0g					
Monounsaturated Fat 0g		Vitamin A 0% Vitamin C 0%		Calcium 0% Iron 4%	

Applegate Farms, Antibiotic-Free Smoked Turkey Breast

2 oz

Amount per serving	%DV	Amount per serving	%DV	Amount per serving	%DV
Calories 50		**Cholesterol** 30mg	10%	**Total Carbohydrate** 0g	0%
Total Fat 0g	0%	**Sodium** 360mg	15%	Dietary Fiber 0g	0%
Saturated Fat 0g	0%	**Protein** 12g		Sugars 0g	
Polyunsaturated Fat 0g					
Monounsaturated Fat 0g		Vitamin A 0% Vitamin C 0%		Calcium 0% Iron 4%	

Applegate Farms, Antibiotic-Free Turkey Bacon

1 pan fried slice

Amount per serving	%DV	Amount per serving	%DV	Amount per serving	%DV
Calories 35		**Cholesterol** 25mg	8%	**Total Carbohydrate** 0g	0%
Total Fat 1.5g	2%	**Sodium** 200mg	8%	Dietary Fiber 0g	0%
Saturated Fat 0g	0%	**Protein** 6g		Sugars 0g	
Polyunsaturated Fat 0g					
Monounsaturated Fat 0g		Vitamin A 0% Vitamin C 0%		Calcium 0% Iron 2%	

Applegate Farms, Antibiotic-Free Uncured Black Forest Ham

2 oz

Amount per serving	%DV	Amount per serving	%DV	Amount per serving	%DV
Calories 50		**Cholesterol** 35mg	12%	**Total Carbohydrate** 0g	0%
Total Fat 1.5g	2%	**Sodium** 480mg	20%	Dietary Fiber 0g	0%
Saturated Fat 0.5g	3%	**Protein** 10g		Sugars 0g	
Polyunsaturated Fat 0g					
Monounsaturated Fat 0g		Vitamin A 0% Vitamin C 0%		Calcium 0% Iron 2%	

Applegate Farms, Chipotle Chicken

2 oz

Amount per serving	%DV	Amount per serving	%DV	Amount per serving	%DV
Calories 60		**Cholesterol** 30mg	10%	**Total Carbohydrate** 1g	0%
Total Fat 0.5g	1%	**Sodium** 400mg	17%	Dietary Fiber 0g	0%
Saturated Fat 0g	0%	**Protein** 12g		Sugars 0g	
Polyunsaturated Fat 0g					
Monounsaturated Fat 0g		Vitamin A 0% Vitamin C 0%		Calcium 2% Iron 2%	

Applegate Farms, Herb Turkey Breast

2 oz

Amount per serving	%DV	Amount per serving	%DV	Amount per serving	%DV
Calories 50		**Cholesterol** 30mg	10%	**Total Carbohydrate** 0g	0%
Total Fat 0g	0%	**Sodium** 400mg	17%	Dietary Fiber 0g	0%
Saturated Fat 0g	0%	**Protein** 12g		Sugars 0g	
Polyunsaturated Fat 0g					
Monounsaturated Fat 0g		Vitamin A 0% Vitamin C 0%		Calcium 2% Iron 4%	

Applegate Farms, Honey Maple Turkey Breast

2 oz

Amount per serving	%DV	Amount per serving	%DV	Amount per serving	%DV
Calories 50		**Cholesterol** 25mg	8%	**Total Carbohydrate** 3g	1%
Total Fat 0g	0%	**Sodium** 450mg	19%	Dietary Fiber 0g	0%
Saturated Fat 0g	0%	**Protein** 12g		Sugars 2g	
Polyunsaturated Fat 0g					
Monounsaturated Fat 0g		Vitamin A 0% Vitamin C 0%		Calcium 0% Iron 2%	

Applegate Farms, Natural Slow Cooked Ham

2 oz

Amount per serving	%DV	Amount per serving	%DV	Amount per serving	%DV
Calories 60		**Cholesterol** 35mg	12%	**Total Carbohydrate** 0g	0%
Total Fat 1.5g	2%	**Sodium** 480mg	20%	Dietary Fiber 0g	0%
Saturated Fat 0.5g	3%	**Protein** 11g		Sugars 0g	
Polyunsaturated Fat 0g					
Monounsaturated Fat 0g		Vitamin A 0% Vitamin C 0%		Calcium 0% Iron 4%	

Applegate Farms, No Salt Turkey

2 oz

Amount per serving	%DV	Amount per serving	%DV	Amount per serving	%DV
Calories 60		**Cholesterol** 35mg	12%	**Total Carbohydrate** 0g	0%
Total Fat 0g	0%	**Sodium** 30mg	1%	Dietary Fiber 0g	0%
Saturated Fat 0g	0%	**Protein** 15g		Sugars 0g	
Polyunsaturated Fat 0g					
Monounsaturated Fat 0g		Vitamin A 0% Vitamin C 0%		Calcium 0% Iron 4%	

Applegate Farms, Organic Herb Turkey Breast

2 oz

Amount per serving	%DV	Amount per serving	%DV	Amount per serving	%DV
Calories 50		**Cholesterol** 25mg	8%	**Total Carbohydrate** 0g	0%
Total Fat 0g	0%	**Sodium** 360mg	15%	Dietary Fiber 0g	0%
Saturated Fat 0g	0%	**Protein** 10g		Sugars 0g	
Polyunsaturated Fat 0g					
Monounsaturated Fat 0g		Vitamin A 0% Vitamin C 0%		Calcium 0% Iron 4%	

Applegate Farms, Organic Oven-Roasted Chicken Breast

2 oz

Amount per serving	%DV	Amount per serving	%DV	Amount per serving	%DV
Calories 60		**Cholesterol** 30mg	10%	**Total Carbohydrate** 1g	0%
Total Fat 1.5g	2%	**Sodium** 360mg	15%	Dietary Fiber 0g	0%
Saturated Fat 0g	0%	**Protein** 10g		Sugars 1g	
Polyunsaturated Fat 0g					
Monounsaturated Fat 0g		Vitamin A 0% Vitamin C 0%		Calcium 0% Iron 2%	

Applegate Farms, Organic Roast Beef

2 oz

Amount per serving	%DV	Amount per serving	%DV	Amount per serving	%DV
Calories 80		**Cholesterol** 35mg	12%	**Total Carbohydrate** 0g	0%
Total Fat 3g	5%	**Sodium** 320mg	13%	Dietary Fiber 0g	0%
Saturated Fat 1g	5%	**Protein** 12g		Sugars 0g	
Polyunsaturated Fat 0g					
Monounsaturated Fat 0g		Vitamin A 0% Vitamin C 0%		Calcium 0% Iron 6%	

Applegate Farms, Organic Roasted Chicken Breast

2 oz

Amount per serving	%DV	Amount per serving	%DV	Amount per serving	%DV
Calories 60		**Cholesterol** 30mg	10%	**Total Carbohydrate** 1g	0%
Total Fat 1.5g	2%	**Sodium** 360mg	15%	Dietary Fiber 0g	0%
Saturated Fat 0.5g	2%	**Protein** 10g		Sugars 1g	
Polyunsaturated Fat 0g					
Monounsaturated Fat 0g		Vitamin A 0% Vitamin C 0%		Calcium 0% Iron 2%	

Applegate Farms, Organic Roasted Turkey Breast

2 oz

Amount per serving	%DV	Amount per serving	%DV	Amount per serving	%DV
Calories 50		**Cholesterol** 25mg	8%	**Total Carbohydrate** 0g	0%
Total Fat 0g	0%	**Sodium** 360mg	15%	Dietary Fiber 0g	0%
Saturated Fat 0g	0%	**Protein** 10g		Sugars 0g	
Polyunsaturated Fat 0g					
Monounsaturated Fat 0g		Vitamin A 0% Vitamin C 0%		Calcium 0% Iron 4%	

Applegate Farms, Organic Oven-Roasted Smoked Chicken Breast

2 oz

Amount per serving	%DV	Amount per serving	%DV	Amount per serving	%DV
Calories 60		**Cholesterol** 30mg	10%	**Total Carbohydrate** 1g	0%
Total Fat 1.5g	2%	**Sodium** 360mg	15%	Dietary Fiber 0g	0%
Saturated Fat 0.5g	2%	**Protein** 10g		Sugars 1g	
Polyunsaturated Fat 0g					
Monounsaturated Fat 0g		Vitamin A 0% Vitamin C 0%		Calcium 0% Iron 2%	

Applegate Farms, Organic Smoked Turkey Breast

2 oz

Amount per serving	%DV	Amount per serving	%DV	Amount per serving	%DV
Calories 50		**Cholesterol** 25mg	8%	**Total Carbohydrate** 0g	0%
Total Fat 0g	0%	**Sodium** 360mg	15%	Dietary Fiber 0g	0%
Saturated Fat 0g	0%	**Protein** 10g		Sugars 0g	
Polyunsaturated Fat 0g					
Monounsaturated Fat 0g		Vitamin A 0% Vitamin C 0%		Calcium 0% Iron 2%	

Applegate Farms, Oven Roasted Turkey Breast

2 oz

Amount per serving	%DV	Amount per serving	%DV	Amount per serving	%DV
Calories 50		**Cholesterol** 30mg	10%	**Total Carbohydrate** 0g	0%
Total Fat 0g	0%	**Sodium** 400mg	17%	Dietary Fiber 0g	0%
Saturated Fat 0g	0%	**Protein** 12g		Sugars 0g	
Polyunsaturated Fat 0g					
Monounsaturated Fat 0g		Vitamin A 0% Vitamin C 0%		Calcium 0% Iron 4%	

Applegate Farms, Peppered Eye Round Roast Beef

2 oz

Amount per serving	%DV	Amount per serving	%DV	Amount per serving	%DV
Calories 80		**Cholesterol** 30mg	10%	**Total Carbohydrate** 0g	0%
Total Fat 3g	5%	**Sodium** 200mg	8%	Dietary Fiber 0g	0%
Saturated Fat 1g	5%	**Protein** 12g		Sugars 0g	
Polyunsaturated Fat 0g					
Monounsaturated Fat 0g		Vitamin A 0% Vitamin C 0%		Calcium 0% Iron 8%	

Applegate Farms, Peppered Turkey Breast

2 oz

Amount per serving	%DV	Amount per serving	%DV	Amount per serving	%DV
Calories 50		**Cholesterol** 30mg	10%	**Total Carbohydrate** 0g	0%
Total Fat 0g	0%	**Sodium** 360mg	15%	Dietary Fiber 0g	0%
Saturated Fat 0g	0%	**Protein** 12g		Sugars 0g	
Polyunsaturated Fat 0g					
Monounsaturated Fat 0g		Vitamin A 0% Vitamin C 0%		Calcium 0% Iron 4%	

Applegate Farms, Roast Beef

2 oz

Amount per serving	%DV	Amount per serving	%DV	Amount per serving	%DV
Calories 80		**Cholesterol** 30mg	10%	**Total Carbohydrate** 0g	0%
Total Fat 3g	5%	**Sodium** 200mg	8%	Dietary Fiber 0g	0%
Saturated Fat 1g	5%	**Protein** 12g		Sugars 0g	
Polyunsaturated Fat 0g					
Monounsaturated Fat 0g		Vitamin A 0% Vitamin C 0%		Calcium 0% Iron 8%	

Applegate Farms, Slow Cooked Ham

2 oz

Amount per serving	%DV	Amount per serving	%DV	Amount per serving	%DV
Calories 60		**Cholesterol** 35mg	12%	**Total Carbohydrate** 0g	0%
Total Fat 1.5g	2%	**Sodium** 480mg	20%	Dietary Fiber 0g	0%
Saturated Fat 0.5g	3%	**Protein** 11g		Sugars 0g	
Polyunsaturated Fat 0g					
Monounsaturated Fat 0g		Vitamin A 0% Vitamin C 0%		Calcium 0% Iron 4%	

Applegate Farms, Smoked Chicken Breast

2 oz

Amount per serving	%DV	Amount per serving	%DV	Amount per serving	%DV
Calories 60		**Cholesterol** 30mg	10%	**Total Carbohydrate** 2g	1%
Total Fat 1.5g	2%	**Sodium** 310mg	13%	Dietary Fiber 0g	0%
Saturated Fat 0g	0%	**Protein** 12g		Sugars 1g	
Polyunsaturated Fat 0g					
Monounsaturated Fat 0g		Vitamin A 2% Vitamin C 2%		Calcium 2% Iron 2%	

Applegate Farms, Smoked Turkey Breast

2 oz

Amount per serving	%DV	Amount per serving	%DV	Amount per serving	%DV
Calories 50		**Cholesterol** 30mg	10%	**Total Carbohydrate** 0g	0%
Total Fat 0g	0%	**Sodium** 400mg	17%	Dietary Fiber 0g	0%
Saturated Fat 0g	0%	**Protein** 12g		Sugars 0g	
Polyunsaturated Fat 0g					
Monounsaturated Fat 0g		Vitamin A 0% Vitamin C 0%		Calcium 0% Iron 2%	

Applegate Farms, Southwestern Turkey Breast

2 oz

Amount per serving	%DV	Amount per serving	%DV	Amount per serving	%DV
Calories 50		**Cholesterol** 25mg	8%	**Total Carbohydrate** 1g	0%
Total Fat 0g	0%	**Sodium** 420mg	18%	Dietary Fiber 0g	0%
Saturated Fat 0g	0%	**Protein** 11g		Sugars 0g	
Polyunsaturated Fat 0g					
Monounsaturated Fat 0g		Vitamin A 2% Vitamin C 0%		Calcium 0% Iron 4%	

Applegate Farms, Turkey Pastrami

2 oz

Amount per serving	%DV	Amount per serving	%DV	Amount per serving	%DV
Calories 50		**Cholesterol** 30mg	10%	**Total Carbohydrate** 0g	0%
Total Fat 0g	0%	**Sodium** 360mg	15%	Dietary Fiber 0g	0%
Saturated Fat 0g	0%	**Protein** 12g		Sugars 0g	
Polyunsaturated Fat 0g					
Monounsaturated Fat 0g		Vitamin A 0% Vitamin C 0%		Calcium 0% Iron 4%	

Applegate Farms, Uncured Turkey Salami

2 oz

Amount per serving	%DV	Amount per serving	%DV	Amount per serving	%DV
Calories 70		**Cholesterol** 30mg	10%	**Total Carbohydrate** 0g	0%
Total Fat 2g	3%	**Sodium** 360mg	15%	Dietary Fiber 0g	0%
Saturated Fat 1g	5%	**Protein** 11g		Sugars 0g	
Polyunsaturated Fat 0g					
Monounsaturated Fat 0g		Vitamin A 0% Vitamin C 0%		Calcium 0% Iron 4%	

Boar's Head, 1st Cut Cooked Corned Beef Brisket

2 oz

Amount per serving	%DV	Amount per serving	%DV	Amount per serving	%DV
Calories 80		**Cholesterol** 40mg	13%	**Total Carbohydrate** 0g	0%
Total Fat 4g	6%	**Sodium** 460mg	19%	Dietary Fiber 0g	0%
Saturated Fat 1.5g	8%	**Protein** 12g		Sugars 0g	
Polyunsaturated Fat 0g					
Monounsaturated Fat 2g		Vitamin A 0% Vitamin C 0%		Calcium 0% Iron 8%	

Boar's Head, All American BBQ Seasoned Roasted Chicken Breast

2 oz

Amount per serving	%DV	Amount per serving	%DV	Amount per serving	%DV
Calories 60		**Cholesterol** 35mg	12%	**Total Carbohydrate** 2g	1%
Total Fat 0.5g	1%	**Sodium** 340mg	14%	Dietary Fiber 0g	0%
Saturated Fat 0g	0%	**Protein** 13g		Sugars 2g	
Polyunsaturated Fat 0g					
Monounsaturated Fat 0g		Vitamin A 0% Vitamin C 2%		Calcium 0% Iron 4%	

Boar's Head, All Natural Applewood Smoked Uncured Ham

2 oz / 56g

Amount per serving	%DV	Amount per serving	%DV	Amount per serving	%DV
Calories 70		**Cholesterol** 35mg	12%	**Total Carbohydrate** 1g	0%
Total Fat 2g	3%	**Sodium** 440mg	18%	Dietary Fiber 0g	0%
Saturated Fat 0.5g	2%	**Protein** 11g		Sugars 1g	
Polyunsaturated Fat 0g					
Monounsaturated Fat 1g		Vitamin A 0% Vitamin C 0%		Calcium 0% Iron 2%	

Boar's Head, All Natural Cap-Off Top Round Oven-Roasted Beef

2 oz

Amount per serving	%DV	Amount per serving	%DV	Amount per serving	%DV
Calories 80		**Cholesterol** 40mg	13%	**Total Carbohydrate** 0g	0%
Total Fat 3g	5%	**Sodium** 140mg	6%	Dietary Fiber 0g	0%
Saturated Fat 1g	5%	**Protein** 14g		Sugars 0g	
Polyunsaturated Fat 0g					
Monounsaturated Fat 1g		Vitamin A 0% Vitamin C 2%		Calcium 0% Iron 6%	

Boar's Head, All Natural Roasted Turkey Breast

2 oz / 56g

Amount per serving	%DV	Amount per serving	%DV	Amount per serving	%DV
Calories 60		**Cholesterol** 30mg	10%	**Total Carbohydrate** 1g	0%
Total Fat 1g	2%	**Sodium** 330mg	14%	Dietary Fiber 0g	0%
Saturated Fat 0g	0%	**Protein** 13g		Sugars 0g	
Polyunsaturated Fat 0g					
Monounsaturated Fat 0g		Vitamin A 0% Vitamin C 0%		Calcium 0% Iron 2%	

Boar's Head, All Natural Roasted Turkey Breast with Lemon & Herb

2 oz / 56g

Amount per serving	%DV	Amount per serving	%DV	Amount per serving	%DV
Calories 60		**Cholesterol** 30mg	10%	**Total Carbohydrate** 0g	0%
Total Fat 1g	2%	**Sodium** 400mg	17%	Dietary Fiber 0g	0%
Saturated Fat 0g	0%	**Protein** 12g		Sugars 1g	
Polyunsaturated Fat 0g					
Monounsaturated Fat 0g		Vitamin A 0% Vitamin C 0%		Calcium 0% Iron 2%	

Boar's Head, All Natural Smoked Turkey Breast

2 oz / 56g

Amount per serving	%DV	Amount per serving	%DV	Amount per serving	%DV
Calories 60		**Cholesterol** 30mg	10%	**Total Carbohydrate** 0g	0%
Total Fat 1g	2%	**Sodium** 390mg	16%	Dietary Fiber 0g	0%
Saturated Fat 0g	0%	**Protein** 14g		Sugars 0g	
Polyunsaturated Fat 0g					
Monounsaturated Fat 0g		Vitamin A 0% Vitamin C 2%		Calcium 0% Iron 2%	

Boar's Head, All Natural Smoked Uncured Ham

2 oz

Amount per serving	%DV	Amount per serving	%DV	Amount per serving	%DV
Calories 70		**Cholesterol** 35mg	12%	**Total Carbohydrate** 1g	0%
Total Fat 2g	3%	**Sodium** 440mg	18%	Dietary Fiber 0g	0%
Saturated Fat 0.5g	3%	**Protein** 12g		Sugars 1g	
Polyunsaturated Fat 0g					
Monounsaturated Fat 1g		Vitamin A 0% Vitamin C 4%		Calcium 0% Iron 2%	

Boar's Head, All Natural Tuscan Brand Roasted Turkey Breast

2 oz / 56g

Amount per serving	%DV	Amount per serving	%DV	Amount per serving	%DV
Calories 60		**Cholesterol** 30mg	10%	**Total Carbohydrate** 0g	0%
Total Fat 1g	2%	**Sodium** 380mg	16%	Dietary Fiber 0g	0%
Saturated Fat 0g	0%	**Protein** 15g		Sugars 0g	
Polyunsaturated Fat 0g					
Monounsaturated Fat 0g		Vitamin A 0% Vitamin C 2%		Calcium 0% Iron 2%	

Boar's Head, All Natural Uncured Ham

2 oz / 56g

Amount per serving	%DV	Amount per serving	%DV	Amount per serving	%DV
Calories 70		**Cholesterol** 30mg	10%	**Total Carbohydrate** 1g	0%
Total Fat 2g	3%	**Sodium** 440mg	18%	Dietary Fiber 0g	0%
Saturated Fat 0.5g	2%	**Protein** 11g		Sugars 1g	
Polyunsaturated Fat 0g					
Monounsaturated Fat 0.5g		Vitamin A 0% Vitamin C 0%		Calcium 0% Iron 2%	

Boar's Head, Black Forest Brand Boneless Smoked Ham, 25% Lower Sodium

2 oz

Amount per serving	%DV	Amount per serving	%DV	Amount per serving	%DV
Calories 60		**Cholesterol** 30mg	10%	**Total Carbohydrate** 2g	1%
Total Fat 1g	2%	**Sodium** 440mg	18%	Dietary Fiber 0g	0%
Saturated Fat 0g	0%	**Protein** 10g		Sugars 2g	
Polyunsaturated Fat 0g					
Monounsaturated Fat 0g		Vitamin A 0% Vitamin C 0%		Calcium 0% Iron 4%	

Boar's Head, Blazing Buffalo Style, Roasted Chicken Breast

2 oz

Amount per serving	%DV	Amount per serving	%DV	Amount per serving	%DV
Calories 60		**Cholesterol** 35mg	12%	**Total Carbohydrate** 0g	0%
Total Fat 1g	2%	**Sodium** 460mg	19%	Dietary Fiber 0g	0%
Saturated Fat 0g	0%	**Protein** 13g		Sugars 0g	
Polyunsaturated Fat 0g					
Monounsaturated Fat 0g		Vitamin A 2% Vitamin C 2%		Calcium 0% Iron 2%	

Boar's Head, Branded Deluxe Ham, 42% Lower Sodium

2 oz

Amount per serving	%DV	Amount per serving	%DV	Amount per serving	%DV
Calories 60		**Cholesterol** 25mg	8%	**Total Carbohydrate** 2g	1%
Total Fat 1g	2%	**Sodium** 460mg	19%	Dietary Fiber 0g	0%
Saturated Fat 0g	0%	**Protein** 10g		Sugars 2g	
Polyunsaturated Fat 0g					
Monounsaturated Fat 0g		Vitamin A 0% Vitamin C 0%		Calcium 0% Iron 2%	

Boar's Head, Cajun Style Seasoned, Cap-Off Top Round

2 oz

Amount per serving	%DV	Amount per serving	%DV	Amount per serving	%DV
Calories 80		**Cholesterol** 35mg	12%	**Total Carbohydrate** 0g	0%
Total Fat 3g	5%	**Sodium** 330mg	14%	Dietary Fiber 0g	0%
Saturated Fat 1g	5%	**Protein** 12g		Sugars 0g	
Polyunsaturated Fat 0g					
Monounsaturated Fat 1.5g		Vitamin A 2% Vitamin C 0%		Calcium 0% Iron 8%	

Boar's Head, Chipotle Chicken Breast

2 oz

Amount per serving	%DV	Amount per serving	%DV	Amount per serving	%DV
Calories 60		**Cholesterol** 40mg	13%	**Total Carbohydrate** 1g	0%
Total Fat 1g	2%	**Sodium** 420mg	18%	Dietary Fiber 0g	0%
Saturated Fat 0g	0%	**Protein** 13g		Sugars 0g	
Polyunsaturated Fat 0g					
Monounsaturated Fat 0g		Vitamin A 0% Vitamin C 2%		Calcium 0% Iron 2%	

Boar's Head, Cracked Pepper Mill Smoked Turkey Breast

2 oz / 56g

Amount per serving	%DV	Amount per serving	%DV	Amount per serving	%DV
Calories 60		**Cholesterol** 30mg	10%	**Total Carbohydrate** 0g	0%
Total Fat 1g	2%	**Sodium** 460mg	19%	Dietary Fiber 0g	0%
Saturated Fat 0g	0%	**Protein** 13g		Sugars 1g	
Polyunsaturated Fat 0g					
Monounsaturated Fat 0g		Vitamin A 0% Vitamin C 0%		Calcium 0% Iron 2%	

Boar's Head, Cracked Pepper Mill, Smoked Turkey Breast

2 oz

Amount per serving	%DV	Amount per serving	%DV	Amount per serving	%DV
Calories 60		**Cholesterol** 30mg	10%	**Total Carbohydrate** 0g	0%
Total Fat 1g	2%	**Sodium** 460mg	19%	Dietary Fiber 0g	0%
Saturated Fat 0g	0%	**Protein** 13g		Sugars 1g	
Polyunsaturated Fat 0g					
Monounsaturated Fat 0g		Vitamin A 0% Vitamin C 0%		Calcium 0% Iron 2%	

Boar's Head, Deluxe Low Sodium Oven-Roasted Beef, Cap-Off Round

2 oz

Amount per serving	%DV	Amount per serving	%DV	Amount per serving	%DV
Calories 80		**Cholesterol** 30mg	10%	**Total Carbohydrate** 1g	0%
Total Fat 2.5g	4%	**Sodium** 80mg	3%	Dietary Fiber 0g	0%
Saturated Fat 1g	5%	**Protein** 15g		Sugars 0g	
Polyunsaturated Fat 0g					
Monounsaturated Fat 0g		Vitamin A 0% Vitamin C 0%		Calcium 0% Iron 8%	

Boar's Head, EverRoast, Oven-Roasted Chicken Breast

2 oz

Amount per serving	%DV	Amount per serving	%DV	Amount per serving	%DV
Calories 50		**Cholesterol** 30mg	10%	**Total Carbohydrate** 1g	0%
Total Fat 0.5g	1%	**Sodium** 440mg	18%	Dietary Fiber 0g	0%
Saturated Fat 0g	0%	**Protein** 13g		Sugars 1g	
Polyunsaturated Fat 0g					
Monounsaturated Fat 0g		Vitamin A 0%	Vitamin C 0%	Calcium 2%	Iron 2%

Boar's Head, Golden Catering Style Oven-Roasted Turkey Breast - 47% Lower Sodium

2 oz / 56g

Amount per serving	%DV	Amount per serving	%DV	Amount per serving	%DV
Calories 60		**Cholesterol** 25mg	8%	**Total Carbohydrate** 0g	0%
Total Fat 1g	2%	**Sodium** 340mg	14%	Dietary Fiber 0g	0%
Saturated Fat 0g	0%	**Protein** 13g		Sugars 0g	
Polyunsaturated Fat 0g					
Monounsaturated Fat 0g		Vitamin A 0%	Vitamin C 0%	Calcium 0%	Iron 2%

Boar's Head, Golden Classic Oven-Roasted 42% Lower Sodium Chicken Breast

2 oz / 56g

Amount per serving	%DV	Amount per serving	%DV	Amount per serving	%DV
Calories 60		**Cholesterol** 35mg	12%	**Total Carbohydrate** 0g	0%
Total Fat 1g	2%	**Sodium** 350mg	15%	Dietary Fiber 0g	0%
Saturated Fat 0g	0%	**Protein** 13g		Sugars 0g	
Polyunsaturated Fat 0g					
Monounsaturated Fat 0g		Vitamin A 0%	Vitamin C 0%	Calcium 0%	Iron 2%

Boar's Head, Hickory Smoked Black Forest Turkey Breast - 40% Less Sodium

2 oz / 56g

Amount per serving	%DV	Amount per serving	%DV	Amount per serving	%DV
Calories 60		**Cholesterol** 25mg	8%	**Total Carbohydrate** 0g	0%
Total Fat 1g	2%	**Sodium** 390mg	16%	Dietary Fiber 0g	0%
Saturated Fat 0g	0%	**Protein** 13g		Sugars 0g	
Polyunsaturated Fat 0g					
Monounsaturated Fat 0g		Vitamin A 0%	Vitamin C 0%	Calcium 0%	Iron 2%

Boar's Head, Hickory Smoked Boneless Skinless Chicken Breast

2 oz / 56g

Amount per serving	%DV	Amount per serving	%DV	Amount per serving	%DV
Calories 60		**Cholesterol** 35mg	12%	**Total Carbohydrate** 0g	0%
Total Fat 1g	2%	**Sodium** 360mg	15%	Dietary Fiber 0g	0%
Saturated Fat 0g	0%	**Protein** 13g		Sugars 0g	
Polyunsaturated Fat 0g					
Monounsaturated Fat 0g		Vitamin A 0%	Vitamin C 0%	Calcium 0%	Iron 2%

Boar's Head, Hickory Smoked Chicken Breast

2 oz

Amount per serving	%DV	Amount per serving	%DV	Amount per serving	%DV
Calories 60		**Cholesterol** 35mg	12%	**Total Carbohydrate** 0g	0%
Total Fat 1g	2%	**Sodium** 360mg	15%	Dietary Fiber 0g	0%
Saturated Fat 0g	0%	**Protein** 13g		Sugars 0g	
Polyunsaturated Fat 0g					
Monounsaturated Fat 0g		Vitamin A 0%	Vitamin C 0%	Calcium 0%	Iron 2%

Boar's Head, Honey Smoked Turkey Breast, Skinless

2 oz

Amount per serving	%DV	Amount per serving	%DV	Amount per serving	%DV
Calories 70		**Cholesterol** 25mg	8%	**Total Carbohydrate** 2g	1%
Total Fat 1g	2%	**Sodium** 480mg	20%	Dietary Fiber 0g	0%
Saturated Fat 0g	0%	**Protein** 13g		Sugars 2g	
Polyunsaturated Fat 0g					
Monounsaturated Fat 0g		Vitamin A 0%	Vitamin C 0%	Calcium 0%	Iron 2%

Boar's Head, Italian Style Seasoned Beef with Braciole Seasoning

2 oz

Amount per serving	%DV	Amount per serving	%DV	Amount per serving	%DV
Calories 70		**Cholesterol** 35mg	12%	**Total Carbohydrate** 0g	0%
Total Fat 2g	3%	**Sodium** 370mg	15%	Dietary Fiber 0g	0%
Saturated Fat 1g	5%	**Protein** 13g		Sugars 0g	
Polyunsaturated Fat 0g					
Monounsaturated Fat 0g		Vitamin A 0%	Vitamin C 0%	Calcium 0%	Iron 6%

Boar's Head, Jerk Turkey Breast

2 oz

Amount per serving	%DV	Amount per serving	%DV	Amount per serving	%DV
Calories 60		**Cholesterol** 25mg	8%	**Total Carbohydrate** 0g	0%
Total Fat 1g	2%	**Sodium** 370mg	15%	Dietary Fiber 0g	0%
Saturated Fat 0g	0%	**Protein** 12g		Sugars 0g	
Polyunsaturated Fat 0g					
Monounsaturated Fat 0g		Vitamin A 0%	Vitamin C 0%	Calcium 0%	Iron 2%

Boar's Head, Lemon Pepper Boneless Skinless Roasted Chicken Breast

2 oz / 56g

Amount per serving	%DV	Amount per serving	%DV	Amount per serving	%DV
Calories 60		**Cholesterol** 35mg	12%	**Total Carbohydrate** 1g	0%
Total Fat 1g	2%	**Sodium** 360mg	15%	Dietary Fiber 0g	0%
Saturated Fat 0g	0%	**Protein** 13g		Sugars 0g	
Polyunsaturated Fat 0g					
Monounsaturated Fat 0g		Vitamin A 0%	Vitamin C 0%	Calcium 0%	Iron 2%

Boar's Head, London Broil

2 oz

Amount per serving	%DV	Amount per serving	%DV	Amount per serving	%DV
Calories 70		**Cholesterol** 25mg	8%	**Total Carbohydrate** 0g	0%
Total Fat 3g	5%	**Sodium** 310mg	13%	Dietary Fiber 0g	0%
Saturated Fat 1g	5%	**Protein** 12g		Sugars 0g	
Polyunsaturated Fat 0g					
Monounsaturated Fat 1.5g		Vitamin A 0%	Vitamin C 0%	Calcium 0%	Iron 8%

Boar's Head, Londonport Top Round Seasoned Roast Beef

2 oz / 56g

Amount per serving	%DV	Amount per serving	%DV	Amount per serving	%DV
Calories 80		**Cholesterol** 40mg	13%	**Total Carbohydrate** 2g	1%
Total Fat 2.5g	4%	**Sodium** 350mg	15%	Dietary Fiber 0g	0%
Saturated Fat 1g	5%	**Protein** 13g		Sugars 2g	
Polyunsaturated Fat 0g					
Monounsaturated Fat 0g		Vitamin A 0%	Vitamin C 0%	Calcium 0%	Iron 8%

Boar's Head, Maple Glazed Honey Coat Cured Turkey Breast

2 oz / 56g

Amount per serving	%DV	Amount per serving	%DV	Amount per serving	%DV
Calories 70		**Cholesterol** 30mg	10%	**Total Carbohydrate** 2g	1%
Total Fat 0.5g	1%	**Sodium** 440mg	18%	Dietary Fiber 0g	0%
Saturated Fat 0g	0%	**Protein** 14g		Sugars 2g	
Polyunsaturated Fat 0g					
Monounsaturated Fat 0g		Vitamin A 0%	Vitamin C 0%	Calcium 0%	Iron 2%

Boar's Head, Maple Glazed Oven- Roasted Chicken Breast

2 oz / 56g

Amount per serving	%DV	Amount per serving	%DV	Amount per serving	%DV
Calories 60		**Cholesterol** 30mg	10%	**Total Carbohydrate** 2g	1%
Total Fat 1g	2%	**Sodium** 340mg	14%	Dietary Fiber 0g	0%
Saturated Fat 0g	0%	**Protein** 12g		Sugars 2g	
Polyunsaturated Fat 0g					
Monounsaturated Fat 0g		Vitamin A 0%	Vitamin C 0%	Calcium 0%	Iron 0%

Boar's Head, Mesquite Wood Smoked Skinless Roasted Breast of Turkey

2 oz / 56g

Amount per serving	%DV	Amount per serving	%DV	Amount per serving	%DV
Calories 60		**Cholesterol** 25mg	8%	**Total Carbohydrate** 0g	0%
Total Fat 1g	2%	**Sodium** 440mg	18%	Dietary Fiber 0g	0%
Saturated Fat 0g	0%	**Protein** 12g		Sugars 0g	
Polyunsaturated Fat 0g					
Monounsaturated Fat 0g		Vitamin A 0%	Vitamin C 0%	Calcium 0%	Iron 2%

Boar's Head, No Salt Added Oven-Roasted Turkey Breast

2 oz / 56g

Amount per serving	%DV	Amount per serving	%DV	Amount per serving	%DV
Calories 70		**Cholesterol** 40mg	13%	**Total Carbohydrate** 0g	0%
Total Fat 1g	2%	**Sodium** 55mg	2%	Dietary Fiber 0g	0%
Saturated Fat 0g	0%	**Protein** 15g		Sugars 0g	
Polyunsaturated Fat 0g					
Monounsaturated Fat 0g		Vitamin A 0%	Vitamin C 0%	Calcium 0%	Iron 2%

Boar's Head, Ovengold Roasted Breast of Turkey - Skinless

2 oz / 56g

Amount per serving	%DV	Amount per serving	%DV	Amount per serving	%DV
Calories 60		**Cholesterol** 20mg	7%	**Total Carbohydrate** 0g	0%
Total Fat 1g	2%	**Sodium** 350mg	15%	Dietary Fiber 0g	0%
Saturated Fat 0g	0%	**Protein** 13g		Sugars 0g	
Polyunsaturated Fat 0g					
Monounsaturated Fat 0g		Vitamin A 0%	Vitamin C 0%	Calcium 0%	Iron 2%

Boar's Head, Pancetta Bacon Topped Oven-Roasted Turkey Breast

2 oz / 56g

Amount per serving	%DV	Amount per serving	%DV	Amount per serving	%DV
Calories 60		**Cholesterol** 20mg	7%	**Total Carbohydrate** 0g	0%
Total Fat 1.5g	2%	**Sodium** 350mg	15%	Dietary Fiber 0g	0%
Saturated Fat 0.5g	2%	**Protein** 13g		Sugars 0g	
Polyunsaturated Fat 0g					
Monounsaturated Fat 0.5g		Vitamin A 0%	Vitamin C 2%	Calcium 0%	Iron 2%

Boar's Head, Pastrami Seasoned Turkey Breast

2 oz / 56g

Amount per serving	%DV	Amount per serving	%DV	Amount per serving	%DV
Calories 60		**Cholesterol** 25mg	8%	**Total Carbohydrate** 1g	0%
Total Fat 0.5g	1%	**Sodium** 440mg	18%	Dietary Fiber 0g	0%
Saturated Fat 0g	0%	**Protein** 13g		Sugars 0g	
Polyunsaturated Fat 0g					
Monounsaturated Fat 0g		Vitamin A 0%	Vitamin C 0%	Calcium 0%	Iron 2%

Boar's Head, Porketta

2 oz

Amount per serving	%DV	Amount per serving	%DV	Amount per serving	%DV
Calories 80		**Cholesterol** 25mg	8%	**Total Carbohydrate** 1g	0%
Total Fat 3.5g	5%	**Sodium** 440mg	18%	Dietary Fiber 0g	0%
Saturated Fat 1g	5%	**Protein** 12g		Sugars 1g	
Polyunsaturated Fat 0.5g					
Monounsaturated Fat 1.5g		Vitamin A 0%	Vitamin C 0%	Calcium 0%	Iron 2%

Boar's Head, Premium 47% Lower Sodium Oven-Roasted Turkey Breast

2 oz / 56g

Amount per serving	%DV	Amount per serving	%DV	Amount per serving	%DV
Calories 60		**Cholesterol** 20mg	7%	**Total Carbohydrate** 0g	0%
Total Fat 0.5g	1%	**Sodium** 340mg	14%	Dietary Fiber 0g	0%
Saturated Fat 0g	0%	**Protein** 12g		Sugars 0g	
Polyunsaturated Fat 0g					
Monounsaturated Fat 0g		Vitamin A 0%	Vitamin C 0%	Calcium 0%	Iron 2%

Boar's Head, Rotisserie Seasoned Oven-Roasted Chicken Breast

2 oz / 56g

Amount per serving	%DV	Amount per serving	%DV	Amount per serving	%DV
Calories 60		**Cholesterol** 35mg	12%	**Total Carbohydrate** 0g	0%
Total Fat 1g	2%	**Sodium** 400mg	17%	Dietary Fiber 0g	0%
Saturated Fat 0g	0%	**Protein** 13g		Sugars 0g	
Polyunsaturated Fat 0g					
Monounsaturated Fat 0g		Vitamin A 0%	Vitamin C 0%	Calcium 4%	Iron 2%

Boar's Head, Salsalito Roasted Turkey Breast

2 oz / 56g

Amount per serving	%DV	Amount per serving	%DV	Amount per serving	%DV
Calories 60		**Cholesterol** 25mg	8%	**Total Carbohydrate** 1g	0%
Total Fat 0.5g	1%	**Sodium** 480mg	20%	Dietary Fiber 0g	0%
Saturated Fat 0g	0%	**Protein** 13g		Sugars 0g	
Polyunsaturated Fat 0g					
Monounsaturated Fat 0g		Vitamin A 0%	Vitamin C 0%	Calcium 2%	Iron 2%

Boar's Head, Seasoned Filet of Roast Beef, Cap-Off Top Round

2 oz

Amount per serving	%DV	Amount per serving	%DV	Amount per serving	%DV
Calories 90		**Cholesterol** 40mg	13%	**Total Carbohydrate** 0g	0%
Total Fat 3g	5%	**Sodium** 230mg	10%	Dietary Fiber 0g	0%
Saturated Fat 1.5g	8%	**Protein** 14g		Sugars 0g	
Polyunsaturated Fat 0g					
Monounsaturated Fat 1.5g		Vitamin A 0%	Vitamin C 0%	Calcium 0%	Iron 10%

Buddig Deli Cuts, Baked Honey Ham

6 slices / 56g

Amount per serving	%DV	Amount per serving	%DV	Amount per serving	%DV
Calories 70		**Cholesterol** 20mg	7%	**Total Carbohydrate** 3g	1%
Total Fat 1.5g	2%	**Sodium** 460mg	19%	Dietary Fiber 0g	0%
Saturated Fat 0.5g	3%	**Protein** 10g		Sugars 3g	
Polyunsaturated Fat 0g					
Monounsaturated Fat 0g		Vitamin A 0%	Vitamin C 0%	Calcium 0%	Iron 8%

Buddig Deli Cuts, Baked Honey Ham, Water Added

6 slices / 2 oz / 56g

Amount per serving	%DV	Amount per serving	%DV	Amount per serving	%DV
Calories 90		**Cholesterol** 20mg	7%	**Total Carbohydrate** 3g	1%
Total Fat 3g	5%	**Sodium** 460mg	19%	Dietary Fiber 0g	0%
Saturated Fat 1g	5%	**Protein** 10g		Sugars 3g	
Polyunsaturated Fat 0g					
Monounsaturated Fat 0g		Vitamin A 0%	Vitamin C 0%	Calcium 0%	Iron 8%

Buddig Deli Cuts, Brown Sugar Baked Ham, Water Added

6 slices / 2oz / 56g

Amount per serving	%DV	Amount per serving	%DV	Amount per serving	%DV
Calories 70		**Cholesterol** 20mg	7%	**Total Carbohydrate** 3g	1%
Total Fat 2g	3%	**Sodium** 460mg	19%	Dietary Fiber 0g	0%
Saturated Fat 1g	5%	**Protein** 10g		Sugars 3g	
Polyunsaturated Fat 0g					
Monounsaturated Fat 0g		Vitamin A 0%	Vitamin C 0%	Calcium 0%	Iron 8%

Buddig Deli Cuts, Hickory Smoked Turkey & White Turkey

6 slices / 56g

Amount per serving	%DV	Amount per serving	%DV	Amount per serving	%DV
Calories 70		**Cholesterol** 20mg	7%	**Total Carbohydrate** 2g	1%
Total Fat 3g	5%	**Sodium** 460mg	19%	Dietary Fiber 0g	0%
Saturated Fat 1g	5%	**Protein** 10g		Sugars 1g	
Polyunsaturated Fat 0g					
Monounsaturated Fat 0g		Vitamin A 0%	Vitamin C 0%	Calcium 0%	Iron 2%

Buddig Deli Cuts, Honey-Roasted Turkey

6 slices / 56g

Amount per serving	%DV	Amount per serving	%DV	Amount per serving	%DV
Calories 80		**Cholesterol** 20mg	7%	**Total Carbohydrate** 4g	1%
Total Fat 2.5g	4%	**Sodium** 460mg	19%	Dietary Fiber 0g	0%
Saturated Fat 1g	5%	**Protein** 9g		Sugars 3g	
Polyunsaturated Fat 0g					
Monounsaturated Fat 0g		Vitamin A 0%	Vitamin C 0%	Calcium 0%	Iron 9%

Buddig Deli Cuts, Honey-Roasted Turkey Breast & White Turkey

6 slices / 56oz

Amount per serving	%DV	Amount per serving	%DV	Amount per serving	%DV
Calories 80		**Cholesterol** 30mg	10%	**Total Carbohydrate** 3g	1%
Total Fat 4g	6%	**Sodium** 0mg	0%	Dietary Fiber 0g	0%
Saturated Fat 1g	5%	**Protein** 9g		Sugars 3g	
Polyunsaturated Fat 0g					
Monounsaturated Fat 0g		Vitamin A 0%	Vitamin C 0%	Calcium 0%	Iron 0%

Buddig Deli Cuts, Oven-Roasted Turkey

2 oz

Amount per serving	%DV	Amount per serving	%DV	Amount per serving	%DV
Calories 70		**Cholesterol** 20mg	7%	**Total Carbohydrate** 2g	1%
Total Fat 2.5g	4%	**Sodium** 460mg	19%	Dietary Fiber 0g	0%
Saturated Fat 1g	5%	**Protein** 10g		Sugars 1g	
Polyunsaturated Fat 0g					
Monounsaturated Fat 0g		Vitamin A 0% Vitamin C 0%		Calcium 0% Iron 2%	

Buddig Deli Cuts, Oven-Roasted Turkey Breast & White Turkey

6 slices / 57g

Amount per serving	%DV	Amount per serving	%DV	Amount per serving	%DV
Calories 60		**Cholesterol** 20mg	7%	**Total Carbohydrate** 1g	0%
Total Fat 1.5g	2%	**Sodium** 460mg	19%	Dietary Fiber 0g	0%
Saturated Fat 0.5g	3%	**Protein** 10g		Sugars 1g	
Polyunsaturated Fat 0g					
Monounsaturated Fat 0g		Vitamin A 0% Vitamin C 0%		Calcium 0% Iron 2%	

Buddig Deli Cuts, Rotisserie Chicken

6 slices / 56g

Amount per serving	%DV	Amount per serving	%DV	Amount per serving	%DV
Calories 70		**Cholesterol** 20mg	7%	**Total Carbohydrate** 1g	0%
Total Fat 1.5g	2%	**Sodium** 460mg	19%	Dietary Fiber 0g	0%
Saturated Fat 0.5g	3%	**Protein** 10g		Sugars 1g	
Polyunsaturated Fat 0g					
Monounsaturated Fat 0g		Vitamin A 0% Vitamin C 0%		Calcium 0% Iron 4%	

Buddig Deli Cuts, Rotisserie Flavored Chicken Breast

6 slices / 57g

Amount per serving	%DV	Amount per serving	%DV	Amount per serving	%DV
Calories 70		**Cholesterol** 20mg	7%	**Total Carbohydrate** 2g	1%
Total Fat 2.5g	4%	**Sodium** 460mg	19%	Dietary Fiber 0g	0%
Saturated Fat 0.6g	3%	**Protein** 10g		Sugars 1g	
Polyunsaturated Fat 0g					
Monounsaturated Fat 0g		Vitamin A 0% Vitamin C 0%		Calcium 0% Iron 2%	

Buddig Deli Cuts, Smoked Ham

6 slices / 56g

Amount per serving	%DV	Amount per serving	%DV	Amount per serving	%DV
Calories 70		**Cholesterol** 20mg	7%	**Total Carbohydrate** 1g	0%
Total Fat 2.5g	4%	**Sodium** 460mg	19%	Dietary Fiber 0g	0%
Saturated Fat 1g	5%	**Protein** 10g		Sugars 1g	
Polyunsaturated Fat 0g					
Monounsaturated Fat 0g		Vitamin A 0% Vitamin C 0%		Calcium 0% Iron 8%	

Buddig Fix Quix, Oven-Roasted Turkey Breast

43g

Amount per serving	%DV	Amount per serving	%DV	Amount per serving	%DV
Calories 50		**Cholesterol** 15mg	5%	**Total Carbohydrate** 2g	1%
Total Fat 2g	3%	**Sodium** 350mg	15%	Dietary Fiber 0g	0%
Saturated Fat 1g	5%	**Protein** 7g		Sugars 1g	
Polyunsaturated Fat 0g					
Monounsaturated Fat 0g		Vitamin A 0% Vitamin C 0%		Calcium 0% Iron 2%	

Buddig Fix Quix, Smoked Ham Cubes

2 oz / 56g

Amount per serving	%DV	Amount per serving	%DV	Amount per serving	%DV
Calories 70		**Cholesterol** 20mg	7%	**Total Carbohydrate** 1g	0%
Total Fat 3g	5%	**Sodium** 460mg	19%	Dietary Fiber 0g	0%
Saturated Fat 1g	5%	**Protein** 10g		Sugars 1g	
Polyunsaturated Fat 0g					
Monounsaturated Fat 0g		Vitamin A 0% Vitamin C 0%		Calcium 0% Iron 6%	

Buddig, Original Chicken

2 oz

Amount per serving	%DV	Amount per serving	%DV	Amount per serving	%DV
Calories 90		**Cholesterol** 0mg	0%	**Total Carbohydrate** 2g	1%
Total Fat 5g	8%	**Sodium** 0mg	0%	Dietary Fiber 0g	0%
Saturated Fat 0g	0%	**Protein** 10g		Sugars 0g	
Polyunsaturated Fat 0g					
Monounsaturated Fat 0g		Vitamin A 0% Vitamin C 0%		Calcium 0% Iron 4%	

Buddig, Original Ham

2 oz

Amount per serving	%DV	Amount per serving	%DV	Amount per serving	%DV
Calories 90		**Cholesterol** 0mg	0%	**Total Carbohydrate** 2g	1%
Total Fat 5g	8%	**Sodium** 0mg	0%	Dietary Fiber 0g	0%
Saturated Fat 0g	0%	**Protein** 10g		Sugars 0g	
Polyunsaturated Fat 0g					
Monounsaturated Fat 0g		Vitamin A 0% Vitamin C 0%		Calcium 0% Iron 6%	

Buddig, Original Mesquite Turkey

2 oz

Amount per serving	%DV	Amount per serving	%DV	Amount per serving	%DV
Calories 90		**Cholesterol** 0mg	0%	**Total Carbohydrate** 2g	1%
Total Fat 5g	8%	**Sodium** 0mg	0%	Dietary Fiber 0g	0%
Saturated Fat 0g	0%	**Protein** 10g		Sugars 0g	
Polyunsaturated Fat 0g					
Monounsaturated Fat 0g		Vitamin A 0% Vitamin C 0%		Calcium 0% Iron 2%	

Buddig, Original Turkey

2 oz

Amount per serving	%DV	Amount per serving	%DV	Amount per serving	%DV
Calories 90		**Cholesterol** 0mg	0%	**Total Carbohydrate** 2g	1%
Total Fat 5g	8%	**Sodium** 0mg	0%	Dietary Fiber 0g	0%
Saturated Fat 0g	0%	**Protein** 10g		Sugars 0g	
Polyunsaturated Fat 0g					
Monounsaturated Fat 0g		Vitamin A 0% Vitamin C 0%		Calcium 0% Iron 2%	

Butterball 40% Less Sodium Turkey Breast

2 oz / 56g

Amount per serving	%DV	Amount per serving	%DV	Amount per serving	%DV
Calories 50		**Cholesterol** 30mg	10%	**Total Carbohydrate** 1g	0%
Total Fat 1g	2%	**Sodium** 330mg	14%	Dietary Fiber 0g	0%
Saturated Fat 0g	0%	**Protein** 11g		Sugars 0g	
Polyunsaturated Fat 0g					
Monounsaturated Fat 0g		Vitamin A 0% Vitamin C 0%		Calcium 0% Iron 4%	

Butterball Deep Fried Honey Turkey Breast

2 oz

Amount per serving	%DV	Amount per serving	%DV	Amount per serving	%DV
Calories 60		**Cholesterol** 25mg	8%	**Total Carbohydrate** 4g	1%
Total Fat 1g	2%	**Sodium** 460mg	19%	Dietary Fiber 0g	0%
Saturated Fat 0g	0%	**Protein** 10g		Sugars 4g	
Polyunsaturated Fat 0g					
Monounsaturated Fat 0g		Vitamin A 0% Vitamin C 0%		Calcium 0% Iron 4%	

Butterball Original 40% Less Sodium Turkey Breast

2 oz / 56g

Amount per serving	%DV	Amount per serving	%DV	Amount per serving	%DV
Calories 50		**Cholesterol** 30mg	10%	**Total Carbohydrate** 1g	0%
Total Fat 1g	2%	**Sodium** 330mg	14%	Dietary Fiber 0g	0%
Saturated Fat 0g	0%	**Protein** 11g		Sugars 0g	
Polyunsaturated Fat 0g					
Monounsaturated Fat 0g		Vitamin A 0% Vitamin C 0%		Calcium 0% Iron 4%	

Butterball Original Cajun Style Turkey Breast

2 oz / 56g

Amount per serving	%DV	Amount per serving	%DV	Amount per serving	%DV
Calories 60		**Cholesterol** 25mg	8%	**Total Carbohydrate** 2g	1%
Total Fat 1g	2%	**Sodium** 480mg	20%	Dietary Fiber 0g	0%
Saturated Fat 0g	0%	**Protein** 11g		Sugars 1g	
Polyunsaturated Fat 0g					
Monounsaturated Fat 0g		Vitamin A 0% Vitamin C 0%		Calcium 0% Iron 2%	

Butterball Original Deep Fried Flavored Chicken Breast Buffalo Style

2 oz

Amount per serving	%DV	Amount per serving	%DV	Amount per serving	%DV
Calories 50		**Cholesterol** 25mg	8%	**Total Carbohydrate** 1g	0%
Total Fat 0.5g	1%	**Sodium** 450mg	19%	Dietary Fiber 0g	0%
Saturated Fat 0g	0%	**Protein** 10g		Sugars 1g	
Polyunsaturated Fat 0g					
Monounsaturated Fat 0g		Vitamin A 4% Vitamin C 0%		Calcium 0% Iron 0%	

Butterball Original Deep Fried Flavored Turkey Breast Thanksgiving Style

2 oz

Amount per serving	%DV	Amount per serving	%DV	Amount per serving	%DV
Calories 50		**Cholesterol** 25mg	8%	**Total Carbohydrate** 2g	1%
Total Fat 1g	2%	**Sodium** 470mg	20%	Dietary Fiber 0g	0%
Saturated Fat 0g	0%	**Protein** 10g		Sugars 1g	
Polyunsaturated Fat 0g					
Monounsaturated Fat 0g		Vitamin A 0% Vitamin C 0%		Calcium 0% Iron 4%	

Chicken Breast, Fat-Free, Mesquite Flavor, Sliced

1 serving, 2 slices / 42g

Amount per serving	%DV	Amount per serving	%DV	Amount per serving	%DV
Calories 34		**Cholesterol** 15mg	5%	**Total Carbohydrate** 0.9g	0%
Total Fat 0g	0%	**Sodium** 437mg	18%	Dietary Fiber 0g	0%
Saturated Fat 0g	0%	**Protein** 7.1g		Sugars 0.1g	
Polyunsaturated Fat 0g					
Monounsaturated Fat 0g		Vitamin A 0% Vitamin C 0%		Calcium 0% Iron 1%	

Columbus Farm to Fork Naturals Honey Roasted Turkey Breast

2 slices

Amount per serving	%DV	Amount per serving	%DV	Amount per serving	%DV
Calories 70		**Cholesterol** 30mg	10%	**Total Carbohydrate** 3g	1%
Total Fat 0.5g	1%	**Sodium** 380mg	16%	Dietary Fiber 0g	0%
Saturated Fat 0g	0%	**Protein** 13g		Sugars 2g	
Polyunsaturated Fat 0g					
Monounsaturated Fat 0g		Vitamin A 0% Vitamin C 0%		Calcium 0% Iron 4%	

Columbus Farm to Fork Naturals Oven-Roasted Chicken Breast

2 oz / 56g

Amount per serving	%DV	Amount per serving	%DV	Amount per serving	%DV
Calories 60		**Cholesterol** 30mg	10%	**Total Carbohydrate** 0g	0%
Total Fat 1g	2%	**Sodium** 460mg	19%	Dietary Fiber 0g	0%
Saturated Fat 0g	0%	**Protein** 11g		Sugars 0g	
Polyunsaturated Fat 0g					
Monounsaturated Fat 0g		Vitamin A 0% Vitamin C 0%		Calcium 0% Iron 2%	

Columbus Farm to Fork Naturals Oven-Roasted Turkey Breast

2 slices

Amount per serving	%DV	Amount per serving	%DV	Amount per serving	%DV
Calories 60		**Cholesterol** 35mg	12%	**Total Carbohydrate** 1g	0%
Total Fat 0.5g	1%	**Sodium** 370mg	15%	Dietary Fiber 0g	0%
Saturated Fat 0g	0%	**Protein** 13g		Sugars 0g	
Polyunsaturated Fat 0g					
Monounsaturated Fat 0g		Vitamin A 0% Vitamin C 0%		Calcium 0% Iron 4%	

Columbus Farm to Fork Naturals Smoked Turkey Breast

2 slices

Amount per serving	%DV	Amount per serving	%DV	Amount per serving	%DV
Calories 60		**Cholesterol** 35mg	12%	**Total Carbohydrate** 1g	0%
Total Fat 0.5g	1%	**Sodium** 370mg	15%	Dietary Fiber 0g	0%
Saturated Fat 0g	0%	**Protein** 13g		Sugars 0g	
Polyunsaturated Fat 0g					
Monounsaturated Fat 0g		Vitamin A 0% Vitamin C 0%		Calcium 0% Iron 4%	

Columbus Herb Turkey Breast

2 oz / 56g

Amount per serving	%DV	Amount per serving	%DV	Amount per serving	%DV
Calories 60		**Cholesterol** 20mg	7%	**Total Carbohydrate** 1g	0%
Total Fat 0.5g	1%	**Sodium** 260mg	11%	Dietary Fiber 0g	0%
Saturated Fat 0g	0%	**Protein** 13g		Sugars 0g	
Polyunsaturated Fat 0g					
Monounsaturated Fat 0g		Vitamin A 2% Vitamin C 0%		Calcium 0% Iron 4%	

Columbus Oven Roasted Chicken Breast

2 oz / 56g

Amount per serving	%DV	Amount per serving	%DV	Amount per serving	%DV
Calories 60		**Cholesterol** 30mg	10%	**Total Carbohydrate** 0g	0%
Total Fat 1g	2%	**Sodium** 460mg	19%	Dietary Fiber 0g	0%
Saturated Fat 0g	0%	**Protein** 11g		Sugars 0g	
Polyunsaturated Fat 0g					
Monounsaturated Fat 0g		Vitamin A 0% Vitamin C 0%		Calcium 2% Iron 2%	

Columbus Pan Roasted Turkey Breast

2 oz / 56g

Amount per serving	%DV	Amount per serving	%DV	Amount per serving	%DV
Calories 60		**Cholesterol** 35mg	12%	**Total Carbohydrate** 1g	0%
Total Fat 1g	2%	**Sodium** 460mg	19%	Dietary Fiber 0g	0%
Saturated Fat 0g	0%	**Protein** 12g		Sugars 1g	
Polyunsaturated Fat 0g					
Monounsaturated Fat 0g		Vitamin A 0% Vitamin C 0%		Calcium 4% Iron 4%	

Columbus Peppered Turkey Breast

2 oz / 56g

Amount per serving	%DV	Amount per serving	%DV	Amount per serving	%DV
Calories 60		**Cholesterol** 20mg	7%	**Total Carbohydrate** 1g	0%
Total Fat 0.5g	1%	**Sodium** 260mg	11%	Dietary Fiber 0g	0%
Saturated Fat 0g	0%	**Protein** 13g		Sugars 0g	
Polyunsaturated Fat 0g					
Monounsaturated Fat 0g		Vitamin A 0% Vitamin C 0%		Calcium 0% Iron 6%	

Columbus Reduced Sodium Honey Ham

2 slices / 56g

Amount per serving	%DV	Amount per serving	%DV	Amount per serving	%DV
Calories 70		**Cholesterol** 30mg	10%	**Total Carbohydrate** 4g	1%
Total Fat 2.5g	4%	**Sodium** 360mg	15%	Dietary Fiber 0g	0%
Saturated Fat 1g	5%	**Protein** 10g		Sugars 0g	
Polyunsaturated Fat 0g					
Monounsaturated Fat 0g		Vitamin A 0% Vitamin C 0%		Calcium 0% Iron 2%	

Columbus, Reduced Sodium Turkey Breast

2 oz / 56g

Amount per serving	%DV	Amount per serving	%DV	Amount per serving	%DV
Calories 60		**Cholesterol** 20mg	7%	**Total Carbohydrate** 0g	0%
Total Fat 0.5g	1%	**Sodium** 220mg	9%	Dietary Fiber 0g	0%
Saturated Fat 0g	0%	**Protein** 13g		Sugars 0g	
Polyunsaturated Fat 0g					
Monounsaturated Fat 0g		Vitamin A 0% Vitamin C 0%		Calcium 4% Iron 0%	

Fit & Active Deli Thin Sliced Oven-Roasted Turkey Breast

2 oz / 56g

Amount per serving	%DV	Amount per serving	%DV	Amount per serving	%DV
Calories 60		**Cholesterol** 25mg	8%	**Total Carbohydrate** 3g	1%
Total Fat 1g	2%	**Sodium** 400mg	17%	Dietary Fiber 0g	0%
Saturated Fat 0g	0%	**Protein** 10g		Sugars 1g	
Polyunsaturated Fat 0g					
Monounsaturated Fat 0g		Vitamin A 0% Vitamin C 0%		Calcium 0% Iron 2%	

Fit & Active Deli Thin Sliced Smoked Honey Ham

2 oz / 56g

Amount per serving	%DV	Amount per serving	%DV	Amount per serving	%DV
Calories 70		**Cholesterol** 20mg	7%	**Total Carbohydrate** 3g	1%
Total Fat 1.5g	2%	**Sodium** 460mg	19%	Dietary Fiber 0g	0%
Saturated Fat 0.5g	3%	**Protein** 10g		Sugars 3g	
Polyunsaturated Fat 0g					
Monounsaturated Fat 0g		Vitamin A 0% Vitamin C 0%		Calcium 0% Iron 8%	

Healthy Ones, 97% Fat-Free Brown Chicken Breast, 7 oz Thin-Sliced Tub

6 slices

Amount per serving	%DV	Amount per serving	%DV	Amount per serving	%DV
Calories 50		**Cholesterol** 25mg	8%	**Total Carbohydrate** 2g	1%
Total Fat 1g	2%	**Sodium** 320mg	13%	Dietary Fiber 0g	0%
Saturated Fat 0g	0%	**Protein** 10g		Sugars 1g	
Polyunsaturated Fat 0g					
Monounsaturated Fat 0g		Vitamin A 0%	Vitamin C 0%	Calcium 0%	Iron 2%

Healthy Ones, 97% Fat-Free Brown Chicken Breast, Deli Sliced

56g

Amount per serving	%DV	Amount per serving	%DV	Amount per serving	%DV
Calories 50		**Cholesterol** 25mg	8%	**Total Carbohydrate** 1g	0%
Total Fat 1g	2%	**Sodium** 350mg	15%	Dietary Fiber 0g	0%
Saturated Fat 0.5g	3%	**Protein** 11g		Sugars 1g	
Polyunsaturated Fat 0g					
Monounsaturated Fat 0g		Vitamin A 0%	Vitamin C 0%	Calcium 0%	Iron 2%

Healthy Ones, 97% Fat-Free Cooked Ham

1 slice

Amount per serving	%DV	Amount per serving	%DV	Amount per serving	%DV
Calories 30		**Cholesterol** 15mg	5%	**Total Carbohydrate** 1g	0%
Total Fat 1g	2%	**Sodium** 230mg	10%	Dietary Fiber 0g	0%
Saturated Fat 0.5g	2%	**Protein** 5g		Sugars 1g	
Polyunsaturated Fat 0g					
Monounsaturated Fat 0g		Vitamin A 0%	Vitamin C 0%	Calcium 0%	Iron 2%

Healthy Ones, 97% Fat-Free Cooked Ham, Deli Sliced

2 oz

Amount per serving	%DV	Amount per serving	%DV	Amount per serving	%DV
Calories 60		**Cholesterol** 25mg	8%	**Total Carbohydrate** 1g	0%
Total Fat 1.5g	2%	**Sodium** 340mg	14%	Dietary Fiber 0g	0%
Saturated Fat 0.5g	3%	**Protein** 10g		Sugars 1g	
Polyunsaturated Fat 0g					
Monounsaturated Fat 0g		Vitamin A 0%	Vitamin C 0%	Calcium 0%	Iron 2%

Healthy Ones, 97% Fat-Free Golden Oven Roasted Turkey Breast, 10 oz Hearty Sliced

1 slice / 28 g

Amount per serving	%DV	Amount per serving	%DV	Amount per serving	%DV
Calories 30		**Cholesterol** 10mg	3%	**Total Carbohydrate** 1g	0%
Total Fat 1g	2%	**Sodium** 160mg	7%	Dietary Fiber 0g	0%
Saturated Fat 0.5g	3%	**Protein** 5g		Sugars 1g	
Polyunsaturated Fat 0g					
Monounsaturated Fat 0g		Vitamin A 0%	Vitamin C 0%	Calcium 0%	Iron 2%

Healthy Ones, 97% Fat-Free Golden Oven Roasted Turkey Breast, 5 oz Deli Thin

4 slices / 52g

Amount per serving	%DV	Amount per serving	%DV	Amount per serving	%DV
Calories 60		**Cholesterol** 20mg	7%	**Total Carbohydrate** 1g	0%
Total Fat 1.5g	2%	**Sodium** 310mg	13%	Dietary Fiber 0g	0%
Saturated Fat 0.5g	3%	**Protein** 10g		Sugars 1g	
Polyunsaturated Fat 0g					
Monounsaturated Fat 0g		Vitamin A 0% Vitamin C 0%		Calcium 0% Iron 2%	

Healthy Ones, 97% Fat-Free Golden Oven Roasted Turkey Breast, 7 oz Thin Sliced

6 slices / 54g

Amount per serving	%DV	Amount per serving	%DV	Amount per serving	%DV
Calories 60		**Cholesterol** 25mg	8%	**Total Carbohydrate** 1g	0%
Total Fat 1.5g	2%	**Sodium** 320mg	13%	Dietary Fiber 0g	0%
Saturated Fat 0.5g	3%	**Protein** 10g		Sugars 1g	
Polyunsaturated Fat 0g					
Monounsaturated Fat 0g		Vitamin A 2% Vitamin C 0%		Calcium 0% Iron 2%	

Healthy Ones, 97% Fat-Free Golden Oven Roasted Turkey Breast, Deli Sliced

56g

Amount per serving	%DV	Amount per serving	%DV	Amount per serving	%DV
Calories 50		**Cholesterol** 25mg	8%	**Total Carbohydrate** 1g	0%
Total Fat 1g	2%	**Sodium** 330mg	14%	Dietary Fiber 0g	0%
Saturated Fat 0.5g	3%	**Protein** 10g		Sugars 1g	
Polyunsaturated Fat 0g					
Monounsaturated Fat 0g		Vitamin A 0% Vitamin C 0%		Calcium 0% Iron 0%	

Healthy Ones, 97% Fat-Free Honey Ham, 10 oz Deli-Thin Package

1 slice / 28g

Amount per serving	%DV	Amount per serving	%DV	Amount per serving	%DV
Calories 35		**Cholesterol** 10mg	3%	**Total Carbohydrate** 1g	0%
Total Fat 0.5g	1%	**Sodium** 180mg	8%	Dietary Fiber 0g	0%
Saturated Fat 0.5g	3%	**Protein** 6g		Sugars 1g	
Polyunsaturated Fat 0g					
Monounsaturated Fat 0g		Vitamin A 0% Vitamin C 0%		Calcium 0% Iron 2%	

Healthy Ones, 97% Fat-Free Honey Ham, 5 oz Deli-Thin Package

4 slices

Amount per serving	%DV	Amount per serving	%DV	Amount per serving	%DV
Calories 60		**Cholesterol** 20mg	7%	**Total Carbohydrate** 3g	1%
Total Fat 1g	2%	**Sodium** 330mg	14%	Dietary Fiber 0g	0%
Saturated Fat 0.5g	3%	**Protein** 10g		Sugars 3g	
Polyunsaturated Fat 0g					
Monounsaturated Fat 0g		Vitamin A 0% Vitamin C 0%		Calcium 0% Iron 2%	

Healthy Ones, 97% Fat-Free Honey Ham, 7 oz Thin-Sliced Tub

6 slices

Amount per serving	%DV	Amount per serving	%DV	Amount per serving	%DV
Calories 70		Cholesterol 25mg	8%	Total Carbohydrate 3g	1%
Total Fat 1.5g	2%	Sodium 340mg	14%	Dietary Fiber 0g	0%
Saturated Fat 0.5g	3%	Protein 10g		Sugars 3g	
Polyunsaturated Fat 0g					
Monounsaturated Fat 0g		Vitamin A 0%	Vitamin C 0%	Calcium 0%	Iron 2%

Healthy Ones, 97% Fat-Free Honey Ham, Deli Sliced

56g

Amount per serving	%DV	Amount per serving	%DV	Amount per serving	%DV
Calories 60		Cholesterol 25mg	8%	Total Carbohydrate 2g	1%
Total Fat 1.5g	2%	Sodium 360mg	15%	Dietary Fiber 0g	0%
Saturated Fat 0.5g	3%	Protein 10g		Sugars 2g	
Polyunsaturated Fat 0g					
Monounsaturated Fat 0g		Vitamin A 0%	Vitamin C 0%	Calcium 0%	Iron 2%

Healthy Ones, 97% Fat-Free Mesquite Smoked Chicken Breast

56g

Amount per serving	%DV	Amount per serving	%DV	Amount per serving	%DV
Calories 50		Cholesterol 25mg	8%	Total Carbohydrate 1g	0%
Total Fat 1g	2%	Sodium 340mg	14%	Dietary Fiber 0g	0%
Saturated Fat 0.5g	3%	Protein 11g		Sugars 1g	
Polyunsaturated Fat 0g					
Monounsaturated Fat 0g		Vitamin A 0%	Vitamin C 0%	Calcium 0%	Iron 2%

Healthy Ones, Deli 97% Fat-Free Virginia Brand Ham

56g

Amount per serving	%DV	Amount per serving	%DV	Amount per serving	%DV
Calories 60		Cholesterol 25mg	8%	Total Carbohydrate 1g	0%
Total Fat 1.5g	2%	Sodium 330mg	14%	Dietary Fiber 0g	0%
Saturated Fat 0.5g	3%	Protein 10g		Sugars 1g	
Polyunsaturated Fat 0g					
Monounsaturated Fat 0g		Vitamin A 0%	Vitamin C 0%	Calcium 0%	Iron 2%

Healthy Ones, Deli 98% Fat-Free Mesquite Smoked Turkey Breast

56g

Amount per serving	%DV	Amount per serving	%DV	Amount per serving	%DV
Calories 50		Cholesterol 25mg	8%	Total Carbohydrate 1g	0%
Total Fat 1g	2%	Sodium 340mg	14%	Dietary Fiber 0g	0%
Saturated Fat 0.5g	3%	Protein 10g		Sugars 0g	
Polyunsaturated Fat 0g					
Monounsaturated Fat 0g		Vitamin A 0%	Vitamin C 0%	Calcium 0%	Iron 0%

Healthy Ones, Deli 98% Fat-Free Smoked Turkey Breast

56g

Amount per serving	%DV	Amount per serving	%DV	Amount per serving	%DV
Calories 50		**Cholesterol** 25mg	8%	**Total Carbohydrate** 1g	0%
Total Fat 1g	2%	**Sodium** 340mg	14%	Dietary Fiber 0g	0%
Saturated Fat 0.5g	3%	**Protein** 10g		Sugars 0g	
Polyunsaturated Fat 0g					
Monounsaturated Fat 0g		Vitamin A 0% Vitamin C 0%		Calcium 0% Iron 0%	

Healthy Ones, Deli Black Forest Brand Ham, 7 oz Thin Sliced Tub

6 slices

Amount per serving	%DV	Amount per serving	%DV	Amount per serving	%DV
Calories 60		**Cholesterol** 25mg	8%	**Total Carbohydrate** 1g	0%
Total Fat 1.5g	2%	**Sodium** 360mg	15%	Dietary Fiber 0g	0%
Saturated Fat 0.5g	3%	**Protein** 10g		Sugars 1g	
Polyunsaturated Fat 0g					
Monounsaturated Fat 0g		Vitamin A 0% Vitamin C 0%		Calcium 0% Iron 2%	

Healthy Ones, Deli Black Forest Brand Ham, Deli Sliced

2 oz

Amount per serving	%DV	Amount per serving	%DV	Amount per serving	%DV
Calories 60		**Cholesterol** 25mg	8%	**Total Carbohydrate** 1g	0%
Total Fat 1.5g	2%	**Sodium** 360mg	15%	Dietary Fiber 0g	0%
Saturated Fat 0.5g	3%	**Protein** 11g		Sugars 1g	
Polyunsaturated Fat 0g					
Monounsaturated Fat 0g		Vitamin A 0% Vitamin C 0%		Calcium 0% Iron 2%	

Healthy Ones, Deli Buffalo Style Chicken, Deli Sliced

56g

Amount per serving	%DV	Amount per serving	%DV	Amount per serving	%DV
Calories 60		**Cholesterol** 30mg	10%	**Total Carbohydrate** 1g	0%
Total Fat 1g	2%	**Sodium** 380mg	16%	Dietary Fiber 0g	0%
Saturated Fat 0.5g	3%	**Protein** 11g		Sugars 1g	
Polyunsaturated Fat 0g					
Monounsaturated Fat 0g		Vitamin A 0% Vitamin C 0%		Calcium 0% Iron 0%	

Healthy Ones, Deli Ham Off The Bone, Deli Sliced

56g

Amount per serving	%DV	Amount per serving	%DV	Amount per serving	%DV
Calories 60		**Cholesterol** 25mg	8%	**Total Carbohydrate** 2g	1%
Total Fat 1.5g	2%	**Sodium** 370mg	15%	Dietary Fiber 0g	0%
Saturated Fat 0.5g	3%	**Protein** 11g		Sugars 2g	
Polyunsaturated Fat 0g					
Monounsaturated Fat 0g		Vitamin A 0% Vitamin C 0%		Calcium 0% Iron 2%	

Healthy Ones, Deli Maple Ham, Deli Sliced

56g

Amount per serving	%DV	Amount per serving	%DV	Amount per serving	%DV
Calories 70		**Cholesterol** 25mg	8%	**Total Carbohydrate** 5g	2%
Total Fat 1.5g	2%	**Sodium** 390mg	16%	Dietary Fiber 0g	0%
Saturated Fat 0.5g	3%	**Protein** 11g		Sugars 4g	
Polyunsaturated Fat 0g					
Monounsaturated Fat 0g		Vitamin A 0%	Vitamin C 0%	Calcium 0%	Iron 4%

Healthy Ones, Deli Rotisserie Seasoned Chicken, 7 oz Thin-Sliced Tub

6 slices / 54g

Amount per serving	%DV	Amount per serving	%DV	Amount per serving	%DV
Calories 50		**Cholesterol** 25mg	8%	**Total Carbohydrate** 2g	1%
Total Fat 1g	2%	**Sodium** 320mg	13%	Dietary Fiber 0g	0%
Saturated Fat 0g	0%	**Protein** 10g		Sugars 1g	
Polyunsaturated Fat 0g					
Monounsaturated Fat 0g		Vitamin A 0%	Vitamin C 0%	Calcium 0%	Iron 2%

Healthy Ones, Deli Rotisserie Seasoned Chicken, Deli Sliced

56g

Amount per serving	%DV	Amount per serving	%DV	Amount per serving	%DV
Calories 50		**Cholesterol** 25mg	8%	**Total Carbohydrate** 1g	0%
Total Fat 1g	2%	**Sodium** 350mg	15%	Dietary Fiber 0g	0%
Saturated Fat 0.5g	2%	**Protein** 11g		Sugars 1g	
Polyunsaturated Fat 0g					
Monounsaturated Fat 0g		Vitamin A 0%	Vitamin C 0%	Calcium 0%	Iron 2%

Healthy Ones, Deli Thin-Sliced Honey Smoked Turkey Breast, 5 oz Deli Thin Package

4 slices / 52g

Amount per serving	%DV	Amount per serving	%DV	Amount per serving	%DV
Calories 60		**Cholesterol** 20mg	7%	**Total Carbohydrate** 3g	1%
Total Fat 1.5g	2%	**Sodium** 280mg	12%	Dietary Fiber 0g	0%
Saturated Fat 0.5g	3%	**Protein** 10g		Sugars 3g	
Polyunsaturated Fat 0g					
Monounsaturated Fat 0g		Vitamin A 0%	Vitamin C 0%	Calcium 0%	Iron 2%

Healthy Ones, Deli Thin-Sliced Honey Smoked Turkey Breast, 7 oz Thin-Sliced Tub

6 slices / 54g

Amount per serving	%DV	Amount per serving	%DV	Amount per serving	%DV
Calories 60		**Cholesterol** 20mg	7%	**Total Carbohydrate** 3g	1%
Total Fat 1.5g	2%	**Sodium** 290mg	12%	Dietary Fiber 0g	0%
Saturated Fat 0.5g	3%	**Protein** 10g		Sugars 3g	
Polyunsaturated Fat 0g					
Monounsaturated Fat 0g		Vitamin A 0%	Vitamin C 0%	Calcium 0%	Iron 2%

Healthy Ones, Deli Thin-Sliced Oven-Roasted Chicken Breast, 5 oz Deli Thin Package

4 slices / 52g

Amount per serving	%DV	Amount per serving	%DV	Amount per serving	%DV
Calories 45		**Cholesterol** 25mg	8%	**Total Carbohydrate** 1g	0%
Total Fat 0.5g	1%	**Sodium** 310mg	13%	Dietary Fiber 0g	0%
Saturated Fat 0g	0%	**Protein** 10g		Sugars 0g	
Polyunsaturated Fat 0g					
Monounsaturated Fat 0g		Vitamin A 0%	Vitamin C 0%	Calcium 0%	Iron 2%

Healthy Ones, Deli Thin-Sliced Oven-Roasted Chicken Breast, 7 oz Thin-Sliced Tub

6 slices / 54g

Amount per serving	%DV	Amount per serving	%DV	Amount per serving	%DV
Calories 60		**Cholesterol** 25mg	8%	**Total Carbohydrate** 1g	0%
Total Fat 1.5g	2%	**Sodium** 320mg	13%	Dietary Fiber 0g	0%
Saturated Fat 0.5g	3%	**Protein** 10g		Sugars 1g	
Polyunsaturated Fat 0g					
Monounsaturated Fat 0g		Vitamin A 2%	Vitamin C 0%	Calcium 0%	Iron 2%

Healthy Ones, Thin-Sliced Variety Pack Honey Ham/Oven-Roasted Turkey Breast

6 slices / 54g

Amount per serving	%DV	Amount per serving	%DV	Amount per serving	%DV
Calories 60		**Cholesterol** 25mg	8%	**Total Carbohydrate** 1g	0%
Total Fat 1.5g	2%	**Sodium** 330mg	14%	Dietary Fiber 0g	0%
Saturated Fat 0.5g	3%	**Protein** 10g		Sugars 1g	
Polyunsaturated Fat 0g					
Monounsaturated Fat 0g		Vitamin A 0%	Vitamin C 0%	Calcium 4%	Iron 2%

Hillshire Farm Lower Sodium Honey Ham with Natural Juices

2 oz / 56g

Amount per serving	%DV	Amount per serving	%DV	Amount per serving	%DV
Calories 80		**Cholesterol** 30mg	10%	**Total Carbohydrate** 5g	2%
Total Fat 1.5g	2%	**Sodium** 450mg	19%	Dietary Fiber 0g	0%
Saturated Fat 1g	5%	**Protein** 10g		Sugars 4g	
Polyunsaturated Fat 0g					
Monounsaturated Fat 0g		Vitamin A 0%	Vitamin C 0%	Calcium 0%	Iron 2%

Hillshire Farm Lower Sodium Honey-Roasted Turkey Breast

2 oz / 56g

Amount per serving	%DV	Amount per serving	%DV	Amount per serving	%DV
Calories 70		**Cholesterol** 25mg	8%	**Total Carbohydrate** 5g	2%
Total Fat 0.5g	1%	**Sodium** 410mg	17%	Dietary Fiber 0g	0%
Saturated Fat 0g	0%	**Protein** 10g		Sugars 3g	
Polyunsaturated Fat 0g					
Monounsaturated Fat 0g		Vitamin A 0%	Vitamin C 0%	Calcium 0%	Iron 4%

Hillshire Farm Lower Sodium Oven-Roasted Turkey Breast

2 oz / 56g

Amount per serving	%DV	Amount per serving	%DV	Amount per serving	%DV
Calories 60		**Cholesterol** 30mg	10%	**Total Carbohydrate** 3g	1%
Total Fat 0.5g	1%	**Sodium** 420mg	18%	Dietary Fiber 0g	0%
Saturated Fat 0g	0%	**Protein** 11g		Sugars 1g	
Polyunsaturated Fat 0g					
Monounsaturated Fat 0g		Vitamin A 0%	Vitamin C 0%	Calcium 0%	Iron 4%

Hillshire Farm Lower Sodium Smoked Ham with Natural Juices

2 oz / 56g

Amount per serving	%DV	Amount per serving	%DV	Amount per serving	%DV
Calories 80		**Cholesterol** 30mg	10%	**Total Carbohydrate** 3g	1%
Total Fat 1.5g	2%	**Sodium** 450mg	19%	Dietary Fiber 0g	0%
Saturated Fat 1g	5%	**Protein** 10g		Sugars 2g	
Polyunsaturated Fat 0g					
Monounsaturated Fat 0g		Vitamin A 0%	Vitamin C 0%	Calcium 0%	Iron 2%

Hormel Natural Choice, Rotisserie Style Deli Chicken Breast

2 oz / 56g

Amount per serving	%DV	Amount per serving	%DV	Amount per serving	%DV
Calories 50		**Cholesterol** 35mg	12%	**Total Carbohydrate** 0g	0%
Total Fat 1g	2%	**Sodium** 470mg	20%	Dietary Fiber 0g	0%
Saturated Fat 0g	0%	**Protein** 11g		Sugars 0g	
Polyunsaturated Fat 0g					
Monounsaturated Fat 0g		Vitamin A 0%	Vitamin C 0%	Calcium 0%	Iron 2%

Hormel Natural, Packaged Deli Sandwich Meats, Honey Deli Turkey

56g

Amount per serving	%DV	Amount per serving	%DV	Amount per serving	%DV
Calories 60		**Cholesterol** 25mg	8%	**Total Carbohydrate** 2g	1%
Total Fat 1g	2%	**Sodium** 450mg	19%	Dietary Fiber 0g	0%
Saturated Fat 0g	0%	**Protein** 11g		Sugars 2g	
Polyunsaturated Fat 0g					
Monounsaturated Fat 0g		Vitamin A 0%	Vitamin C 0%	Calcium 0%	Iron 0%

Hormel Natural, Packaged Deli Sandwich Meats, Mesquite Deli Turkey

56g

Amount per serving	%DV	Amount per serving	%DV	Amount per serving	%DV
Calories 60		**Cholesterol** 25mg	8%	**Total Carbohydrate** 1g	0%
Total Fat 1g	2%	**Sodium** 450mg	19%	Dietary Fiber 0g	0%
Saturated Fat 0g	0%	**Protein** 11g		Sugars 1g	
Polyunsaturated Fat 0g					
Monounsaturated Fat 0g		Vitamin A 0%	Vitamin C 0%	Calcium 0%	Iron 0%

Hormel Natural, Packaged Deli Sandwich Meats, Oven-Roasted Deli Turkey

56g

Amount per serving	%DV	Amount per serving	%DV	Amount per serving	%DV
Calories 60		**Cholesterol** 25mg	8%	**Total Carbohydrate** 1g	0%
Total Fat 1g	2%	**Sodium** 460mg	19%	Dietary Fiber 0g	0%
Saturated Fat 0g	0%	**Protein** 11g		Sugars 1g	
Polyunsaturated Fat 0g					
Monounsaturated Fat 0g		Vitamin A 0% Vitamin C 0%		Calcium 0% Iron 0%	

Hormel Natural, Packaged Deli Sandwich Meats, Rotisserie Style Chicken Breast

56g

Amount per serving	%DV	Amount per serving	%DV	Amount per serving	%DV
Calories 50		**Cholesterol** 35mg	12%	**Total Carbohydrate** 0g	0%
Total Fat 1g	2%	**Sodium** 470mg	20%	Dietary Fiber 0g	0%
Saturated Fat 0g	0%	**Protein** 11g		Sugars 0g	
Polyunsaturated Fat 0g					
Monounsaturated Fat 0g		Vitamin A 0% Vitamin C 0%		Calcium 0% Iron 0%	

Hormel Natural, Packaged Deli Sandwich Meats, Smoked Deli Turkey

56g

Amount per serving	%DV	Amount per serving	%DV	Amount per serving	%DV
Calories 60		**Cholesterol** 25mg	8%	**Total Carbohydrate** 1g	0%
Total Fat 1g	2%	**Sodium** 450mg	19%	Dietary Fiber 0g	0%
Saturated Fat 0g	0%	**Protein** 11g		Sugars 1g	
Polyunsaturated Fat 0g					
Monounsaturated Fat 0g		Vitamin A 0% Vitamin C 0%		Calcium 0% Iron 0%	

Jennie-O Turkey, Deli Favorites, Sliced Roasted Turkey Breast Reduced Sodium

56g

Amount per serving	%DV	Amount per serving	%DV	Amount per serving	%DV
Calories 70		**Cholesterol** 30mg	10%	**Total Carbohydrate** 0g	0%
Total Fat 1.5g	2%	**Sodium** 440mg	18%	Dietary Fiber 0g	0%
Saturated Fat 0g	0%	**Protein** 13g		Sugars 0g	
Polyunsaturated Fat 0g					
Monounsaturated Fat 0g		Vitamin A 0% Vitamin C 0%		Calcium 2% Iron 0%	

Kirkland Signature Oven Browned Turkey Breast

2 oz / 56g

Amount per serving	%DV	Amount per serving	%DV	Amount per serving	%DV
Calories 60		**Cholesterol** 25mg	8%	**Total Carbohydrate** 0g	0%
Total Fat 0.5g	1%	**Sodium** 290mg	12%	Dietary Fiber 0g	0%
Saturated Fat 0g	0%	**Protein** 12g		Sugars 0g	
Polyunsaturated Fat 0g					
Monounsaturated Fat 0g		Vitamin A 0% Vitamin C 0%		Calcium 10% Iron 4%	

Kirkland Signature Smoked Honey Ham

4 slices / 56g

Amount per serving	%DV	Amount per serving	%DV	Amount per serving	%DV
Calories 70		**Cholesterol** 30mg	10%	**Total Carbohydrate** 5g	2%
Total Fat 1.5g	2%	**Sodium** 420mg	18%	Dietary Fiber 0g	0%
Saturated Fat 0.5g	2%	**Protein** 10g		Sugars 4g	
Polyunsaturated Fat 0g					
Monounsaturated Fat 0g		Vitamin A 0%	Vitamin C 0%	Calcium 2%	Iron 4%

Krakus Reduced Sodium Polish Ham

2 oz / 56g

Amount per serving	%DV	Amount per serving	%DV	Amount per serving	%DV
Calories 60		**Cholesterol** 25mg	8%	**Total Carbohydrate** 1g	0%
Total Fat 1g	2%	**Sodium** 460mg	19%	Dietary Fiber 0g	0%
Saturated Fat 0.5g	3%	**Protein** 11g		Sugars 1g	
Polyunsaturated Fat 0g					
Monounsaturated Fat 0g		Vitamin A 0%	Vitamin C 0%	Calcium 0%	Iron 2%

Kroger, Lower Sodium Traditional Ham

3 slices / 56g

Amount per serving	%DV	Amount per serving	%DV	Amount per serving	%DV
Calories 45		**Cholesterol** 30mg	10%	**Total Carbohydrate** 1g	0%
Total Fat 0.5g	1%	**Sodium** 400mg	17%	Dietary Fiber 0g	0%
Saturated Fat 0g	0%	**Protein** 9g		Sugars 0g	
Polyunsaturated Fat 0g					
Monounsaturated Fat 0.5g		Vitamin A 0%	Vitamin C 0%	Calcium 4%	Iron 2%

Kroger, Lower Sodium Turkey Breast

2 oz / 1 serving

Amount per serving	%DV	Amount per serving	%DV	Amount per serving	%DV
Calories 60		**Cholesterol** 30mg	10%	**Total Carbohydrate** 1g	0%
Total Fat 1g	2%	**Sodium** 340mg	14%	Dietary Fiber 0g	0%
Saturated Fat 0g	0%	**Protein** 11g		Sugars 1g	
Polyunsaturated Fat 0g					
Monounsaturated Fat 0g		Vitamin A 0%	Vitamin C 0%	Calcium 2%	Iron 4%

Market Pantry Healthy Oven-Roasted Turkey Breast

3 slices / 56.8g

Amount per serving	%DV	Amount per serving	%DV	Amount per serving	%DV
Calories 61		**Cholesterol** 30mg	10%	**Total Carbohydrate** 4g	1%
Total Fat 1g	2%	**Sodium** 365mg	15%	Dietary Fiber 0g	0%
Saturated Fat 0g	0%	**Protein** 9g		Sugars 3g	
Polyunsaturated Fat 0g					
Monounsaturated Fat 0g		Vitamin A 0%	Vitamin C 0%	Calcium 0%	Iron 4%

Market Pantry Healthy Smoked Honey Turkey Breast

2 oz / 57.0g

Amount per serving	%DV	Amount per serving	%DV	Amount per serving	%DV
Calories 70		**Cholesterol** 30mg	10%	**Total Carbohydrate** 4g	1%
Total Fat 1g	2%	**Sodium** 400mg	17%	Dietary Fiber 0g	0%
Saturated Fat 0g	0%	**Protein** 10g		Sugars 3g	
Polyunsaturated Fat 0g					
Monounsaturated Fat 0g		Vitamin A 0%　Vitamin C 0%		Calcium 2%　Iron 4%	

Plumrose Deli Sliced 98% Fat-Free Honey Turkey Breast

1 slice / 28g

Amount per serving	%DV	Amount per serving	%DV	Amount per serving	%DV
Calories 25		**Cholesterol** 15mg	5%	**Total Carbohydrate** 0g	0%
Total Fat 0.5g	1%	**Sodium** 280mg	12%	Dietary Fiber 0g	0%
Saturated Fat 0g	0%	**Protein** 5g		Sugars 1g	
Polyunsaturated Fat 0g					
Monounsaturated Fat 0g		Vitamin A 0%　Vitamin C 0%		Calcium 0%　Iron 2%	

Plumrose, Deli Shaved 97% Fat-Free Premium Ham

6 slices / 56g

Amount per serving	%DV	Amount per serving	%DV	Amount per serving	%DV
Calories 55		**Cholesterol** 20mg	7%	**Total Carbohydrate** 1g	0%
Total Fat 1.5g	2%	**Sodium** 480mg	20%	Dietary Fiber 0g	0%
Saturated Fat 0.5g	2%	**Protein** 9g		Sugars 1g	
Polyunsaturated Fat 0g					
Monounsaturated Fat 0g		Vitamin A 0%　Vitamin C 0%		Calcium 0%　Iron 2%	

Plumrose, Deli Sliced 97% Fat-Free Premium Honey Ham, Water Added

6 slices / 56g

Amount per serving	%DV	Amount per serving	%DV	Amount per serving	%DV
Calories 55		**Cholesterol** 20mg	7%	**Total Carbohydrate** 1g	0%
Total Fat 1.5g	2%	**Sodium** 480mg	20%	Dietary Fiber 0g	0%
Saturated Fat 0.5g	2%	**Protein** 9g		Sugars 1g	
Polyunsaturated Fat 0g					
Monounsaturated Fat 0g		Vitamin A 0%　Vitamin C 0%		Calcium 0%　Iron 2%	

Plumrose, Deli Sliced 97% Fat-Free Smoked Virginia Brand Ham

1 slice / 28g

Amount per serving	%DV	Amount per serving	%DV	Amount per serving	%DV
Calories 25		**Cholesterol** 15mg	5%	**Total Carbohydrate** 0g	0%
Total Fat 1g	2%	**Sodium** 230mg	10%	Dietary Fiber 0g	0%
Saturated Fat 0g	0%	**Protein** 4g		Sugars 0g	
Polyunsaturated Fat 0g					
Monounsaturated Fat 0g		Vitamin A 0%　Vitamin C 0%		Calcium 0%　Iron 2%	

Private Selection, Aged Bourbon Chicken Breast

2 oz / 56g

Amount per serving	%DV	Amount per serving	%DV	Amount per serving	%DV
Calories 60		**Cholesterol** 25mg	8%	**Total Carbohydrate** 2g	1%
Total Fat 0.5g	1%	**Sodium** 430mg	18%	Dietary Fiber 0g	0%
Saturated Fat 0g	0%	**Protein** 11g		Sugars 1g	
Polyunsaturated Fat 0g					
Monounsaturated Fat 0g		Vitamin A 0%	Vitamin C 0%	Calcium 0%	Iron 0%

Private Selection, Buffalo Style Chicken Breast

2 oz / 56g

Amount per serving	%DV	Amount per serving	%DV	Amount per serving	%DV
Calories 60		**Cholesterol** 30mg	10%	**Total Carbohydrate** 1g	0%
Total Fat 0.5g	1%	**Sodium** 420mg	18%	Dietary Fiber 0g	0%
Saturated Fat 0g	0%	**Protein** 13g		Sugars 0g	
Polyunsaturated Fat 0g					
Monounsaturated Fat 0g		Vitamin A 0%	Vitamin C 0%	Calcium 0%	Iron 0%

Private Selection, Cracked Pepper Turkey Breast

2 oz / 56g

Amount per serving	%DV	Amount per serving	%DV	Amount per serving	%DV
Calories 60		**Cholesterol** 30mg	10%	**Total Carbohydrate** 1g	0%
Total Fat 0.5g	1%	**Sodium** 450mg	19%	Dietary Fiber 0g	0%
Saturated Fat 0g	0%	**Protein** 11g		Sugars 1g	
Polyunsaturated Fat 0g					
Monounsaturated Fat 0g		Vitamin A 0%	Vitamin C 0%	Calcium 0%	Iron 0%

Private Selection, Golden Roasted Chicken Breast

2 oz / 56g

Amount per serving	%DV	Amount per serving	%DV	Amount per serving	%DV
Calories 60		**Cholesterol** 30mg	10%	**Total Carbohydrate** 0g	0%
Total Fat 1g	2%	**Sodium** 460mg	19%	Dietary Fiber 0g	0%
Saturated Fat 0g	0%	**Protein** 11g		Sugars 0g	
Polyunsaturated Fat 0g					
Monounsaturated Fat 0g		Vitamin A 0%	Vitamin C 0%	Calcium 0%	Iron 0%

Private Selection, Golden Roasted Turkey Breast

2 oz / 56g

Amount per serving	%DV	Amount per serving	%DV	Amount per serving	%DV
Calories 70		**Cholesterol** 35mg	12%	**Total Carbohydrate** 0g	0%
Total Fat 1g	2%	**Sodium** 380mg	16%	Dietary Fiber 0g	0%
Saturated Fat 0g	0%	**Protein** 13g		Sugars 0g	
Polyunsaturated Fat 0g					
Monounsaturated Fat 0g		Vitamin A 0%	Vitamin C 0%	Calcium 0%	Iron 0%

Private Selection, Golden Roasted Turkey Breast Lower Sodium

2 oz / 56g

Amount per serving	%DV	Amount per serving	%DV	Amount per serving	%DV
Calories 60		**Cholesterol** 30mg	10%	**Total Carbohydrate** 1g	0%
Total Fat 1g	2%	**Sodium** 340mg	14%	Dietary Fiber 0g	0%
Saturated Fat 0g	0%	**Protein** 11g		Sugars 1g	
Polyunsaturated Fat 0g					
Monounsaturated Fat 0g		Vitamin A 0% Vitamin C 0%		Calcium 0% Iron 0%	

Private Selection, Maple Cured Turkey Breast

2 oz / 56g

Amount per serving	%DV	Amount per serving	%DV	Amount per serving	%DV
Calories 60		**Cholesterol** 25mg	8%	**Total Carbohydrate** 3g	1%
Total Fat 0g	0%	**Sodium** 420mg	18%	Dietary Fiber 0g	0%
Saturated Fat 0g	0%	**Protein** 10g		Sugars 3g	
Polyunsaturated Fat 0g					
Monounsaturated Fat 0g		Vitamin A 0% Vitamin C 0%		Calcium 0% Iron 0%	

Private Selection, Rottiserie Seasoned Chicken Breast

2 oz / 56g

Amount per serving	%DV	Amount per serving	%DV	Amount per serving	%DV
Calories 60		**Cholesterol** 30mg	10%	**Total Carbohydrate** 1g	0%
Total Fat 1g	2%	**Sodium** 440mg	18%	Dietary Fiber 0g	0%
Saturated Fat 0g	0%	**Protein** 12g		Sugars 1g	
Polyunsaturated Fat 0g					
Monounsaturated Fat 0g		Vitamin A 0% Vitamin C 0%		Calcium 0% Iron 0%	

Private Selection, Savory Herb & Garlic Chicken Breast

2 oz / 56g

Amount per serving	%DV	Amount per serving	%DV	Amount per serving	%DV
Calories 60		**Cholesterol** 30mg	10%	**Total Carbohydrate** 0g	0%
Total Fat 0.5g	1%	**Sodium** 400mg	17%	Dietary Fiber 0g	0%
Saturated Fat 0g	0%	**Protein** 11g		Sugars 0g	
Polyunsaturated Fat 0g					
Monounsaturated Fat 0g		Vitamin A 0% Vitamin C 0%		Calcium 0% Iron 0%	

Private Selection, USDA Choice Roast Beef Top Round Low Sodium

2 oz / 56g

Amount per serving	%DV	Amount per serving	%DV	Amount per serving	%DV
Calories 80		**Cholesterol** 25mg	8%	**Total Carbohydrate** 1g	0%
Total Fat 3g	5%	**Sodium** 90mg	4%	Dietary Fiber 0g	0%
Saturated Fat 1g	5%	**Protein** 11g		Sugars 0g	
Polyunsaturated Fat 0g					
Monounsaturated Fat 0g		Vitamin A 0% Vitamin C 0%		Calcium 0% Iron 0%	

Private Selection, Wildflower Honey Ham Lower Sodium

2 oz / 56g

Amount per serving	%DV	Amount per serving	%DV	Amount per serving	%DV
Calories 80		**Cholesterol** 30mg	10%	**Total Carbohydrate** 4g	1%
Total Fat 1.5g	2%	**Sodium** 370mg	15%	Dietary Fiber 0g	0%
Saturated Fat 0.5g	3%	**Protein** 10g		Sugars 4g	
Polyunsaturated Fat 0g					
Monounsaturated Fat 0g		Vitamin A 0%	Vitamin C 0%	Calcium 0%	Iron 0%

Sara Lee Black Forest Ham with Natural Juices

2 oz

Amount per serving	%DV	Amount per serving	%DV	Amount per serving	%DV
Calories 60		**Cholesterol** 25mg	8%	**Total Carbohydrate** 1g	0%
Total Fat 1.5g	2%	**Sodium** 440mg	18%	Dietary Fiber 0g	0%
Saturated Fat 0g	0%	**Protein** 10g		Sugars 1g	
Polyunsaturated Fat 0g					
Monounsaturated Fat 0g		Vitamin A 0%	Vitamin C 0%	Calcium 0%	Iron 2%

Sara Lee Basil Pesto Chicken Breast

2 oz

Amount per serving	%DV	Amount per serving	%DV	Amount per serving	%DV
Calories 50		**Cholesterol** 20mg	7%	**Total Carbohydrate** 1g	0%
Total Fat 0.5g	1%	**Sodium** 430mg	18%	Dietary Fiber 0g	0%
Saturated Fat 0g	0%	**Protein** 11g		Sugars 1g	
Polyunsaturated Fat 0g					
Monounsaturated Fat 0g		Vitamin A 0%	Vitamin C 2%	Calcium 0%	Iron 2%

Sara Lee Brown Sugar Ham, Pre-Sliced

2 oz

Amount per serving	%DV	Amount per serving	%DV	Amount per serving	%DV
Calories 70		**Cholesterol** 25mg	8%	**Total Carbohydrate** 5g	2%
Total Fat 1.5g	2%	**Sodium** 420mg	18%	Dietary Fiber 0g	0%
Saturated Fat 0.5g	3%	**Protein** 9g		Sugars 4g	
Polyunsaturated Fat 0g					
Monounsaturated Fat 0g		Vitamin A 0%	Vitamin C 0%	Calcium 2%	Iron 2%

Sara Lee Brown Sugar Ham, Water Added

2 oz

Amount per serving	%DV	Amount per serving	%DV	Amount per serving	%DV
Calories 70		**Cholesterol** 25mg	8%	**Total Carbohydrate** 5g	2%
Total Fat 1.5g	2%	**Sodium** 420mg	18%	Dietary Fiber 0g	0%
Saturated Fat 0.5g	3%	**Protein** 9g		Sugars 4g	
Polyunsaturated Fat 0g					
Monounsaturated Fat 0g		Vitamin A 0%	Vitamin C 0%	Calcium 0%	Iron 2%

Sara Lee Cajun Style Turkey Breast

2 oz

Amount per serving	%DV	Amount per serving	%DV	Amount per serving	%DV
Calories 60		**Cholesterol** 30mg	10%	**Total Carbohydrate** 2g	1%
Total Fat 0.5g	1%	**Sodium** 450mg	19%	Dietary Fiber 0g	0%
Saturated Fat 0g	0%	**Protein** 11g		Sugars 1g	
Polyunsaturated Fat 0g					
Monounsaturated Fat 0g		Vitamin A 2%　　Vitamin C 0%		Calcium 0%　　Iron 4%	

Sara Lee Chipotle Seasoned Turkey Breast

2 oz

Amount per serving	%DV	Amount per serving	%DV	Amount per serving	%DV
Calories 60		**Cholesterol** 30mg	10%	**Total Carbohydrate** 1g	0%
Total Fat 1g	2%	**Sodium** 440mg	18%	Dietary Fiber 0g	0%
Saturated Fat 0g	0%	**Protein** 11g		Sugars 1g	
Polyunsaturated Fat 0g					
Monounsaturated Fat 0g		Vitamin A 0%　　Vitamin C 0%		Calcium 0%　　Iron 4%	

Sara Lee Cracked Pepper Turkey Breast

2 oz

Amount per serving	%DV	Amount per serving	%DV	Amount per serving	%DV
Calories 60		**Cholesterol** 30mg	10%	**Total Carbohydrate** 2g	1%
Total Fat 0.5g	1%	**Sodium** 420mg	18%	Dietary Fiber 0g	0%
Saturated Fat 0g	0%	**Protein** 11g		Sugars 1g	
Polyunsaturated Fat 0g					
Monounsaturated Fat 0g		Vitamin A 0%　　Vitamin C 0%		Calcium 0%　　Iron 4%	

Sara Lee Cracked Pepper Turkey Breast, Pre-Sliced

2 slices

Amount per serving	%DV	Amount per serving	%DV	Amount per serving	%DV
Calories 45		**Cholesterol** 25mg	8%	**Total Carbohydrate** 1g	0%
Total Fat 0.5g	1%	**Sodium** 380mg	16%	Dietary Fiber 0g	0%
Saturated Fat 0g	0%	**Protein** 9g		Sugars 1g	
Polyunsaturated Fat 0g					
Monounsaturated Fat 0g		Vitamin A 0%　　Vitamin C 0%		Calcium 0%　　Iron 2%	

Sara Lee Hardwood Smoked Chicken Breast

2 oz

Amount per serving	%DV	Amount per serving	%DV	Amount per serving	%DV
Calories 50		**Cholesterol** 25mg	8%	**Total Carbohydrate** 0g	0%
Total Fat 0g	0%	**Sodium** 410mg	17%	Dietary Fiber 0g	0%
Saturated Fat 0g	0%	**Protein** 11g		Sugars 0g	
Polyunsaturated Fat 0g					
Monounsaturated Fat 0g		Vitamin A 0%　　Vitamin C 0%		Calcium 0%　　Iron 2%	

Sara Lee Hardwood Smoked Turkey Breast, Pre-Sliced

2 slices

Amount per serving	%DV	Amount per serving	%DV	Amount per serving	%DV
Calories 45		**Cholesterol** 25mg	8%	**Total Carbohydrate** 1g	0%
Total Fat 0g	0%	**Sodium** 370mg	15%	Dietary Fiber 0g	0%
Saturated Fat 0g	0%	**Protein** 9g		Sugars 1g	
Polyunsaturated Fat 0g					
Monounsaturated Fat 0g		Vitamin A 0% Vitamin C 0%		Calcium 0% Iron 2%	

Sara Lee Honey Ham, Pre-Sliced

2 slices

Amount per serving	%DV	Amount per serving	%DV	Amount per serving	%DV
Calories 50		**Cholesterol** 20mg	7%	**Total Carbohydrate** 3g	1%
Total Fat 1g	2%	**Sodium** 380mg	16%	Dietary Fiber 0g	0%
Saturated Fat 0g	0%	**Protein** 8g		Sugars 2g	
Polyunsaturated Fat 0g					
Monounsaturated Fat 0g		Vitamin A 0% Vitamin C 0%		Calcium 0% Iron 2%	

Sara Lee Honey-Roasted Turkey Breast

2 oz

Amount per serving	%DV	Amount per serving	%DV	Amount per serving	%DV
Calories 60		**Cholesterol** 30mg	10%	**Total Carbohydrate** 3g	1%
Total Fat 0.5g	1%	**Sodium** 420mg	18%	Dietary Fiber 0g	0%
Saturated Fat 0g	0%	**Protein** 11g		Sugars 2g	
Polyunsaturated Fat 0g					
Monounsaturated Fat 0g		Vitamin A 0% Vitamin C 0%		Calcium 0% Iron 2%	

Sara Lee Honey-Roasted Turkey Breast, Pre-Sliced

2 slices

Amount per serving	%DV	Amount per serving	%DV	Amount per serving	%DV
Calories 50		**Cholesterol** 25mg	8%	**Total Carbohydrate** 2g	1%
Total Fat 0g	0%	**Sodium** 350mg	15%	Dietary Fiber 0g	0%
Saturated Fat 0g	0%	**Protein** 9g		Sugars 2g	
Polyunsaturated Fat 0g					
Monounsaturated Fat 0g		Vitamin A 0% Vitamin C 0%		Calcium 0% Iron 2%	

Sara Lee Lower Sodium Honey Ham

2 oz

Amount per serving	%DV	Amount per serving	%DV	Amount per serving	%DV
Calories 60		**Cholesterol** 25mg	8%	**Total Carbohydrate** 3g	1%
Total Fat 1.5g	2%	**Sodium** 400mg	17%	Dietary Fiber 0g	0%
Saturated Fat 0.5g	2%	**Protein** 10g		Sugars 3g	
Polyunsaturated Fat 0g					
Monounsaturated Fat 0g		Vitamin A 0% Vitamin C 0%		Calcium 0% Iron 2%	

Sara Lee Lower Sodium Honey-Roasted Turkey Breast

2 oz

Amount per serving	%DV	Amount per serving	%DV	Amount per serving	%DV
Calories 70		**Cholesterol** 30mg	10%	**Total Carbohydrate** 3g	1%
Total Fat 1g	2%	**Sodium** 430mg	18%	Dietary Fiber 0g	0%
Saturated Fat 0g	0%	**Protein** 11g		Sugars 3g	
Polyunsaturated Fat 0g					
Monounsaturated Fat 0g		Vitamin A 0% Vitamin C 0%		Calcium 0% Iron 2%	

Sara Lee Lower Sodium Honey-Roasted Turkey Breast, Pre-Sliced

2 slices

Amount per serving	%DV	Amount per serving	%DV	Amount per serving	%DV
Calories 60		**Cholesterol** 25mg	8%	**Total Carbohydrate** 3g	1%
Total Fat 0.5g	1%	**Sodium** 300mg	12%	Dietary Fiber 0g	0%
Saturated Fat 0g	0%	**Protein** 10g		Sugars 3g	
Polyunsaturated Fat 0g					
Monounsaturated Fat 0g		Vitamin A 0% Vitamin C 0%		Calcium 0% Iron 2%	

Sara Lee Lower Sodium Oven-Roasted Chicken Breast

2 oz

Amount per serving	%DV	Amount per serving	%DV	Amount per serving	%DV
Calories 50		**Cholesterol** 30mg	10%	**Total Carbohydrate** 0g	0%
Total Fat 0.5g	1%	**Sodium** 350mg	15%	Dietary Fiber 0g	0%
Saturated Fat 0g	0%	**Protein** 11g		Sugars 0g	
Polyunsaturated Fat 0g					
Monounsaturated Fat 0g		Vitamin A 0% Vitamin C 0%		Calcium 0% Iron 2%	

Sara Lee Lower Sodium Oven-Roasted Turkey Breast

2 oz

Amount per serving	%DV	Amount per serving	%DV	Amount per serving	%DV
Calories 60		**Cholesterol** 30mg	10%	**Total Carbohydrate** 1g	0%
Total Fat 1g	2%	**Sodium** 340mg	14%	Dietary Fiber 0g	0%
Saturated Fat 0g	0%	**Protein** 12g		Sugars 1g	
Polyunsaturated Fat 0g					
Monounsaturated Fat 0g		Vitamin A 2% Vitamin C 0%		Calcium 0% Iron 2%	

Sara Lee Lower Sodium Roast Beef

2 oz

Amount per serving	%DV	Amount per serving	%DV	Amount per serving	%DV
Calories 70		**Cholesterol** 35mg	12%	**Total Carbohydrate** 2g	1%
Total Fat 2.5g	4%	**Sodium** 360mg	15%	Dietary Fiber 0g	0%
Saturated Fat 1g	5%	**Protein** 11g		Sugars 1g	
Polyunsaturated Fat 0g					
Monounsaturated Fat 0g		Vitamin A 0% Vitamin C 0%		Calcium 0% Iron 4%	

Sara Lee Maple Honey Ham, Water Added

2 oz

Amount per serving	%DV	Amount per serving	%DV	Amount per serving	%DV
Calories 70		**Cholesterol** 25mg	8%	**Total Carbohydrate** 4g	1%
Total Fat 1.5g	2%	**Sodium** 450mg	19%	Dietary Fiber 0g	0%
Saturated Fat 0.5g	3%	**Protein** 9g		Sugars 4g	
Polyunsaturated Fat 0g					
Monounsaturated Fat 0g		Vitamin A 0%	Vitamin C 0%	Calcium 0%	Iron 2%

Sara Lee Oven-Roasted Chicken Breast

2 oz

Amount per serving	%DV	Amount per serving	%DV	Amount per serving	%DV
Calories 50		**Cholesterol** 25mg	8%	**Total Carbohydrate** 0g	0%
Total Fat 0g	0%	**Sodium** 410mg	17%	Dietary Fiber 0g	0%
Saturated Fat 0g	0%	**Protein** 11g		Sugars 0g	
Polyunsaturated Fat 0g					
Monounsaturated Fat 0g		Vitamin A 0%	Vitamin C 0%	Calcium 0%	Iron 2%

Sara Lee Oven-Roasted Turkey Breast, Pre-Sliced

2 slices

Amount per serving	%DV	Amount per serving	%DV	Amount per serving	%DV
Calories 60		**Cholesterol** 30mg	10%	**Total Carbohydrate** 1g	0%
Total Fat 0.5g	1%	**Sodium** 470mg	20%	Dietary Fiber 0g	0%
Saturated Fat 0g	0%	**Protein** 12g		Sugars 0g	
Polyunsaturated Fat 0g					
Monounsaturated Fat 0g		Vitamin A 0%	Vitamin C 0%	Calcium 0%	Iron 2%

Sara Lee Roast Beef, Pre-Sliced

2 slices

Amount per serving	%DV	Amount per serving	%DV	Amount per serving	%DV
Calories 60		**Cholesterol** 25mg	8%	**Total Carbohydrate** 1g	0%
Total Fat 2g	3%	**Sodium** 380mg	16%	Dietary Fiber 0g	0%
Saturated Fat 1g	5%	**Protein** 9g		Sugars 0g	
Polyunsaturated Fat 0g					
Monounsaturated Fat 0g		Vitamin A 0%	Vitamin C 0%	Calcium 0%	Iron 4%

Sara Lee Rosemary & Sage Turkey Breast

2 oz

Amount per serving	%DV	Amount per serving	%DV	Amount per serving	%DV
Calories 60		**Cholesterol** 30mg	10%	**Total Carbohydrate** 2g	1%
Total Fat 1g	2%	**Sodium** 460mg	19%	Dietary Fiber 0g	0%
Saturated Fat 0g	0%	**Protein** 11g		Sugars 2g	
Polyunsaturated Fat 0g					
Monounsaturated Fat 0g		Vitamin A 0%	Vitamin C 0%	Calcium 0%	Iron 4%

Sara Lee Virginia Brand Baked Ham, Pre-Sliced

2 slices

Amount per serving	%DV	Amount per serving	%DV	Amount per serving	%DV
Calories 50		**Cholesterol** 20mg	7%	**Total Carbohydrate** 3g	1%
Total Fat 1g	2%	**Sodium** 380mg	16%	Dietary Fiber 0g	0%
Saturated Fat 0g	0%	**Protein** 8g		Sugars 3g	
Polyunsaturated Fat 0g					
Monounsaturated Fat 0g		Vitamin A 0% Vitamin C 0%		Calcium 0% Iron 2%	

Sara Lee Virginia Brand Ham, with Natural Juices

2 oz

Amount per serving	%DV	Amount per serving	%DV	Amount per serving	%DV
Calories 60		**Cholesterol** 25mg	8%	**Total Carbohydrate** 2g	1%
Total Fat 1.5g	2%	**Sodium** 440mg	18%	Dietary Fiber 0g	0%
Saturated Fat 0.5g	3%	**Protein** 10g		Sugars 2g	
Polyunsaturated Fat 0g					
Monounsaturated Fat 0g		Vitamin A 0% Vitamin C 0%		Calcium 0% Iron 2%	

Sara Lee, BBQ Seasoned Chicken Breast

2 oz

Amount per serving	%DV	Amount per serving	%DV	Amount per serving	%DV
Calories 60		**Cholesterol** 20mg	7%	**Total Carbohydrate** 3g	1%
Total Fat 0.5g	1%	**Sodium** 420mg	18%	Dietary Fiber 0g	0%
Saturated Fat 0g	0%	**Protein** 11g		Sugars 2g	
Polyunsaturated Fat 0g					
Monounsaturated Fat 0g		Vitamin A 2% Vitamin C 2%		Calcium 0% Iron 2%	

Sara Lee, Buffalo Style Chicken Breast

2 oz

Amount per serving	%DV	Amount per serving	%DV	Amount per serving	%DV
Calories 50		**Cholesterol** 20mg	7%	**Total Carbohydrate** 1g	0%
Total Fat 0.5g	1%	**Sodium** 470mg	20%	Dietary Fiber 0g	0%
Saturated Fat 0g	0%	**Protein** 11g		Sugars 0g	
Polyunsaturated Fat 0g					
Monounsaturated Fat 0g		Vitamin A 2% Vitamin C 2%		Calcium 0% Iron 2%	

Sara Lee, Lower Sodium Virginia Brand Ham, Pre-Sliced

2 slices

Amount per serving	%DV	Amount per serving	%DV	Amount per serving	%DV
Calories 50		**Cholesterol** 20mg	7%	**Total Carbohydrate** 2g	1%
Total Fat 1g	2%	**Sodium** 310mg	13%	Dietary Fiber 0g	0%
Saturated Fat 0g	0%	**Protein** 8g		Sugars 2g	
Polyunsaturated Fat 0g					
Monounsaturated Fat 0g		Vitamin A 0% Vitamin C 0%		Calcium 0% Iron 2%	

Swanson Premium Chunk White & Dark Chicken in Water

2 oz / 57 g

Amount per serving	%DV	Amount per serving	%DV	Amount per serving	%DV
Calories 60		**Cholesterol** 30mg	10%	**Total Carbohydrate** 0g	0%
Total Fat 2g	3%	**Sodium** 250mg	10%	Dietary Fiber 0g	0%
Saturated Fat 0.5g	3%	**Protein** 10g		Sugars 0g	
Polyunsaturated Fat 0g					
Monounsaturated Fat 0g		Vitamin A 0% Vitamin C 0%		Calcium 0% Iron 0%	

Swanson Premium Chunk White Chicken Breast in Water

2 oz / drained / 56g

Amount per serving	%DV	Amount per serving	%DV	Amount per serving	%DV
Calories 60		**Cholesterol** 25mg	8%	**Total Carbohydrate** 1g	0%
Total Fat 1g	2%	**Sodium** 260mg	11%	Dietary Fiber 0g	0%
Saturated Fat 0g	0%	**Protein** 12g		Sugars 0g	
Polyunsaturated Fat 0g					
Monounsaturated Fat 0g		Vitamin A 0% Vitamin C 0%		Calcium 0% Iron 0%	

Thumann's Buffalo Style Oven-Roasted Chicken Breast

2 oz / 56g

Amount per serving	%DV	Amount per serving	%DV	Amount per serving	%DV
Calories 60		**Cholesterol** 30mg	10%	**Total Carbohydrate** 0g	0%
Total Fat 1g	2%	**Sodium** 260mg	11%	Dietary Fiber 0g	0%
Saturated Fat 0g	0%	**Protein** 13g		Sugars 0g	
Polyunsaturated Fat 0g					
Monounsaturated Fat 0g		Vitamin A 0% Vitamin C 0%		Calcium 0% Iron 4%	

Thumann's Deluxe Cooked Ham - Lower Sodium

2 oz / 56g

Amount per serving	%DV	Amount per serving	%DV	Amount per serving	%DV
Calories 60		**Cholesterol** 21mg	7%	**Total Carbohydrate** 1g	0%
Total Fat 1g	2%	**Sodium** 400mg	17%	Dietary Fiber 0g	0%
Saturated Fat 0g	0%	**Protein** 10g		Sugars 1g	
Polyunsaturated Fat 0g					
Monounsaturated Fat 0g		Vitamin A 0% Vitamin C 0%		Calcium 4% Iron 4%	

Thumann's Filet of Turkey - Rotisserie Flavor

2 oz / 56g

Amount per serving	%DV	Amount per serving	%DV	Amount per serving	%DV
Calories 40		**Cholesterol** 25mg	8%	**Total Carbohydrate** 0g	0%
Total Fat 0.5g	1%	**Sodium** 350mg	15%	Dietary Fiber 0g	0%
Saturated Fat 0g	0%	**Protein** 13g		Sugars 0g	
Polyunsaturated Fat 0g					
Monounsaturated Fat 0g		Vitamin A 0% Vitamin C 0%		Calcium 10% Iron 4%	

Thumann's Oven-Roasted Premium Chicken Breast

2 oz / 56g

Amount per serving	%DV	Amount per serving	%DV	Amount per serving	%DV
Calories 60		**Cholesterol** 30mg	10%	**Total Carbohydrate** 0g	0%
Total Fat 1g	2%	**Sodium** 260mg	11%	Dietary Fiber 0g	0%
Saturated Fat 0g	0%	**Protein** 13g		Sugars 0g	
Polyunsaturated Fat 0g					
Monounsaturated Fat 0g		Vitamin A 0% Vitamin C 0%		Calcium 0% Iron 4%	

Thumann's Roasted Gourmet Turkey Breast

2 oz / 56g

Amount per serving	%DV	Amount per serving	%DV	Amount per serving	%DV
Calories 40		**Cholesterol** 25mg	8%	**Total Carbohydrate** 0g	0%
Total Fat 0.5g	1%	**Sodium** 280mg	12%	Dietary Fiber 0g	0%
Saturated Fat 0g	0%	**Protein** 13g		Sugars 0g	
Polyunsaturated Fat 0g					
Monounsaturated Fat 0g		Vitamin A 0% Vitamin C 0%		Calcium 0% Iron 4%	

Thumann's, All Natural Black Angus Cooked Corned Beef Round

2 oz

Amount per serving	%DV	Amount per serving	%DV	Amount per serving	%DV
Calories 70		**Cholesterol** 32mg	11%	**Total Carbohydrate** 0g	0%
Total Fat 2g	3%	**Sodium** 450mg	19%	Dietary Fiber 0g	0%
Saturated Fat 1g	5%	**Protein** 12g		Sugars 0g	
Polyunsaturated Fat 0g					
Monounsaturated Fat 0g		Vitamin A 0% Vitamin C 0%		Calcium 0% Iron 4%	

Thumann's, All Natural Black Forest Brand Ham

2 oz

Amount per serving	%DV	Amount per serving	%DV	Amount per serving	%DV
Calories 60		**Cholesterol** 21mg	7%	**Total Carbohydrate** 1g	0%
Total Fat 1g	2%	**Sodium** 400mg	17%	Dietary Fiber 0g	0%
Saturated Fat 0g	0%	**Protein** 10g		Sugars 1g	
Polyunsaturated Fat 0g					
Monounsaturated Fat 0g		Vitamin A 0% Vitamin C 25%		Calcium 4% Iron 0%	

Thumann's, All Natural Oven-Roasted Gourmet Chicken Breast

2 oz

Amount per serving	%DV	Amount per serving	%DV	Amount per serving	%DV
Calories 40		**Cholesterol** 25mg	8%	**Total Carbohydrate** 0g	0%
Total Fat 0.5g	1%	**Sodium** 350mg	15%	Dietary Fiber 0g	0%
Saturated Fat 0g	0%	**Protein** 13g		Sugars 0g	
Polyunsaturated Fat 0g					
Monounsaturated Fat 0g		Vitamin A 0% Vitamin C 0%		Calcium 0% Iron 4%	

Thumann's, All Natural Oven-Roasted Gourmet Turkey Breast

2 oz

Amount per serving	%DV	Amount per serving	%DV	Amount per serving	%DV
Calories 40		**Cholesterol** 25mg	8%	**Total Carbohydrate** 0g	0%
Total Fat 0.5g	1%	**Sodium** 350mg	15%	Dietary Fiber 0g	0%
Saturated Fat 0g	0%	**Protein** 13g		Sugars 0g	
Polyunsaturated Fat 0g					
Monounsaturated Fat 0g		Vitamin A 0% · Vitamin C 0%		Calcium 0% · Iron 4%	

Thumann's, All Natural Oven-Roasted Top Round

2 oz

Amount per serving	%DV	Amount per serving	%DV	Amount per serving	%DV
Calories 70		**Cholesterol** 25mg	8%	**Total Carbohydrate** 0g	0%
Total Fat 1g	2%	**Sodium** 160mg	7%	Dietary Fiber 0g	0%
Saturated Fat 0.5g	2%	**Protein** 15g		Sugars 0g	
Polyunsaturated Fat 0g					
Monounsaturated Fat 0g		Vitamin A 0% · Vitamin C 0%		Calcium 0% · Iron 2%	

Thumann's, Buffalo Style, Oven-Roasted Chicken Breast

2 oz

Amount per serving	%DV	Amount per serving	%DV	Amount per serving	%DV
Calories 60		**Cholesterol** 30mg	10%	**Total Carbohydrate** 0g	0%
Total Fat 1g	2%	**Sodium** 260mg	11%	Dietary Fiber 0g	0%
Saturated Fat 0g	0%	**Protein** 13g		Sugars 0g	
Polyunsaturated Fat 0g					
Monounsaturated Fat 0g		Vitamin A 0% · Vitamin C 0%		Calcium 0% · Iron 4%	

Thumann's, Capless Roast Beef

2 oz / 56g

Amount per serving	%DV	Amount per serving	%DV	Amount per serving	%DV
Calories 70		**Cholesterol** 20mg	7%	**Total Carbohydrate** 0g	0%
Total Fat 1.5g	2%	**Sodium** 160mg	7%	Dietary Fiber 0g	0%
Saturated Fat 0.5g	3%	**Protein** 14g		Sugars 0g	
Polyunsaturated Fat 0g					
Monounsaturated Fat 0g		Vitamin A 0% · Vitamin C 0%		Calcium 0% · Iron 4%	

Thumann's, Deluxe Cooked Ham, Lower Sodium

2 oz

Amount per serving	%DV	Amount per serving	%DV	Amount per serving	%DV
Calories 60		**Cholesterol** 21mg	7%	**Total Carbohydrate** 1g	0%
Total Fat 1g	2%	**Sodium** 400mg	17%	Dietary Fiber 0g	0%
Saturated Fat 0g	0%	**Protein** 10g		Sugars 1g	
Polyunsaturated Fat 0g					
Monounsaturated Fat 0g		Vitamin A 0% · Vitamin C 25%		Calcium 0% · Iron 4%	

Thumann's, Filet of Turkey, Rotisserie Flavor

2 oz

Amount per serving	%DV	Amount per serving	%DV	Amount per serving	%DV
Calories 40		**Cholesterol** 25mg	8%	**Total Carbohydrate** 0g	0%
Total Fat 0.5g	1%	**Sodium** 350mg	15%	Dietary Fiber 0g	0%
Saturated Fat 0g	0%	**Protein** 13g		Sugars 0g	
Polyunsaturated Fat 0g					
Monounsaturated Fat 0g		Vitamin A 0% Vitamin C 0%		Calcium 0% Iron 4%	

Thumann's, Golden Roasted Gourmet, Turkey Breast

2 oz

Amount per serving	%DV	Amount per serving	%DV	Amount per serving	%DV
Calories 40		**Cholesterol** 25mg	8%	**Total Carbohydrate** 0g	0%
Total Fat 0.5g	1%	**Sodium** 280mg	12%	Dietary Fiber 0g	0%
Saturated Fat 0g	0%	**Protein** 13g		Sugars 0g	
Polyunsaturated Fat 0g					
Monounsaturated Fat 0g		Vitamin A 0% Vitamin C 0%		Calcium 0% Iron 4%	

Thumann's, Oven-Roasted Premium Chicken Breast

2 oz

Amount per serving	%DV	Amount per serving	%DV	Amount per serving	%DV
Calories 60		**Cholesterol** 30mg	10%	**Total Carbohydrate** 0g	0%
Total Fat 1g	2%	**Sodium** 260mg	11%	Dietary Fiber 0g	0%
Saturated Fat 0g	0%	**Protein** 13g		Sugars 0g	
Polyunsaturated Fat 0g					
Monounsaturated Fat 0g		Vitamin A 0% Vitamin C 0%		Calcium 0% Iron 4%	

Turkey Breast, Low Salt, Prepackaged or Deli, Luncheon Meat

1 slice / 28g

Amount per serving	%DV	Amount per serving	%DV	Amount per serving	%DV
Calories 28		**Cholesterol** 12mg	4%	**Total Carbohydrate** 0g	0%
Total Fat 0g	0%	**Sodium** 216mg	9%	Dietary Fiber 0g	0%
Saturated Fat 0g	0%	**Protein** 6g		Sugars 1g	
Polyunsaturated Fat 0g					
Monounsaturated Fat 0g		Vitamin A 0% Vitamin C 0%		Calcium 0% Iron 1%	

Turkey Breast, Sliced, Oven-Roasted, Luncheon Meat

1 slice / 21g

Amount per serving	%DV	Amount per serving	%DV	Amount per serving	%DV
Calories 22		**Cholesterol** 9mg	3%	**Total Carbohydrate** 1g	0%
Total Fat 0g	0%	**Sodium** 213mg	9%	Dietary Fiber 0g	0%
Saturated Fat 0g	0%	**Protein** 4g		Sugars 1g	
Polyunsaturated Fat 0g					
Monounsaturated Fat 0g		Vitamin A 0% Vitamin C 2%		Calcium 0% Iron 2%	

Seafood

Bass, Fresh Water, Mixed Species, Cooked, Dry Heat

3 oz / 85g

Amount per serving	%DV	Amount per serving	%DV	Amount per serving	%DV
Calories 105		Cholesterol 45mg	15%	Total Carbohydrate 0g	0%
Total Fat 2.1g	3%	Sodium 74mg	3%	Dietary Fiber 0g	0%
Saturated Fat 0g	0%	Protein 20g		Sugars 0g	
Polyunsaturated Fat 0.8g					
Monounsaturated Fat 0.4g		Vitamin A 3%	Vitamin C 0%	Calcium 1%	Iron 2%

Bass, Striped, Cooked, Dry Heat

3 oz / 85g

Amount per serving	%DV	Amount per serving	%DV	Amount per serving	%DV
Calories 106		Cholesterol 88mg	29%	Total Carbohydrate 0g	0%
Total Fat 2.5g	4%	Sodium 75mg	3%	Dietary Fiber 0g	0%
Saturated Fat 0.5g	3%	Protein 19.3g		Sugars 0g	
Polyunsaturated Fat 0.8g					
Monounsaturated Fat 0.6g		Vitamin A 2%	Vitamin C 0%	Calcium 1%	Iron 5%

Bluefish, Cooked, Dry Heat

3 oz / 85g

Amount per serving	%DV	Amount per serving	%DV	Amount per serving	%DV
Calories 135		Cholesterol 65mg	22%	Total Carbohydrate 0g	0%
Total Fat 4.6g	7%	Sodium 65mg	3%	Dietary Fiber 0g	0%
Saturated Fat 1g	5%	Protein 21.8g		Sugars 0g	
Polyunsaturated Fat 1.1g					
Monounsaturated Fat 1.9g		Vitamin A 8%	Vitamin C 0%	Calcium 1%	Iron 3%

Bumble Bee, Chunk Light Tuna in Water

1 can drained / 2.7 oz / 62g

Amount per serving	%DV	Amount per serving	%DV	Amount per serving	%DV
Calories 50		Cholesterol 30mg	10%	Total Carbohydrate 0g	0%
Total Fat 0g	0%	Sodium 200mg	8%	Dietary Fiber 0g	0%
Saturated Fat 0g	0%	Protein 12g		Sugars 0g	
Polyunsaturated Fat 0g					
Monounsaturated Fat 0g		Vitamin A 0%	Vitamin C 0%	Calcium 0%	Iron 2%

Bumble Bee, Prime Fillet Solid White Albacore in Water

2 oz drained / about 1/4 cup / 56g

Amount per serving	%DV	Amount per serving	%DV	Amount per serving	%DV
Calories 60		Cholesterol 25mg	8%	Total Carbohydrate 0g	0%
Total Fat 0g	0%	Sodium 250mg	10%	Dietary Fiber 0g	0%
Saturated Fat 0g	0%	Protein 13g		Sugars 0g	
Polyunsaturated Fat 0g					
Monounsaturated Fat 0g		Vitamin A 0%	Vitamin C 0%	Calcium 0%	Iron 2%

Bumble Bee, Chunk White Albacore in Water

2 oz drained / about 1/4 cup / 56g

Amount per serving	%DV	Amount per serving	%DV	Amount per serving	%DV
Calories 60		**Cholesterol** 30mg	10%	**Total Carbohydrate** 0g	0%
Total Fat 1g	2%	**Sodium** 140mg	6%	Dietary Fiber 0g	0%
Saturated Fat 0g	0%	**Protein** 13g		Sugars 0g	
Polyunsaturated Fat 0g					
Monounsaturated Fat 0g		Vitamin A 0%	Vitamin C 0%	Calcium 0%	Iron 2%

Bumble Bee, Chunk White Albacore in Water

1 can drained / 2.6 oz / 62g

Amount per serving	%DV	Amount per serving	%DV	Amount per serving	%DV
Calories 70		**Cholesterol** 30mg	10%	**Total Carbohydrate** 0g	0%
Total Fat 1g	2%	**Sodium** 160mg	7%	Dietary Fiber 0g	0%
Saturated Fat 0g	0%	**Protein** 13g		Sugars 0g	
Polyunsaturated Fat 0g					
Monounsaturated Fat 0g		Vitamin A 0%	Vitamin C 0%	Calcium 0%	Iron 2%

Bumble Bee, Chunk Light Tuna in Water

2 oz drained / about 1/4 cup / 56g

Amount per serving	%DV	Amount per serving	%DV	Amount per serving	%DV
Calories 50		**Cholesterol** 30mg	10%	**Total Carbohydrate** 0g	0%
Total Fat 0.5g	1%	**Sodium** 180mg	8%	Dietary Fiber 0g	0%
Saturated Fat 0g	0%	**Protein** 11g		Sugars 0g	
Polyunsaturated Fat 0g					
Monounsaturated Fat 0g		Vitamin A 0%	Vitamin C 0%	Calcium 0%	Iron 2%

Bumble Bee, Premium Albacore Tuna in Water

1 pouch

Amount per serving	%DV	Amount per serving	%DV	Amount per serving	%DV
Calories 80		**Cholesterol** 35mg	12%	**Total Carbohydrate** 0g	0%
Total Fat 2g	3%	**Sodium** 140mg	6%	Dietary Fiber 0g	0%
Saturated Fat 1g	5%	**Protein** 16g		Sugars 0g	
Polyunsaturated Fat 1g					
Monounsaturated Fat 0g		Vitamin A 0%	Vitamin C 0%	Calcium 0%	Iron 2%

Bumble Bee, Premium Albacore Tuna in Water

2 oz / about 1/4 cup / 56g

Amount per serving	%DV	Amount per serving	%DV	Amount per serving	%DV
Calories 70		**Cholesterol** 30mg	10%	**Total Carbohydrate** 0g	0%
Total Fat 1.5g	2%	**Sodium** 140mg	6%	Dietary Fiber 0g	0%
Saturated Fat 0.5g	3%	**Protein** 13g		Sugars 0g	
Polyunsaturated Fat 0g					
Monounsaturated Fat 0g		Vitamin A 0%	Vitamin C 0%	Calcium 0%	Iron 2%

Bumble Bee, Premium Light Tuna in Water

1 pouch / 71g

Amount per serving	%DV	Amount per serving	%DV	Amount per serving	%DV
Calories 70		**Cholesterol** 35mg	12%	**Total Carbohydrate** 0g	0%
Total Fat 1g	2%	**Sodium** 240mg	10%	Dietary Fiber 0g	0%
Saturated Fat 1g	5%	**Protein** 16g		Sugars 0g	
Polyunsaturated Fat 0g					
Monounsaturated Fat 0g		Vitamin A 0% Vitamin C 0%		Calcium 0% Iron 4%	

Bumble Bee, Premium Light Tuna in Water

2 oz / about 1/4 cup / 56g

Amount per serving	%DV	Amount per serving	%DV	Amount per serving	%DV
Calories 60		**Cholesterol** 30mg	10%	**Total Carbohydrate** 0g	0%
Total Fat 0.5g	1%	**Sodium** 180mg	8%	Dietary Fiber 0g	0%
Saturated Fat 0g	0%	**Protein** 13g		Sugars 0g	
Polyunsaturated Fat 0g					
Monounsaturated Fat 0g		Vitamin A 0% Vitamin C 0%		Calcium 0% Iron 2%	

Bumble Bee, Prime Filet Atlantic Salmon

2 oz drained / about 1/4 cup / 56g

Amount per serving	%DV	Amount per serving	%DV	Amount per serving	%DV
Calories 80		**Cholesterol** 30mg	10%	**Total Carbohydrate** 0g	0%
Total Fat 4g	6%	**Sodium** 180mg	8%	Dietary Fiber 0g	0%
Saturated Fat 1g	5%	**Protein** 12g		Sugars 0g	
Polyunsaturated Fat 2g					
Monounsaturated Fat 1g		Vitamin A 0% Vitamin C 0%		Calcium 0% Iron 0%	

Bumble Bee, Prime Fillet Solid White Albacore in Water

1 can drained / 2.2 oz / 62g

Amount per serving	%DV	Amount per serving	%DV	Amount per serving	%DV
Calories 60		**Cholesterol** 25mg	8%	**Total Carbohydrate** 0g	0%
Total Fat 0g	0%	**Sodium** 160mg	7%	Dietary Fiber 0g	0%
Saturated Fat 0g	0%	**Protein** 15g		Sugars 0g	
Polyunsaturated Fat 0g					
Monounsaturated Fat 0g		Vitamin A 0% Vitamin C 0%		Calcium 0% Iron 2%	

Bumble Bee, Prime Fillet Solid White Albacore in Water

2 oz drained / about 1/4 cup / 56g

Amount per serving	%DV	Amount per serving	%DV	Amount per serving	%DV
Calories 60		**Cholesterol** 25mg	8%	**Total Carbohydrate** 0g	0%
Total Fat 0g	0%	**Sodium** 140mg	6%	Dietary Fiber 0g	0%
Saturated Fat 0g	0%	**Protein** 13g		Sugars 0g	
Polyunsaturated Fat 0g					
Monounsaturated Fat 0g		Vitamin A 0% Vitamin C 0%		Calcium 0% Iron 2%	

Bumble Bee, Prime Fillet Very Low Sodium Solid White Albacore in Water

2 oz drained / about 1/4 cup / 56g

Amount per serving	%DV	Amount per serving	%DV	Amount per serving	%DV
Calories 70		**Cholesterol** 25mg	8%	**Total Carbohydrate** 0g	0%
Total Fat 0.5g	1%	**Sodium** 35mg	1%	Dietary Fiber 0g	0%
Saturated Fat 0g	0%	**Protein** 16g		Sugars 0g	
Polyunsaturated Fat 0g					
Monounsaturated Fat 0g		Vitamin A 0%	Vitamin C 0%	Calcium 0%	Iron 0%

Bumble Bee, Skinless & Boneless Pink Salmon

2 oz drained / about 1/4 cup / 56g

Amount per serving	%DV	Amount per serving	%DV	Amount per serving	%DV
Calories 60		**Cholesterol** 30mg	10%	**Total Carbohydrate** 0g	0%
Total Fat 1.5g	2%	**Sodium** 180mg	8%	Dietary Fiber 0g	0%
Saturated Fat 0.5g	2%	**Protein** 12g		Sugars 0g	
Polyunsaturated Fat 1g					
Monounsaturated Fat 0g		Vitamin A 0%	Vitamin C 0%	Calcium 0%	Iron 2%

Bumble Bee, Solid White Albacore in Water

1 can drained / 2.2 oz /62g

Amount per serving	%DV	Amount per serving	%DV	Amount per serving	%DV
Calories 60		**Cholesterol** 25mg	8%	**Total Carbohydrate** 0g	0%
Total Fat 0g	0%	**Sodium** 160mg	7%	Dietary Fiber 0g	0%
Saturated Fat 0g	0%	**Protein** 15g		Sugars 0g	
Polyunsaturated Fat 0g					
Monounsaturated Fat 0g		Vitamin A 0%	Vitamin C 0%	Calcium 30%	Iron 2%

Bumble Bee, Solid White Albacore in Water

2 oz drained /about 1/4 cup /56g

Amount per serving	%DV	Amount per serving	%DV	Amount per serving	%DV
Calories 60		**Cholesterol** 25mg	8%	**Total Carbohydrate** 0g	0%
Total Fat 0g	0%	**Sodium** 250mg	10%	Dietary Fiber 0g	0%
Saturated Fat 0g	0%	**Protein** 13g		Sugars 0g	
Polyunsaturated Fat 0g					
Monounsaturated Fat 0g		Vitamin A 0%	Vitamin C 0%	Calcium 30%	Iron 2%

Bumble Bee, Wild Alaska Blueback Salmon

2.2 oz / about 1/4 cup / 63g

Amount per serving	%DV	Amount per serving	%DV	Amount per serving	%DV
Calories 100		**Cholesterol** 40mg	13%	**Total Carbohydrate** 0g	0%
Total Fat 5g	8%	**Sodium** 220mg	9%	Dietary Fiber 0g	0%
Saturated Fat 1g	5%	**Protein** 13g		Sugars 0g	
Polyunsaturated Fat 2.5g					
Monounsaturated Fat 1.5g		Vitamin A 4%	Vitamin C 0%	Calcium 2%	Iron 4%

Bumble Bee, Wild Alaska Red Salmon

2.2 oz / about 1/4 cup / 63g

Amount per serving	%DV	Amount per serving	%DV	Amount per serving	%DV
Calories 100		**Cholesterol** 40mg	13%	**Total Carbohydrate** 0g	0%
Total Fat 5g	8%	**Sodium** 220mg	9%	Dietary Fiber 0g	0%
Saturated Fat 1g	5%	**Protein** 13g		Sugars 0g	
Polyunsaturated Fat 2.5g					
Monounsaturated Fat 1.5g		Vitamin A 4% Vitamin C 0%		Calcium 2% Iron 4%	

Burbot, Cooked, Dry Heat

3 oz / 85g

Amount per serving	%DV	Amount per serving	%DV	Amount per serving	%DV
Calories 98		**Cholesterol** 65mg	22%	**Total Carbohydrate** 0g	0%
Total Fat 0g	0%	**Sodium** 106mg	4%	Dietary Fiber 0g	0%
Saturated Fat 0g	0%	**Protein** 21g		Sugars 0g	
Polyunsaturated Fat 0g					
Monounsaturated Fat 0g		Vitamin A 0% Vitamin C 0%		Calcium 6% Iron 6%	

Catfish, Channel, Wild, Cooked, Dry Heat

3 oz / 85g

Amount per serving	%DV	Amount per serving	%DV	Amount per serving	%DV
Calories 89		**Cholesterol** 61mg	20%	**Total Carbohydrate** 0g	0%
Total Fat 2g	3%	**Sodium** 43mg	2%	Dietary Fiber 0g	0%
Saturated Fat 1g	5%	**Protein** 15.6g		Sugars 0g	
Polyunsaturated Fat 0g					
Monounsaturated Fat 0g		Vitamin A 1% Vitamin C 1%		Calcium 1% Iron 2%	

Clams, Mixed Species, Canned, Drained Solid

3 oz / 85g

Amount per serving	%DV	Amount per serving	%DV	Amount per serving	%DV
Calories 126		**Cholesterol** 57mg	19%	**Total Carbohydrate** 4.4g	1%
Total Fat 1.7g	3%	**Sodium** 95mg	4%	Dietary Fiber 0g	0%
Saturated Fat 0g	0%	**Protein** 21.7g		Sugars 0g	
Polyunsaturated Fat 0g					
Monounsaturated Fat 0g		Vitamin A 10% Vitamin C 31%		Calcium 8% Iron 132%	

Clams, Mixed Species, Canned, Liquid

3 oz / 85g

Amount per serving	%DV	Amount per serving	%DV	Amount per serving	%DV
Calories 2		**Cholesterol** 3mg	1%	**Total Carbohydrate** 0g	0%
Total Fat 0g	0%	**Sodium** 183mg	8%	Dietary Fiber 0g	0%
Saturated Fat 0g	0%	**Protein** 0g		Sugars 0g	
Polyunsaturated Fat 0g					
Monounsaturated Fat 0g		Vitamin A 1% Vitamin C 1%		Calcium 1% Iron 1%	

Clearwater Sea Scallops

110g

Amount per serving	%DV	Amount per serving	%DV	Amount per serving	%DV
Calories 90		**Cholesterol** 30mg	10%	**Total Carbohydrate** 2g	1%
Total Fat 0g	0%	**Sodium** 210mg	9%	Dietary Fiber 0g	0%
Saturated Fat 0g	0%	**Protein** 20g		Sugars 0g	
Polyunsaturated Fat 0g					
Monounsaturated Fat 0g		Vitamin A 0% Vitamin C 0%		Calcium 2% Iron 2%	

Cod, Atlantic, Canned, Solids and Liquid

3 oz / 85g

Amount per serving	%DV	Amount per serving	%DV	Amount per serving	%DV
Calories 89		**Cholesterol** 47mg	16%	**Total Carbohydrate** 0g	0%
Total Fat 1g	2%	**Sodium** 185mg	8%	Dietary Fiber 0g	0%
Saturated Fat 0g	0%	**Protein** 19.4g		Sugars 0g	
Polyunsaturated Fat 0g					
Monounsaturated Fat 0g		Vitamin A 1% Vitamin C 1%		Calcium 2% Iron 2%	

Cod, Atlantic, Cooked, Dry Heat

3 oz / 85g

Amount per serving	%DV	Amount per serving	%DV	Amount per serving	%DV
Calories 89		**Cholesterol** 47mg	16%	**Total Carbohydrate** 0g	0%
Total Fat 1g	2%	**Sodium** 66mg	3%	Dietary Fiber 0g	0%
Saturated Fat 0g	0%	**Protein** 19.4g		Sugars 0g	
Polyunsaturated Fat 0g					
Monounsaturated Fat 0g		Vitamin A 1% Vitamin C 1%		Calcium 1% Iron 2%	

Cod, Pacific, Cooked, Dry Heat

3 oz / 85g

Amount per serving	%DV	Amount per serving	%DV	Amount per serving	%DV
Calories 90		**Cholesterol** 40mg	13%	**Total Carbohydrate** 0g	0%
Total Fat 0g	0%	**Sodium** 77mg	3%	Dietary Fiber 0g	0%
Saturated Fat 0g	0%	**Protein** 19.5g		Sugars 0g	
Polyunsaturated Fat 0g					
Monounsaturated Fat 0g		Vitamin A 1% Vitamin C 5%		Calcium 1% Iron 2%	

Coral, Chunk Light Tuna in Water

2 oz drained / about 1/4 cup / 56g

Amount per serving	%DV	Amount per serving	%DV	Amount per serving	%DV
Calories 50		**Cholesterol** 30mg	10%	**Total Carbohydrate** 0g	0%
Total Fat 0g	0%	**Sodium** 180mg	8%	Dietary Fiber 0g	0%
Saturated Fat 0g	0%	**Protein** 11g		Sugars 0g	
Polyunsaturated Fat 0g					
Monounsaturated Fat 0g		Vitamin A 0% Vitamin C 0%		Calcium 0% Iron 2%	

Crab, Blue, Canned

1 oz / 28.35g

Amount per serving	%DV	Amount per serving	%DV	Amount per serving	%DV
Calories 84		**Cholesterol** 76mg	25%	**Total Carbohydrate** 0g	0%
Total Fat 1g	2%	**Sodium** 283mg	12%	Dietary Fiber 0g	0%
Saturated Fat 0g	0%	**Protein** 17.4g		Sugars 0g	
Polyunsaturated Fat 0g					
Monounsaturated Fat 0g		Vitamin A 0%	Vitamin C 4%	Calcium 9%	Iron 4%

Crab, Blue, Crab Cakes

1 cake / 60g

Amount per serving	%DV	Amount per serving	%DV	Amount per serving	%DV
Calories 93		**Cholesterol** 90mg	30%	**Total Carbohydrate** 0g	0%
Total Fat 5g	8%	**Sodium** 198mg	8%	Dietary Fiber 0g	0%
Saturated Fat 1g	5%	**Protein** 12g		Sugars 0g	
Polyunsaturated Fat 1g					
Monounsaturated Fat 1g		Vitamin A 3%	Vitamin C 3%	Calcium 6%	Iron 4%

Cusk, Cooked, Dry Heat

3 oz / 85g

Amount per serving	%DV	Amount per serving	%DV	Amount per serving	%DV
Calories 95		**Cholesterol** 45mg	15%	**Total Carbohydrate** 0g	0%
Total Fat 1g	2%	**Sodium** 34mg	1%	Dietary Fiber 0g	0%
Saturated Fat 0g	0%	**Protein** 21g		Sugars 0g	
Polyunsaturated Fat 0g					
Monounsaturated Fat 0g		Vitamin A 1%	Vitamin C 0%	Calcium 1%	Iron 5%

Dolphinfish, Cooked, Dry Heat

3 oz / 85g

Amount per serving	%DV	Amount per serving	%DV	Amount per serving	%DV
Calories 93		**Cholesterol** 80mg	27%	**Total Carbohydrate** 0g	0%
Total Fat 1g	2%	**Sodium** 96mg	4%	Dietary Fiber 0g	0%
Saturated Fat 0g	0%	**Protein** 20g		Sugars 0g	
Polyunsaturated Fat 0g					
Monounsaturated Fat 0g		Vitamin A 4%	Vitamin C 0%	Calcium 2%	Iron 7%

Dr. Praeger's Sensible Foods, Potato Crusted Fishies

4 fishies

Amount per serving	%DV	Amount per serving	%DV	Amount per serving	%DV
Calories 80		**Cholesterol** 25mg	8%	**Total Carbohydrate** 7g	2%
Total Fat 4g	6%	**Sodium** 220mg	9%	Dietary Fiber 1g	4%
Saturated Fat 0.5g	2%	**Protein** 4g		Sugars 0g	
Polyunsaturated Fat 0g					
Monounsaturated Fat 0g		Vitamin A 4%	Vitamin C 0%	Calcium 0%	Iron 6%

Drum, Fresh Water, Cooked, Dry Heat

3 oz / 85g

Amount per serving	%DV	Amount per serving	%DV	Amount per serving	%DV
Calories 130		**Cholesterol** 70mg	23%	**Total Carbohydrate** 0g	0%
Total Fat 5g	8%	**Sodium** 82mg	3%	Dietary Fiber 0g	0%
Saturated Fat 1g	5%	**Protein** 19g		Sugars 0g	
Polyunsaturated Fat 0g					
Monounsaturated Fat 0g		Vitamin A 3%	Vitamin C 1%	Calcium 7%	Iron 5%

Flatfish (Flounder and Sole Species), Cooked, Dry Heat

3 oz / 85g

Amount per serving	%DV	Amount per serving	%DV	Amount per serving	%DV
Calories 100		**Cholesterol** 58mg	19%	**Total Carbohydrate** 0g	0%
Total Fat 1g	2%	**Sodium** 89mg	4%	Dietary Fiber 0g	0%
Saturated Fat 0g	0%	**Protein** 20g		Sugars 0g	
Polyunsaturated Fat 0g					
Monounsaturated Fat 0g		Vitamin A 1%	Vitamin C 0%	Calcium 1%	Iron 1%

Gefilte Fish, Commercial, Sweet Recipe

1 piece / 42g

Amount per serving	%DV	Amount per serving	%DV	Amount per serving	%DV
Calories 35		**Cholesterol** 13mg	4%	**Total Carbohydrate** 3.1g	1%
Total Fat 0.7g	1%	**Sodium** 220mg	9%	Dietary Fiber 0g	0%
Saturated Fat 0.2g	1%	**Protein** 3.8g		Sugars 0g	
Polyunsaturated Fat 0.1g					
Monounsaturated Fat 0.3g		Vitamin A 1%	Vitamin C 1%	Calcium 1%	Iron 6%

Grouper, Mixed Species, Cooked, Dry Heat

3 oz / 85g

Amount per serving	%DV	Amount per serving	%DV	Amount per serving	%DV
Calories 100		**Cholesterol** 40mg	13%	**Total Carbohydrate** 0g	0%
Total Fat 1g	2%	**Sodium** 45mg	2%	Dietary Fiber 0g	0%
Saturated Fat 0g	0%	**Protein** 21g		Sugars 0g	
Polyunsaturated Fat 0g					
Monounsaturated Fat 0g		Vitamin A 3%	Vitamin C 0%	Calcium 2%	Iron 5%

Haddock, Cooked, Dry Heat

3 oz / 85g

Amount per serving	%DV	Amount per serving	%DV	Amount per serving	%DV
Calories 95		**Cholesterol** 63mg	21%	**Total Carbohydrate** 0g	0%
Total Fat 0g	0%	**Sodium** 74mg	3%	Dietary Fiber 0g	0%
Saturated Fat 0g	0%	**Protein** 20g		Sugars 0g	
Polyunsaturated Fat 0g					
Monounsaturated Fat 0g		Vitamin A 1%	Vitamin C 0%	Calcium 3%	Iron 6%

Halibut, Atlantic and Pacific, Cooked, Dry Heat

3 oz / 85g

Amount per serving	%DV	Amount per serving	%DV	Amount per serving	%DV
Calories 119		**Cholesterol** 35mg	12%	**Total Carbohydrate** 0g	0%
Total Fat 2g	3%	**Sodium** 59mg	2%	Dietary Fiber 0g	0%
Saturated Fat 0g	0%	**Protein** 22g		Sugars 0g	
Polyunsaturated Fat 0g					
Monounsaturated Fat 0g		Vitamin A 3%	Vitamin C 0%	Calcium 5%	Iron 5%

Herring, Atlantic, Kippered

1 small filet / 20g

Amount per serving	%DV	Amount per serving	%DV	Amount per serving	%DV
Calories 43		**Cholesterol** 16mg	5%	**Total Carbohydrate** 0g	0%
Total Fat 2g	3%	**Sodium** 184mg	8%	Dietary Fiber 0g	0%
Saturated Fat 1g	5%	**Protein** 5g		Sugars 0g	
Polyunsaturated Fat 0g					
Monounsaturated Fat 0g		Vitamin A 1%	Vitamin C 0%	Calcium 2%	Iron 2%

Ian's Natural Foods, Allergy Friendly Fish Sticks

6 sticks

Amount per serving	%DV	Amount per serving	%DV	Amount per serving	%DV
Calories 190		**Cholesterol** 35mg	12%	**Total Carbohydrate** 24g	8%
Total Fat 5g	8%	**Sodium** 170mg	7%	Dietary Fiber 1g	4%
Saturated Fat 0g	0%	**Protein** 11g		Sugars 0g	
Polyunsaturated Fat 0g					
Monounsaturated Fat 0g		Vitamin A 0%	Vitamin C 2%	Calcium 2%	Iron 2%

Lingcod, Cooked, Dry Heat

3 oz / 85g

Amount per serving	%DV	Amount per serving	%DV	Amount per serving	%DV
Calories 93		**Cholesterol** 57mg	19%	**Total Carbohydrate** 0g	0%
Total Fat 1g	2%	**Sodium** 65mg	3%	Dietary Fiber 0g	0%
Saturated Fat 0g	0%	**Protein** 19g		Sugars 0g	
Polyunsaturated Fat 0g					
Monounsaturated Fat 0g		Vitamin A 1%	Vitamin C 0%	Calcium 2%	Iron 2%

Mackerel, King, Cooked, Dry Heat

3 oz / 85g

Amount per serving	%DV	Amount per serving	%DV	Amount per serving	%DV
Calories 114		**Cholesterol** 58mg	19%	**Total Carbohydrate** 0g	0%
Total Fat 2.1g	3%	**Sodium** 173mg	7%	Dietary Fiber 0g	0%
Saturated Fat 0g	0%	**Protein** 22g		Sugars 0g	
Polyunsaturated Fat 0g					
Monounsaturated Fat 0g		Vitamin A 14%	Vitamin C 2%	Calcium 3%	Iron 11%

Mackerel, Spanish, Cooked, Dry Heat

3 oz / 85g

Amount per serving	%DV	Amount per serving	%DV	Amount per serving	%DV
Calories 134		**Cholesterol** 62mg	21%	**Total Carbohydrate** 0g	0%
Total Fat 5g	8%	**Sodium** 56mg	2%	Dietary Fiber 0g	0%
Saturated Fat 1.5g	8%	**Protein** 20g		Sugars 0g	
Polyunsaturated Fat 1g					
Monounsaturated Fat 1g		Vitamin A 2%	Vitamin C 2%	Calcium 1%	Iron 3%

Mollusks, Clam, Mixed Species, Canned, Liquid

3 oz / 85g

Amount per serving	%DV	Amount per serving	%DV	Amount per serving	%DV
Calories 1.5		**Cholesterol** 2.5mg	1%	**Total Carbohydrate** 0g	0%
Total Fat 0g	0%	**Sodium** 183mg	8%	Dietary Fiber 0g	0%
Saturated Fat 0g	0%	**Protein** 0.5g		Sugars 0g	
Polyunsaturated Fat 0g					
Monounsaturated Fat 0g		Vitamin A 25.5%	Vitamin C 1%	Calcium 11%	Iron 0.5%

Mollusks, Clam, Mixed Species, Raw

1 large / 20g

Amount per serving	%DV	Amount per serving	%DV	Amount per serving	%DV
Calories 17		**Cholesterol** 6mg	2%	**Total Carbohydrate** 0.5g	0%
Total Fat 0g	0%	**Sodium** 120mg	5%	Dietary Fiber 0g	0%
Saturated Fat 0g	0%	**Protein** 3g		Sugars 0g	
Polyunsaturated Fat 0g					
Monounsaturated Fat 0g		Vitamin A 60%	Vitamin C 0%	Calcium 8%	Iron 0.5%

Monkfish, Cooked, Dry Heat

3 oz / 85g

Amount per serving	%DV	Amount per serving	%DV	Amount per serving	%DV
Calories 82		**Cholesterol** 27mg	9%	**Total Carbohydrate** 0g	0%
Total Fat 2g	3%	**Sodium** 20mg	1%	Dietary Fiber 0g	0%
Saturated Fat 0g	0%	**Protein** 16g		Sugars 0g	
Polyunsaturated Fat 0g					
Monounsaturated Fat 0g		Vitamin A 1%	Vitamin C 1%	Calcium 1%	Iron 2%

Mullet, Striped, Cooked, Dry Heat

3 oz / 85g

Amount per serving	%DV	Amount per serving	%DV	Amount per serving	%DV
Calories 128		**Cholesterol** 54mg	18%	**Total Carbohydrate** 0g	0%
Total Fat 4g	6%	**Sodium** 60mg	2%	Dietary Fiber 0g	0%
Saturated Fat 1g	5%	**Protein** 21g		Sugars 0g	
Polyunsaturated Fat 0g					
Monounsaturated Fat 0g		Vitamin A 2%	Vitamin C 2%	Calcium 3%	Iron 7%

Mussels, Blue, Cooked, Moist Heat

3 oz / 85g

Amount per serving	%DV	Amount per serving	%DV	Amount per serving	%DV
Calories 146		**Cholesterol** 48mg	16%	**Total Carbohydrate** 6g	2%
Total Fat 3.8g	6%	**Sodium** 314mg	13%	Dietary Fiber 0g	0%
Saturated Fat 0g	0%	**Protein** 20g		Sugars 0g	
Polyunsaturated Fat 1g					
Monounsaturated Fat 0g		Vitamin A 5%	Vitamin C 19%	Calcium 3%	Iron 32%

Octopus, Common, Cooked, Moist Heat

3 oz / 85g

Amount per serving	%DV	Amount per serving	%DV	Amount per serving	%DV
Calories 139		**Cholesterol** 82mg	27%	**Total Carbohydrate** 4g	1%
Total Fat 2g	3%	**Sodium** 391mg	16%	Dietary Fiber 0g	0%
Saturated Fat 0g	0%	**Protein** 25g		Sugars 0g	
Polyunsaturated Fat 0g					
Monounsaturated Fat 0g		Vitamin A 5%	Vitamin C 11%	Calcium 9%	Iron 45%

Oysters, Eastern, Farmed, Cooked, Dry Heat

6 medium / 59g

Amount per serving	%DV	Amount per serving	%DV	Amount per serving	%DV
Calories 47		**Cholesterol** 22mg	7%	**Total Carbohydrate** 4g	1%
Total Fat 1g	2%	**Sodium** 96mg	4%	Dietary Fiber 0g	0%
Saturated Fat 0g	0%	**Protein** 4.1g		Sugars 0g	
Polyunsaturated Fat 0g					
Monounsaturated Fat 0g		Vitamin A 1%	Vitamin C 16%	Calcium 3%	Iron 25%

Oysters, Eastern, Farmed, Raw

6 medium / 84g

Amount per serving	%DV	Amount per serving	%DV	Amount per serving	%DV
Calories 47		**Cholesterol** 21mg	7%	**Total Carbohydrate** 5g	2%
Total Fat 1g	2%	**Sodium** 96mg	4%	Dietary Fiber 0g	0%
Saturated Fat 0g	0%	**Protein** 4.1g		Sugars 0g	
Polyunsaturated Fat 0g					
Monounsaturated Fat 0g		Vitamin A 1%	Vitamin C 6%	Calcium 3%	Iron 25%

Oysters, Eastern, Wild, Cooked, Dry Heat

6 medium / 59g

Amount per serving	%DV	Amount per serving	%DV	Amount per serving	%DV
Calories 42		**Cholesterol** 29mg	10%	**Total Carbohydrate** 3g	1%
Total Fat 1g	2%	**Sodium** 144mg	6%	Dietary Fiber 0g	0%
Saturated Fat 0g	0%	**Protein** 5g		Sugars 0g	
Polyunsaturated Fat 0g					
Monounsaturated Fat 0g		Vitamin A 0%	Vitamin C 4%	Calcium 3%	Iron 14%

Oysters, Eastern, Wild, Cooked, Moist Heat

6 medium / 42g

Amount per serving	%DV	Amount per serving	%DV	Amount per serving	%DV
Calories 57		**Cholesterol** 44mg	15%	**Total Carbohydrate** 3.2g	1%
Total Fat 2g	3%	**Sodium** 177mg	7%	Dietary Fiber 0g	0%
Saturated Fat 0g	0%	**Protein** 5.9g		Sugars 0g	
Polyunsaturated Fat 0g					
Monounsaturated Fat 0g		Vitamin A 1% Vitamin C 4%		Calcium 4% Iron 28%	

Oysters, Pacific, Cooked, Moist Heat

3 oz / 85g

Amount per serving	%DV	Amount per serving	%DV	Amount per serving	%DV
Calories 139		**Cholesterol** 85mg	28%	**Total Carbohydrate** 8g	3%
Total Fat 4g	6%	**Sodium** 180mg	8%	Dietary Fiber 0g	0%
Saturated Fat 1g	5%	**Protein** 16g		Sugars 0g	
Polyunsaturated Fat 0g					
Monounsaturated Fat 0g		Vitamin A 8% Vitamin C 18%		Calcium 1% Iron 43%	

Oysters, Pacific, Raw

3 oz / 85g

Amount per serving	%DV	Amount per serving	%DV	Amount per serving	%DV
Calories 69		**Cholesterol** 42mg	14%	**Total Carbohydrate** 4g	1%
Total Fat 2g	3%	**Sodium** 90mg	4%	Dietary Fiber 0g	0%
Saturated Fat 0g	0%	**Protein** 8g		Sugars 0g	
Polyunsaturated Fat 0g					
Monounsaturated Fat 0g		Vitamin A 5% Vitamin C 11%		Calcium 1% Iron 24%	

Pike, Northern, Cooked, Dry Heat

3 oz / 85g

Amount per serving	%DV	Amount per serving	%DV	Amount per serving	%DV
Calories 96		**Cholesterol** 42mg	14%	**Total Carbohydrate** 0g	0%
Total Fat 1g	2%	**Sodium** 42mg	2%	Dietary Fiber 0g	0%
Saturated Fat 0g	0%	**Protein** 21g		Sugars 0g	
Polyunsaturated Fat 0g					
Monounsaturated Fat 0g		Vitamin A 1% Vitamin C 5%		Calcium 6% Iron 3%	

Pike, Walleye, Cooked, Dry Heat

3 oz / 85g

Amount per serving	%DV	Amount per serving	%DV	Amount per serving	%DV
Calories 101		**Cholesterol** 93mg	31%	**Total Carbohydrate** 0g	0%
Total Fat 1g	2%	**Sodium** 55mg	2%	Dietary Fiber 0g	0%
Saturated Fat 0g	0%	**Protein** 21g		Sugars 0g	
Polyunsaturated Fat 0g					
Monounsaturated Fat 0g		Vitamin A 1% Vitamin C 0%		Calcium 12% Iron 8%	

Pollock, Atlantic, Cooked, Dry Heat

3 oz / 85g

Amount per serving	%DV	Amount per serving	%DV	Amount per serving	%DV
Calories 100		**Cholesterol** 77mg	26%	**Total Carbohydrate** 0g	0%
Total Fat 1g	2%	**Sodium** 94mg	4%	Dietary Fiber 0g	0%
Saturated Fat 0g	0%	**Protein** 21g		Sugars 0g	
Polyunsaturated Fat 0g					
Monounsaturated Fat 0g		Vitamin A 1%	Vitamin C 0%	Calcium 7%	Iron 3%

Pollock, Walleye, Cooked, Dry Heat

3 oz / 85g

Amount per serving	%DV	Amount per serving	%DV	Amount per serving	%DV
Calories 96		**Cholesterol** 82mg	27%	**Total Carbohydrate** 0g	0%
Total Fat 1g	2%	**Sodium** 88mg	4%	Dietary Fiber 0g	0%
Saturated Fat 0g	0%	**Protein** 20g		Sugars 0g	
Polyunsaturated Fat 0g					
Monounsaturated Fat 0g		Vitamin A 1%	Vitamin C 0%	Calcium 1%	Iron 1%

Pout, Ocean, Cooked, Dry Heat

3 oz / 85g

Amount per serving	%DV	Amount per serving	%DV	Amount per serving	%DV
Calories 87		**Cholesterol** 57mg	19%	**Total Carbohydrate** 0g	0%
Total Fat 1g	2%	**Sodium** 66mg	3%	Dietary Fiber 0g	0%
Saturated Fat 0g	0%	**Protein** 18g		Sugars 0g	
Polyunsaturated Fat 0g					
Monounsaturated Fat 0g		Vitamin A 1%	Vitamin C 0%	Calcium 1%	Iron 2%

Rockfish, Pacific, Mixed Species, Cooked, Dry Heat

3 oz / 85g

Amount per serving	%DV	Amount per serving	%DV	Amount per serving	%DV
Calories 103		**Cholesterol** 38mg	13%	**Total Carbohydrate** 0g	0%
Total Fat 1.7g	3%	**Sodium** 66mg	3%	Dietary Fiber 0g	0%
Saturated Fat 0g	0%	**Protein** 20g		Sugars 0g	
Polyunsaturated Fat 0g					
Monounsaturated Fat 0g		Vitamin A 4%	Vitamin C 0%	Calcium 1%	Iron 2%

Roughy, Orange, Cooked, Dry Heat

3 oz / 85g

Amount per serving	%DV	Amount per serving	%DV	Amount per serving	%DV
Calories 89		**Cholesterol** 68mg	23%	**Total Carbohydrate** 0g	0%
Total Fat 0g	0%	**Sodium** 59mg	2%	Dietary Fiber 0g	0%
Saturated Fat 0g	0%	**Protein** 19g		Sugars 0g	
Polyunsaturated Fat 0g					
Monounsaturated Fat 0g		Vitamin A 1%	Vitamin C 0%	Calcium 1%	Iron 5%

Salmon, Chum, Canned, without Salt, Drained Solid with Bone

3 oz / 85g

Amount per serving	%DV	Amount per serving	%DV	Amount per serving	%DV
Calories 89		**Cholesterol** 68mg	23%	**Total Carbohydrate** 0g	0%
Total Fat 0g	0%	**Sodium** 59mg	2%	Dietary Fiber 0g	0%
Saturated Fat 0g	0%	**Protein** 19.2g		Sugars 0g	
Polyunsaturated Fat 0g					
Monounsaturated Fat 0g		Vitamin A 1% Vitamin C 0%		Calcium 1% Iron 5%	

Salmon, Chum, Cooked, Dry Heat

3 oz / 85g

Amount per serving	%DV	Amount per serving	%DV	Amount per serving	%DV
Calories 131		**Cholesterol** 81mg	27%	**Total Carbohydrate** 0g	0%
Total Fat 4g	6%	**Sodium** 55mg	2%	Dietary Fiber 0g	0%
Saturated Fat 0g	0%	**Protein** 21.9g		Sugars 0g	
Polyunsaturated Fat 0g					
Monounsaturated Fat 1g		Vitamin A 2% Vitamin C 0%		Calcium 1% Iron 3%	

Salmon, Chum, Drained Solid with Bone

3 oz / 85g

Amount per serving	%DV	Amount per serving	%DV	Amount per serving	%DV
Calories 120		**Cholesterol** 33mg	11%	**Total Carbohydrate** 0g	0%
Total Fat 5g	8%	**Sodium** 414mg	17%	Dietary Fiber 0g	0%
Saturated Fat 1g	5%	**Protein** 18g		Sugars 0g	
Polyunsaturated Fat 0g					
Monounsaturated Fat 0g		Vitamin A 1% Vitamin C 0%		Calcium 21% Iron 3%	

Salmon, Coho, Wild, Cooked, Dry Heat

3 oz / 85g

Amount per serving	%DV	Amount per serving	%DV	Amount per serving	%DV
Calories 118		**Cholesterol** 47mg	16%	**Total Carbohydrate** 0g	0%
Total Fat 4g	6%	**Sodium** 49mg	2%	Dietary Fiber 0g	0%
Saturated Fat 1g	5%	**Protein** 20g		Sugars 0g	
Polyunsaturated Fat 0g					
Monounsaturated Fat 0g		Vitamin A 2% Vitamin C 2%		Calcium 4% Iron 3%	

Salmon, Pink, Canned, Solids with Bone and Liquid

3 oz / 85g

Amount per serving	%DV	Amount per serving	%DV	Amount per serving	%DV
Calories 118		**Cholesterol** 47mg	16%	**Total Carbohydrate** 0g	0%
Total Fat 5g	8%	**Sodium** 471mg	20%	Dietary Fiber 0g	0%
Saturated Fat 1g	5%	**Protein** 16.8g		Sugars 0g	
Polyunsaturated Fat 1g					
Monounsaturated Fat 1g		Vitamin A 1% Vitamin C 0%		Calcium 18% Iron 4%	

Salmon, Pink, Canned, without Salt, Solids with Bone and Liquid

3 oz / 85g

Amount per serving	%DV	Amount per serving	%DV	Amount per serving	%DV
Calories 118		**Cholesterol** 47mg	16%	**Total Carbohydrate** 0g	0%
Total Fat 5g	8%	**Sodium** 64mg	3%	Dietary Fiber 0g	0%
Saturated Fat 1g	5%	**Protein** 17g		Sugars 0g	
Polyunsaturated Fat 0g					
Monounsaturated Fat 0g		Vitamin A 1%	Vitamin C 0%	Calcium 18%	Iron 4%

Sea Bass, Mixed Species, Cooked, Dry Heat

3 oz / 85g

Amount per serving	%DV	Amount per serving	%DV	Amount per serving	%DV
Calories 105		**Cholesterol** 45mg	15%	**Total Carbohydrate** 0g	0%
Total Fat 2g	3%	**Sodium** 74mg	3%	Dietary Fiber 0g	0%
Saturated Fat 1g	5%	**Protein** 20g		Sugars 0g	
Polyunsaturated Fat 0g					
Monounsaturated Fat 0g		Vitamin A 4%	Vitamin C 0%	Calcium 1%	Iron 2%

Sea Trout, Mixed Species, Cooked, Dry Heat

3 oz / 85g

Amount per serving	%DV	Amount per serving	%DV	Amount per serving	%DV
Calories 113		**Cholesterol** 90mg	30%	**Total Carbohydrate** 0g	0%
Total Fat 4g	6%	**Sodium** 63mg	3%	Dietary Fiber 0g	0%
Saturated Fat 1g	5%	**Protein** 18g		Sugars 0g	
Polyunsaturated Fat 0g					
Monounsaturated Fat 0g		Vitamin A 2%	Vitamin C 0%	Calcium 2%	Iron 2%

Smelt, Rainbow, Cooked, Dry Heat

3 oz / 85g

Amount per serving	%DV	Amount per serving	%DV	Amount per serving	%DV
Calories 105		**Cholesterol** 77mg	26%	**Total Carbohydrate** 0g	0%
Total Fat 2.6g	4%	**Sodium** 65mg	3%	Dietary Fiber 0g	0%
Saturated Fat 0g	0%	**Protein** 19g		Sugars 0g	
Polyunsaturated Fat 1g					
Monounsaturated Fat 0g		Vitamin A 1%	Vitamin C 0%	Calcium 7%	Iron 5%

Snapper, Mixed Species, Cooked, Dry Heat

3 oz / 85g

Amount per serving	%DV	Amount per serving	%DV	Amount per serving	%DV
Calories 109		**Cholesterol** 40mg	13%	**Total Carbohydrate** 0g	0%
Total Fat 1.4g	2%	**Sodium** 49mg	2%	Dietary Fiber 0g	0%
Saturated Fat 0g	0%	**Protein** 22.3g		Sugars 0g	
Polyunsaturated Fat 0g					
Monounsaturated Fat 0g		Vitamin A 2% Vitamin C 3%		Calcium 4% Iron 1%	

Spiny Lobster, Mixed Species, Cooked, Moist Heat

3 oz / 85g

Amount per serving	%DV	Amount per serving	%DV	Amount per serving	%DV
Calories 122		**Cholesterol** 77mg	26%	**Total Carbohydrate** 3g	1%
Total Fat 2g	3%	**Sodium** 193mg	8%	Dietary Fiber 0g	0%
Saturated Fat 0g	0%	**Protein** 22g		Sugars 0g	
Polyunsaturated Fat 0g					
Monounsaturated Fat 0g		Vitamin A 0% Vitamin C 3%		Calcium 5% Iron 7%	

Spot, Cooked, Dry Heat

3 oz / 85g

Amount per serving	%DV	Amount per serving	%DV	Amount per serving	%DV
Calories 134		**Cholesterol** 66mg	22%	**Total Carbohydrate** 0g	0%
Total Fat 5g	8%	**Sodium** 32mg	1%	Dietary Fiber 0g	0%
Saturated Fat 1.5g	8%	**Protein** 20g		Sugars 0g	
Polyunsaturated Fat 1g					
Monounsaturated Fat 1g		Vitamin A 2% Vitamin C 0%		Calcium 2% Iron 2%	

StarKist Albacore White Tuna in Water

1 can / 85g / 3 oz

Amount per serving	%DV	Amount per serving	%DV	Amount per serving	%DV
Calories 90		**Cholesterol** 35mg	12%	**Total Carbohydrate** 0g	0%
Total Fat 1g	2%	**Sodium** 250mg	10%	Dietary Fiber 0g	0%
Saturated Fat 0.5g	2%	**Protein** 20g		Sugars 0g	
Polyunsaturated Fat 0.5g					
Monounsaturated Fat 0g		Vitamin A 0% Vitamin C 0%		Calcium 0% Iron 4%	

StarKist Chunk Light Tuna in Water

1 can / 85g / 3 oz

Amount per serving	%DV	Amount per serving	%DV	Amount per serving	%DV
Calories 70		**Cholesterol** 30mg	10%	**Total Carbohydrate** 0g	0%
Total Fat 0.5g	1%	**Sodium** 320mg	13%	Dietary Fiber 0g	0%
Saturated Fat 0g	0%	**Protein** 16g		Sugars 0g	
Polyunsaturated Fat 0g					
Monounsaturated Fat 0g		Vitamin A 0% Vitamin C 0%		Calcium 0% Iron 6%	

StarKist Chunk White Albacore Tuna in Water

1 can drained / 2.8 oz / 79g

Amount per serving	%DV	Amount per serving	%DV	Amount per serving	%DV
Calories 80		**Cholesterol** 25mg	8%	**Total Carbohydrate** 0g	0%
Total Fat 0.5g	1%	**Sodium** 200mg	8%	Dietary Fiber 0g	0%
Saturated Fat 0g	0%	**Protein** 16g		Sugars 0g	
Polyunsaturated Fat 0g					
Monounsaturated Fat 0g		Vitamin A 0% Vitamin C 0%		Calcium 0% Iron 4%	

StarKist Low Sodium Chunk Light Tuna in Water

2 oz drained / about 1/4 cup / 56g

Amount per serving	%DV	Amount per serving	%DV	Amount per serving	%DV
Calories 60		**Cholesterol** 25mg	8%	**Total Carbohydrate** 0g	0%
Total Fat 0.5g	1%	**Sodium** 100mg	4%	Dietary Fiber 0g	0%
Saturated Fat 0g	0%	**Protein** 15g		Sugars 0g	
Polyunsaturated Fat 0g					
Monounsaturated Fat 0g		Vitamin A 0% Vitamin C 0%		Calcium 0% Iron 2%	

StarKist Selects Chunk Light Tuna in Water

2 oz drained / about 1/4 cup / 56g

Amount per serving	%DV	Amount per serving	%DV	Amount per serving	%DV
Calories 50		**Cholesterol** 25mg	8%	**Total Carbohydrate** 0g	0%
Total Fat 0.5g	1%	**Sodium** 170mg	7%	Dietary Fiber 0g	0%
Saturated Fat 0g	0%	**Protein** 12g		Sugars 0g	
Polyunsaturated Fat 0g					
Monounsaturated Fat 0g		Vitamin A 0% Vitamin C 0%		Calcium 0% Iron 4%	

StarKist Selects Low Sodium Chunk Light Tuna in Water

2 oz drained / about 1/4 cup / 56g

Amount per serving	%DV	Amount per serving	%DV	Amount per serving	%DV
Calories 60		**Cholesterol** 25mg	8%	**Total Carbohydrate** 0g	0%
Total Fat 0.5g	1%	**Sodium** 100mg	4%	Dietary Fiber 0g	0%
Saturated Fat 0g	0%	**Protein** 15g		Sugars 0g	
Polyunsaturated Fat 0g					
Monounsaturated Fat 0g		Vitamin A 0% Vitamin C 0%		Calcium 0% Iron 2%	

StarKist Selects Solid Light Tuna in Water

2 oz drained / about 1/4 cup / 56g

Amount per serving	%DV	Amount per serving	%DV	Amount per serving	%DV
Calories 60		**Cholesterol** 30mg	10%	**Total Carbohydrate** 0g	0%
Total Fat 0.5g	1%	**Sodium** 150mg	6%	Dietary Fiber 0g	0%
Saturated Fat 0g	0%	**Protein** 15g		Sugars 0g	
Polyunsaturated Fat 0g					
Monounsaturated Fat 0g		Vitamin A 0% Vitamin C 0%		Calcium 0% Iron 4%	

StarKist Selects Solid White Albacore Tuna in Water

2 oz drained / about 1/4 cup / 56g

Amount per serving	%DV	Amount per serving	%DV	Amount per serving	%DV
Calories 60		**Cholesterol** 25mg	8%	**Total Carbohydrate** 0g	0%
Total Fat 0.5g	1%	**Sodium** 170mg	7%	Dietary Fiber 0g	0%
Saturated Fat 0g	0%	**Protein** 15g		Sugars 0g	
Polyunsaturated Fat 0g					
Monounsaturated Fat 0g		Vitamin A 0% Vitamin C 0%		Calcium 0% Iron 0%	

StarKist Selects Very Low Sodium Chunk White Albacore Tuna in Water

2 oz drained / about 1/4 cup / 56g

Amount per serving	%DV	Amount per serving	%DV	Amount per serving	%DV
Calories 70		**Cholesterol** 25mg	8%	**Total Carbohydrate** 0g	0%
Total Fat 1g	2%	**Sodium** 35mg	1%	Dietary Fiber 0g	0%
Saturated Fat 0g	0%	**Protein** 16g		Sugars 0g	
Polyunsaturated Fat 0g					
Monounsaturated Fat 0g		Vitamin A 0% Vitamin C 0%		Calcium 0% Iron 2%	

StarKist Solid White Albacore Tuna in Water

1 can / 85g / 3 oz

Amount per serving	%DV	Amount per serving	%DV	Amount per serving	%DV
Calories 90		**Cholesterol** 35mg	12%	**Total Carbohydrate** 0g	0%
Total Fat 1g	2%	**Sodium** 250mg	10%	Dietary Fiber 0g	0%
Saturated Fat 0.5g	3%	**Protein** 20g		Sugars 0g	
Polyunsaturated Fat 0.5g					
Monounsaturated Fat 0g		Vitamin A 0% Vitamin C 0%		Calcium 0% Iron 4%	

StarKist Tuna Creations Premium Chunk Light Tuna in Hickory Smoke Flavors

2.6 oz / 74g

Amount per serving	%DV	Amount per serving	%DV	Amount per serving	%DV
Calories 110		**Cholesterol** 35mg	12%	**Total Carbohydrate** 0g	0%
Total Fat 3.5g	5%	**Sodium** 340mg	14%	Dietary Fiber 0g	0%
Saturated Fat 0.5g	2%	**Protein** 19g		Sugars 0g	
Polyunsaturated Fat 2g					
Monounsaturated Fat 1g		Vitamin A 0% Vitamin C 0%		Calcium 0% Iron 4%	

StarKist Tuna Creations Premium Chunk Light Tuna with Sweet & Spicy Flavors

1 pouch

Amount per serving	%DV	Amount per serving	%DV	Amount per serving	%DV
Calories 90		**Cholesterol** 35mg	12%	**Total Carbohydrate** 4g	1%
Total Fat 0.5g	1%	**Sodium** 380mg	16%	Dietary Fiber 0g	0%
Saturated Fat 0g	0%	**Protein** 16g		Sugars 3.5g	
Polyunsaturated Fat 0.5g					
Monounsaturated Fat 0g		Vitamin A 2% Vitamin C 0%		Calcium 30% Iron 2%	

StarKist Tuna Creations Premium Chunk Light Tuna with Zesty Lemon Pepper Flavors

1 pouch / 74g

Amount per serving	%DV	Amount per serving	%DV	Amount per serving	%DV
Calories 80		**Cholesterol** 35mg	12%	**Total Carbohydrate** 1g	0%
Total Fat 0.5g	1%	**Sodium** 340mg	14%	Dietary Fiber 0g	0%
Saturated Fat 0g	0%	**Protein** 18g		Sugars 0g	
Polyunsaturated Fat 0g					
Monounsaturated Fat 0g		Vitamin A 0% Vitamin C 0%		Calcium 30% Iron 4%	

StarKist, Chunk Light Tuna in Vegetable Oil

2 oz drained / 56g / about 1/4 cup

Amount per serving	%DV	Amount per serving	%DV	Amount per serving	%DV
Calories 80		**Cholesterol** 20mg	7%	**Total Carbohydrate** 0.5g	0%
Total Fat 4.5g	7%	**Sodium** 170mg	7%	Dietary Fiber 0g	0%
Saturated Fat 1g	5%	**Protein** 10g		Sugars 0g	
Polyunsaturated Fat 2.5g					
Monounsaturated Fat 1g		Vitamin A 0% Vitamin C 0%		Calcium 0% Iron 2%	

Sucker, White, Cooked, Dry Heat

3 oz / 85g

Amount per serving	%DV	Amount per serving	%DV	Amount per serving	%DV
Calories 101		**Cholesterol** 45mg	15%	**Total Carbohydrate** 0g	0%
Total Fat 2.5g	4%	**Sodium** 43mg	2%	Dietary Fiber 0g	0%
Saturated Fat 0g	0%	**Protein** 18g		Sugars 0g	
Polyunsaturated Fat 0g					
Monounsaturated Fat 0g		Vitamin A 3% Vitamin C 0%		Calcium 8% Iron 8%	

Sunfish, Pumpkin Seed, Cooked, Dry Heat

3 oz / 85g

Amount per serving	%DV	Amount per serving	%DV	Amount per serving	%DV
Calories 97		**Cholesterol** 73mg	24%	**Total Carbohydrate** 0g	0%
Total Fat 1g	2%	**Sodium** 88mg	4%	Dietary Fiber 0g	0%
Saturated Fat 0g	0%	**Protein** 21g		Sugars 0g	
Polyunsaturated Fat 0g					
Monounsaturated Fat 0g		Vitamin A 1% Vitamin C 1%		Calcium 9% Iron 7%	

Surimi

3 oz / 85g

Amount per serving	%DV	Amount per serving	%DV	Amount per serving	%DV
Calories 84		**Cholesterol** 26mg	9%	**Total Carbohydrate** 5.8g	2%
Total Fat 1g	2%	**Sodium** 122mg	5%	Dietary Fiber 0g	0%
Saturated Fat 0g	0%	**Protein** 12.9g		Sugars 0g	
Polyunsaturated Fat 0g					
Monounsaturated Fat 0g		Vitamin A 1% Vitamin C 0%		Calcium 1% Iron 1%	

Tilefish, Cooked, Dry Heat

3 oz / 85g

Amount per serving	%DV	Amount per serving	%DV	Amount per serving	%DV
Calories 125		**Cholesterol** 54mg	18%	**Total Carbohydrate** 0g	0%
Total Fat 4g	6%	**Sodium** 50mg	2%	Dietary Fiber 0g	0%
Saturated Fat 1g	5%	**Protein** 21g		Sugars 0g	
Polyunsaturated Fat 1g					
Monounsaturated Fat 1g		Vitamin A 1%	Vitamin C 0%	Calcium 2%	Iron 1%

TransOcean, Crab Classic Chunk Style

1/2 cup / 85g

Amount per serving	%DV	Amount per serving	%DV	Amount per serving	%DV
Calories 80		**Cholesterol** 15mg	5%	**Total Carbohydrate** 11g	4%
Total Fat 0g	0%	**Sodium** 450mg	19%	Dietary Fiber 0g	0%
Saturated Fat 0g	0%	**Protein** 8g		Sugars 3g	
Polyunsaturated Fat 0g					
Monounsaturated Fat 0g		Vitamin A 0%	Vitamin C 0%	Calcium 0%	Iron 0%

TransOcean, Crab Classic Flake Style

1/2 cup / 85g

Amount per serving	%DV	Amount per serving	%DV	Amount per serving	%DV
Calories 80		**Cholesterol** 5mg	2%	**Total Carbohydrate** 14g	5%
Total Fat 0g	0%	**Sodium** 450mg	19%	Dietary Fiber 0g	0%
Saturated Fat 0g	0%	**Protein** 6g		Sugars 3g	
Polyunsaturated Fat 0g					
Monounsaturated Fat 0g		Vitamin A 4%	Vitamin C 15%	Calcium 2%	Iron 2%

TransOcean, Crab Classic Leg Style

1/2 cup / 85g

Amount per serving	%DV	Amount per serving	%DV	Amount per serving	%DV
Calories 90		**Cholesterol** 10mg	3%	**Total Carbohydrate** 15g	5%
Total Fat 0g	0%	**Sodium** 450mg	19%	Dietary Fiber 0g	0%
Saturated Fat 0g	0%	**Protein** 6g		Sugars 3g	
Polyunsaturated Fat 0g					
Monounsaturated Fat 0g		Vitamin A 0%	Vitamin C 0%	Calcium 2%	Iron 0%

TransOcean, Crab Classic Single Serving

1 package / 64g

Amount per serving	%DV	Amount per serving	%DV	Amount per serving	%DV
Calories 60		**Cholesterol** 5mg	2%	**Total Carbohydrate** 11g	4%
Total Fat 0g	0%	**Sodium** 340mg	14%	Dietary Fiber 0g	0%
Saturated Fat 0g	0%	**Protein** 5g		Sugars 3g	
Polyunsaturated Fat 0g					
Monounsaturated Fat 0g		Vitamin A 0%	Vitamin C 0%	Calcium 0%	Iron 0%

TransOcean, Crab Supreme / Jaiba Supremo Flake Style

1/2 cup / 85g

Amount per serving	%DV	Amount per serving	%DV	Amount per serving	%DV
Calories 70		**Cholesterol** 10mg	3%	**Total Carbohydrate** 12g	4%
Total Fat 0g	0%	**Sodium** 450mg	19%	Dietary Fiber 0g	0%
Saturated Fat 0g	0%	**Protein** 6g		Sugars 4g	
Polyunsaturated Fat 0g					
Monounsaturated Fat 0g		Vitamin A 0% Vitamin C 0%		Calcium 0% Iron 0%	

TransOcean, Crab Supreme / Jaiba Supremo Leg Style

2 pieces / 72g

Amount per serving	%DV	Amount per serving	%DV	Amount per serving	%DV
Calories 60		**Cholesterol** 10mg	3%	**Total Carbohydrate** 10g	3%
Total Fat 0g	0%	**Sodium** 380mg	16%	Dietary Fiber 0g	0%
Saturated Fat 0g	0%	**Protein** 5g		Sugars 3g	
Polyunsaturated Fat 0g					
Monounsaturated Fat 0g		Vitamin A 0% Vitamin C 0%		Calcium 0% Iron 0%	

TransOcean, Lobster Classic Chunk Style

1/2 cup / 85g

Amount per serving	%DV	Amount per serving	%DV	Amount per serving	%DV
Calories 80		**Cholesterol** 15mg	5%	**Total Carbohydrate** 11g	4%
Total Fat 0g	0%	**Sodium** 450mg	19%	Dietary Fiber 0g	0%
Saturated Fat 0g	0%	**Protein** 8g		Sugars 3g	
Polyunsaturated Fat 0g					
Monounsaturated Fat 0g		Vitamin A 0% Vitamin C 0%		Calcium 0% Iron 0%	

TransOcean, Seafood Snackers

1 package / 85g

Amount per serving	%DV	Amount per serving	%DV	Amount per serving	%DV
Calories 80		**Cholesterol** 5mg	2%	**Total Carbohydrate** 14g	5%
Total Fat 0g	0%	**Sodium** 450mg	19%	Dietary Fiber 0g	0%
Saturated Fat 0g	0%	**Protein** 6g		Sugars 3g	
Polyunsaturated Fat 0g					
Monounsaturated Fat 0g		Vitamin A 0% Vitamin C 0%		Calcium 2% Iron 0%	

Trout, Rainbow, Wild, Cooked, Dry Heat

3 oz / 85g

Amount per serving	%DV	Amount per serving	%DV	Amount per serving	%DV
Calories 128		**Cholesterol** 59mg	20%	**Total Carbohydrate** 0g	0%
Total Fat 4.9g	8%	**Sodium** 48mg	2%	Dietary Fiber 0g	0%
Saturated Fat 1g	5%	**Protein** 19.4g		Sugars 0g	
Polyunsaturated Fat 1g					
Monounsaturated Fat 1g		Vitamin A 1% Vitamin C 3%		Calcium 7% Iron 2%	

Tuna, Skipjack, Fresh, Cooked, Dry Heat

3 oz / 85g

Amount per serving	%DV	Amount per serving	%DV	Amount per serving	%DV
Calories 112		**Cholesterol** 51mg	17%	**Total Carbohydrate** 0g	0%
Total Fat 1g	2%	**Sodium** 40mg	2%	Dietary Fiber 0g	0%
Saturated Fat 0g	0%	**Protein** 24g		Sugars 0g	
Polyunsaturated Fat 0g					
Monounsaturated Fat 0g		Vitamin A 1%	Vitamin C 1%	Calcium 3%	Iron 8%

Tuna, White, Canned in Water, Drained Solid

3 oz / 85g

Amount per serving	%DV	Amount per serving	%DV	Amount per serving	%DV
Calories 109		**Cholesterol** 36mg	12%	**Total Carbohydrate** 0g	0%
Total Fat 3g	5%	**Sodium** 320mg	13%	Dietary Fiber 0g	0%
Saturated Fat 1g	5%	**Protein** 20g		Sugars 0g	
Polyunsaturated Fat 0g					
Monounsaturated Fat 0g		Vitamin A 0%	Vitamin C 0%	Calcium 1%	Iron 5%

Tuna, White, Canned in Water, without Salt, Drained Solid

3 oz / 85g

Amount per serving	%DV	Amount per serving	%DV	Amount per serving	%DV
Calories 109		**Cholesterol** 36mg	12%	**Total Carbohydrate** 0g	0%
Total Fat 3g	5%	**Sodium** 43mg	2%	Dietary Fiber 0g	0%
Saturated Fat 1g	5%	**Protein** 20g		Sugars 0g	
Polyunsaturated Fat 0g					
Monounsaturated Fat 0g		Vitamin A 0%	Vitamin C 0%	Calcium 1%	Iron 5%

Tuna, Yellowfin, Fresh, Cooked, Dry Heat

3 oz / 85g

Amount per serving	%DV	Amount per serving	%DV	Amount per serving	%DV
Calories 118		**Cholesterol** 49mg	16%	**Total Carbohydrate** 0g	0%
Total Fat 1g	2%	**Sodium** 40mg	2%	Dietary Fiber 0g	0%
Saturated Fat 0g	0%	**Protein** 25g		Sugars 0g	
Polyunsaturated Fat 0g					
Monounsaturated Fat 0g		Vitamin A 1%	Vitamin C 1%	Calcium 2%	Iron 4%

Whiting, Mixed Species, Cooked, Dry Heat

3 oz / 85g

Amount per serving	%DV	Amount per serving	%DV	Amount per serving	%DV
Calories 99		**Cholesterol** 71mg	24%	**Total Carbohydrate** 0g	0%
Total Fat 1g	2%	**Sodium** 112mg	5%	Dietary Fiber 0g	0%
Saturated Fat 0g	0%	**Protein** 20g		Sugars 0g	
Polyunsaturated Fat 0g					
Monounsaturated Fat 0g		Vitamin A 2%	Vitamin C 0%	Calcium 5%	Iron 2%

Wolffish, Atlantic, Cooked, Dry Heat

3 oz / 85g

Amount per serving	%DV	Amount per serving	%DV	Amount per serving	%DV
Calories 105		**Cholesterol** 50mg	17%	**Total Carbohydrate** 0g	0%
Total Fat 3g	5%	**Sodium** 93mg	4%	Dietary Fiber 0g	0%
Saturated Fat 0g	0%	**Protein** 19g		Sugars g	
Polyunsaturated Fat 0g					
Monounsaturated Fat 0g		Vitamin A 7%	Vitamin C 0%	Calcium 1%	Iron 1%

Soy Products

Mori-nu, Tofu, Silken, Firm

1 slice / 84g

Amount per serving	%DV	Amount per serving	%DV	Amount per serving	%DV
Calories 50		**Cholesterol** 0mg	0%	**Total Carbohydrate** 2g	1%
Total Fat 2.5g	4%	**Sodium** 30mg	1%	Dietary Fiber 0g	0%
Saturated Fat 0g	0%	**Protein** 6g		Sugars 0g	
Polyunsaturated Fat 0g					
Monounsaturated Fat 0g		Vitamin A 0%	Vitamin C 0%	Calcium 2%	Iron 4%

Mori-nu, Tofu, Silken, Lite Firm

1 slice / 84g

Amount per serving	%DV	Amount per serving	%DV	Amount per serving	%DV
Calories 30		**Cholesterol** 0mg	0%	**Total Carbohydrate** 1g	0%
Total Fat 1g	2%	**Sodium** 70mg	3%	Dietary Fiber 0g	0%
Saturated Fat 0g	0%	**Protein** 5g		Sugars 0g	
Polyunsaturated Fat 0g					
Monounsaturated Fat 0g		Vitamin A 0%	Vitamin C 0%	Calcium 2%	Iron 4%

Mori-nu, Tofu, Silken, Soft

1 slice / 84g

Amount per serving	%DV	Amount per serving	%DV	Amount per serving	%DV
Calories 45		**Cholesterol** 0mg	0%	**Total Carbohydrate** 2g	1%
Total Fat 2.5g	4%	**Sodium** 0mg	0%	Dietary Fiber 0g	0%
Saturated Fat 0g	0%	**Protein** 4g		Sugars 0g	
Polyunsaturated Fat 0g					
Monounsaturated Fat 0g		Vitamin A 0%	Vitamin C 0%	Calcium 2%	Iron 4%

Mori-nu, Tofu, Silken, Extra Firm

1 slice / 84g

Amount per serving	%DV	Amount per serving	%DV	Amount per serving	%DV
Calories 45		**Cholesterol** 0mg	0%	**Total Carbohydrate** 2g	1%
Total Fat 1.5g	2%	**Sodium** 53mg	2%	Dietary Fiber 0g	0%
Saturated Fat 0g	0%	**Protein** 6g		Sugars 0g	
Polyunsaturated Fat 0g					
Monounsaturated Fat 0g		Vitamin A 0%	Vitamin C 0%	Calcium 2%	Iron 4%

MorningStar Farms, Breakfast Pattie, Made with Organic Soy

1 patty / 38g

Amount per serving	%DV	Amount per serving	%DV	Amount per serving	%DV
Calories 80		**Cholesterol** 0mg	0%	**Total Carbohydrate** 4g	1%
Total Fat 3g	5%	**Sodium** 240mg	10%	Dietary Fiber 1g	4%
Saturated Fat 0.5g	3%	**Protein** 8g		Sugars 1g	
Polyunsaturated Fat 1.5g					
Monounsaturated Fat 1g		Vitamin A 0% Vitamin C 0%		Calcium 0% Iron 6%	

MorningStar Farms, Garden Veggie Patties

1 pattie / 67g

Amount per serving	%DV	Amount per serving	%DV	Amount per serving	%DV
Calories 110		**Cholesterol** 0mg	0%	**Total Carbohydrate** 9g	3%
Total Fat 3.5g	5%	**Sodium** 350mg	15%	Dietary Fiber 3g	12%
Saturated Fat 0.5g	2%	**Protein** 10g		Sugars 1g	
Polyunsaturated Fat 1.5g					
Monounsaturated Fat 0.5g		Vitamin A 4% Vitamin C 0%		Calcium 4% Iron 4%	

MorningStar Farms, Grillers Vegan Veggie Burgers

1 burger / 71g

Amount per serving	%DV	Amount per serving	%DV	Amount per serving	%DV
Calories 100		**Cholesterol** 0mg	0%	**Total Carbohydrate** 7g	2%
Total Fat 2.5g	4%	**Sodium** 280mg	12%	Dietary Fiber 4g	16%
Saturated Fat 0g	0%	**Protein** 12g		Sugars 1g	
Polyunsaturated Fat 1g					
Monounsaturated Fat 1g		Vitamin A 0% Vitamin C 0%		Calcium 4% Iron 10%	

VitaSoy USA, Organic Nasoya Extra Firm Tofu

1/5 pkg / 79g

Amount per serving	%DV	Amount per serving	%DV	Amount per serving	%DV
Calories 80		**Cholesterol** 0mg	0%	**Total Carbohydrate** 2g	1%
Total Fat 4g	6%	**Sodium** 0mg	0%	Dietary Fiber 1g	4%
Saturated Fat 0.5g	2%	**Protein** 8g		Sugars 0g	
Polyunsaturated Fat 2.5g					
Monounsaturated Fat 1g		Vitamin A 0% Vitamin C 0%		Calcium 6% Iron 8%	

VitaSoy USA, Organic Nasoya Firm Tofu

1/5 pkg / 79g

Amount per serving	%DV	Amount per serving	%DV	Amount per serving	%DV
Calories 70		**Cholesterol** 0mg	0%	**Total Carbohydrate** 2g	1%
Total Fat 3g	5%	**Sodium** 0mg	0%	Dietary Fiber 1g	4%
Saturated Fat 0g	0%	**Protein** 7g		Sugars 0g	
Polyunsaturated Fat 2g					
Monounsaturated Fat 1g		Vitamin A 0% Vitamin C 0%		Calcium 10% Iron 6%	

Vegetables

Why Eat Vegetables?

Eating a diet rich in vegetables and fruits as part of an overall healthy diet may reduce the risk for heart disease, including heart attack and stroke. Most vegetables are naturally low in fat, calories, and sodium, and none have cholesterol, although added sauces or seasonings may add fat, calories, sodium, and cholesterol. Vegetables are important sources of many nutrients, including potassium, dietary fiber, folate (folic acid), vitamin A, and vitamin C. Diets rich in potassium may help to maintain healthy blood pressure. Vitamin A keeps eyes and skin healthy and helps to protect against infections. Vitamin C helps heal cuts and wounds, keeps teeth and gums healthy, and aids in iron absorption.

Daily Goal

2½ cups for an adult on a 2,000-calorie diet

    1 cup equivalents:
        1 cup cooked vegetable
        2 cups raw vegetables
        2 medium carrots
        3" tomato
        1 cup cooked dry peas or beans
        1 cup starchy vegetable

Heart-Healthy Nutrients in Vegetables

Potassium helps your heart beat as it squeezes blood through your body. If you have high blood pressure, heart failure, or heart rhythm problems, getting enough potassium is especially important. Although potassium and cholesterol aren't directly related, eating a potassium-rich diet might lower your cholesterol, too.

Good vegetable sources of potassium are tomatoes, potatoes, spinach, beans, acorn squash, broccoli, artichokes, butternut squash, Brussels sprouts, carrots, kale, lentils, legumes, mushrooms, okra, parsnips, pumpkin, spinach, and peas.

Check out the FDA-approved Health Claim for potassium and high blood pressure and stroke on page 27.

ary fiber is the term for several materials that make up vegetables that your body can't digest. Fiber is classified as soluble or insoluble.

Soluble fiber, when eaten regularly as part of a diet low in saturated fat, trans fat, and cholesterol, has been associated with a decreased risk of cardiovascular disease. Soluble fibers modestly reduce LDL ("bad") cholesterol. Vegetables high in soluble fiber include cucumbers, celery, and carrots.

Check out the FDA-approved Health Claim for Soluble Fiber and risk of heart disease on page 26.

Insoluble fiber has been associated with decreased risk of heart disease. Foods high in insoluble fiber include cabbage, beets, carrots, Brussels sprouts, turnips, and cauliflower.

Antioxidants can help prevent artery damage by fighting free radicals produced in the process of oxidation. Natural food sources of antioxidants are often found to be more effective than taking antioxidant supplements. The major antioxidants found in vegetables are:

Antioxidant	Food Sources
Lycopene	Tomatoes, red cabbage, asparagus, parsley, basil, watermelon
Vitamin E	Spinach, broccoli, turnip greens
Beta carotene	Brightly colored orange and yellow foods such as carrots, winter squash, sweet potatoes, pumpkin, and tomatoes. Also found in kale, spinach, turnip greens, romaine lettuce, broccoli, collard greens, and cilantro.

Heart-Healthy Shopping Tips for Vegetables

- Look for these FDA-Approved Heart Health Claims on Vegetables:

Potassium and the Risk of High Blood Pressure and Stroke
"Diets containing foods that are a good source of potassium and that are low in sodium may reduce the risk of high blood pressure and stroke."

Products carrying this claim must be low in sodium, total fat, saturated fat, and cholesterol and contain a good source of potassium (350 mg/10% Daily Value or higher).

Fruits, Vegetables, and Grain Products that Contain Fiber, Particularly Soluble Fiber, and Risk of Coronary Heart Disease

"Diets low in saturated fat and cholesterol and rich in fruits, vegetables, and grain products that contain some types of dietary fiber, particularly soluble fiber, may reduce the risk of heart disease, a disease associated with many factors."

A vegetable that contains this claim must be low in total fat, saturated fat, and cholesterol and contain at least 0.6 grams of soluble fiber per serving (without fortification). The soluble fiber content must be provided on label.

- Look for the American Heart Association's Heart Check mark on fresh, canned, and frozen vegetable products and vegetable juices. For more information on the Heart-Check mark, go to www.heartcheckmark.org.

- Be sure to buy and eat plenty of vegetables. Choose vegetables that are deeply colored throughout such as spinach, carrots, broccoli, and tomatoes. They tend to be higher in vitamins and minerals than others, such as potatoes and corn.

- Buy fresh vegetables in season.

- Purchase locally grown vegetables when possible.

- When fresh vegetables aren't available, choose frozen without sauces or canned in water without added sugars, saturated and trans fat, or salt.

- Canned vegetables can be high in sodium. Look for salt-free canned vegetables or rinse canned vegetables before using.

- Frozen vegetables may have sauces that add calories, fat, and salt. Choose frozen and canned vegetables without sauces and seasonings.

- Buy vegetables that are good sources of fiber, including green beans, broccoli, and carrots.

- Choose raw vegetables for snacks, such as carrot and celery sticks, broccoli, cherry tomatoes, and cauliflower.

- Stock up on plain frozen or canned vegetables for fast preparation.

- Remember that over a quarter of your plate should be vegetables.

Shopping List Essentials for Heart Health

Asparagus
Broccoli
Carrots
Cilantro
Collard Greens

Kale
Pumpkin
Red Cabbage
Romaine Lettuce
Spinach

Sweet
Potatoes/Yams
Tomatoes
Turnip Greens
Winter Squash

Criteria for Vegetables

Using the FDA guidelines for Heart Health Claims, the foods listed meet the following criteria:

- Total fat–3 grams or less

- Saturated fat–1 gram or less

- Trans fat–0.5 grams or less (Trans Fat is not listed in the charts because all items report 0 grams Trans Fat. Since foods with less than 0.5 grams of trans fat can list 0 grams in the Nutrition Facts, be sure to check the ingredients for partially hydrogenated fats to determine if a product contains any trans fats.)

- Cholesterol–20 mg or less

- Beneficial Nutrients–10% Daily Value or higher of one beneficial nutrient (vitamin A, vitamin C, iron, calcium, protein, or dietary fiber). Raw, canned, or frozen vegetables do not necessarily need to meet these criteria and can be labeled "healthy" if they do not contain ingredients that change the nutritional profile and do not contain more than 360 mg of sodium.

- Sodium–360 mg or less for fresh, frozen, and canned plain vegetables and juices. Look for lower sodium levels to help reduce high blood pressure.

- Vegetable juices must be 100% juice

Herbs, spices, seasonings, and salsas may not meet the 10% Beneficial Nutrient requirement given above because the serving size is so small. Be sure to choose those that are lowest in sodium.

Foods that are not included in this list are canned and frozen vegetables with added salt and high fat sauces and vegetable juice beverages that are not 100% vegetable juice. It does not mean that these are bad foods and beverages; they should be eaten only occasionally while you focus on fresh vegetables.

Salsa

505 Southwestern, Salsa

2 tbsp / 30ml

Amount per serving	%DV	Amount per serving	%DV	Amount per serving	%DV
Calories 10		**Cholesterol** 0mg	0%	**Total Carbohydrate** 2g	1%
Total Fat 0g	0%	**Sodium** 190mg	8%	Dietary Fiber 0g	0%
Saturated Fat 0g	0%	**Protein** 0g		Sugars 1g	
Polyunsaturated Fat 0g					
Monounsaturated Fat 0g		Vitamin A 2%	Vitamin C 40%	Calcium 0%	Iron 0%

Amy's, Black Bean & Corn Salsa

2 tbsp

Amount per serving	%DV	Amount per serving	%DV	Amount per serving	%DV
Calories 15		**Cholesterol** 0mg	0%	**Total Carbohydrate** 3g	1%
Total Fat 0g	0%	**Sodium** 170mg	7%	Dietary Fiber 1g	4%
Saturated Fat 0g	0%	**Protein** 1g		Sugars 1g	
Polyunsaturated Fat 0g					
Monounsaturated Fat 0g		Vitamin A 2%	Vitamin C 4%	Calcium 0%	Iron 2%

Amy's, Medium Salsa

2 tbsp

Amount per serving	%DV	Amount per serving	%DV	Amount per serving	%DV
Calories 10		**Cholesterol** 0mg	0%	**Total Carbohydrate** 2g	1%
Total Fat 0g	0%	**Sodium** 190mg	8%	Dietary Fiber 0g	0%
Saturated Fat 0g	0%	**Protein** 0g		Sugars 1g	
Polyunsaturated Fat 0g					
Monounsaturated Fat 0g		Vitamin A 2%	Vitamin C 4%	Calcium 2%	Iron 2%

Amy's, Mild Salsa

2 tbsp

Amount per serving	%DV	Amount per serving	%DV	Amount per serving	%DV
Calories 10		**Cholesterol** 0mg	0%	**Total Carbohydrate** 2g	1%
Total Fat 0g	0%	**Sodium** 190mg	8%	Dietary Fiber 0g	0%
Saturated Fat 0g	0%	**Protein** 0g		Sugars 1g	
Polyunsaturated Fat 0g					
Monounsaturated Fat 0g		Vitamin A 2%	Vitamin C 4%	Calcium 2%	Iron 2%

Newman's Own, Black Bean and Corn Salsa

2 tbsp / 32g

Amount per serving	%DV	Amount per serving	%DV	Amount per serving	%DV
Calories 20		**Cholesterol** 0mg	0%	**Total Carbohydrate** 5g	2%
Total Fat 0g	0%	**Sodium** 140mg	6%	Dietary Fiber 2g	8%
Saturated Fat 0g	0%	**Protein** 1g		Sugars 1g	
Polyunsaturated Fat 0g					
Monounsaturated Fat 0g		Vitamin A 2%	Vitamin C 0%	Calcium 2%	Iron 2%

Newman's Own, Farmer's Garden Salsa

2 tbsp / 32g

Amount per serving	%DV	Amount per serving	%DV	Amount per serving	%DV
Calories 15		**Cholesterol** 0mg	0%	**Total Carbohydrate** 4g	1%
Total Fat 0g	0%	**Sodium** 220mg	9%	Dietary Fiber 0g	0%
Saturated Fat 0g	0%	**Protein** 1g		Sugars 2g	
Polyunsaturated Fat 0g					
Monounsaturated Fat 0g		Vitamin A 6% Vitamin C 0%		Calcium 2% Iron 2%	

Newman's Own, Hot Salsa

2 tbsp / 32g

Amount per serving	%DV	Amount per serving	%DV	Amount per serving	%DV
Calories 10		**Cholesterol** 0mg	0%	**Total Carbohydrate** 2g	1%
Total Fat 0g	0%	**Sodium** 150mg	6%	Dietary Fiber 1g	4%
Saturated Fat 0g	0%	**Protein** 0g		Sugars 1g	
Polyunsaturated Fat 0g					
Monounsaturated Fat 0g		Vitamin A 4% Vitamin C 0%		Calcium 0% Iron 0%	

Newman's Own, Mango Salsa

2 tbsp / 32g

Amount per serving	%DV	Amount per serving	%DV	Amount per serving	%DV
Calories 20		**Cholesterol** 0mg	0%	**Total Carbohydrate** 5g	2%
Total Fat 0g	0%	**Sodium** 180mg	8%	Dietary Fiber 0g	0%
Saturated Fat 0g	0%	**Protein** 0g		Sugars 3g	
Polyunsaturated Fat 0g					
Monounsaturated Fat 0g		Vitamin A 4% Vitamin C 0%		Calcium 2% Iron 2%	

Newman's Own, Medium Salsa

2 tbsp / 32g

Amount per serving	%DV	Amount per serving	%DV	Amount per serving	%DV
Calories 10		**Cholesterol** 0mg	0%	**Total Carbohydrate** 2g	1%
Total Fat 0g	0%	**Sodium** 105mg	4%	Dietary Fiber 1g	4%
Saturated Fat 0g	0%	**Protein** 0g		Sugars 1g	
Polyunsaturated Fat 0g					
Monounsaturated Fat 0g		Vitamin A 4% Vitamin C 0%		Calcium 0% Iron 0%	

Newman's Own, Mild Salsa

2 tbsp / 32g

Amount per serving	%DV	Amount per serving	%DV	Amount per serving	%DV
Calories 10		**Cholesterol** 0mg	0%	**Total Carbohydrate** 2g	1%
Total Fat 0g	0%	**Sodium** 65mg	3%	Dietary Fiber 1g	4%
Saturated Fat 0g	0%	**Protein** 0g		Sugars 1g	
Polyunsaturated Fat 0g					
Monounsaturated Fat 0g		Vitamin A 4% Vitamin C 0%		Calcium 0% Iron 0%	

Newman's Own, Peach Chunky Salsa

2 tbsp / 32g

Amount per serving	%DV	Amount per serving	%DV	Amount per serving	%DV
Calories 25		**Cholesterol** 0mg	0%	**Total Carbohydrate** 6g	2%
Total Fat 0g	0%	**Sodium** 90mg	4%	Dietary Fiber 1g	4%
Saturated Fat 0g	0%	**Protein** 0g		Sugars 5g	
Polyunsaturated Fat 0g					
Monounsaturated Fat 0g		Vitamin A 15%　Vitamin C 0%		Calcium 0%　Iron 0%	

Newman's Own, Pineapple Salsa

2 tbsp / 32g

Amount per serving	%DV	Amount per serving	%DV	Amount per serving	%DV
Calories 15		**Cholesterol** 0mg	0%	**Total Carbohydrate** 3g	1%
Total Fat 0g	0%	**Sodium** 90mg	4%	Dietary Fiber 1g	4%
Saturated Fat 0g	0%	**Protein** 0g		Sugars 3g	
Polyunsaturated Fat 0g					
Monounsaturated Fat 0g		Vitamin A 15%　Vitamin C 0%		Calcium 0%　Iron 0%	

Newman's Own, Roasted Garlic Chunky Salsa

2 tbsp / 32g

Amount per serving	%DV	Amount per serving	%DV	Amount per serving	%DV
Calories 10		**Cholesterol** 0mg	0%	**Total Carbohydrate** 2g	1%
Total Fat 0g	0%	**Sodium** 150mg	6%	Dietary Fiber 1g	4%
Saturated Fat 0g	0%	**Protein** 1g		Sugars 1g	
Polyunsaturated Fat 0g					
Monounsaturated Fat 0g		Vitamin A 10%　Vitamin C 0%		Calcium 0%　Iron 0%	

Newman's Own, Tequila Lime Salsa

2 tbsp / 32g

Amount per serving	%DV	Amount per serving	%DV	Amount per serving	%DV
Calories 15		**Cholesterol** 0mg	0%	**Total Carbohydrate** 3g	1%
Total Fat 0g	0%	**Sodium** 170mg	7%	Dietary Fiber 0g	0%
Saturated Fat 0g	0%	**Protein** 0g		Sugars 2g	
Polyunsaturated Fat 0g					
Monounsaturated Fat 0g		Vitamin A 4%　Vitamin C 0%		Calcium 2%　Iron 2%	

Pace, Chunky Salsa

2 tbsp / 30g

Amount per serving	%DV	Amount per serving	%DV	Amount per serving	%DV
Calories 10		**Cholesterol** 0mg	0%	**Total Carbohydrate** 3g	1%
Total Fat 0g	0%	**Sodium** 230mg	10%	Dietary Fiber 1g	4%
Saturated Fat 0g	0%	**Protein** 0g		Sugars 2g	
Polyunsaturated Fat 0g					
Monounsaturated Fat 0g		Vitamin A 2%　Vitamin C 0%		Calcium 0%　Iron 0%	

Pace, Garlic & Lime Verde Restaurant Salsa

2 tbsp / 30 ml

Amount per serving	%DV	Amount per serving	%DV	Amount per serving	%DV
Calories 10		**Cholesterol** 0mg	0%	**Total Carbohydrate** 2g	1%
Total Fat 0g	0%	**Sodium** 130mg	5%	Dietary Fiber 0g	0%
Saturated Fat 0g	0%	**Protein** 0g		Sugars 1g	
Polyunsaturated Fat 0g					
Monounsaturated Fat 0g		Vitamin A 2%	Vitamin C 0%	Calcium 0%	Iron 0%

Pace, Salsas, Restaurant Style Salsa

2 tbsp

Amount per serving	%DV	Amount per serving	%DV	Amount per serving	%DV
Calories 10		**Cholesterol** 0mg	0%	**Total Carbohydrate** 2g	1%
Total Fat 0g	0%	**Sodium** 130mg	5%	Dietary Fiber 0g	0%
Saturated Fat 0g	0%	**Protein** 0g		Sugars 0g	
Polyunsaturated Fat 0g					
Monounsaturated Fat 0g		Vitamin A 2%	Vitamin C 0%	Calcium 0%	Iron 0%

Pace, Salsas, Southwest Chipotle Restaurant Style Salsa

2 tbsp

Amount per serving	%DV	Amount per serving	%DV	Amount per serving	%DV
Calories 10		**Cholesterol** 0mg	0%	**Total Carbohydrate** 2g	1%
Total Fat 0g	0%	**Sodium** 140mg	6%	Dietary Fiber 0g	0%
Saturated Fat 0g	0%	**Protein** 0g		Sugars 1g	
Polyunsaturated Fat 0g					
Monounsaturated Fat 0g		Vitamin A 2%	Vitamin C 0%	Calcium 0%	Iron 0%

Sabra, Chunky Pico De Gallo Salsa

2 tbsp / 1 oz / 30g

Amount per serving	%DV	Amount per serving	%DV	Amount per serving	%DV
Calories 10		**Cholesterol** 0mg	0%	**Total Carbohydrate** 2g	1%
Total Fat 0g	0%	**Sodium** 200mg	8%	Dietary Fiber 0g	0%
Saturated Fat 0g	0%	**Protein** 0g		Sugars 1g	
Polyunsaturated Fat 0g					
Monounsaturated Fat 0g		Vitamin A 2%	Vitamin C 10%	Calcium 2%	Iron 2%

Sabra, Mild Homestyle Salsa

2 tbsp / 1 oz / 30g

Amount per serving	%DV	Amount per serving	%DV	Amount per serving	%DV
Calories 10		**Cholesterol** 0mg	0%	**Total Carbohydrate** 2g	1%
Total Fat 0g	0%	**Sodium** 170mg	7%	Dietary Fiber 0g	0%
Saturated Fat 0g	0%	**Protein** 0g		Sugars 1g	
Polyunsaturated Fat 0g					
Monounsaturated Fat 0g		Vitamin A 2%	Vitamin C 6%	Calcium 0%	Iron 0%

Sabra, Southwestern Style Salsa

2 tbsp

Amount per serving	%DV	Amount per serving	%DV	Amount per serving	%DV
Calories 15		**Cholesterol** 0mg	0%	**Total Carbohydrate** 3g	1%
Total Fat 0g	0%	**Sodium** 115mg	5%	Dietary Fiber 1g	4%
Saturated Fat 0g	0%	**Protein** 0g		Sugars 2g	
Polyunsaturated Fat 0g					
Monounsaturated Fat 0g		Vitamin A 0%	Vitamin C 6%	Calcium 0%	Iron 2%

Simply Organic Foods, Salsa Mix

1/2 tsp

Amount per serving	%DV	Amount per serving	%DV	Amount per serving	%DV
Calories 5		**Cholesterol** 0mg	0%	**Total Carbohydrate** 1g	0%
Total Fat 0g	0%	**Sodium** 60mg	3%	Dietary Fiber 0g	0%
Saturated Fat 0g	0%	**Protein** 0g		Sugars 0g	
Polyunsaturated Fat 0g					
Monounsaturated Fat 0g		Vitamin A 2%	Vitamin C 2%	Calcium 0%	Iron 0%

Wholly Salsa, Avocado Verde Dip

2 tbsp / 30g

Amount per serving	%DV	Amount per serving	%DV	Amount per serving	%DV
Calories 25		**Cholesterol** 0mg	0%	**Total Carbohydrate** 2g	1%
Total Fat 1.5g	2%	**Sodium** 135mg	6%	Dietary Fiber 1g	4%
Saturated Fat 0g	0%	**Protein** 0g		Sugars 1g	
Polyunsaturated Fat 0g					
Monounsaturated Fat 0g		Vitamin A 2%	Vitamin C 150%	Calcium 2%	Iron 0%

Wholly Salsa, Classic Hot Dip

2 tbsp / 30g

Amount per serving	%DV	Amount per serving	%DV	Amount per serving	%DV
Calories 10		**Cholesterol** 0mg	0%	**Total Carbohydrate** 2g	1%
Total Fat 0g	0%	**Sodium** 160mg	7%	Dietary Fiber 0g	0%
Saturated Fat 0g	0%	**Protein** 0g		Sugars 1g	
Polyunsaturated Fat 0g					
Monounsaturated Fat 0g		Vitamin A 4%	Vitamin C 15%	Calcium 0%	Iron 0%

Wholly Salsa, Classic Medium Dip

2 tbsp / 30g

Amount per serving	%DV	Amount per serving	%DV	Amount per serving	%DV
Calories 10		**Cholesterol** 0mg	0%	**Total Carbohydrate** 2g	1%
Total Fat 0g		**Sodium** 160mg	7%	Dietary Fiber 0g	0%
Saturated Fat 0g	0%	**Protein** 0g		Sugars 1g	
Polyunsaturated Fat 0g	0%				
Monounsaturated Fat 0g		Vitamin A 4%	Vitamin C 15%	Calcium 0%	Iron 0%

Wholly Salsa, Classic Mild Dip

2 tbsp / 30g

Amount per serving	%DV	Amount per serving	%DV	Amount per serving	%DV
Calories 10		**Cholesterol** 0mg	0%	**Total Carbohydrate** 2g	1%
Total Fat 0g	0%	**Sodium** 160mg	7%	Dietary Fiber 0g	0%
Saturated Fat 0g	0%	**Protein** 0g		Sugars 1g	
Polyunsaturated Fat 0g					
Monounsaturated Fat 0g		Vitamin A 4%	Vitamin C 15%	Calcium 0%	Iron 0%

Wholly Salsa, Guacamole & Spicy Pico Dip

2 tbsp / 30g

Amount per serving	%DV	Amount per serving	%DV	Amount per serving	%DV
Calories 35		**Cholesterol** 0mg	0%	**Total Carbohydrate** 2g	1%
Total Fat 2.5g	4%	**Sodium** 115mg	5%	Dietary Fiber 1g	4%
Saturated Fat 0g	0%	**Protein** 0g		Sugars 0g	
Polyunsaturated Fat 0g					
Monounsaturated Fat 0g		Vitamin A 4%	Vitamin C 6%	Calcium 0%	Iron 0%

Wholly Salsa, Pineapple Dip

2 tbsp / 30g

Amount per serving	%DV	Amount per serving	%DV	Amount per serving	%DV
Calories 15		**Cholesterol** 0mg	0%	**Total Carbohydrate** 4g	1%
Total Fat 0g	0%	**Sodium** 25mg	1%	Dietary Fiber 0g	0%
Saturated Fat 0g	0%	**Protein** 0g		Sugars 3g	
Polyunsaturated Fat 0g					
Monounsaturated Fat 0g		Vitamin A 2%	Vitamin C 8%	Calcium 0%	Iron 0%

Wholly Salsa, Red Pepper Mango Dip

2 tbsp / 30g

Amount per serving	%DV	Amount per serving	%DV	Amount per serving	%DV
Calories 25		**Cholesterol** 0mg	0%	**Total Carbohydrate** 6g	2%
Total Fat 0g	0%	**Sodium** 25mg	1%	Dietary Fiber 0g	0%
Saturated Fat 0g	0%	**Protein** 0g		Sugars 5g	
Polyunsaturated Fat 0g					
Monounsaturated Fat 0g		Vitamin A 6%	Vitamin C 20%	Calcium 0%	Iron 0%

Wholly Salsa, Roasted Tomato Dip

2 tbsp / 30g

Amount per serving	%DV	Amount per serving	%DV	Amount per serving	%DV
Calories 10		**Cholesterol** 0mg	0%	**Total Carbohydrate** 3g	1%
Total Fat 0g	0%	**Sodium** 120mg	5%	Dietary Fiber 0g	0%
Saturated Fat 0g	0%	**Protein** 0g		Sugars 2g	
Polyunsaturated Fat 0g					
Monounsaturated Fat 0g		Vitamin A 4%	Vitamin C 15%	Calcium 0%	Iron 0%

Spices and Herbs

Allspice, Ground

1 tbsp / 6g

Amount per serving	%DV	Amount per serving	%DV	Amount per serving	%DV
Calories 16		**Cholesterol** 0mg	0%	**Total Carbohydrate** 4g	1%
Total Fat 1g	2%	**Sodium** 5mg	0%	Dietary Fiber 1g	4%
Saturated Fat 0g	0%	**Protein** 0g		Sugars 0g	
Polyunsaturated Fat 0g					
Monounsaturated Fat 0g		Vitamin A 1% Vitamin C 4%		Calcium 4% Iron 2%	

Anise Seed

1 tsp / whole / 6g

Amount per serving	%DV	Amount per serving	%DV	Amount per serving	%DV
Calories 22		**Cholesterol** 0mg	0%	**Total Carbohydrate** 1g	0%
Total Fat 1g	2%	**Sodium** 1mg	0%	Dietary Fiber 1g	4%
Saturated Fat 0g	0%	**Protein** 1g		Sugars 0g	
Polyunsaturated Fat 0g					
Monounsaturated Fat 0g		Vitamin A 0% Vitamin C 2%		Calcium 4% Iron 13%	

Basil, Dried

1 tsp, leaves / 0g

Amount per serving	%DV	Amount per serving	%DV	Amount per serving	%DV
Calories 1		**Cholesterol** 0mg	0%	**Total Carbohydrate** 1g	0%
Total Fat 0g	0%	**Sodium** 0mg	0%	Dietary Fiber 0g	0%
Saturated Fat 0g	0%	**Protein** 0g		Sugars 0g	
Polyunsaturated Fat 0g					
Monounsaturated Fat 0g		Vitamin A 1% Vitamin C 1%		Calcium 1% Iron 1%	

Basil, Fresh

5 leaves / 2.5g

Amount per serving	%DV	Amount per serving	%DV	Amount per serving	%DV
Calories 1		**Cholesterol** 0mg	0%	**Total Carbohydrate** 0g	0%
Total Fat 0g	0%	**Sodium** 0mg	0%	Dietary Fiber 0g	0%
Saturated Fat 0g	0%	**Protein** 0g		Sugars 0g	
Polyunsaturated Fat 0g					
Monounsaturated Fat 0g		Vitamin A 3% Vitamin C 1%		Calcium 0% Iron 0%	

Bay Leaf

1 tsp, crumbled / 2g

Amount per serving	%DV	Amount per serving	%DV	Amount per serving	%DV
Calories 5		**Cholesterol** 0mg	0%	**Total Carbohydrate** 1g	0%
Total Fat 0g	0%	**Sodium** 0mg	0%	Dietary Fiber 0g	0%
Saturated Fat 0g	0%	**Protein** 0g		Sugars 0g	
Polyunsaturated Fat 0g					
Monounsaturated Fat 0g		Vitamin A 2% Vitamin C 1%		Calcium 1% Iron 4%	

Caraway Seed

1 tbsp / 6g

Amount per serving	%DV	Amount per serving	%DV	Amount per serving	%DV
Calories 22		**Cholesterol** 0mg	0%	**Total Carbohydrate** 3g	1%
Total Fat 1g	2%	**Sodium** 1mg	0%	Dietary Fiber 2g	8%
Saturated Fat 0g	0%	**Protein** 1g		Sugars 0g	
Polyunsaturated Fat 0g					
Monounsaturated Fat 0g		Vitamin A 0% Vitamin C 2%		Calcium 4% Iron 6%	

Cardamom

1 tsp, ground / 6g

Amount per serving	%DV	Amount per serving	%DV	Amount per serving	%DV
Calories 18		**Cholesterol** 0mg	0%	**Total Carbohydrate** 4g	1%
Total Fat 0g	0%	**Sodium** 1mg	0%	Dietary Fiber 2g	8%
Saturated Fat 0g	0%	**Protein** 1g		Sugars 0g	
Polyunsaturated Fat 0g					
Monounsaturated Fat 0g		Vitamin A 0% Vitamin C 2%		Calcium 2% Iron 4%	

Celery Seed

1 tbsp / 6g

Amount per serving	%DV	Amount per serving	%DV	Amount per serving	%DV
Calories 25		**Cholesterol** 0mg	0%	**Total Carbohydrate** 3g	1%
Total Fat 2g	3%	**Sodium** 10mg	0%	Dietary Fiber 1g	4%
Saturated Fat 0g	0%	**Protein** 1g		Sugars 0g	
Polyunsaturated Fat 0g					
Monounsaturated Fat 0g		Vitamin A 0% Vitamin C 2%		Calcium 11% Iron 16%	

Chervil, Dried

1 tbsp / 2g

Amount per serving	%DV	Amount per serving	%DV	Amount per serving	%DV
Calories 4		**Cholesterol** 0mg	0%	**Total Carbohydrate** 1g	0%
Total Fat 0g	0%	**Sodium** 1mg	0%	Dietary Fiber 0g	0%
Saturated Fat 0g	0%	**Protein** 0g		Sugars 0g	
Polyunsaturated Fat 0g					
Monounsaturated Fat 0g		Vitamin A 2% Vitamin C 1%		Calcium 2% Iron 3%	

Chili Powder

1 tbsp / 8g

Amount per serving	%DV	Amount per serving	%DV	Amount per serving	%DV
Calories 24		**Cholesterol** 0mg	0%	**Total Carbohydrate** 4g	1%
Total Fat 1g	2%	**Sodium** 76mg	3%	Dietary Fiber 3g	12%
Saturated Fat 0g	0%	**Protein** 1g		Sugars 1g	
Polyunsaturated Fat 0g					
Monounsaturated Fat 0g		Vitamin A 44% Vitamin C 8%		Calcium 2% Iron 6%	

Cinnamon, Ground

1 tbsp / 8g

Amount per serving	%DV	Amount per serving	%DV	Amount per serving	%DV
Calories 19		**Cholesterol** 0mg	0%	**Total Carbohydrate** 6g	2%
Total Fat 0g	0%	**Sodium** 1mg	0%	Dietary Fiber 4g	16%
Saturated Fat 0g	0%	**Protein** 0g		Sugars 0g	
Polyunsaturated Fat 0g					
Monounsaturated Fat 0g		Vitamin A 0%	Vitamin C 0%	Calcium 8%	Iron 4%

Cloves, Ground

1 tbsp / 6g

Amount per serving	%DV	Amount per serving	%DV	Amount per serving	%DV
Calories 21		**Cholesterol** 0mg	0%	**Total Carbohydrate** 4g	1%
Total Fat 1g	2%	**Sodium** 16mg	1%	Dietary Fiber 2g	8%
Saturated Fat 0g	0%	**Protein** 0g		Sugars 0g	
Polyunsaturated Fat 0g					
Monounsaturated Fat 0g		Vitamin A 1%	Vitamin C 9%	Calcium 4%	Iron 3%

Coriander Leaf, Dried (Chinese Parsley, Cilantro)

1 tbsp / 2g

Amount per serving	%DV	Amount per serving	%DV	Amount per serving	%DV
Calories 5		**Cholesterol** 0mg	0%	**Total Carbohydrate** 1g	0%
Total Fat 0g	0%	**Sodium** 4mg	0%	Dietary Fiber 0g	0%
Saturated Fat 0g	0%	**Protein** 0g		Sugars 0g	
Polyunsaturated Fat 0g					
Monounsaturated Fat 0g		Vitamin A 2%	Vitamin C 17%	Calcium 2%	Iron 4%

Coriander Seed

1 tbsp / 5.0g

Amount per serving	%DV	Amount per serving	%DV	Amount per serving	%DV
Calories 15		**Cholesterol** 0mg	0%	**Total Carbohydrate** 3g	1%
Total Fat 1g	2%	**Sodium** 2mg	0%	Dietary Fiber 2g	8%
Saturated Fat 0g	0%	**Protein** 1g		Sugars 0g	
Polyunsaturated Fat 0g					
Monounsaturated Fat 0g		Vitamin A 0%	Vitamin C 2%	Calcium 4%	Iron 5%

Cumin Seed

1 tbsp, whole / 6g

Amount per serving	%DV	Amount per serving	%DV	Amount per serving	%DV
Calories 22		**Cholesterol** 0mg	0%	**Total Carbohydrate** 3g	1%
Total Fat 1g	2%	**Sodium** 10mg	0%	Dietary Fiber 1g	4%
Saturated Fat 0g	0%	**Protein** 1g		Sugars 0g	
Polyunsaturated Fat 0g					
Monounsaturated Fat 0g		Vitamin A 2%	Vitamin C 1%	Calcium 6%	Iron 22%

Curry Powder

1 tbsp / 6g

Amount per serving	%DV	Amount per serving	%DV	Amount per serving	%DV
Calories 20		**Cholesterol** 0mg	0%	**Total Carbohydrate** 4g	1%
Total Fat 1g	2%	**Sodium** 3mg	0%	Dietary Fiber 2g	8%
Saturated Fat 0g	0%	**Protein** 1g		Sugars 0g	
Polyunsaturated Fat 0g					
Monounsaturated Fat 0g		Vitamin A 1% Vitamin C 1%		Calcium 3% Iron 10%	

Dill Seed

1 tbsp / 6g

Amount per serving	%DV	Amount per serving	%DV	Amount per serving	%DV
Calories 20		**Cholesterol** 0mg	0%	**Total Carbohydrate** 4g	1%
Total Fat 1g	2%	**Sodium** 1mg	0%	Dietary Fiber 1g	4%
Saturated Fat 0g	0%	**Protein** 1g		Sugars 0g	
Polyunsaturated Fat 0g					
Monounsaturated Fat 0g		Vitamin A 0% Vitamin C 2%		Calcium 10% Iron 6%	

Dill Weed, Dried

1 tbsp / 3g

Amount per serving	%DV	Amount per serving	%DV	Amount per serving	%DV
Calories 8		**Cholesterol** 0mg	0%	**Total Carbohydrate** 2g	1%
Total Fat 0g	0%	**Sodium** 6mg	0%	Dietary Fiber 0g	0%
Saturated Fat 0g	0%	**Protein** 1g		Sugars 0g	
Polyunsaturated Fat 0g					
Monounsaturated Fat 0g		Vitamin A 4% Vitamin C 2%		Calcium 5% Iron 8%	

Eden Foods, Dulse Flakes, Sea Vegetable, Organic, Wild, Hand Harvested, Raw

1 tsp

Amount per serving	%DV	Amount per serving	%DV	Amount per serving	%DV
Calories 3		**Cholesterol** 0mg	0%	**Total Carbohydrate** 0g	0%
Total Fat 0g	0%	**Sodium** 15mg	1%	Dietary Fiber 0g	0%
Saturated Fat 0g	0%	**Protein** 0g		Sugars 0g	
Polyunsaturated Fat 0g					
Monounsaturated Fat 0g		Vitamin A 0% Vitamin C 0%		Calcium 0% Iron 2%	

Eden Foods, Dulse Whole Leaf, Sea Vegetable, Organic, Wild, Hand Harvested

1/4 cup / 4g

Amount per serving	%DV	Amount per serving	%DV	Amount per serving	%DV
Calories 10		**Cholesterol** 0mg	0%	**Total Carbohydrate** 2g	1%
Total Fat 0g	0%	**Sodium** 60mg	3%	Dietary Fiber 1g	4%
Saturated Fat 0g	0%	**Protein** 1g		Sugars 0g	
Polyunsaturated Fat 0g					
Monounsaturated Fat 0g		Vitamin A 0% Vitamin C 0%		Calcium 0% Iron 2%	

Eden Foods, Yansen (Dandelion Root Concentrate)

1/4 tsp / 2g

Amount per serving	%DV	Amount per serving	%DV	Amount per serving	%DV
Calories 5		**Cholesterol** 0mg	0%	**Total Carbohydrate** 1g	0%
Total Fat 0g	0%	**Sodium** 0mg	0%	Dietary Fiber 0g	0%
Saturated Fat 0g	0%	**Protein** 0g		Sugars 1g	
Polyunsaturated Fat 0g					
Monounsaturated Fat 0g		Vitamin A 0% Vitamin C 0%		Calcium 0% Iron 0%	

Fennel Seed

1 tbsp, whole / 6g

Amount per serving	%DV	Amount per serving	%DV	Amount per serving	%DV
Calories 20		**Cholesterol** 0mg	0%	**Total Carbohydrate** 3g	1%
Total Fat 1g	2%	**Sodium** 5mg	0%	Dietary Fiber 2g	8%
Saturated Fat 0g	0%	**Protein** 1g		Sugars 0g	
Polyunsaturated Fat 0g					
Monounsaturated Fat 0g		Vitamin A 0% Vitamin C 2%		Calcium 7% Iron 6%	

Fenugreek Seed

1 tbsp / 11g

Amount per serving	%DV	Amount per serving	%DV	Amount per serving	%DV
Calories 36		**Cholesterol** 0mg	0%	**Total Carbohydrate** 6g	2%
Total Fat 1g	2%	**Sodium** 7mg	0%	Dietary Fiber 3g	12%
Saturated Fat 0g	0%	**Protein** 3g		Sugars 0g	
Polyunsaturated Fat 0g					
Monounsaturated Fat 0g		Vitamin A 0% Vitamin C 1%		Calcium 2% Iron 20%	

Garlic Powder

1 tbsp / 8.25g

Amount per serving	%DV	Amount per serving	%DV	Amount per serving	%DV
Calories 27		**Cholesterol** 0mg	0%	**Total Carbohydrate** 6g	2%
Total Fat 0g	0%	**Sodium** 2mg	0%	Dietary Fiber 1g	4%
Saturated Fat 0g	0%	**Protein** 1g		Sugars 2g	
Polyunsaturated Fat 0g					
Monounsaturated Fat 0g		Vitamin A 0% Vitamin C 2%		Calcium 1% Iron 1%	

Ginger, Ground

1 tsp / 2g

Amount per serving	%DV	Amount per serving	%DV	Amount per serving	%DV
Calories 18		**Cholesterol** 0mg	0%	**Total Carbohydrate** 4g	1%
Total Fat 0g	0%	**Sodium** 2mg	0%	Dietary Fiber 1g	4%
Saturated Fat 0g	0%	**Protein** 0g		Sugars 0g	
Polyunsaturated Fat 0g					
Monounsaturated Fat 0g		Vitamin A 0% Vitamin C 1%		Calcium 1% Iron 3%	

Horseradish, Prepared

1 tbsp / 15g

Amount per serving	%DV	Amount per serving	%DV	Amount per serving	%DV
Calories 7		**Cholesterol** 0mg	0%	**Total Carbohydrate** 2g	1%
Total Fat 0g	0%	**Sodium** 47mg	2%	Dietary Fiber 0g	0%
Saturated Fat 0g	0%	**Protein** 0g		Sugars 1g	
Polyunsaturated Fat 0g					
Monounsaturated Fat 0g		Vitamin A 0%	Vitamin C 6%	Calcium 1%	Iron 0%

Mace, Ground

1 tbsp / 5g

Amount per serving	%DV	Amount per serving	%DV	Amount per serving	%DV
Calories 25		**Cholesterol** 0mg	0%	**Total Carbohydrate** 3g	1%
Total Fat 2g	3%	**Sodium** 4mg	0%	Dietary Fiber 1g	4%
Saturated Fat 0g	0%	**Protein** 0g		Sugars 0g	
Polyunsaturated Fat 0g					
Monounsaturated Fat 0g		Vitamin A 1%	Vitamin C 2%	Calcium 1%	Iron 4%

Marjoram, Dried

1 tbsp / 2g

Amount per serving	%DV	Amount per serving	%DV	Amount per serving	%DV
Calories 4		**Cholesterol** 0mg	0%	**Total Carbohydrate** 1g	0%
Total Fat 0g	0%	**Sodium** 1mg	0%	Dietary Fiber 1g	4%
Saturated Fat 0g	0%	**Protein** 0g		Sugars 0g	
Polyunsaturated Fat 0g					
Monounsaturated Fat 0g		Vitamin A 2%	Vitamin C 1%	Calcium 3%	Iron 7%

Onion Powder

1 tbsp / 7g

Amount per serving	%DV	Amount per serving	%DV	Amount per serving	%DV
Calories 23		**Cholesterol** 0mg	0%	**Total Carbohydrate** 5g	2%
Total Fat 0g	0%	**Sodium** 4mg	0%	Dietary Fiber 0g	0%
Saturated Fat 0g	0%	**Protein** 1g		Sugars 0g	
Polyunsaturated Fat 0g					
Monounsaturated Fat 0g		Vitamin A 0%	Vitamin C 2%	Calcium 2%	Iron 1%

Oregano, Dried

1 tsp, ground / 2g

Amount per serving	%DV	Amount per serving	%DV	Amount per serving	%DV
Calories 5		**Cholesterol** 0mg	0%	**Total Carbohydrate** 1g	0%
Total Fat 0g	0%	**Sodium** 0.5mg	0%	Dietary Fiber 1g	4%
Saturated Fat 0g	0%	**Protein** 0g		Sugars 0g	
Polyunsaturated Fat 0g					
Monounsaturated Fat 0g		Vitamin A 2%	Vitamin C 1%	Calcium 3%	Iron 4%

Paprika

1 tbsp / 7g

Amount per serving	%DV
Calories 20	
Total Fat 1g	2%
Saturated Fat 0g	0%
Polyunsaturated Fat 0g	
Monounsaturated Fat 0g	

Amount per serving	%DV
Cholesterol 0mg	0%
Sodium 2mg	0%
Protein 1g	
Vitamin A 71% Vitamin C 8%	

Amount per serving	%DV
Total Carbohydrate 4g	1%
Dietary Fiber 3g	12%
Sugars 1g	
Calcium 1% Iron 9%	

Parsley, Dried

1 tbsp / 2g

Amount per serving	%DV
Calories 4	
Total Fat 0g	0%
Saturated Fat 0g	0%
Polyunsaturated Fat 0g	
Monounsaturated Fat 0g	

Amount per serving	%DV
Cholesterol 0mg	0%
Sodium 7mg	0%
Protein 0.5g	
Vitamin A 3% Vitamin C 3%	

Amount per serving	%DV
Total Carbohydrate 1g	0%
Dietary Fiber 0g	0%
Sugars 0g	
Calcium 2% Iron 8%	

Parsley, Fresh

1 tbsp / 4g

Amount per serving	%DV
Calories 1	
Total Fat 0g	0%
Saturated Fat 0g	0%
Polyunsaturated Fat 0g	
Monounsaturated Fat 0g	

Amount per serving	%DV
Cholesterol 0mg	0%
Sodium 2mg	0%
Protein 0g	
Vitamin A 6% Vitamin C 8%	

Amount per serving	%DV
Total Carbohydrate 0g	0%
Dietary Fiber 0g	0%
Sugars 0g	
Calcium 1% Iron 1%	

Pepper, Black

1 tbsp, ground / 6g

Amount per serving	%DV
Calories 16	
Total Fat 0g	0%
Saturated Fat 0g	0%
Polyunsaturated Fat 0g	
Monounsaturated Fat 0g	

Amount per serving	%DV
Cholesterol 0mg	0%
Sodium 3mg	0%
Protein 1g	
Vitamin A 0% Vitamin C 2%	

Amount per serving	%DV
Total Carbohydrate 4g	1%
Dietary Fiber 2g	8%
Sugars 0g	
Calcium 3% Iron 10%	

Pepper, Red or Cayenne

1 tbsp / 5g

Amount per serving	%DV
Calories 17	
Total Fat 0g	0%
Saturated Fat 0g	0%
Polyunsaturated Fat 0g	
Monounsaturated Fat 0g	

Amount per serving	%DV
Cholesterol 0mg	0%
Sodium 2mg	0%
Protein 1g	
Vitamin A 44% Vitamin C 7%	

Amount per serving	%DV
Total Carbohydrate 3g	1%
Dietary Fiber 1g	4%
Sugars 1g	
Calcium 1% Iron 2%	

Pepper, White

1 tbsp, ground / 7g

Amount per serving	%DV	Amount per serving	%DV	Amount per serving	%DV
Calories 21		**Cholesterol** 0mg	0%	**Total Carbohydrate** 5g	2%
Total Fat 0g	0%	**Sodium** 0mg	0%	Dietary Fiber 2g	8%
Saturated Fat 0g	0%	**Protein** 1g		Sugars g	
Polyunsaturated Fat 0g					
Monounsaturated Fat 0g		Vitamin A 0%	Vitamin C 2%	Calcium 2%	Iron 6%

Peppermint, Fresh

2 leaves / 0g

Amount per serving	%DV	Amount per serving	%DV	Amount per serving	%DV
Calories 0		**Cholesterol** 0mg	0%	**Total Carbohydrate** 0g	0%
Total Fat 0g	0%	**Sodium** 0mg	0%	Dietary Fiber 0g	0%
Saturated Fat 0g	0%	**Protein** 0g		Sugars 0g	
Polyunsaturated Fat 0g					
Monounsaturated Fat 0g		Vitamin A 0%	Vitamin C 0%	Calcium 0%	Iron 0%

Poultry Seasoning

1 tbsp / 4g

Amount per serving	%DV	Amount per serving	%DV	Amount per serving	%DV
Calories 13		**Cholesterol** 0mg	0%	**Total Carbohydrate** 3g	1%
Total Fat 0g	0%	**Sodium** 1mg	0%	Dietary Fiber 0g	0%
Saturated Fat 0g	0%	**Protein** 0g		Sugars 0g	
Polyunsaturated Fat 0g					
Monounsaturated Fat 0g		Vitamin A 2%	Vitamin C 1%	Calcium 4%	Iron 8%

Pumpkin Pie Spice

1 tbsp / 6g

Amount per serving	%DV	Amount per serving	%DV	Amount per serving	%DV
Calories 19		**Cholesterol** 0mg	0%	**Total Carbohydrate** 4g	1%
Total Fat 1g	2%	**Sodium** 3mg	0%	Dietary Fiber 1g	4%
Saturated Fat 0g	0%	**Protein** 0g		Sugars 0g	
Polyunsaturated Fat 0g					
Monounsaturated Fat 0g		Vitamin A 0%	Vitamin C 2%	Calcium 4%	Iron 6%

Rosemary, Dried

1 tbsp / 3g

Amount per serving	%DV	Amount per serving	%DV	Amount per serving	%DV
Calories 11		**Cholesterol** 0mg	0%	**Total Carbohydrate** 2g	1%
Total Fat 0g	0%	**Sodium** 2mg	0%	Dietary Fiber 1g	4%
Saturated Fat 0g	0%	**Protein** 0g		Sugars 0g	
Polyunsaturated Fat 0g					
Monounsaturated Fat 0g		Vitamin A 2%	Vitamin C 3%	Calcium 4%	Iron 5%

Rosemary, Fresh

1 tbsp / 2g

Amount per serving	%DV	Amount per serving	%DV	Amount per serving	%DV
Calories 2		**Cholesterol** 0mg	0%	**Total Carbohydrate** 0g	0%
Total Fat 0g	0%	**Sodium** 0mg	0%	Dietary Fiber 0g	0%
Saturated Fat 0g	0%	**Protein** 0g		Sugars 0g	
Polyunsaturated Fat 0g					
Monounsaturated Fat 0g		Vitamin A 1%	Vitamin C 1%	Calcium 0%	Iron 1%

Saffron

1 tbsp / 2g

Amount per serving	%DV	Amount per serving	%DV	Amount per serving	%DV
Calories 6		**Cholesterol** 0mg	0%	**Total Carbohydrate** 1g	0%
Total Fat 0g	0%	**Sodium** 3mg	0%	Dietary Fiber 0g	0%
Saturated Fat 0g	0%	**Protein** 0g		Sugars 0g	
Polyunsaturated Fat 0g					
Monounsaturated Fat 0g		Vitamin A 0%	Vitamin C 3%	Calcium 0%	Iron 1%

Sage, Ground

1 tbsp / 2g

Amount per serving	%DV	Amount per serving	%DV	Amount per serving	%DV
Calories 6		**Cholesterol** 0mg	0%	**Total Carbohydrate** 1g	0%
Total Fat 0g	0%	**Sodium** 0mg	0%	Dietary Fiber 1g	4%
Saturated Fat 0g	0%	**Protein** 0g		Sugars 0g	
Polyunsaturated Fat 0g					
Monounsaturated Fat 0g		Vitamin A 2%	Vitamin C 1%	Calcium 3%	Iron 3%

Savory, Ground

1 tbsp / 4g

Amount per serving	%DV	Amount per serving	%DV	Amount per serving	%DV
Calories 12		**Cholesterol** 0mg	0%	**Total Carbohydrate** 3g	1%
Total Fat 0g	0%	**Sodium** 1mg	0%	Dietary Fiber 2g	8%
Saturated Fat 0g	0%	**Protein** 0g		Sugars 0g	
Polyunsaturated Fat 0g					
Monounsaturated Fat 0g		Vitamin A 4%	Vitamin C 4%	Calcium 9%	Iron 9%

Simply Organic Foods, Sweet Basil Pesto

2 tsp / 4g

Amount per serving	%DV	Amount per serving	%DV	Amount per serving	%DV
Calories 10		**Cholesterol** 0mg	0%	**Total Carbohydrate** 2g	1%
Total Fat 0g	0%	**Sodium** 200mg	8%	Dietary Fiber 0g	0%
Saturated Fat 0g	0%	**Protein** 0g		Sugars 0g	
Polyunsaturated Fat 0g					
Monounsaturated Fat 0g		Vitamin A 0%	Vitamin C 0%	Calcium 2%	Iron 6%

Spearmint, Dried

1 tsp / 0g

Amount per serving	%DV	Amount per serving	%DV	Amount per serving	%DV
Calories 1		**Cholesterol** 0mg	0%	**Total Carbohydrate** 0g	0%
Total Fat 0g	0%	**Sodium** 2mg	0%	Dietary Fiber 0g	0%
Saturated Fat 0g	0%	**Protein** 0g		Sugars 0g	
Polyunsaturated Fat 0g					
Monounsaturated Fat 0g		Vitamin A 1% Vitamin C 0%		Calcium 1% Iron 2%	

Spearmint, Fresh

2 tbsp / 11g

Amount per serving	%DV	Amount per serving	%DV	Amount per serving	%DV
Calories 0		**Cholesterol** 0mg	0%	**Total Carbohydrate** 0g	0%
Total Fat 0g	0%	**Sodium** 3mg	0%	Dietary Fiber 0g	0%
Saturated Fat 0g	0%	**Protein** 0g		Sugars 0g	
Polyunsaturated Fat 0g					
Monounsaturated Fat 0g		Vitamin A 9% Vitamin C 2%		Calcium 2% Iron 7%	

Tarragon, Dried

1 tbsp, ground / 5g

Amount per serving	%DV	Amount per serving	%DV	Amount per serving	%DV
Calories 14		**Cholesterol** 0mg	0%	**Total Carbohydrate** 2g	1%
Total Fat 0g	0%	**Sodium** 3mg	0%	Dietary Fiber 0g	0%
Saturated Fat 0g	0%	**Protein** 1g		Sugars 0g	
Polyunsaturated Fat 0g					
Monounsaturated Fat 0g		Vitamin A 4% Vitamin C 4%		Calcium 5% Iron 9%	

Thyme, Dried

1 tbsp, ground / 4g

Amount per serving	%DV	Amount per serving	%DV	Amount per serving	%DV
Calories 12		**Cholesterol** 0mg	0%	**Total Carbohydrate** 3g	1%
Total Fat 0g	0%	**Sodium** 2mg	0%	Dietary Fiber 2g	8%
Saturated Fat 0g	0%	**Protein** 0g		Sugars 0g	
Polyunsaturated Fat 0g					
Monounsaturated Fat 0g		Vitamin A 3% Vitamin C 4%		Calcium 8% Iron 29%	

Thyme, Fresh

1 tsp / 1g

Amount per serving	%DV	Amount per serving	%DV	Amount per serving	%DV
Calories 1		**Cholesterol** 0mg	0%	**Total Carbohydrate** 0g	0%
Total Fat 0g	0%	**Sodium** 0mg	0%	Dietary Fiber 0g	0%
Saturated Fat 0g	0%	**Protein** 0g		Sugars 0g	
Polyunsaturated Fat 0g					
Monounsaturated Fat 0g		Vitamin A 1% Vitamin C 2%		Calcium 0% Iron 1%	

Turmeric, Ground

1 tbsp / 7g

Amount per serving	%DV	Amount per serving	%DV	Amount per serving	%DV
Calories 24		**Cholesterol** 0mg	0%	**Total Carbohydrate** 4g	1%
Total Fat 1g	2%	**Sodium** 3mg	0%	Dietary Fiber 1g	4%
Saturated Fat 0g	0%	**Protein** 1g		Sugars 0g	
Polyunsaturated Fat 0g					
Monounsaturated Fat 0g		Vitamin A 0%	Vitamin C 3%	Calcium 1%	Iron 16%

Potatoes

Del Monte, Diced Potatoes

1/2 cup / 122g

Amount per serving	%DV	Amount per serving	%DV	Amount per serving	%DV
Calories 60		**Cholesterol** 0mg	0%	**Total Carbohydrate** 13g	4%
Total Fat 0g	0%	**Sodium** 21mg	1%	Dietary Fiber 1g	4%
Saturated Fat 0g	0%	**Protein** 1g		Sugars 1g	
Polyunsaturated Fat 0g					
Monounsaturated Fat 0g		Vitamin A 0%	Vitamin C 10%	Calcium 2%	Iron 2%

Del Monte, Fresh Cut Sliced New Potatoes

2/3 cup / 155g

Amount per serving	%DV	Amount per serving	%DV	Amount per serving	%DV
Calories 80		**Cholesterol** 0mg	0%	**Total Carbohydrate** 13g	4%
Total Fat 0g	0%	**Sodium** 280mg	12%	Dietary Fiber 2g	8%
Saturated Fat 0g	0%	**Protein** 1g		Sugars 0g	
Polyunsaturated Fat 0g					
Monounsaturated Fat 0g		Vitamin A 0%	Vitamin C 15%	Calcium 2%	Iron 2%

Del Monte, Whole New Potatoes

2 medium potatoes / 158g

Amount per serving	%DV	Amount per serving	%DV	Amount per serving	%DV
Calories 70		**Cholesterol** 0mg	0%	**Total Carbohydrate** 15g	5%
Total Fat 0g	0%	**Sodium** 240mg	10%	Dietary Fiber 1g	4%
Saturated Fat 0g	0%	**Protein** 2g		Sugars 1g	
Polyunsaturated Fat 0g					
Monounsaturated Fat 0g		Vitamin A 0%	Vitamin C 15%	Calcium 4%	Iron 2%

Dole, Fresh Vegetables, Potatoes

1 potato / 5.3 oz / 148g

Amount per serving	%DV	Amount per serving	%DV	Amount per serving	%DV
Calories 110		**Cholesterol** 0mg	0%	**Total Carbohydrate** 26g	9%
Total Fat 0g	0%	**Sodium** 0mg	0%	Dietary Fiber 2g	8%
Saturated Fat 0g	0%	**Protein** 3g		Sugars 1g	
Polyunsaturated Fat 0g					
Monounsaturated Fat 0g		Vitamin A 0%	Vitamin C 45%	Calcium 2%	Iron 6%

Dole, Fresh Vegetables, Sweet Potatoes

200g

Amount per serving	%DV	Amount per serving	%DV	Amount per serving	%DV
Calories 180		**Cholesterol** 0mg	0%	**Total Carbohydrate** 41g	14%
Total Fat 0g	0%	**Sodium** 72mg	3%	Dietary Fiber 7g	28%
Saturated Fat 0g	0%	**Protein** 4g		Sugars 13g	
Polyunsaturated Fat 0g					
Monounsaturated Fat 0g		Vitamin A 769% Vitamin C 65%		Calcium 8% Iron 8%	

Dr. Praeger's Sensible Foods, Sweet Potato Littles

2 pieces / 37g

Amount per serving	%DV	Amount per serving	%DV	Amount per serving	%DV
Calories 60		**Cholesterol** 0mg	0%	**Total Carbohydrate** 9g	3%
Total Fat 2g	3%	**Sodium** 85mg	4%	Dietary Fiber 1g	4%
Saturated Fat 0g	0%	**Protein** 1g		Sugars 2g	
Polyunsaturated Fat 0g					
Monounsaturated Fat 0g		Vitamin A 16% Vitamin C 3%		Calcium 1% Iron 3%	

Dr. Praeger's Sensible Foods, Sweet Potato Pancakes

1 pancake / 57g

Amount per serving	%DV	Amount per serving	%DV	Amount per serving	%DV
Calories 80		**Cholesterol** 0mg	0%	**Total Carbohydrate** 12g	4%
Total Fat 2g	3%	**Sodium** 140mg	6%	Dietary Fiber 3g	12%
Saturated Fat 0g	0%	**Protein** 2g		Sugars 6g	
Polyunsaturated Fat 0g					
Monounsaturated Fat 0g		Vitamin A 25% Vitamin C 4%		Calcium 2% Iron 4%	

Edward & Sons, Organic Home Style Mashed Potatoes

1/2 cup / prepared / 25g

Amount per serving	%DV	Amount per serving	%DV	Amount per serving	%DV
Calories 150		**Cholesterol** 0mg	0%	**Total Carbohydrate** 20g	7%
Total Fat 0g	0%	**Sodium** 190mg	8%	Dietary Fiber 2g	8%
Saturated Fat 0g	0%	**Protein** 2g		Sugars 1g	
Polyunsaturated Fat 0g					
Monounsaturated Fat 0g		Vitamin A 6% Vitamin C 8%		Calcium 6% Iron 2%	

Edward & Sons, Organic Roasted Garlic Mashed Potatoes

1/2 cup / prepared / 25g

Amount per serving	%DV	Amount per serving	%DV	Amount per serving	%DV
Calories 150		**Cholesterol** 0mg	0%	**Total Carbohydrate** 20g	7%
Total Fat 0g	0%	**Sodium** 190mg	8%	Dietary Fiber 2g	8%
Saturated Fat 0g	0%	**Protein** 2g		Sugars 1g	
Polyunsaturated Fat 0g					
Monounsaturated Fat 0g		Vitamin A 6% Vitamin C 8%		Calcium 6% Iron 4%	

Farm Pak Barnes, Farming Premium Sweet Potatoes

1 medium / 114g baked, no salt

Amount per serving	%DV	Amount per serving	%DV	Amount per serving	%DV
Calories 103		**Cholesterol** 0mg	0%	**Total Carbohydrate** 24g	8%
Total Fat 0g	0%	**Sodium** 40mg	2%	Dietary Fiber 4g	16%
Saturated Fat 0g	0%	**Protein** 0g		Sugars 0g	
Polyunsaturated Fat 0g					
Monounsaturated Fat 0g		Vitamin A 438% Vitamin C 0%		Calcium 0% Iron 4%	

Ian's Natural Foods, Allergy Friendly Sweet Potato Fries

about 15 pieces / 3 oz / 85g

Amount per serving	%DV	Amount per serving	%DV	Amount per serving	%DV
Calories 180		**Cholesterol** 0mg	0%	**Total Carbohydrate** 37g	12%
Total Fat 2g	3%	**Sodium** 50mg	2%	Dietary Fiber 3g	12%
Saturated Fat 0g	0%	**Protein** 3g		Sugars 14g	
Polyunsaturated Fat 0g					
Monounsaturated Fat 0g		Vitamin A 80% Vitamin C 8%		Calcium 4% Iron 2%	

Idaho Potato

1 potato / 148g / 5.3 oz

Amount per serving	%DV	Amount per serving	%DV	Amount per serving	%DV
Calories 110		**Cholesterol** 0mg	0%	**Total Carbohydrate** 26g	9%
Total Fat 0g	0%	**Sodium** 0mg	0%	Dietary Fiber 2g	8%
Saturated Fat 0g	0%	**Protein** 2g		Sugars 1g	
Polyunsaturated Fat 0g					
Monounsaturated Fat 0g		Vitamin A 0% Vitamin C 0%		Calcium 0% Iron 6%	

Idaho Red Potato

1 medium potato

Amount per serving	%DV	Amount per serving	%DV	Amount per serving	%DV
Calories 154		**Cholesterol** 0mg	0%	**Total Carbohydrate** 34g	11%
Total Fat 0.5g	1%	**Sodium** 21mg	1%	Dietary Fiber 3g	12%
Saturated Fat 0g	0%	**Protein** 4g		Sugars 2.5g	
Polyunsaturated Fat 0g					
Monounsaturated Fat 0g		Vitamin A 0% Vitamin C 0%		Calcium 0% Iron 7%	

Idahoan, Honest Earth All Natural Creamy Mashed Potatoes

1/2 cup

Amount per serving	%DV	Amount per serving	%DV	Amount per serving	%DV
Calories 180		**Cholesterol** 0mg	0%	**Total Carbohydrate** 17g	6%
Total Fat 1g	2%	**Sodium** 270mg	11%	Dietary Fiber 2g	8%
Saturated Fat 0g	0%	**Protein** 2g		Sugars 1g	
Polyunsaturated Fat 0g					
Monounsaturated Fat 0g		Vitamin A 6% Vitamin C 8%		Calcium 4% Iron 2%	

Idahoan, Original Mashed Potatoes

1/2 cup

Amount per serving	%DV	Amount per serving	%DV	Amount per serving	%DV
Calories 180		**Cholesterol** 0mg	0%	**Total Carbohydrate** 17g	6%
Total Fat 0g	0%	**Sodium** 15mg	1%	Dietary Fiber 1g	4%
Saturated Fat 0g	0%	**Protein** 2g		Sugars 1g	
Polyunsaturated Fat 0g					
Monounsaturated Fat 0g		Vitamin A 2% Vitamin C 6%		Calcium 8% Iron 0%	

Mountain Yam, Hawaii, Cooked, Steamed, with Salt

1 cup, cubes / 145g

Amount per serving	%DV	Amount per serving	%DV	Amount per serving	%DV
Calories 119		**Cholesterol** 0mg	0%	**Total Carbohydrate** 29g	10%
Total Fat 0g	0%	**Sodium** 360mg	15%	Dietary Fiber 0g	0%
Saturated Fat 0g	0%	**Protein** 3g		Sugars 0g	
Polyunsaturated Fat 0g					
Monounsaturated Fat 0g		Vitamin A 0% Vitamin C 0%		Calcium 1% Iron 3%	

Mountain Yam, Hawaii, Cooked, Steamed, without Salt

1 cup, cubes / 145g

Amount per serving	%DV	Amount per serving	%DV	Amount per serving	%DV
Calories 119		**Cholesterol** 0mg	0%	**Total Carbohydrate** 29g	10%
Total Fat 0g	0%	**Sodium** 17mg	1%	Dietary Fiber 0g	0%
Saturated Fat 0g	0%	**Protein** 2.5g		Sugars 0g	
Polyunsaturated Fat 0g					
Monounsaturated Fat 0g		Vitamin A 0% Vitamin C 0%		Calcium 1% Iron 3%	

Mountain Yam, Hawaii, Raw

1/2 cup, cubes / 68g

Amount per serving	%DV	Amount per serving	%DV	Amount per serving	%DV
Calories 46		**Cholesterol** 0mg	0%	**Total Carbohydrate** 11g	4%
Total Fat 0g	0%	**Sodium** 9mg	0%	Dietary Fiber 0g	0%
Saturated Fat 0g	0%	**Protein** 1g		Sugars 0g	
Polyunsaturated Fat 0g					
Monounsaturated Fat 0g		Vitamin A 0% Vitamin C 3%		Calcium 2% Iron 2%	

Potato, Baked, Flesh and Skin, without Salt

1 potato, medium / 173g

Amount per serving	%DV	Amount per serving	%DV	Amount per serving	%DV
Calories 161		**Cholesterol** 0mg	0%	**Total Carbohydrate** 37g	12%
Total Fat 0g	0%	**Sodium** 17mg	1%	Dietary Fiber 4g	16%
Saturated Fat 0g	0%	**Protein** 4g		Sugars 2g	
Polyunsaturated Fat 0g					
Monounsaturated Fat 0g		Vitamin A 0% Vitamin C 28%		Calcium 3% Iron 10%	

Potatoes, Baked, Flesh and Skin, with Salt

1 cup / 61g

Amount per serving	%DV	Amount per serving	%DV	Amount per serving	%DV
Calories 57		**Cholesterol** 0mg	0%	**Total Carbohydrate** 13g	4%
Total Fat 0g	0%	**Sodium** 149mg	6%	Dietary Fiber 1g	4%
Saturated Fat 0g	0%	**Protein** 2g		Sugars 1g	
Polyunsaturated Fat 0g					
Monounsaturated Fat 0g		Vitamin A 0% Vitamin C 10%		Calcium 1% Iron 4%	

Potatoes, Baked, Flesh, with Salt

1/2 cup / 61g

Amount per serving	%DV	Amount per serving	%DV	Amount per serving	%DV
Calories 57		**Cholesterol** 0mg	0%	**Total Carbohydrate** 13g	4%
Total Fat 0g	0%	**Sodium** 147mg	6%	Dietary Fiber 1g	4%
Saturated Fat 0g	0%	**Protein** 1g		Sugars 1g	
Polyunsaturated Fat 0g					
Monounsaturated Fat 0g		Vitamin A 0% Vitamin C 13%		Calcium 0% Iron 1%	

Potatoes, Baked, Flesh, without Salt

1 potato, 2-1/3" x 4-3/4" / 156g

Amount per serving	%DV	Amount per serving	%DV	Amount per serving	%DV
Calories 145		**Cholesterol** 0mg	0%	**Total Carbohydrate** 34g	11%
Total Fat 0g	0%	**Sodium** 8mg	0%	Dietary Fiber 2g	8%
Saturated Fat 0g	0%	**Protein** 3g		Sugars 3g	
Polyunsaturated Fat 0g					
Monounsaturated Fat 0g		Vitamin A 0% Vitamin C 33%		Calcium 1% Iron 3%	

Potatoes, Baked, Skin, with Salt

1 skin / 58g

Amount per serving	%DV	Amount per serving	%DV	Amount per serving	%DV
Calories 115		**Cholesterol** 0mg	0%	**Total Carbohydrate** 27g	9%
Total Fat 0g	0%	**Sodium** 149mg	6%	Dietary Fiber 5g	20%
Saturated Fat 0g	0%	**Protein** 2g		Sugars 1g	
Polyunsaturated Fat 0g					
Monounsaturated Fat 0g		Vitamin A 0% Vitamin C 13%		Calcium 2% Iron 23%	

Potatoes, Baked, Skin, without Salt

1 skin / 58g

Amount per serving	%DV	Amount per serving	%DV	Amount per serving	%DV
Calories 115		**Cholesterol** 0mg	0%	**Total Carbohydrate** 27g	9%
Total Fat 0g	0%	**Sodium** 12mg	0%	Dietary Fiber 5g	20%
Saturated Fat 0g	0%	**Protein** 2g		Sugars 1g	
Polyunsaturated Fat 0g					
Monounsaturated Fat 0g		Vitamin A 0% Vitamin C 13%		Calcium 2% Iron 23%	

Potatoes, Boiled, Cooked in Skin, Flesh, with Salt

1/2 cup / 78g

Amount per serving	%DV	Amount per serving	%DV	Amount per serving	%DV
Calories 68		**Cholesterol** 0mg	0%	**Total Carbohydrate** 16g	5%
Total Fat 0g	0%	**Sodium** 187mg	8%	Dietary Fiber 2g	8%
Saturated Fat 0g	0%	**Protein** 1g		Sugars 1g	
Polyunsaturated Fat 0g					
Monounsaturated Fat 0g		Vitamin A 0%	Vitamin C 17%	Calcium 0%	Iron 1%

Potatoes, Boiled, Cooked in Skin, Flesh, without Salt

1 potato, 2-1/2″ diameter, sphere / 136g

Amount per serving	%DV	Amount per serving	%DV	Amount per serving	%DV
Calories 118		**Cholesterol** 0mg	0%	**Total Carbohydrate** 27g	9%
Total Fat 0g	0%	**Sodium** 5mg	0%	Dietary Fiber 2g	8%
Saturated Fat 0g	0%	**Protein** 3g		Sugars 1g	
Polyunsaturated Fat 0g					
Monounsaturated Fat 0g		Vitamin A 0%	Vitamin C 29%	Calcium 1%	Iron 2%

Potatoes, Boiled, Cooked in Skin, with Salt

1 skin / 34g

Amount per serving	%DV	Amount per serving	%DV	Amount per serving	%DV
Calories 27		**Cholesterol** 0mg	0%	**Total Carbohydrate** 6g	2%
Total Fat 0g	0%	**Sodium** 85mg	4%	Dietary Fiber 1g	4%
Saturated Fat 0g	0%	**Protein** 1g		Sugars g	
Polyunsaturated Fat 0g					
Monounsaturated Fat 0g		Vitamin A 0%	Vitamin C 3%	Calcium 2%	Iron 11%

Potatoes, Boiled, Cooked in Skin, without Salt

1 skin / 34g

Amount per serving	%DV	Amount per serving	%DV	Amount per serving	%DV
Calories 27		**Cholesterol** 0mg	0%	**Total Carbohydrate** 6g	2%
Total Fat 0g	0%	**Sodium** 5mg	0%	Dietary Fiber 1g	4%
Saturated Fat 0g	0%	**Protein** 1g		Sugars 0g	
Polyunsaturated Fat 0g					
Monounsaturated Fat 0g		Vitamin A 0%	Vitamin C 3%	Calcium 2%	Iron 11%

Potatoes, Boiled, Cooked without Skin, Flesh, with Salt

1 small (1-3/4″ to 2-1/2″ diameter) / 125g

Amount per serving	%DV	Amount per serving	%DV	Amount per serving	%DV
Calories 107		**Cholesterol** 0mg	0%	**Total Carbohydrate** 25g	8%
Total Fat 0g	0%	**Sodium** 301mg	13%	Dietary Fiber 2g	8%
Saturated Fat 0g	0%	**Protein** 2g		Sugars 1g	
Polyunsaturated Fat 0g					
Monounsaturated Fat 0g		Vitamin A 0%	Vitamin C 15%	Calcium 1%	Iron 2%

Potatoes, Boiled, Cooked without Skin, Flesh, without Salt

1 medium, 2-1/4" to 3-1/4" diameter / 167g

Amount per serving	%DV	Amount per serving	%DV	Amount per serving	%DV
Calories 144		**Cholesterol** 0mg	0%	**Total Carbohydrate** 33g	11%
Total Fat 0g	0%	**Sodium** 8mg	0%	Dietary Fiber 3g	12%
Saturated Fat 0g	0%	**Protein** 3g		Sugars 1g	
Polyunsaturated Fat 0g					
Monounsaturated Fat 0g		Vitamin A 0%	Vitamin C 21%	Calcium 1%	Iron 3%

Potatoes, Canned, Drained Solids

1 potato / 35g

Amount per serving	%DV	Amount per serving	%DV	Amount per serving	%DV
Calories 21		**Cholesterol** 0mg	0%	**Total Carbohydrate** 5g	2%
Total Fat 0g	0%	**Sodium** 77mg	3%	Dietary Fiber 1g	4%
Saturated Fat 0g	0%	**Protein** 0g		Sugars 0g	
Polyunsaturated Fat 0g					
Monounsaturated Fat 0g		Vitamin A 0%	Vitamin C 3%	Calcium 0%	Iron 2%

Potatoes, Red, Flesh and Skin, Baked

1 medium, 2-1/4" to 3-1/4" diameter /173g

Amount per serving	%DV	Amount per serving	%DV	Amount per serving	%DV
Calories 154		**Cholesterol** 0mg	0%	**Total Carbohydrate** 34g	11%
Total Fat 0g	0%	**Sodium** 21mg	1%	Dietary Fiber 3g	12%
Saturated Fat 0g	0%	**Protein** 4g		Sugars 2g	
Polyunsaturated Fat 0g					
Monounsaturated Fat 0g		Vitamin A 0%	Vitamin C 36%	Calcium 2%	Iron 7%

Potatoes, Red, Flesh and Skin, Raw

1 medium potato, 2-1/4" to 3-1/4" diameter / 213g

Amount per serving	%DV	Amount per serving	%DV	Amount per serving	%DV
Calories 149		**Cholesterol** 0mg	0%	**Total Carbohydrate** 34g	11%
Total Fat 0g	0%	**Sodium** 13mg	1%	Dietary Fiber 4g	16%
Saturated Fat 0g	0%	**Protein** 4g		Sugars 2g	
Polyunsaturated Fat 0g					
Monounsaturated Fat 0g		Vitamin A 0%	Vitamin C 31%	Calcium 2%	Iron 9%

Potatoes, Russet, Flesh and Skin, Baked

1 medium potato, 2-1/4" to 3-1/4" diameter / 173g

Amount per serving	%DV	Amount per serving	%DV	Amount per serving	%DV
Calories 168		**Cholesterol** 0mg	0%	**Total Carbohydrate** 37g	12%
Total Fat 0g	0%	**Sodium** 0mg	0%	Dietary Fiber 4g	16%
Saturated Fat 0g	0%	**Protein** 5g		Sugars 2g	
Polyunsaturated Fat 0g					
Monounsaturated Fat 0g		Vitamin A 0%	Vitamin C 37%	Calcium 3%	Iron 10%

Potatoes, Russet, Flesh and Skin, Raw

1 medium potato, 2-1/4" to 3-1/4" diameter / 213g

Amount per serving	%DV	Amount per serving	%DV	Amount per serving	%DV
Calories 134		**Cholesterol** 0mg	0%	**Total Carbohydrate** 31g	10%
Total Fat 0g	0%	**Sodium** 9mg	0%	Dietary Fiber 2g	8%
Saturated Fat 0g	0%	**Protein** 4g		Sugars 1g	
Polyunsaturated Fat 0g					
Monounsaturated Fat 0g		Vitamin A 0%	Vitamin C 16%	Calcium 2%	Iron 8%

Potatoes, White, Flesh and Skin, Baked

1 medium potato, 2-1/4" to 3-1/4" diameter / 173g

Amount per serving	%DV	Amount per serving	%DV	Amount per serving	%DV
Calories 130		**Cholesterol** 0mg	0%	**Total Carbohydrate** 30g	10%
Total Fat 0g	0%	**Sodium** 10mg	0%	Dietary Fiber 3g	12%
Saturated Fat 0g	0%	**Protein** 3g		Sugars 2g	
Polyunsaturated Fat 0g					
Monounsaturated Fat 0g		Vitamin A 0%	Vitamin C 29%	Calcium 1%	Iron 5%

Potatoes, White, Flesh and Skin, Raw

1 medium potato, 2-1/4" to 3-1/4" diameter / 213g

Amount per serving	%DV	Amount per serving	%DV	Amount per serving	%DV
Calories 147		**Cholesterol** 0mg	0%	**Total Carbohydrate** 36g	12%
Total Fat 0g	0%	**Sodium** 13mg	1%	Dietary Fiber 5g	20%
Saturated Fat 0g	0%	**Protein** 4g		Sugars 2g	
Polyunsaturated Fat 0g					
Monounsaturated Fat 0g		Vitamin A 0%	Vitamin C 70%	Calcium 2%	Iron 6%

Sweet Potato, Canned, Vacuum Pack

1 cup, pieces / 200g

Amount per serving	%DV	Amount per serving	%DV	Amount per serving	%DV
Calories 182		**Cholesterol** 0mg	0%	**Total Carbohydrate** 42g	14%
Total Fat 0g	0%	**Sodium** 106mg	4%	Dietary Fiber 4g	16%
Saturated Fat 0g	0%	**Protein** 3g		Sugars 10g	
Polyunsaturated Fat 0g					
Monounsaturated Fat 0g		Vitamin A 319%	Vitamin C 88%	Calcium 4%	Iron 10%

Sweet Potato, Cooked, Baked in Skin, with Salt

1/2 cup, mashed / 100g

Amount per serving	%DV	Amount per serving	%DV	Amount per serving	%DV
Calories 92		**Cholesterol** 0mg	0%	**Total Carbohydrate** 21g	7%
Total Fat 0g	0%	**Sodium** 246mg	10%	Dietary Fiber 3g	12%
Saturated Fat 0g	0%	**Protein** 2g		Sugars 11g	
Polyunsaturated Fat 0g					
Monounsaturated Fat 0g		Vitamin A 384%	Vitamin C 33%	Calcium 4%	Iron 4%

Sweet Potato, Cooked, Baked in Skin, without Salt

1 medium / 114g

Amount per serving	%DV	Amount per serving	%DV	Amount per serving	%DV
Calories 103		**Cholesterol** 0mg	0%	**Total Carbohydrate** 24g	8%
Total Fat 0g	0%	**Sodium** 41mg	2%	Dietary Fiber 4g	16%
Saturated Fat 0g	0%	**Protein** 2g		Sugars 7g	
Polyunsaturated Fat 0g					
Monounsaturated Fat 0g		Vitamin A 438% Vitamin C 37%		Calcium 4% Iron 4%	

Sweet Potato, Cooked, Boiled, without Skin

1 medium / 151g

Amount per serving	%DV	Amount per serving	%DV	Amount per serving	%DV
Calories 115		**Cholesterol** 0mg	0%	**Total Carbohydrate** 27g	9%
Total Fat 0g	0%	**Sodium** 41mg	2%	Dietary Fiber 4g	16%
Saturated Fat 0g	0%	**Protein** 2g		Sugars 9g	
Polyunsaturated Fat 0g					
Monounsaturated Fat 0g		Vitamin A 475% Vitamin C 32%		Calcium 4% Iron 6%	

Sweet Potato, Cooked, Boiled, without Skin, with Salt

1 cup mashed / 328g

Amount per serving	%DV	Amount per serving	%DV	Amount per serving	%DV
Calories 249		**Cholesterol** 0mg	0%	**Total Carbohydrate** 58g	19%
Total Fat 0g	0%	**Sodium** 89mg	4%	Dietary Fiber 8g	32%
Saturated Fat 0g	0%	**Protein** 4g		Sugars 19g	
Polyunsaturated Fat 0g					
Monounsaturated Fat 0g		Vitamin A 1033% Vitamin C 70%		Calcium 9% Iron 13%	

Sweet Potato, Frozen, Cooked, Baked, without Salt

1 cup, cubes / 176g

Amount per serving	%DV	Amount per serving	%DV	Amount per serving	%DV
Calories 176		**Cholesterol** 0mg	0%	**Total Carbohydrate** 41g	14%
Total Fat 0g	0%	**Sodium** 14mg	1%	Dietary Fiber 3g	12%
Saturated Fat 0g	0%	**Protein** 3g		Sugars 16g	
Polyunsaturated Fat 0g					
Monounsaturated Fat 0g		Vitamin A 735% Vitamin C 27%		Calcium 6% Iron 5%	

Sweet Potato, Raw, Unprepared

1 cup, cubes / 133g

Amount per serving	%DV	Amount per serving	%DV	Amount per serving	%DV
Calories 114		**Cholesterol** 0mg	0%	**Total Carbohydrate** 27g	9%
Total Fat 0g	0%	**Sodium** 73mg	3%	Dietary Fiber 4g	16%
Saturated Fat 0g	0%	**Protein** 2g		Sugars 6g	
Polyunsaturated Fat 0g					
Monounsaturated Fat 0g		Vitamin A 377% Vitamin C 5%		Calcium 4% Iron 5%	

Yam, Cooked, Boiled, Drained or Baked, without Salt

1 cup, cubes / 136g

Amount per serving	%DV	Amount per serving	%DV	Amount per serving	%DV
Calories 158		**Cholesterol** 0mg	0%	**Total Carbohydrate** 37g	12%
Total Fat 0g	0%	**Sodium** 11mg	0%	Dietary Fiber 5g	20%
Saturated Fat 0g	0%	**Protein** 2g		Sugars 1g	
Polyunsaturated Fat 0g					
Monounsaturated Fat 0g		Vitamin A 3%	Vitamin C 27%	Calcium 2%	Iron 4%

Yam, Cooked, Boiled, Drained, or Baked, with Salt

1/2 cup, cubes / 68g

Amount per serving	%DV	Amount per serving	%DV	Amount per serving	%DV
Calories 78		**Cholesterol** 0mg	0%	**Total Carbohydrate** 18g	6%
Total Fat 0g	0%	**Sodium** 166mg	7%	Dietary Fiber 3g	12%
Saturated Fat 0g	0%	**Protein** 1g		Sugars 0g	
Polyunsaturated Fat 0g					
Monounsaturated Fat 0g		Vitamin A 2%	Vitamin C 14%	Calcium 1%	Iron 2%

Yam, Raw

1 cup, cubes / 150g

Amount per serving	%DV	Amount per serving	%DV	Amount per serving	%DV
Calories 177		**Cholesterol** 0mg	0%	**Total Carbohydrate** 42g	14%
Total Fat 0g	0%	**Sodium** 13mg	1%	Dietary Fiber 6g	24%
Saturated Fat 0g	0%	**Protein** 2g		Sugars 1g	
Polyunsaturated Fat 0g					
Monounsaturated Fat 0g		Vitamin A 4%	Vitamin C 43%	Calcium 3%	Iron 4%

Seasonings

Simply Organic Foods, Citrus 'n Herb Seasoning

1/4 tsp / 0.6g

Amount per serving	%DV	Amount per serving	%DV	Amount per serving	%DV
Calories 5		**Cholesterol** 0mg	0%	**Total Carbohydrate** 0g	0%
Total Fat 0g	0%	**Sodium** 0mg	0%	Dietary Fiber 0g	0%
Saturated Fat 0g	0%	**Protein** 0g		Sugars 0g	
Polyunsaturated Fat 0g					
Monounsaturated Fat 0g		Vitamin A 0%	Vitamin C 2%	Calcium 0%	Iron 0%

Simply Organic Foods, Orange Ginger Seasoning

1/4 tsp / 0.9g

Amount per serving	%DV	Amount per serving	%DV	Amount per serving	%DV
Calories 5		**Cholesterol** 0mg	0%	**Total Carbohydrate** 1g	0%
Total Fat 0g	0%	**Sodium** 60mg	3%	Dietary Fiber 0g	0%
Saturated Fat 0g	0%	**Protein** 0g		Sugars 0g	
Polyunsaturated Fat 0g					
Monounsaturated Fat 0g		Vitamin A 0%	Vitamin C 0%	Calcium 0%	Iron 0%

Simply Organic Foods, Red Bean Seasoning Mix

2 tsp / 4.5g

Amount per serving	%DV	Amount per serving	%DV	Amount per serving	%DV
Calories 15		**Cholesterol** 0mg	0%	**Total Carbohydrate** 3g	1%
Total Fat 0g	0%	**Sodium** 250mg	10%	Dietary Fiber 1g	4%
Saturated Fat 0g	0%	**Protein** 0g		Sugars 0g	
Polyunsaturated Fat 0g					
Monounsaturated Fat 0g		Vitamin A 6%	Vitamin C 2%	Calcium 0%	Iron 2%

Simply Organic Foods, Salsa Verde Seasoning

1/2 tsp / 1.7g

Amount per serving	%DV	Amount per serving	%DV	Amount per serving	%DV
Calories 5		**Cholesterol** 0mg	0%	**Total Carbohydrate** 1g	0%
Total Fat 0g	0%	**Sodium** 80mg	3%	Dietary Fiber 0g	0%
Saturated Fat 0g	0%	**Protein** 0g		Sugars 0g	
Polyunsaturated Fat 0g					
Monounsaturated Fat 0g		Vitamin A 0%	Vitamin C 0%	Calcium 2%	Iron 0%

Simply Organic Foods, Seafood Seasoning

1/4 tsp / 0.6g

Amount per serving	%DV	Amount per serving	%DV	Amount per serving	%DV
Calories 0		**Cholesterol** 0mg	0%	**Total Carbohydrate** 0g	0%
Total Fat 0g	0%	**Sodium** 40mg	2%	Dietary Fiber 0g	0%
Saturated Fat 0g	0%	**Protein** 0g		Sugars 0g	
Polyunsaturated Fat 0g					
Monounsaturated Fat 0g		Vitamin A 0%	Vitamin C 0%	Calcium 0%	Iron 0%

Simply Organic Foods, Spicy Steak Seasoning

1/4 tsp / 0.7g

Amount per serving	%DV	Amount per serving	%DV	Amount per serving	%DV
Calories 0		**Cholesterol** 0mg	0%	**Total Carbohydrate** 0g	0%
Total Fat 0g	0%	**Sodium** 35mg	1%	Dietary Fiber 0g	0%
Saturated Fat 0g	0%	**Protein** 0g		Sugars 0g	
Polyunsaturated Fat 0g					
Monounsaturated Fat 0g		Vitamin A 0%	Vitamin C 0%	Calcium 0%	Iron 0%

Simply Organic Foods, Steak Seasoning

1/4 tsp / 0.8g

Amount per serving	%DV	Amount per serving	%DV	Amount per serving	%DV
Calories 0		**Cholesterol** 0mg	0%	**Total Carbohydrate** 0g	0%
Total Fat 0g	0%	**Sodium** 85mg	4%	Dietary Fiber 0g	0%
Saturated Fat 0g	0%	**Protein** 0g		Sugars 0g	
Polyunsaturated Fat 0g					
Monounsaturated Fat 0g		Vitamin A 0%	Vitamin C 0%	Calcium 0%	Iron 0%

Simply Organic Foods, Vegetable Seasoning

1/4 tsp / 0.7g

Amount per serving	%DV	Amount per serving	%DV	Amount per serving	%DV
Calories 0		**Cholesterol** 0mg	0%	**Total Carbohydrate** 0g	0%
Total Fat 0g	0%	**Sodium** 40mg	2%	Dietary Fiber 0g	0%
Saturated Fat 0g	0%	**Protein** 0g		Sugars 0g	
Polyunsaturated Fat 0g					
Monounsaturated Fat 0g		Vitamin A 0% Vitamin C 2%		Calcium 0% Iron 0%	

Vegetables

Artichokes (Globe or French), Cooked, Boiled, Drained, with Salt

1 artichoke, medium / 120g

Amount per serving	%DV	Amount per serving	%DV	Amount per serving	%DV
Calories 64		**Cholesterol** 0mg	0%	**Total Carbohydrate** 10g	3%
Total Fat 0.4g	1%	**Sodium** 72mg	3%	Dietary Fiber 10.3g	41%
Saturated Fat 0.1g	0%	**Protein** 3.5g		Sugars 1.2g	
Polyunsaturated Fat 0.2g					
Monounsaturated Fat 0g		Vitamin A 0% Vitamin C 15%		Calcium 3% Iron 4%	

Artichokes (Globe or French), Cooked, Boiled, Drained, without Salt

1 artichoke, medium / 120g

Amount per serving	%DV	Amount per serving	%DV	Amount per serving	%DV
Calories 64		**Cholesterol** 0mg	0%	**Total Carbohydrate** 14.3g	5%
Total Fat 0.4g	1%	**Sodium** 72mg	3%	Dietary Fiber 10.3g	41%
Saturated Fat 0.1g	0%	**Protein** 3.5g		Sugars 1.2g	
Polyunsaturated Fat 0.2g					
Monounsaturated Fat 0g		Vitamin A 0% Vitamin C 15%		Calcium 3% Iron 4%	

Artichokes (Globe or French), Raw

1 artichoke, large / 162g

Amount per serving	%DV	Amount per serving	%DV	Amount per serving	%DV
Calories 76		**Cholesterol** 0mg	0%	**Total Carbohydrate** 17g	6%
Total Fat 0.2g	0%	**Sodium** 152mg	6%	Dietary Fiber 8.7g	35%
Saturated Fat 0.1g	0%	**Protein** 5.3g		Sugars 1.6g	
Polyunsaturated Fat 0.1g					
Monounsaturated Fat 0g		Vitamin A 0% Vitamin C 32%		Calcium 7% Iron 12%	

Arugula, Raw

1/2 cup / 10g

Amount per serving	%DV	Amount per serving	%DV	Amount per serving	%DV
Calories 3		**Cholesterol** 0mg	0%	**Total Carbohydrate** 0.4g	0%
Total Fat 0.1g	0%	**Sodium** 3mg	0%	Dietary Fiber 0.2g	1%
Saturated Fat 0g	0%	**Protein** 0.3g		Sugars 0.2g	
Polyunsaturated Fat 0g					
Monounsaturated Fat 0g		Vitamin A 5% Vitamin C 3%		Calcium 2% Iron 1%	

Asparagus, Cooked, Boiled, Drained, with Salt

4 spears, 1/2″ base / 60g

Amount per serving	%DV	Amount per serving	%DV	Amount per serving	%DV
Calories 13		**Cholesterol** 0mg	0%	**Total Carbohydrate** 2g	1%
Total Fat 0g	0%	**Sodium** 144mg	6%	Dietary Fiber 1g	4%
Saturated Fat 0g	0%	**Protein** 1g		Sugars 1g	
Polyunsaturated Fat 0g					
Monounsaturated Fat 0g		Vitamin A 12% Vitamin C 8%		Calcium 1% Iron 3%	

Asparagus, Frozen, Cooked, Boiled, Drained, without Salt

1 package, 10 oz yields / 293g

Amount per serving	%DV	Amount per serving	%DV	Amount per serving	%DV
Calories 53		**Cholesterol** 0mg	0%	**Total Carbohydrate** 6g	2%
Total Fat 1g	2%	**Sodium** 9mg	0%	Dietary Fiber 5g	20%
Saturated Fat 0g	0%	**Protein** 9g		Sugars 1g	
Polyunsaturated Fat 0g					
Monounsaturated Fat 0g		Vitamin A 47% Vitamin C 119%		Calcium 5% Iron 9%	

Asparagus, Frozen, Unprepared

4 spears / 58g

Amount per serving	%DV	Amount per serving	%DV	Amount per serving	%DV
Calories 14		**Cholesterol** 0mg	0%	**Total Carbohydrate** 2g	1%
Total Fat 0g	0%	**Sodium** 5mg	0%	Dietary Fiber 1g	4%
Saturated Fat 0g	0%	**Protein** 2g		Sugars 0g	
Polyunsaturated Fat 0g					
Monounsaturated Fat 0g		Vitamin A 11% Vitamin C 31%		Calcium 1% Iron 2%	

Asparagus, Raw

1 spear, small, 5″ long or less / 12g

Amount per serving	%DV	Amount per serving	%DV	Amount per serving	%DV
Calories 2		**Cholesterol** 0mg	0%	**Total Carbohydrate** 0g	0%
Total Fat 0g	0%	**Sodium** 0mg	0%	Dietary Fiber 0g	0%
Saturated Fat 0g	0%	**Protein** 0g		Sugars 0g	
Polyunsaturated Fat 0g					
Monounsaturated Fat 0g		Vitamin A 2% Vitamin C 1%		Calcium 0% Iron 1%	

Beans, Snap, Green, Canned, No Salt Added, Drained Solids

1 cup / 135g

Amount per serving	%DV	Amount per serving	%DV	Amount per serving	%DV
Calories 27		**Cholesterol** 0mg	0%	**Total Carbohydrate** 6g	2%
Total Fat 0g	0%	**Sodium** 3mg	0%	Dietary Fiber 3g	12%
Saturated Fat 0g	0%	**Protein** 2g		Sugars 1g	
Polyunsaturated Fat 0g					
Monounsaturated Fat 0g		Vitamin A 10% Vitamin C 11%		Calcium 4% Iron 7%	

Beans, Snap, Green, Frozen, All Styles, Unprepared

1 cup / 121g

Amount per serving	%DV	Amount per serving	%DV	Amount per serving	%DV
Calories 47		**Cholesterol** 0mg	0%	**Total Carbohydrate** 9g	3%
Total Fat 0g	0%	**Sodium** 4mg	0%	Dietary Fiber 3g	12%
Saturated Fat 0g	0%	**Protein** 2g		Sugars 3g	
Polyunsaturated Fat 0g					
Monounsaturated Fat 0g		Vitamin A 13% Vitamin C 26%		Calcium 5% Iron 6%	

Beans, Snap, Green, Frozen, Cooked, Boiled, Drained, without Salt

1 cup / 135g

Amount per serving	%DV	Amount per serving	%DV	Amount per serving	%DV
Calories 38		**Cholesterol** 0mg	0%	**Total Carbohydrate** 9g	3%
Total Fat 0g	0%	**Sodium** 1mg	0%	Dietary Fiber 4g	16%
Saturated Fat 0g	0%	**Protein** 2g		Sugars 2g	
Polyunsaturated Fat 0g					
Monounsaturated Fat 0g		Vitamin A 15% Vitamin C 9%		Calcium 6% Iron 5%	

Beans, Snap, Green, Raw

1 cup / 110g

Amount per serving	%DV	Amount per serving	%DV	Amount per serving	%DV
Calories 34		**Cholesterol** 0mg	0%	**Total Carbohydrate** 8g	3%
Total Fat 0g	0%	**Sodium** 7mg	0%	Dietary Fiber 4g	16%
Saturated Fat 0g	0%	**Protein** 2g		Sugars 2g	
Polyunsaturated Fat 0g					
Monounsaturated Fat 0g		Vitamin A 15% Vitamin C 30%		Calcium 4% Iron 6%	

Beans, Snap, Yellow, Canned, No Salt Added, Drained Solids

1/2 cup / 68g

Amount per serving	%DV	Amount per serving	%DV	Amount per serving	%DV
Calories 14		**Cholesterol** 0mg	0%	**Total Carbohydrate** 3g	1%
Total Fat 0g	0%	**Sodium** 1mg	0%	Dietary Fiber 1g	4%
Saturated Fat 0g	0%	**Protein** 1g		Sugars 1g	
Polyunsaturated Fat 0g					
Monounsaturated Fat 0g		Vitamin A 1% Vitamin C 5%		Calcium 2% Iron 3%	

Beans, Snap, Yellow, Cooked, Boiled, Drained, without Salt

1 cup / 125g

Amount per serving	%DV	Amount per serving	%DV	Amount per serving	%DV
Calories 44		**Cholesterol** 0mg	0%	**Total Carbohydrate** 10g	3%
Total Fat 0g	0%	**Sodium** 4mg	0%	Dietary Fiber 4g	16%
Saturated Fat 0g	0%	**Protein** 2g		Sugars 2g	
Polyunsaturated Fat 0g					
Monounsaturated Fat 0g		Vitamin A 2% Vitamin C 20%		Calcium 6% Iron 9%	

Beans, Snap, Yellow, Frozen, All Styles, Unprepared

1 cup / 124g

Amount per serving	%DV	Amount per serving	%DV	Amount per serving	%DV
Calories 41		**Cholesterol** 0mg	0%	**Total Carbohydrate** 9g	3%
Total Fat 0g	0%	**Sodium** 4mg	0%	Dietary Fiber 3g	12%
Saturated Fat 0g	0%	**Protein** 2g		Sugars 0g	
Polyunsaturated Fat 0g					
Monounsaturated Fat 0g		Vitamin A 3%	Vitamin C 27%	Calcium 5%	Iron 6%

Beans, Snap, Yellow, Raw

1 cup / 110g

Amount per serving	%DV	Amount per serving	%DV	Amount per serving	%DV
Calories 34		**Cholesterol** 0mg	0%	**Total Carbohydrate** 8g	3%
Total Fat 0g	0%	**Sodium** 7mg	0%	Dietary Fiber 4g	16%
Saturated Fat 0g	0%	**Protein** 2g		Sugars 0g	
Polyunsaturated Fat 0g					
Monounsaturated Fat 0g		Vitamin A 2%	Vitamin C 30%	Calcium 4%	Iron 6%

Beet Greens, Cooked, Boiled, Drained, without Salt

1/2 cup, 1″ pieces / 72g

Amount per serving	%DV	Amount per serving	%DV	Amount per serving	%DV
Calories 19		**Cholesterol** 0mg	0%	**Total Carbohydrate** 4g	1%
Total Fat 0g	0%	**Sodium** 174mg	7%	Dietary Fiber 2g	8%
Saturated Fat 0g	0%	**Protein** 2g		Sugars 0g	
Polyunsaturated Fat 0g					
Monounsaturated Fat 0g		Vitamin A 110%	Vitamin C 30%	Calcium 8%	Iron 8%

Beet Greens, Raw

1 cup / 38g

Amount per serving	%DV	Amount per serving	%DV	Amount per serving	%DV
Calories 8		**Cholesterol** 0mg	0%	**Total Carbohydrate** 2g	1%
Total Fat 0g	0%	**Sodium** 86mg	4%	Dietary Fiber 1g	4%
Saturated Fat 0g	0%	**Protein** 1g		Sugars 0g	
Polyunsaturated Fat 0g					
Monounsaturated Fat 0g		Vitamin A 48%	Vitamin C 19%	Calcium 4%	Iron 5%

Beets, Canned, Drained Solids

1 cup, diced / 157g

Amount per serving	%DV	Amount per serving	%DV	Amount per serving	%DV
Calories 49		**Cholesterol** 0mg	0%	**Total Carbohydrate** 11g	4%
Total Fat 0g	0%	**Sodium** 305mg	13%	Dietary Fiber 3g	12%
Saturated Fat 0g	0%	**Protein** 1g		Sugars 9g	
Polyunsaturated Fat 0g					
Monounsaturated Fat 0g		Vitamin A 1%	Vitamin C 11%	Calcium 2%	Iron 16%

Beets, Cooked, Boiled, Drained

1/2 cup slices / 85g

Amount per serving	%DV	Amount per serving	%DV	Amount per serving	%DV
Calories 37		**Cholesterol** 0mg	0%	**Total Carbohydrate** 8g	3%
Total Fat 0g	0%	**Sodium** 65mg	3%	Dietary Fiber 2g	8%
Saturated Fat 0g	0%	**Protein** 1g		Sugars 7g	
Polyunsaturated Fat 0g					
Monounsaturated Fat 0g		Vitamin A 1% Vitamin C 5%		Calcium 1% Iron 4%	

Beets, Cooked, Boiled, Drained, with Salt

1/2 cup slices / 85g

Amount per serving	%DV	Amount per serving	%DV	Amount per serving	%DV
Calories 37		**Cholesterol** 0mg	0%	**Total Carbohydrate** 8g	3%
Total Fat 0g	0%	**Sodium** 242mg	10%	Dietary Fiber 2g	8%
Saturated Fat 0g	0%	**Protein** 1g		Sugars 7g	
Polyunsaturated Fat 0g					
Monounsaturated Fat 0g		Vitamin A 1% Vitamin C 5%		Calcium 1% Iron 4%	

Beets, Raw

1 cup / 136g

Amount per serving	%DV	Amount per serving	%DV	Amount per serving	%DV
Calories 58		**Cholesterol** 0mg	0%	**Total Carbohydrate** 13g	4%
Total Fat 0g	0%	**Sodium** 106mg	4%	Dietary Fiber 4g	16%
Saturated Fat 0g	0%	**Protein** 2g		Sugars 9g	
Polyunsaturated Fat 0g					
Monounsaturated Fat 0g		Vitamin A 1% Vitamin C 11%		Calcium 2% Iron 6%	

Broadbeans, Immature Seeds, Raw

1 cup / 109g

Amount per serving	%DV	Amount per serving	%DV	Amount per serving	%DV
Calories 78		**Cholesterol** 0mg	0%	**Total Carbohydrate** 13g	4%
Total Fat 1g	2%	**Sodium** 54mg	2%	Dietary Fiber 5g	20%
Saturated Fat 0g	0%	**Protein** 6g		Sugars 0g	
Polyunsaturated Fat 0g					
Monounsaturated Fat 0g		Vitamin A 8% Vitamin C 60%		Calcium 2% Iron 12%	

Broccoli, Cooked, Boiled, Drained, with Salt

1/2 cup, chopped / 78g

Amount per serving	%DV	Amount per serving	%DV	Amount per serving	%DV
Calories 27		**Cholesterol** 0mg	0%	**Total Carbohydrate** 6g	2%
Total Fat 0g	0%	**Sodium** 204mg	8%	Dietary Fiber 3g	12%
Saturated Fat 0g	0%	**Protein** 2g		Sugars 1g	
Polyunsaturated Fat 0.5g					
Monounsaturated Fat 0g		Vitamin A 24% Vitamin C 84%		Calcium 3% Iron 3%	

Broccoli, Cooked, Boiled, Drained, without Salt

1 medium stalk, 7-1/2″ - 8″ long / 180g

Amount per serving	%DV	Amount per serving	%DV	Amount per serving	%DV
Calories 63		**Cholesterol** 0mg	0%	**Total Carbohydrate** 13g	4%
Total Fat 1g	2%	**Sodium** 74mg	3%	Dietary Fiber 6g	24%
Saturated Fat 0g	0%	**Protein** 4g		Sugars 3g	
Polyunsaturated Fat 0g					
Monounsaturated Fat 0g		Vitamin A 56% Vitamin C 195% Calcium 7% Iron 7%			

Broccoli, Frozen, Spears, Cooked, Boiled, Drained, with Salt

1/2 cup / 92g

Amount per serving	%DV	Amount per serving	%DV	Amount per serving	%DV
Calories 26		**Cholesterol** 0mg	0%	**Total Carbohydrate** 5g	2%
Total Fat 0g	0%	**Sodium** 239mg	10%	Dietary Fiber 3g	12%
Saturated Fat 0g	0%	**Protein** 3g		Sugars 1g	
Polyunsaturated Fat 0g					
Monounsaturated Fat 0g		Vitamin A 21% Vitamin C 61% Calcium 5% Iron 3%			

Broccoli, Frozen, Spears, Cooked, Boiled, Drained, without Salt

1 package, 10 oz yields / 250g

Amount per serving	%DV	Amount per serving	%DV	Amount per serving	%DV
Calories 70		**Cholesterol** 0mg	0%	**Total Carbohydrate** 13g	4%
Total Fat 0g	0%	**Sodium** 60mg	2%	Dietary Fiber 8g	32%
Saturated Fat 0g	0%	**Protein** 8g		Sugars 4g	
Polyunoaturated Fat 0g					
Monounsaturated Fat 0g		Vitamin A 51% Vitamin C 167% Calcium 13% Iron 8%			

Broccoli, Frozen, Spears, Unprepared

1 package, 10 oz / 284g

Amount per serving	%DV	Amount per serving	%DV	Amount per serving	%DV
Calories 82		**Cholesterol** 0mg	0%	**Total Carbohydrate** 15g	5%
Total Fat 1g	2%	**Sodium** 48mg	2%	Dietary Fiber 9g	36%
Saturated Fat 0g	0%	**Protein** 9g		Sugars 4g	
Polyunsaturated Fat 0g					
Monounsaturated Fat 0g		Vitamin A 65% Vitamin C 323% Calcium 12% Iron 11%			

Broccoli, Raw

1 cup chopped / 91g

Amount per serving	%DV	Amount per serving	%DV	Amount per serving	%DV
Calories 31		**Cholesterol** 0mg	0%	**Total Carbohydrate** 6g	2%
Total Fat 0g	0%	**Sodium** 30mg	1%	Dietary Fiber 2g	8%
Saturated Fat 0g	0%	**Protein** 3g		Sugars 2g	
Polyunsaturated Fat 0g					
Monounsaturated Fat 0g		Vitamin A 11% Vitamin C 135% Calcium 4% Iron 4%			

Broccoli, Stalks, Raw

1 stalk / 114g

Amount per serving	%DV	Amount per serving	%DV	Amount per serving	%DV
Calories 32		**Cholesterol** 0mg	0%	**Total Carbohydrate** 6g	2%
Total Fat 0g	0%	**Sodium** 31mg	1%	Dietary Fiber g	%
Saturated Fat 0g	0%	**Protein** 3g		Sugars g	
Polyunsaturated Fat 0g					
Monounsaturated Fat 0g		Vitamin A 9%	Vitamin C 177%	Calcium 5%	Iron 6%

Brussels Sprouts, Cooked, Boiled, Drained, with Salt

1/2 cup / 78g

Amount per serving	%DV	Amount per serving	%DV	Amount per serving	%DV
Calories 28		**Cholesterol** 0mg	0%	**Total Carbohydrate** 6g	2%
Total Fat 0g	0%	**Sodium** 200mg	8%	Dietary Fiber 2g	8%
Saturated Fat 0g	0%	**Protein** 2g		Sugars 1g	
Polyunsaturated Fat 0g					
Monounsaturated Fat 0g		Vitamin A 12%	Vitamin C 81%	Calcium 3%	Iron 5%

Brussels Sprouts, Cooked, Boiled, Drained, without Salt

1/2 cup / 78g

Amount per serving	%DV	Amount per serving	%DV	Amount per serving	%DV
Calories 28		**Cholesterol** 0mg	0%	**Total Carbohydrate** 6g	2%
Total Fat 0g	0%	**Sodium** 16mg	1%	Dietary Fiber 2g	8%
Saturated Fat 0g	0%	**Protein** 2g		Sugars 1g	
Polyunsaturated Fat 0g					
Monounsaturated Fat 0g		Vitamin A 12%	Vitamin C 81%	Calcium 3%	Iron 5%

Brussels Sprouts, Frozen, Cooked, Boiled, Drained, without Salt

1 cup / 155g

Amount per serving	%DV	Amount per serving	%DV	Amount per serving	%DV
Calories 65		**Cholesterol** 0mg	0%	**Total Carbohydrate** 13g	4%
Total Fat 1g	2%	**Sodium** 23mg	1%	Dietary Fiber 6g	24%
Saturated Fat 0g	0%	**Protein** 6g		Sugars 3g	
Polyunsaturated Fat 0g					
Monounsaturated Fat 0g		Vitamin A 29%	Vitamin C 118%	Calcium 4%	Iron 4%

Brussels Sprouts, Frozen, Unprepared

1 package, 10 oz / 284g

Amount per serving	%DV	Amount per serving	%DV	Amount per serving	%DV
Calories 116		**Cholesterol** 0mg	0%	**Total Carbohydrate** 22g	7%
Total Fat 1g	2%	**Sodium** 28mg	1%	Dietary Fiber 11g	44%
Saturated Fat 0g	0%	**Protein** 11g		Sugars 0g	
Polyunsaturated Fat 0g					
Monounsaturated Fat 0g		Vitamin A 35%	Vitamin C 351%	Calcium 7%	Iron 15%

Brussels Sprouts, Raw

1 cup / 88g

Amount per serving	%DV	Amount per serving	%DV	Amount per serving	%DV
Calories 38		**Cholesterol** 0mg	0%	**Total Carbohydrate** 8g	3%
Total Fat 0g	0%	**Sodium** 22mg	1%	Dietary Fiber 3g	12%
Saturated Fat 0g	0%	**Protein** 3g		Sugars 2g	
Polyunsaturated Fat 0g					
Monounsaturated Fat 0g		Vitamin A 13%	Vitamin C 125%	Calcium 4%	Iron 7%

Cabbage, Common, Cooked, Boiled, Drained, with Salt

1/2 cup, shredded / 75g

Amount per serving	%DV	Amount per serving	%DV	Amount per serving	%DV
Calories 17		**Cholesterol** 0mg	0%	**Total Carbohydrate** 4g	1%
Total Fat 0g	0%	**Sodium** 191mg	8%	Dietary Fiber 1g	4%
Saturated Fat 0g	0%	**Protein** 1g		Sugars 2g	
Polyunsaturated Fat 0g					
Monounsaturated Fat 0g		Vitamin A 1%	Vitamin C 47%	Calcium 4%	Iron 1%

Cabbage, Common (Danish, Domestic, and Pointed Types), Stored, Raw

1/2 cup, shredded / 35g

Amount per serving	%DV	Amount per serving	%DV	Amount per serving	%DV
Calories 8		**Cholesterol** 0mg	0%	**Total Carbohydrate** 1.9g	1%
Total Fat 0g	0%	**Sodium** 6mg	0%	Dietary Fiber 8g	32%
Saturated Fat 0g	0%	**Protein** 0g		Sugars 0g	
Polyunsaturated Fat 0g					
Monounsaturated Fat 0g		Vitamin A 1%	Vitamin C 25%	Calcium 2%	Iron 1%

Cabbage, Cooked, Boiled, Drained, without Salt

1/2 cup, shredded / 75g

Amount per serving	%DV	Amount per serving	%DV	Amount per serving	%DV
Calories 17		**Cholesterol** 0mg	0%	**Total Carbohydrate** 4g	1%
Total Fat 0g	0%	**Sodium** 6mg	0%	Dietary Fiber 1g	4%
Saturated Fat 0g	0%	**Protein** 1g		Sugars 2g	
Polyunsaturated Fat 0g					
Monounsaturated Fat 0g		Vitamin A 1%	Vitamin C 47%	Calcium 4%	Iron 1%

Cabbage, Raw

1 cup, chopped / 89g

Amount per serving	%DV	Amount per serving	%DV	Amount per serving	%DV
Calories 22		**Cholesterol** 0mg	0%	**Total Carbohydrate** 5g	2%
Total Fat 0g	0%	**Sodium** 16mg	1%	Dietary Fiber 2g	8%
Saturated Fat 0g	0%	**Protein** 1g		Sugars 3g	
Polyunsaturated Fat 0g					
Monounsaturated Fat 0g		Vitamin A 2%	Vitamin C 54%	Calcium 4%	Iron 2%

Cabbage, Red, Cooked, Boiled, Drained, with Salt

1/2 cup, shredded / 75g

Amount per serving	%DV	Amount per serving	%DV	Amount per serving	%DV
Calories 22		**Cholesterol** 0mg	0%	**Total Carbohydrate** 5g	2%
Total Fat 0g	0%	**Sodium** 183mg	8%	Dietary Fiber 2g	8%
Saturated Fat 0g	0%	**Protein** 1g		Sugars 2g	
Polyunsaturated Fat 0g					
Monounsaturated Fat 0g		Vitamin A 0%	Vitamin C 14%	Calcium 3%	Iron 3%

Cabbage, Red, Cooked, Boiled, Drained, without Salt

1/2 cup, shredded / 75g

Amount per serving	%DV	Amount per serving	%DV	Amount per serving	%DV
Calories 22		**Cholesterol** 0mg	0%	**Total Carbohydrate** 5g	2%
Total Fat 0g	0%	**Sodium** 21mg	1%	Dietary Fiber 2g	8%
Saturated Fat 0g	0%	**Protein** 1g		Sugars 2g	
Polyunsaturated Fat 0g					
Monounsaturated Fat 0g		Vitamin A 0%	Vitamin C 43%	Calcium 3%	Iron 3%

Cabbage, Red, Raw

1 cup, chopped / 89g

Amount per serving	%DV	Amount per serving	%DV	Amount per serving	%DV
Calories 28		**Cholesterol** 0mg	0%	**Total Carbohydrate** 7g	2%
Total Fat 0g	0%	**Sodium** 24mg	1%	Dietary Fiber 2g	8%
Saturated Fat 0g	0%	**Protein** 1g		Sugars 3g	
Polyunsaturated Fat 0g					
Monounsaturated Fat 0g		Vitamin A 20%	Vitamin C 85%	Calcium 4%	Iron 4%

Carrots, Baby, Raw

1 oz / 28g

Amount per serving	%DV	Amount per serving	%DV	Amount per serving	%DV
Calories 10		**Cholesterol** 0mg	0%	**Total Carbohydrate** 2g	1%
Total Fat 0g	0%	**Sodium** 22mg	1%	Dietary Fiber 1g	4%
Saturated Fat 0g	0%	**Protein** 0g		Sugars 1g	
Polyunsaturated Fat 0g					
Monounsaturated Fat 0g		Vitamin A 77%	Vitamin C 1%	Calcium 1%	Iron 1%

Carrots, Canned, No Salt Added, Drained Solids

1 cup, sliced / 146g

Amount per serving	%DV	Amount per serving	%DV	Amount per serving	%DV
Calories 36		**Cholesterol** 0mg	0%	**Total Carbohydrate** 8g	3%
Total Fat 0g	0%	**Sodium** 61mg	3%	Dietary Fiber 2g	8%
Saturated Fat 0g	0%	**Protein** 1g		Sugars 4g	
Polyunsaturated Fat 0g					
Monounsaturated Fat 0g		Vitamin A 326%	Vitamin C 7%	Calcium 4%	Iron 5%

Carrots, Canned, No Salt Added, Solids and Liquids

1/2 cup slices / 123g

Amount per serving	%DV	Amount per serving	%DV	Amount per serving	%DV
Calories 28		**Cholesterol** 0mg	0%	**Total Carbohydrate** 7g	2%
Total Fat 0g	0%	**Sodium** 42mg	2%	Dietary Fiber 2g	8%
Saturated Fat 0g	0%	**Protein** 1g		Sugars 3g	
Polyunsaturated Fat 0g					
Monounsaturated Fat 0g		Vitamin A 275% Vitamin C 4%		Calcium 4% Iron 4%	

Carrots, Canned, No Salt, Drained Solid

1 cup, sliced / 146g

Amount per serving	%DV	Amount per serving	%DV	Amount per serving	%DV
Calories 37		**Cholesterol** 0mg	0%	**Total Carbohydrate** 8.1g	3%
Total Fat 0.3g	0%	**Sodium** 61mg	3%	Dietary Fiber 2.2g	9%
Saturated Fat 0.1g	1%	**Protein** 0.9g		Sugars 3.6g	
Polyunsaturated Fat 0.1g					
Monounsaturated Fat 0g		Vitamin A 326% Vitamin C 7%		Calcium 4% Iron 5%	

Carrots, Canned, No Salt, Solids and Liquids

1 cup, slices

Amount per serving	%DV	Amount per serving	%DV	Amount per serving	%DV
Calories 28		**Cholesterol** 0mg	0%	**Total Carbohydrate** 6.6g	2%
Total Fat 0.2g	0%	**Sodium** 42mg	2%	Dietary Fiber 2.2g	9%
Saturated Fat 0g	0%	**Protein** 0.7g		Sugars 3g	
Polyunsaturated Fat 0.1g					
Monounsaturated Fat 0g		Vitamin A 275% Vitamin C 4%		Calcium 4% Iron 4%	

Carrots, Canned, Regular Pack, Drained Solids

1 oz / 28g

Amount per serving	%DV	Amount per serving	%DV	Amount per serving	%DV
Calories 7		**Cholesterol** 0mg	0%	**Total Carbohydrate** 2g	1%
Total Fat 0g	0%	**Sodium** 68mg	3%	Dietary Fiber 0g	0%
Saturated Fat 0g	0%	**Protein** 0g		Sugars 1g	
Polyunsaturated Fat 0g					
Monounsaturated Fat 0g		Vitamin A 63% Vitamin C 1%		Calcium 1% Iron 1%	

Carrots, Cooked, Boiled, Drained, with Salt

1 carrot / 46g

Amount per serving	%DV	Amount per serving	%DV	Amount per serving	%DV
Calories 16		**Cholesterol** 0mg	0%	**Total Carbohydrate** 4g	1%
Total Fat 0g	0%	**Sodium** 139mg	6%	Dietary Fiber 1g	4%
Saturated Fat 0g	0%	**Protein** 0g		Sugars 2g	
Polyunsaturated Fat 0g					
Monounsaturated Fat 0g		Vitamin A 157% Vitamin C 3%		Calcium 1% Iron 1%	

Carrots, Cooked, Boiled, Drained, without Salt

1/2 cup slices / 78g

Amount per serving	%DV	Amount per serving	%DV	Amount per serving	%DV
Calories 27		**Cholesterol** 0mg	0%	**Total Carbohydrate** 6g	2%
Total Fat 0g	0%	**Sodium** 45mg	2%	Dietary Fiber 2g	8%
Saturated Fat 0g	0%	**Protein** 1g		Sugars 3g	
Polyunsaturated Fat 0g					
Monounsaturated Fat 0g		Vitamin A 266% Vitamin C 5%		Calcium 2% Iron 1%	

Carrots, Frozen, Cooked, Boiled, Drained, without Salt

1 cup, sliced / 146g

Amount per serving	%DV	Amount per serving	%DV	Amount per serving	%DV
Calories 54		**Cholesterol** 0mg	0%	**Total Carbohydrate** 11g	4%
Total Fat 1g	2%	**Sodium** 86mg	4%	Dietary Fiber 5g	20%
Saturated Fat 0g	0%	**Protein** 1g		Sugars 6g	
Polyunsaturated Fat 0g					
Monounsaturated Fat 0g		Vitamin A 494% Vitamin C 6%		Calcium 4% Iron 5%	

Carrots, Frozen, Unprepared

1 package, 10 oz / 284g

Amount per serving	%DV	Amount per serving	%DV	Amount per serving	%DV
Calories 102		**Cholesterol** 0mg	0%	**Total Carbohydrate** 24g	8%
Total Fat 1g	2%	**Sodium** 193mg	8%	Dietary Fiber 9g	36%
Saturated Fat 0g	0%	**Protein** 2g		Sugars 14g	
Polyunsaturated Fat 0g					
Monounsaturated Fat 0g		Vitamin A 807% Vitamin C 12%		Calcium 10% Iron 7%	

Carrots, Raw

1 cup, grated / 110g

Amount per serving	%DV	Amount per serving	%DV	Amount per serving	%DV
Calories 45		**Cholesterol** 0mg	0%	**Total Carbohydrate** 11g	4%
Total Fat 0.5g	1%	**Sodium** 76mg	3%	Dietary Fiber 3g	12%
Saturated Fat 0g	0%	**Protein** 1g		Sugars 5g	
Polyunsaturated Fat 0g					
Monounsaturated Fat 0g		Vitamin A 368% Vitamin C 11%		Calcium 4% Iron 2%	

Cauliflower, Cooked, Boiled, Drained, with Salt

3 flowerets / 54g

Amount per serving	%DV	Amount per serving	%DV	Amount per serving	%DV
Calories 12		**Cholesterol** 0mg	0%	**Total Carbohydrate** 2g	1%
Total Fat 0g	0%	**Sodium** 131mg	5%	Dietary Fiber 1g	4%
Saturated Fat 0g	0%	**Protein** 1g		Sugars 1g	
Polyunsaturated Fat 0g					
Monounsaturated Fat 0g		Vitamin A 0% Vitamin C 40%		Calcium 1% Iron 1%	

Cauliflower, Cooked, Boiled, Drained, without Salt

3 flowerets / 54g

Amount per serving	%DV	Amount per serving	%DV	Amount per serving	%DV
Calories 12		**Cholesterol** 0mg	0%	**Total Carbohydrate** 2g	1%
Total Fat 0g	0%	**Sodium** 8mg	0%	Dietary Fiber 1g	4%
Saturated Fat 0g	0%	**Protein** 1g		Sugars 1g	
Polyunsaturated Fat 0g					
Monounsaturated Fat 0g		Vitamin A 0% Vitamin C 40%		Calcium 1% Iron 1%	

Cauliflower, Frozen, Unprepared

1/2 cup, 1″ pieces / 66g

Amount per serving	%DV	Amount per serving	%DV	Amount per serving	%DV
Calories 16		**Cholesterol** 0mg	0%	**Total Carbohydrate** 3g	1%
Total Fat 0g	0%	**Sodium** 16mg	1%	Dietary Fiber 2g	8%
Saturated Fat 0g	0%	**Protein** 1g		Sugars 1g	
Polyunsaturated Fat 0g					
Monounsaturated Fat 0g		Vitamin A 0% Vitamin C 54%		Calcium 1% Iron 2%	

Cauliflower, Green, Cooked, No Salt Added

1/2 head / 90g

Amount per serving	%DV	Amount per serving	%DV	Amount per serving	%DV
Calories 29		**Cholesterol** 0mg	0%	**Total Carbohydrate** 6g	2%
Total Fat 0g	0%	**Sodium** 21mg	1%	Dietary Fiber 3g	12%
Saturated Fat 0g	0%	**Protein** 3g		Sugars 0g	
Polyunsaturated Fat 0g					
Monounsaturated Fat 0g		Vitamin A 3% Vitamin C 109%		Calcium 3% Iron 4%	

Cauliflower, Green, Cooked, with Salt

1/2 cup, 1″ pieces / 62g

Amount per serving	%DV	Amount per serving	%DV	Amount per serving	%DV
Calories 20		**Cholesterol** 0mg	0%	**Total Carbohydrate** 4g	1%
Total Fat 0g	0%	**Sodium** 161mg	7%	Dietary Fiber 2g	8%
Saturated Fat 0g	0%	**Protein** 2g		Sugars 0g	
Polyunsaturated Fat 0g					
Monounsaturated Fat 0g		Vitamin A 2% Vitamin C 75%		Calcium 2% Iron 2%	

Cauliflower, Green, Raw

1 cup / 64g

Amount per serving	%DV	Amount per serving	%DV	Amount per serving	%DV
Calories 20		**Cholesterol** 0mg	0%	**Total Carbohydrate** 4g	1%
Total Fat 0g	0%	**Sodium** 15mg	1%	Dietary Fiber 2g	8%
Saturated Fat 0g	0%	**Protein** 2g		Sugars 2g	
Polyunsaturated Fat 0g					
Monounsaturated Fat 0g		Vitamin A 2% Vitamin C 94%		Calcium 2% Iron 3%	

Cauliflower, Raw

1 cup / 100g

Amount per serving	%DV	Amount per serving	%DV	Amount per serving	%DV
Calories 25		**Cholesterol** 0mg	0%	**Total Carbohydrate** 5g	2%
Total Fat 0g	0%	**Sodium** 30mg	1%	Dietary Fiber 3g	12%
Saturated Fat 0g	0%	**Protein** 2g		Sugars 2g	
Polyunsaturated Fat 0g					
Monounsaturated Fat 0g		Vitamin A 0%	Vitamin C 77%	Calcium 2%	Iron 2%

Celery, Cooked, Boiled, Drained, with Salt

1 oz / 28g

Amount per serving	%DV	Amount per serving	%DV	Amount per serving	%DV
Calories 5		**Cholesterol** 0mg	0%	**Total Carbohydrate** 1g	0%
Total Fat 0g	0%	**Sodium** 92mg	4%	Dietary Fiber 0g	0%
Saturated Fat 0g	0%	**Protein** 0g		Sugars 1g	
Polyunsaturated Fat 0g					
Monounsaturated Fat 0g		Vitamin A 3%	Vitamin C 3%	Calcium 1%	Iron 1%

Celery, Cooked, Boiled, Drained, without Salt

1 cup, diced / 150g / 75g

Amount per serving	%DV	Amount per serving	%DV	Amount per serving	%DV
Calories 27		**Cholesterol** 0mg	0%	**Total Carbohydrate** 6g	2%
Total Fat 0g	0%	**Sodium** 136mg	6%	Dietary Fiber 2g	8%
Saturated Fat 0g	0%	**Protein** 1g		Sugars 4g	
Polyunsaturated Fat 0g					
Monounsaturated Fat 0g		Vitamin A 16%	Vitamin C 15%	Calcium 6%	Iron 4%

Celery, Raw

1 stalk, medium, 7 1/2 x 8" long / 40g

Amount per serving	%DV	Amount per serving	%DV	Amount per serving	%DV
Calories 6		**Cholesterol** 0mg	0%	**Total Carbohydrate** 1g	0%
Total Fat 0g	0%	**Sodium** 32mg	1%	Dietary Fiber 1g	4%
Saturated Fat 0g	0%	**Protein** 0g		Sugars 1g	
Polyunsaturated Fat 0g					
Monounsaturated Fat 0g		Vitamin A 4%	Vitamin C 2%	Calcium 2%	Iron 0%

Chayote, Fruit, Raw

1 chayote, 5-3/4" / 203g

Amount per serving	%DV	Amount per serving	%DV	Amount per serving	%DV
Calories 39		**Cholesterol** 0mg	0%	**Total Carbohydrate** 9g	3%
Total Fat 0g	0%	**Sodium** 4mg	0%	Dietary Fiber 3g	12%
Saturated Fat 0g	0%	**Protein** 2g		Sugars 3g	
Polyunsaturated Fat 0g					
Monounsaturated Fat 0g		Vitamin A 0%	Vitamin C 26%	Calcium 3%	Iron 4%

Chives, Raw

1 tbsp, chopped / 3g

Amount per serving	%DV	Amount per serving	%DV	Amount per serving	%DV
Calories 1		**Cholesterol** 0mg	0%	**Total Carbohydrate** 0g	0%
Total Fat 0g	0%	**Sodium** 0mg	0%	Dietary Fiber 0g	0%
Saturated Fat 0g	0%	**Protein** 0g		Sugars 0g	
Polyunsaturated Fat 0g					
Monounsaturated Fat 0g		Vitamin A 3% Vitamin C 3%		Calcium 0% Iron 0%	

Cole Slaw, Home-Prepared

1/2 cup / 60g

Amount per serving	%DV	Amount per serving	%DV	Amount per serving	%DV
Calories 47		**Cholesterol** 5mg	2%	**Total Carbohydrate** 7g	2%
Total Fat 2g	3%	**Sodium** 14mg	1%	Dietary Fiber 1g	4%
Saturated Fat 0g	0%	**Protein** 1g		Sugars 0g	
Polyunsaturated Fat 1g					
Monounsaturated Fat 0.5g		Vitamin A 4% Vitamin C 33%		Calcium 3% Iron 2%	

Collards, Cooked, Boiled, Drained, without Salt

1 cup, chopped / 190g

Amount per serving	%DV	Amount per serving	%DV	Amount per serving	%DV
Calories 49		**Cholesterol** 0mg	0%	**Total Carbohydrate** 9g	3%
Total Fat 1g	2%	**Sodium** 30mg	1%	Dietary Fiber 5g	20%
Saturated Fat 0g	0%	**Protein** 4g		Sugars 1g	
Polyunsaturated Fat 0g					
Monounsaturated Fat 0g		Vitamin A 308% Vitamin C 58%		Calcium 27% Iron 12%	

Collards, Frozen, Chopped, Cooked, Boiled, Drained, without Salt

1 cup, chopped / 170g

Amount per serving	%DV	Amount per serving	%DV	Amount per serving	%DV
Calories 61		**Cholesterol** 0mg	0%	**Total Carbohydrate** 12g	4%
Total Fat 1g	2%	**Sodium** 85mg	4%	Dietary Fiber 5g	20%
Saturated Fat 0g	0%	**Protein** 5g		Sugars 1g	
Polyunsaturated Fat 0g					
Monounsaturated Fat 0g		Vitamin A 391% Vitamin C 75%		Calcium 36% Iron 11%	

Collards, Raw

1 cup, chopped / 36g

Amount per serving	%DV	Amount per serving	%DV	Amount per serving	%DV
Calories 11		**Cholesterol** 0mg	0%	**Total Carbohydrate** 2g	1%
Total Fat 0g	0%	**Sodium** 7mg	0%	Dietary Fiber 1g	4%
Saturated Fat 0g	0%	**Protein** 1g		Sugars 0g	
Polyunsaturated Fat 0g					
Monounsaturated Fat 0g		Vitamin A 48% Vitamin C 21%		Calcium 5% Iron 0%	

Corn, Sweet, White, Cooked, Boiled, Drained, with Salt

1 medium ear, 6-3/4" to 7-1/2" long / 103g

Amount per serving	%DV	Amount per serving	%DV	Amount per serving	%DV
Calories 111		**Cholesterol** 0mg	0%	**Total Carbohydrate** 26g	9%
Total Fat 1g	2%	**Sodium** 261mg	11%	Dietary Fiber 3g	12%
Saturated Fat 0g	0%	**Protein** 3g		Sugars 4g	
Polyunsaturated Fat 0g					
Monounsaturated Fat 0g		Vitamin A 0% Vitamin C 0%		Calcium 0% Iron 3%	

Corn, Sweet, White, Cooked, Boiled, Drained, without Salt

1 ear / 77g

Amount per serving	%DV	Amount per serving	%DV	Amount per serving	%DV
Calories 83		**Cholesterol** 0mg	0%	**Total Carbohydrate** 19.3g	6%
Total Fat 1g	2%	**Sodium** 13mg	1%	Dietary Fiber 2.1g	8%
Saturated Fat 0.2g	1%	**Protein** 2.6g		Sugars 3.1g	
Polyunsaturated Fat 0.5g					
Monounsaturated Fat 0.3g		Vitamin A 0% Vitamin C 8%		Calcium 0% Iron 3%	

Corn, Sweet, Yellow, Cooked, Boiled, Drained, with Salt

1 small ear, 5 1/2 to 6-1/2" long / 89g

Amount per serving	%DV	Amount per serving	%DV	Amount per serving	%DV
Calories 96		**Cholesterol** 0mg	0%	**Total Carbohydrate** 22g	7%
Total Fat 1g	2%	**Sodium** 225mg	9%	Dietary Fiber 2g	8%
Saturated Fat 0g	0%	**Protein** 3g		Sugars 3g	
Polyunsaturated Fat 0g					
Monounsaturated Fat 0g		Vitamin A 5% Vitamin C 9%		Calcium 0% Iron 3%	

Corn, Sweet, Yellow, Cooked, Boiled, Drained, without Salt

1 cup cut / 164g

Amount per serving	%DV	Amount per serving	%DV	Amount per serving	%DV
Calories 177		**Cholesterol** 0mg	0%	**Total Carbohydrate** 41g	14%
Total Fat 2g	3%	**Sodium** 0mg	0%	Dietary Fiber 5g	20%
Saturated Fat 0g	0%	**Protein** 5g		Sugars 5g	
Polyunsaturated Fat 0g					
Monounsaturated Fat 0g		Vitamin A 9% Vitamin C 17%		Calcium 0% Iron 4%	

Corn, Sweet, Yellow, Frozen, Kernels Cut Off Cob, Boiled, Drained, without Salt

1 cup / 82g

Amount per serving	%DV	Amount per serving	%DV	Amount per serving	%DV
Calories 66		**Cholesterol** 0mg	0%	**Total Carbohydrate** 16g	5%
Total Fat 1g	2%	**Sodium** 1mg	0%	Dietary Fiber 2g	8%
Saturated Fat 0g	0%	**Protein** 2g		Sugars 3g	
Polyunsaturated Fat 0g					
Monounsaturated Fat 0g		Vitamin A 3% Vitamin C 5%		Calcium 0% Iron 2%	

Corn, Sweet, Yellow, Frozen, Kernels On Cob, Cooked, Boiled, Drained, with Salt

1 ear, yields / 63g

Amount per serving	%DV	Amount per serving	%DV	Amount per serving	%DV
Calories 59		**Cholesterol** 0mg	0%	**Total Carbohydrate** 14g	5%
Total Fat 0g	0%	**Sodium** 151mg	6%	Dietary Fiber 2g	8%
Saturated Fat 0g	0%	**Protein** 2g		Sugars 2g	
Polyunsaturated Fat 0g					
Monounsaturated Fat 0g		Vitamin A 3%	Vitamin C 5%	Calcium 0%	Iron 2%

Corn, Sweet, Yellow, Frozen, Kernels On Cob, Cooked, Boiled, Drained, without Salt

1 ear, yields / 63g

Amount per serving	%DV	Amount per serving	%DV	Amount per serving	%DV
Calories 59		**Cholesterol** 0mg	0%	**Total Carbohydrate** 14g	5%
Total Fat 0g	0%	**Sodium** 3mg	0%	Dietary Fiber 2g	8%
Saturated Fat 0g	0%	**Protein** 2g		Sugars 2g	
Polyunsaturated Fat 0g					
Monounsaturated Fat 0g		Vitamin A 3%	Vitamin C 5%	Calcium 0%	Iron 2%

Corn, Sweet, Yellow, Frozen, Kernels On Cob, Unprepared

1 package / 284g

Amount per serving	%DV	Amount per serving	%DV	Amount per serving	%DV
Calories 250		**Cholesterol** 0mg	0%	**Total Carbohydrate** 59g	20%
Total Fat 2g	3%	**Sodium** 9mg	0%	Dietary Fiber 6g	24%
Saturated Fat 0g	0%	**Protein** 9g		Sugars 7g	
Polyunsaturated Fat 0g					
Monounsaturated Fat 0g		Vitamin A 11%	Vitamin C 30%	Calcium 1%	Iron 7%

Cucumber, Peeled, Raw

1 cup, sliced / 119g

Amount per serving	%DV	Amount per serving	%DV	Amount per serving	%DV
Calories 14		**Cholesterol** 0mg	0%	**Total Carbohydrate** 3g	1%
Total Fat 0g	0%	**Sodium** 2mg	0%	Dietary Fiber 1g	4%
Saturated Fat 0g	0%	**Protein** 1g		Sugars 2g	
Polyunsaturated Fat 0g					
Monounsaturated Fat 0g		Vitamin A 2%	Vitamin C 6%	Calcium 2%	Iron 1%

Cucumber, with Peel, Raw

1 cucumber, 8-1/4" / 301g

Amount per serving	%DV	Amount per serving	%DV	Amount per serving	%DV
Calories 45		**Cholesterol** 0mg	0%	**Total Carbohydrate** 11g	4%
Total Fat 0g	0%	**Sodium** 6mg	0%	Dietary Fiber 2g	8%
Saturated Fat 0g	0%	**Protein** 2g		Sugars 5g	
Polyunsaturated Fat 0g					
Monounsaturated Fat 0g		Vitamin A 6%	Vitamin C 14%	Calcium 5%	Iron 5%

Dandelion, Greens, Cooked, Boiled, Drained, without Salt

1 cup, chopped / 105g

Amount per serving	%DV	Amount per serving	%DV	Amount per serving	%DV
Calories 35		**Cholesterol** 0mg	0%	**Total Carbohydrate** 7g	2%
Total Fat 1g	2%	**Sodium** 46mg	2%	Dietary Fiber 3g	12%
Saturated Fat 0g	0%	**Protein** 2g		Sugars 1g	
Polyunsaturated Fat 0g					
Monounsaturated Fat 0g		Vitamin A 144% Vitamin C 32%		Calcium 15% Iron 10%	

Dandelion, Greens, Raw

1 cup, chopped / 55g

Amount per serving	%DV	Amount per serving	%DV	Amount per serving	%DV
Calories 25		**Cholesterol** 0mg	0%	**Total Carbohydrate** 5g	2%
Total Fat 0g	0%	**Sodium** 42mg	2%	Dietary Fiber 2g	8%
Saturated Fat 0g	0%	**Protein** 1g		Sugars 0g	
Polyunsaturated Fat 0g					
Monounsaturated Fat 0g		Vitamin A 112% Vitamin C 32%		Calcium 10% Iron 9%	

Eggplant, Cooked, Boiled, Drained, with Salt

1 cup, 1″ cubes / 99g

Amount per serving	%DV	Amount per serving	%DV	Amount per serving	%DV
Calories 33		**Cholesterol** 0mg	0%	**Total Carbohydrate** 8g	3%
Total Fat 0g	0%	**Sodium** 237mg	10%	Dietary Fiber 2.5g	10%
Saturated Fat 0g	0%	**Protein** 1g		Sugars 3g	
Polyunsaturated Fat 0g					
Monounsaturated Fat 0g		Vitamin A 1% Vitamin C 2%		Calcium 1% Iron 1%	

Eggplant, Cooked, Boiled, Drained, without Salt

1 cup, 1″ cubes / 99g

Amount per serving	%DV	Amount per serving	%DV	Amount per serving	%DV
Calories 35		**Cholesterol** 0mg	0%	**Total Carbohydrate** 9g	3%
Total Fat 0g	0%	**Sodium** 1mg	0%	Dietary Fiber 2g	8%
Saturated Fat 0g	0%	**Protein** 1g		Sugars 3g	
Polyunsaturated Fat 0g					
Monounsaturated Fat 0g		Vitamin A 1% Vitamin C 2%		Calcium 1% Iron 1%	

Eggplant, Raw

1 eggplant, peeled, yield from 1-1/4 lb / 458g

Amount per serving	%DV	Amount per serving	%DV	Amount per serving	%DV
Calories 110		**Cholesterol** 0mg	0%	**Total Carbohydrate** 26g	9%
Total Fat 1g	2%	**Sodium** 9mg	0%	Dietary Fiber 16g	64%
Saturated Fat 0g	0%	**Protein** g		Sugars 11g	
Polyunsaturated Fat 0g					
Monounsaturated Fat 0g		Vitamin A 2% Vitamin C 17%		Calcium 4% Iron 6%	

Endive, Raw

1/2 cup, chopped / 25g

Amount per serving	%DV	Amount per serving	%DV	Amount per serving	%DV
Calories 4		**Cholesterol** 0mg	0%	**Total Carbohydrate** 1g	0%
Total Fat 0g	0%	**Sodium** 5mg	0%	Dietary Fiber 1g	4%
Saturated Fat 0g	0%	**Protein** 0g		Sugars 0g	
Polyunsaturated Fat 0g					
Monounsaturated Fat 0g		Vitamin A 11%	Vitamin C 3%	Calcium 1%	Iron 0%

Fennel, Bulb, Raw

1 cup, sliced / 87g

Amount per serving	%DV	Amount per serving	%DV	Amount per serving	%DV
Calories 27		**Cholesterol** 0mg	0%	**Total Carbohydrate** 6g	2%
Total Fat 0g	0%	**Sodium** 45mg	2%	Dietary Fiber 3g	12%
Saturated Fat 0g	0%	**Protein** 1g		Sugars 0g	
Polyunsaturated Fat 0g					
Monounsaturated Fat 0g		Vitamin A 2%	Vitamin C 17%	Calcium 4%	Iron 4%

Garden Cress Cooked, Boiled, Drained, without Salt

1 cup / 135g

Amount per serving	%DV	Amount per serving	%DV	Amount per serving	%DV
Calories 31		**Cholesterol** 0mg	0%	**Total Carbohydrate** 5g	2%
Total Fat 1g	2%	**Sodium** 11mg	0%	Dietary Fiber 1g	4%
Saturated Fat 0g	0%	**Protein** 3g		Sugars 4g	
Polyunsaturated Fat 0g					
Monounsaturated Fat 0g		Vitamin A 126%	Vitamin C 52%	Calcium 8%	Iron 6%

Garden Cress Raw

1 oz / 28g

Amount per serving	%DV	Amount per serving	%DV	Amount per serving	%DV
Calories 9		**Cholesterol** 0mg	0%	**Total Carbohydrate** 2g	1%
Total Fat 0g	0%	**Sodium** 4mg	0%	Dietary Fiber 0g	0%
Saturated Fat 0g	0%	**Protein** 1g		Sugars 1g	
Polyunsaturated Fat 0g					
Monounsaturated Fat 0g		Vitamin A 39%	Vitamin C 32%	Calcium 2%	Iron 2%

Garlic, Raw

1 clove / 3g

Amount per serving	%DV	Amount per serving	%DV	Amount per serving	%DV
Calories 4		**Cholesterol** 0mg	0%	**Total Carbohydrate** 1g	0%
Total Fat 0g	0%	**Sodium** 1mg	0%	Dietary Fiber 0g	0%
Saturated Fat 0g	0%	**Protein** 0g		Sugars 0g	
Polyunsaturated Fat 0g					
Monounsaturated Fat 0g		Vitamin A 0%	Vitamin C 2%	Calcium 1%	Iron 0%

Ginger Root, Raw

1/4 cup, slices, 1″ diameter / 24g

Amount per serving	%DV	Amount per serving	%DV	Amount per serving	%DV
Calories 19		**Cholesterol** 0mg	0%	**Total Carbohydrate** 4g	1%
Total Fat 0g	0%	**Sodium** 3mg	0%	Dietary Fiber 0g	0%
Saturated Fat 0g	0%	**Protein** 0g		Sugars 0g	
Polyunsaturated Fat 0g					
Monounsaturated Fat 0g		Vitamin A 0% Vitamin C 2%		Calcium 0% Iron 1%	

Grape Leaves, Raw

1 oz / 28g

Amount per serving	%DV	Amount per serving	%DV	Amount per serving	%DV
Calories 26		**Cholesterol** 0mg	0%	**Total Carbohydrate** 5g	2%
Total Fat 1g	2%	**Sodium** 3mg	0%	Dietary Fiber 3g	12%
Saturated Fat 0g	0%	**Protein** 2g		Sugars 2g	
Polyunsaturated Fat 0g					
Monounsaturated Fat 0g		Vitamin A 154% Vitamin C 5%		Calcium 10% Iron 4%	

Hearts of Palm, Canned

1 piece / 33g

Amount per serving	%DV	Amount per serving	%DV	Amount per serving	%DV
Calories 9		**Cholesterol** 0mg	0%	**Total Carbohydrate** 2g	1%
Total Fat 0g	0%	**Sodium** 141mg	6%	Dietary Fiber 1g	4%
Saturated Fat 0g	0%	**Protein** 1g		Sugars 0g	
Polyunsaturated Fat 0g					
Monounsaturated Fat 0g		Vitamin A 0% Vitamin C 4%		Calcium 2% Iron 6%	

Jerusalem Artichokes, Raw

1 cup, slices / 150g

Amount per serving	%DV	Amount per serving	%DV	Amount per serving	%DV
Calories 110		**Cholesterol** 0mg	0%	**Total Carbohydrate** 26.2g	9%
Total Fat 0g	0%	**Sodium** 6mg	0%	Dietary Fiber 2.4g	10%
Saturated Fat 0g	0%	**Protein** 3g		Sugars 14.4g	
Polyunsaturated Fat 0g					
Monounsaturated Fat 0g		Vitamin A 1% Vitamin C 10%		Calcium 2% Iron 28%	

Kale, Cooked, Boiled, Drained, with Salt

1 cup, chopped / 130g

Amount per serving	%DV	Amount per serving	%DV	Amount per serving	%DV
		Cholesterol 0mg	0%	**Total Carbohydrate** 7g	2%
	2%	**Sodium** 337mg	14%	Dietary Fiber 3g	12%
0g	0%	**Protein** 2g		Sugars 2g	
Fat 0g					
Fat 0g		Vitamin A 354% Vitamin C 89%		Calcium 9% Iron 6%	

Kale, Cooked, Boiled, Drained, without Salt

1 cup, chopped / 130g

Amount per serving	%DV	Amount per serving	%DV	Amount per serving	%DV
Calories 36		**Cholesterol** 0mg	0%	**Total Carbohydrate** 7g	2%
Total Fat 1g	2%	**Sodium** 30mg	1%	Dietary Fiber 3g	12%
Saturated Fat 0g	0%	**Protein** 2g		Sugars 2g	
Polyunsaturated Fat 0g					
Monounsaturated Fat 0g		Vitamin A 354% Vitamin C 89%		Calcium 9% Iron 6%	

Kale, Frozen, Cooked, Boiled, Drained, with Salt

1 cup, chopped / 130g

Amount per serving	%DV	Amount per serving	%DV	Amount per serving	%DV
Calories 39		**Cholesterol** 0mg	0%	**Total Carbohydrate** 7g	2%
Total Fat 1g	2%	**Sodium** 326mg	14%	Dietary Fiber 3g	12%
Saturated Fat 0g	0%	**Protein** 4g		Sugars 2g	
Polyunsaturated Fat 0g					
Monounsaturated Fat 0g		Vitamin A 382% Vitamin C 55%		Calcium 18% Iron 7%	

Kale, Frozen, Cooked, Boiled, Drained, without Salt

1 cup, chopped / 130g

Amount per serving	%DV	Amount per serving	%DV	Amount per serving	%DV
Calories 39		**Cholesterol** 0mg	0%	**Total Carbohydrate** 7g	2%
Total Fat 1g	2%	**Sodium** 19mg	1%	Dietary Fiber 3g	12%
Saturated Fat 0g	0%	**Protein** 4g		Sugars 2g	
Polyunsaturated Fat 0g					
Monounsaturated Fat 0g		Vitamin A 382% Vitamin C 55%		Calcium 18% Iron 7%	

Kale, Raw

1 cup, chopped / 67g

Amount per serving	%DV	Amount per serving	%DV	Amount per serving	%DV
Calories 33		**Cholesterol** 0mg	0%	**Total Carbohydrate** 7g	2%
Total Fat 0g	0%	**Sodium** 29mg	1%	Dietary Fiber 1g	4%
Saturated Fat 0g	0%	**Protein** 2g		Sugars 0g	
Polyunsaturated Fat 0g					
Monounsaturated Fat 0g		Vitamin A 206% Vitamin C 134%		Calcium 9% Iron 6%	

Leeks, (Bulb and Lower Leaf-Portion), Cooked, Boiled, Drained, with Salt

1/4 cup, chopped / 26g

Amount per serving	%DV	Amount per serving	%DV	Amount per serving	%DV
Calories 8		**Cholesterol** 0mg	0%	**Total Carbohydrate** 2g	1%
Total Fat 0g	0%	**Sodium** 64mg	3%	Dietary Fiber 0g	0%
Saturated Fat 0g	0%	**Protein** 0g		Sugars 1g	
Polyunsaturated Fat 0g					
Monounsaturated Fat 0g		Vitamin A 4% Vitamin C 2%		Calcium 1% Iron 2%	

Leeks, (Bulb and Lower Leaf-Portion), Cooked, Boiled, Drained, without Salt

1/4 cup, chopped or diced / 26g

Amount per serving	%DV	Amount per serving	%DV	Amount per serving	%DV
Calories 8		**Cholesterol** 0mg	0%	**Total Carbohydrate** 2g	1%
Total Fat 0g	0%	**Sodium** 3mg	0%	Dietary Fiber 0g	0%
Saturated Fat 0g	0%	**Protein** 0g		Sugars 1g	
Polyunsaturated Fat 0g					
Monounsaturated Fat 0g		Vitamin A 4%	Vitamin C 2%	Calcium 1%	Iron 2%

Lemon Grass (Citronella), Raw

1 tbsp / 4.8g

Amount per serving	%DV	Amount per serving	%DV	Amount per serving	%DV
Calories 5		**Cholesterol** 0mg	0%	**Total Carbohydrate** 1g	0%
Total Fat 0g	0%	**Sodium** 0mg	0%	Dietary Fiber 0g	0%
Saturated Fat 0g	0%	**Protein** 0g		Sugars 0g	
Polyunsaturated Fat 0g					
Monounsaturated Fat 0g		Vitamin A 0%	Vitamin C 0%	Calcium 0%	Iron 2%

Lettuce, Butterhead (Includes Boston and Bibb Types), Raw

1 cup, shredded or chopped / 55g

Amount per serving	%DV	Amount per serving	%DV	Amount per serving	%DV
Calories 7		**Cholesterol** 0mg	0%	**Total Carbohydrate** 1g	0%
Total Fat 0g	0%	**Sodium** 3mg	0%	Dietary Fiber 1g	4%
Saturated Fat 0g	0%	**Protein** 1g		Sugars 1g	
Polyunsaturated Fat 0g					
Monounsaturated Fat 0g		Vitamin A 36%	Vitamin C 3%	Calcium 2%	Iron 4%

Lettuce, Cos or Romaine, Raw

1 leaf, outter / 28g

Amount per serving	%DV	Amount per serving	%DV	Amount per serving	%DV
Calories 5		**Cholesterol** 0mg	0%	**Total Carbohydrate** 0g	0%
Total Fat 0g	0%	**Sodium** 2mg	0%	Dietary Fiber 0g	0%
Saturated Fat 0g	0%	**Protein** 0g		Sugars 0g	
Polyunsaturated Fat 0g					
Monounsaturated Fat 0g		Vitamin A 49%	Vitamin C 11%	Calcium 1%	Iron 2%

Lettuce, Green Leaf, Raw

1 head / 360g

Amount per serving	%DV	Amount per serving	%DV	Amount per serving	%DV
Calories 54		**Cholesterol** 0mg	0%	**Total Carbohydrate** 10g	3%
Total Fat 1g	2%	**Sodium** 101mg	4%	Dietary Fiber 5g	20%
Saturated Fat 0g	0%	**Protein** 5g		Sugars 3g	
Polyunsaturated Fat 0g					
Monounsaturated Fat 0g		Vitamin A 533%	Vitamin C 108%	Calcium 13%	Iron 17%

Lettuce, Iceberg (Includes Crisphead Types), Raw

1 large leaf / 15g

Amount per serving	%DV	Amount per serving	%DV	Amount per serving	%DV
Calories 2		**Cholesterol** 0mg	0%	**Total Carbohydrate** 0g	0%
Total Fat 0g	0%	**Sodium** 1mg	0%	Dietary Fiber 0g	0%
Saturated Fat 0g	0%	**Protein** 0g		Sugars 0g	
Polyunsaturated Fat 0g					
Monounsaturated Fat 0g		Vitamin A 2% Vitamin C 1%		Calcium 0% Iron 0%	

Lettuce, Red Leaf, Raw

1 oz / 28g

Amount per serving	%DV	Amount per serving	%DV	Amount per serving	%DV
Calories 4		**Cholesterol** 0mg	0%	**Total Carbohydrate** 0g	0%
Total Fat 0g	0%	**Sodium** 7mg	0%	Dietary Fiber 0g	0%
Saturated Fat 0g	0%	**Protein** 0g		Sugars 0g	
Polyunsaturated Fat 0g					
Monounsaturated Fat 0g		Vitamin A 42% Vitamin C 2%		Calcium 1% Iron 2%	

Lima Beans, Immature Seeds, Canned, No Salt Added, Solids and Liquids

1/2 cup / 124g

Amount per serving	%DV	Amount per serving	%DV	Amount per serving	%DV
Calories 88		**Cholesterol** 0mg	0%	**Total Carbohydrate** 17g	6%
Total Fat 0g	0%	**Sodium** 5mg	0%	Dietary Fiber 4g	16%
Saturated Fat 0g	0%	**Protein** 5g		Sugars 1g	
Polyunsaturated Fat 0g					
Monounsaturated Fat 0g		Vitamin A 4% Vitamin C 18%		Calcium 3% Iron 11%	

Lima Beans, Immature Seeds, Frozen, Baby, Cooked, Boiled, Drained, without Salt

1 package, 10 oz yields / 311g

Amount per serving	%DV	Amount per serving	%DV	Amount per serving	%DV
Calories 326.5		**Cholesterol** 0mg	0%	**Total Carbohydrate** 60.5g	20%
Total Fat 1g	2%	**Sodium** 90mg	4%	Dietary Fiber 18.5g	74%
Saturated Fat 0g	0%	**Protein** 20.5g		Sugars 4.5g	
Polyunsaturated Fat 0.5g					
Monounsaturated Fat 0g		Vitamin A 519.5% Vitamin C 18% Calcium 87% Iron 6%			

Lima Beans, Immature, Frozen, Fordhook, Boiled, Drained, without Salt

1 package, 10 oz yields / 311g

Amount per serving	%DV	Amount per serving	%DV	Amount per serving	%DV
Calories 320.5		**Cholesterol** 0mg	0%	**Total Carbohydrate** 60g	20%
Total Fat 1g	2%	**Sodium** 214.5mg	9%	Dietary Fiber 18g	72%
Saturated Fat 0g	0%	**Protein** 19g		Sugars 4g	
Polyunsaturated Fat 0.5g					
Monounsaturated Fat 0g		Vitamin A 591% Vitamin C 40% Calcium 93.5% Iron 5.5%			

Lotus Root, Cooked, Boiled, Drained, with Salt

1/2 cup / 60g

Amount per serving	%DV	Amount per serving	%DV	Amount per serving	%DV
Calories 40		**Cholesterol** 0mg	0%	**Total Carbohydrate** 10g	3%
Total Fat 0g	0%	**Sodium** 169mg	7%	Dietary Fiber 2g	8%
Saturated Fat 0g	0%	**Protein** 1g		Sugars 0g	
Polyunsaturated Fat 0g					
Monounsaturated Fat 0g		Vitamin A 0%	Vitamin C 27%	Calcium 2%	Iron 3%

Lotus Root, Cooked, Boiled, Drained, without Salt

10 slices, 2-1/2″ diameter / 89g

Amount per serving	%DV	Amount per serving	%DV	Amount per serving	%DV
Calories 59		**Cholesterol** 0mg	0%	**Total Carbohydrate** 14g	5%
Total Fat 0g	0%	**Sodium** 40mg	2%	Dietary Fiber 3g	12%
Saturated Fat 0g	0%	**Protein** 1g		Sugars 0g	
Polyunsaturated Fat 0g					
Monounsaturated Fat 0g		Vitamin A 0%	Vitamin C 41%	Calcium 2%	Iron 4%

Lotus Root, Raw

1 root, 9-1/2″ long / 115g

Amount per serving	%DV	Amount per serving	%DV	Amount per serving	%DV
Calories 85		**Cholesterol** 0mg	0%	**Total Carbohydrate** 20g	7%
Total Fat 0g	0%	**Sodium** 46mg	2%	Dietary Fiber 6g	24%
Saturated Fat 0g	0%	**Protein** 3g		Sugars 0g	
Polyunsaturated Fat 0g					
Monounsaturated Fat 0g		Vitamin A 0%	Vitamin C 84%	Calcium 5%	Iron 7%

Malabar Spinach, Cooked

1 cup / 44g

Amount per serving	%DV	Amount per serving	%DV	Amount per serving	%DV
Calories 10		**Cholesterol** 0mg	0%	**Total Carbohydrate** 1g	0%
Total Fat 0g	0%	**Sodium** 24mg	1%	Dietary Fiber 1g	4%
Saturated Fat 0g	0%	**Protein** 1g		Sugars 0g	
Polyunsaturated Fat 0g					
Monounsaturated Fat 0g		Vitamin A 10%	Vitamin C 4%	Calcium 5%	Iron 4%

Mung Beans, Mature Seeds, Sprouted, Raw

1 cup / 104g

Amount per serving	%DV	Amount per serving	%DV	Amount per serving	%DV
Calories 31		**Cholesterol** 0mg	0%	**Total Carbohydrate** 6g	2%
Total Fat 0g	0%	**Sodium** 6mg	0%	Dietary Fiber 2g	8%
Saturated Fat 0g	0%	**Protein** 3g		Sugars 4g	
Polyunsaturated Fat 0g					
Monounsaturated Fat 0g		Vitamin A 0%	Vitamin C 23%	Calcium 1%	Iron 5%

Mushrooms, Brown, Italian, or Crimini, Raw

1 cup, sliced / 72g

Amount per serving	%DV	Amount per serving	%DV	Amount per serving	%DV
Calories 19		Cholesterol 0mg	0%	Total Carbohydrate 3g	1%
Total Fat 0g	0%	Sodium 4mg	0%	Dietary Fiber 0.4g	2%
Saturated Fat 0g	0%	Protein 1.8g		Sugars 1.2g	
Polyunsaturated Fat 0g					
Monounsaturated Fat 0g		Vitamin A 0%	Vitamin C 0%	Calcium 1%	Iron 2%

Mushrooms, Enoki, Raw

1 large / 5g

Amount per serving	%DV	Amount per serving	%DV	Amount per serving	%DV
Calories 2		Cholesterol 0mg	0%	Total Carbohydrate 0g	0%
Total Fat 0g	0%	Sodium 0mg	0%	Dietary Fiber 0g	0%
Saturated Fat 0g	0%	Protein 0g		Sugars 0g	
Polyunsaturated Fat 0g					
Monounsaturated Fat 0g		Vitamin A 0%	Vitamin C 0%	Calcium 0%	Iron 0%

Mushrooms, Maitake, Raw

1 cup diced / 70g

Amount per serving	%DV	Amount per serving	%DV	Amount per serving	%DV
Calories 26		Cholesterol 0mg	0%	Total Carbohydrate 5g	2%
Total Fat 0g	0%	Sodium 1mg	0%	Dietary Fiber 2g	8%
Saturated Fat 0g	0%	Protein 1g		Sugars 1g	
Polyunsaturated Fat 0g					
Monounsaturated Fat 0g		Vitamin A 0%	Vitamin C 0%	Calcium 0%	Iron 1%

Mushrooms, Oyster, Raw

1 cup, sliced / 86g

Amount per serving	%DV	Amount per serving	%DV	Amount per serving	%DV
Calories 37		Cholesterol 0mg	0%	Total Carbohydrate 5.6g	2%
Total Fat 0g	0%	Sodium 15mg	1%	Dietary Fiber 2g	8%
Saturated Fat 0g	0%	Protein 2.8g		Sugars 1g	
Polyunsaturated Fat 0g					
Monounsaturated Fat 0g		Vitamin A 1%	Vitamin C 0%	Calcium 0%	Iron 6%

Mushrooms, Portobello, Raw

1 cup / sliced / 84g

Amount per serving	%DV	Amount per serving	%DV	Amount per serving	%DV
Calories 22		Cholesterol 0mg	0%	Total Carbohydrate 4g	1%
Total Fat 0g	0%	Sodium 5mg	0%	Dietary Fiber 1g	4%
Saturated Fat 0g	0%	Protein 2g		Sugars 2g	
Polyunsaturated Fat 0g					
Monounsaturated Fat 0g		Vitamin A 0%	Vitamin C 0%	Calcium 1%	Iron 3%

Mushrooms, Shiitake, Cooked, with Salt

4 mushrooms / 72g

Amount per serving	%DV	Amount per serving	%DV	Amount per serving	%DV
Calories 39		**Cholesterol** 0mg	0%	**Total Carbohydrate** 10g	3%
Total Fat 0g	0%	**Sodium** 173mg	7%	Dietary Fiber 2g	8%
Saturated Fat 0g	0%	**Protein** 1g		Sugars 3g	
Polyunsaturated Fat 0g					
Monounsaturated Fat 0g		Vitamin A 0% Vitamin C 0%		Calcium 0% Iron 2%	

Mushrooms, Shiitake, Dried

1 mushroom / 15g

Amount per serving	%DV	Amount per serving	%DV	Amount per serving	%DV
Calories 44		**Cholesterol** 0mg	0%	**Total Carbohydrate** 11.3g	4%
Total Fat 0g	0%	**Sodium** 2mg	0%	Dietary Fiber 1.7g	7%
Saturated Fat 0g	0%	**Protein** 1.4g		Sugars 0g	
Polyunsaturated Fat 0g					
Monounsaturated Fat 0g		Vitamin A 0% Vitamin C 1%		Calcium 0% Iron 1%	

Mushrooms, Shiitake, Stir-Fried

1 cup, sliced / 97g

Amount per serving	%DV	Amount per serving	%DV	Amount per serving	%DV
Calories 47		**Cholesterol** 0mg	0%	**Total Carbohydrate** 7g	2%
Total Fat 0g	0%	**Sodium** 5mg	0%	Dietary Fiber 3g	12%
Saturated Fat 0g	0%	**Protein** 3g		Sugars 0g	
Polyunsaturated Fat 0g					
Monounsaturated Fat 0g		Vitamin A 0% Vitamin C 0%		Calcium 0% Iron 3%	

Mushrooms, Straw, Canned, Drained Solids

1 oz / 28g

Amount per serving	%DV	Amount per serving	%DV	Amount per serving	%DV
Calories 9		**Cholesterol** 0mg	0%	**Total Carbohydrate** 1g	0%
Total Fat 0g	0%	**Sodium** 108mg	4%	Dietary Fiber 0g	0%
Saturated Fat 0g	0%	**Protein** 1g		Sugars 0g	
Polyunsaturated Fat 0g					
Monounsaturated Fat 0g		Vitamin A 0% Vitamin C 0%		Calcium 0% Iron 2%	

Mushrooms, White, Raw

1 cup, pieces or slices / 70g

Amount per serving	%DV	Amount per serving	%DV	Amount per serving	%DV
Calories 15		**Cholesterol** 0mg	0%	**Total Carbohydrate** 2g	1%
Total Fat 0g	0%	**Sodium** 4mg	0%	Dietary Fiber 1g	4%
Saturated Fat 0g	0%	**Protein** 2g		Sugars 1g	
Polyunsaturated Fat 0g					
Monounsaturated Fat 0g		Vitamin A 0% Vitamin C 2%		Calcium 0% Iron 2%	

Mushrooms, White, Stir-Fried

1 cup / sliced / 108g

Amount per serving	%DV	Amount per serving	%DV	Amount per serving	%DV
Calories 28		**Cholesterol** 0mg	0%	**Total Carbohydrate** 4g	1%
Total Fat 0g	0%	**Sodium** 13mg	1%	Dietary Fiber 2g	8%
Saturated Fat 0g	0%	**Protein** 0g		Sugars 0g	
Polyunsaturated Fat 0g					
Monounsaturated Fat 0g		Vitamin A 0% Vitamin C 0%		Calcium 0% Iron 2%	

Mustard Greens, Frozen, Cooked, Boiled, Drained, without Salt

1 cup, chopped / 150g

Amount per serving	%DV	Amount per serving	%DV	Amount per serving	%DV
Calories 28		**Cholesterol** 0mg	0%	**Total Carbohydrate** 5g	2%
Total Fat 0g	0%	**Sodium** 37mg	2%	Dietary Fiber 4g	16%
Saturated Fat 0g	0%	**Protein** 3g		Sugars 0g	
Polyunsaturated Fat 0g					
Monounsaturated Fat 0g		Vitamin A 212% Vitamin C 35%		Calcium 15% Iron 9%	

Mustard Greens, Frozen, Unprepared

1 cup, chopped / 146g

Amount per serving	%DV	Amount per serving	%DV	Amount per serving	%DV
Calories 29		**Cholesterol** 0mg	0%	**Total Carbohydrate** 5g	2%
Total Fat 0g	0%	**Sodium** 151mg	6%	Dietary Fiber 5g	20%
Saturated Fat 0g	0%	**Protein** 4g		Sugars 0g	
Polyunsaturated Fat 0g					
Monounsaturated Fat 0g		Vitamin A 151% Vitamin C 62%		Calcium 17% Iron 10%	

Mustard Greens, Raw

1 cup, chopped / 56g

Amount per serving	%DV	Amount per serving	%DV	Amount per serving	%DV
Calories 15		**Cholesterol** 0mg	0%	**Total Carbohydrate** 2.7g	1%
Total Fat 0g	0%	**Sodium** 14mg	1%	Dietary Fiber 1.8g	7%
Saturated Fat 0g	0%	**Protein** 1.5g		Sugars 0g	
Polyunsaturated Fat 0g					
Monounsaturated Fat 0g		Vitamin A 118% Vitamin C 65%		Calcium 6% Iron 5%	

Mustard Spinach, Tendergreen, Raw

1 cup, chopped / 150g

Amount per serving	%DV	Amount per serving	%DV	Amount per serving	%DV
Calories 33		**Cholesterol** 0mg	0%	**Total Carbohydrate** 5.8g	2%
Total Fat 0g	0%	**Sodium** 32mg	1%	Dietary Fiber 4.2g	17%
Saturated Fat 0g	0%	**Protein** 3.3g		Sugars 0g	
Polyunsaturated Fat 0.1g					
Monounsaturated Fat 0.2g		Vitamin A 297% Vitamin C 325%		Calcium 32% Iron 13%	

New Zealand Spinach, Cooked, Boiled, Drained, without Salt

1 cup, chopped / 180g

Amount per serving	%DV	Amount per serving	%DV	Amount per serving	%DV
Calories 22		**Cholesterol** 0mg	0%	**Total Carbohydrate** 4g	1%
Total Fat 0g	0%	**Sodium** 193mg	8%	Dietary Fiber 0g	0%
Saturated Fat 0g	0%	**Protein** 2.3g		Sugars 0g	
Polyunsaturated Fat 0g					
Monounsaturated Fat 0g		Vitamin A 130% Vitamin C 48%		Calcium 9% Iron 7%	

New Zealand Spinach, Raw

1 cup, chopped / 56g

Amount per serving	%DV	Amount per serving	%DV	Amount per serving	%DV
Calories 8		**Cholesterol** 0mg	0%	**Total Carbohydrate** 1.4g	0%
Total Fat 0g	0%	**Sodium** 73mg	3%	Dietary Fiber 0g	0%
Saturated Fat 0g	0%	**Protein** 0.8g		Sugars 0g	
Polyunsaturated Fat 0g					
Monounsaturated Fat 0g		Vitamin A 49% Vitamin C 28%		Calcium 3% Iron 2%	

Nopales, Cooked, without Salt

1 cup / 149g

Amount per serving	%DV	Amount per serving	%DV	Amount per serving	%DV
Calories 22		**Cholesterol** 0mg	0%	**Total Carbohydrate** 1g	0%
Total Fat 0g	0%	**Sodium** 30mg	1%	Dietary Fiber 3g	12%
Saturated Fat 0g	0%	**Protein** 2g		Sugars 2g	
Polyunsaturated Fat 0g					
Monounsaturated Fat 0g		Vitamin A 13% Vitamin C 13%		Calcium 24% Iron 4%	

Okra, Cooked, Boiled, Drained, with Salt

1/2 cup, slices / 80g

Amount per serving	%DV	Amount per serving	%DV	Amount per serving	%DV
Calories 18		**Cholesterol** 0mg	0%	**Total Carbohydrate** 4g	1%
Total Fat 0g	0%	**Sodium** 193mg	8%	Dietary Fiber 2g	8%
Saturated Fat 0g	0%	**Protein** 1g		Sugars 2g	
Polyunsaturated Fat 0g					
Monounsaturated Fat 0g		Vitamin A 5% Vitamin C 22%		Calcium 6% Iron 1%	

Okra, Cooked, Boiled, Drained, without Salt

1/2 cup, slices / 80g

Amount per serving	%DV	Amount per serving	%DV	Amount per serving	%DV
Calories 18		**Cholesterol** 0mg	0%	**Total Carbohydrate** 4g	1%
Total Fat 0g	0%	**Sodium** 5mg	0%	Dietary Fiber 2g	8%
Saturated Fat 0g	0%	**Protein** 1g		Sugars 2g	
Polyunsaturated Fat 0g					
Monounsaturated Fat 0g		Vitamin A 5% Vitamin C 22%		Calcium 6% Iron 1%	

Okra, Frozen, Cooked, Boiled, Drained, with Salt

1/2 cup, slices / 92g

Amount per serving	%DV	Amount per serving	%DV	Amount per serving	%DV
Calories 71		**Cholesterol** 0mg	0%	**Total Carbohydrate** 15g	5%
Total Fat 1g	2%	**Sodium** 220mg	9%	Dietary Fiber 7g	28%
Saturated Fat 0g	0%	**Protein** 5g		Sugars 7g	
Polyunsaturated Fat 0g					
Monounsaturated Fat 0g		Vitamin A 280.5%	Vitamin C 9%	Calcium 68%	Iron 0.5%

Okra, Frozen, Cooked, Boiled, Drained, without Salt

1/2 cup, slices / 92g

Amount per serving	%DV	Amount per serving	%DV	Amount per serving	%DV
Calories 26		**Cholesterol** 0mg	0%	**Total Carbohydrate** 5g	2%
Total Fat 0g	0%	**Sodium** 3mg	0%	Dietary Fiber 3g	12%
Saturated Fat 0g	0%	**Protein** 2g		Sugars 3g	
Polyunsaturated Fat 0g					
Monounsaturated Fat 0g		Vitamin A 6%	Vitamin C 19%	Calcium 9%	Iron 3%

Okra, Frozen, Unprepared

1 oz / 28g

Amount per serving	%DV	Amount per serving	%DV	Amount per serving	%DV
Calories 8		**Cholesterol** 0mg	0%	**Total Carbohydrate** 2g	1%
Total Fat 0g	0%	**Sodium** 1mg	0%	Dietary Fiber 1g	4%
Saturated Fat 0g	0%	**Protein** 0g		Sugars 1g	
Polyunsaturated Fat 0g					
Monounsaturated Fat 0g		Vitamin A 2%	Vitamin C 6%	Calcium 2%	Iron 1%

Okra, Raw

1 cup / 100g

Amount per serving	%DV	Amount per serving	%DV	Amount per serving	%DV
Calories 31		**Cholesterol** 0mg	0%	**Total Carbohydrate** 7g	2%
Total Fat 0g	0%	**Sodium** 8mg	0%	Dietary Fiber 3g	12%
Saturated Fat 0g	0%	**Protein** 2g		Sugars 1g	
Polyunsaturated Fat 0g					
Monounsaturated Fat 0g		Vitamin A 7%	Vitamin C 35%	Calcium 8%	Iron 4%

Onions, Canned, Solids and Liquids

1 oz / 28g

Amount per serving	%DV	Amount per serving	%DV	Amount per serving	%DV
Calories 5		**Cholesterol** 0mg	0%	**Total Carbohydrate** 1g	0%
Total Fat 0g	0%	**Sodium** 104mg	4%	Dietary Fiber 0g	0%
Saturated Fat 0g	0%	**Protein** 0g		Sugars 1g	
Polyunsaturated Fat 0g					
Monounsaturated Fat 0g		Vitamin A 0%	Vitamin C 0%	Calcium 1%	Iron 0%

Onions, Cooked, Boiled, Drained, with Salt

1 small / 60g

Amount per serving	%DV	Amount per serving	%DV	Amount per serving	%DV
Calories 25		**Cholesterol** 0mg	0%	**Total Carbohydrate** 6g	2%
Total Fat 0g	0%	**Sodium** 143mg	6%	Dietary Fiber 1g	4%
Saturated Fat 0g	0%	**Protein** 1g		Sugars 3g	
Polyunsaturated Fat 0g					
Monounsaturated Fat 0g		Vitamin A 0% Vitamin C 5%		Calcium 1% Iron 1%	

Onions, Cooked, Boiled, Drained, without Salt

1 cup / 210g

Amount per serving	%DV	Amount per serving	%DV	Amount per serving	%DV
Calories 92		**Cholesterol** 0mg	0%	**Total Carbohydrate** 21g	7%
Total Fat 0g	0%	**Sodium** 6mg	0%	Dietary Fiber 3g	12%
Saturated Fat 0g	0%	**Protein** 0g		Sugars 10g	
Polyunsaturated Fat 0g					
Monounsaturated Fat 0g		Vitamin A 0% Vitamin C 18%		Calcium 5% Iron 3%	

Onions, Dehydrated Flakes

1/4 cup / 14g

Amount per serving	%DV	Amount per serving	%DV	Amount per serving	%DV
Calories 49		**Cholesterol** 0mg	0%	**Total Carbohydrate** 12g	4%
Total Fat 0g	0%	**Sodium** 3mg	0%	Dietary Fiber 1g	4%
Saturated Fat 0g	0%	**Protein** 1g		Sugars 5g	
Polyunsaturated Fat 0g					
Monounsaturated Fat 0g		Vitamin A 0% Vitamin C 17%		Calcium 4% Iron 1%	

Onions, Frozen, Chopped, Cooked, Boiled, Drained, with Salt

1 tbsp chopped / 15g

Amount per serving	%DV	Amount per serving	%DV	Amount per serving	%DV
Calories 4		**Cholesterol** 0mg	0%	**Total Carbohydrate** 1g	0%
Total Fat 0g	0%	**Sodium** 37mg	2%	Dietary Fiber 0g	0%
Saturated Fat 0g	0%	**Protein** 0g		Sugars 0g	
Polyunsaturated Fat 0g					
Monounsaturated Fat 0g		Vitamin A 0% Vitamin C 1%		Calcium 0% Iron 0%	

Onions, Frozen, Chopped, Cooked, Boiled, Drained, without Salt

1 tbsp chopped / 15g

Amount per serving	%DV	Amount per serving	%DV	Amount per serving	%DV
Calories 4		**Cholesterol** 0mg	0%	**Total Carbohydrate** 1g	0%
Total Fat 0g	0%	**Sodium** 2mg	0%	Dietary Fiber 0g	0%
Saturated Fat 0g	0%	**Protein** 0g		Sugars 0g	
Polyunsaturated Fat 0g					
Monounsaturated Fat 0g		Vitamin A 0% Vitamin C 1%		Calcium 0% Iron 0%	

Onions, Raw

1 cup, chopped / 160g

Amount per serving	%DV	Amount per serving	%DV	Amount per serving	%DV
Calories 64		**Cholesterol** 0mg	0%	**Total Carbohydrate** 15g	5%
Total Fat 0g	0%	**Sodium** 6mg	0%	Dietary Fiber 3g	12%
Saturated Fat 0g	0%	**Protein** 2g		Sugars 7g	
Polyunsaturated Fat 0g					
Monounsaturated Fat 0g		Vitamin A 0%	Vitamin C 20%	Calcium 4%	Iron 2%

Onions, Spring or Scallions (Includes Tops and Bulb), Raw

1 cup, chopped / 100g

Amount per serving	%DV	Amount per serving	%DV	Amount per serving	%DV
Calories 32		**Cholesterol** 0mg	0%	**Total Carbohydrate** 7g	2%
Total Fat 0g	0%	**Sodium** 16mg	1%	Dietary Fiber 3g	12%
Saturated Fat 0g	0%	**Protein** 2g		Sugars 2g	
Polyunsaturated Fat 0g					
Monounsaturated Fat 0g		Vitamin A 20%	Vitamin C 31%	Calcium 7%	Iron 8%

Onions, Sweet, Raw

1 onion / 331g

Amount per serving	%DV	Amount per serving	%DV	Amount per serving	%DV
Calories 106		**Cholesterol** 0mg	0%	**Total Carbohydrate** 25g	8%
Total Fat 0g	0%	**Sodium** 26mg	1%	Dietary Fiber 3g	12%
Saturated Fat 0g	0%	**Protein** 3g		Sugars 17g	
Polyunsaturated Fat 0g					
Monounsaturated Fat 0g		Vitamin A 0%	Vitamin C 26%	Calcium 29.5%	Iron 0.5%

Parsnips, Cooked, Boiled, Drained, with Salt

1 oz / 28g

Amount per serving	%DV	Amount per serving	%DV	Amount per serving	%DV
Calories 20		**Cholesterol** 0mg	0%	**Total Carbohydrate** 5g	2%
Total Fat 0g	0%	**Sodium** 69mg	3%	Dietary Fiber 1g	4%
Saturated Fat 0g	0%	**Protein** 0g		Sugars 1g	
Polyunsaturated Fat 0g					
Monounsaturated Fat 0g		Vitamin A 0%	Vitamin C 6%	Calcium 1%	Iron 1%

Parsnips, Cooked, Boiled, Drained, without Salt

1/2 cup, slices / 78g

Amount per serving	%DV	Amount per serving	%DV	Amount per serving	%DV
Calories 55		**Cholesterol** 0mg	0%	**Total Carbohydrate** 13g	4%
Total Fat 0g	0%	**Sodium** 8mg	0%	Dietary Fiber 3g	12%
Saturated Fat 0g	0%	**Protein** 1g		Sugars 4g	
Polyunsaturated Fat 0g					
Monounsaturated Fat 0g		Vitamin A 0%	Vitamin C 17%	Calcium 3%	Iron 3%

Parsnips, Raw

1 cup, slices / 133g

Amount per serving	%DV	Amount per serving	%DV	Amount per serving	%DV
Calories 100		**Cholesterol** 0mg	0%	**Total Carbohydrate** 23.9g	8%
Total Fat 0g	0%	**Sodium** 13mg	1%	Dietary Fiber 6.5g	26%
Saturated Fat 0g	0%	**Protein** 1.6g		Sugars 6.4g	
Polyunsaturated Fat 0g					
Monounsaturated Fat 0g		Vitamin A 0% Vitamin C 38%		Calcium 5% Iron 4%	

Peas and Carrots, Frozen, Cooked, Boiled, Drained, without Salt

1/2 cup / 80g

Amount per serving	%DV	Amount per serving	%DV	Amount per serving	%DV
Calories 38		**Cholesterol** 0mg	0%	**Total Carbohydrate** 8g	3%
Total Fat 0g	0%	**Sodium** 54mg	2%	Dietary Fiber 2g	8%
Saturated Fat 0g	0%	**Protein** 2g		Sugars 3g	
Polyunsaturated Fat 0g					
Monounsaturated Fat 0g		Vitamin A 52% Vitamin C 11%		Calcium 2% Iron 4%	

Peas, Edible-Podded, Frozen, Cooked, Boiled, Drained, without Salt

1 cup / 160g

Amount per serving	%DV	Amount per serving	%DV	Amount per serving	%DV
Calories 83		**Cholesterol** 0mg	0%	**Total Carbohydrate** 14g	5%
Total Fat 1g	2%	**Sodium** 8mg	0%	Dietary Fiber 5g	20%
Saturated Fat 0g	0%	**Protein** 6g		Sugars 8g	
Polyunsaturated Fat 0g					
Monounsaturated Fat 0g		Vitamin A 42% Vitamin C 59%		Calcium 9% Iron 21%	

Peas, Edible-Podded, Frozen, Unprepared

1/2 cup / 72g

Amount per serving	%DV	Amount per serving	%DV	Amount per serving	%DV
Calories 30		**Cholesterol** 0mg	0%	**Total Carbohydrate** 5g	2%
Total Fat 0g	0%	**Sodium** 3mg	0%	Dietary Fiber 2g	8%
Saturated Fat 0g	0%	**Protein** 2g		Sugars 0g	
Polyunsaturated Fat 0g					
Monounsaturated Fat 0g		Vitamin A 2% Vitamin C 26%		Calcium 4% Iron 8%	

Peas, Edible-Podded, Raw

1 cup, whole / 63g

Amount per serving	%DV	Amount per serving	%DV	Amount per serving	%DV
Calories 26		**Cholesterol** 0mg	0%	**Total Carbohydrate** 5g	2%
Total Fat 0g	0%	**Sodium** 3mg	0%	Dietary Fiber 2g	8%
Saturated Fat 0g	0%	**Protein** 2g		Sugars 3g	
Polyunsaturated Fat 0g					
Monounsaturated Fat 0g		Vitamin A 14% Vitamin C 63%		Calcium 3% Iron 7%	

Peas, Green, Canned, No Salt Added, Drained Solids

1/2 cup / 85g

Amount per serving	%DV	Amount per serving	%DV	Amount per serving	%DV
Calories 59		**Cholesterol** 0mg	0%	**Total Carbohydrate** 11g	4%
Total Fat 0g	0%	**Sodium** 2mg	0%	Dietary Fiber 3g	12%
Saturated Fat 0g	0%	**Protein** 4g		Sugars 4g	
Polyunsaturated Fat 0.5g					
Monounsaturated Fat 0g		Vitamin A 9%	Vitamin C 14%	Calcium 2%	Iron 4%

Peas, Green, Canned, No Salt Added, Solids and Liquids

1/2 cup / 124g

Amount per serving	%DV	Amount per serving	%DV	Amount per serving	%DV
Calories 66		**Cholesterol** 0mg	0%	**Total Carbohydrate** 12g	4%
Total Fat 0g	0%	**Sodium** 11mg	0%	Dietary Fiber 4g	16%
Saturated Fat 0g	0%	**Protein** 4g		Sugars 4g	
Polyunsaturated Fat 0g					
Monounsaturated Fat 0g		Vitamin A 36%	Vitamin C 20%	Calcium 2%	Iron 7%

Peas, Green, Canned, Seasoned, Solids and Liquids

1/2 cup / 114g

Amount per serving	%DV	Amount per serving	%DV	Amount per serving	%DV
Calories 57		**Cholesterol** 0mg	0%	**Total Carbohydrate** 11g	4%
Total Fat 0g	0%	**Sodium** 290mg	12%	Dietary Fiber 2g	8%
Saturated Fat 0g	0%	**Protein** 4g		Sugars 0g	
Polyunsaturated Fat 0g					
Monounsaturated Fat 0g		Vitamin A 10%	Vitamin C 22%	Calcium 2%	Iron 8%

Peas, Green, Frozen, Cooked, Boiled, Drained, without Salt

1/2 cup / 80g

Amount per serving	%DV	Amount per serving	%DV	Amount per serving	%DV
Calories 62		**Cholesterol** 0mg	0%	**Total Carbohydrate** 11g	4%
Total Fat 0g	0%	**Sodium** 58mg	2%	Dietary Fiber 4g	16%
Saturated Fat 0g	0%	**Protein** 4g		Sugars 4g	
Polyunsaturated Fat 0g					
Monounsaturated Fat 0g		Vitamin A 34%	Vitamin C 13%	Calcium 2%	Iron 7%

Peas, Green, Frozen, Unprepared

1 cup / 134g

Amount per serving	%DV	Amount per serving	%DV	Amount per serving	%DV
Calories 103		**Cholesterol** 0mg	0%	**Total Carbohydrate** 18g	6%
Total Fat 1g	2%	**Sodium** 55mg	2%	Dietary Fiber 6g	24%
Saturated Fat 0g	0%	**Protein** 7g		Sugars 7g	
Polyunsaturated Fat 0g					
Monounsaturated Fat 0g		Vitamin A 55%	Vitamin C 40%	Calcium 3%	Iron 11%

Peas, Green, Raw

1 cup / 145g

Amount per serving	%DV	Amount per serving	%DV	Amount per serving	%DV
Calories 117		Cholesterol 0mg	0%	Total Carbohydrate 21g	7%
Total Fat 1g	2%	Sodium 7mg	0%	Dietary Fiber 7.4g	30%
Saturated Fat 0g	0%	Protein 7.9g		Sugars 8.2g	
Polyunsaturated Fat 0g					
Monounsaturated Fat 0g		Vitamin A 22% Vitamin C 97%		Calcium 4% Iron 12%	

Peppers, Hot Chili, Green, Raw

1/2 cup, chopped or diced / 75g

Amount per serving	%DV	Amount per serving	%DV	Amount per serving	%DV
Calories 30		Cholesterol 0mg	0%	Total Carbohydrate 7g	2%
Total Fat 0g	0%	Sodium 5mg	0%	Dietary Fiber 1g	4%
Saturated Fat 0g	0%	Protein 1g		Sugars 4g	
Polyunsaturated Fat 0g					
Monounsaturated Fat 0g		Vitamin A 18% Vitamin C 303%		Calcium 1% Iron 5%	

Peppers, Hot Chili, Red, Raw

1/2 cup, chopped or diced / 75g

Amount per serving	%DV	Amount per serving	%DV	Amount per serving	%DV
Calories 30		Cholesterol 0mg	0%	Total Carbohydrate 7g	2%
Total Fat 0.5g	1%	Sodium 7mg	0%	Dietary Fiber 1g	4%
Saturated Fat 0g	0%	Protein 1g		Sugars 4g	
Polyunsaturated Fat 0g					
Monounsaturated Fat 0g		Vitamin A 14% Vitamin C 180%		Calcium 1% Iron 4%	

Peppers, Hot Chili, Sun-Dried

1 cup / 37g

Amount per serving	%DV	Amount per serving	%DV	Amount per serving	%DV
Calories 120		Cholesterol 0mg	0%	Total Carbohydrate 26g	9%
Total Fat 0g	0%	Sodium 34mg	1%	Dietary Fiber 11g	44%
Saturated Fat 0g	0%	Protein 4g		Sugars 15g	
Polyunsaturated Fat 0g					
Monounsaturated Fat 0g		Vitamin A 196% Vitamin C 19%		Calcium 2% Iron 12%	

Peppers, Hungarian, Raw

1 pepper / 27g

Amount per serving	%DV	Amount per serving	%DV	Amount per serving	%DV
Calories 8		Cholesterol 0mg	0%	Total Carbohydrate 1.8g	1%
Total Fat 0g	0%	Sodium 0mg	0%	Dietary Fiber 0g	0%
Saturated Fat 0g	0%	Protein 0g		Sugars 0g	
Polyunsaturated Fat 0g					
Monounsaturated Fat 0g		Vitamin A 1% Vitamin C 42%		Calcium 0% Iron 1%	

Peppers, Jalapeno, Raw

1 pepper / 14g

Amount per serving	%DV	Amount per serving	%DV	Amount per serving	%DV
Calories 4		**Cholesterol** 0mg	0%	**Total Carbohydrate** 1g	0%
Total Fat 0g	0%	**Sodium** 0mg	0%	Dietary Fiber 0g	0%
Saturated Fat 0g	0%	**Protein** 0g		Sugars 0g	
Polyunsaturated Fat 0g					
Monounsaturated Fat 0g		Vitamin A 2%	Vitamin C 10%	Calcium 0%	Iron 1%

Peppers, Serrano, Raw

1 pepper / 6g

Amount per serving	%DV	Amount per serving	%DV	Amount per serving	%DV
Calories 2		**Cholesterol** 0mg	0%	**Total Carbohydrate** 0g	0%
Total Fat 0g	0%	**Sodium** 1mg	0%	Dietary Fiber 0g	0%
Saturated Fat 0g	0%	**Protein** 0g		Sugars 0g	
Polyunsaturated Fat 0g					
Monounsaturated Fat 0g		Vitamin A 1%	Vitamin C 4%	Calcium 0%	Iron 0%

Peppers, Sweet, Green, Cooked, Boiled, Drained, with Salt

1 tbsp / 12g

Amount per serving	%DV	Amount per serving	%DV	Amount per serving	%DV
Calories 3		**Cholesterol** 0mg	0%	**Total Carbohydrate** 1g	0%
Total Fat 0g	0%	**Sodium** 27mg	1%	Dietary Fiber 0g	0%
Saturated Fat 0g	0%	**Protein** 0g		Sugars 0g	
Polyunsaturated Fat 0g					
Monounsaturated Fat 0g		Vitamin A 1%	Vitamin C 14%	Calcium 0%	Iron 0%

Peppers, Sweet, Green, Cooked, Boiled, Drained, without Salt

1 cup, chopped or strips / 135g

Amount per serving	%DV	Amount per serving	%DV	Amount per serving	%DV
Calories 38		**Cholesterol** 0mg	0%	**Total Carbohydrate** 9g	3%
Total Fat 0g	0%	**Sodium** 3mg	0%	Dietary Fiber 2g	8%
Saturated Fat 0g	0%	**Protein** 1g		Sugars 4g	
Polyunsaturated Fat 0g					
Monounsaturated Fat 0g		Vitamin A 13%	Vitamin C 167%	Calcium 1%	Iron 3%

Peppers, Sweet, Green, Freeze-Dried

1/4 cup / 2g

Amount per serving	%DV	Amount per serving	%DV	Amount per serving	%DV
Calories 5		**Cholesterol** 0mg	0%	**Total Carbohydrate** 1g	0%
Total Fat 0g	0%	**Sodium** 3mg	0%	Dietary Fiber 0g	0%
Saturated Fat 0g	0%	**Protein** 0g		Sugars 1g	
Polyunsaturated Fat 0g					
Monounsaturated Fat 0g		Vitamin A 2%	Vitamin C 48%	Calcium 0%	Iron 1%

Peppers, Sweet, Green, Frozen, Chopped, Cooked, Boiled, Drained, with Salt

1 tbsp, chopped / 12g

Amount per serving	%DV	Amount per serving	%DV	Amount per serving	%DV
Calories 2		**Cholesterol** 0mg	0%	**Total Carbohydrate** 0g	0%
Total Fat 0g	0%	**Sodium** 28mg	1%	Dietary Fiber 0g	0%
Saturated Fat 0g	0%	**Protein** 0g		Sugars 0g	
Polyunsaturated Fat 0g					
Monounsaturated Fat 0g		Vitamin A 0%	Vitamin C 8%	Calcium 0%	Iron 0%

Peppers, Sweet, Green, Frozen, Chopped, Unprepared

1 package, 10 oz / 284g

Amount per serving	%DV	Amount per serving	%DV	Amount per serving	%DV
Calories 57		**Cholesterol** 0mg	0%	**Total Carbohydrate** 13g	4%
Total Fat 1g	2%	**Sodium** 14mg	1%	Dietary Fiber 5g	20%
Saturated Fat 0g	0%	**Protein** 3g		Sugars 0g	
Polyunsaturated Fat 0g					
Monounsaturated Fat 0g		Vitamin A 21%	Vitamin C 278%	Calcium 3%	Iron 10%

Peppers, Sweet, Green, Raw

1 cup, chopped / 149g

Amount per serving	%DV	Amount per serving	%DV	Amount per serving	%DV
Calories 30		**Cholesterol** 0mg	0%	**Total Carbohydrate** 7g	2%
Total Fat 0g	0%	**Sodium** 4mg	0%	Dietary Fiber 3g	12%
Saturated Fat 0g	0%	**Protein** 1g		Sugars 4g	
Polyunsaturated Fat 0g					
Monounsaturated Fat 0g		Vitamin A 11%	Vitamin C 200%	Calcium 1%	Iron 3%

Peppers, Sweet, Red, Cooked, Boiled, Drained, without Salt

1/2 cup, chopped / 68g

Amount per serving	%DV	Amount per serving	%DV	Amount per serving	%DV
Calories 19		**Cholesterol** 0mg	0%	**Total Carbohydrate** 5g	2%
Total Fat 0g	0%	**Sodium** 0mg	0%	Dietary Fiber 0g	0%
Saturated Fat 0g	0%	**Protein** 0g		Sugars 3g	
Polyunsaturated Fat 0g					
Monounsaturated Fat 0g		Vitamin A 40%	Vitamin C 194%	Calcium 1%	Iron 2%

Peppers, Sweet, Red, Freeze-Dried

1/4 cup / 2g

Amount per serving	%DV	Amount per serving	%DV	Amount per serving	%DV
Calories 5		**Cholesterol** 0mg	0%	**Total Carbohydrate** 1g	0%
Total Fat 0g	0%	**Sodium** 3mg	0%	Dietary Fiber 0g	0%
Saturated Fat 0g	0%	**Protein** 0g		Sugars 1g	
Polyunsaturated Fat 0g					
Monounsaturated Fat 0g		Vitamin A 23%	Vitamin C 48%	Calcium 0%	Iron 1%

Peppers, Sweet, Red, Frozen, Chopped, Boiled, Drained, with Salt

1 tbsp, chopped / 12g

Amount per serving	%DV	Amount per serving	%DV	Amount per serving	%DV
Calories 2		**Cholesterol** 0mg	0%	**Total Carbohydrate** 0g	0%
Total Fat 0g	0%	**Sodium** 28mg	1%	Dietary Fiber 0g	0%
Saturated Fat 0g	0%	**Protein** 0g		Sugars 0g	
Polyunsaturated Fat 0g					
Monounsaturated Fat 0g		Vitamin A 8%	Vitamin C 8%	Calcium 0%	Iron 0%

Peppers, Sweet, Red, Frozen, Chopped, Boiled, Drained, without Salt

1/2 cup, chopped / 68g

Amount per serving	%DV	Amount per serving	%DV	Amount per serving	%DV
Calories 19		**Cholesterol** 0mg	0%	**Total Carbohydrate** 5g	2%
Total Fat 0g	0%	**Sodium** 1mg	0%	Dietary Fiber 0g	0%
Saturated Fat 0g	0%	**Protein** 1g		Sugars 3g	
Polyunsaturated Fat 0g					
Monounsaturated Fat 0g		Vitamin A 40%	Vitamin C 194%	Calcium 1%	Iron 2%

Peppers, Sweet, Red, Frozen, Chopped, Unprepared

1 / 10 oz pkg / 28g

Amount per serving	%DV	Amount per serving	%DV	Amount per serving	%DV
Calories 6		**Cholesterol** 0mg	0%	**Total Carbohydrate** 1g	0%
Total Fat 0g	0%	**Sodium** 1mg	0%	Dietary Fiber 0g	0%
Saturated Fat 0g	0%	**Protein** 0g		Sugars 1g	
Polyunsaturated Fat 0g					
Monounsaturated Fat 0g		Vitamin A 14%	Vitamin C 27%	Calcium 0%	Iron 1%

Peppers, Sweet, Red, Raw

1 cup, sliced / 92g

Amount per serving	%DV	Amount per serving	%DV	Amount per serving	%DV
Calories 29		**Cholesterol** 0mg	0%	**Total Carbohydrate** 6g	2%
Total Fat 0g	0%	**Sodium** 4mg	0%	Dietary Fiber 2g	8%
Saturated Fat 0g	0%	**Protein** 1g		Sugars 4g	
Polyunsaturated Fat 0g					
Monounsaturated Fat 0g		Vitamin A 58%	Vitamin C 196%	Calcium 1%	Iron 2%

Peppers, Sweet, Yellow, Raw

1 pepper, large (3-3/4″ long, 3″ diameter) / 186g

Amount per serving	%DV	Amount per serving	%DV	Amount per serving	%DV
Calories 50		**Cholesterol** 0mg	0%	**Total Carbohydrate** 12g	4%
Total Fat 0g	0%	**Sodium** 4mg	0%	Dietary Fiber 2g	8%
Saturated Fat 0g	0%	**Protein** 2g		Sugars 0g	
Polyunsaturated Fat 0g					
Monounsaturated Fat 0g		Vitamin A 7%	Vitamin C 569%	Calcium 2%	Iron 5%

Pimento, Canned

1 cup / 192g

Amount per serving	%DV	Amount per serving	%DV	Amount per serving	%DV
Calories 44		**Cholesterol** 0mg	0%	**Total Carbohydrate** 10g	3%
Total Fat 1g	2%	**Sodium** 27mg	1%	Dietary Fiber 4g	16%
Saturated Fat 0g	0%	**Protein** 2g		Sugars 5g	
Polyunsaturated Fat 0g					
Monounsaturated Fat 0g		Vitamin A 102% Vitamin C 272% Calcium 1% Iron 18%			

Pumpkin Flowers, Cooked, Boiled, Drained, without Salt

1 cup / 134g

Amount per serving	%DV	Amount per serving	%DV	Amount per serving	%DV
Calories 20		**Cholesterol** 0mg	0%	**Total Carbohydrate** 4.4g	1%
Total Fat 0g	0%	**Sodium** 8mg	0%	Dietary Fiber 1.2g	5%
Saturated Fat 0g	0%	**Protein** 1.5g		Sugars 3.2g	
Polyunsaturated Fat 0g					
Monounsaturated Fat 0g		Vitamin A 46% Vitamin C 11% Calcium 5% Iron 7%			

Pumpkin Leaves, Cooked, Boiled, Drained, with Salt

1 cup / 71g

Amount per serving	%DV	Amount per serving	%DV	Amount per serving	%DV
Calories 15		**Cholesterol** 0mg	0%	**Total Carbohydrate** 2.4g	1%
Total Fat 0.2g	0%	**Sodium** 173mg	7%	Dietary Fiber 1.9g	8%
Saturated Fat 0.1g	0%	**Protein** 1.9g		Sugars 0.5g	
Polyunsaturated Fat 0g					
Monounsaturated Fat 0g		Vitamin A 23% Vitamin C 1% Calcium 3% Iron 13%			

Pumpkin Leaves, Cooked, Boiled, Drained, without Salt

1 cup / 71g

Amount per serving	%DV	Amount per serving	%DV	Amount per serving	%DV
Calories 15		**Cholesterol** 0mg	0%	**Total Carbohydrate** 2.4g	1%
Total Fat 0.2g	0%	**Sodium** 6mg	0%	Dietary Fiber 1.9g	8%
Saturated Fat 0.1g	0%	**Protein** 1.9g		Sugars 0.5g	
Polyunsaturated Fat 0g					
Monounsaturated Fat 0g		Vitamin A 23% Vitamin C 1% Calcium 3% Iron 13%			

Pumpkin, Canned, without Salt

1 cup / 245g

Amount per serving	%DV	Amount per serving	%DV	Amount per serving	%DV
Calories 83		**Cholesterol** 0mg	0%	**Total Carbohydrate** 19.8g	7%
Total Fat 0.7g	1%	**Sodium** 12mg	0%	Dietary Fiber 7.1g	28%
Saturated Fat 0.4g	2%	**Protein** 2.7g		Sugars 8.1g	
Polyunsaturated Fat 0g					
Monounsaturated Fat 0.1g		Vitamin A 763% Vitamin C 17% Calcium 6% Iron 19%			

Pumpkin, Cooked, Boiled, Drained, without Salt

1 cup, mashed / 245g

Amount per serving	%DV	Amount per serving	%DV	Amount per serving	%DV
Calories 49		**Cholesterol** 0mg	0%	**Total Carbohydrate** 12g	4%
Total Fat 0g	0%	**Sodium** 2mg	0%	Dietary Fiber 2.5g	10%
Saturated Fat 0g	0%	**Protein** 2g		Sugars 2g	
Polyunsaturated Fat 0g					
Monounsaturated Fat 0g		Vitamin A 245% Vitamin C 19%		Calcium 4% Iron 8%	

Pumpkin, Flowers, Cooked, Boiled, Drained, with Salt

1 cup / 134g

Amount per serving	%DV	Amount per serving	%DV	Amount per serving	%DV
Calories 20		**Cholesterol** 0mg	0%	**Total Carbohydrate** 4g	1%
Total Fat 0g	0%	**Sodium** 324mg	14%	Dietary Fiber 1g	4%
Saturated Fat 0g	0%	**Protein** 1g		Sugars 3g	
Polyunsaturated Fat 0g					
Monounsaturated Fat 0g		Vitamin A 46% Vitamin C 11%		Calcium 5% Iron 7%	

Pumpkin, Raw

1 cup, 1″ cubes / 116g

Amount per serving	%DV	Amount per serving	%DV	Amount per serving	%DV
Calories 30		**Cholesterol** 0mg	0%	**Total Carbohydrate** 8g	3%
Total Fat 0g	0%	**Sodium** 1mg	0%	Dietary Fiber 1g	4%
Saturated Fat 0g	0%	**Protein** 1g		Sugars 2g	
Polyunsaturated Fat 0g					
Monounsaturated Fat 0g		Vitamin A 171% Vitamin C 17%		Calcium 2% Iron 5%	

Purslane, Cooked, Boiled, Drained, without salt

1 cup / 115g

Amount per serving	%DV	Amount per serving	%DV	Amount per serving	%DV
Calories 21		**Cholesterol** 0mg	0%	**Total Carbohydrate** 4g	1%
Total Fat 0g	0%	**Sodium** 51mg	2%	Dietary Fiber 0g	0%
Saturated Fat 0g	0%	**Protein** 2g		Sugars 0g	
Polyunsaturated Fat 0g					
Monounsaturated Fat 0g		Vitamin A 43% Vitamin C 20%		Calcium 9% Iron 5%	

Purslane, Raw

1 cup / 43g

Amount per serving	%DV	Amount per serving	%DV	Amount per serving	%DV
Calories 7		**Cholesterol** 0mg	0%	**Total Carbohydrate** 0g	0%
Total Fat 0g	0%	**Sodium** 19mg	1%	Dietary Fiber 0g	0%
Saturated Fat 0g	0%	**Protein** 0g		Sugars 0g	
Polyunsaturated Fat 0g					
Monounsaturated Fat 0g		Vitamin A 11% Vitamin C 15%		Calcium 3% Iron 5%	

Radicchio, Raw

1 oz / 28g

Amount per serving	%DV	Amount per serving	%DV	Amount per serving	%DV
Calories 6		**Cholesterol** 0mg	0%	**Total Carbohydrate** 1g	0%
Total Fat 0g	0%	**Sodium** 6mg	0%	Dietary Fiber 0g	0%
Saturated Fat 0g	0%	**Protein** 0g		Sugars 0g	
Polyunsaturated Fat 0g					
Monounsaturated Fat 0g		Vitamin A 0% Vitamin C 4%		Calcium 1% Iron 1%	

Radish Seeds, Sprouted, Raw

1 cup / 38g

Amount per serving	%DV	Amount per serving	%DV	Amount per serving	%DV
Calories 16		**Cholesterol** 0mg	0%	**Total Carbohydrate** 1g	0%
Total Fat 1g	2%	**Sodium** 2mg	0%	Dietary Fiber 0g	0%
Saturated Fat 0g	0%	**Protein** 1g		Sugars 0g	
Polyunsaturated Fat 0g					
Monounsaturated Fat 0g		Vitamin A 3% Vitamin C 18%		Calcium 2% Iron 2%	

Radishes, Oriental, Cooked, Boiled, Drained, without Salt

1 cup, sliced / 147g

Amount per serving	%DV	Amount per serving	%DV	Amount per serving	%DV
Calories 25		**Cholesterol** 0mg	0%	**Total Carbohydrate** 5g	2%
Total Fat 0g	0%	**Sodium** 19mg	1%	Dietary Fiber 2.5g	10%
Saturated Fat 0g	0%	**Protein** 1g		Sugars 3g	
Polyunsaturated Fat 0g					
Monounsaturated Fat 0g		Vitamin A 0% Vitamin C 37%		Calcium 2% Iron 1%	

Radishes, Oriental, Dried

1 cup / 116g

Amount per serving	%DV	Amount per serving	%DV	Amount per serving	%DV
Calories 314		**Cholesterol** 0mg	0%	**Total Carbohydrate** 74g	25%
Total Fat 1g	2%	**Sodium** 323mg	13%	Dietary Fiber 0g	%
Saturated Fat 0g	0%	**Protein** 9g		Sugars 0g	
Polyunsaturated Fat 0g					
Monounsaturated Fat 0g		Vitamin A 0% Vitamin C 0%		Calcium 73% Iron 43%	

Radishes, Oriental, Raw

1 radish, 7" long / 338g

Amount per serving	%DV	Amount per serving	%DV	Amount per serving	%DV
Calories 61		**Cholesterol** 0mg	0%	**Total Carbohydrate** 14g	5%
Total Fat 0g	0%	**Sodium** 71mg	3%	Dietary Fiber 5g	20%
Saturated Fat 0g	0%	**Protein** 2g		Sugars 8g	
Polyunsaturated Fat 0g					
Monounsaturated Fat 0g		Vitamin A 0% Vitamin C 124%		Calcium 9% Iron 8%	

Radishes, Raw

1 large, 1" to 1-1/4" diameter / 9g

Amount per serving	%DV	Amount per serving	%DV	Amount per serving	%DV
Calories 1		**Cholesterol** 0mg	0%	**Total Carbohydrate** 0g	0%
Total Fat 0g	0%	**Sodium** 4mg	0%	Dietary Fiber 0g	0%
Saturated Fat 0g	0%	**Protein** 0g		Sugars 0g	
Polyunsaturated Fat 0g					
Monounsaturated Fat 0g		Vitamin A 0% Vitamin C 2%		Calcium 0% Iron 0%	

Radishes, White Icicle, Raw

1 radish, 7" long / 17g

Amount per serving	%DV	Amount per serving	%DV	Amount per serving	%DV
Calories 7		**Cholesterol** 0mg	0%	**Total Carbohydrate** 1g	0%
Total Fat 0g	0%	**Sodium** 8mg	0%	Dietary Fiber 1g	4%
Saturated Fat 0g	0%	**Protein** 1g		Sugars 0g	
Polyunsaturated Fat 0g					
Monounsaturated Fat 0g		Vitamin A 0% Vitamin C 24%		Calcium 1% Iron 2%	

Rhubarb, Frozen, Uncooked

1 cup, diced / 137g

Amount per serving	%DV	Amount per serving	%DV	Amount per serving	%DV
Calories 29		**Cholesterol** 0mg	0%	**Total Carbohydrate** 7g	2%
Total Fat 0g	0%	**Sodium** 3mg	0%	Dietary Fiber 2g	8%
Saturated Fat 0g	0%	**Protein** 1g		Sugars 2g	
Polyunsaturated Fat 0g					
Monounsaturated Fat 0g		Vitamin A 3% Vitamin C 11%		Calcium 27% Iron 2%	

Roselle, Raw

1 cup, without refuse / 57g

Amount per serving	%DV	Amount per serving	%DV	Amount per serving	%DV
Calories 28		**Cholesterol** 0mg	0%	**Total Carbohydrate** 6g	2%
Total Fat 0g	0%	**Sodium** 3mg	0%	Dietary Fiber 0g	0%
Saturated Fat 0g	0%	**Protein** 1g		Sugars 0g	
Polyunsaturated Fat 0g					
Monounsaturated Fat 0g		Vitamin A 3% Vitamin C 11%		Calcium 12% Iron 5%	

Rutabagas, Cooked, Boiled, Drained, with Salt

1/2 cup, mashed / 120g

Amount per serving	%DV	Amount per serving	%DV	Amount per serving	%DV
Calories 47		**Cholesterol** 0mg	0%	**Total Carbohydrate** 10g	3%
Total Fat 0g	0%	**Sodium** 305mg	13%	Dietary Fiber 0g	0%
Saturated Fat 0g	0%	**Protein** 2g		Sugars 7g	
Polyunsaturated Fat 0.1g					
Monounsaturated Fat 0g		Vitamin A 0% Vitamin C 38%		Calcium 6% Iron 4%	

Rutabagas, Cooked, Boiled, Drained, without Salt

1 cup, cubes / 170g

Amount per serving	%DV	Amount per serving	%DV	Amount per serving	%DV
Calories 66		**Cholesterol** 0mg	0%	**Total Carbohydrate** 15g	5%
Total Fat 0g	0%	**Sodium** 34mg	1%	Dietary Fiber 3g	12%
Saturated Fat 0g	0%	**Protein** 2g		Sugars 10g	
Polyunsaturated Fat 0g					
Monounsaturated Fat 0g		Vitamin A 0%	Vitamin C 53%	Calcium 8%	Iron 5%

Rutabagas, Raw

1 small / 192g

Amount per serving	%DV	Amount per serving	%DV	Amount per serving	%DV
Calories 69		**Cholesterol** 0mg	0%	**Total Carbohydrate** 16g	5%
Total Fat 0g	0%	**Sodium** 38mg	2%	Dietary Fiber 5g	20%
Saturated Fat 0g	0%	**Protein** 2g		Sugars 11g	
Polyunsaturated Fat 0g					
Monounsaturated Fat 0g		Vitamin A 0%	Vitamin C 80%	Calcium 9%	Iron 6%

Salsify (Vegetable Oyster), Raw

1 cup, slices / 133g

Amount per serving	%DV	Amount per serving	%DV	Amount per serving	%DV
Calories 109		**Cholesterol** 0mg	0%	**Total Carbohydrate** 25g	8%
Total Fat 0g	0%	**Sodium** 27mg	1%	Dietary Fiber 4g	16%
Saturated Fat 0g	0%	**Protein** 4g		Sugars 0g	
Polyunsaturated Fat 0g					
Monounsaturated Fat 0g		Vitamin A 0%	Vitamin C 18%	Calcium 8%	Iron 5%

Salsify, Cooked, Boiled, Drained, without Salt

1 cup, sliced / 135g

Amount per serving	%DV	Amount per serving	%DV	Amount per serving	%DV
Calories 92		**Cholesterol** 0mg	0%	**Total Carbohydrate** 21g	7%
Total Fat 0g	0%	**Sodium** 22mg	1%	Dietary Fiber 4g	16%
Saturated Fat 0g	0%	**Protein** 4g		Sugars 4g	
Polyunsaturated Fat 0g					
Monounsaturated Fat 0g		Vitamin A 0%	Vitamin C 10%	Calcium 6%	Iron 4%

Seaweed, Laver, Raw

10 sheets / 26g

Amount per serving	%DV	Amount per serving	%DV	Amount per serving	%DV
Calories 9		**Cholesterol** 0mg	0%	**Total Carbohydrate** 1g	0%
Total Fat 0g	0%	**Sodium** 12mg	0%	Dietary Fiber 0g	0%
Saturated Fat 0g	0%	**Protein** 2g		Sugars 0g	
Polyunsaturated Fat 0g					
Monounsaturated Fat 0g		Vitamin A 27%	Vitamin C 17%	Calcium 2%	Iron 3%

Seaweed, Spirulina, Dried

1 tbsp / 7g

Amount per serving	%DV	Amount per serving	%DV	Amount per serving	%DV
Calories 20		**Cholesterol** 0mg	0%	**Total Carbohydrate** 2g	1%
Total Fat 1g	2%	**Sodium** 73mg	3%	Dietary Fiber 0g	0%
Saturated Fat 0g	0%	**Protein** 4g		Sugars 0g	
Polyunsaturated Fat 0g					
Monounsaturated Fat 0g		Vitamin A 1% Vitamin C 1%		Calcium 1% Iron 11%	

Shallots, Freeze-Dried

1 oz / 28g

Amount per serving	%DV	Amount per serving	%DV	Amount per serving	%DV
Calories 20		**Cholesterol** 0mg	0%	**Total Carbohydrate** 5g	2%
Total Fat 0g	0%	**Sodium** 3mg	0%	Dietary Fiber 0g	0%
Saturated Fat 0g	0%	**Protein** 1g		Sugars 0g	
Polyunsaturated Fat 0g					
Monounsaturated Fat 0g		Vitamin A 7% Vitamin C 4%		Calcium 1% Iron 2%	

Shallots, Raw

1 tbsp, chopped / 10g

Amount per serving	%DV	Amount per serving	%DV	Amount per serving	%DV
Calories 7		**Cholesterol** 0mg	0%	**Total Carbohydrate** 2g	1%
Total Fat 0g	0%	**Sodium** 1mg	0%	Dietary Fiber 0g	0%
Saturated Fat 0g	0%	**Protein** 0g		Sugars 0g	
Polyunsaturated Fat 0g					
Monounsaturated Fat 0g		Vitamin A 2% Vitamin C 1%		Calcium 0% Iron 1%	

Soybeans, Mature Seeds, Sprouted, Raw

1/2 cup / 35g

Amount per serving	%DV	Amount per serving	%DV	Amount per serving	%DV
Calories 43		**Cholesterol** 0mg	0%	**Total Carbohydrate** 3g	1%
Total Fat 2g	3%	**Sodium** 5mg	0%	Dietary Fiber 0g	0%
Saturated Fat 0g	0%	**Protein** 5g		Sugars 0g	
Polyunsaturated Fat 0g					
Monounsaturated Fat 0g		Vitamin A 0% Vitamin C 9%		Calcium 2% Iron 4%	

Spinach, Canned, No Salt, Solids and Liquids

1 cup / 234g

Amount per serving	%DV	Amount per serving	%DV	Amount per serving	%DV
Calories 44		**Cholesterol** 0mg	0%	**Total Carbohydrate** 7g	2%
Total Fat 1g	2%	**Sodium** 175mg	7%	Dietary Fiber 5g	20%
Saturated Fat 0g	0%	**Protein** 5g		Sugars 0g	
Polyunsaturated Fat 0g					
Monounsaturated Fat 0g		Vitamin A 301% Vitamin C 53%		Calcium 19% Iron 21%	

Spinach, Cooked, Boiled, Drained, without Salt

1 cup / 180g

Amount per serving	%DV	Amount per serving	%DV	Amount per serving	%DV
Calories 41		**Cholesterol** 0mg	0%	**Total Carbohydrate** 7g	2%
Total Fat 0g	0%	**Sodium** 126mg	5%	Dietary Fiber 4g	16%
Saturated Fat 0g	0%	**Protein** 5g		Sugars 1g	
Polyunsaturated Fat 0g					
Monounsaturated Fat 0g		Vitamin A 377% Vitamin C 29%		Calcium 24% Iron 36%	

Spinach, Frozen, Chopped or Leaf, Cooked, Boiled, Drained, with Salt

1/2 cup / 95g

Amount per serving	%DV	Amount per serving	%DV	Amount per serving	%DV
Calories 32		**Cholesterol** 0mg	0%	**Total Carbohydrate** 5g	2%
Total Fat 1g	2%	**Sodium** 306mg	13%	Dietary Fiber 4g	16%
Saturated Fat 0g	0%	**Protein** 4g		Sugars 0g	
Polyunsaturated Fat 0g					
Monounsaturated Fat 0g		Vitamin A 229% Vitamin C 3%		Calcium 15% Iron 10%	

Spinach, Frozen, Chopped or Leaf, Cooked, Boiled, Drained, without Salt

1/2 cup / 95g

Amount per serving	%DV	Amount per serving	%DV	Amount per serving	%DV
Calories 32		**Cholesterol** 0mg	0%	**Total Carbohydrate** 5g	2%
Total Fat 1g	2%	**Sodium** 92mg	4%	Dietary Fiber 4g	16%
Saturated Fat 0g	0%	**Protein** 4g		Sugars 0g	
Polyunsaturated Fat 0g					
Monounsaturated Fat 0g		Vitamin A 229% Vitamin C 3%		Calcium 15% Iron 10%	

Spinach, Frozen, Chopped or Leaf, Unprepared

1 cup, / 156g

Amount per serving	%DV	Amount per serving	%DV	Amount per serving	%DV
Calories 45		**Cholesterol** 0mg	0%	**Total Carbohydrate** 7g	2%
Total Fat 1g	2%	**Sodium** 115mg	5%	Dietary Fiber 5g	20%
Saturated Fat 0g	0%	**Protein** 6g		Sugars 1g	
Polyunsaturated Fat 0g					
Monounsaturated Fat 0g		Vitamin A 366% Vitamin C 14%		Calcium 20% Iron 16%	

Spinach, Raw

1 cup / 30g

Amount per serving	%DV	Amount per serving	%DV	Amount per serving	%DV
Calories 7		**Cholesterol** 0mg	0%	**Total Carbohydrate** 1g	0%
Total Fat 0g	0%	**Sodium** 24mg	1%	Dietary Fiber 1g	4%
Saturated Fat 0g	0%	**Protein** 1g		Sugars 0g	
Polyunsaturated Fat 0g					
Monounsaturated Fat 0g		Vitamin A 56% Vitamin C 14%		Calcium 3% Iron 5%	

Squash, Summer, All Varieties, Cooked, Boiled, Drained, without Salt

1 cup, sliced / 180g

Amount per serving	%DV	Amount per serving	%DV	Amount per serving	%DV
Calories 36		**Cholesterol** 0mg	0%	**Total Carbohydrate** 8g	3%
Total Fat 1g	2%	**Sodium** 2mg	0%	Dietary Fiber 3g	12%
Saturated Fat 0g	0%	**Protein** 2g		Sugars 5g	
Polyunsaturated Fat 0g					
Monounsaturated Fat 0g		Vitamin A 8%	Vitamin C 16%	Calcium 5%	Iron 4%

Squash, Summer, All Varieties, Raw

1 cup, sliced / 113g

Amount per serving	%DV	Amount per serving	%DV	Amount per serving	%DV
Calories 18		**Cholesterol** 0mg	0%	**Total Carbohydrate** 4g	1%
Total Fat 0g	0%	**Sodium** 2mg	0%	Dietary Fiber 1g	4%
Saturated Fat 0g	0%	**Protein** 1g		Sugars 2g	
Polyunsaturated Fat 0g					
Monounsaturated Fat 0g		Vitamin A 5%	Vitamin C 32%	Calcium 2%	Iron 2%

Squash, Summer, Crookneck & Straightneck, Boiled, Drained, without Salt

1 cup, slices / 192g

Amount per serving	%DV	Amount per serving	%DV	Amount per serving	%DV
Calories 48		**Cholesterol** 0mg	0%	**Total Carbohydrate** 11g	4%
Total Fat 0g	0%	**Sodium** 12mg	0%	Dietary Fiber 3g	12%
Saturated Fat 0g	0%	**Protein** 2g		Sugars 4g	
Polyunsaturated Fat 0g					
Monounsaturated Fat 0g		Vitamin A 8%	Vitamin C 22%	Calcium 4%	Iron 6%

Squash, Summer, Crookneck and Straightneck, Canned, Drained, Solid, without Salt

1 cup, mashed / 240g

Amount per serving	%DV	Amount per serving	%DV	Amount per serving	%DV
Calories 31		**Cholesterol** 0mg	0%	**Total Carbohydrate** 7g	2%
Total Fat 0g	0%	**Sodium** 12mg	1%	Dietary Fiber 3g	12%
Saturated Fat 0g	0%	**Protein** 1g		Sugars 3g	
Polyunsaturated Fat 0g					
Monounsaturated Fat 0g		Vitamin A 5%	Vitamin C 11%	Calcium 3%	Iron 9%

Squash, Summer, Crookneck and Straightneck, Cooked, Boiled, Drained, without Salt

1 cup, slices / 180g

Amount per serving	%DV	Amount per serving	%DV	Amount per serving	%DV
Calories 36		**Cholesterol** 0mg	0%	**Total Carbohydrate** 8g	3%
Total Fat 1g	2%	**Sodium** 0mg	0%	Dietary Fiber 3g	12%
Saturated Fat 0g	0%	**Protein** 2g		Sugars 3g	
Polyunsaturated Fat 0g					
Monounsaturated Fat 0g		Vitamin A 6%	Vitamin C 16%	Calcium 4%	Iron 4%

Squash, Summer, Crookneck and Straightneck, Frozen, Unprepared

1 cup, slices / 130g

Amount per serving	%DV	Amount per serving	%DV	Amount per serving	%DV
Calories 26		**Cholesterol** 0mg	0%	**Total Carbohydrate** 6g	2%
Total Fat 0g	0%	**Sodium** 7mg	0%	Dietary Fiber 2g	8%
Saturated Fat 0g	0%	**Protein** 1g		Sugars 0g	
Polyunsaturated Fat 0g					
Monounsaturated Fat 0g		Vitamin A 7% Vitamin C 14%		Calcium 2% Iron 3%	

Squash, Summer, Crookneck and Straightneck, Raw

1 cup, sliced / 130g

Amount per serving	%DV	Amount per serving	%DV	Amount per serving	%DV
Calories 25		**Cholesterol** 0mg	0%	**Total Carbohydrate** 5g	2%
Total Fat 0g	0%	**Sodium** 3mg	0%	Dietary Fiber 2g	8%
Saturated Fat 0g	0%	**Protein** 1g		Sugars 4g	
Polyunsaturated Fat 0g					
Monounsaturated Fat 0g		Vitamin A 4% Vitamin C 18%		Calcium 3% Iron 3%	

Squash, Summer, Scallop, Cooked, Boiled, Drained, without Salt

1 cup, sliced / 180g

Amount per serving	%DV	Amount per serving	%DV	Amount per serving	%DV
Calories 29		**Cholesterol** 0mg	0%	**Total Carbohydrate** 6g	2%
Total Fat 0g	0%	**Sodium** 2mg	0%	Dietary Fiber 3g	12%
Saturated Fat 0g	0%	**Protein** 2g		Sugars 3g	
Polyunsaturated Fat 0g					
Monounsaturated Fat 0g		Vitamin A 3% Vitamin C 32%		Calcium 3% Iron 3%	

Squash, Summer, Scallop, Raw

1 cup, slices / 130g

Amount per serving	%DV	Amount per serving	%DV	Amount per serving	%DV
Calories 23		**Cholesterol** 0mg	0%	**Total Carbohydrate** 5g	2%
Total Fat 0g	0%	**Sodium** 1mg	0%	Dietary Fiber 0g	0%
Saturated Fat 0g	0%	**Protein** 2g		Sugars 0g	
Polyunsaturated Fat 0g					
Monounsaturated Fat 0g		Vitamin A 3% Vitamin C 39%		Calcium 2% Iron 3%	

Squash, Summer, Zucchini, Includes Skin, Cooked, Boiled, Drained, without Salt

1 cup, sliced / 180g

Amount per serving	%DV	Amount per serving	%DV	Amount per serving	%DV
Calories 29		**Cholesterol** 0mg	0%	**Total Carbohydrate** 7g	2%
Total Fat 0g	0%	**Sodium** 5mg	0%	Dietary Fiber 3g	12%
Saturated Fat 0g	0%	**Protein** 1g		Sugars 3g	
Polyunsaturated Fat 0g					
Monounsaturated Fat 0g		Vitamin A 40% Vitamin C 14%		Calcium 2% Iron 4%	

Squash, Summer, Zucchini, Includes Skin, Raw

1 cup, sliced / 113g

Amount per serving	%DV	Amount per serving	%DV	Amount per serving	%DV
Calories 18		**Cholesterol** 0mg	0%	**Total Carbohydrate** 4g	1%
Total Fat 0g	0%	**Sodium** 11mg	0%	Dietary Fiber 1g	4%
Saturated Fat 0g	0%	**Protein** 0g		Sugars 0g	
Polyunsaturated Fat 0g					
Monounsaturated Fat 0g		Vitamin A 5%	Vitamin C 32%	Calcium 2%	Iron 2%

Squash, Summer, Zucchini, Including Skin, Frozen, Boiled, Drained, without Salt

1 cup / 223g

Amount per serving	%DV	Amount per serving	%DV	Amount per serving	%DV
Calories 38		**Cholesterol** 0mg	0%	**Total Carbohydrate** 8g	3%
Total Fat 0g	0%	**Sodium** 4mg	0%	Dietary Fiber 3g	12%
Saturated Fat 0g	0%	**Protein** 3g		Sugars 4g	
Polyunsaturated Fat 0g					
Monounsaturated Fat 0g		Vitamin A 8%	Vitamin C 14%	Calcium 4%	Iron 6%

Squash, Summer, Zucchini, Including Skin, Frozen, Unprepared

10 oz / 284g

Amount per serving	%DV	Amount per serving	%DV	Amount per serving	%DV
Calories 48		**Cholesterol** 0mg	0%	**Total Carbohydrate** 10g	3%
Total Fat 0g	0%	**Sodium** 6mg	0%	Dietary Fiber 4g	16%
Saturated Fat 0g	0%	**Protein** 3g		Sugars 5g	
Polyunsaturated Fat 0g					
Monounsaturated Fat 0g		Vitamin A 11%	Vitamin C 25%	Calcium 5%	Iron 8%

Squash, Summer, Zucchini, Including Skin, Raw

1 cup, chopped / 124g

Amount per serving	%DV	Amount per serving	%DV	Amount per serving	%DV
Calories 20		**Cholesterol** 0mg	0%	**Total Carbohydrate** 4g	1%
Total Fat 0g	0%	**Sodium** 12mg	0%	Dietary Fiber 1g	4%
Saturated Fat 0g	0%	**Protein** 2g		Sugars 2g	
Polyunsaturated Fat 0g					
Monounsaturated Fat 0g		Vitamin A 5%	Vitamin C 32%	Calcium 2%	Iron 2%

Squash, Winter, Acorn, Cooked, Baked, without Salt

1 cup, cubes / 205g

Amount per serving	%DV	Amount per serving	%DV	Amount per serving	%DV
Calories 115		**Cholesterol** 0mg	0%	**Total Carbohydrate** 30g	10%
Total Fat 0g	0%	**Sodium** 8mg	0%	Dietary Fiber 9g	36%
Saturated Fat 0g	0%	**Protein** 2g		Sugars 0g	
Polyunsaturated Fat 0g					
Monounsaturated Fat 0g		Vitamin A 18%	Vitamin C 37%	Calcium 9%	Iron 11%

Squash, Winter, Acorn, Cooked, Boiled, Mashed, without Salt

1 cup, mashed / 245g

Amount per serving	%DV	Amount per serving	%DV	Amount per serving	%DV
Calories 83		**Cholesterol** 0mg	0%	**Total Carbohydrate** 22g	7%
Total Fat 0g	0%	**Sodium** 7mg	0%	Dietary Fiber 6g	24%
Saturated Fat 0g	0%	**Protein** 2g		Sugars 0g	
Polyunsaturated Fat 0g					
Monounsaturated Fat 0g		Vitamin A 40% Vitamin C 27%		Calcium 6% Iron 8%	

Squash, Winter, All Varieties, Cooked, Baked, without Salt

1 cup, cubes / 205g

Amount per serving	%DV	Amount per serving	%DV	Amount per serving	%DV
Calories 76		**Cholesterol** 0mg	0%	**Total Carbohydrate** 18g	6%
Total Fat 1g	2%	**Sodium** 2mg	0%	Dietary Fiber 6g	24%
Saturated Fat 0g	0%	**Protein** 2g		Sugars 7g	
Polyunsaturated Fat 0g					
Monounsaturated Fat 0g		Vitamin A 214% Vitamin C 33%		Calcium 5% Iron 5%	

Squash, Winter, All Varieties, Raw

1 cup, cubes / 116g

Amount per serving	%DV	Amount per serving	%DV	Amount per serving	%DV
Calories 39		**Cholesterol** 0mg	0%	**Total Carbohydrate** 10g	3%
Total Fat 0g	0%	**Sodium** 5mg	0%	Dietary Fiber 1.5g	6%
Saturated Fat 0g	0%	**Protein** 1g		Sugars 3g	
Polyunsaturated Fat 0g					
Monounsaturated Fat 0g		Vitamin A 32% Vitamin C 24%		Calcium 24% Iron 4%	

Squash, Winter, Butternut, Cooked, Baked, without Salt

1 cup, cubes / 205g

Amount per serving	%DV	Amount per serving	%DV	Amount per serving	%DV
Calories 82		**Cholesterol** 0mg	0%	**Total Carbohydrate** 22g	7%
Total Fat 0g	0%	**Sodium** 8mg	0%	Dietary Fiber 6.5g	26%
Saturated Fat 0g	0%	**Protein** 2g		Sugars 4g	
Polyunsaturated Fat 0g					
Monounsaturated Fat 0g		Vitamin A 457% Vitamin C 52%		Calcium 8% Iron 7%	

Squash, Winter, Butternut, Frozen, Cooked, Boiled, without Salt

1 cup, mashed / 240g

Amount per serving	%DV	Amount per serving	%DV	Amount per serving	%DV
Calories 94		**Cholesterol** 0mg	0%	**Total Carbohydrate** 24g	8%
Total Fat 0g	0%	**Sodium** 5mg	0%	Dietary Fiber 0g	0%
Saturated Fat 0g	0%	**Protein** 3g		Sugars 0g	
Polyunsaturated Fat 0g					
Monounsaturated Fat 0g		Vitamin A 160% Vitamin C 14%		Calcium 5% Iron 8%	

Squash, Winter, Butternut, Frozen, Unprepared

1 package, 12 oz / 340g

Amount per serving	%DV	Amount per serving	%DV	Amount per serving	%DV
Calories 194		**Cholesterol** 0mg	0%	**Total Carbohydrate** 49g	16%
Total Fat 0g	0%	**Sodium** 7mg	0%	Dietary Fiber 4g	16%
Saturated Fat 0g	0%	**Protein** 6g		Sugars 10g	
Polyunsaturated Fat 0g					
Monounsaturated Fat 0g		Vitamin A 326% Vitamin C 35%		Calcium 10% Iron 17%	

Squash, Winter, Butternut, Raw

1 cup, cubes / 140g

Amount per serving	%DV	Amount per serving	%DV	Amount per serving	%DV
Calories 63		**Cholesterol** 0mg	0%	**Total Carbohydrate** 16g	5%
Total Fat 0g	0%	**Sodium** 6mg	0%	Dietary Fiber 3g	12%
Saturated Fat 0g	0%	**Protein** 1g		Sugars 3g	
Polyunsaturated Fat 0g					
Monounsaturated Fat 0g		Vitamin A 298% Vitamin C 49%		Calcium 7% Iron 5%	

Squash, Winter, Hubbard, Cooked, Baked, without Salt

1 cup, cubes / 205g

Amount per serving	%DV	Amount per serving	%DV	Amount per serving	%DV
Calories 102		**Cholesterol** 0mg	0%	**Total Carbohydrate** 22g	7%
Total Fat 1g	2%	**Sodium** 16mg	1%	Dietary Fiber 0g	0%
Saturated Fat 0g	0%	**Protein** 5g		Sugars 0g	
Polyunsaturated Fat 0g					
Monounsaturated Fat 0g		Vitamin A 247% Vitamin C 32%		Calcium 3% Iron 5%	

Squash, Winter, Hubbard, Cooked, Boiled, Mashed, without Salt

1 cup, mashed / 236g

Amount per serving	%DV	Amount per serving	%DV	Amount per serving	%DV
Calories 71		**Cholesterol** 0mg	0%	**Total Carbohydrate** 15g	5%
Total Fat 1g	2%	**Sodium** 12mg	0%	Dietary Fiber 7g	28%
Saturated Fat 0g	0%	**Protein** 3g		Sugars 7g	
Polyunsaturated Fat 0g					
Monounsaturated Fat 0g		Vitamin A 189% Vitamin C 26%		Calcium 2% Iron 4%	

Squash, Winter, Hubbard, Raw

1 cup, cubes / 116g

Amount per serving	%DV	Amount per serving	%DV	Amount per serving	%DV
Calories 46		**Cholesterol** 0mg	0%	**Total Carbohydrate** 10g	3%
Total Fat 1g	2%	**Sodium** 8mg	0%	Dietary Fiber 0g	0%
Saturated Fat 0g	0%	**Protein** 2g		Sugars 0g	
Polyunsaturated Fat 0g					
Monounsaturated Fat 0g		Vitamin A 32% Vitamin C 21%		Calcium 2% Iron 3%	

Squash, Winter, Spaghetti, Cooked, Boiled, Drained or Baked, without Salt

1 cup / 155g

Amount per serving	%DV	Amount per serving	%DV	Amount per serving	%DV
Calories 42		**Cholesterol** 0mg	0%	**Total Carbohydrate** 10g	3%
Total Fat 0g	0%	**Sodium** 28mg	1%	Dietary Fiber 2g	8%
Saturated Fat 0g	0%	**Protein** 1g		Sugars 4g	
Polyunsaturated Fat 0g					
Monounsaturated Fat 0g		Vitamin A 3% Vitamin C 9%		Calcium 3% Iron 3%	

Squash, Winter, Spaghetti, Raw

1 cup, cubes / 101g

Amount per serving	%DV	Amount per serving	%DV	Amount per serving	%DV
Calories 31		**Cholesterol** 0mg	0%	**Total Carbohydrate** 7g	2%
Total Fat 1g	2%	**Sodium** 17mg	1%	Dietary Fiber 0g	0%
Saturated Fat 0g	0%	**Protein** 1g		Sugars 0g	
Polyunsaturated Fat 0g					
Monounsaturated Fat 0g		Vitamin A 1% Vitamin C 4%		Calcium 2% Iron 2%	

Squash, Zucchini, Baby, Raw

1 medium / 11g

Amount per serving	%DV	Amount per serving	%DV	Amount per serving	%DV
Calories 2		**Cholesterol** 0mg	0%	**Total Carbohydrate** 0g	0%
Total Fat 0g	0%	**Sodium** 0mg	0%	Dietary Fiber 0g	0%
Saturated Fat 0g	0%	**Protein** 0g		Sugars 0g	
Polyunsaturated Fat 0g					
Monounsaturated Fat 0g		Vitamin A 1% Vitamin C 6%		Calcium 0% Iron 0%	

Succotash (Corn and Limas), Cooked, Boiled, Drained, without Salt

1 cup / 192g

Amount per serving	%DV	Amount per serving	%DV	Amount per serving	%DV
Calories 221		**Cholesterol** 0mg	0%	**Total Carbohydrate** 47g	16%
Total Fat 2g	3%	**Sodium** 33mg	1%	Dietary Fiber 9g	36%
Saturated Fat 0g	0%	**Protein** 10g		Sugars 0g	
Polyunsaturated Fat 0g					
Monounsaturated Fat 0g		Vitamin A 11% Vitamin C 26%		Calcium 3% Iron 16%	

Succotash (Corn and Limas), Frozen, Cooked, Boiled, Drained, without Salt

1 cup / 170g

Amount per serving	%DV	Amount per serving	%DV	Amount per serving	%DV
Calories 158		**Cholesterol** 0mg	0%	**Total Carbohydrate** 34g	11%
Total Fat 2g	3%	**Sodium** 76mg	3%	Dietary Fiber 7g	28%
Saturated Fat 0g	0%	**Protein** 7g		Sugars 4g	
Polyunsaturated Fat 0g					
Monounsaturated Fat 0g		Vitamin A 7% Vitamin C 17%		Calcium 3% Iron 8%	

Succotash (Corn and Limas), Frozen, Unprepared

1 cup / 156g

Amount per serving	%DV	Amount per serving	%DV	Amount per serving	%DV
Calories 145		**Cholesterol** 0mg	0%	**Total Carbohydrate** 31g	10%
Total Fat 1g	2%	**Sodium** 70mg	3%	Dietary Fiber 6g	24%
Saturated Fat 0g	0%	**Protein** 7g		Sugars 0g	
Polyunsaturated Fat 0g					
Monounsaturated Fat 0g		Vitamin A 8%	Vitamin C 22%	Calcium 2%	Iron 8%

Taro Leaves, Cooked, Steamed, without Salt

1 cup / 145g

Amount per serving	%DV	Amount per serving	%DV	Amount per serving	%DV
Calories 35		**Cholesterol** 0mg	0%	**Total Carbohydrate** 6g	2%
Total Fat 1g	2%	**Sodium** 3mg	0%	Dietary Fiber 3g	12%
Saturated Fat 0g	0%	**Protein** 4g		Sugars 0g	
Polyunsaturated Fat 0g					
Monounsaturated Fat 0g		Vitamin A 123%	Vitamin C 86%	Calcium 12%	Iron 10%

Taro, Cooked, with Salt

1 cup, slices / 132g

Amount per serving	%DV	Amount per serving	%DV	Amount per serving	%DV
Calories 187		**Cholesterol** 0mg	0%	**Total Carbohydrate** 46g	15%
Total Fat 0g	0%	**Sodium** 331mg	14%	Dietary Fiber 6.5g	26%
Saturated Fat 0g	0%	**Protein** 1g		Sugars 1g	
Polyunsaturated Fat 0g					
Monounsaturated Fat 0g		Vitamin A 2%	Vitamin C 11%	Calcium 2%	Iron 5%

Taro, Leaves, Cooked, Steamed, with Salt

1 cup / 145g

Amount per serving	%DV	Amount per serving	%DV	Amount per serving	%DV
Calories 35		**Cholesterol** 0mg	0%	**Total Carbohydrate** 6g	2%
Total Fat 0g	0%	**Sodium** 345mg	14%	Dietary Fiber 3g	12%
Saturated Fat 0g	0%	**Protein** 4g		Sugars 0g	
Polyunsaturated Fat 0g					
Monounsaturated Fat 0g		Vitamin A 123%	Vitamin C 86%	Calcium 12%	Iron 10%

Taro, Raw

1 cup, sliced / 104g

Amount per serving	%DV	Amount per serving	%DV	Amount per serving	%DV
Calories 116		**Cholesterol** 0mg	0%	**Total Carbohydrate** 28g	9%
Total Fat 0g	0%	**Sodium** 11mg	0%	Dietary Fiber 4.5g	18%
Saturated Fat 0g	0%	**Protein** 2g		Sugars 0g	
Polyunsaturated Fat 0g					
Monounsaturated Fat 0g		Vitamin A 2%	Vitamin C 8%	Calcium 4%	Iron 3%

Taro, Shoots, Cooked, with Salt

1 cup, slices / 140g

Amount per serving	%DV	Amount per serving	%DV	Amount per serving	%DV
Calories 20		**Cholesterol** 0mg	0%	**Total Carbohydrate** 4g	1%
Total Fat 0g	0%	**Sodium** 333mg	14%	Dietary Fiber 0g	0%
Saturated Fat 0g	0%	**Protein** 1g		Sugars 0g	
Polyunsaturated Fat 0g					
Monounsaturated Fat 0g		Vitamin A 1%	Vitamin C 44%	Calcium 2%	Iron 3%

Taro, Tahitian, Cooked, without Salt

1 cup, slices / 137g

Amount per serving	%DV	Amount per serving	%DV	Amount per serving	%DV
Calories 60		**Cholesterol** 0mg	0%	**Total Carbohydrate** 9g	3%
Total Fat 1g	2%	**Sodium** 74mg	3%	Dietary Fiber 0g	0%
Saturated Fat 0g	0%	**Protein** 6g		Sugars 0g	
Polyunsaturated Fat 0g					
Monounsaturated Fat 0g		Vitamin A 48%	Vitamin C 87%	Calcium 20%	Iron 12%

Taro, Tahitian, Raw

1 cup, slices / 125g

Amount per serving	%DV	Amount per serving	%DV	Amount per serving	%DV
Calories 55		**Cholesterol** 0mg	0%	**Total Carbohydrate** 9g	3%
Total Fat 1g	2%	**Sodium** 62mg	3%	Dietary Fiber 0g	0%
Saturated Fat 0g	0%	**Protein** 3g		Sugars 0g	
Polyunsaturated Fat 0g					
Monounsaturated Fat 0g		Vitamin A 51%	Vitamin C 200%	Calcium 16%	Iron 9%

Tomatillos, Raw

1 medium / 34g

Amount per serving	%DV	Amount per serving	%DV	Amount per serving	%DV
Calories 11		**Cholesterol** 0mg	0%	**Total Carbohydrate** 2g	1%
Total Fat 0g	0%	**Sodium** 0mg	0%	Dietary Fiber 1g	4%
Saturated Fat 0g	0%	**Protein** 0g		Sugars 1g	
Polyunsaturated Fat 0g					
Monounsaturated Fat 0g		Vitamin A 1%	Vitamin C 7%	Calcium 0%	Iron 1%

Tomatoes, Green, Raw

1 medium / 123g

Amount per serving	%DV	Amount per serving	%DV	Amount per serving	%DV
Calories 28		**Cholesterol** 0mg	0%	**Total Carbohydrate** 6g	2%
Total Fat 0g	0%	**Sodium** 16mg	1%	Dietary Fiber 1g	4%
Saturated Fat 0g	0%	**Protein** 1g		Sugars 5g	
Polyunsaturated Fat 0g					
Monounsaturated Fat 0g		Vitamin A 16%	Vitamin C 48%	Calcium 2%	Iron 3%

Tomatoes, Orange, Raw

1 tomato / 111g

Amount per serving	%DV	Amount per serving	%DV	Amount per serving	%DV
Calories 25		**Cholesterol** 0mg	0%	**Total Carbohydrate** 5g	2%
Total Fat 0g	0%	**Sodium** 66mg	3%	Dietary Fiber 1g	4%
Saturated Fat 0g	0%	**Protein** 2g		Sugars 0g	
Polyunsaturated Fat 0g					
Monounsaturated Fat 0g		Vitamin A 47%	Vitamin C 42%	Calcium 1%	Iron 4%

Tomatoes, Red, Ripe, Canned, Packed in Tomato Juice

1 medium / 111g

Amount per serving	%DV	Amount per serving	%DV	Amount per serving	%DV
Calories 19		**Cholesterol** 0mg	0%	**Total Carbohydrate** 4g	1%
Total Fat 0g	0%	**Sodium** 159mg	7%	Dietary Fiber 1g	4%
Saturated Fat 0g	0%	**Protein** 1g		Sugars 3g	
Polyunsaturated Fat 0g					
Monounsaturated Fat 0g		Vitamin A 3%	Vitamin C 17%	Calcium 3%	Iron 6%

Tomatoes, Red, Ripe, Canned, Packed in Tomato Juice, No Salt Added

1 cup / 240g

Amount per serving	%DV	Amount per serving	%DV	Amount per serving	%DV
Calories 41		**Cholesterol** 0mg	0%	**Total Carbohydrate** 10g	3%
Total Fat 0g	0%	**Sodium** 24mg	1%	Dietary Fiber 2g	8%
Saturated Fat 0g	0%	**Protein** 2g		Sugars 6g	
Polyunsaturated Fat 0g					
Monounsaturated Fat 0g		Vitamin A 6%	Vitamin C 37%	Calcium 7%	Iron 13%

Tomatoes, Red, Ripe, Cooked

2 medium / 246g

Amount per serving	%DV	Amount per serving	%DV	Amount per serving	%DV
Calories 44		**Cholesterol** 0mg	0%	**Total Carbohydrate** 10g	3%
Total Fat 0g	0%	**Sodium** 27mg	1%	Dietary Fiber 2g	8%
Saturated Fat 0g	0%	**Protein** 2g		Sugars 6g	
Polyunsaturated Fat 0g					
Monounsaturated Fat 0g		Vitamin A 24%	Vitamin C 93%	Calcium 3%	Iron 9%

Tomatoes, Red, Ripe, Cooked, with Salt

1 oz / 28g

Amount per serving	%DV	Amount per serving	%DV	Amount per serving	%DV
Calories 5		**Cholesterol** 0mg	0%	**Total Carbohydrate** 1g	0%
Total Fat 0g	0%	**Sodium** 69mg	3%	Dietary Fiber 0g	0%
Saturated Fat 0g	0%	**Protein** 0g		Sugars 1g	
Polyunsaturated Fat 0g					
Monounsaturated Fat 0g		Vitamin A 3%	Vitamin C 11%	Calcium 0%	Iron 1%

Tomatoes, Red, Ripe, Raw

1 cup, chopped or sliced / 180g

Amount per serving	%DV	Amount per serving	%DV	Amount per serving	%DV
Calories 32		**Cholesterol** 0mg	0%	**Total Carbohydrate** 7g	2%
Total Fat 0g	0%	**Sodium** 9mg	0%	Dietary Fiber 2g	8%
Saturated Fat 0g	0%	**Protein** 2g		Sugars 5g	
Polyunsaturated Fat 0g					
Monounsaturated Fat 0g		Vitamin A 30% Vitamin C 38%		Calcium 2% Iron 3%	

Tomatoes, Red, Ripe, Raw, Year Round Average

1 medium whole / 2-3/5″ diameter / 123g

Amount per serving	%DV	Amount per serving	%DV	Amount per serving	%DV
Calories 22		**Cholesterol** 0mg	0%	**Total Carbohydrate** 5g	2%
Total Fat 0g	0%	**Sodium** 6mg	0%	Dietary Fiber 1g	4%
Saturated Fat 0g	0%	**Protein** 1g		Sugars 3g	
Polyunsaturated Fat 0g					
Monounsaturated Fat 0g		Vitamin A 20% Vitamin C 26%		Calcium 18% Iron 2%	

Tomatoes, Sun-Dried

1 piece / 2g

Amount per serving	%DV	Amount per serving	%DV	Amount per serving	%DV
Calories 5		**Cholesterol** 0mg	0%	**Total Carbohydrate** 1g	0%
Total Fat 0g	0%	**Sodium** 42mg	2%	Dietary Fiber 0g	0%
Saturated Fat 0g	0%	**Protein** 0g		Sugars 1g	
Polyunsaturated Fat 0g					
Monounsaturated Fat 0g		Vitamin A 0% Vitamin C 1%		Calcium 0% Iron 1%	

Tomatoes, Sun-Dried, Packed in Oil, Drained

1 piece / 3g

Amount per serving	%DV	Amount per serving	%DV	Amount per serving	%DV
Calories 6		**Cholesterol** 0mg	0%	**Total Carbohydrate** 1g	0%
Total Fat 0g	0%	**Sodium** 8mg	0%	Dietary Fiber 0g	0%
Saturated Fat 0g	0%	**Protein** 0g		Sugars 0g	
Polyunsaturated Fat 0g					
Monounsaturated Fat 0g		Vitamin A 1% Vitamin C 5%		Calcium 0% Iron 0%	

Tomatoes, Yellow, Raw

1 tomato / 212g

Amount per serving	%DV	Amount per serving	%DV	Amount per serving	%DV
Calories 32		**Cholesterol** 0mg	0%	**Total Carbohydrate** 6g	2%
Total Fat 1g	2%	**Sodium** 49mg	2%	Dietary Fiber 1g	4%
Saturated Fat 0g	0%	**Protein** 2g		Sugars 0g	
Polyunsaturated Fat 0g					
Monounsaturated Fat 0g		Vitamin A 0% Vitamin C 32%		Calcium 2% Iron 6%	

Turnip Greens and Turnips, Frozen, Cooked, Boiled, Drained, with Salt

1/2 cup / 86g

Amount per serving	%DV	Amount per serving	%DV	Amount per serving	%DV
Calories 29		**Cholesterol** 0mg	0%	**Total Carbohydrate** 4g	1%
Total Fat 0g	0%	**Sodium** 219mg	9%	Dietary Fiber 3g	12%
Saturated Fat 0g	0%	**Protein** 3g		Sugars 1g	
Polyunsaturated Fat 0g					
Monounsaturated Fat 0g		Vitamin A 148% Vitamin C 26%		Calcium 11% Iron 8%	

Turnip Greens and Turnips, Frozen, Cooked, Boiled, Drained, without Salt

1 cup / 163g

Amount per serving	%DV	Amount per serving	%DV	Amount per serving	%DV
Calories 57		**Cholesterol** 0mg	0%	**Total Carbohydrate** 8g	3%
Total Fat 1g	2%	**Sodium** 31mg	1%	Dietary Fiber 5g	20%
Saturated Fat 0g	0%	**Protein** 5g		Sugars 2g	
Polyunsaturated Fat 0g					
Monounsaturated Fat 0g		Vitamin A 281% Vitamin C 49%		Calcium 21% Iron 16%	

Turnip Greens and Turnips, Frozen, Unprepared

1 package / 10 oz / 284g

Amount per serving	%DV	Amount per serving	%DV	Amount per serving	%DV
Calories 60		**Cholesterol** 0mg	0%	**Total Carbohydrate** 10g	3%
Total Fat 1g	2%	**Sodium** 51mg	2%	Dietary Fiber 7g	28%
Saturated Fat 0g	0%	**Protein** 7g		Sugars 0g	
Polyunsaturated Fat 0g					
Monounsaturated Fat 0g		Vitamin A 347% Vitamin C 122%		Calcium 32% Iron 26%	

Turnip Greens, Canned, No Salt

1 cup / 144g

Amount per serving	%DV	Amount per serving	%DV	Amount per serving	%DV
Calories 27		**Cholesterol** 0mg	0%	**Total Carbohydrate** 4g	1%
Total Fat 0g	0%	**Sodium** 42mg	2%	Dietary Fiber 2g	8%
Saturated Fat 0g	0%	**Protein** 2g		Sugars 1g	
Polyunsaturated Fat 0g					
Monounsaturated Fat 0g		Vitamin A 171% Vitamin C 37%.		Calcium 17% Iron 12%	

Turnip Greens, Cooked, Boiled, Drained, without Salt

1 cup, chopped / 144g

Amount per serving	%DV	Amount per serving	%DV	Amount per serving	%DV
Calories 29		**Cholesterol** 0mg	0%	**Total Carbohydrate** 6g	2%
Total Fat 0g	0%	**Sodium** 42mg	2%	Dietary Fiber 5g	20%
Saturated Fat 0g	0%	**Protein** 2g		Sugars 1g	
Polyunsaturated Fat 0g					
Monounsaturated Fat 0g		Vitamin A 220% Vitamin C 66%		Calcium 20% Iron 6%	

Turnip Greens, Frozen, Cooked, Boiled, Drained, with Salt

1/2 cup / 82g

Amount per serving	%DV	Amount per serving	%DV	Amount per serving	%DV
Calories 24		**Cholesterol** 0mg	0%	**Total Carbohydrate** 4g	1%
Total Fat 0g	1%	**Sodium** 206mg	9%	Dietary Fiber 3g	11%
Saturated Fat 0g	0%	**Protein** 3g		Sugars 1g	
Polyunsaturated Fat 0g					
Monounsaturated Fat 0g		Vitamin A 177%	Vitamin C 30%	Calcium 12%	Iron 9%

Turnip Greens, Frozen, Cooked, Boiled, Drained, without Salt

1 cup / 163g

Amount per serving	%DV	Amount per serving	%DV	Amount per serving	%DV
Calories 57		**Cholesterol** 0mg	0%	**Total Carbohydrate** 8g	3%
Total Fat 1g	2%	**Sodium** 31mg	1%	Dietary Fiber 5g	20%
Saturated Fat 0g	0%	**Protein** 5g		Sugars 2g	
Polyunsaturated Fat 0g					
Monounsaturated Fat 0g		Vitamin A 281%	Vitamin C 49%	Calcium 21%	Iron 16%

Turnip Greens, Frozen, Unprepared

1 package, 10 oz / 284g

Amount per serving	%DV	Amount per serving	%DV	Amount per serving	%DV
Calories 660		**Cholesterol** 0mg	0%	**Total Carbohydrate** 10g	3%
Total Fat 1g	2%	**Sodium** 51mg	2%	Dietary Fiber 7g	28%
Saturated Fat 0g	0%	**Protein** 7g		Sugars 0g	
Polyunsaturated Fat 0g					
Monounsaturated Fat 0g		Vitamin A 347%	Vitamin C 122%	Calcium 32%	Iron 26%

Turnip Greens, Raw

1 cup, chopped / 55g

Amount per serving	%DV	Amount per serving	%DV	Amount per serving	%DV
Calories 18		**Cholesterol** 0mg	0%	**Total Carbohydrate** 4g	1%
Total Fat 0g	0%	**Sodium** 22mg	1%	Dietary Fiber 2g	8%
Saturated Fat 0g	0%	**Protein** 1g		Sugars 0g	
Polyunsaturated Fat 0g					
Monounsaturated Fat 0g		Vitamin A 127%	Vitamin C 55%	Calcium 10%	Iron 3%

Turnips, Cooked, Boiled, Drained, without Salt

1 cup, mashed / 230g

Amount per serving	%DV	Amount per serving	%DV	Amount per serving	%DV
Calories 51		**Cholesterol** 0mg	0%	**Total Carbohydrate** 12g	4%
Total Fat 0g	0%	**Sodium** 37mg	2%	Dietary Fiber 5g	20%
Saturated Fat 0g	0%	**Protein** 2g		Sugars 7g	
Polyunsaturated Fat 0g					
Monounsaturated Fat 0g		Vitamin A 0%	Vitamin C 44%	Calcium 8%	Iron 2%

Turnips, Frozen, Cooked, Boiled, Drained, without Salt

1 cup / 156g

Amount per serving	%DV	Amount per serving	%DV	Amount per serving	%DV
Calories 36		**Cholesterol** 0mg	0%	**Total Carbohydrate** 7g	2%
Total Fat 0g	0%	**Sodium** 56mg	2%	Dietary Fiber 3g	12%
Saturated Fat 0g	0%	**Protein** 2g		Sugars 4g	
Polyunsaturated Fat 0g					
Monounsaturated Fat 0g		Vitamin A 0%	Vitamin C 10%	Calcium 5%	Iron 8%

Turnips, Frozen, Unprepared

1/3 package, mashed / 10 oz / 94g

Amount per serving	%DV	Amount per serving	%DV	Amount per serving	%DV
Calories 15		**Cholesterol** 0mg	0%	**Total Carbohydrate** 3g	1%
Total Fat 0g	0%	**Sodium** 23mg	1%	Dietary Fiber 2g	8%
Saturated Fat 0g	0%	**Protein** 1g		Sugars 0g	
Polyunsaturated Fat 0g					
Monounsaturated Fat 0g		Vitamin A 0%	Vitamin C 7%	Calcium 2%	Iron 4%

Turnips, Raw

1 medium / 122g

Amount per serving	%DV	Amount per serving	%DV	Amount per serving	%DV
Calories 34		**Cholesterol** 0mg	0%	**Total Carbohydrate** 8g	3%
Total Fat 0g	0%	**Sodium** 82mg	3%	Dietary Fiber 2g	8%
Saturated Fat 0g	0%	**Protein** 1g		Sugars 5g	
Polyunsaturated Fat 0g					
Monounsaturated Fat 0g		Vitamin A 0%	Vitamin C 43%	Calcium 4%	Iron 2%

Vegetables, Mixed (Corn, Lima Beans, Peas, Green Beans, Carrots) Canned, No Salt

1 cup / 182g

Amount per serving	%DV	Amount per serving	%DV	Amount per serving	%DV
Calories 67		**Cholesterol** 0mg	0%	**Total Carbohydrate** 13g	4%
Total Fat 0g	0%	**Sodium** 47mg	2%	Dietary Fiber 6g	24%
Saturated Fat 0g	0%	**Protein** 3g		Sugars 4g	
Polyunsaturated Fat 0g					
Monounsaturated Fat 0g		Vitamin A 424%	Vitamin C 12%	Calcium 4%	Iron 7%

Vegetables, Mixed, Canned, Drained, Solids

1 cup / 163g

Amount per serving	%DV	Amount per serving	%DV	Amount per serving	%DV
Calories 80		**Cholesterol** 0mg	0%	**Total Carbohydrate** 15g	5%
Total Fat 0g	0%	**Sodium** 243mg	10%	Dietary Fiber 5g	20%
Saturated Fat 0g	0%	**Protein** 4g		Sugars 4g	
Polyunsaturated Fat 0g					
Monounsaturated Fat 0g		Vitamin A 380%	Vitamin C 14%	Calcium 4%	Iron 10%

Vegetables, Mixed, Frozen, Cooked, Boiled, Drained, with Salt

1/2 cup / 91g

Amount per serving	%DV	Amount per serving	%DV	Amount per serving	%DV
Calories 55		Cholesterol 0mg	0%	Total Carbohydrate 12g	4%
Total Fat 0g	0%	Sodium 247mg	10%	Dietary Fiber 4g	16%
Saturated Fat 0g	0%	Protein 3g		Sugars 3g	
Polyunsaturated Fat 0g					
Monounsaturated Fat 0g		Vitamin A 78%	Vitamin C 5%	Calcium 2%	Iron 4%

Vegetables, Mixed, Frozen, Cooked, Boiled, Drained, without Salt

1/2 cup / 91g

Amount per serving	%DV	Amount per serving	%DV	Amount per serving	%DV
Calories 59		Cholesterol 0mg	0%	Total Carbohydrate 12g	4%
Total Fat 0g	0%	Sodium 32mg	1%	Dietary Fiber 4g	16%
Saturated Fat 0g	0%	Protein 3g		Sugars 3g	
Polyunsaturated Fat 0g					
Monounsaturated Fat 0g		Vitamin A 78%	Vitamin C 5%	Calcium 2%	Iron 4%

Wasabi, Root, Raw

1 cup, sliced / 130g

Amount per serving	%DV	Amount per serving	%DV	Amount per serving	%DV
Calories 142		Cholesterol 0mg	0%	Total Carbohydrate 31g	10%
Total Fat 1g	2%	Sodium 22mg	1%	Dietary Fiber 10g	40%
Saturated Fat 0g	0%	Protein 6g		Sugars 0g	
Polyunsaturated Fat 0g					
Monounsaturated Fat 0g		Vitamin A 1%	Vitamin C 91%	Calcium 17%	Iron 7%

Water Chestnuts, Chinese (Matai), Raw

4 water chestnuts / 36g

Amount per serving	%DV	Amount per serving	%DV	Amount per serving	%DV
Calories 35		Cholesterol 0mg	0%	Total Carbohydrate 9g	3%
Total Fat 0g	0%	Sodium 5mg	0%	Dietary Fiber 1g	4%
Saturated Fat 0g	0%	Protein 1g		Sugars 2g	
Polyunsaturated Fat 0g					
Monounsaturated Fat 0g		Vitamin A 0%	Vitamin C 2%	Calcium 0%	Iron 0%

Water Chestnuts, Chinese, Canned, Solids and Liquids

4 water chestnuts / 28g

Amount per serving	%DV	Amount per serving	%DV	Amount per serving	%DV
Calories 14		Cholesterol 0mg	0%	Total Carbohydrate 3g	1%
Total Fat 0g	0%	Sodium 2mg	0%	Dietary Fiber 1g	4%
Saturated Fat 0g	0%	Protein 0g		Sugars 1g	
Polyunsaturated Fat 0g					
Monounsaturated Fat 0g		Vitamin A 0%	Vitamin C 1%	Calcium 0%	Iron 1%

Watercress, Raw

1 cup, chopped / 34g

Amount per serving	%DV	Amount per serving	%DV	Amount per serving	%DV
Calories 4		**Cholesterol** 0mg	0%	**Total Carbohydrate** 0g	0%
Total Fat 0g	0%	**Sodium** 14mg	1%	Dietary Fiber 0g	0%
Saturated Fat 0g	0%	**Protein** 0g		Sugars 0g	
Polyunsaturated Fat 0g					
Monounsaturated Fat 0g		Vitamin A 22%	Vitamin C 24%	Calcium 4%	Iron 0%

Waxgourd (Chinese Preserving Melon), Cooked, Boiled, Drained, without Salt

1 cup, cubes / 175g

Amount per serving	%DV	Amount per serving	%DV	Amount per serving	%DV
Calories 24		**Cholesterol** 0mg	0%	**Total Carbohydrate** 5g	2%
Total Fat 0g	0%	**Sodium** 187mg	8%	Dietary Fiber 2g	8%
Saturated Fat 0g	0%	**Protein** 1g		Sugars 2g	
Polyunsaturated Fat 0g					
Monounsaturated Fat 0g		Vitamin A 0%	Vitamin C 31%	Calcium 3%	Iron 4%

Winged Bean, Immature Seeds, Cooked, Boiled, Drained, with Salt

1 cup / 62g

Amount per serving	%DV	Amount per serving	%DV	Amount per serving	%DV
Calories 23		**Cholesterol** 0mg	0%	**Total Carbohydrate** 2g	1%
Total Fat 0g	0%	**Sodium** 149mg	6%	Dietary Fiber 0g	0%
Saturated Fat 0g	0%	**Protein** 3g		Sugars 0g	
Polyunsaturated Fat 0g					
Monounsaturated Fat 0g		Vitamin A 1%	Vitamin C 10%	Calcium 4%	Iron 4%

Winged Beans, Immature Seeds, Raw

1 cup slices / 44g

Amount per serving	%DV	Amount per serving	%DV	Amount per serving	%DV
Calories 22		**Cholesterol** 0mg	0%	**Total Carbohydrate** 2g	1%
Total Fat 0g	0%	**Sodium** 2mg	0%	Dietary Fiber 0g	0%
Saturated Fat 0g	0%	**Protein** 3g		Sugars 0g	
Polyunsaturated Fat 0g					
Monounsaturated Fat 0g		Vitamin A 1%	Vitamin C 13%	Calcium 4%	Iron 4%

Yambean (Jicama), Raw

1 cup slices / 120g

Amount per serving	%DV	Amount per serving	%DV	Amount per serving	%DV
Calories 46		**Cholesterol** 0mg	0%	**Total Carbohydrate** 11g	4%
Total Fat 0g	0%	**Sodium** 5mg	0%	Dietary Fiber 6g	24%
Saturated Fat 0g	0%	**Protein** 1g		Sugars 2g	
Polyunsaturated Fat 0g					
Monounsaturated Fat 0g		Vitamin A 1%	Vitamin C 40%	Calcium 1%	Iron 4%

Yardlong Bean, Cooked, Boiled, Drained, with Salt

1 cup slices / 104g

Amount per serving	%DV	Amount per serving	%DV	Amount per serving	%DV
Calories 49		**Cholesterol** 0mg	0%	**Total Carbohydrate** 10g	3%
Total Fat 0g	0%	**Sodium** 250mg	10%	Dietary Fiber 0g	0%
Saturated Fat 0g	0%	**Protein** 3g		Sugars 0g	
Polyunsaturated Fat 0g					
Monounsaturated Fat 0g		Vitamin A 9%	Vitamin C 28%	Calcium 5%	Iron 6%

Yardlong Bean, Cooked, Boiled, Drained, without Salt

1 cup sliced / 104g

Amount per serving	%DV	Amount per serving	%DV	Amount per serving	%DV
Calories 49		**Cholesterol** 0mg	0%	**Total Carbohydrate** 10g	3%
Total Fat 0g	0%	**Sodium** 4mg	0%	Dietary Fiber 0g	0%
Saturated Fat 0g	0%	**Protein** 3g		Sugars 0g	
Polyunsaturated Fat 0g					
Monounsaturated Fat 0g		Vitamin A 9%	Vitamin C 28%	Calcium 5%	Iron 6%

Yardlong Bean, Raw

1 cup slices / 91g

Amount per serving	%DV	Amount per serving	%DV	Amount per serving	%DV
Calories 43		**Cholesterol** 0mg	0%	**Total Carbohydrate** 8g	3%
Total Fat 0g	0%	**Sodium** 4mg	0%	Dietary Fiber 0g	0%
Saturated Fat 0g	0%	**Protein** 3g		Sugars 0g	
Polyunsaturated Fat 0g					
Monounsaturated Fat 0g		Vitamin A 16%	Vitamin C 29%	Calcium 5%	Iron 2%

Yautia (Tannier), Raw

1 cup, sliced / 135g

Amount per serving	%DV	Amount per serving	%DV	Amount per serving	%DV
Calories 132		**Cholesterol** 0mg	0%	**Total Carbohydrate** 32g	11%
Total Fat 1g	2%	**Sodium** 28mg	1%	Dietary Fiber 2g	8%
Saturated Fat 0g	0%	**Protein** 2g		Sugars 0g	
Polyunsaturated Fat 0g					
Monounsaturated Fat 0g		Vitamin A 0%	Vitamin C 12%	Calcium 1%	Iron 7%

Vegetable Juices

Bolthouse Farms, 100% Carrot Juice

8 fl oz / 240 ml

Amount per serving	%DV	Amount per serving	%DV	Amount per serving	%DV
Calories 70		**Cholesterol** 0mg	0%	**Total Carbohydrate** 14g	5%
Total Fat 0g	0%	**Sodium** 170mg	7%	Dietary Fiber 1g	4%
Saturated Fat 0g	0%	**Protein** 1g		Sugars 13g	
Polyunsaturated Fat 0g					
Monounsaturated Fat 0g		Vitamin A 700%	Vitamin C 4%	Calcium 4%	Iron 2%

Bolthouse Farms, 100% Orange + Carrot Juice

8 fl oz / 240ml

Amount per serving	%DV	Amount per serving	%DV	Amount per serving	%DV
Calories 120		**Cholesterol** 0mg	0%	**Total Carbohydrate** 27g	9%
Total Fat 0g	0%	**Sodium** 95mg	4%	Dietary Fiber 2g	8%
Saturated Fat 0g	0%	**Protein** 2g		Sugars 23g	
Polyunsaturated Fat 0g					
Monounsaturated Fat 0g		Vitamin A 300% Vitamin C 100%		Calcium 6% Iron 2%	

Bolthouse Farms, 100% Organic Carrot Juice

8 fl oz / 240ml

Amount per serving	%DV	Amount per serving	%DV	Amount per serving	%DV
Calories 70		**Cholesterol** 0mg	0%	**Total Carbohydrate** 13g	4%
Total Fat 0g	0%	**Sodium** 135mg	6%	Dietary Fiber 2g	8%
Saturated Fat 0g	0%	**Protein** 2g		Sugars 13g	
Polyunsaturated Fat 0g					
Monounsaturated Fat 0g		Vitamin A 700% Vitamin C 4%		Calcium 4% Iron 2%	

Bolthouse Farms, Daily Greens Juice

8 fl oz / 240ml

Amount per serving	%DV	Amount per serving	%DV	Amount per serving	%DV
Calories 90		**Cholesterol** 0mg	0%	**Total Carbohydrate** 23g	8%
Total Fat 0g	0%	**Sodium** 65mg	3%	Dietary Fiber 3g	12%
Saturated Fat 0g	0%	**Protein** 1g		Sugars 19g	
Polyunsaturated Fat 0g					
Monounsaturated Fat 0g		Vitamin A 100% Vitamin C 110%		Calcium 25% Iron 50%	

Campbell's Low Sodium, Tomato Juice

1 serving / 243g

Amount per serving	%DV	Amount per serving	%DV	Amount per serving	%DV
Calories 50		**Cholesterol** 0mg	0%	**Total Carbohydrate** 10g	3%
Total Fat 0g	0%	**Sodium** 140mg	6%	Dietary Fiber 2g	8%
Saturated Fat 0g	0%	**Protein** 2g		Sugars 0g	
Polyunsaturated Fat 0g					
Monounsaturated Fat 0g		Vitamin A 10% Vitamin C 120%		Calcium 2% Iron 2%	

Campbell's V8 Low Sodium 100% Vegetable Juice

8 fl oz / 240 ml

Amount per serving	%DV	Amount per serving	%DV	Amount per serving	%DV
Calories 50		**Cholesterol** 0mg	0%	**Total Carbohydrate** 10g	3%
Total Fat 0g	0%	**Sodium** 140mg	6%	Dietary Fiber 2g	8%
Saturated Fat 0g	0%	**Protein** 2g		Sugars 7g	
Polyunsaturated Fat 0g					
Monounsaturated Fat 0g		Vitamin A 40% Vitamin C 0%		Calcium 4% Iron 2%	

Campbell's, V8 Low Sodium Spicy Hot 100% Vegetable Juice

8 fl oz / 240 ml

Amount per serving	%DV	Amount per serving	%DV	Amount per serving	%DV
Calories 50		**Cholesterol** 0mg	0%	**Total Carbohydrate** 11g	4%
Total Fat 0g	0%	**Sodium** 140mg	6%	Dietary Fiber 2g	8%
Saturated Fat 0g	0%	**Protein** 2g		Sugars 8g	
Polyunsaturated Fat 0g					
Monounsaturated Fat 0g		Vitamin A 40% Vitamin C 0%		Calcium 0% Iron 2%	

Tomato and Vegetable Juice, Low Sodium

1 cup / 242g

Amount per serving	%DV	Amount per serving	%DV	Amount per serving	%DV
Calories 53		**Cholesterol** 0mg	0%	**Total Carbohydrate** 11g	4%
Total Fat 0g	0%	**Sodium** 169mg	7%	Dietary Fiber 2g	8%
Saturated Fat 0g	0%	**Protein** 1g		Sugars 9g	
Polyunsaturated Fat 0g					
Monounsaturated Fat 0g		Vitamin A 75% Vitamin C 112%		Calcium 3% Iron 6%	

Tomato Juice, Canned, without Salt

1 fl oz / 30.4g

Amount per serving	%DV	Amount per serving	%DV	Amount per serving	%DV
Calories 5		**Cholesterol** 0mg	0%	**Total Carbohydrate** 1g	0%
Total Fat 0g	0%	**Sodium** 3mg	0%	Dietary Fiber 0g	0%
Saturated Fat 0g	0%	**Protein** 0g		Sugars 1g	
Polyunsaturated Fat 0g					
Monounsaturated Fat 0g		Vitamin A 3% Vitamin C 9%		Calcium 0% Iron 1%	

Tomato Juice, Canned, without Salt Added

1 cup / 243g

Amount per serving	%DV	Amount per serving	%DV	Amount per serving	%DV
Calories 41		**Cholesterol** 0mg	0%	**Total Carbohydrate** 10g	3%
Total Fat 0g	0%	**Sodium** 24mg	1%	Dietary Fiber 1g	4%
Saturated Fat 0g	0%	**Protein** 2g		Sugars 9g	
Polyunsaturated Fat 0g					
Monounsaturated Fat 0g		Vitamin A 22% Vitamin C 74%		Calcium 2% Iron 6%	

Vegetable Products

Bolthouse Farms, Baby Cut Carrots

3 oz / 85g

Amount per serving	%DV	Amount per serving	%DV	Amount per serving	%DV
Calories 35		**Cholesterol** 0mg	0%	**Total Carbohydrate** 8g	3%
Total Fat 0g	0%	**Sodium** 65mg	3%	Dietary Fiber 2g	8%
Saturated Fat 0g	0%	**Protein** 1g		Sugars 5g	
Polyunsaturated Fat 0g					
Monounsaturated Fat 0g		Vitamin A 120% Vitamin C 0%		Calcium 2% Iron 2%	

Bolthouse Farms, Premium Carrot Chips

3 oz / 85g

Amount per serving	%DV	Amount per serving	%DV	Amount per serving	%DV
Calories 35		**Cholesterol** 0mg	0%	**Total Carbohydrate** 8g	3%
Total Fat 0g	0%	**Sodium** 65mg	3%	Dietary Fiber 2g	8%
Saturated Fat 0g	0%	**Protein** 1g		Sugars 5g	
Polyunsaturated Fat 0g					
Monounsaturated Fat 0g		Vitamin A 120% Vitamin C 10%		Calcium 2% Iron 2%	

Bolthouse Farms, Premium Carrot Matchstix

3 oz / 85g

Amount per serving	%DV	Amount per serving	%DV	Amount per serving	%DV
Calories 35		**Cholesterol** 0mg	0%	**Total Carbohydrate** 8g	3%
Total Fat 0g	0%	**Sodium** 65mg	3%	Dietary Fiber 2g	8%
Saturated Fat 0g	0%	**Protein** 1g		Sugars 5g	
Polyunsaturated Fat 0g					
Monounsaturated Fat 0g		Vitamin A 120% Vitamin C 10%		Calcium 2% Iron 2%	

Bolthouse Farms, Premium Sweet Carrot Petites

3 oz / 85g

Amount per serving	%DV	Amount per serving	%DV	Amount per serving	%DV
Calories 35		**Cholesterol** 0mg	0%	**Total Carbohydrate** 8g	3%
Total Fat 0g	0%	**Sodium** 65mg	3%	Dietary Fiber 2g	8%
Saturated Fat 0g	0%	**Protein** 1g		Sugars 5g	
Polyunsaturated Fat 0g					
Monounsaturated Fat 0g		Vitamin A 120% Vitamin C 10%		Calcium 6% Iron 2%	

Del Monte, Chopped Spinach

1/2 cup / 115g

Amount per serving	%DV	Amount per serving	%DV	Amount per serving	%DV
Calories 30		**Cholesterol** 0mg	0%	**Total Carbohydrate** 4g	1%
Total Fat 0g	0%	**Sodium** 360mg	15%	Dietary Fiber 2g	8%
Saturated Fat 0g	0%	**Protein** 2g		Sugars 0g	
Polyunsaturated Fat 0g					
Monounsaturated Fat 0g		Vitamin A 50% Vitamin C 25%		Calcium 10% Iron 6%	

Del Monte, Cream Style White Corn

1/2 cup / 125g

Amount per serving	%DV	Amount per serving	%DV	Amount per serving	%DV
Calories 70		**Cholesterol** 0mg	0%	**Total Carbohydrate** 16g	5%
Total Fat 0g	0%	**Sodium** 240mg	10%	Dietary Fiber 1g	4%
Saturated Fat 0g	0%	**Protein** 1g		Sugars 7g	
Polyunsaturated Fat 0g					
Monounsaturated Fat 0g		Vitamin A 0% Vitamin C 0%		Calcium 0% Iron 2%	

Del Monte, Leaf Spinach

1/2 cup / 115g

Amount per serving	%DV	Amount per serving	%DV	Amount per serving	%DV
Calories 30		**Cholesterol** 0mg	0%	**Total Carbohydrate** 4g	1%
Total Fat 0g	0%	**Sodium** 360mg	15%	Dietary Fiber 2g	8%
Saturated Fat 0g	0%	**Protein** 2g		Sugars 0g	
Polyunsaturated Fat 0g					
Monounsaturated Fat 0g		Vitamin A 50% Vitamin C 25%		Calcium 10% Iron 6%	

Del Monte, Leaf Spinach, No Salt Added

1/2 cup / 115g

Amount per serving	%DV	Amount per serving	%DV	Amount per serving	%DV
Calories 30		**Cholesterol** 0mg	0%	**Total Carbohydrate** 4g	1%
Total Fat 0g	0%	**Sodium** 85mg	4%	Dietary Fiber 2g	8%
Saturated Fat 0g	0%	**Protein** 2g		Sugars 0g	
Polyunsaturated Fat 0g					
Monounsaturated Fat 0g		Vitamin A 50% Vitamin C 25%		Calcium 10% Iron 6%	

Del Monte, Mixed Vegetables

1/2 cup / 124g

Amount per serving	%DV	Amount per serving	%DV	Amount per serving	%DV
Calories 40		**Cholesterol** 0mg	0%	**Total Carbohydrate** 8g	3%
Total Fat 0g	0%	**Sodium** 360mg	15%	Dietary Fiber 3g	12%
Saturated Fat 0g	0%	**Protein** 2g		Sugars 2g	
Polyunsaturated Fat 0g					
Monounsaturated Fat 0g		Vitamin A 30% Vitamin C 2%		Calcium 2% Iron 4%	

Del Monte, Mixed Vegetables, No Salt Added

1/2 cup / 124g

Amount per serving	%DV	Amount per serving	%DV	Amount per serving	%DV
Calories 40		**Cholesterol** 0mg	0%	**Total Carbohydrate** 8g	3%
Total Fat 0g	0%	**Sodium** 25mg	1%	Dietary Fiber 2g	8%
Saturated Fat 0g	0%	**Protein** 2g		Sugars 3g	
Polyunsaturated Fat 0g					
Monounsaturated Fat 0g		Vitamin A 45% Vitamin C 4%		Calcium 2% Iron 4%	

Del Monte, Peas and Carrots

1/2 cup / 128g

Amount per serving	%DV	Amount per serving	%DV	Amount per serving	%DV
Calories 60		**Cholesterol** 0mg	0%	**Total Carbohydrate** 13g	4%
Total Fat 0g	0%	**Sodium** 0mg	0%	Dietary Fiber 4g	16%
Saturated Fat 0g	0%	**Protein** 3g		Sugars 4g	
Polyunsaturated Fat 0g					
Monounsaturated Fat 0g		Vitamin A 80% Vitamin C 10%		Calcium 2% Iron 6%	

Del Monte, Sliced Carrots

1/2 cup / 123g

Amount per serving	%DV	Amount per serving	%DV	Amount per serving	%DV
Calories 35		**Cholesterol** 0mg	0%	**Total Carbohydrate** 8g	3%
Total Fat 0g	0%	**Sodium** 270mg	11%	Dietary Fiber 3g	12%
Saturated Fat 0g	0%	**Protein** 0g		Sugars 5g	
Polyunsaturated Fat 0g					
Monounsaturated Fat 0g		Vitamin A 300% Vitamin C 6%		Calcium 2% Iron 2%	

Del Monte, Summer Crisp, Whole Kernel Corn, No Salt Added

1/2 cup / 125g

Amount per serving	%DV	Amount per serving	%DV	Amount per serving	%DV
Calories 90		**Cholesterol** 0mg	0%	**Total Carbohydrate** 18g	6%
Total Fat 1g	2%	**Sodium** 10mg	0%	Dietary Fiber 3g	12%
Saturated Fat 0g	0%	**Protein** 2g		Sugars 6g	
Polyunsaturated Fat 0g					
Monounsaturated Fat 0g		Vitamin A 0% Vitamin C 10%		Calcium 0% Iron 2%	

Del Monte, Sweet Peas

1/2 cup / 125g

Amount per serving	%DV	Amount per serving	%DV	Amount per serving	%DV
Calories 60		**Cholesterol** 0mg	0%	**Total Carbohydrate** 13g	4%
Total Fat 0g	0%	**Sodium** 350mg	15%	Dietary Fiber 3g	12%
Saturated Fat 0g	0%	**Protein** 3g		Sugars 6g	
Polyunsaturated Fat 0g					
Monounsaturated Fat 0g		Vitamin A 10% Vitamin C 16%		Calcium 2% Iron 8%	

Del Monte, Sweet Peas, No Salt Added

1/2 cup / 125g

Amount per serving	%DV	Amount per serving	%DV	Amount per serving	%DV
Calories 60		**Cholesterol** 0mg	0%	**Total Carbohydrate** 13g	4%
Total Fat 0g	0%	**Sodium** 10mg	0%	Dietary Fiber 3g	12%
Saturated Fat 0g	0%	**Protein** 3g		Sugars 6g	
Polyunsaturated Fat 0g					
Monounsaturated Fat 0g		Vitamin A 10% Vitamin C 16%		Calcium 6% Iron 8%	

Del Monte, Sweet Peas, Low Sodium

1/2 cup / 125g

Amount per serving	%DV	Amount per serving	%DV	Amount per serving	%DV
Calories 60		**Cholesterol** 0mg	0%	**Total Carbohydrate** 13g	4%
Total Fat 0g	0%	**Sodium** 350mg	15%	Dietary Fiber 3g	12%
Saturated Fat 0g	0%	**Protein** 3g		Sugars 6g	
Polyunsaturated Fat 0g					
Monounsaturated Fat 0g		Vitamin A 10% Vitamin C 16%		Calcium 2% Iron 8%	

Del Monte, Very Young & Small Sweet Peas

1/2 cup / 125g

Amount per serving	%DV	Amount per serving	%DV	Amount per serving	%DV
Calories 60		**Cholesterol** 0mg	0%	**Total Carbohydrate** 13g	4%
Total Fat 0g	0%	**Sodium** 360mg	15%	Dietary Fiber 3g	12%
Saturated Fat 0g	0%	**Protein** 3g		Sugars 6g	
Polyunsaturated Fat 0g					
Monounsaturated Fat 0g		Vitamin A 10% Vitamin C 16%		Calcium 2% Iron 8%	

Del Monte, Whole Kernel Corn

1/2 cup / 125g

Amount per serving	%DV	Amount per serving	%DV	Amount per serving	%DV
Calories 90		**Cholesterol** 0mg	0%	**Total Carbohydrate** 18g	6%
Total Fat 1g	2%	**Sodium** 360mg	15%	Dietary Fiber 3g	12%
Saturated Fat 0g	0%	**Protein** 2g		Sugars 6g	
Polyunsaturated Fat 0g					
Monounsaturated Fat 0g		Vitamin A 0% Vitamin C 6%		Calcium 0% Iron 2%	

Del Monte, Whole Kernel Corn, Low Sodium

1/2 cup / 125g

Amount per serving	%DV	Amount per serving	%DV	Amount per serving	%DV
Calories 60		**Cholesterol** 0mg	0%	**Total Carbohydrate** 11g	4%
Total Fat 1g	2%	**Sodium** 180mg	8%	Dietary Fiber 3g	12%
Saturated Fat 0g	0%	**Protein** 2g		Sugars 7g	
Polyunsaturated Fat 0g					
Monounsaturated Fat 0g		Vitamin A 0% Vitamin C 6%		Calcium 0% Iron 2%	

Del Monte, Whole Kernel Corn, No Salt Added

1/2 cup / 125g

Amount per serving	%DV	Amount per serving	%DV	Amount per serving	%DV
Calories 90		**Cholesterol** 0mg	0%	**Total Carbohydrate** 18g	6%
Total Fat 1g	2%	**Sodium** 10mg	0%	Dietary Fiber 3g	12%
Saturated Fat 0g	0%	**Protein** 2g		Sugars 6g	
Polyunsaturated Fat 0g					
Monounsaturated Fat 0g		Vitamin A 0% Vitamin C 10%		Calcium 0% Iron 2%	

Del Monte, Whole Kernel Gold & White Corn

1/2 cup / 125g

Amount per serving	%DV	Amount per serving	%DV	Amount per serving	%DV
Calories 70		**Cholesterol** 0mg	0%	**Total Carbohydrate** 13g	4%
Total Fat 1g	2%	**Sodium** 240mg	10%	Dietary Fiber 2g	8%
Saturated Fat 0g	0%	**Protein** 1g		Sugars 3g	
Polyunsaturated Fat 0g					
Monounsaturated Fat 0g		Vitamin A 0% Vitamin C 0%		Calcium 2% Iron 2%	

Del Monte, Whole Kernel White Corn

1/2 cup / 125g

Amount per serving	%DV	Amount per serving	%DV	Amount per serving	%DV
Calories 60		**Cholesterol** 0mg	0%	**Total Carbohydrate** 13g	4%
Total Fat 1g	2%	**Sodium** 240mg	10%	Dietary Fiber 3g	12%
Saturated Fat 0g	0%	**Protein** 2g		Sugars 6g	
Polyunsaturated Fat 0g					
Monounsaturated Fat 0g		Vitamin A 0% Vitamin C 0%		Calcium 0% Iron 2%	

Dole Salads, American Blend

3 oz / about 1-1/2 cups / 85g

Amount per serving	%DV	Amount per serving	%DV	Amount per serving	%DV
Calories 15		**Cholesterol** 0mg	0%	**Total Carbohydrate** 3g	1%
Total Fat 0g	0%	**Sodium** 10mg	0%	Dietary Fiber 2g	8%
Saturated Fat 0g	0%	**Protein** 1g		Sugars 1g	
Polyunsaturated Fat 0g					
Monounsaturated Fat 0g		Vitamin A 100% Vitamin C 35%		Calcium 2% Iron 2%	

Dole Salads, Angel Hair Coleslaw

3 oz / about 1-1/2 cups / 85g

Amount per serving	%DV	Amount per serving	%DV	Amount per serving	%DV
Calories 20		**Cholesterol** 0mg	0%	**Total Carbohydrate** 5g	2%
Total Fat 0g	0%	**Sodium** 15mg	1%	Dietary Fiber 2g	8%
Saturated Fat 0g	0%	**Protein** 1g		Sugars 3g	
Polyunsaturated Fat 0g					
Monounsaturated Fat 0g		Vitamin A 2% Vitamin C 50%		Calcium 4% Iron 2%	

Dole Salads, Arugula

3 oz / about 3 cups / 85g

Amount per serving	%DV	Amount per serving	%DV	Amount per serving	%DV
Calories 20		**Cholesterol** 0mg	0%	**Total Carbohydrate** 3g	1%
Total Fat 0g	0%	**Sodium** 25mg	1%	Dietary Fiber 1g	4%
Saturated Fat 0g	0%	**Protein** 2g		Sugars 2g	
Polyunsaturated Fat 0g					
Monounsaturated Fat 0g		Vitamin A 40% Vitamin C 20%		Calcium 15% Iron 6%	

Dole Salads, Baby Garden Blend

3 oz / about 1-1/2 cups / 85g

Amount per serving	%DV	Amount per serving	%DV	Amount per serving	%DV
Calories 25		**Cholesterol** 0mg	0%	**Total Carbohydrate** 3g	1%
Total Fat 0g	0%	**Sodium** 45mg	2%	Dietary Fiber 2g	8%
Saturated Fat 0g	0%	**Protein** 2g		Sugars 0g	
Polyunsaturated Fat 0g					
Monounsaturated Fat 0g		Vitamin A 30% Vitamin C 35%		Calcium 6% Iron 2%	

Dole Salads, Baby Romaine

3 oz / about 1-1/2 cups / 85g

Amount per serving	%DV	Amount per serving	%DV	Amount per serving	%DV
Calories 25		**Cholesterol** 0mg	0%	**Total Carbohydrate** 4g	1%
Total Fat 0g	0%	**Sodium** 110mg	5%	Dietary Fiber 2g	8%
Saturated Fat 0g	0%	**Protein** 2g		Sugars 0g	
Polyunsaturated Fat 0g					
Monounsaturated Fat 0g		Vitamin A 100% Vitamin C 15%		Calcium 4%	Iron 4%

Dole Salads, Baby Spinach

3 oz / about 1-1/2 cups / 85g

Amount per serving	%DV	Amount per serving	%DV	Amount per serving	%DV
Calories 20		**Cholesterol** 0mg	0%	**Total Carbohydrate** 3g	1%
Total Fat 0g	0%	**Sodium** 65mg	3%	Dietary Fiber 2g	8%
Saturated Fat 0g	0%	**Protein** 2g		Sugars 0g	
Polyunsaturated Fat 0g					
Monounsaturated Fat 0g		Vitamin A 110% Vitamin C 40%		Calcium 8%	Iron 15%

Dole Salads, Baby Spinach Clamshell

3 oz / about 1-1/2 cups / 85g

Amount per serving	%DV	Amount per serving	%DV	Amount per serving	%DV
Calories 20		**Cholesterol** 0mg	0%	**Total Carbohydrate** 3g	1%
Total Fat 0g	0%	**Sodium** 65mg	3%	Dietary Fiber 2g	8%
Saturated Fat 0g	0%	**Protein** 2g		Sugars 0g	
Polyunsaturated Fat 0g					
Monounsaturated Fat 0g		Vitamin A 160% Vitamin C 40%		Calcium 8%	Iron 15%

Dole Salads, Baby Spinach with Tender Reds

3 oz / about 1-1/2 cups / 85g

Amount per serving	%DV	Amount per serving	%DV	Amount per serving	%DV
Calories 50		**Cholesterol** 0mg	0%	**Total Carbohydrate** 12g	4%
Total Fat 0g	0%	**Sodium** 210mg	9%	Dietary Fiber 6g	24%
Saturated Fat 0g	0%	**Protein** 3g		Sugars 0g	
Polyunsaturated Fat 0g					
Monounsaturated Fat 0g		Vitamin A 120% Vitamin C 30%		Calcium 10%	Iron 20%

Dole Salads, Butter Bliss

3 oz / about 1-1/2 cups / 85g

Amount per serving	%DV	Amount per serving	%DV	Amount per serving	%DV
Calories 15		**Cholesterol** 0mg	0%	**Total Carbohydrate** 2g	1%
Total Fat 0g	0%	**Sodium** 15mg	1%	Dietary Fiber 1g	4%
Saturated Fat 0g	0%	**Protein** 1g		Sugars 1g	
Polyunsaturated Fat 0g					
Monounsaturated Fat 0g		Vitamin A 60% Vitamin C 10%		Calcium 2%	Iron 6%

Dole Salads, Chopped Romaine

3 oz / about 1-1/2 cups / 85g

Amount per serving	%DV	Amount per serving	%DV	Amount per serving	%DV
Calories 15		**Cholesterol** 0mg	0%	**Total Carbohydrate** 3g	1%
Total Fat 0g	0%	**Sodium** 5mg	0%	Dietary Fiber 1g	4%
Saturated Fat 0g	0%	**Protein** 1g		Sugars 2g	
Polyunsaturated Fat 0g					
Monounsaturated Fat 0g		Vitamin A 45%	Vitamin C 35%	Calcium 4%	Iron 6%

Dole Salads, Classic Coleslaw

3 oz / about 1-1/2 cups / 85g

Amount per serving	%DV	Amount per serving	%DV	Amount per serving	%DV
Calories 20		**Cholesterol** 0mg	0%	**Total Carbohydrate** 5g	2%
Total Fat 0g	0%	**Sodium** 20mg	1%	Dietary Fiber 2g	8%
Saturated Fat 0g	0%	**Protein** 1g		Sugars 3g	
Polyunsaturated Fat 0g					
Monounsaturated Fat 0g		Vitamin A 30%	Vitamin C 40%	Calcium 4%	Iron 2%

Dole Salads, Classic Iceberg

3 oz / about 1-1/2 cups / 85g

Amount per serving	%DV	Amount per serving	%DV	Amount per serving	%DV
Calories 15		**Cholesterol** 0mg	0%	**Total Carbohydrate** 4g	1%
Total Fat 0g	0%	**Sodium** 15mg	1%	Dietary Fiber 1g	4%
Saturated Fat 0g	0%	**Protein** 1g		Sugars 2g	
Polyunsaturated Fat 0g					
Monounsaturated Fat 0g		Vitamin A 50%	Vitamin C 10%	Calcium 2%	Iron 2%

Dole Salads, Classic Spring Mix with Garden Vegetables

3 oz /servings per container 3

Amount per serving	%DV	Amount per serving	%DV	Amount per serving	%DV
Calories 0		**Cholesterol** 0mg	0%	**Total Carbohydrate** 16g	5%
Total Fat 0g	0%	**Sodium** 125mg	5%	Dietary Fiber 6g	24%
Saturated Fat 0g	0%	**Protein** 5g		Sugars 5g	
Polyunsaturated Fat 0g					
Monounsaturated Fat 0g		Vitamin A 230%	Vitamin C 70%	Calcium 15%	Iron 10%

Dole Salads, European Blend

3 oz / about 1-1/21 cups / 85g

Amount per serving	%DV	Amount per serving	%DV	Amount per serving	%DV
Calories 15		**Cholesterol** 0mg	0%	**Total Carbohydrate** 3g	1%
Total Fat 0g	0%	**Sodium** 10mg	0%	Dietary Fiber 1g	4%
Saturated Fat 0g	0%	**Protein** 1g		Sugars 1g	
Polyunsaturated Fat 0g					
Monounsaturated Fat 0g		Vitamin A 50%	Vitamin C 15%	Calcium 2%	Iron 4%

Dole Salads, Extra Veggie, Baby Spinach & Spring Mix with Grape Tomatoes

3 oz / serving per container 2.5

Amount per serving	%DV	Amount per serving	%DV	Amount per serving	%DV
Calories 20		**Cholesterol** 0mg	0%	**Total Carbohydrate** 3g	1%
Total Fat 0g	0%	**Sodium** 35mg	1%	Dietary Fiber 2g	8%
Saturated Fat 0g	0%	**Protein** 2g		Sugars 1g	
Polyunsaturated Fat 0g					
Monounsaturated Fat 0g		Vitamin A 70% Vitamin C 30%		Calcium 4% Iron 4%	

Dole Salads, Extra Veggies, Veggie Spring Mix with Snap Peas

3 oz / serving per container 2.5

Amount per serving	%DV	Amount per serving	%DV	Amount per serving	%DV
Calories 20		**Cholesterol** 0mg	0%	**Total Carbohydrate** 5g	2%
Total Fat 0g	0%	**Sodium** 65mg	3%	Dietary Fiber 2g	8%
Saturated Fat 0g	0%	**Protein** 1g		Sugars 2g	
Polyunsaturated Fat 0g					
Monounsaturated Fat 0g		Vitamin A 90% Vitamin C 20%		Calcium 4% Iron 2%	

Dole Salads, Field Greens

3 oz / about 1-1/2 cups / 85g

Amount per serving	%DV	Amount per serving	%DV	Amount per serving	%DV
Calories 20		**Cholesterol** 0mg	0%	**Total Carbohydrate** 4g	1%
Total Fat 0g	0%	**Sodium** 20mg	1%	Dietary Fiber 2g	8%
Saturated Fat 0g	0%	**Protein** 1g		Sugars 1g	
Polyunsaturated Fat 0g					
Monounsaturated Fat 0g		Vitamin A 100% Vitamin C 20%		Calcium 4% Iron 4%	

Dole Salads, Greener Selection

3 oz / about 1-1/2 cups / 85g

Amount per serving	%DV	Amount per serving	%DV	Amount per serving	%DV
Calories 15		**Cholesterol** 0mg	0%	**Total Carbohydrate** 4g	1%
Total Fat 0g	0%	**Sodium** 15mg	1%	Dietary Fiber 1g	4%
Saturated Fat 0g	0%	**Protein** 1g		Sugars 2g	
Polyunsaturated Fat 0g					
Monounsaturated Fat 0g		Vitamin A 60% Vitamin C 20%		Calcium 2% Iron 4%	

Dole Salads, Hearts of Romaine

3 oz / about 1-1/2 cups / 85g

Amount per serving	%DV	Amount per serving	%DV	Amount per serving	%DV
Calories 15		**Cholesterol** 0mg	0%	**Total Carbohydrate** 3g	1%
Total Fat 0g	0%	**Sodium** 10mg	0%	Dietary Fiber 1g	4%
Saturated Fat 0g	0%	**Protein** 1g		Sugars 2g	
Polyunsaturated Fat 0g					
Monounsaturated Fat 0g		Vitamin A 100% Vitamin C 30%		Calcium 2% Iron 4%	

Dole Salads, Italian Blend

3 oz / about 1-1/2 cups / 85g

Amount per serving	%DV	Amount per serving	%DV	Amount per serving	%DV
Calories 15		**Cholesterol** 0mg	0%	**Total Carbohydrate** 3g	1%
Total Fat 0g	0%	**Sodium** 10mg	0%	Dietary Fiber 1g	4%
Saturated Fat 0g	0%	**Protein** 1g		Sugars 2g	
Polyunsaturated Fat 0g					
Monounsaturated Fat 0g		Vitamin A 90%	Vitamin C 30%	Calcium 2%	Iron 4%

Dole Salads, Just Lettuce

3 oz / about 1-1/2 cups / 85g

Amount per serving	%DV	Amount per serving	%DV	Amount per serving	%DV
Calories 15		**Cholesterol** 0mg	0%	**Total Carbohydrate** 3g	1%
Total Fat 0g	0%	**Sodium** 10mg	0%	Dietary Fiber 1g	4%
Saturated Fat 0g	0%	**Protein** 1g		Sugars 1g	
Polyunsaturated Fat 0g					
Monounsaturated Fat 0g		Vitamin A 60%	Vitamin C 15%	Calcium 2%	Iron 2%

Dole Salads, Leafy Romaine

3 oz / about 1-1/2 cups / 85g

Amount per serving	%DV	Amount per serving	%DV	Amount per serving	%DV
Calories 15		**Cholesterol** 0mg	0%	**Total Carbohydrate** 3g	1%
Total Fat 0g	0%	**Sodium** 15mg	1%	Dietary Fiber 1g	4%
Saturated Fat 0g	0%	**Protein** 1g		Sugars 2g	
Polyunsaturated Fat 0g					
Monounsaturated Fat 0g		Vitamin A 100%	Vitamin C 30%	Calcium 2%	Iron 4%

Dole Salads, Mediterranean Blend

3 oz / about 1-1/2 cups / 85g

Amount per serving	%DV	Amount per serving	%DV	Amount per serving	%DV
Calories 15		**Cholesterol** 0mg	0%	**Total Carbohydrate** 3g	1%
Total Fat 0g	0%	**Sodium** 20mg	1%	Dietary Fiber 2g	8%
Saturated Fat 0g	0%	**Protein** 1g		Sugars 1g	
Polyunsaturated Fat 0g					
Monounsaturated Fat 0g		Vitamin A 50%	Vitamin C 8%	Calcium 4%	Iron 4%

Dole Salads, Seven Lettuces

3 oz / about 1-1/2 cups / 85g

Amount per serving	%DV	Amount per serving	%DV	Amount per serving	%DV
Calories 20		**Cholesterol** 0mg	0%	**Total Carbohydrate** 4g	1%
Total Fat 0g	0%	**Sodium** 10mg	0%	Dietary Fiber 1g	4%
Saturated Fat 0g	0%	**Protein** 1g		Sugars 1g	
Polyunsaturated Fat 0g					
Monounsaturated Fat 0g		Vitamin A 50%	Vitamin C 25%	Calcium 2%	Iron 4%

Dole Salads, Shredded Carrots

3 oz / about 1-1/2 cups / 85g

Amount per serving	%DV	Amount per serving	%DV	Amount per serving	%DV
Calories 35		**Cholesterol** 0mg	0%	**Total Carbohydrate** 9g	3%
Total Fat 0g	0%	**Sodium** 60mg	3%	Dietary Fiber 2g	8%
Saturated Fat 0g	0%	**Protein** 1g		Sugars 4g	
Polyunsaturated Fat 0g					
Monounsaturated Fat 0g		Vitamin A 290% Vitamin C 8%		Calcium 2% Iron 2%	

Dole Salads, Shredded Lettuce

3 oz / about 1-1/2 cups / 85g

Amount per serving	%DV	Amount per serving	%DV	Amount per serving	%DV
Calories 10		**Cholesterol** 0mg	0%	**Total Carbohydrate** 3g	1%
Total Fat 0g	0%	**Sodium** 10mg	0%	Dietary Fiber 1g	4%
Saturated Fat 0g	0%	**Protein** 1g		Sugars 1g	
Polyunsaturated Fat 0g					
Monounsaturated Fat 0g		Vitamin A 8% Vitamin C 4%		Calcium 2% Iron 2%	

Dole Salads, Shredded Red Cabbage

3 oz / about 1-1/2 cups / 85g

Amount per serving	%DV	Amount per serving	%DV	Amount per serving	%DV
Calories 25		**Cholesterol** 0mg	0%	**Total Carbohydrate** 6g	2%
Total Fat 0g	0%	**Sodium** 25mg	1%	Dietary Fiber 2g	8%
Saturated Fat 0g	0%	**Protein** 1g		Sugars 3g	
Polyunsaturated Fat 0g					
Monounsaturated Fat 0g		Vitamin A 20% Vitamin C 80%		Calcium 4% Iron 4%	

Dole Salads, Spinach

3 oz / about 1-1/2 cups / 85g

Amount per serving	%DV	Amount per serving	%DV	Amount per serving	%DV
Calories 20		**Cholesterol** 0mg	0%	**Total Carbohydrate** 3g	1%
Total Fat 0g	0%	**Sodium** 67mg	3%	Dietary Fiber 2g	8%
Saturated Fat 0g	0%	**Protein** 2g		Sugars 0g	
Polyunsaturated Fat 0g					
Monounsaturated Fat 0g		Vitamin A 160% Vitamin C 40%		Calcium 8% Iron 15%	

Dole Salads, Spring Mix

3 oz / about 1-1/2 cups / 85g

Amount per serving	%DV	Amount per serving	%DV	Amount per serving	%DV
Calories 20		**Cholesterol** 0mg	0%	**Total Carbohydrate** 3g	1%
Total Fat 0g	0%	**Sodium** 95mg	4%	Dietary Fiber 2g	8%
Saturated Fat 0g	0%	**Protein** 2g		Sugars 2g	
Polyunsaturated Fat 0g					
Monounsaturated Fat 0g		Vitamin A 80% Vitamin C 8%		Calcium 4% Iron 4%	

Dole Salads, Spring Mix

3 oz / about 1-1/2 cups / 85g

Amount per serving	%DV	Amount per serving	%DV	Amount per serving	%DV
Calories 20		**Cholesterol** 0mg	0%	**Total Carbohydrate** 3g	1%
Total Fat 0g	0%	**Sodium** 95mg	4%	Dietary Fiber 2g	8%
Saturated Fat 0g	0%	**Protein** 2g		Sugars 0g	
Polyunsaturated Fat 0g					
Monounsaturated Fat 0g		Vitamin A 80% Vitamin C 8%		Calcium 4% Iron 4%	

Dole Salads, Sweet Baby Lettuce

3 oz

Amount per serving	%DV	Amount per serving	%DV	Amount per serving	%DV
Calories 20		**Cholesterol** 0mg	0%	**Total Carbohydrate** 4g	1%
Total Fat 0g	0%	**Sodium** 60mg	2%	Dietary Fiber 2g	8%
Saturated Fat 0g	0%	**Protein** 2g		Sugars 0g	
Polyunsaturated Fat 0g					
Monounsaturated Fat 0g		Vitamin A 80% Vitamin C 10%		Calcium 4% Iron 4%	

Dole Salads, Tender Greens

3 oz

Amount per serving	%DV	Amount per serving	%DV	Amount per serving	%DV
Calories 25		**Cholesterol** 0mg	0%	**Total Carbohydrate** 4g	1%
Total Fat 0g	0%	**Sodium** 75mg	3%	Dietary Fiber 2g	8%
Saturated Fat 0g	0%	**Protein** 2g		Sugars 1g	
Polyunsaturated Fat 0g					
Monounsaturated Fat 0g		Vitamin A 160% Vitamin C 20%		Calcium 6% Iron 6%	

Dole Salads, Very Veggie

3 oz / about 1-1/2 cups / 85g

Amount per serving	%DV	Amount per serving	%DV	Amount per serving	%DV
Calories 20		**Cholesterol** 0mg	0%	**Total Carbohydrate** 4g	1%
Total Fat 0g	0%	**Sodium** 20mg	1%	Dietary Fiber 2g	8%
Saturated Fat 0g	0%	**Protein** 1g		Sugars 2g	
Polyunsaturated Fat 0g					
Monounsaturated Fat 0g		Vitamin A 80% Vitamin C 30%		Calcium 2% Iron 4%	

Dole, Fresh Vegetable, Onions

1 medium onion / 148g

Amount per serving	%DV	Amount per serving	%DV	Amount per serving	%DV
Calories 45		**Cholesterol** 0mg	0%	**Total Carbohydrate** 11g	4%
Total Fat 0g	0%	**Sodium** 5mg	0%	Dietary Fiber 3g	12%
Saturated Fat 0g	0%	**Protein** 1g		Sugars 9g	
Polyunsaturated Fat 0g					
Monounsaturated Fat 0g		Vitamin A 0% Vitamin C 20%		Calcium 4% Iron 4%	

Dole, Fresh Vegetables, Artichokes

2/3 medium artichoke / 85g

Amount per serving	%DV	Amount per serving	%DV	Amount per serving	%DV
Calories 40		**Cholesterol** 0mg	0%	**Total Carbohydrate** 9g	3%
Total Fat 0g	0%	**Sodium** 80mg	3%	Dietary Fiber 4g	16%
Saturated Fat 0g	0%	**Protein** 3g		Sugars 0g	
Polyunsaturated Fat 0g					
Monounsaturated Fat 0g		Vitamin A 2% Vitamin C 15%		Calcium 4% Iron 6%	

Dole, Fresh Vegetables, Asparagus

5 medium spears / 80g

Amount per serving	%DV	Amount per serving	%DV	Amount per serving	%DV
Calories 15		**Cholesterol** 0mg	0%	**Total Carbohydrate** 3g	1%
Total Fat 0g	0%	**Sodium** 0mg	0%	Dietary Fiber 2g	8%
Saturated Fat 0g	0%	**Protein** 2g		Sugars 2g	
Polyunsaturated Fat 0g					
Monounsaturated Fat 0g		Vitamin A 10% Vitamin C 8%		Calcium 2% Iron 10%	

Dole, Fresh Vegetables, Broccoli

1 medium stalk / 148g

Amount per serving	%DV	Amount per serving	%DV	Amount per serving	%DV
Calories 50		**Cholesterol** 0mg	0%	**Total Carbohydrate** 10g	3%
Total Fat 1g	2%	**Sodium** 50mg	2%	Dietary Fiber 4g	16%
Saturated Fat 0g	0%	**Protein** 4g		Sugars 3g	
Polyunsaturated Fat 0g					
Monounsaturated Fat 0g		Vitamin A 20% Vitamin C 220%		Calcium 8% Iron 6%	

Dole, Fresh Vegetables, Brussels Sprouts

4 sprouts / 84g

Amount per serving	%DV	Amount per serving	%DV	Amount per serving	%DV
Calories 30		**Cholesterol** 0mg	0%	**Total Carbohydrate** 6g	2%
Total Fat 0g	0%	**Sodium** 20mg	1%	Dietary Fiber 3g	12%
Saturated Fat 0g	0%	**Protein** 2g		Sugars 1g	
Polyunsaturated Fat 0g					
Monounsaturated Fat 0g		Vitamin A 15% Vitamin C 90%		Calcium 4% Iron 6%	

Dole, Fresh Vegetables, Butter Lettuce

1/2 head / 85g

Amount per serving	%DV	Amount per serving	%DV	Amount per serving	%DV
Calories 10		**Cholesterol** 0mg	0%	**Total Carbohydrate** 1g	0%
Total Fat 0g	0%	**Sodium** 0mg	0%	Dietary Fiber 0g	0%
Saturated Fat 0g	0%	**Protein** 1g		Sugars 0g	
Polyunsaturated Fat 0g					
Monounsaturated Fat 0g		Vitamin A 60% Vitamin C 6%		Calcium 4% Iron 6%	

Dole, Fresh Vegetables, Carrots

1 medium carrot / 72g

Amount per serving	%DV	Amount per serving	%DV	Amount per serving	%DV
Calories 30		**Cholesterol** 0mg	0%	**Total Carbohydrate** 7g	2%
Total Fat 0g	0%	**Sodium** 50mg	2%	Dietary Fiber 2g	8%
Saturated Fat 0g	0%	**Protein** 1g		Sugars 3g	
Polyunsaturated Fat 0g					
Monounsaturated Fat 0g		Vitamin A 240% Vitamin C 8%		Calcium 2% Iron 2%	

Dole, Fresh Vegetables, Cauliflower

1/6 medium head / about 1 cup / 96g

Amount per serving	%DV	Amount per serving	%DV	Amount per serving	%DV
Calories 25		**Cholesterol** 0mg	0%	**Total Carbohydrate** 5g	2%
Total Fat 0g	0%	**Sodium** 30mg	1%	Dietary Fiber 2g	8%
Saturated Fat 0g	0%	**Protein** 2g		Sugars 2g	
Polyunsaturated Fat 0g					
Monounsaturated Fat 0g		Vitamin A 0% Vitamin C 70%		Calcium 2% Iron 2%	

Dole, Fresh Vegetables, Celery

2 medium stalks / 110g

Amount per serving	%DV	Amount per serving	%DV	Amount per serving	%DV
Calories 15		**Cholesterol** 0mg	0%	**Total Carbohydrate** 3g	1%
Total Fat 0g	0%	**Sodium** 90mg	4%	Dietary Fiber 2g	8%
Saturated Fat 0g	0%	**Protein** 1g		Sugars 0g	
Polyunsaturated Fat 0g					
Monounsaturated Fat 0g		Vitamin A 10% Vitamin C 6%		Calcium 4% Iron 2%	

Dole, Fresh Vegetables, Green Leaf Lettuce

1/4 head / about 4 outer leaves / 90g

Amount per serving	%DV	Amount per serving	%DV	Amount per serving	%DV
Calories 15		**Cholesterol** 0mg	0%	**Total Carbohydrate** 3g	1%
Total Fat 0g	0%	**Sodium** 25mg	1%	Dietary Fiber 1g	4%
Saturated Fat 0g	0%	**Protein** 1g		Sugars 1g	
Polyunsaturated Fat 0g					
Monounsaturated Fat 0g		Vitamin A 130% Vitamin C 25%		Calcium 4% Iron 4%	

Dole, Fresh Vegetables, Iceberg Lettuce

1/6 medium head / 89g

Amount per serving	%DV	Amount per serving	%DV	Amount per serving	%DV
Calories 10		**Cholesterol** 0mg	0%	**Total Carbohydrate** 3g	1%
Total Fat 0g	0%	**Sodium** 10mg	0%	Dietary Fiber 1g	4%
Saturated Fat 0g	0%	**Protein** 1g		Sugars 2g	
Polyunsaturated Fat 0g					
Monounsaturated Fat 0g		Vitamin A 8% Vitamin C 4%		Calcium 2% Iron 2%	

Dole, Fresh Vegetables, Mushrooms

1/2 cup raw / 35g

Amount per serving	%DV	Amount per serving	%DV	Amount per serving	%DV
Calories 9		**Cholesterol** 0mg	0%	**Total Carbohydrate** 1g	0%
Total Fat 0g	0%	**Sodium** 0mg	0%	Dietary Fiber 0g	0%
Saturated Fat 0g	0%	**Protein** 0g		Sugars 0g	
Polyunsaturated Fat 0g					
Monounsaturated Fat 0g		Vitamin A 0%	Vitamin C 0%	Calcium 0%	Iron 0%

Dole, Fresh Vegetables, Radish

9 large radishes / 81g

Amount per serving	%DV	Amount per serving	%DV	Amount per serving	%DV
Calories 0		**Cholesterol** 0mg	0%	**Total Carbohydrate** 0g	0%
Total Fat 0g	0%	**Sodium** 30mg	1%	Dietary Fiber 4g	16%
Saturated Fat 0g	0%	**Protein** 1g		Sugars 21g	
Polyunsaturated Fat 0g					
Monounsaturated Fat 0g		Vitamin A 0%	Vitamin C 20%	Calcium 2%	Iron 2%

Dole, Fresh Vegetables, Romaine Lettuce

3 outer leaves / 85g

Amount per serving	%DV	Amount per serving	%DV	Amount per serving	%DV
Calories 15		**Cholesterol** 0mg	0%	**Total Carbohydrate** 3g	1%
Total Fat 0g	0%	**Sodium** 1mg	0%	Dietary Fiber 2g	8%
Saturated Fat 0g	0%	**Protein** 1g		Sugars 1g	
Polyunsaturated Fat 0g					
Monounsaturated Fat 0g		Vitamin A 100%	Vitamin C 35%	Calcium 2%	Iron 4%

Dr. Praeger's Sensible Foods, Broccoli Littles

2 pieces / 34g

Amount per serving	%DV	Amount per serving	%DV	Amount per serving	%DV
Calories 40		**Cholesterol** 0mg	0%	**Total Carbohydrate** 4g	1%
Total Fat 2.5g	4%	**Sodium** 100mg	4%	Dietary Fiber 1g	4%
Saturated Fat 0g	0%	**Protein** 1g		Sugars 0g	
Polyunsaturated Fat 0g					
Monounsaturated Fat 0g		Vitamin A 1%	Vitamin C 9%	Calcium 0%	Iron 5%

Eden Foods, Crushed Tomatoes with Basil, Organic

1/4 cup / 61g

Amount per serving	%DV	Amount per serving	%DV	Amount per serving	%DV
Calories 20		**Cholesterol** 0mg	0%	**Total Carbohydrate** 3g	1%
Total Fat 0g	0%	**Sodium** 0mg	0%	Dietary Fiber 1g	4%
Saturated Fat 0g	0%	**Protein** 1g		Sugars 2g	
Polyunsaturated Fat 0g					
Monounsaturated Fat 0g		Vitamin A 15%	Vitamin C 15%	Calcium 2%	Iron 4%

Eden Foods, Crushed Tomatoes with Onions and Garlic, Organic

1/4 cup / 61g

Amount per serving	%DV	Amount per serving	%DV	Amount per serving	%DV
Calories 20		**Cholesterol** 0mg	0%	**Total Carbohydrate** 3g	1%
Total Fat 0g	0%	**Sodium** 0mg	0%	Dietary Fiber 1g	4%
Saturated Fat 0g	0%	**Protein** 1g		Sugars 2g	
Polyunsaturated Fat 0g					
Monounsaturated Fat 0g		Vitamin A 15%	Vitamin C 15%	Calcium 2%	Iron 4%

Eden Foods, Crushed Tomatoes with Roasted Onion, Organic

1/4 cup / 61g

Amount per serving	%DV	Amount per serving	%DV	Amount per serving	%DV
Calories 20		**Cholesterol** 0mg	0%	**Total Carbohydrate** 3g	1%
Total Fat 0g	0%	**Sodium** 0mg	0%	Dietary Fiber 1g	4%
Saturated Fat 0g	0%	**Protein** 1g		Sugars 2g	
Polyunsaturated Fat 0g					
Monounsaturated Fat 0g		Vitamin A 15%	Vitamin C 15%	Calcium 2%	Iron 4%

Eden Foods, Crushed Tomatoes with Sweet Basil, Organic

1/4 cup / 60g

Amount per serving	%DV	Amount per serving	%DV	Amount per serving	%DV
Calories 20		**Cholesterol** 0mg	0%	**Total Carbohydrate** 3g	1%
Total Fat 0g	0%	**Sodium** 0mg	0%	Dietary Fiber 1g	4%
Saturated Fat 0g	0%	**Protein** 1g		Sugars 2g	
Polyunsaturated Fat 0g					
Monounsaturated Fat 0g		Vitamin A 15%	Vitamin C 15%	Calcium 2%	Iron 4%

Eden Foods, Crushed Tomatoes, Organic

1/4 cup / 61g

Amount per serving	%DV	Amount per serving	%DV	Amount per serving	%DV
Calories 20		**Cholesterol** 0mg	0%	**Total Carbohydrate** 3g	1%
Total Fat 0g	0%	**Sodium** 0mg	0%	Dietary Fiber 1g	4%
Saturated Fat 0g	0%	**Protein** 1g		Sugars 2g	
Polyunsaturated Fat 0g					
Monounsaturated Fat 0g		Vitamin A 15%	Vitamin C 15%	Calcium 2%	Iron 4%

Eden Foods, Daikon Radish, Shredded and Dried

2 tbsp / 14g

Amount per serving	%DV	Amount per serving	%DV	Amount per serving	%DV
Calories 45		**Cholesterol** 0mg	0%	**Total Carbohydrate** 9g	3%
Total Fat 0g	0%	**Sodium** 20mg	1%	Dietary Fiber 3g	12%
Saturated Fat 0g	0%	**Protein** 1g		Sugars 6g	
Polyunsaturated Fat 0g					
Monounsaturated Fat 0g		Vitamin A 0%	Vitamin C 0%	Calcium 6%	Iron 4%

Eden Foods, Diced Tomatoes with Basil, Organic

1/2 cup / 130g

Amount per serving	%DV	Amount per serving	%DV	Amount per serving	%DV
Calories 30		**Cholesterol** 0mg	0%	**Total Carbohydrate** 6g	2%
Total Fat 0g	0%	**Sodium** 5mg	0%	Dietary Fiber 2g	8%
Saturated Fat 0g	0%	**Protein** 1g		Sugars 4g	
Polyunsaturated Fat 0g					
Monounsaturated Fat 0g		Vitamin A 20% Vitamin C 30%		Calcium 2% Iron 2%	

Eden Foods, Diced Tomatoes with Green Chiles, Organic

1/2 cup / 130g

Amount per serving	%DV	Amount per serving	%DV	Amount per serving	%DV
Calories 30		**Cholesterol** 0mg	0%	**Total Carbohydrate** 5g	2%
Total Fat 0g	0%	**Sodium** 35mg	1%	Dietary Fiber 2g	8%
Saturated Fat 0g	0%	**Protein** 2g		Sugars 3g	
Polyunsaturated Fat 0g					
Monounsaturated Fat 0g		Vitamin A 20% Vitamin C 15%		Calcium 2% Iron 2%	

Eden Foods, Diced Tomatoes with Roasted Onion, Organic

1/2 cup / 130g

Amount per serving	%DV	Amount per serving	%DV	Amount per serving	%DV
Calories 30		**Cholesterol** 0mg	0%	**Total Carbohydrate** 6g	2%
Total Fat 0g	0%	**Sodium** 5mg	0%	Dietary Fiber 2g	8%
Saturated Fat 0g	0%	**Protein** 1g		Sugars 4g	
Polyunsaturated Fat 0g					
Monounsaturated Fat 0g		Vitamin A 20% Vitamin C 30%		Calcium 2% Iron 2%	

Eden Foods, Diced Tomatoes, Organic

1/2 cup / 130g

Amount per serving	%DV	Amount per serving	%DV	Amount per serving	%DV
Calories 30		**Cholesterol** 0mg	0%	**Total Carbohydrate** 6g	2%
Total Fat 0g	0%	**Sodium** 5mg	0%	Dietary Fiber 2g	8%
Saturated Fat 0g	0%	**Protein** 1g		Sugars 4g	
Polyunsaturated Fat 0g					
Monounsaturated Fat 0g		Vitamin A 20% Vitamin C 30%		Calcium 2% Iron 2%	

Eden Foods, Lotus Root

About 5 slices / dried

Amount per serving	%DV	Amount per serving	%DV	Amount per serving	%DV
Calories 35		**Cholesterol** 0mg	0%	**Total Carbohydrate** 8g	3%
Total Fat 0g	0%	**Sodium** 25mg	1%	Dietary Fiber 2g	8%
Saturated Fat 0g	0%	**Protein** 1g		Sugars 1g	
Polyunsaturated Fat 0g					
Monounsaturated Fat 0g		Vitamin A 0% Vitamin C 0%		Calcium 0% Iron 2%	

Eden Foods, Maitake Mushrooms, Dried

About 10 pieces

Amount per serving	%DV	Amount per serving	%DV	Amount per serving	%DV
Calories 35		**Cholesterol** 0mg	0%	**Total Carbohydrate** 7g	2%
Total Fat 0g	0%	**Sodium** 0mg	0%	Dietary Fiber 4g	16%
Saturated Fat 0g	0%	**Protein** 2g		Sugars 0g	
Polyunsaturated Fat 0g					
Monounsaturated Fat 0g		Vitamin A 0% Vitamin C 0%		Calcium 0% Iron 2%	

Eden Foods, Nori Krinkles, Sea Vegetables, Cultivated, Toasted

1/2 cup / 2.5g

Amount per serving	%DV	Amount per serving	%DV	Amount per serving	%DV
Calories 10		**Cholesterol** 0mg	0%	**Total Carbohydrate** 1g	0%
Total Fat 0g	0%	**Sodium** 5mg	0%	Dietary Fiber 1g	4%
Saturated Fat 0g	0%	**Protein** 1g		Sugars 0g	
Polyunsaturated Fat 0g					
Monounsaturated Fat 0g		Vitamin A 8% Vitamin C 10%		Calcium 0% Iron 0%	

Eden Foods, Nori, Sea Vegetable, Cultivated, Raw

1 sheet / 2.5g

Amount per serving	%DV	Amount per serving	%DV	Amount per serving	%DV
Calories 10		**Cholesterol** 0mg	0%	**Total Carbohydrate** 0g	0%
Total Fat 0g	0%	**Sodium** 5mg	0%	Dietary Fiber 1g	4%
Saturated Fat 0g	0%	**Protein** 1g		Sugars 0g	
Polyunsaturated Fat 0g					
Monounsaturated Fat 0g		Vitamin A 8% Vitamin C 10%		Calcium 0% Iron 0%	

Eden Foods, Sauerkraut, Organic

1/4 cup / 30g

Amount per serving	%DV	Amount per serving	%DV	Amount per serving	%DV
Calories 5		**Cholesterol** 0mg	0%	**Total Carbohydrate** 2g	1%
Total Fat 0g	0%	**Sodium** 150mg	6%	Dietary Fiber 1g	4%
Saturated Fat 0g	0%	**Protein** 0g		Sugars 0g	
Polyunsaturated Fat 0g					
Monounsaturated Fat 0g		Vitamin A 0% Vitamin C 6%		Calcium 0% Iron 0%	

Eden Foods, Shiitake Mushrooms, Dried Sliced

about 6 slices / 10g

Amount per serving	%DV	Amount per serving	%DV	Amount per serving	%DV
Calories 35		**Cholesterol** 0mg	0%	**Total Carbohydrate** 7g	2%
Total Fat 0g	0%	**Sodium** 0mg	0%	Dietary Fiber 5g	20%
Saturated Fat 0g	0%	**Protein** 2g		Sugars 2g	
Polyunsaturated Fat 0g					
Monounsaturated Fat 0g		Vitamin A 0% Vitamin C 0%		Calcium 0% Iron 4%	

Eden Foods, Shiitake Mushrooms, Whole Dried

3 mushrooms / 10g

Amount per serving	%DV	Amount per serving	%DV	Amount per serving	%DV
Calories 35		**Cholesterol** 0mg	0%	**Total Carbohydrate** 7g	2%
Total Fat 0g	0%	**Sodium** 0mg	0%	Dietary Fiber 5g	20%
Saturated Fat 0g	0%	**Protein** 2g		Sugars 2g	
Polyunsaturated Fat 0g					
Monounsaturated Fat 0g		Vitamin A 0% Vitamin C 0%		Calcium 0% Iron 4%	

Eden Foods, Sushi Nori, Sea Vegetable, Cultivated

1 toasted sheet / 2.5g

Amount per serving	%DV	Amount per serving	%DV	Amount per serving	%DV
Calories 5		**Cholesterol** 0mg	0%	**Total Carbohydrate** 0g	0%
Total Fat 0g	0%	**Sodium** 5mg	0%	Dietary Fiber 1g	4%
Saturated Fat 0g	0%	**Protein** 1g		Sugars 0g	
Polyunsaturated Fat 0g					
Monounsaturated Fat 0g		Vitamin A 8% Vitamin C 10%		Calcium 0% Iron 0%	

Eden Foods, Whole Roma Tomatoes with Sweet Basil, Organic

1/2 cup

Amount per serving	%DV	Amount per serving	%DV	Amount per serving	%DV
Calories 30		**Cholesterol** 0mg	0%	**Total Carbohydrate** 4g	1%
Total Fat 0g	0%	**Sodium** 10mg	0%	Dietary Fiber 1g	4%
Saturated Fat 0g	0%	**Protein** 1g		Sugars 2g	
Polyunsaturated Fat 0g					
Monounsaturated Fat 0g		Vitamin A 25% Vitamin C 35%		Calcium 0% Iron 4%	

Glory Foods Sensibly Seasoned Lower Sodium Tomatoes, Okra & Corn

1/2 cup / 117g

Amount per serving	%DV	Amount per serving	%DV	Amount per serving	%DV
Calories 35		**Cholesterol** 0mg	0%	**Total Carbohydrate** 8g	3%
Total Fat 0g	0%	**Sodium** 150mg	6%	Dietary Fiber 2g	8%
Saturated Fat 0g	0%	**Protein** 1g		Sugars 4g	
Polyunsaturated Fat 0g					
Monounsaturated Fat 0g		Vitamin A 6% Vitamin C 15%		Calcium 4% Iron 2%	

Glory Foods, Sensibly Seasoned Lower Sodium Mixed Greens

1/2 cup / 118g

Amount per serving	%DV	Amount per serving	%DV	Amount per serving	%DV
Calories 20		**Cholesterol** 0mg	0%	**Total Carbohydrate** 4g	1%
Total Fat 0g	0%	**Sodium** 240mg	10%	Dietary Fiber 2g	8%
Saturated Fat 0g	0%	**Protein** 1g		Sugars 1g	
Polyunsaturated Fat 0g					
Monounsaturated Fat 0g		Vitamin A 110% Vitamin C 35%		Calcium 6% Iron 4%	

Glory Foods, Sensibly Seasoned Lower Sodium Tomatoes & Okra

1/2 cup

Amount per serving	%DV	Amount per serving	%DV	Amount per serving	%DV
Calories 25		**Cholesterol** 0mg	0%	**Total Carbohydrate** 6g	2%
Total Fat 0g	0%	**Sodium** 150mg	6%	Dietary Fiber 1g	4%
Saturated Fat 0g	0%	**Protein** 1g		Sugars 4g	
Polyunsaturated Fat 0g					
Monounsaturated Fat 0g		Vitamin A 6%	Vitamin C 15%	Calcium 4%	Iron 2%

Glory Foods, Sensibly Seasoned Lower Sodium Turnip Greens

1/2 cup / 118g

Amount per serving	%DV	Amount per serving	%DV	Amount per serving	%DV
Calories 20		**Cholesterol** 0mg	0%	**Total Carbohydrate** 4g	1%
Total Fat 0g	0%	**Sodium** 240mg	10%	Dietary Fiber 2g	8%
Saturated Fat 0g	0%	**Protein** 1g		Sugars 1g	
Polyunsaturated Fat 0g					
Monounsaturated Fat 0g		Vitamin A 60%	Vitamin C 15%	Calcium 10%	Iron 4%

Hunt's, Tomato Puree

1/4 cup / 62g

Amount per serving	%DV	Amount per serving	%DV	Amount per serving	%DV
Calories 40		**Cholesterol** 0mg	0%	**Total Carbohydrate** 8g	3%
Total Fat 0g	0%	**Sodium** 125mg	5%	Dietary Fiber 3g	12%
Saturated Fat 0g	0%	**Protein** 2g		Sugars 4g	
Polyunsaturated Fat 0g					
Monounsaturated Fat 0g		Vitamin A 10%	Vitamin C 6%	Calcium 0%	Iron 2%

Hunt's, Tomatoes Crushed

1/2 cup / 121g

Amount per serving	%DV	Amount per serving	%DV	Amount per serving	%DV
Calories 45		**Cholesterol** 0mg	0%	**Total Carbohydrate** 9g	3%
Total Fat 0g	0%	**Sodium** 230mg	10%	Dietary Fiber 3g	12%
Saturated Fat 0g	0%	**Protein** 2g		Sugars 4g	
Polyunsaturated Fat 0g					
Monounsaturated Fat 0g		Vitamin A 10%	Vitamin C 0%	Calcium 0%	Iron 8%

Hunt's, Tomatoes Crushed Basil

1/2 cup / 121g

Amount per serving	%DV	Amount per serving	%DV	Amount per serving	%DV
Calories 45		**Cholesterol** 0mg	0%	**Total Carbohydrate** 9g	3%
Total Fat 0g	0%	**Sodium** 230mg	10%	Dietary Fiber 3g	12%
Saturated Fat 0g	0%	**Protein** 2g		Sugars 4g	
Polyunsaturated Fat 0g					
Monounsaturated Fat 0g		Vitamin A 10%	Vitamin C 0%	Calcium 0%	Iron 8%

Hunt's, Tomatoes Diced in Sauce

1/2 cup / 122g

Amount per serving	%DV	Amount per serving	%DV	Amount per serving	%DV
Calories 35		**Cholesterol** 0mg	0%	**Total Carbohydrate** 7g	2%
Total Fat 0g	0%	**Sodium** 310mg	13%	Dietary Fiber 2g	8%
Saturated Fat 0g	0%	**Protein** 1g		Sugars 3g	
Polyunsaturated Fat 0g					
Monounsaturated Fat 0g		Vitamin A 10%	Vitamin C 20%	Calcium 4%	Iron 6%

Hunt's, Tomatoes Diced Roasted Garlic

1/2 cup / 121g

Amount per serving	%DV	Amount per serving	%DV	Amount per serving	%DV
Calories 35		**Cholesterol** 0mg	0%	**Total Carbohydrate** 8g	3%
Total Fat 0g	0%	**Sodium** 260mg	11%	Dietary Fiber 2g	8%
Saturated Fat 0g	0%	**Protein** 1g		Sugars 4g	
Polyunsaturated Fat 0g					
Monounsaturated Fat 0g		Vitamin A 6%	Vitamin C 20%	Calcium 4%	Iron 4%

Hunt's, Tomatoes Diced Sweet Onion

1/2 cup / 123g

Amount per serving	%DV	Amount per serving	%DV	Amount per serving	%DV
Calories 35		**Cholesterol** 0mg	0%	**Total Carbohydrate** 8g	3%
Total Fat 0g	0%	**Sodium** 320mg	13%	Dietary Fiber 2g	8%
Saturated Fat 0g	0%	**Protein** 1g		Sugars 4g	
Polyunsaturated Fat 0g					
Monounsaturated Fat 0g		Vitamin A 8%	Vitamin C 15%	Calcium 4%	Iron 6%

Hunt's, Tomatoes No Salt Added Stewed

1/2 cup / 121g

Amount per serving	%DV	Amount per serving	%DV	Amount per serving	%DV
Calories 40		**Cholesterol** 0mg	0%	**Total Carbohydrate** 8g	3%
Total Fat 0g	0%	**Sodium** 30mg	1%	Dietary Fiber 2g	8%
Saturated Fat 0g	0%	**Protein** 1g		Sugars 5g	
Polyunsaturated Fat 0g					
Monounsaturated Fat 0g		Vitamin A 6%	Vitamin C 20%	Calcium 4%	Iron 4%

Hunt's, Tomatoes Petite Diced

1/2 cup / 121g

Amount per serving	%DV	Amount per serving	%DV	Amount per serving	%DV
Calories 30		**Cholesterol** 0mg	0%	**Total Carbohydrate** 6g	2%
Total Fat 0g	0%	**Sodium** 220mg	9%	Dietary Fiber 2g	8%
Saturated Fat 0g	0%	**Protein** 1g		Sugars 3g	
Polyunsaturated Fat 0g					
Monounsaturated Fat 0g		Vitamin A 8%	Vitamin C 20%	Calcium 2%	Iron 4%

Hunt's, Tomatoes Whole Peeled Plum Tomatoes

1/2 cup / about 2 small / 121g

Amount per serving	%DV	Amount per serving	%DV	Amount per serving	%DV
Calories 30		**Cholesterol** 0mg	0%	**Total Carbohydrate** 5g	2%
Total Fat 0g	0%	**Sodium** 190mg	8%	Dietary Fiber 2g	8%
Saturated Fat 0g	0%	**Protein** 1g		Sugars 3g	
Polyunsaturated Fat 0g					
Monounsaturated Fat 0g		Vitamin A 6%	Vitamin C 20%	Calcium 4%	Iron 0%

Hunt's, Tomatoes Whole Peeled Plum Tomatoes Basil

1/2 cup / about 2 small / 121g

Amount per serving	%DV	Amount per serving	%DV	Amount per serving	%DV
Calories 30		**Cholesterol** 0mg	0%	**Total Carbohydrate** 5g	2%
Total Fat 0g	0%	**Sodium** 190mg	8%	Dietary Fiber 2g	8%
Saturated Fat 0g	0%	**Protein** 1g		Sugars 3g	
Polyunsaturated Fat 0g					
Monounsaturated Fat 0g		Vitamin A 6%	Vitamin C 20%	Calcium 4%	Iron 0%

Hunt's, Tomatoes, Diced Green Pepper, Celery & Onion

1/2 cup / 123g

Amount per serving	%DV	Amount per serving	%DV	Amount per serving	%DV
Calories 45		**Cholesterol** 0mg	0%	**Total Carbohydrate** 10g	3%
Total Fat 0g	0%	**Sodium** 250mg	10%	Dietary Fiber 2g	8%
Saturated Fat 0g	0%	**Protein** 1g		Sugars 5g	
Polyunsaturated Fat 0g					
Monounsaturated Fat 0g		Vitamin A 6%	Vitamin C 20%	Calcium 4%	Iron 4%

Jovial Foods, Organic Tomatoes, Including Diced, Whole Peeled, and Crushed

1/2 cup / 124g

Amount per serving	%DV	Amount per serving	%DV	Amount per serving	%DV
Calories 30		**Cholesterol** 0mg	0%	**Total Carbohydrate** 6g	2%
Total Fat 0g	0%	**Sodium** 30mg	1%	Dietary Fiber 1g	4%
Saturated Fat 0g	0%	**Protein** 1g		Sugars 4g	
Polyunsaturated Fat 0g					
Monounsaturated Fat 0g		Vitamin A 25%	Vitamin C 35%	Calcium 2%	Iron 2%

Ketchup

1 tbsp / 15g

Amount per serving	%DV	Amount per serving	%DV	Amount per serving	%DV
Calories 15		**Cholesterol** 0mg	0%	**Total Carbohydrate** 4.5g	2%
Total Fat 0g	0%	**Sodium** 167mg	7%	Dietary Fiber 0g	0%
Saturated Fat 0g	0%	**Protein** 0g		Sugars 3.5g	
Polyunsaturated Fat 0g					
Monounsaturated Fat 0g		Vitamin A 3%	Vitamin C 4%	Calcium 0%	Iron 0%

Ketchup, Low Sodium

1 tbsp / 15g

Amount per serving	%DV	Amount per serving	%DV	Amount per serving	%DV
Calories 15		**Cholesterol** 0mg	0%	**Total Carbohydrate** 4g	1%
Total Fat 0g	0%	**Sodium** 3mg	0%	Dietary Fiber 0g	0%
Saturated Fat 0g	0%	**Protein** 0g		Sugars 3g	
Polyunsaturated Fat 0g					
Monounsaturated Fat 0g		Vitamin A 3% Vitamin C 4%		Calcium 0% Iron 0%	

Lucini, Hearty Artichoke Tomato Sauce

1/2 cup / 125g

Amount per serving	%DV	Amount per serving	%DV	Amount per serving	%DV
Calories 50		**Cholesterol** 0mg	0%	**Total Carbohydrate** 7g	2%
Total Fat 1.5g	2%	**Sodium** 230mg	10%	Dietary Fiber 3g	12%
Saturated Fat 0g	0%	**Protein** 2g		Sugars 1g	
Polyunsaturated Fat 0g					
Monounsaturated Fat 0g		Vitamin A 0% Vitamin C 15%		Calcium 2% Iron 6%	

Lucini, Tuscan Harvest Plum Tomatoes, Diced Peeled 100% Organic

1/2 cup / 125g

Amount per serving	%DV	Amount per serving	%DV	Amount per serving	%DV
Calories 19		**Cholesterol** 0mg	0%	**Total Carbohydrate** 4g	1%
Total Fat 0g	0%	**Sodium** 80mg	3%	Dietary Fiber 3g	12%
Saturated Fat 0g	0%	**Protein** 1g		Sugars 4g	
Polyunsaturated Fat 0g					
Monounsaturated Fat 0g		Vitamin A 14% Vitamin C 15%		Calcium 8% Iron 4%	

Lucini, Tuscan Harvest Plum Tomatoes, Whole Peeled 100% Organic

1/2 cup / 125g

Amount per serving	%DV	Amount per serving	%DV	Amount per serving	%DV
Calories 19		**Cholesterol** 0mg	0%	**Total Carbohydrate** 4g	1%
Total Fat 0g	0%	**Sodium** 80mg	3%	Dietary Fiber 3g	12%
Saturated Fat 0g	0%	**Protein** 1g		Sugars 4g	
Polyunsaturated Fat 0g					
Monounsaturated Fat 0g		Vitamin A 14% Vitamin C 15%		Calcium 8% Iron 4%	

Mariani, Premium Sun-Dried Tomatoes, Tomato Halves

1 tbsp / 5g

Amount per serving	%DV	Amount per serving	%DV	Amount per serving	%DV
Calories 15		**Cholesterol** 0mg	0%	**Total Carbohydrate** 3g	1%
Total Fat 0g	0%	**Sodium** 10mg	0%	Dietary Fiber 1g	4%
Saturated Fat 0g	0%	**Protein** 0g		Sugars 2g	
Polyunsaturated Fat 0g					
Monounsaturated Fat 0g		Vitamin A 10% Vitamin C 2%		Calcium 0% Iron 0%	

Mariani, Premium Sun-Dried Tomatoes, Tomatoes Julienne

1 tbsp / 5g

Amount per serving	%DV	Amount per serving	%DV	Amount per serving	%DV
Calories 15		**Cholesterol** 0mg	0%	**Total Carbohydrate** 3g	1%
Total Fat 0g	0%	**Sodium** 10mg	0%	Dietary Fiber 1g	4%
Saturated Fat 0g	0%	**Protein** 0g		Sugars 2g	
Polyunsaturated Fat 0g					
Monounsaturated Fat 0g		Vitamin A 10% Vitamin C 2%		Calcium 0% Iron 0%	

Mezzetta, Artichoke Hearts

2 pieces

Amount per serving	%DV	Amount per serving	%DV	Amount per serving	%DV
Calories 20		**Cholesterol** 0mg	0%	**Total Carbohydrate** 2g	1%
Total Fat 2g	3%	**Sodium** 80mg	3%	Dietary Fiber 1g	4%
Saturated Fat 0g	0%	**Protein** 0g		Sugars 0g	
Polyunsaturated Fat 0g					
Monounsaturated Fat 0g		Vitamin A 0% Vitamin C 10%		Calcium 0% Iron 0%	

Mezzetta, Banana Peppers, Sweet

3 peppers

Amount per serving	%DV	Amount per serving	%DV	Amount per serving	%DV
Calories 10		**Cholesterol** 0mg	0%	**Total Carbohydrate** 1g	0%
Total Fat 0g	0%	**Sodium** 320mg	13%	Dietary Fiber 0g	0%
Saturated Fat 0g	0%	**Protein** 0g		Sugars 0g	
Polyunsaturated Fat 0g					
Monounsaturated Fat 0g		Vitamin A 0% Vitamin C 20%		Calcium 0% Iron 2%	

Mezzetta, California Red Hot Chili Peppers

5 pieces

Amount per serving	%DV	Amount per serving	%DV	Amount per serving	%DV
Calories 10		**Cholesterol** 0mg	0%	**Total Carbohydrate** 1g	0%
Total Fat 0g	0%	**Sodium** 330mg	14%	Dietary Fiber 0g	0%
Saturated Fat 0g	0%	**Protein** 0g		Sugars 1g	
Polyunsaturated Fat 0g					
Monounsaturated Fat 0g		Vitamin A 0% Vitamin C 20%		Calcium 2% Iron 15%	

Mezzetta, Cherry Peppers, Sweet

3.5 oz

Amount per serving	%DV	Amount per serving	%DV	Amount per serving	%DV
Calories 15		**Cholesterol** 0mg	0%	**Total Carbohydrate** 2g	1%
Total Fat 0g	0%	**Sodium** 340mg	14%	Dietary Fiber 1g	4%
Saturated Fat 0g	0%	**Protein** 1g		Sugars 1g	
Polyunsaturated Fat 0g					
Monounsaturated Fat 0g		Vitamin A 10% Vitamin C 20%		Calcium 0% Iron 4%	

Mezzetta, Grape Leaves

1 grape leaf

Amount per serving	%DV	Amount per serving	%DV	Amount per serving	%DV
Calories 5		**Cholesterol** 0mg	0%	**Total Carbohydrate** 1g	0%
Total Fat 0g	0%	**Sodium** 120mg	5%	Dietary Fiber 0g	0%
Saturated Fat 0g	0%	**Protein** 0g		Sugars 0g	
Polyunsaturated Fat 0g					
Monounsaturated Fat 0g		Vitamin A 0%	Vitamin C 0%	Calcium 0%	Iron 0%

Mezzetta, Green Chili Peppers

2 tbsp

Amount per serving	%DV	Amount per serving	%DV	Amount per serving	%DV
Calories 10		**Cholesterol** 0mg	0%	**Total Carbohydrate** 2g	1%
Total Fat 0g	0%	**Sodium** 180mg	8%	Dietary Fiber 0g	0%
Saturated Fat 0g	0%	**Protein** 0g		Sugars 1g	
Polyunsaturated Fat 0g					
Monounsaturated Fat 0g		Vitamin A 6%	Vitamin C 90%	Calcium 2%	Iron 2%

Mezzetta, Imported Cocktail Onions

8 onions

Amount per serving	%DV	Amount per serving	%DV	Amount per serving	%DV
Calories 5		**Cholesterol** 0mg	0%	**Total Carbohydrate** 1g	0%
Total Fat 0g	0%	**Sodium** 300mg	12%	Dietary Fiber 0g	0%
Saturated Fat 0g	0%	**Protein** 0g		Sugars 1g	
Polyunsaturated Fat 0g					
Monounsaturated Fat 0g		Vitamin A 0%	Vitamin C 0%	Calcium 0%	Iron 0%

Native Forest, Artichoke Hearts, Marinated

8 pieces

Amount per serving	%DV	Amount per serving	%DV	Amount per serving	%DV
Calories 15		**Cholesterol** 0mg	0%	**Total Carbohydrate** 2g	1%
Total Fat 1g	2%	**Sodium** 140mg	6%	Dietary Fiber 1g	4%
Saturated Fat 0g	0%	**Protein** 0g		Sugars 0g	
Polyunsaturated Fat 0g					
Monounsaturated Fat 0g		Vitamin A 0%	Vitamin C 10%	Calcium 0%	Iron 0%

Native Forest, Organic Bamboo Shoots

1/2 cup

Amount per serving	%DV	Amount per serving	%DV	Amount per serving	%DV
Calories 15		**Cholesterol** 0mg	0%	**Total Carbohydrate** 3g	1%
Total Fat 0g	0%	**Sodium** 5mg	0%	Dietary Fiber 1g	4%
Saturated Fat 0g	0%	**Protein** 1g		Sugars 2g	
Polyunsaturated Fat 0g					
Monounsaturated Fat 0g		Vitamin A 0%	Vitamin C 0%	Calcium 0%	Iron 0%

Native Forest, Organic Cut Baby Corn

1/2 cup

Amount per serving	%DV	Amount per serving	%DV	Amount per serving	%DV
Calories 25		**Cholesterol** 0mg	0%	**Total Carbohydrate** 4g	1%
Total Fat 0g	0%	**Sodium** 280mg	12%	Dietary Fiber 2g	8%
Saturated Fat 0g	0%	**Protein** 2g		Sugars 1g	
Polyunsaturated Fat 0g					
Monounsaturated Fat 0g		Vitamin A 4% Vitamin C 2%		Calcium 0% Iron 4%	

Native Forest, Organic Hearts of Palm

1 oz

Amount per serving	%DV	Amount per serving	%DV	Amount per serving	%DV
Calories 10		**Cholesterol** 0mg	0%	**Total Carbohydrate** 1g	0%
Total Fat 0g	0%	**Sodium** 75mg	3%	Dietary Fiber 1g	4%
Saturated Fat 0g	0%	**Protein** 1g		Sugars 0g	
Polyunsaturated Fat 0g					
Monounsaturated Fat 0g		Vitamin A 0% Vitamin C 0%		Calcium 2% Iron 2%	

Nestlé, Libby's, 100% Pure Pumpkin

1/2 cup

Amount per serving	%DV	Amount per serving	%DV	Amount per serving	%DV
Calories 40		**Cholesterol** 0mg	0%	**Total Carbohydrate** 9g	3%
Total Fat 1g	2%	**Sodium** 5mg	0%	Dietary Fiber 5g	20%
Saturated Fat 0g	0%	**Protein** 2g		Sugars 4g	
Polyunsaturated Fat 0g					
Monounsaturated Fat 0g		Vitamin A 300% Vitamin C 2%		Calcium 2% Iron 4%	

Pero Family Farms, Mini Sweet Peppers

3 peppers / 85g

Amount per serving	%DV	Amount per serving	%DV	Amount per serving	%DV
Calories 25		**Cholesterol** 0mg	0%	**Total Carbohydrate** 5g	2%
Total Fat 0g	0%	**Sodium** 0mg	0%	Dietary Fiber 1g	4%
Saturated Fat 0g	0%	**Protein** 1g		Sugars 3g	
Polyunsaturated Fat 0g					
Monounsaturated Fat 0g		Vitamin A 35% Vitamin C 270%		Calcium 0% Iron 2%	

Sabra, Moroccan Matbuch

2 tbsp / 1 oz / 28g

Amount per serving	%DV	Amount per serving	%DV	Amount per serving	%DV
Calories 30		**Cholesterol** 0mg	0%	**Total Carbohydrate** 2g	1%
Total Fat 0.5g	1%	**Sodium** 180mg	8%	Dietary Fiber 0g	0%
Saturated Fat 0g	0%	**Protein** 1g		Sugars 1g	
Polyunsaturated Fat 0g					
Monounsaturated Fat 0g		Vitamin A 4% Vitamin C 4%		Calcium 0% Iron 2%	

Thumann's, Sweet Roasted Peppers

1 oz / 28g

Amount per serving	%DV	Amount per serving	%DV	Amount per serving	%DV
Calories 15		**Cholesterol** 0mg	0%	**Total Carbohydrate** 5g	2%
Total Fat 0g	0%	**Sodium** 250mg	10%	Dietary Fiber 1g	4%
Saturated Fat 0g	0%	**Protein** 1g		Sugars 4g	
Polyunsaturated Fat 0g					
Monounsaturated Fat 0g		Vitamin A 0% Vitamin C 4%		Calcium 0% Iron 0%	

Dining Out

Heart-Healthy Eating Out Tips

Eating out can be a dietary danger zone if you are attempting to follow a heart-healthy diet. The goal is to enjoy your meal with control. The problem with eating out is that you lose control of portion sizes, ingredients, and preparation methods. Here are some tips for heart-healthy eating in restaurants. The good news is that you can eat heart healthy if you plan ahead and know what to look for.

Plan Ahead

- Set some reasonable goals for your meal:
    - Focus on just a few goals that are realistic.
- No butter on your bread or skipping the bread completely.
- Skip dessert.
- Drink only one glass of wine.
- Eat half your entrée and take the other half home.
    - Decide on a portion sizes of meat, bread, etc. Be sure to have a visual reference such as the palm of your hand for a 3 to 4 oz. portion of meat, a dice for 1 oz. of cheese, and what 4 oz. of wine looks like in a wine glass.
    - Resolve to eat only half the bun, have wine but no dessert, or limit yourself to 10 French fries or tortilla chips.
- Never arrive at a restaurant hungry. Hungry people make bad ordering decisions. Don't skip meals thinking that this will give you more food to eat. Eat an apple and drink a glass of water before you go out. This will help you control your hunger and make better decisions.

Choose the Right Restaurant

- Many restaurants offer meals that are low in total fat, saturated fat, cholesterol, and sodium, or will prepare your food to order. If they have little heart icons on the menu, be sure to ask what they mean. Don't take anything for granted.

- Know your restaurant and be familiar with the menu:
  - Go to a restaurant that you are familiar with and know the menu options.
  - If the restaurant is new to you, go online and print out a copy of the menu.
  - Decide on dishes at home before you are tempted by the sight of the food or what others are ordering.
  - Call the restaurant ahead of time if you have questions on sauces, portion sizes, and preparation, as well as possible substitutions.
- Avoid restaurants that offer all-you-can-eat buffets or specials because you are more likely to eat more food and calories than you need.

Ask Questions

- If you feel awkward doing this at the table, call the restaurant ahead of time and ask to speak to the chef or a waiter.
- How are items prepared? Can they alter the preparation?
  - Baked rather than fried?
  - Sauté in broth rather than oil?
  - Sauces on the side rather than on top?
  - Plain bread rather than buttered?
- What substitutions can be made?
- What are the portion sizes of meat, etc?

Control Portion Sizes

- Order a main dish from the appetizer menu.
- Plan to take half the entrée home for a future meal. Ask your waiter to put half in a to-go box and just to serve you the other half.
- Stay away from buffets, especially an all-you-can-eat buffet.

Savor your food. Try to never finish everything on your plate. Always leave a bite or two to prove to yourself that you are in control of your food rather than the food controlling you. You don't have to clean your plate!

Decipher the Menu

- Look for a diet, light, or heart-healthy section of the menu. Make sure that you understand exactly what this means. "Light" may mean smaller portions but not lower calories or fat.
- Avoid ordering before-meal extras like cocktails, appetizers, and bread and butter because these are often sources of extra fat, sodium, and calories.

- Look for terms like "grilled" or "broiled" not "fried" or "crispy."
- Ask about sides—potatoes, vegetables, etc. Request substitutions if the choice is high in fat like French fries or fried onion rings.
- Look for smaller portions. Lunch portions are usually smaller. Appetizer portions are smaller and can make a tasty entrée. If you prefer the full entree, ask if you can split an entrée or ask for a to-go box and take half home for another meal.

Course by Course Suggestions

Beverages
- Drink plenty of water
- Alcoholic beverages can stimulate your appetite. Plus the calories (about 200 calories per ounce) in alcohol can add up fast. The best choice is a glass of wine sipped slowly.
- Stick to water, reduced-fat milk, tea, coffee, or diet soda.

Starters
- Soup can fill you up. A clear, broth-based soup with vegetables is good as an appetizer because a soup in general tends to decrease your appetite. Soup takes a long time to eat, is filling and low in calories, and good for you, but it can be high in sodium.
- Salads are a great way to start a meal because they can take the edge off your appetite. Order a tossed green or spinach salad with the dressing served on the side. You decide how much salad dressing you will eat. Dipping your fork into the dressing and then spearing some veggies can cut down on the amount of dressing you eat. Avoid bacon bits, cheese, croutons, meats, and prepared salads like potato salad.
    - 1 tablespoon of grated cheese adds 28 calories and 2 grams of fat.
    - 1 tablespoon of bacon bits adds 30 calories and 1 gram of fat.
    - 1 tablespoon of salad dressing adds 60 to 90 calories and 6 to 9 gram——s of fat.

Entrees
- Choose baked, broiled, grilled, poached, roasted, or steamed entrees. Ask that dishes be prepared without extra salt, butter, or oil.
- Meats and vegetables sautéed or stir-fried in a small amount of oil, broth, or water are usually lower in fat.
- Choose fish often. Some fish are higher in fat than others, but the type of fat is good for you. Ask that the fish be steamed, grilled, broiled, or poached.

- Choose white meat chicken over dark meat. Ask for the skin to be removed or remove it yourself. Order poultry steamed, poached, roasted, broiled, boiled, grilled, or baked.
- Allow yourself red meat a few times a week. Be sure to choose lean cuts of meat like loin, flank, or tenderloin.
- Request sauces on the side so that you can determine if they contain fat, and then decide how much you will eat.
- "Dry" is a good term to use when ordering.

Side Dishes
  - Choose vegetables and ask for them to be steamed.
  - Baked potatoes, boiled new potatoes, and rice also may be good options if they are prepared without added fats.
  - Top your baked potato with salsa instead of butter or sour cream.
  - Skip the French fries, potato chips, and onion rings, as well as vegetables slathered in cheese or cream sauces.

Dessert
  - Leave a little time for your food to digest before ordering dessert. It takes about 20 minutes for your stomach to feel full and send a "full" message to your brain.
  - If you still want dessert, consider splitting the dessert with a friend. Half the dessert is half the calories.
  - Healthy dessert choices include berries, melon, sorbet, or frozen yogurt.

Types of Restaurants

Fast Food—You can eat heart healthy at a fast food restaurant if you know what to look for and order.

  - Most fast food chains are required to have nutrition information available for menu items. Look for a posted chart or nutrition information brochures. Ask if you can't find the information.
  - Pass on "value-size" specials that provide more food for less money. "Super-sizing" a menu item usually increases the amount of fat, sodium, and calories.
  - Skip the sides that are usually fried and ask for healthier options—fruit cups or a salad.
  - Choose a grilled chicken sandwich over a breaded or fried chicken sandwich or a hamburger.
  - Avoid double-meat sandwiches.
  - Hold the mayo and special sauces that are usually fat based.

- Order pickles, onions, lettuce, tomatoes, mustard, and ketchup on your sandwich.
- Ask for a whole-wheat bun.
- Drink water, diet soda, or skim or low-fat milk. Regular sodas are loaded with sugars and calories.
- Skip the smoothie or shake.

Breakfast Restaurants–Breakfast menus can be loaded with high-fat and high-sodium items like bacon and sausage and baked goods that are high in trans fats. Instead, look for choices that include fresh fruit and whole grains.

- Choose a bagel rather than a Danish.
- Ask for low-fat cream cheese with your bagel.
- Order whole-grain rather than white toast. Skip the butter and spread on a little jam.
- Choose a whole-grain cereal like oatmeal.
- Skip the high-fat granola.
- Enjoy fat-free or low-fat yogurt with fruit.

Steakhouse–Even steak can fit in a heart-healthy diet. Just make sure it is a lean cut of beef and a reasonable portion.

- Look for a lean cut of beef like a tenderloin, London broil, filet mignon, round, flank steak, or sirloin tip.
- Choose the smallest portion they have—this is usually 6 oz., which is the recommended daily amount. If you eat it all, go vegetarian for the rest of the day.
- Ask that all visible fat be removed from the meat.
- Choose sides wisely—a salad with the dressing on the side or a steamed vegetable.
- If you choose a baked potato, be stingy with the extras or eat the potato dry.

Ethnic Restaurants

Cajun–Cajun cuisine is spicy and deep fried, but almost all dishes have a low-fat counterpart.

- Avoid fried foods—seafood and hushpuppies—and ask for boiled crawfish or shrimp.
- Stay away from the Cajun sausages that are high in fat.
- Gumbo, etouffe, and sauces made with a roux (flour and butter) are high in fat.
- Sidestep dirty rice (contains chicken gizzards and livers high in cholesterol

and butter), and ask for white rice or whole-grain brown or wild rice.
- Choose red beans and rice without the sausage.

Chinese–Chinese food has lots of health benefits with its emphasis on stir-frying lots of vegetables and small portions of lean meats. Unfortunately, the U.S. version of Chinese food is high in sodium and fat.

- Choose entrees with lots of vegetables.
- Ask for steamed brown rice rather than fried rice.
- Substitute chicken for duck if possible.
- Select steamed dumplings instead of egg rolls or fried wontons.
- Look for terms like "boiled," "steamed," or "lightly stir-fried."
- Try dishes with water chestnuts rather than dishes with cashews and peanuts.
- Choose wonton or hot-and-sour soup rather than egg drop soup.
- Ask for low-sodium soy sauce.

French–French food traditionally uses a lot of butter in sauces and desserts. "Nouvelle cuisine" has introduced a new, lighter way of cooking with a French flair.

- Choose simple dishes with sauces on the side.
- Select French bread rather than a croissant.
- Look for the term "Bordelaise" or a wine-based sauce rather than a Hollandaise, Mornay, béchamel, or Bernaise sauce.
- Request lightly sautéed vegetables rather than creamy "au gratin" potatoes.
- Choose a poached pear or peaches rather than a crème caramel or chocolate mousse.
- Start with a mixed green salad with a vinaigrette dressing rather than French onion soup.

Greek–Greece borders the Mediterranean and naturally eats what we call a Mediterranean diet that uses lots of heart-healthy olive oil with a focus on vegetables.

- Limit the olives and feta cheese if you are trying to cut down on sodium.
- Olive oil is healthy but a concentrated source of calories. Ask for dishes to be prepared with less olive oil.
- Low-fat items to look for are "dolmas," a rice mixture wrapped in grape leaves, and "tzatziki," yogurt and cucumber appetizer.
- Shish kabobs, pieces of vegetables and lean meats grilled on a stick, are a low-fat choice
- Couscous or bulgur wheat with vegetables or chicken is a heart-healthy choice.
- Choose a chicken pita sandwich rather than a Gyro.
- Plaki, fish cooked in tomatoes, onions, and garlic, is a healthy choice.

- Skip phyllo pastry dishes like Baklava that are high in butter.
- Choose fruit for dessert.

Indian–Indian food has good and bad points. It includes lots of high-fiber grains with vegetables and legumes while limiting animal protein. The problem is that much of the food is prepared with ghee (clarified butter) or is fried. Coconut oil and milk, which are high in saturated fat, are also often used.

- Choose chicken, seafood or vegetable dishes rather than beef or lamb.
- Select dishes prepared without ghee.
- If sodium is a concern, skip the soups.
- Start with a salad or yogurt with chopped or shredded vegetables.
- Low-fat preparation terms to look for are "tikka" (roasted in an oven with spices), "tandoori" (baked in a clay oven), "shish kabob" (vegetables and small pieces of lean meat grilled on a stick), "gobhi matar tamatar" (cauliflower with peas and tomatoes), "matar pulao" (rice pilaf with peas), and o "riata" (a sauce of chopped cucumbers and yogurt.)

Italian–Most people think of pasta or pizza when they think of Italian cuisine. It's the full-fat cheese and sauces that are the problem.

- Ask for pasta made with whole grains.
- Choose a marinara sauce rather than a cream sauce.
- Limit the cheese and bacon.
- If you order pizza, choose toppings like spinach, mushrooms, broccoli, and roasted peppers to cut down on the saturated fat.
- Choose minestrone soup rather than fried calamari for an appetizer.
- Pasta primavera (with sautéed vegetables) or pasta with white or red clam sauce is a low-fat dish.
- For dessert, try an Italian ice rather than a high-fat Italian pastry.

Japanese–Japanese cuisine highlights rice and vegetables and uses food preparation methods that require little or no fat or oil. High-sodium sauces need to be avoided.

- Ask for steamed vegetables rather than vegetable tempura (lightly battered and fried vegetables).
- Tempura means fried and can be a vegetable or meat dish.
- Teriyaki is grilled chicken or beef.
- Avoid dishes that are battered, breaded, and fried.
- Sushi is raw fish and vegetables rolled in a layer of cooked rice and covered with seaweed.

Mexican–A lot of Mexican food is fried with lard and topped with cheese, so it's high in saturated fat and sodium. But healthful choices can be found.

- Ask for baked tortilla chips rather than fried tortilla chips.
- Corn tortillas are lower in fat than flour tortillas.
- Veracruz or other tomato-based sauces are better than cream or cheese sauces.
- High-fat terms on the menu are "carnitas" (fried beef or pork), "chorizo" (sausage), "refried" beans, "quesadillas" (fried flour tortillas filled with meat and cheese), "flautas" (fried, rolled tortillas stuffed with shredded meat and topped with a sauce), "chimichangas" (fried flour tortillas filled with spicy meat and Monterey Jack cheese), "burrito" (large flour tortilla filled with beans or meat and topped with shredded cheese).
- Low-fat menu terms are "frijoles a la charra" or "borracho beans" (low-fat beans), and "fajitas" (marinated chicken or beef grilled with onions and green peppers).

Vietnamese–This blend of Far East and French cuisine makes a tasty dining experience.

- Start off with "canh chua tom" (spicy and sour shrimp soup) or "goi cuon" (fresh spring roll).
- Low-fat preparation can be found in "go xa lui nuong" (grilled beef with lemon grass in rice paper with vegetables), "ca hap" (steamed whole fish), or "ca kho to" (fish steamed with caramel sauce in a clay pot).
- For dessert, choose Lychee (fruit in syrup) rather than coconut flan with caramel ("banh dua car a men").

Green Flag Menu Terms
Baked, broiled, boiled, poached, grilled, roasted, steamed, lean, dry, fat free, low fat, fresh, light, marinated, reduced, vinaigrette, high fiber, whole grain, multi-grain, vegetarian.

Red Flag Menu Terms
Fried, creamed or creamy, buttered or buttery, oil, au gratin, breaded, Alfredo, battered or batter-dipped, gravy, smothered, fried, fricasseed, creamed, sautéed, stir-fried, stuffed, breaded, basted, alfredo, parmigiana, béarnaise or hollandaise, crispy, crunchy, giant, loaded, super-sized,

Appendix

Heart-Healthy Food Companies

8th Continent
Stremicks Heritage Foods
4002 Westminster Avenue
Santa Ana, CA 92703
Phone: (800) 247-6458
www.8thcontinent.com

505 Southwestern
P.O. Box 7067
Boise, ID 83707
Phone: (800) 292-9900
Email: *info@flagshipfood.com*
www.505chile.com

Almond Board of California
1150 Ninth Street, Suite 1500
Modesto, CA 95354
Phone: (209) 549-8262
Email: *staff@almondboard.com*
www.almondboard.com

Alpine Lace
Divison of Land O'Lakes Inc.
Company has online contact form
www.alpinelace.com

American Custom Meats
4276 North Tracy Blvd
Tracy, CA 95304
Phone: (209) 839-8800
www.acmeats.com

American Italian Pasta Company
1251 N.W. Briarcliff Parkway,
Suite 500
Kansas City, MO 64116
Phone: (816) 584-5000
www.aipc.com

American Pistachio Growers
9 River Park Place East, Suite 410
Fresno, CA 93720
Phone: (559) 475-0435
www.AmericanPistachios.org

Amick Farms, LLC
2079 Batesburg Highway
Batesburg, SC 29006
Phone: (800) 926-4257

274 Nealson Street
Hurlock, MD 21643
Phone: (410) 943-3989

Amy's Kitchen
P.O. Box 449
Petaluma, CA 94953
Phone: (707) 781-7535
www.amys.com

Ancient Harvest
P.O. Box 279
Gardena, CA 90248-0279
Phone: (310) 217-8125
(8am-4pm PST)
www.quinoa.net

Andean Dream
P.O. Box 411404
Loa Angeles, CA 90041
Phone: (310) 281-6036
www.andeandream.com

Annie Chun's
P.O. Box 911170
Los Angeles, CA 90091
Email: info@anniechun.com
www.anniechun.com

Annie's
1610 Fifth Street
Berkeley, CA 94710
Phone: (800) 288-1089
www.annies.com

Applegate Farms
750 Rt. 202 South, Suite 300
Bridgewater, NJ 08807-5530
www.applegate.com

AriZona Teas
Arizona Beverage Co.
644 Linn Street, Suite 318
Cincinnati, OH 45203
Phone: (800) 832-3775
www.drinkarizona.com

Armour-Eckrich Meats LLC
John Morrell Food Group
Consumer Affairs
P.O. Box 405020
Cincinnati, OH 45240-5020
Phone: 1 (800) 722-1127
(M-F, 8:30am-4:30pm EST)
or by using the website electronic form
www.johnmorrellfoodgroup.com

Arnold
Bimbo Bakeries
P.O. Box 976
Horsham, PA 19044
Phone: (800) 984-0989
www.arnoldbread.com

ARO Pistachios, Inc.
Orandi Ranch
19570 Avenue 88
Terra Bella, CA 93270
Phone: (559) 535-1500;
(559) 535-4401
www.aropistachio.com

Artisan Bistro
Home of Helen's Kitchen
and Artisan Bistro
1882 Mcgaw Avenue, Suite A
Irvine, CA 92614
Phone: (866) 328-8638
www.theartisanbistro.com

Artisan Lettuce
Tanimura & Antle
1 Harris Road
Salinas, CA 93908
Phone: (877) 827-7388
www.artisanlettuce.com

Anthony's
American Italian Pasta Company
1251 N.W. Briarcliff Parkway,
Suite 500
Kansas City, MO 64116
Phone: (816) 584-500 or
(877) EAT-PASTA
www.aipc.com

Arrowhead Mills
The Hain Celestial Group, Inc.
4600 Sleepytime Drive
Boulder, CO 80301
Phone: (800) 434-4246
(M-F, 9am-7pm EST)
www.arrowheadmills.com

Attune Foods
Company has online contact form
www.attunefoods.com

Back to Nature
10 Mayer Avenue
Madison, WI 53701
Company has online email
www.backtonaturefoods.com

Barbara's Bakery, Inc.
3900 Cypress Drive
Petaluma, CA 94954
Phone: (800) 343-0590
www.barbarasbakery.com

Bay Valley Foods, LLC
Customer Solutions
1555 East Highway 151
Platteville, WI 53818
Phone: (800) 236-1119

Better 'n Eggs
301 Carlson Parkway, Suite 400
Minnetonka, MN 55305
Phone: (877) 727-3884
www.betterneggs.com

Bigelow Teas
R.C. Bigelow Inc.
201 Black Rock Turnpike
Fairfield, VT 06825
Phone: (888) 244-3569
(M-Fri, 9am-5pm EST)
www.bigelowtea.com

BBU, Inc.
Bimbo Bakeries USA
255 Business Center Drive
Horsham, PA 19044
Phone (toll free) 1-800-984-0989
www.bimbobakeriesusa.com

Bird's Eye
Pinnacle Consumer Relations
P.O. Box 3900
Peoria, IL 61612
Company has online contact form
www.birdseye.com

Blue Diamond Growers
Phone: (800) 987-2329
Company has online contact form
www.bluediamond.com

Boar's Head
Phone: (800) 352-6277
www.boarshead.com

Bob's Red Mill
Phone: (503) 654-3215
or (800) 349-2173
Company has online contact form
www.bobsredmill.com

Bolthouse Farms, Inc.
Phone: (800) 467-4683
Company has online contact form
www.bolthouse.com

Borden Dairy Farmers of America, Inc.
Global Dairy Products Group
10220 North Ambassador Drive
Kansas City, MO 64153
Phone: (888) 337-2407
www.bordendairy.com

Boulangerie St-Methode Inc.
14, rue Principale, Est
Adstock (Qc)
G0N 1S0
Phone: (418) 422-2246
(M-F, 8am-5pm)
Toll Free: 1 (800) 463-6317
Email: info@bstm.ca
www.boulangeriestmethode.com/en

Breyer's
490 Old Connecticut Path
Framingham, MA 01701-4577
Phone: (508) 620-4300
www.breyers.com

Brownberry
Bimbo Bakeries
P.O. Box 976
Horsham, PA 19044
Phone: (800) 984-0989
(M-F, 8am-8pm EST)
www.brownberry.com

Brown Cow Farms
Phone (888) 429-5459 (HAY-LILY)
(M-F, 6am-3pm PST)
www.browncowfarms.com

Bruce Foods Corporation
P.O. Drawer 1030
New Iberia, LA 70562-1030
Phone: (337) 365-8101
Fax: (337) 369-9026
www.brucefoods.com

Brummel & Brown
920 Sylvan Avenue
Englewood Cliffs, NJ 07632
Phone: (866) 204-9750
www.brummelandbrown.com

Bubba Foods, LLC
P.O. Box 2823
Jacksonville, FL 32203
Phone: 1 (877) TRY-BUBBA
E-mail: csr@bubbafoods.com
www.bubba-burger.com

Buddig
Consumer Affairs
950 West 175 Street
Homewood, IL 60430
Toll Free: 888-633-5684
www.buddig.com

Bumble Bee Foods LLC
P.O. Box 85362
San Diego, CA 92186
Att: Consumer Affairs
Company has online contact form
www.bumblebee.com

Bushwick Potato Commission
201 Northwest Drive
Farmingdale, NY 11735
Phone: (516) 249-6030 or
(800) 645-9470
www.bushwickpotato.com

Butterball, LLC
Consumer Affairs
P.O. Box 1547
Kings Mountain, NC 28086
Phone: (800) 288-8372
(M-F, 10am-7pm CST)
www.butterball.com

Cabot
1 Home Farm Way
Montpleier, VT 05602
Phone: (888) 792-2268
www.cabotcheese.com

California Date Commission
P.O. Box 1736
Indio, CA 92202
Toll Free: 1 (800) 223-8748
Phone: (760) 347-4510
Email: info@datesaregreat.com
www.datesaregreat.com

California Walnut Board
California Walnut Commission
101 Parkshore Drive, Suite 250
Folsom, CA 95630
Phone: (916) 932-7070
Email: info@walnuts.org
www.walnuts.org

**Campbell Soup Company/
Campbell's V8**
1 Campbell Place
Camden, NJ 08103-1701
Phone: 1 (800) 257-8443
(M-F, 9am-7pm EST)
www.campbellsoup.com

Cardini's
T. Marzetti Company
P.O. Box 29163
Columbus, OH 43229-0163
Phone: (800) 999-1835
www.cardinissaladdressing.com

Carl Buddig & Company
Consumer Affairs
950 West 175 Street
Homewood, IL 60430
Phone (Toll Free): (888) 633-5684
www.buddig.com

Cheerios
P.O. Box 9452
Minneapolis, MN 55440
Phone: (800) 828-32902
www.cheerios.com

Classico
P.O. Box 57
Pittsburgh, PA 15230-0057
Phone: (888) 337-2420
Company has contact online form
www.classico.com

Clearwater Seafoods Limited Partnership
757 Bedford Highway
Bedford, Nova Scotia
Canada, B4A 3Z7
Phone: (902) 443-0550
www.clearwater.ca/en

Clougherty Packing, LLC
a subsidiary of Hormel Foods Corp
1 Hormel Place
Austin, MN 55912
Phone: (507) 434-6300
www.farmerjohn.com

Coleman Natural Foods, LLC
Consumer Affairs
P.O. Box 768
Kings Mountain, NC 28086

Phone: (800) 442-8666
www.colemannatural.com

Columbus Foods, Inc.
30977 San Antonio Road
Hayward, CA 94544
Company has online contact form
www.columbussalame.com

Conte's
Phone: (856) 697-3400
Toll Free: (800) 211-6607
Company has online contact form
Email:
customer_service@contepasta.com

Country Choice
P.O. Box 44247
Eden Prairie, MN 55344
Phone: (952) 829-8824
www.countrychoicenaturals.com

Cream of Wheat
Company has online contact form
www.creamofwheat.com

Crunchmaster
T.H. Foods, Inc.
2154 Harlem Road
Loves Park, IL 61111
Phone: (800) 896-2396
www.crunchmaster.com

Crystal Farms
6465 Wayzata Blvd., Suite 200
Minneapolis, MN 55426-1723
Phone: (952) 544-8101
www.crystalfarms.com

Dr. Praeger's Sensible Foods
Phone: (877)-PRAEGER
or (201) 703-1300
Company has online contact form
www.drpraegers.com

Daily Chef
Sam's Club
Member Service
2101 S.E. Simple Savings Drive
Bentonville, AR 72716-0745
Phone: (888) 746-7726
(Mon-Fri, 7am-8pm; Sat, 9am-5pm;
Sun, 10am-6pm CST)

Damascus Bakery, Inc.
56 Gold Street
Brooklyn, NY 11201
Phone: (800) 367-7482
(1-800-FOR-PITA)
Email: *info@damascusbakery.com*
www.damascusbakery.com

Dannon
100 Hillside Avenue, 3rd Floor
White Plains, NY 10603
Phone: (914) 872-8400
www.dannon.com

DeBoles
Phone: (800) 434-4246
(M-F, 9am-7pm EST)
www.deboles.com

Del Monte
Company has online form
www.delmontefoods.com

DiGiorno
Phone: (800) 225-2270
M-F, 8am-8pm)
Company has online contact form
www.digiorno.com

DiLuigi Inc.
41 Popes Lane
Danvers, MA 01923
Phone: (978) 750-9900
Company has online contact form
www.diluigisausage.com

Dole Food Company
P.O. Box 5700
Thousand Oaks, CA 91359-5700
Phone: (800) 356-3111
(Mon-Fri, 8am-3pm PT)
www.delmontefoods.com

Driscoll's Strawberry Associates, Inc.
345 Westridge Drive
Watsonville, CA 95076
www.driscolls.com

Dr. McDougall's
Right Foods, Inc.
105 Associated Road
South San Francisco, CA 94080-6013
Phone: (800) 367-3844
www.rightfoods.com

Earth Balance
7102 LaVista Place, Suite 200
Longmont Colorado, 80503
Phone: (201) 568-9300
www.earthbalancenatural.com

Earth's Best
4600 Sleepytime Drive
Boulder, CO 80301
Phone: (800) 434-4246
www.earthbest.com

Eating Right Turkey Burger
www.eating-right.ca

Eden Foods
701 Tecumseh Road
Clinton, MI 49236
Phone: (888) 424-3336
www.edenfoods.com

Edward & Sons
P.O. Box 1326
Carpinteria, CA 93014
Phone: (805) 684-8500
www.edwardandsons.com

Egg Beaters
Company has online form
U.S. Consumer Affairs
1 (877) 266-2472
www.eggbeaters.com

Eggland's Best, Inc.
1400 South Trooper Road,
Suite 201
Jeffersonville, PA 19403
Phone: (800) 922-EGGS (3447)
www.egglandsbest.com

Ener-G Foods, Inc.
5960 1st Ave South
Seattle, WA 98108
Phone: (800) 331-5222
www.ener-g.com

Enjoy Life Foods
Phone: (847) 260-0300
www.enjoylifefoods.com

Erewhon
535 Pacific Ave., 3rd Floor
San Francisco, CA 94133
Phone: (800) 641-4508
www.usmillsinc.com

Fage
25-26 50th Street
Woodside, NY 11377
Phone: (866) 962-5912
(M-F, 9am-5pm EST)
www.fageusa.com

Farmer John
Consumer Response
3049 East Vernon Avenue
Los Angeles, CA 90058
Phone: (800) 846-7635
(M-F, 8am-4pm CST),
excluding holidays.
Summer hours may vary.
www.farmerjohn.com

Farm-Pak
7840 Old Bailey Highway
Spring Hope, NC 27882
Phone: (252) 459-3101
or 1 (800) 367-2799
Email: *sales@farmpak.com*
www.farmpak.com

Fieldale Farms Corporation
P.O. Box 558
Baldwin, GA 30511
Phone: 1 (706) 778-5100
(M-F, 8am-5pm EST)
www.fieldale.com

Fit & Active
Eckenbergstrasse 16
Essen 45307, Germany
Phone: +49 201-85-93-0
www.aldi.com

Fleischmann's
Company has online form
www.conagrafoods.com

Florida's Natural Growers
A Division of Citrus World, Inc.
20205 US Highway 27 North
Lake Wales, FL 33853
Phone: 1 (888) 657-6600
www.floridasnatural.com

Food for Life
Phone (Customer Service):
(951) 279-5090
www.foodforlife.com

Foster Poultry Farms
Phone: (800) 255-7227
(M-F, 8am-5pm PST)
www.fosterfarms.com

FPL Foods, LLC
1301 New Savannah Road
Augusta, GA 30901
Phone: (706) 722-2694
Email: *customerservice@fplfood.com*
www.fplfood.net

Francesco Rinaldi
815 West Whitney Road
Fairport, NY 14450
Phone: (585) 377-7700
www.francescorinaldi.com

Frieda's
4465 Corporate Center Drive
Los Alamitos, CA 90720-2561
Phone: (714) 826-6100
www.friedas.com

Galaxy Nutritional Foods
2441 Viscount Row
Orlando, FL 32809
Phone: (407) 855-5500
Company has online contact form
www.galaxyfoods.com

Gardenburger
Kellogg's Consumer Affairs
P.O. Box CAMB
Battle Creek, MI 49016
Phone: (800) 962-1413
www.gardenburger.com

Garden Lites
165-35 145th Drive
Jamaica, NY 11434
Phone: (718) 439-0200, ext. 624
Email:
customerservice@garden-lites.com
www.garden-lites.com

General Mills, Inc.
P.O. Box 9452
Minneapolis, MN 55440
Phone: (800) 248-7310
(M-F, 7:30am-5:30pm CT)
www.generalmills.com

Georgia Pecan Commission
www.georgiapecans.org

GFA Brands, Inc.
Boulder Brands, Inc.
115 West Century Road, Suite 260
Paramus, NJ 07652-1432
Phone (Consumer Affairs):
(201) 421-3970
www.smartbalance.com

Girardi's
P.O. Box 29163
Columbus, OH 43229-0163
Phone: (614) 846-2232
www.marzetti.com

Glory Foods, Inc.
www.gloryfoods.com

Golden Grain
Company has online contact form
www.goldengrainpasta.com

Good Karma
Phone: (800) 550-6731
www.GoodKarmaFoods.com

Green Giant
P.O. Box 9452
Minneapolis, MN 55440
Phone: (800) 998-9996
(M-F, 7:30am-5:30pm CT)
www.greengiant.com

Grower Direct Nut Co. Inc.
164 Hampden Road
Somers, CT, 06071
Phone: (860) 763-2335
www.growerdirectfarms.com

Hadley Date Gardens
83-555 Airport Boulevard
Thermal, CA 92274
Phone: (760) 399-5191
www.hadleys.com

The Hain Celestial Group
Consumer Relations
4600 Sleepytime Drive
Boulder, CO 80301
Phone: 1 (800) 434-4246
(M-F, 7am–5pm MT)
www.hain-celestial.com

Hansel 'n Gretel Brand, Inc.
The Healthy Deli
79-36 Cooper Avenue
Glendale, NY 11385
Phone: (718) 326-0041
Email: infor@healthydeli.com
www.healthydeli.com

Hansen's Natural
550 Monica Circle, Suite 201
Corona, CA 92880
Phone: (800) 426-7367
(M-F, 9am-5pm)
Company has online contact form
www.hansens.com

Harrell Nut Company
P.O. Box 508
Camilla, GA 31730
Email: info@harrellnut.com
www.harrellnut.com

Healthy Choice
ConAgra Foods
Phone: (877) 266-2472
www.healthychoice.com

Healthy Ones
Armour-Eckrich Consumer Affairs
P.O. Box 405020
Cincinnati, OH 45240-5020
Phone: 1 (800) 722-1127
(M-F, 8:30am-4:30pm EST)
www.healthy-ones.com

Healthy Valley Organic
Phone: 1 (866) 595-8917
(8-5pm CT, M-F)
www.healthvalley.com

Heartland
1583 Sulphur Spring Road, Suite 108
Baltimore, MD 21227
Phone: (800) 492-5592
www.heartlandfoods.com

High Plains Bison
Phone: 1 (877) 526-7375
(Mon-Fri, 9am-4pm MT)
www.highplainsbison.com

Hillshire Brands Company
Consumer Affairs
P.O. Box 3901
Peoria, IL 61612
Company has online contact form
www.hillshirebrands.com

Honest Tea/Honest Ade
4827 Bethesda Avenue
Bethesda, MD 20814
Phone: (800) 865-4736
or (301) 652-3556
www.honestea.com

Horizon
12002 Airport Way
Broomfield, CO 80021
Phone: (888) 494-3020
(M-F, 8am-5pm CT, excluding holidays)
www.horizondairy.com/cheese

Hormel Foods Corporation
Consumer Response
1 Hormel Place
Austin, MN 55912
Phone: 1 (800) 523-4635
(M-F, 8am-4pm CT, excluding holidays)
Summer hours may vary.

House Foods America Corporation
7351 Orangewood Avenue
Garden Grove, CA 92841
Phone: (877) 333-7077
Company has online contact form
www.house-foods.com

Hunt's
ConAgra Foods, Inc.
U.S. Consumer Affairs
Phone: (877) 266-2472
www.hunts.com

Ian's Natural Foods
190 Fountain Street
Framington, MA 01702
Phone: (800) 54-FOODS (36637)
www.iansnaturalfoods.com

Idahoan Foods, LLC
357 Constitution Way
Idaho Falls, ID 83402
Phone: (208) 542-3700
or (800) 746-7999
www.idahoanfoods.com

Idaho Potato Commission
661 South Rivershore Lane,
Suite 230
Eagle, ID 83616
Phone: (208) 334-2350
www.idahopotato.com

Jennie-O Turkey Store, Inc.
Hormel Foods Corporation
Consumer Response
1 Hormel Place
Austin, MN 55912
Phone: 1 (800) 621-3505
(M-F, 8am-4pm CST)
Excludes holidays.
Summer hours may vary.

Jovial Foods
5 Tyler Drive
North Franklin, CT 06254
Phone: (877) 642-0644
(M-F, 8:30-4:30 EST)
www.jovialfoods.com

Kansas City Steak Company
100 Osage Avenue
Kansas City, KS 66105
Phone: 1 (800) 98STEAK
(1-800-987-8325)
Email:
customerservice@kansascitysteaks.com
www.kansascitysteaks.com

Kashi Company
P.O. Box 8557
La Jolla, CA 92038
Phone: (877) 747-2467
(M-F, 5am-4pm PST)
www.kashi.com

Kedem Food Products
63 Lefante Way
Bayonne, NJ 07002
Phone: (800) 382-8299
www.kedem.com

Keenan Farms, Inc.
P.O. Box 99
Avenal, CA 93204-0099
Phone: (559) 945-1400
Email: info@keenanpistachio.com
www.keenanpistachio.com

Kellogg's
Consumer Affairs
P.O. Box CAMB
Battle Creek, MI 49016
Phone: (800) 962-1413
www.kelloggs.com

Ken's Foods
Company has online contact form
www.kensfoods.com

Kettle Cuisine
270 Second Street
Chelsea, MA 02150
Phone: (617) 409-1100
www.kettlecuisine.com

Kirkland Signature
Costco
P.O. Box 34331
Seattle, WA 98124
Phone: (800) 955-2292
www.costco.com

Kitchen Basics, Inc.
Phone: 1 (800) 632-5847
Company has online form
www.mccormickgourmet.com

Kraft Foods Group
Consumer Relations
1 Kraft Court, Glenview, IL 60025
Phone: 1 (877) 535-5666
www.kraftrecipes.com

Krakus
Armour-Eckrich
P.O. Box 405020
Cincinnati, OH 45240-5020
1 (800) 722-1127
(Mon-Fri, 8:30am-4:30pm EST)

The Kroger Co.
1014 Vine Street
Cincinnati, OH 45202-1100
Phone: (800) 576-4377
www.kroger.com

Laura's Lean Beef Company
1517 Bull Lea Road, Suite 210
Lexington, Kentucky 40511
Phone: 1 (800) ITS-LEAN
(1-800-487-5326)
(M-F, 8am-5pm EST)
Email:
LLBcustomers@laurasleanbeef.com
www.laurasleanbeef.com

Lean Cuisine
Consumer Service Center
P.O. Box 2178
Wilkes-Barre, PA 18703
Phone: (800) 993-8625
www.LeanCuisine.com

Lifeway Foods, Inc.
6431 West Oakton Street
Morton Grove, IL 60053
Phone: (877) 281-3874
www.lifeway.net

Lighthouse
1109 North Ella
Sandpoint, ID 83864
Phone: (800) 669-3169
www.litehousefoods.com

Loma Linda
Kellogg's Consumer Affairs
P.O. Box CAMB
Battle Creek, MI 49016
Phone: (800) 962-1413
www.worthingtonfoods.com

Lucini
Phone: (888) 5-LUCINI
Email: info@lucini.com
Company has online contact form
www.lucini.com

Lundberg Family Farms
Phone: (530) 538-3500
(M-F, 8:30am-5pm PT)
www.lundberg.com

Luxury Pasta
Company has online form
www.luxurypasta.com

Malt-O-Meal
P.O. Box 1025
Lakeville, MN 55044
Phone: (800) 743-3029
(M-F, 8am-4pm CST)
www.malt-o-meal.com

Maple Grove Farms
Company has online contact form
www.maplegrove.com

Market Pantry
Products brand by Target
Phone: (800) 440-0680
www.target.com

Mariani Packing Company
500 Crocker Drive
Vacaville, CA 95688-8706
Phone: (707) 452-2800
www.marianifruit.com

Marie's
P.O. Box 1105, Brea, CA 92822
Phone: (800) 339-1051
www.maries.com

Marzetti
T. Marzetti Company
P.O. Box 29163
Columbus, OH 43229-0163
Phone: (800) 999-1835
(M-F, 8am-5pm)
www.marzetti.com

Member's Mark
(a division of Sam's Club)
Member Service
2101 S.E. Simple Savings Drive
Bentonville, AR 72716-0745
Company has online form
Phone: (888) 746-7726
(Mon-Fri, 7am-8pm; Sat,
9am-5pm; Sun, 10am-6pm CST)

Mezzetta
G.L. Mezzetta, Inc.
105 Mazzetta Court
American Canyon, CA 94503
Phone: (800) 941-7044
(M-F, 7:30am-4:30pm PST)
www.mezzetta.com

Michigan Turkey Producers
1100 Hall Street SW
Grand Rapids, MI 49503
Phone: (616) 245-2221
Email: info@miturkey.com
www.miturkey.com

**Milton's Baking Company/
Milton's Healthy/Milton's Craft Bakers**
Company has online contact form
www.miltonsbaking.com

Minute Maid
The Coca-Cola Company
P.O. Box 1734
Atlanta, GA 30301
(800) 438-2653
www.minutemaid.com

**Mississippi Peanut Growers
Association**
P.O. Box 284
Petal, MS 39465
Phone: 601-606-3547
www.peanuts.msstate.edu

Morningstar Farms
4504 State Road 83
Hartford, WI 53027
Phone: (262) 670-6561
www.morningstarfarms.com

MountainKing Potatoes
P.O. Box 14532
Houston, TX 77221
Phone: (800) 395-2004
Company has online contact form
www.mtnking.com

Mueller's
Company has online contact form
www.mullerspasta.com

Murray's Chicken
5190 Main Street
South Fallsburg, NY 12779
Phone: 1 (800) 770-6347
www.murrayschicken.com

National Beef Packing Company, LLC
12200 North Ambassador Drive,
Suite 500
Kansas City, MO 64163
Phone: 1 (800) 449-BEEF
Company has online contact form
www.nationalbeef.com

National Cattlemen's Beef Association
9110 East Nichols Avenue, #300
Centennial, CO 80112
Phone: (303) 694-0305
www.beef.org

National Pecan Shellers Association
1100 Johnson Ferry Road,
Suite 300
Atlanta, GA 30342
Phone: (404) 252-3663
Email: npsa@kellencompany.com
www.ilovepecans.org

National Pork Board
1776 NW 114th Street
Des Moines, IA 50325
Phone: (515) 223-2600
Toll-Free: 1-800-456-7675
Email: info@pork.org
www.pork.org

National Watermelon Promotion Board
3361 Rouse Road, Suite 150
Orlando, FL 32817
Phone: (407) 657-0261
Toll-Free: (877) 599-9595
www.watermelon.org

Native Forest/Nature Factor
Edward & Sons Trading Company, Inc.
P.O. Box 1326
Carpinteria, CA 93014
Phone: (805) 684-8220
www.edwardandsons.com

Nature's Path
9100 Van Horne Way
Richmond, BC Canada V6X 1W3
Phone: (866) 880-7284 (
M-F, 12pm-8pm EST)
www.naturespath.com

Nestle's
Phone: (818) 549-7131
www.nestleusa.com

Newman's Own/ Newman's Own Organics
7010 Soquel Drive, Ste 200
Aptos, CA 95003-3671
Phone: (831) 685-2866
Company has on-line contact form
www.newmansown.com

Nonpareil Farms
40 North 400
WestBlackfoot, ID 83221
Phone: (208) 785-3030
Toll-Free: (800) 522-2223
www.nonpareilfarms.com

North Coast Seafoods
Europarc Innovation Centre
Innovation Way, Grimsby
North East Lincolnshire
DN37 9TT, UK
Tel: +44 (0) 1472 350 666
Fax: +44 (0) 1472 350 777
E-mail: info@northcoastseafoods.co.uk
www.northcoastseafoods.net

Old Orchard Brands, LLC.
P.O. Box 66
Sparta MI 49345
Phone: (800) 330-2173
Company has online contact form
www.oldorchard.com

Olivio Premium Products
867 Boylston Street
Boston, MA 02116
Phone: (617) 266-5522
www.olivioproducts.com

Omega Farms
Phone: (541) 935-1588
Email: info@omega-farms.com
www.omega-farms.com

Organic Bistro
1882 Mcgaw Avenue, Suite A
Irvine, CA 92614
Phone: (866) 328-8638
www.theartisanbistro.com

Oroweat
Bimbo Bakeries
Consumer Relations Department
P.O. Box 976
Horsham, PA 19044
www.oroweat.com

Pace
Phone: (800) 257-8443
(M-F, 9am-7pm EST)
www.campbellsoupcomany.com

Pacific Natural Foods/Pacific Organic
19480 SW 97th Avenue
Tualatin, OR 97062
Phone: (503) 692-9610
Company has online contact form
www.pacificfoods.com

Paramount Farms International
Phone: (877) 450-9493
Company has online contact form
www.paramountfarms.com

The Peanut Institute
Phone: 1 (888) 873-2688
or 1 (888) 8PEANUT)
Organization has online contact form
www.peanut-institute.org

Pepperidge Farm
Company has online contact form
www.pepperidgefarm.com

Perdue Farms, Inc.
Consumer Relations
P.O. Box 788
Kings Mountain, NC 28086
Phone: 1-800-4-PERDUE
or 1 (800) 473-7383
(M-F, 9:30am-6pm EST)

Pero Vegetable Company, LLC
Company has online contact form
www.perofamilyfarms.com

Peterson Farms, Inc.
3104 West Baseline Road
P.O. Box 95
Shelby, MI 49455
Phone: (231) 861-7101
www.petersonfarmsinc.com

Pilgrim's Pride Corporation
1770 Promontory Circle
Greeley, CO 80634
General Inquiries: (800) 727-5366
Consumer Relations: (800) 321-1470
Company has online contact form
www.pilgrimspride.com

Plumrose USA, Inc.
1901 Butterfield Road, Suite 305
Downers Grove IL, 60515
Phone: (732) 257-6600
Toll-Free: 1 (800) 526-4909
Email: consumer@plumroseusa.com
www.plumroseusa.com

Polly-O
www.kraftbrands.com/pollyo

POM Wonderful
Wonderful Call Center
4805 Centennial Plaza Way,
Suite 100
Bakersfield, CA 93312
Phone: (877) 450-9493
Company has online form
www.pomwonderful.com

Porky Products Inc.
400 Port Carteret Drive
Carteret, NJ 07008
Phone: (732) 541-0200
Email: Porky@porkyinc.com
www.porky.com

Post Foods LLC
275 Cliff Street
Battle Creek, MI 49014
Phone: 1 (800) 431-POST
(M-F, 9am–5pm EST, excluding holidays)
Company has online contact form
www.postfoods.com

Potandon Produce, LLC
1210 Pier View Drive
Idaho Falls, ID 83402
Phone: (208) 524-1900
Consumer Inquiry/Comments:
(208) 557-5120
Email: consumer@potandon.com
www.potandon.com

Preferred Brands International, Inc.
4530 Smith Road
Coden, AL 36523
Phone: (251) 873-4062
Email: info@preferredbrandsinc.com
www.preferredbrandsinc.com

Prego
Campbell Soup Company
1 Campbell Place
Camden, NJ 08103-1701
Phone: (800) 257-8443
www.prego.com

Private Selection
Customer Service Center
Phone: (800) 576-4377
(Mon-Fri, 8am-midnight EST)
www.privateselection.com

Produce Packaging, Inc.
7501 Carnegie Avenue
Cleveland, OH 44103
Phone: (216) 391-6129
www.producepackagingltd.com

Progresso
General Mills, Inc.
P.O. Box 9452
Minneapolis, MN 55440
Phone: (800) 200-9377
(M-F, 7:30am-5:30pm CT)
www.progresso.com

Promise
Phone: (800) 298-5018
(Mon-Fri, 8:30am-6pm EST)
www.unileverusa.com

Ragu
Phone: 1 (800) 298-5018
(Mon-Fri, 8:30am-6pm EST)
www.unileverusa.com

Quaker Oats Company
Tropicana Products, Inc.
P.O. Box 049003
Chicago, IL 60604
Phone: 1 (800) 367-6287
(M-F, 9am-5pm EST)
www.quakeroats.com

Rader Farms, Inc.
643 North 98th Street, #133
Omaha, NE 68114
Phone: (866) 890-1004
Email: info@raderfarms.com
www.raderfarms.com

Randall Foods
2900 Ayers Avenue
Vernon, CA 90023
Phone: 800-372-6581
Email: CS@RandallFoods.com
www.randallfarms.com

RMH Foods, LLC
375 Erie Avenue
Morton, IL 61550
Phone: 1(877) RMH-FOODS
(1-877-764-3663)
Email: consumeraffairs@rmhfoods.com
www.rmhfoods.com

Rice Dream
Taste the Dream Customer Care
The Hain Celestial Group, Inc.
4600 Sleepytime Drive
Boulder, CO 80301
Phone: 1 (800) 434-4246
(Mon-Fri, 9am-7pm)

Ronco
American Italian Pasta Company (AIPC)
Phone: 1 (877) EAT-PASTA
www.aipc.com/asp/emailcontact.asp

RPE, Inc.
P.O. Box 330
Bancroft, WI 54921
Phone: (800) 678-2789
Email: rpe@rpespud.com
www.rpespud.com

S&W Fine Foods International Limited
17 Bukit Pasoh Road
Singapore 089831
Phone: (65) 6324 6822
(M-F, 9am-5pm)
www.swpremiumfood.com

Sabra
P.O. Box 660634
Dallas, TX 75266-0634
Phone: (888) 957-2272
(M-F, 9am-4:30pm CT)
www.sabra.com

Sambazon Global Headquarters
1160 Calle Cordillera
San Clemente, CA 92673
Phone: 1 (877) 726-2296
Email: info@sambazon.com
sambazon.com

Sanderson Farms, Inc.
127 Flynt Road
P.O. Box 988
Laurel, MS 39441-0988
Phone: (601) 649-4030
Toll-Free: 1-800-844-4030
www.sandersonfarms.com

San Saba Pecan, LP
2803 West Wallace Street
San Saba, TX 76877
Phone: (325) 372-5727
Toll-Free: (800) 683-2101
Email: blanca@sansabapecan.com
www.sansabapecan.net

Sara Lee
Bimbo Bakeries
Consumer Relations Department
P.O. Box 975
Horsham, PA 19044
Phone: (800) 984-0989
(M-F, 8am-8pm EST)
www.sareleebread.com

Second Nature
Bay Valley Foods Customer Solutions
1555 East Highway 151
Platteville, WI 53818
Phone: (800) 236-1119
Company has online contact form
www.bayvalleyfoods.com

Seeds of Change
P.O. Box 4908
Rancho Dominguez, CA 90220
Phone: (888) 762-7333
(7 days a week, 7am-11pm CT)
Company has online contact form
www.seedsofchange.com

Setton Pistachio of Terra Bella Inc.
9370 Road 234
Terra Bella, CA 93270
Phone: (559) 535-6050
Email: info@settonfarms.com
www.settonfarms.com

Silk
Company has online contact form
www.silk.com

Silver Palate
Company has online contact form
Phone: (201) 568-0110
(M-F, 9am-5pm)
www.silverpalate.com

Simple Orange
www.simpleorangejuice.com

Simply Organic Foods
(800) 437-3301
(Mon-Fri, 7am-6pm CST)
Email:
customercare@simplyorganic.com

Skinner Foods
1010 West Kramer Road
El Centro, CA 92243

Smart Balance
Phone: (201) 421-3970
Company has online contact form
www.smartbalance.com

Smithfield Packing Company
Phone: 1-855-411-PORK (7675)
(M-F, 7:30am-5:30pm EST)
Email: consumeraffairs@smithfield.com
www.smithfield.com

Snapple
Company has online contact form
Phone: (800) 696-5891
www.snapple.com

Soy Dream
Taste the Dream Customer Care
The Hain Celestial Group, Inc.
4600 Sleepytime Drive
Boulder, CO 80301
Phone: (800) 4347-4246
www.tastethedream.com

StarKist Co.
225 North Shore Drive, Suite 400
Pittsburgh, PA 15212
Phone: 1 (412) 323-7400
Toll-Free: 1 (800) 252-1587
(M-F, 9am-5pm EST)
Company has online contact form
www.starkist.com

Sterman Masser, Inc.
2 Fearnot Road
P.O. Box 210
Sacramento, PA 17968
Phone: (570) 682-3709
Email: info@masserspuds.com
www.masserspuds.com

St. Methode Campagnolo
Phone: (800) 463-6317
(M-F, 8am-5pm)
Email: info@bstm.com
www.boulangeriestmethode.com

Stone Meats
1485 Stone Field Way
Pleasant View UT 84404
Phone: (801) 782-9825
www.stonemeats.com

Stonyfield Organic
Stonyfield Farms
10 Burton Drive
Londonderry, NH 03053
Phone: (800) 776-2697
(M-F, 9am-6pm ET)
www.stonyfield.com

Sun Date LLC
Consumer Affairs
85215 Avenue Fifty
Coachella, CA 92236
Phone: (760) 398-6123
(M-F, 8am-12noon; 1pm-4:30pm)
Email: sundate@hotmail.com
www.sundateusa.com

Sun Glo of Idaho, Inc.
378 South 7th West
P.O. Box 300
Sugar City, ID 83448
Phone: (208) 356-7346
www.sungloidaho.com

Sunsweet Growers Inc.
901 North Walton Avenue
Yuba City, CA 95993
Phone: (800) 447-5218 (Mon-Fri,
8am-4pm PST)
Extended holiday hours
Email: sunsweet@casupport.com
Consumer Relations: (800) 417-2253
(Mon-Fri, 9am-6pm EST)

Swanson
Pinnacle Consumer Relations
P.O. Box 3900
Peoria, IL 61612
Phone: (888) 815-6480
www.swansonmeals.com

Swift
JBS Corporate Office
1770 Promontory Circle
Greeley, CO 80634
Phone: (970) 506-8000
Company has online form
www.jbssa.com

Tanimura & Antle
Costumer Relations
1 Harris Road
Salinas, CA 93908
Phone: (877) 827-7388
Company has online contact form
www.taproduce.com

Tasty Bite
1192 Illinois Street
San Francisco, CA 94107
Phone: (866) 972-6879
(M-F, 6am-5pm PT)
Company has online contact form
www.tastybite.com

Tender Choice Pork
151 North Main Street
Wichita, KS 67202
Phone: 1 (800) 328-2823
E-Mail: consumer_affairs@cargill.com
www.tenderchoicepork.com

Thai Kitchen
Simply Asia Foods, LLC
P.O. Box 13242
Berkeley, CA 94712-4242
Phone: 1 (800) 967-8424 (U.S.)
1 (800)-209-8707
(10am-4pm EST, Canada)
www.thaikitchen.com

Thomas'
Bimbo Bakeries
Consumer Relations Department
P.O. Box 976
Horsham, PA 19044
Phone: (800) 984-0986
www.thomasbreads.com

Thumann's Inc.
670 Dell Road
Carlstadt, NJ 07072
Phone: (201) 935-3636
Email:
customer.service@thumanns.com
www.thumanns.com

Toufayan Bakeries, Inc.
175 Railroad Avenue
Ridgefield, NJ 07657
Phone: (201) 941-2000
Toll Free: 1 (800) EAT-PITA
Company has online contact form
www.toufayan.com

Trans-Ocean Products, Inc.
350 West Orchard Drive
Bellingham, WA 98225
Toll Free: (800) 290-2722
Email: info@trans-ocean.com
www.trans-ocean.com

Tropicana Products, Inc.
a division of PepsiCo, Inc.
P.O. Box 049003
Chicago, IL 60604-9003
Phone: 1 (800) 237-7799
(Mon-Fri, 8:30-5:30 EST)
www.tropicana.com

Tyson Sales & Distribution, Inc.
Consumer Relations CP631
P.O. Box 2020
Springdale, AR 72765-2020
Phone: 1-800-233-6332
Company has online contact form
www.tyson.com

The United States Sweet Potato Council, Inc.
12 Nicklaus Lane, Suite 101
Columbia, SC 29229
Phone: (803) 788-7101
Email: CWalker12@bellsouth.net
www.SweetPotatoUSA.org

Vick Family Farms Partnership
11124 Christian Road
Wilson NC 27896-6098
Phone: (252) 237-7313
Company has online contact form
www.vickfamilyfarms.com

Vita Coco
Company has online contact form
www.vitacoc.com

VitaSoy USA
One New England Way
Ayer, MA 01432
Toll Free: 1-800-VITASOY (848-2769)
(Mon-Fri, 8:30am-5pm EST)
E-mail: info@vitasoy-usa.com
www.vitasoy-usa.com

Wada Farms Marketing Group, LLC
326 South 1400 West
Pingree, ID 83262
Phone: (208) 684-9801
Email: info@wadafarms.com
www.wadafarms.com

Weetabix Organic
Company has online contact form
www.weetabixusa.com

Welch Foods, Inc.
Phone: 1 (800) 340-6870
(M-F, 9am-4pm EST)
Company has online contact form
www.welchs.com

Well Pict (berries)
P.O. Box 973
Watsonville, CA 95077
Phone: (831) 722-3871
www.wellpict.com

WestSoy
The Hain Celestial Group
4600 Sleepytime Drive
Boulder, CO 80301
Phone: (800) 434-4246
www.westsoymilk.com

Wholly Guacamole
Company has online contact form
Support hours are M-F, 8am-6pm CST
www.eatwholly.com

Wilcox Farms, Inc.
www.wilcoxfarms.com

WishBone
www.wish-bone.com

Worthington
Kellogg's Consumer Affairs
P.O. Box CAMB
Battle Creek, MI 49016
Phone: (800) 962-1413
www.worthingtonfoods.com

Yoplait
General Mills, Inc.
P.O. Box 9452
Minneapolis, MN 55440
Phone: (800) 248-7310
(M-F, 7:30am-5:30pm CT)
Company has online contact form
www.yoplait.com

ZenSoy
Company has online contact form
www.zensoy.com

Heart-Healthy Resources & Organizations

American Diabetes Association

ATTN: Center for Information
1701 North Beauregard Street
Alexandria, VA 22311
Phone: 1 (800) DIABETES
(800-342-2383)
(Mon-Fri, 8:30am-8pm EST)
www.diabetes.org
American Diabetes Association leads the fight against the deadly consequences of diabetes and fights for those affected by it.

Academy of Nutrition and Dietetics

120 South Riverside Plaza, Suite 2000
Chicago, IL 60606-6995
Phone: (800) 877-1600;
(312) 899-0040
www.eatright.org
Academy of Nutrition and Dietetics is the world's largest organization of food and nutrition professionals.

American Heart Association/ American Stroke Association

7272 Greenville Avenue
Dallas, TX 75231
Phone: 1 (800) AHA-USA-1;
1 (800) 242-8721
www.heart.org
The American Heart Association and American Stroke Association fosters appropriate cardiac care in an effort to reduce disability and deaths caused by cardiovascular disease and stroke.

My Life Check® American Heart Association

mylifecheck.heart.org
My Life Check® is a program designed by the American Heart Association with a goal of improving health through educating the public on how best to live.

Health Check Tools, National Institutes of Health (NIH)

9000 Rockville Pike
Bethesda, MD 20892
nim.nih.gov/medlineplus/healthcheck tools.html
MedlinePlus links to *Health Check Tools* provides information to better understand your health.
The website also allows visitors to assess their health with interactive tools such as calculators, quizzes, and questionnaires.

Heart & Stroke Foundation

222 Queen Street, Suite 1402
Ottawa, ON K1P 5V9
Phone (613) 569-4361
www.heartandstroke.com
The Heart and Stroke Foundation provides general information about heart disease and stroke, and has offices in every province in Canada.

National Cholesterol Education Program (NCEP)

The National Heart, Lung, and Blood Institute
Health Information Center
Attention: Website
P.O. Box 30105
Bethesda, MD 20824-0105
Phone: (301) 592-8573
nhlbi.nih.gov/about/ncep/
The goal of the NCEP is to lower the number of illnesses and deaths from coronary heart disease (CHD) in the U.S. by reducing the percent of Americans with high blood cholesterol.

2010 U.S. Dietary Guidelines

Center for Nutrition Policy and Promotion
3101 Park Center Drive, 10th Floor
Alexandria, VA 22302-1594
cnpp.usda.gov/DietaryGuidelines.htm

The dietary guidelines, provided by the USDA Center for Nutrition Policy and Promotion, is updated every five years, and provides authoritative advice and promotes overall good health.

ChooseMyPlate.gov
Choosemyplate.gov
Provided by the USDA Center for Nutrition Policy and Promotion, the program offers sound advice on building a healthy plate of foods. Included on their website are food plans, meal plans, and SuperTracker, which can help plan, analyze, and track your diet and physical activity.

Heart-Healthy Cookbooks

American Heart Association Quick & Easy Cookbook, 2nd Edition
More Than 200 Healthy Recipes You Can Make in Minutes (2012)

The Healthy Heart Cookbook
Over 700 Recipes for Every Day and Every Occasion by Joseph C. Piscatella and Bernie Piscatella (2003)

American Heart Association Healthy Slow Cooker Cookbook
200 Low-Fuss, Good-for-You Recipes (2012)

Betty Crocker Healthy Heart Cookbook (2013)

The New American Heart Association Cookbook, 8th Edition
Revised and Updated with More Than 150 All-New Recipes (2012)

American Heart Association Healthy Family Meals
150 Recipes Everyone Will Love (2011)

The Everyday DASH Diet Cookbook by
Marla Heller, MS, RD (2013)

Heart-Healthy Recipe Websites

7-Day Heart-Healthy Meal Plan
EatingWell's Heart-Healthy Meal Plan
provides an overall healthy-eating program at five different daily caloric levels.
eatingwell.com/nutrition_health/weight_loss_diet_plans/diet_meal_plans/7_day_heart_healthy_meal_plan

Menus for Heart-Healthy Eating: Cut the Fat and Salt
Do you want to adopt a heart-healthy diet but aren't sure where to start?
mayoclinic.com/health/heart-healthy-diet/HB00039

20-Minute Heart-Healthy Meals–MyRecipes.com
Be good to your heart as well as your appetite in 20 minutes or less.
myrecipes.com/healthy-diet/heart healthy-meals-10000001711371

Healthy Recipes–American Heart Association
heart.org/HEARTORG/GettingHealthy/NutritionCenter/Nutrition-Center_UCM_001184_SubHomePage.jsp

Heart-Healthy Recipes–Better Homes and Gardens
Learn how to boost your heart health with these heart-healthy recipes and meals.
bhg.com/recipes/healthy/heart-healthy/

Heart Healthy Recipes
By making a few changes in your eating habits, you can help lower high blood pressure. Here are some great recipes that show you how.
nhlbi.nih.gov/hbp/prevent/h_eating/h_recip.htm

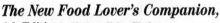

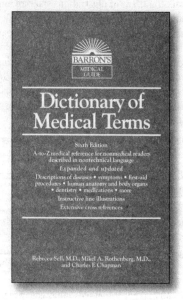